Holland Mania

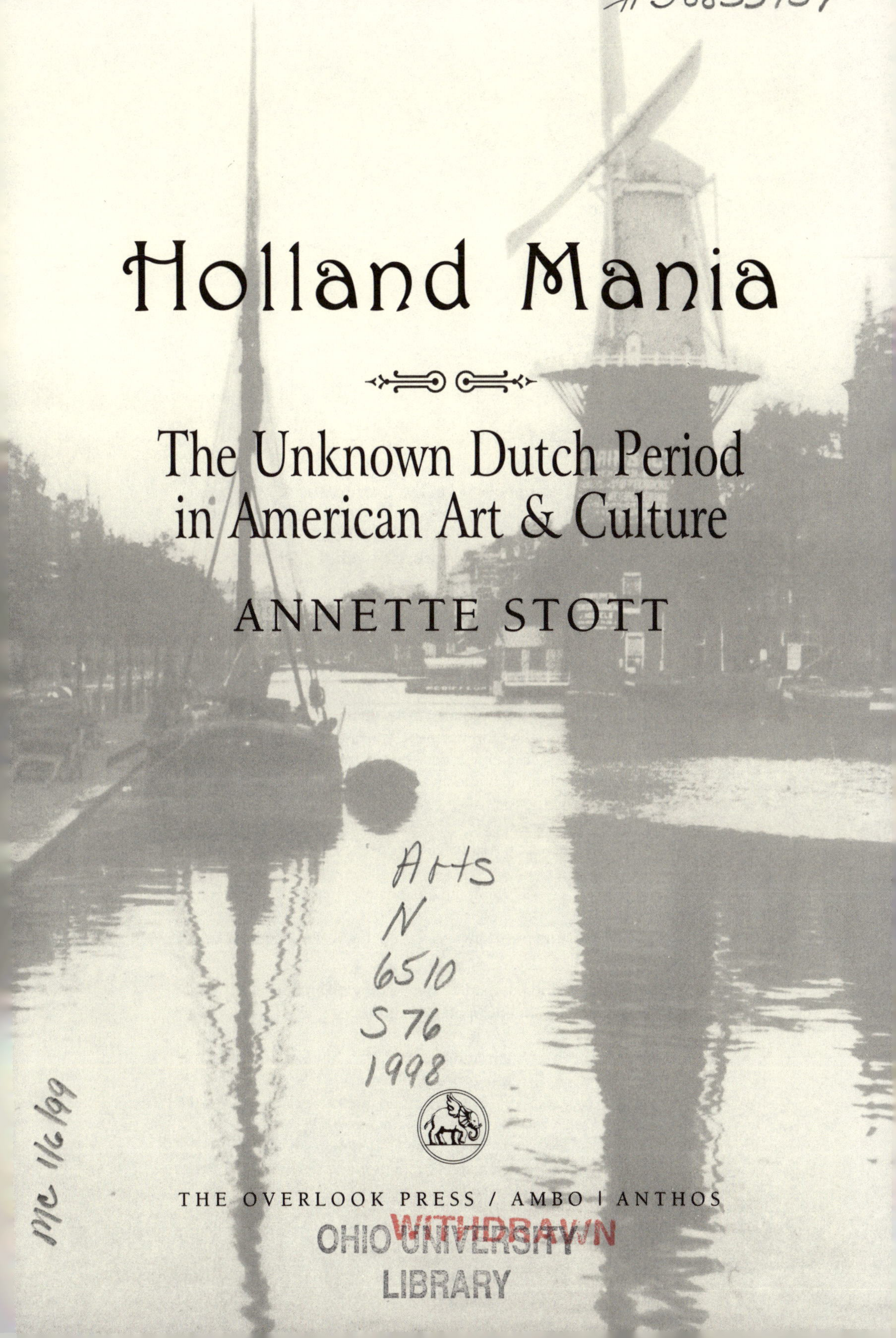

Holland Mania

The Unknown Dutch Period in American Art & Culture

ANNETTE STOTT

THE OVERLOOK PRESS / AMBO | ANTHOS

First published in the United States in 1998 by
The Overlook Press, Peter Mayer Publishers, Inc.
Lewis Hollow Road
Woodstock, New York 12498

Published simultaneously in the Netherlands in Dutch
as an *Olifant Pers* books, in association with Ambo | Anthos publishers

Photo credits begin on page 287

Library of Congress Cataloging-in-Publication Data

Stott, Annette.
Holland mania : the unknown Dutch period in
American art and culture / Annette Stott.
p. cm.
1. Art, American—Dutch influences. 2. Art, Modern—19th century—United States. 3. Art, Modern—20th century—United States. I. Title.
N6510.S76 1998 709'.73'09033—dc21 98-16617

Manufactured in the United States of America
Book design and type formatting by Bernard Schleifer

ISBN 0-87951-906-1
First Edition
1 3 5 7 9 8 6 4 2

Contents

ACKNOWLEDGMENTS

In 1986, I completed a Ph.D. dissertation at Boston University called "American Painters Who Worked in the Netherlands, 1880–1914." It presented primary data about American artists in Holland and a preliminary analysis of their work that provided the foundation for Chapters Two and Four of *Holland Mania.* I want to reaffirm my gratitude to the many people who supported that earlier effort.

Between 1987 and 1991, I pursued the question of what influence all that Dutch-American art and experience had as it entered the United States. What were the implications for American culture, in its broadest definition, of hundreds of artists going to Holland and sending back thousands of pictures? This line of research resulted in a finished book manuscript in 1992. I intended it to provide an introductory overview of the vogue for Holland, hoping that others would be inspired to dig deeper into the various aspects of the phenomenon I call Holland Mania. Unfortunately, publication was delayed, but perhaps the few copies of the manuscript that have circulated among scholars over the years did have something of the intended effect. A number of excellent publications have appeared during the interval and I incorporated this new scholarship when I revised and updated the book manuscript in 1997. The vogue for Holland is still a little-enough known aspect of American history that I hope this long-delayed publication may introduce a broader public to a fascinating era.

The research for major portions of this book was accomplished with the aid of an Andrew W. Mellon Faculty Fellowship in the Humanities at Harvard University in 1989–1990 and a Virginia Steele Scott Foundation Fellowship at the Huntington Library during the summer of 1989. In addition, a Winthrop College Research Grant facilitated my work in Cincinnati and a University of Denver Faculty Research Grant made possible the purchase of many photographs. The author gratefully acknowledges her debt to all four institutions for their support.

The staffs of the Harvard Libraries, Fogg Art Museum, Cincinnati Historical Society, Public Library of Cincinnati and Hamilton County, Cincinnati Art Museum, Archives of American Art, University of Denver libraries, Buffalo and Erie County Public Library and Historical Society, Albright-Knox Art Museum, Library of Congress, National Museum of American Art, the Memorial Gallery and the Library of the University of Rochester, Free Library of Philadelphia, Huntington Library, and Winthrop University Library, have been unfailingly patient and helpful. In particular, I wish to thank Peggy Keeran, arts and humanities reference librarian at the University of Denver, for her expertise in tracking down obscure sources and information. Diane Kotowski graciously photographed many of the illustrations from turn-of-the-century publications and Carol Taylor provided technical expertise in computer map making. Joanna Catron, Curator of Belmont—the Gari Melchers Memorial Estate and Gallery—has helped me find or has provided information for me over the years.

So many individuals have offered me the benefit of their expertise at strategic moments in the process of researching and writing this book. I am indebted to Michael Clark of the University of New Orleans for bringing the germ theory of history to my attention, to Wendy Greenhouse for introducing me to Ruth Elson's work on nineteenth-century children's schoolbooks, to Neil Walker for sending me copies of Dame Laura Knight's autobiographies, to Matt Rohn for architectural references, and to Mary Ellen Perry for bringing Margaret Woodbury Strong's predilection for windmills to my notice. Gerrit Kouwenhoven of the Noord-Veluwe Regional Archives, Ron Van Vleuten and Bart Bult of Egmond, and A. van der Plas and Ing. Jan-Peter Van Brakel of Katwijk facilitated my continuing research in the Netherlands. Many individuals in corporations, agencies, universities, and historical societies responded to my requests for information on far-flung topics, while the owners and managers of numerous commercial galleries and private clubs graciously allowed me to look at archives and paintings. Their help is gratefully acknowledged. I especially appreciate the generosity of Mrs. Arthur Little, August B. Miller, Willem Wouters, Johanna Shotell, Mr. and Mrs. Richard Thayer, Johanna Sibbett, and other families of artists who shared family papers and reminiscences. This book was also enriched by the contributors of illustrations, whose names will be found in the sources of illustrations.

A very special debt of gratitude is owed to Patricia Hills, Hans Kraan, William Truettner, and Barbara Weinberg for their early and continuing support of my work on the Dutch-American connection. Finally, my heartfelt gratitude extends to Gary Schwartz for his unflagging support of this manuscript and to Peter Mayer who not only agreed to publish it, but also made wise suggestions for revision and gently edited it.

Introduction

In October, 1903, the editor of one of the most popular monthly magazines in the United States announced to millions of readers that Holland, not England, was "The Mother of America." Citing evidence of colonial Dutch influence in American politics, cultural institutions, social customs, and language, editor Edward Bok concluded that all truly American characteristics and ideals originated in the Netherlands. This pronouncement in the *Ladies' Home Journal* summed up more than a decade of Dutch influence in American art and history. It came at the height of a craze for Holland that affected Americans from nearly every geographic region of the United States.

The theory that American identity originated in Holland was one of several competing ethnic claims that emerged at the end of the nineteenth century. Inspired partly by the country's centennial, which focused attention on the colonial era, and partly by the "new immigration" of Eastern Europeans, which threatened the cultural identity established by the old settlers, these proliferating ethnic studies attempted to anchor American cultural identity in each of the various nations from which the earliest immigrants had come. Most of them consciously opposed the dominance of England in contemporary theories of American history and culture. As David Gregg, pastor of the Lafayette Avenue Presbyterian Church in Brooklyn, New York explained to his congregation in the early 1890s: "the time has come in the writing of American history when we must give credit to others besides the English, and when we must, for the sake of fairness and for the sake of historic fact, break up the English historical monopoly." Published in 1905 as *Thoughts for the Occasion*, a series of patriotic lectures, Gregg's comments were echoed by many others. Among ethnic studies at that time, claims for Dutch primacy succeeded to a remarkable degree in altering common perceptions of American identity.

Parallels between the history and culture of the Netherlands and the United States supported Holland's promotion to the position of cradle of American civilization. In the search for an alternative to Anglo interpretations of American history, the Netherlands stood out as a country that had enjoyed close economic and political ties with the United States, never had engaged in war against it, and had held a position as an economic and political world leader in the seventeenth century that might have served as a model for the emerging nation. Of all the non-British countries that contributed to the formation of the United States, the majority of late-nineteenth-century Americans had perhaps the least accumulated resentment toward the Netherlands and the most in common with it. Physical appearance, social custom, Protestantism, republicanism, and perceived ideals of democracy and personal freedoms all struck chords of agreement in the two countries. In addition, similarities in the development of the two republics seemed to foretell a dazzling future for the United States. The United Provinces of the Netherlands had risen rapidly to economic superiority and had ruled the seas and colonized the world after freeing itself from the rule of a foreign monarch. Its successor, the United States of America, expected to do the same in its own bid for world power. The relatively inconsequential status of Holland in contemporary world affairs seems to have made no impression on nineteenth-century Americans who viewed the Netherlands almost entirely in terms of its past. In fact, its weak position in nineteenth-century world affairs guaranteed that the Netherlands posed no threat to American ambition. Between 1890 and 1920, the Netherlands became the focal point of many Americans' search for a national past and for a cultural identity in the present.

That search had begun with the declaration of independence from England. Thoroughly stamped with the identity of the country that had ruled them for over one hundred years, residents of the newly constituted United States sought to separate themselves from England, not only politically and economically, but also culturally. Throughout the nineteenth century, a conscious effort went forward to produce an American culture distinctive from, and yet equal to

British culture. Architects, authors, musicians, painters, designers, poets, and sculptors strove to create an American identity through their various art forms by adopting, adapting, and inventing artistic vocabularies. Early endeavors to shape American culture by employing Greek architecture as a symbol of democracy and Roman design as a symbol of republicanism accompanied a wide variety of other approaches. During the eclectic nineteenth century, from time to time an artist or architect looked to Holland, especially in those parts of the country where a Dutch presence was most strongly felt, New York and New Jersey. In the late nineteenth century, however, Holland became a common source of inspiration for visual artists of the United States. Dutch motifs, often reflecting a colonial Dutch-American connection, spread into the popular culture.

The fascination with Holland became so general and so pronounced during this period that it can well be called a period of "Holland Mania." Although this term was not in use at the turn of the century, it is an appropriate name for the phenomenon that occurred then. Consideration of a wide range of cultural indicators, from tourism and advertisements to high fashion and interior design, demonstrates a widespread turn-of-the-century belief in a deeply rooted cultural relationship between the Netherlands and the United States. This belief extended well beyond people of Dutch descent or those living in Dutch-American communities. For a time, the way many Americans imagined themselves and their heritage was shaped partly by the way they viewed Holland.

Appreciation of Dutch cultural values and artifacts at this time was not limited to Americans. A very similar phenomenon can be found in Great Britain and Canada, and minor variations existed in Germany and France. But the particular traits of American character and history, and the cultural affinities between the United States and the Netherlands, produced what might be considered a less tempered vogue for Holland in the United States. The cultural and nationalistic nuances of this vogue differed from those elsewhere, despite the fact that American ideas about Holland sometimes came by way of Germany, France, and England.

This study incorporates art history, historiography, popular culture, and immigrant studies, based on both Dutch and American archival sources, but it focuses on two of the primary ingredients of Holland Mania: visual images and revisionist history. The evidence is presented in a roughly chronological order to demonstrate the complex interrelationship between image and word—between art and history—that created a distinctive and nationalistic interpretation of the Netherlands in the United States.

My central thesis is that a boom in the old Dutch master art market, followed by a rapidly expanding U.S. market for contemporary fine art and popular images of Holland, ushered in an era of increasing Dutch importance in American culture. Before 1880, images of the Netherlands were rare in the work of American artists, but by 1890 the market in the United States for contemporary pictorial interpretations of Holland had grown so strong that it supported six colonies of American artists in the Netherlands. Due to the early influence of the old masters, even these modern pictures often emphasized an old-fashioned, seventeenth-century image of Holland. In the next decade, historians reinterpreted seventeenth-century American history in a Dutch light. Visual images helped shape and disseminate the new historical view. As American history was recast in a Dutch mold, people looked to paintings and illustrations of Holland as models for fashion and interior design. They dug through genealogies in search of a personal Dutch heritage to match that of the nation, or exchanged a less favorable ancestry for a pair of readily available "old Dutch" portraits to hang on the parlor walls. They built or remodeled homes in Dutch and colonial Dutch modes, celebrated Dutch festivals and entertainments, and traveled in Holland, the new Motherland. After the turn of the century, advertisers built on this widespread ideal to market a variety of products. Holland Mania, emerging from the intersection of proliferating representations of Holland and a search for American historical roots, entailed the re-imaging of the American self in terms of this Dutch heritage.

World War I temporarily ended direct contact with the Netherlands for tourists, historians, and artists. During the 1920s, a period of American art sometimes described as isolationist, paintings of Holland fell out of favor and were retired to attics and museum storage. American history, which had never fully accepted Holland as the Motherland, reverted to the theory of a transplanted English culture. Without the theoretical underpinnings, other manifestations of Holland Mania also disappeared. Dutch influence in American culture shriveled to pockets of ethnic celebration within Dutch-American communities, and awareness of past Dutch influence was reduced to the general knowledge that New York City and environs began as a Dutch colony.

Despite the end of widespread national interest in Holland

around 1920, some effects of Holland Mania linger into the present. Most of Americans' cherished stereotypes of Holland originated, or were consolidated, during that period. Contemporary Americans have maintained many of the blinders that allowed their predecessors to look past Holland's technology and modernity to concentrate on its superficial appearance and its historic past. The "land of windmills and wooden shoes" was a commonplace and apt description of the anachronistic, idyllic image fabricated a century ago, to which many continue to cling. In the conclusion of this book I have taken the liberty of speculating about the nature of some continuing Dutch-American cultural relations since 1920.

Because my own reaction to the discovery of a turn-of-the-century Dutch craze in American culture was one of surprise and reluctant but gradual acceptance, it seems natural to me that readers will also wonder how such a phenomenon could have escaped notice. The most obvious connections between Holland and America occurred in the seventeenth century when the Dutch settled the Hudson River area. Because that was the era of greatest economic and political association, most scholarly considerations of Dutch-American relations continue to focus on the colonial period. When historians do examine the late nineteenth and early twentieth centuries, they normally do so primarily in terms of immigration, concentrating on the Dutch-American community. When art historians finally began to examine turn-of-the-century expatriate American art activities, they focused first on France and Germany, the countries at the forefront of nineteenth-century western art. Examination of the Italian-American art connection made a logical next step due to the nineteenth-century exploration of classical design as an expression of nationalism. Not until exhibitions of expatriate art began to turn up numerous paintings of Holland was there any reason to suspect a significant Dutch influence at the turn of the century. As a result of these trends in scholarship, the broader Dutch cultural influence in the United States at the turn of the century and its effects on national identity have gone largely unrecognized.

Several aspects of the following study deserve additional clarification here, beginning with terminology. The word Holland is presently understood by most Americans to refer to the European country wedged between Belgium and Germany, whose official name is the Kingdom of the Netherlands, or *Nederland*. In reality, only two of the eleven provinces that comprise the Netherlands are named Holland, but because the country's population, industry, government, and national institutions are concentrated in those provinces, foreigners have more often called the country Holland than the Netherlands. Throughout this book I use the terms Holland and the Netherlands interchangeably to refer to the entire country; North Holland and South Holland to refer to two specific provinces; and Dutch exclusively in reference to the people, language, and culture of the Netherlands and its colonies.

Likewise, turn-of-the-century writers usually defined Holland, the Netherlands, and Dutch as references to the area presently occupied by the Kingdom of the Netherlands. But they sometimes gave all three names a broader definition. For example, the English word for the people of the Netherlands, Dutch, became confused with the German term for the people of Germany, *Deutsch*. As a result, although Dutch usually designated Holland, it sometimes referred to Germany. The appellation Pennsylvania Dutch to describe the German immigrants of Pennsylvania is a classic example of this problem. In addition, the Netherlands means Lowlands or Low Countries, terms that have traditionally designated the entire region occupied by Belgium, Luxembourg, and Holland, because it lies physically lower than the rest of Europe, near sea level. Turn-of-the-century writers sometimes used the terms Netherlands and Dutch to include this larger area.

The history of the region further complicated its nomenclature. During the sixteenth century, the Spanish Hapsburgs ruled the whole area as a united dependency. Then in 1579, the northern provinces declared their independence from Spain and formed a republic, the United Provinces of the Netherlands. They fought a thirty-year war to secure their independence as a predominantly Protestant, Dutch-speaking nation. The southern provinces, collectively called Flanders, remained under Spanish dominion with a predominantly Roman Catholic, French- and Dutch-speaking culture. In 1795, the United Provinces of the Netherlands lost its independence to Napoleon, becoming the Batavian Republic, a protectorate of France. Less than twenty years later, with Napoleon finally subdued, European heads of state created a new kingdom by joining Flanders with the Netherlands and Luxembourg under the Dutch rule of the House of Orange. Differences in culture and national interests that had solidified during two centuries of separation made this an uneasy alliance and in 1830 the Belgians declared their independence. European powers continued to fight over Luxembourg, continuously reshaping its borders until it gained neutrality in 1867.

For approximately fifty years before the onset of Holland Mania in the United States, the Netherlands and Belgium formed separate political and cultural entities, but the entangled histories and shifting borders of all three countries continued to confuse many Americans. It is not always possible to discern how much of the region American writers intended to include in their comments on "Dutch" art or the history and culture of the "Netherlands." Despite the uncertainty of the language, the balance of evidence indicates that Holland Mania proceeded primarily from Americans' understanding of the history and culture of the northern provinces. They associated both the Netherlands and the United States most closely with the free Protestant republic of the seventeenth century and its colony in North America, only occasionally including aspects of the southern region.

The opposite problem exists with the use of the word American to describe the people and culture of the United States. The term really belongs to the various peoples and cultures of two continents. Increasingly in recent years, it has been used in this broader sense. Because the people of the United States self-identify so strongly as "American," however, and because alternative forms are awkward, throughout this book I have employed American in reference to the geographic area of the United States both before and after the creation of that political entity.

The second matter for clarification concerns the present status of the artists and writers whose work forms the basis of this study. While old masters and famous nineteenth-century artists created many influential images of Holland, rank and file artists who have not, for the most part, acquired positions in the canon of art history also played a vital role in popularizing Dutch influence in the United States. Their magazine illustrations, calendar pages, advertising art, watercolor sketches, china figurines, and picture postcards disseminated images of Holland across America. Their experiences in Holland and their pictorial interpretations of the American qualities embodied in Dutch subjects had some of the most widereaching influence. Therefore, this study considers the full range of images, from tourist souvenirs to fine art, in order to assess the impact of the visual in formulating and distributing ideas about Holland. For the same reasons, this study encompasses the work of nineteenth-century amateur historians whose writings swayed popular opinion, as well as that of professional historians.

Finally, a word should be said about ethnicity in this study. Ethnic diversity among the promoters of Dutch influence in American culture lent credence to their theories. Relatively few of the American artists who drew and painted Holland had any Dutch ancestry and the two historians primarily responsible for the Dutch interpretation of American history were of Scotch-Irish and English descent. While this "diversity" contributed to the credibility and popularity of the argument for Dutch influence, it applied only to western Europe. Plainly, Euro-Americans could more easily identify with the Dutch and more easily see their roots in Holland than could African, Asian, Hispanic, or Native Americans. The development of Holland Mania took place within the dominant Euro-American culture of the United States. Ultimately, its failure to account for the real diversity of formative influences in American culture, both ethnic and racial, contributed to its demise.

Though long forgotten, Holland Mania and its companion ethnic studies at the turn of the century prefigure a contemporary trend, multiculturalism. In the midst of a wave of new immigrants from Eastern Europe one hundred years ago, Americans looked for a cultural anchor among the countries that had contributed to the formation of the United States. In the midst of a wave of new immigrants from Asia and Latin America today, Americans are again looking for a cultural anchor in the country's diverse ethnic composition. Participants in Holland Mania, especially historians, fought the ethnocentric view of American history and identity that was prevalent in their day—a strict adherence to English views and influences. For them, the solution was to recognize the individual claims of minority groups: Dutch, Irish, Scotch, German, and French. Today, all those ethnic groups have been consolidated in the terms Euro-American and white. White is a fairly homogeneous concept that forms a new ethnocentrism, against which the claims of African Americans, Asian Americans, Latinos, and Native Americans are balanced. Just as the recovery of isolated heritages to the mainstream was part of the larger attempt one hundred years ago to define the United States in terms of ethnicity, today African American, Native American, Asian American, and Hispanic cultural contributions are being recovered to the mainstream for the same purpose. The increased scholarship on these ethnic/racial arts and histories during the past twenty years is one indication of this process. Already the struggle to redefine American identity has produced Afro-centrism, a world view centered in the primacy of Africa and the importance of African contributions to the United States. Afro-centrism is a modern equivalent of Holland Mania. This continuous negotiation of ethnic and racial cultures underscores the importance of the multicultural nature of the United States to American identity. As part of the contemporary exploration of multiculturalism, it is worth noting how the changing perceptions of Dutch influence in American culture have shaped and reshaped notions of American identity.

ONE

Dutch Art in America

THE OLD DUTCH MASTERS

IN THE LAST QUARTER OF THE NINETEENTH CENTURY, THE ACCUMULATION of unprecedented wealth among a rising class of industrialists produced a new era in American art collecting. The previous emphasis on contemporary European art yielded to a rapidly expanding market for the old masters. The purchase of old master paintings gave America's new millionaires a socially acceptable way to demonstrate their wealth, taste, and cultural refinement. The perceived democratic nature of the art also appealed to many. Well able to hold their own in the international art market, by the 1880's some of America's wealthiest collectors had focused their attention on the Dutch masters above all other works of art. Paintings by Rembrandt van Rijn, Frans Hals, and Pieter De Hoogh commanded ever higher prices as competition for them increased.

The New York department store magnate Benjamin Altman began buying seventeenth-century Dutch paintings around the turn of the century, rapidly accumulating one of the strongest collections of Dutch art in the United States. He soon owned thirteen Rembrandts, three paintings by Hals, and a variety of scenes by Nicolaes Maes, De Hoogh, Vermeer, Gerrit Dou, Meindert Hobbema, Jacob van Ruysdael, and Albert Cuyp. John Graver Johnson, a Philadelphia lawyer with a growing old master collection of his own, watched in fascination as Altman spent over $750,000 on his new love. "If the price is sufficiently high, he will probably buy," concluded Johnson in a wry comment on his rival's motivation.[1] Johnson collected the paintings of the so-called little

Dutch masters—artists who specialized in small-scale domestic genre scenes, still lifes, and landscapes. He particularly admired the work of Jan Steen, whose picture of *The Doctor's Visit* (FIG. 1c*) is just one of eleven Steens that Johnson acquired. The collector Peter Arrell Brown Widener made headlines when he topped both Johnson and Altman by spending the equivalent of $486,000 on a single painting of a windmill believed to have come from the hand of Rembrandt (FIG. 2c).

Dutch masterpieces appealed to collectors of varied backgrounds. Widener, a Philadelphia financier of German descent, got his start by supplying meat to the United States Army during the Civil War. With the substantial profit from that venture he went on to build the financial empire that supported his enthusiastic art collecting. William Andrews Clark, a Montana senator of Scotch-Irish descent with important mining interests in the west, devoted considerable time to his collection of Dutch paintings and ceramics. Baltimore socialite Mary Frick Jacobs acquired portraits by Rembrandt and Hals. The Dutch-American Martin Antoine Ryerson inherited his father's business interests in the Midwest and his personal love of art made him a governing member of the Art Institute of Chicago at the age of thirty-one. These are just a few of the collectors scattered across the country who helped to secure the fashionability of old Dutch paintings in the United States.

Dealers sometimes bought entire collections as they came on the market, knowing they could sell them in the United States. But wealthy collectors also traveled to the European headquarters of these dealers in their quest for the best. Details of individual purchases are well chronicled by Walter Liedtke and others. Liedtke has hypothesized that the appreciation for Dutch art motivating these collectors was "virtually intuitive." He discusses a tradition of sympathy for seventeenth-century Dutch art throughout the nineteenth century that also manifested in numerous affinities with an emerging national school of American art.[2]

The contest between wealthy American collectors with apparently limitless funds alarmed Europeans. Typically, a Rotterdam newspaper carried an article bemoaning the loss of so many paintings to the United States:

> We often hear with regret, that one or other masterpieces of our greatest artists from the seventeenth or nineteenth century is captured by the dollar kings of North America. How many Rembrandts and works by Maris and Israëls have not been carried by them out

*(Figure numbers followed by the letter "c" are to be found in the color inserts.)

> of our sight! And it is to be feared that this condition of things will grow worse because the number of dollar kings is constantly increasing, who wish to enrich their picture collections with first-class Dutch Art.[3]

Edwin Buijsen has documented the growing concern of Dutch art experts over this loss of national art to American wealth and the campaign to preserve important examples in Dutch institutions. The furor in the Dutch press over the feared loss of part of the Six Collection in 1907 to J.P. Morgan—or any other American millionaire—and the successful effort to have the Dutch government purchase it, provides a good example of the Dutch reaction to America's voracious appetite for Dutch masters.[4]

American collectors focused so much on the Dutch painters that as early as 1890 when an exhibition of old masters from American collections was proposed, the *Art Amateur* questioned:

> . . . what could we show of the Italian masters, of the German school or even of the Flemish school? Next to nothing. . . . it is on the Dutch masters Rembrandt, Franz Hals, Van der Meer of Delft, and Pieter de Hooghe, and on the English painters, Reynolds, Gainsborough, Turner and Constable that we should have to depend. In some of these names we could make a strong showing—of some of the Dutchmen especially.[5]

This prediction proved correct a few years later when the anniversary of Henry Hudson's explorations of the Hudson River coincided with the centennial of Robert Fulton's invention of the steamboat to inspire a gala celebration in New York City. As part of the Hudson–Fulton festivities, the Metropolitan Museum of Art held an exhibition of old masters from American collections. They mustered 146 Dutch paintings, including large numbers of genuine and purported Rembrandts, Ruysdaels, Vermeers, and Hals.

Exhibitions like this, and the publicity generated as each new exorbitantly priced masterpiece left Europe for the United States, raised public awareness of Dutch art. The images became still more accessible to Americans as they moved from private hands to public collections. Between 1888 and 1900, New York financier Henry Marquand gave the Metropolitan Museum of Art a number of Dutch paintings, including *The Smoker* by Hals and *Woman with a Water Jug* by Vermeer, which Marquand had purchased in 1887 as a De Hoogh. Marquand's gifts included landscapes, portraits, and genre scenes by major and minor artists. Benjamin Altman bequeathed his twenty million dollar art collection to the Metropolitan in 1913 and the Dutch part went on permanent display in its own gallery at the museum the next year. John Johnson's collection of nearly twelve hundred old masters, including many authentic Flemish and Dutch examples, became a keystone of the Philadelphia Museum of Art collection when Johnson died in 1917.

Other collectors created their own art institutions. Henry Clay Frick made his first million dollars in the coke and steel industry before he was thirty and began investing his wealth in old masters almost immediately. Between 1900 and 1910, when he gave his collection to the public, Frick acquired some of the finest examples by Rembrandt, Cuyp, and Hobbema, and built a New York mansion to house them. Similarly, the socialite Isabella Stewart Gardner built a palace in Boston to hold her collections, which, by 1900, contained one of the few authentic Vermeers in the United States and excellent examples by Rembrandt. She also bequeathed her collection to the public.

While millionaires endowed the big cities with old Dutch masters, many smaller captains of industry and inheritors of family wealth were busy collecting the work of less well-known seventeenth-century Dutch artists. This enabled smaller cities throughout the country to include old Dutch pictures from local collections in their loan exhibitions. Even people who did not go to art museums were likely to become familiar with the Dutch masters through numerous magazine, newspaper, and lithographic reproductions.

Americans' view of the Netherlands in the late nineteenth century depended largely upon the old Dutch master paintings they collected. As Peter C. Sutton has pointed out in his valuable guide to Dutch art in American museums, collectors at the turn of the century focused on seventeenth-century landscape, genre, and portrait subjects. They passed up most eighteenth- and early nineteenth-century examples and left the history paintings, the literary themes, and pictures by Caravaggio's Dutch followers to European collectors. Scenes of the daily life of Dutch peasants by Adriaen Brouwer and Van Ostade appealed equally as much as genre paintings of the burgher class by Jacob Ochtervelt (FIG. 3) and De Hoogh. The former depicted the farmers and working class upon whose labors the Dutch Republic had depended. The latter reflected the rich material culture and social pursuits of the upper middle class. In both, Americans saw traits with which they identified.

Nineteenth-century art historians formulated a theory of seventeenth-century Dutch art that placed it at the dawn of the modern

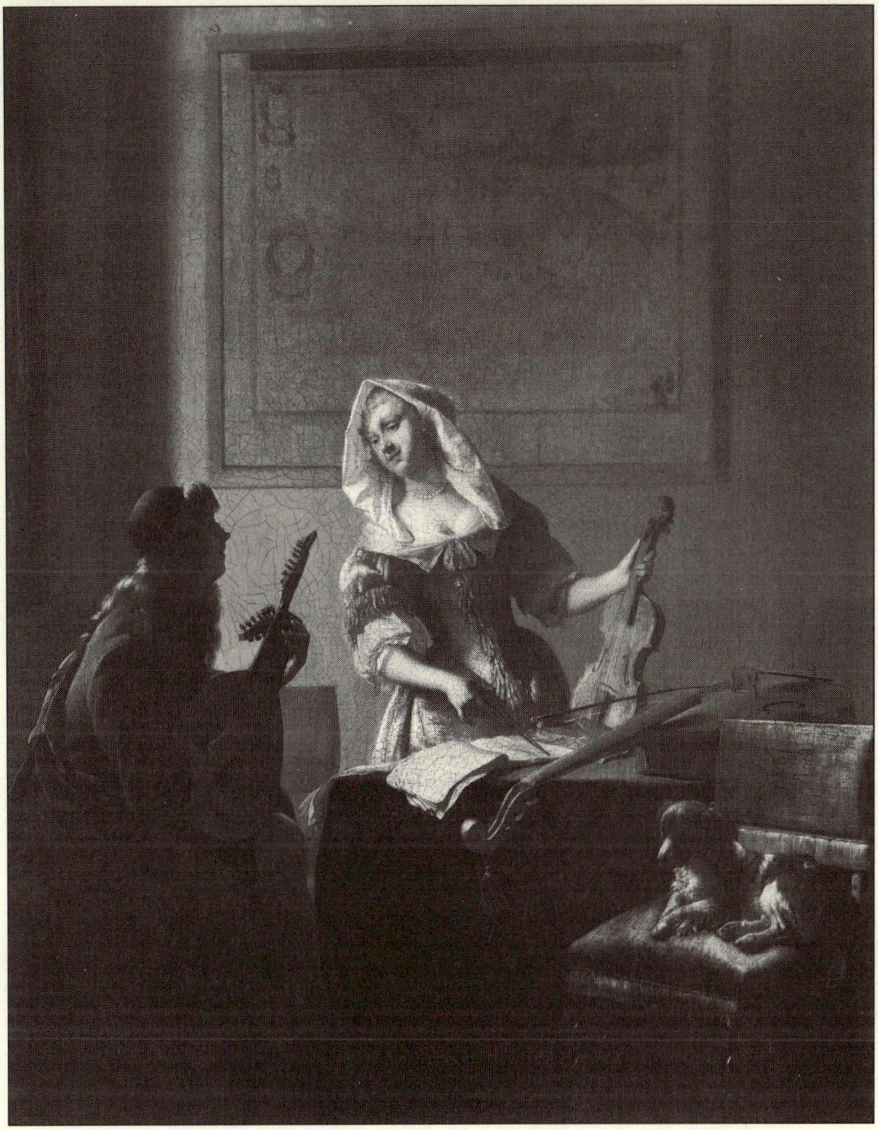

era in art. They associated it with democracy and republican ideals, in the process elevating Dutch art to a position beside, if not above, the art of the Italian Renaissance which had formerly reigned supreme. The eminent French critic Theophile Thoré, also known by his pen name William Bürger; the French philosopher Hippolyte Taine; and the Anglo-American art historian Charles Caffin all contributed to this theory. Thoré-Bürger and Caffin understood the formation of the Dutch republic and its rejection of both Papal authority and Spanish absolutist power as the beginning of an era of

FIG. 3 *Genre scenes like* The Musicians *by Jacob Ochtervelt were popular for their depictions of the life and culture of citizens of the old Dutch Republic. Chicago collector Martin A. Ryerson acquired it and it is now in the Art Institute of Chicago.*

democratic, republican, and egalitarian ideals that would eventually affect all of western society. Explained Caffin:

> As long as society was conditioned by the aristocratic theory, Greek art, and the Renaissance interpretation of its principles, sufficed; but, with the growth and spread of the democratic, a new principle became necessary. Rembrandt conceived it, and our own age is learning to apply it.[6]

Taine was less concerned with the relationship between the old Dutch republic and the modern world, but he, too, saw seventeenth-century Dutch art as the height of artistic expression among Northern European peoples (as the Italian had been among Latin peoples) and a clear demonstration of the principles of liberty and equality at work in the old republic. These three men, writing in the last half of the nineteenth century, explained the effects of the Dutch revolt from Spain as having moved European art away from the Italian model in four distinct areas, and they saw each change in art as an expression of a corresponding change in the political and social order within the Netherlands.

First, according to this theory, the subjects of art changed from a narrow elitist insistence on history painting (including mythology, literary, and Biblical subjects) to an acceptance of the broad realm of human endeavor and environment. The Dutch elevated landscape, still life, genre, and portraiture to a position formerly occupied only by history painting. This democratization of subject matter followed the rejection of Roman Catholicism, with its ornate artistic trappings, and the expulsion of the Spanish aristocracy. It expressed a relatively greater distribution of power and wealth among the Dutch people.

Second, according to these nineteenth-century authorities, Dutch art moved away from an emphasis on the ideal, toward an acceptance of the beauty in all things, even the common, the homely, and the ugly. Instead of seeking perfection, Dutch artists copied nature with as much realism as possible, a trait considered innately democratic by Taine and Caffin. The new, more mundane subjects and the new realism of style produced an art that could be understood by every class of society without special training or education.

The third area of change concerned a shift in power among artists. Instead of a few individual geniuses with circles of lesser followers, the Dutch were considered to have produced large numbers of masters in every subject specialization.

Fourth, these theorists detected a democratization in art patronage.

City burghers, merchants, and even common laborers and farmers replaced the church and aristocracy as the primary patrons of fine art in the old Dutch republic.

Taken together, the picture of Golden Age Dutch art drawn by Thoré-Bürger, Taine, and Caffin suggested an art ideally suited to the political concerns and ideals of the United States. The populist versus elitist patronage and subject matter corresponded to American notions of democracy. The preference for a realistic style easily understood by all, and the opportunity, created through middle-class patronage, for anyone to become an artist appealed to American notions of equality.

The success of the old Dutch masters in the United States owed much to the feelings of national identity they inspired. Whether Americans had read contemporary theories of art or not, one after another described Dutch art in terms of democratic ideals. "Dutch art is of the people and for the people," proclaimed a writer in 1900, "the home, the burghers' home, not the palace, is painted." "Rembrandt, the greatest of them all, studied with incessant assiduity the common people," agreed another. Travel writer Burton Stevenson pointed to the artists' middle-class origins as the source of their preference for democratic themes: "Rembrandt's father was a miller, Hals's father was a merchant, Jan Steen's father was a brewer, de Hooch's father was a butcher, Gerard Dou's father was a glazier . . . . Art, up to that time, had been a thing of saints and madonnas; the Dutch made it a thing of every-day life—an art for the home and fireside." The old Dutch genre paintings, still lifes, portraits, and landscapes (and the absence of the nude) reflected the values of an affluent middle class society with which many nineteenth-century Americans could identify, and which they did not discern in art fostered under European monarchies.[7]

Even individual portraits by seventeenth-century Dutch artists inspired a feeling of affinity in American viewers. As an anonymous turn-of-the-century writer explained, Dutch "portrait painters in the past depicted the faces of men who had done something in the world; painted them solidly, seriously, as they were . . . . Truth, simplicity, dignity, were and are the golden rules of Dutch art."[8] These Dutchmen, common people who had fought for self-government and religious liberty—"men who had done something in the world"—reminded American collectors of themselves and their own ambitions.

A nineteenth-century historian explained the relationship between the old Dutch masters and Americans this way:

> The religious and democratic ideas in which Rembrandt breathed and lived are not more the ideas and feeling only of a poor suffering and struggling people, but they have become the soul and the spirit of the entire great American Commonwealth . . . nobody can be surprised that in our days and especially in America Rembrandt is honored with love and sympathy, that his work is the main attraction in every gallery, and that the holy secret of his art is understood and admired by the staunch and sturdy sons of liberty and democracy.[9]

The writings of the American historian John Lothrop Motley also helped shape the American view of the old Dutch masters. Motley devoted much of his life to a study of the Netherlands in the sixteenth and early seventeenth centuries, the period when the northern provinces began to resist Spanish sovereignty and finally overcame it to create an independent republic of united provinces. He published *The Rise of the Dutch Republic* in 1855 and the *History of the United Netherlands* twelve years later. Both became best sellers in the United States.

Motley couched his interpretation of the Dutch struggle for independence in terms that recalled the American Revolution. He emphasized the bravery, tenacity, and independence of the common Dutch citizens who took up arms and the righteousness of their cause to repel a foreign monarch in favor of a republican form of self-rule. He engaged his audience's sympathy with tales of the great sufferings imposed on Dutch men, women, and children by the occupying Spanish army. Motley reinforced the tendency for Americans to see the paintings of Holland's Golden Age as a reflection of their own ideals and beliefs, their own early struggles, and their subsequent achievement of prosperity.

Old Dutch master paintings of the late sixteenth and seventeenth centuries revealed the people and places that Motley so eloquently described. As the turn-of-the-century art historian George Breed Zug explained: "This whole large group of Dutch painters are the true historians of their period, telling in language plainer than words of the peace that followed the long war, of order, contentment, and of domestic happiness."[10] Collectors focused on this era, not only because it produced the highest quality of art, but because it embodied ideals that they understood to be essentially American. Old Dutch master paintings and Motley's Holland, of which the art was considered a natural expression, became the foundation for the revision of American history that would occur during the 1890s, a revision that placed the Dutch republic as the source of American political and cultural ideals.

In addition to the common notion that the old Dutch masters expressed middle-class democratic and republican values, some people believed that Dutch art had provided the inspiration for American art. Wrote the amateur historian William Elliot Griffis, as he traveled through Holland: "In this Haarlem gallery, as at those in the Hague and Amsterdam, our own American artists, Allston, Vanderlyn, Trumbull, and a host of their successors, have studied and gained inspiration. Indeed, Allston's debt to Netherlandish art is more than that of a student, for one of his distant ancestors was Vanderhorst, a contemporary of Rubens."[11] American genre, still life, landscape, and marine painting all owed a debt to the seventeenth-century Dutch artists' development of these so-called democratic subjects. Virtually all late-nineteenth-century artists studied Frans Hals and Rembrandt, often making a special trip to Holland to do so. The sense of modern American art's debt to Holland echoes throughout Charles Caffin's book *The Story of Dutch Painting*, which begins with the inscription:

TO THE PRESENT AND FUTURE ART
OF THE NEW REPUBLIC OF THE UNITED STATES OF AMERICA
THIS STORY OF THE ART OF THE OLD DUTCH REPUBLIC
IS DEDICATED BY THE AUTHOR

Many late-nineteenth-century American artists felt a special affinity with seventeenth-century Dutch art. Eastman Johnson, known as the American Rembrandt, painted himself in Dutch period costume in 1899 and William Merritt Chase had himself photographed in similar attire. Charles Sheeler remembered that Chase fancied he looked like one of the figures in a painting by Frans Hals and Sheeler thought Chase sported mustachios in an effort to enhance the illusion.[12] Similarly, Jerome Myers painted numerous self-portraits in the guise of Rembrandt. Part of the reason that American artists affiliated themselves with the old Dutch masters and studied and copied their paintings was the belief that Holland provided some of the foundations upon which American art had been built. And if the Dutch masters had inspired American art, then there was all the more reason to collect them, as part of the heritage of the United States.

Unfortunately, the fever for old Dutch masters was matched by the ignorance of most American collectors on the subject, creating a climate ripe for fakes and forgeries. Unscrupulous artists and dealers on both sides of the Atlantic rushed to fill the vacuum created by a limited supply of authentic old masters. The British artist, Sir George Clausen, recalled an incident that occurred while he was studying pictures at the National Gallery in London in the 1880s or 1890s:

> Among the copyists were two old boys who copied Teniers. I could not make them out for a long time: they would copy a figure from one picture, another from another picture and so on, on the same panel, making up a Teniers picture. One day, when washing brushes, I heard one say 'What do you do with your stuff?' 'Oh, I work for the Californian market,' said the other.[13]

News articles regularly exposed forgeries in private collections and museums, and journals such as the *Collector and Art Critic* warned the unwary about the hazards of buying supposed Rembrandts and De Hooghs.

Fear of spending a fortune on a forgery, together with the growing taste for Dutch imagery induced by the old master craze, stimulated the development of the market for contemporary Dutch pictures by artists of the Hague School and by American painters abroad. While not commanding the same prestige, these artists did offer some of the same subjects, in a choice of old-master or modern styles, with authenticity guaranteed. Moreover, for those collectors priced out of the Rembrandt market, contemporary pictures of Holland offered an economical alternative.

THE HAGUE SCHOOL

After the seventeenth century, Dutch art fell into relative obscurity until the second half of the nineteenth century, when Dutch critics began to hail a group of painters based in The Hague as the hope for a new golden age. These artists consciously set out to restore Dutch art to its former glory by painting the common Dutch people and landscape around them. They patterned their art on Rembrandt, Ruysdael, and other old masters, filtered through the lens of French Barbizon art.

The Father of the Hague School, Jozef Israëls, rapidly gained popularity in the United States. Israëls specialized in scenes of the heroic life of peasant farmers and fisherfolk, often painted in dark tonalities reminiscent of Rembrandt. His painting, *The Cottage Madonna* (FIG. 4c), depicts a barefoot peasant woman feeding her child in a detailed rendition of a Dutch cottage. A cross hanging from the mantel symbolizes the Christian piety then commonly supposed to be more intense in country people than in urbanites. Israëls's colleagues, Bernardus Johannes Blommers and Albert Neuhuys, recalled the little Dutch masters with their interior scenes of women performing household tasks and children playing (FIG. 5c).

Other members of the Hague School followed the lead of their seventeenth-century ancestors in further developing the genre of landscape painting. The Maris brothers, Hendrik Willem Mesdag, and Anton Mauve painted Dutch land and sea in misty tones of grey and silver. Mauve became famous for his renditions of sheep on the sandy dunes, while Mesdag popularized tonal seascapes and beach scenes.

In the 1870s French art critics noticed the development of the Hague School and during the eighties its reputation spread through Europe. However, it was American and British collectors who gave contemporary Dutch artists the most concrete financial support. Americans regarded Hague School pictures in the same light as old Dutch masters concerning the content of the pictures. They understood these contemporary paintings to reveal the same virtues as the older pictures.

George Eastman, originator of Eastman Kodak photographic processes, assembled an art collection in his native Rochester, New York. Unable or unwilling to purchase more than one painting each by Rembrandt, Hals, and Jan van de Cappelle in the old master class, the majority of his collection represented contemporary Dutch, French, and American artists. Of the Hague School, he purchased four paintings each by Jacob Maris and Anton Mauve, two Jozef Israëls watercolors, and individual examples by Pieter Stortenbeker, Neuhuys, and Blommers. Eastman rounded out his collection with Dutch scenes by the American painters William Henry Howe and Charles Paul Gruppe. Eastman's combination of contemporary Dutch and American views of Holland was not unusual. American artists actively promoted the work of contemporary Dutch painters.

Residents of Rochester, such as George Eastman, had plenty of opportunity to see the work of contemporary Dutch artists. In 1890, the local artist Emma Lampert, who had studied in the Netherlands and knew many of the Hague School painters, selected work by George Poggenbeek, Jacob Simon Hendrik Kever, and Nicolaas Bastert for the annual art exhibition. Although these men were considered lesser artists in Holland, they were much admired in the United States. Charles Paul Gruppe, who settled in Rochester after many years as an expatriate in Holland, also brought back paintings by Mesdag, Blommers, Maris, and others, which he exhibited in his studio and published in the local newspaper. Two local galleries,

Powers and Rundel's, sold paintings and reproductions by contemporary Dutch artists. Finally, the Rochester Memorial Art Gallery organized loan exhibitions which included contemporary Dutch art from the local collections of Mrs. Jesse Lindsay, Elizabeth Clarke, Mrs. Charles DePuy, and George Eastman. By all of these agencies, contemporary Dutch art became popular in Rochester, in spite of the city's small size and relatively isolated location.

Rochester may have sustained a particularly propitious environment for the marketing of Dutch art. Founded by Dutch colonists in the seventeenth century, a second wave of Dutch immigrants renewed this heritage in the mid-nineteenth century. Rochester's Reformed Churches still performed services in the Dutch language in the first decade of the twentieth century. Nevertheless, the predilection Rochesterians displayed for the purchase of paintings by contemporary Dutch artists and by local artists who painted in the Netherlands may be found in many cities at that time.

Washington, D.C. businessman and real estate financier Thomas E. Waggaman, for example, showcased the modern Dutch school in his collection. He purchased work on his travels and accepted advice from a local artist, Richard Norris Brooke, whose Dutch landscapes Waggaman also purchased. In a special report on private galleries in Washington, D.C., the *American Art Annual* of 1898 admired his oil paintings by Israëls, Mauve, the Maris brothers, and Neuhuys, but concluded:

> It is in the lower gallery, which is exclusively given up to water colors by more than a score of the foremost Dutch artists, that one finds the cream of Mr. Waggaman's collection. ... there is hardly a single artist of prominence who is not represented. There are no less than four subjects by Mauve and there are excellent examples of Bosboom, Israëls, Blommers, Kever, Ter Meulen, Poggenbeek, Valkenburg, Weissenbruch, Mesdag, and Tony Offermans, to enumerate but a few of the names. Certainly it is a choice collection, and a visit seems almost like a trip to Holland.

The reviewer's last statement provides another key to the American appreciation for galleries full of Dutch pictures. For those who had been to Holland, it served to refresh the memories of their travels. For others, a visit to a gallery provided a temporary substitute for a vacation in Holland.

Paintings of the Hague School were readily available to collectors of substance, without leaving the United States. The New York dealer

William Schaus traveled regularly in Holland making contacts with the Dutch artists to provide pictures for his clients. Other American dealers who imported Hague School paintings included Knoedler, James Inglis, the Holland Art Gallery, and Scott and Fowles, all in New York City. Modern Dutch paintings could be seen at all of these establishments, especially at the Holland Art Gallery, the sole purpose of which was to promote Dutch art in the United States.

In addition, the dispersal of some of the original Hague School collections in America gave other collectors a chance to add good examples to their holdings. According to Thomas Waggaman's obituary in the New York Times (28 June 1906), his attempt to place his art collection in trust for the Catholic University revealed a four million dollar debt, leading instead to his bankruptcy and the dispersal of his collection. Others benefited from such auctions. C. K. G. Billings of Fort Tryon Hall (now The Cloisters) in New York City collected paintings by all the major Hague School artists and several of the less well-known Dutch artists who were then popular in the United States. He purchased fifteen of his pictures from the sale of Anna Kendall's extensive modern Dutch collection. Kendall, a resident of Lamoille, Illinois, had assembled an impressive group of twenty-seven Hague School paintings, valued at about $45,000. Other purchasers at the Kendall sale included James G. Shepherd of Scranton, Pennsylvania, whose wholesale collecting of Mathijs Maris had inspired the article in the Rotterdam newspaper quoted earlier, and W. S. Thurber, who spent about $14,000 to acquire three Mauves and examples by Weissenbruck, Bosboom, and Jacob and Willem Maris.[14]

The prices of canvases by even the best known Hague School artists, while substantial, were considerably more modest than prices for old Dutch masters. At the Kendall auction, *First Steps* by Jozef Israëls brought $4,300, and pictures by Jacob Maris, Anton Mauve, and Albert Neuhuys sold for between $3,000 and $3,500 each. Although a few collectors of old masters also bought contemporary work, and vice versa, generally the Hague School provided images for collectors at the next rung down the socioeconomic ladder. The availability of this less expensive Dutch art broadened the range of Americans who could afford to hang fine Dutch paintings on their walls.

An outstanding collection of 332 works by modern Dutch artists at the World's Columbian Exposition in 1893 gave an important boost to the reputation of the Hague School. Millions of people from throughout the United States traveled to Chicago to see the exposition, and many of them took in Holland's exhibits. Reviewing the exhibition later, Lillie Derby noted the same democratic appeal in the art of the Hague School that Americans usually attributed to the old Dutch masters:

> One entered the gray-tinted galleries of Holland with a sigh of restfulness and content. The effort to discriminate between the good and the bad was no longer necessary in the general excellence . . . . For the attractiveness of the Holland pictures had not that conspicuous quality that clamors loudly for admiration; it was a modest loveliness that appealed to all with gentle, although irresistible, insistence.[15]

Since American patrons usually purchased Hague School pictures to decorate their homes, the landscapes with "modest loveliness that appealed to all" and the domesticity of the small figurative pieces suited this art to its decorative purpose.

After the success of their 1893 exhibition, Mesdag and other artists of the Hague School held one-person exhibitions in the United States and often exhibited in the American annuals (FIG. 6). Blommers made two trips to the United States, the first in 1904 to visit Pittsburgh, Chicago, Boston, Philadelphia, Washington, and St. Louis, and the second eight years later to paint a portrait of Andrew Carnegie for the Dutch government. Wherever he went, the local press made much of his visit and Blommers used the opportunity to market his work (FIG. 7).

Blommers understood what the American audience appreciated in his art and he stressed the affinity between his subjects and seventeenth-century subjects, and between the Netherlands and the United States. For example, Blommers told a reporter that he liked New York because of all the Dutch names he saw.

> [They] give me a feeling that the founders of New York must have loved the same soil, the same dunes, canals, and rich 'polders' that I have tried to put on canvas; and that, when they first erected their unpretentious homes on Manhattan, at Albany, and other spots along Hudson's river, the interiors where they dwelt must have been a good deal like the old houses of North Brabant and Zeeland, which I have sometimes painted.[16]

Blommers's statement to the reporter conjured images of the Dutch colonists who founded New York living in the Holland of Rembrandt and Hals. By aligning himself with artists of an earlier age and associating his Dutch subjects with American colonists he

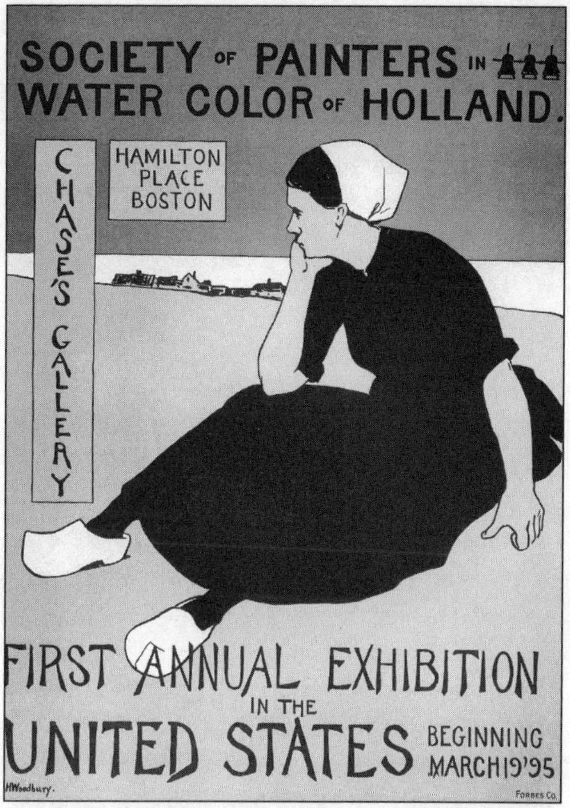

FIG. 6 *Charles Woodbury, a Boston artist who spent much of his time in Holland, designed this poster for the first American exhibition of the Society of Painters in Water Color of Holland. The exhibition traveled to New York and Boston in 1895 and helped familiarize American artists and collectors with contemporary Dutch watercolor techniques.*

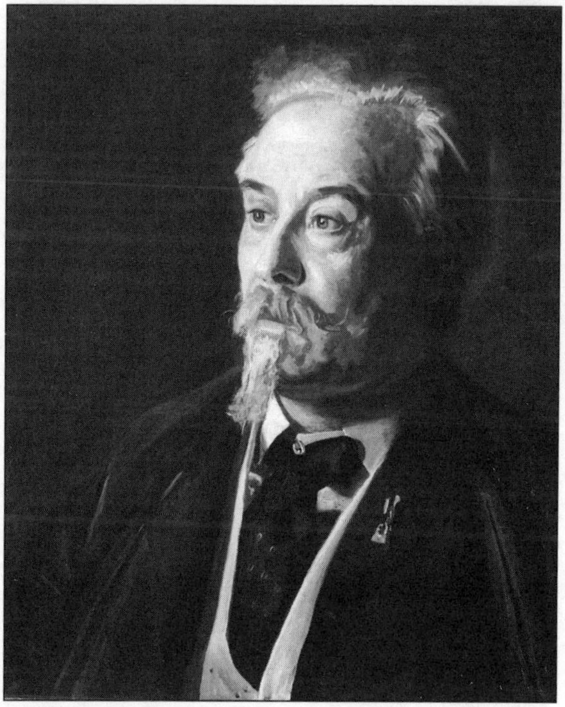

FIG. 7 *Regarded as a lesser master in the Netherlands, Blommers was one of the most popular Hague School artists in the United States. Thomas Eakins painted this portrait of him and inscribed it "To my friend B.J. Blommers."*

endeared himself to his audience. By painting common people in their "unpretentious" homes he convinced Americans that he, like his illustrious predecessors, took a democratic approach to art.

Paintings of the Hague School reinforced the notion instilled in Americans by the old Dutch masters that the Dutch were an honest, democratic, home-loving people. Hague School paintings helped extend Americans' view of seventeenth-century Holland to contemporary Holland.

COPIES AND REPRODUCTIONS

While the prices of work by Blommers and his colleagues suited the purses of some collectors who could not afford old Dutch masters, at the next step down the financial scale, a market existed for copies in all media after Dutch paintings of both the seventeenth and nineteenth centuries. The copy market stands apart from the illicit market for spurious old masters mentioned earlier. Art schools and public institutions such as libraries and athenaeums often desired oil copies after old masters and, less frequently, after modern Dutch painters. Artists also made copies for their own instruction and that of their students. Mary Cassatt, William Merritt Chase, and John Singer Sargent are just a few of the more notable artists who kept such copies in their studios (FIG. 8).

The market for inexpensive copies after the old masters also served to decorate private homes and offices (FIG. 9). Such copies allowed Americans who could not afford the real thing, or who admired an unattainable picture and wanted something better than a color lithograph reproduction of it, to hang Dutch oil paintings on their walls. Benjamin Franklin Landis, a Lancaster, Pennsylvania painter living in Amsterdam, apparently located a good market for copies, for he obtained sixty copy permits from the Rijksmuseum between 1898 and 1913, an extraordinary number for one artist. Since many of the permits allowed him to replicate well known pictures, it seems clear that his patrons sought copies for instruction or decoration, rather than for fraudulent resale.

A closer look at the copy permits obtained from the Rijksmuseum by American artists and art students between 1878 and 1915 reveals their admiration for Frans Hals, Rembrandt, and Vermeer above all others. The painting in the Rijksmuseum most frequently copied by American artists at this time was *De Nar* (The Fool) by Frans Hals. Scholars have long argued over the attribution

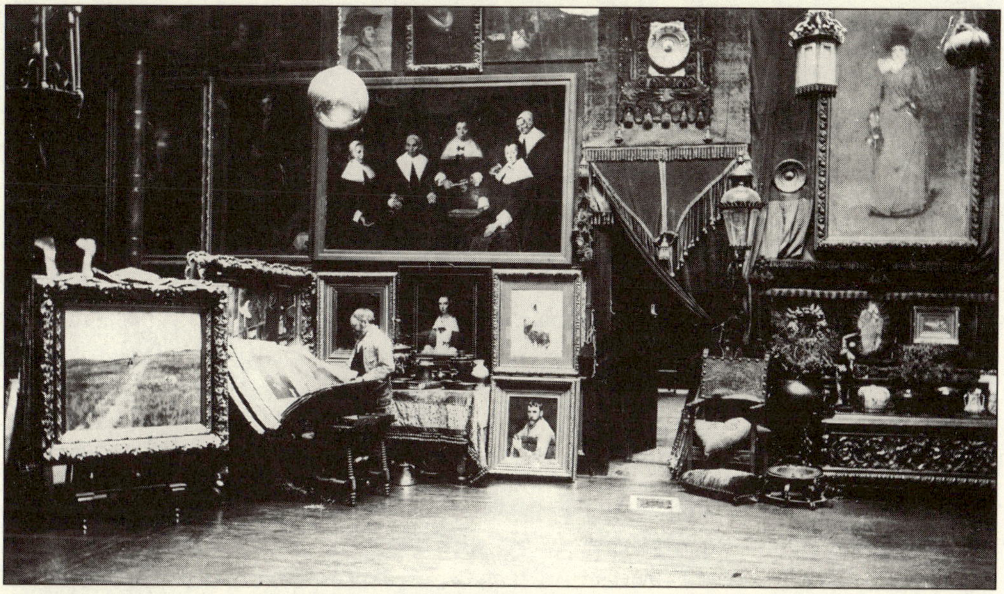

FIG. 8 *William Merritt Chase is one of many American artists who cherished their copies after the old Dutch masters. He is pictured here, c.1895, in his Tenth Street studio in New York City with his copy of Frans Hals's* Regentesses.

FIG. 9 *Edward Bok decorated his office with reproductions after famous old Dutch masters. His influential position as editor of the* Ladies' Home Journal *allowed him to promote the taste for Dutch motifs and decoration in American homes.*

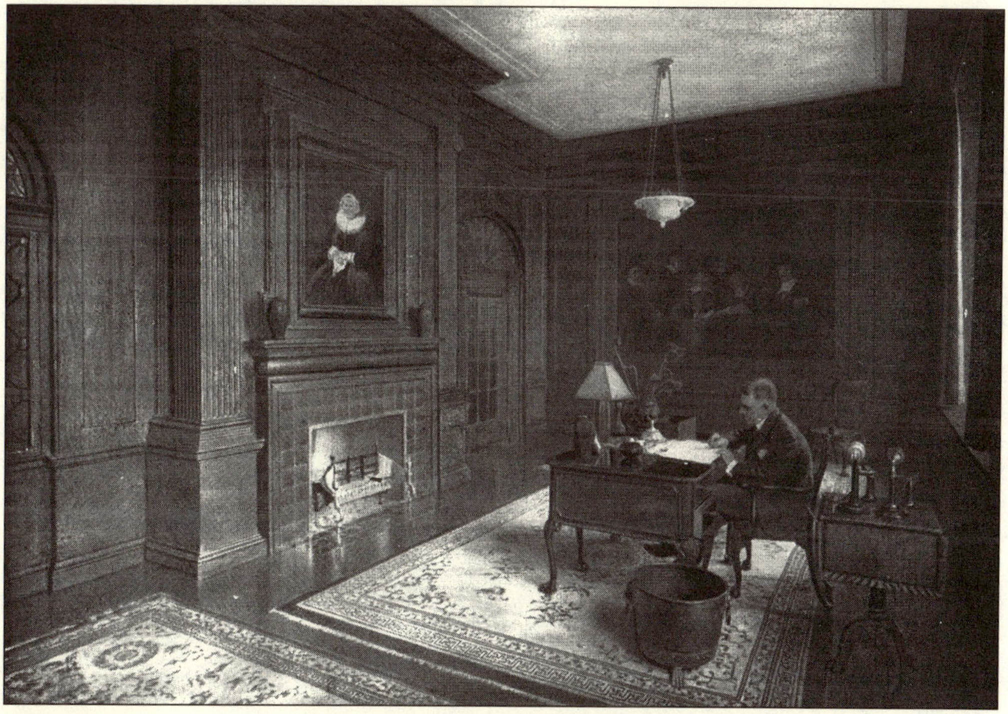

of this picture. The most recent study of Frans Hals by Seymour Slive suggests that it is a copy by an anonymous artist after Frans Hals's *Buffoon Playing a Lute* in the Louvre. The museum listed it as a Frans Hals at that time and most artists had little reason to question it, but the fact that the favorite may have been a copy (making the copies of it copies of copies, at best) highlights the equivocal position the copy has occupied in art history. The next most popular pictures among American artists were *The Merry Drinker* by Frans Hals and *Woman Reading a Letter* by Vermeer. Other frequently copied paintings included *Elizabeth Bas* by Rembrandt (since reattributed to Ferdinand Bol), *The Syndics* by Rembrandt, and *Kitchen Maid* by Vermeer.

The many articles on seventeenth- and nineteenth-century Dutch artists that appeared in art journals and popular magazines at the turn of the century also helped popularize Dutch art in the United States. A British writer observed: "In America artistic matters are treated in the best circles in a far more serious way than in England. The young American reads about each artist of fame, selects the masters he or she personally prefers—for the ladies, having more leisure, enter with completely intelligent zeal into the pursuit—and then study them and their works in the most careful way."[17]

Even if one had not the means to obtain original work or good oil copies, reproductions in these magazines and fine art reproductions by numerous printing firms allowed the decoration of home walls with Dutch pictures. The popular educational magazine *The Chautauquan* advertised portfolios of the work of Mauve, Mesdag, Maris, and Israëls for twenty-five cents apiece. Each portfolio contained fifty halftone pictures by one of the artists. The pictures, available from the Chautauqua Press in 1909, complimented an earlier series of old Dutch masters produced for *Chautauquan* readers by Bates and Guild Company of Boston.

The *Ladies' Home Journal* went into the picture business with even more zeal. As part of a "systematic plan for improving the pictures on the walls of the American home," the *Journal* began printing four-color reproductions of art from American collections, including examples by Rembrandt, Hobbema, Hals, Mauve, and Vermeer from the homes of Morgan, Frick, Widener, Altman, Johnson, and others. The series of forty masterpieces included only one American artist—Whistler, and several Italian, French, and English painters. The strong showing of Dutch masters probably owed much to the fact that the Journal's editor, Edward Bok, had emigrated from the Netherlands to the United States as a child. According to Bok's autobiography, the *Ladies' Home Journal* distributed over 70 million prints from this old master series.

The effect of such cheap illustrations, and of the numerous articles about Dutch art, can be seen in some of the letters to the editor of *The Chautauquan*. One writer stated that after studying the Dutch pictures in the magazine for a year, she and her husband bought several works by contemporary Dutch painters to celebrate this turning point in their lives. But even those who could not afford to buy pictures participated in the vogue for Dutch art. Another correspondent noted that his increased awareness of Dutch art had caused him to develop the picture habit:

> My business requires much traveling and I often have spare time. This year I've hunted up the local picture gallery wherever I could find one and examined the Dutch paintings. In one town where there was no gallery they sent me to a local picture dealer who I found had a hobby for Dutch pictures. He showed me some very interesting things and I spent a delightful hour....I never before realized what an increasing source of pleasure the study of pictures could become. My family take a great interest in these investigations and when I get home almost the first question they ask is about my picture adventures.[18]

As record-breaking prices and blockbuster exhibitions brought the old Dutch masters further into the public eye, as work by modern Dutch artists became more widely available, as magazine illustrations and fine art reproductions brought Dutch art into middle-class homes, more and more Americans became interested in Holland. And the Holland they sought was the one described in genre, landscape, and portrait paintings of the old Dutch republic.

AMERICAN ART

Contemporary Dutch artists' pictures reminiscent of the old Dutch republic certainly attracted Americans, but such scenes painted by American artists held an additional appeal. Besides fulfilling the patron's desire to be in fashion by acquiring pictures of Holland, they allowed viewers and collectors to experience a patriotic pride in native accomplishment and to exercise their patriotism by supporting American artists.

Literally hundreds of American artists went to the Netherlands between 1880 and 1920 to draw and paint the picturesque landscape, people, and architecture. They included the famous (Elizabeth Nourse, John Singer Sargent, James Abbott McNeil Whistler), the unknown (Amy Cross, Pauline Dohn, Parker Mann) and the once famous but now forgotten (Charles Paul Gruppe, George Hitchcock, Walter MacEwen). Some settled in Holland for as long as thirty years, sending their work home to newspapers, magazines, art exhibitions, museums, and private collections throughout the United States. Others stayed only a week or two, filling sketchbooks from which they would later paint pictures of Holland in their American studios. The market was so strong that American dealers sometimes financed artists' trips to the Netherlands in order to replenish their stock. William Merritt Chase, Robert Henri, Emma Lampert, and Alexander Robinson, among others, took classes of pupils to study the old masters and learn to paint Dutch pictures on the spot. A few artists married Hollanders and never returned to the United States, but nearly all brought or sent their pictures home.

The influence of Dutch artists teaching in the United States undoubtedly encouraged some artists to turn to Dutch subjects. In Philadelphia, for instance, young art students took lessons at the Van der Whelen school, where portrait painter Cecilia Beaux remembered the director spoke with such a thick Dutch accent that one had to listen closely to understand his lectures. Beaux went to Holland in the summer of 1900, painting several important pictures in Volendam and Laren, but she concluded that France provided better sketching ground and did not return. Robert Swain Gifford learned marine painting from the Dutch artist Albert van Beest in Fairhaven, Massachusetts before painting his own seascapes in Holland. He exhibited his Dutch marine paintings at the National Academy of Design and the Boston Art Club in 1883, and later painted and etched Dutch landscapes. Aspiring artists in Grand Rapids, Michigan took lessons from the Dutch-born landscape painter Marinus Hartung. These are just a few of the many Dutch artists teaching in the United States who helped inspire their pupils to travel to Holland and paint Dutch subjects.

The excellent American market for Dutch pictures attracted many artists for purely economic reasons. For example, the Reverend James Hogarth Dennis allegedly discovered that he could not make a living in the church and began making long sojourns in the Netherlands where he produced small paintings to sell locally in his native Rochester, New York. His efforts as an amateur painter supplemented his income as a cleric. For other artists, the strong American market for such work brought both fame and wealth. Gari Melchers and George Hitchcock produced pictures in Holland over a period of three decades, establishing solid international reputations with their Dutch paintings, which were much in demand as fine art reproductions (FIG. 10c).

So important was the Dutch experience in American art that magazines like *The Art Amateur* provided artists unable to travel to the Netherlands with instructions for making Dutch pictures at home (FIG. 11). Writing in the *The Art Amateur* in July 1887, Charlotte Adams advised readers to form a costume class for which they should create a Hollandish costume from a discarded fisherman's coat, choose a model with Dutch features, and arrange a pose based on a famous painting or a book illustration. The Palette Art Company of New York offered further aid to the artist at home by selling prints illustrating native Dutch costumes. For the landscape painter, periodicals including *The Art Amateur* and *Palette and Bench* regularly published color plates after Dutch-subject paintings by

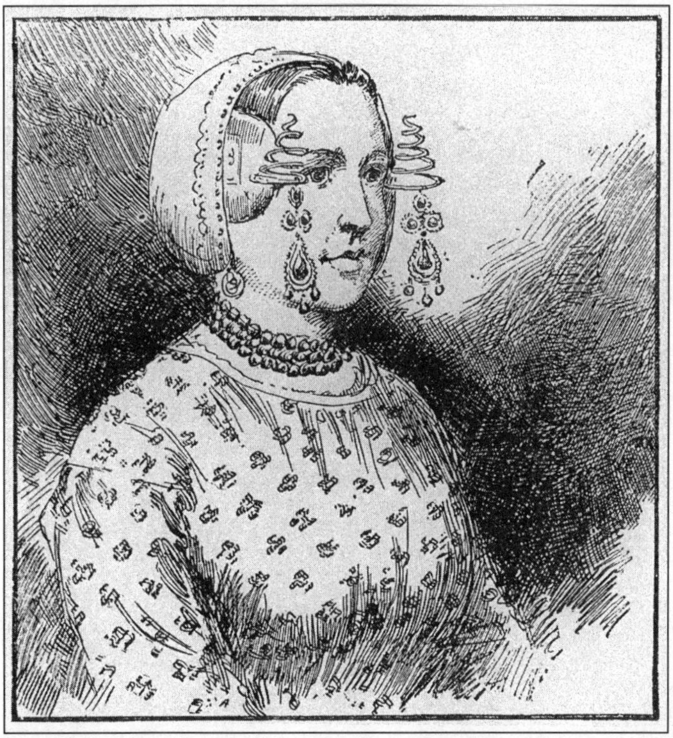

FIG. 11 *The availability of illustrations showing Dutch costumes, like this one from a series published in* The Art Amateur *in 1887, encouraged the production of Dutch genre paintings in American studios.*

American artists with complete instructions for copying them in oils or watercolors (FIG. 12). Such practices resulted in pictures informed more by preconceived notions about Holland derived from prints, photographs, the old masters, the Hague School, and popular literature, than from reality.

More original, but equally improbable compositions resulted from the use of studio props that artists brought back and shared

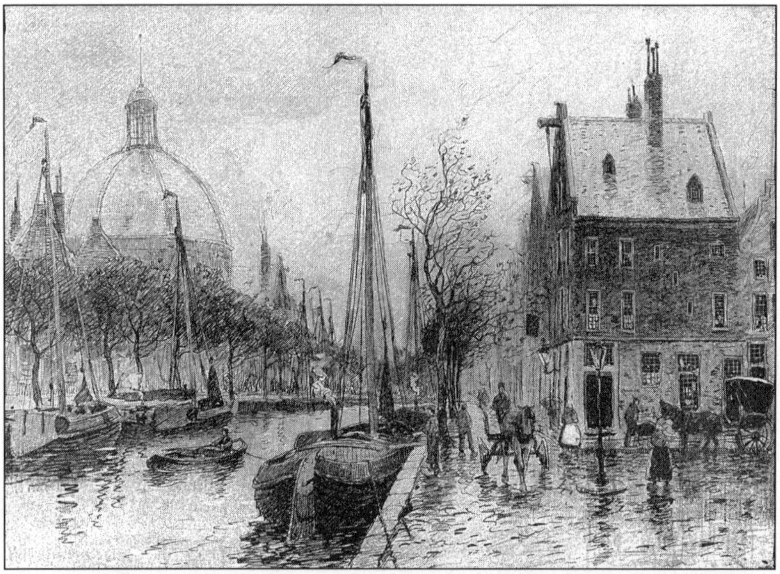

FIG. 12 *Henry Ward Ranger published many articles explaining how to paint in the Dutch method of watercolors. He illustrated them with drawings after his watercolors like* A Wet Day in Amsterdam, *published in 1888.*

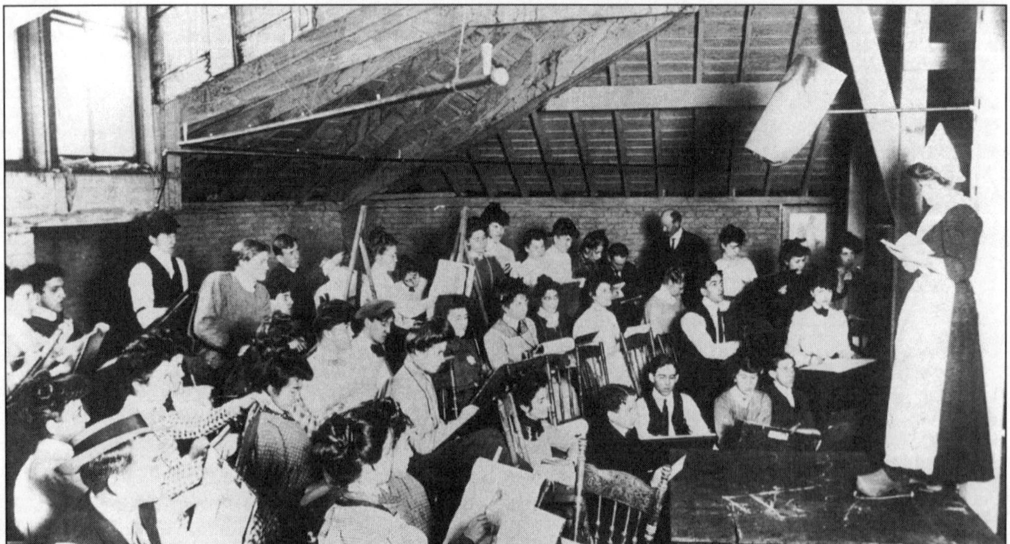

FIG. 13 *Frederick C. Gottwald's class at the Cleveland Institute of Art learned to draw and paint Dutch peasant pictures when a member of the class dressed up in a costume Gottwald brought back from Holland and posed for the others.*

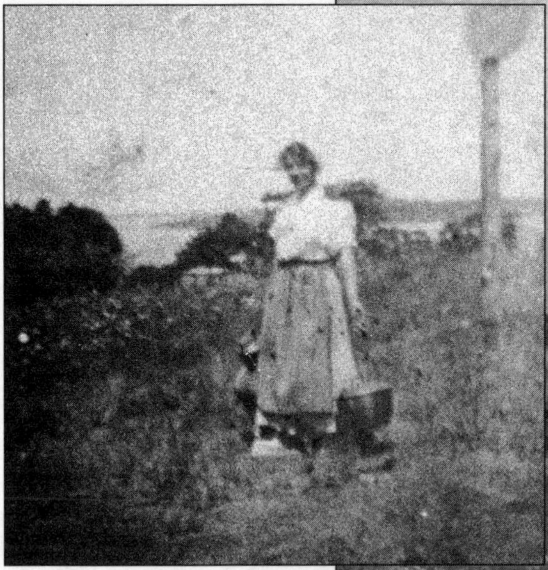

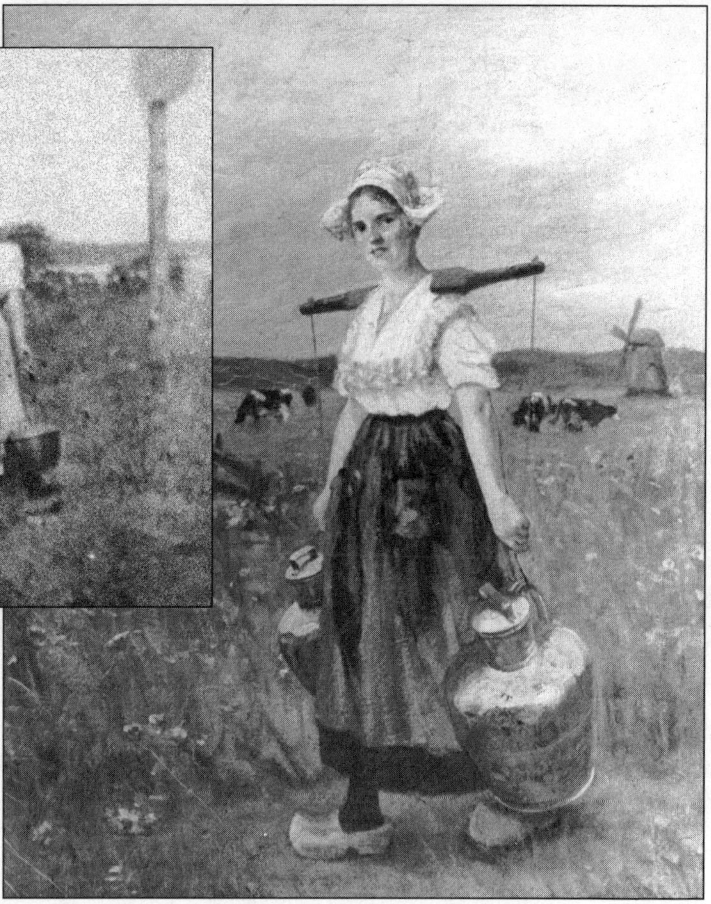

FIG. 14 *A poorly preserved photograph found in Oscar Miller's Portsmouth, Rhode Island studio (inset) reveals that the artist used a local model and American setting to paint his picture of a* Dutch Milkmaid.

with colleagues in their home towns. Frederick C. Gottwald supplied the students of the Cleveland Institute of Art with a complete Dutch costume and the pupils took turns posing in it to give their classmates practice painting and drawing the Dutch peasant (FIG. 13). Emma Lampert purchased crates of Dutch goods with which she stocked the art room of the Mechanics Institute in Rochester. By these methods and the application of creative imagination, many "Dutch" paintings were produced in the United States for the ever-growing market.

Oscar Miller's painting of a Dutch maiden in a typical Holland meadow with cows and a windmill in the background was painted in Bristol Ferry, New Jersey, using an American model dressed in a Dutch cap and wooden shoes and carrying a Dutch yoke and brass jugs (FIG. 14). The distant hills and wood rail fence reflect American rather than Dutch landscape motifs, and of the model's costume, only the headdress is authentic. Similarly, *A Dutch Girl* by Rebekah

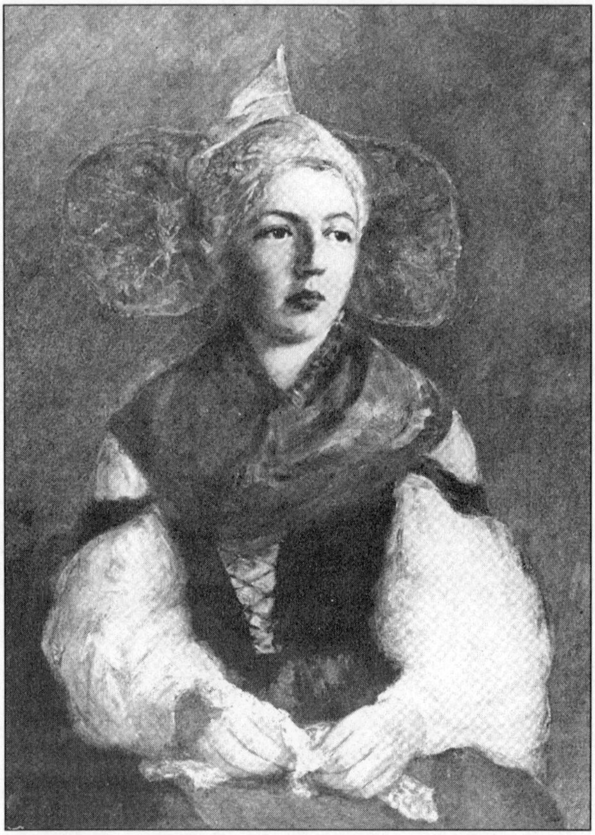

FIG. 15 *The little-known Western artist Rebekah Rogers painted this picture of* A Dutch Girl *from a homemade or imaginary costume. Any sufficiently exotic headdress of lace passed for Dutch in the United States.*

Rogers combines parts of costumes from Volendam and Overijssel with an old English laced bodice, and a liberal dose of imagination (FIG. 15). Homegrown fantasies such as these found favor in the American market as readily as the carefully documented efforts of expatriate artists in the Netherlands.

Through the collection and exhibition of old Dutch masters, related work by the Hague School artists, and scenes of contemporary Holland by American artists at home and abroad, the image of Holland spread across America. It was an image that recalled Motley's heroic Dutch Republic and focused on costumes and customs that were already disappearing in Holland. But, above all, it was an image that Americans related to because it embodied qualities they particularly admired: democratic middle-class values, emphasis on family life, bourgeois ideals and goals, and an affluent consumer culture produced by the industry and genius of the common people.

TWO

American Artists in Holland

Throughout the first three quarters of the nineteenth century, American artists made the Grand Tour of Europe as an essential capstone to their education. Until the last quarter of the century, that journey usually included the briefest of detours through the Netherlands to see the old Dutch masters. The popular illustrator Felix O.C. Darley's experience at mid-century may be taken as representative. Darley stopped only in Amsterdam and The Hague. In a published account of his tour, he described the costume worn by a few rural Dutch visitors to the city, the typical Dutch landscape through which he passed and, at much greater length, the pictures he saw in public and private collections. After mentioning the requisite Rembrandts and Paulus Potter's famous painting of a bull, he summarized, "[their] subjects are often disgusting, but their art, splendid, their power of imitation marvelous, and their color perfect."[19] Seventeenth-century Dutch painting ranked high in the nineteenth-century estimate of art and before the last quarter of the century the best of it could only be seen in quantity in the Netherlands. Thus, generation followed generation of American artists to Holland primarily to study the paintings of the Golden Age.

In the last quarter of the century, when Dutch art became more prevalent in the United States, the goals and experiences of American artists in Holland began to change. Although the old masters remained an attraction, sketching the contemporary Dutch life and landscape became the primary goal. In place of the one- or two-day Grand Tour visit, most artists now stayed for months, and many

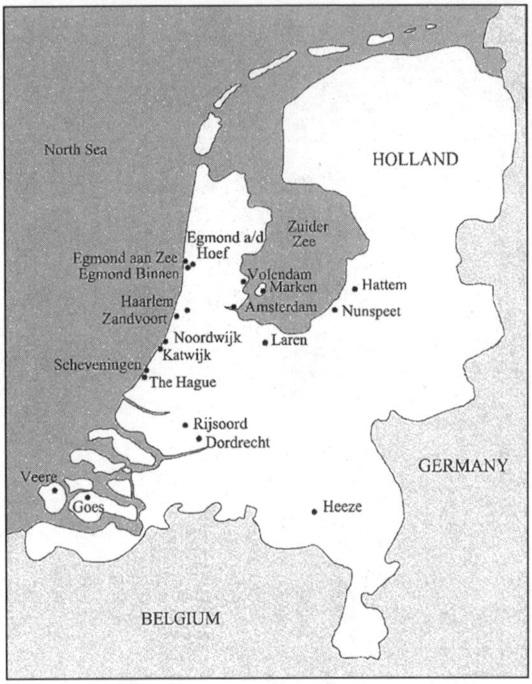

FIG. 16 *Map of the Netherlands around 1900 showing the towns and cities most frequented by American artists.*

returned yearly. Instead of settling in the cities, they gravitated toward small rural villages, away from tourists, railroads, and modern influences. The advent of impressionism and the emphasis on open-air painting in the French schools motivated many to seek out rural sketching grounds for the summers. As word of picturesque subject matter and congenial environments spread, colonies of American artists developed in the small towns of Egmond, Volendam, and Laren in North Holland; Katwijk and Rijsoord in South Holland; and Hattem-Nunspeet in Gelderland (FIG. 16).

The artists' increased contact with Dutch country people contributed to the image they constructed of Holland as a premodern agrarian idyll. At the same time, barriers of language, culture, and occupation between Dutch and American residents in the art colonies furthered the tendency to rely on preconceptions and surface impressions. Each art colony developed its individual subject specializations and preferred style, but all portrayed the general characteristics that Dutch art and American literature had prepared them to see: independence, honesty, piety, strength, and endurance. They often focused on the outer trappings of lace headdresses and wooden shoes, formulating a stereotypical and superficial Dutch image, even when painting portraits of specific people. Nowhere is this more evident than in the art produced at Volendam.

VOLENDAM

Volendam lies eleven miles north of Amsterdam on the very edge of the Zuider Zee. In the 1880s it was an isolated spot, accessible to foreigners only by a slow-moving canalboat or a hired carriage. Its isolation had ensured that it retained those traits most admired by artists. After visiting Holland as a student in one of William Merritt Chase's classes, Charles Sheeler wrote: "Holland was both picturesque and strange. Picturesqueness plus strangeness equaled paintable—then the most overworked word in our vocabulary." Of all the Dutch art colonies, Volendam possessed strangeness and the picturesque in the greatest abundance. Residents wore costumes of almost uniform design, one for men and one for women, with personal variations restricted to the choice of fabrics and placement of patches. The costume delighted figure painters, while the tiny houses, tall dikes, outlying windmill, and little port full of brown-sailed boats provided views for the landscapist. "Not in finding views lies the difficulty, but in selecting them," noted the photographer Florence Albrecht, a sentiment repeated by numerous artists when faced with the abundance of raw art material in Volendam. Because its mien was so strange, even for Holland, Volendam attracted large numbers of artists, and later, tourists.[20]

The extent of Volendam's international character also distinguished it from other colonies. Artists from the Netherlands, France, Germany, and England joined those from Hungary, Austria, the United States, and Japan in recording the life of this fishing village. The town accepted all comers impartially and the Hotel Spaander, begun in 1881 on the main dike, provided accommodation and a place for the artists to mingle. A smiling Volendamer on a painted sign in the doorway announced "Artists Welcome" (FIG. 17).

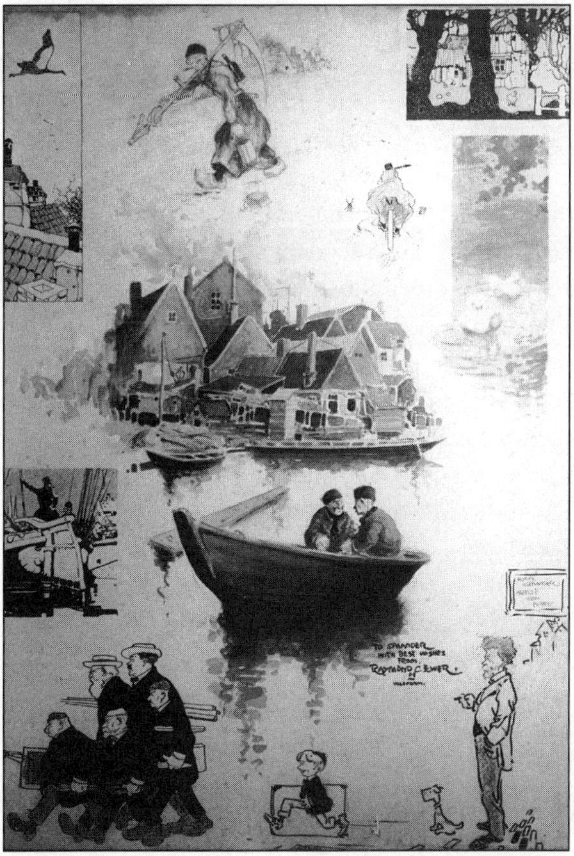

FIG. 17 *Raymond C. Ewer gave Leendert Spaander this multimedia impression of Volendam in 1909. At the bottom, Ewer drew Spaander watching a group of artists leave his hotel for a day of sketching.*

Illustrators did the most to bring Volendam into vogue among English-speaking artists. The Anglo-American painter–illustrator George Henry Boughton and the young American illustrator Edwin Austin Abbey came to Volendam in 1880 on assignment for *Harper's New Monthly Magazine* (FIG. 18). Although this town played only a small part in their Dutch travels, the resulting articles, art prints, and books became so popular that they exerted a beneficial influence in promoting the place. Their brief time in Volendam forced them to give only a surface impression. Abbey described their *modus operandi*:

> We were a little over twenty days in Holland, and visited nearly thirty towns, beside doing a lot of country travel, so you can readily understand that our sketches are of the scantiest description. . . . The mere physical fatigue of travelling at such a rate almost prevented any work at all. At several of the most interesting places we saw we were unable to stop more than an hour. I finally hit upon the plan of buying the complete costume of the peasants of each district, and all the photographs I could get, and these, with the roughest possible notes, some written, some hastily sketched, are all I have had to work from in the drawings sent you.[21]

Although their work received acclaim throughout the United States and became a model of the "real Dutch type" for other artists, by the artist's own admission their images captured only a brief impression of surface appearance. The unique costume, striking color, and other visual oddities of Volendam described by Boughton and Abbey, attracted many other illustrators, who contributed to creating the stereotype of the happy Hollander.

A portfolio of drawings entitled "Three Dutch Types from Volendam" by Ohio artist Iris M. Andrews typifies foreign illustrators' preoccupation with costume and surface appearance. Her types were already familiar to many Americans when they appeared in *Century Magazine* in 1905. *Always Knitting* (FIG. 19) visualized the observation, often repeated in tourists' letters and travel literature, that Dutch females knitted ceaselessly from babyhood to the grave. *Milking-Time* depicted a beaming young Volendamer with a milk pail on her arm, a type interchangeable with the flower seller who usually appeared in illustrations with a flower basket or buckets of flowers on a shoulder yoke. Andrews made no attempt at character portrayal or capturing the spirit of the individual. A visual type sufficed for the magazine audience and she simply repeated the stereo-

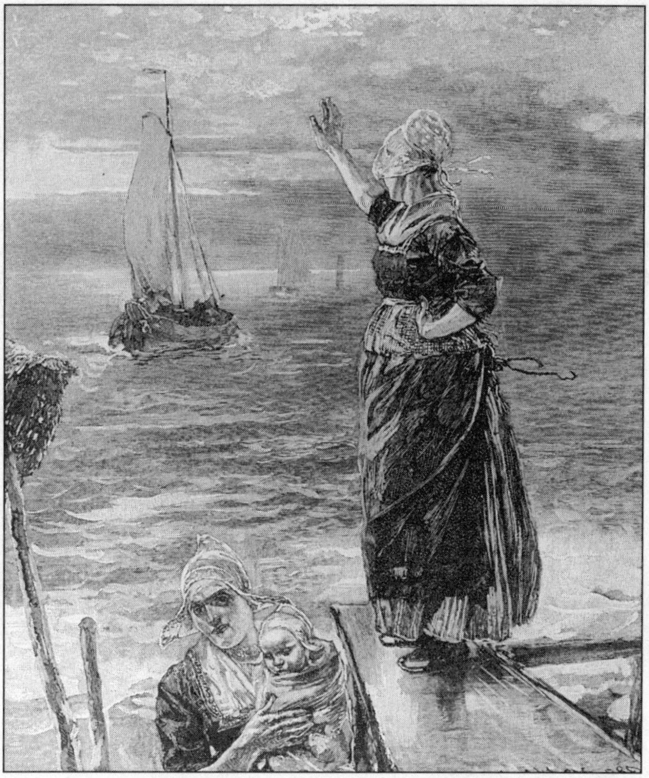

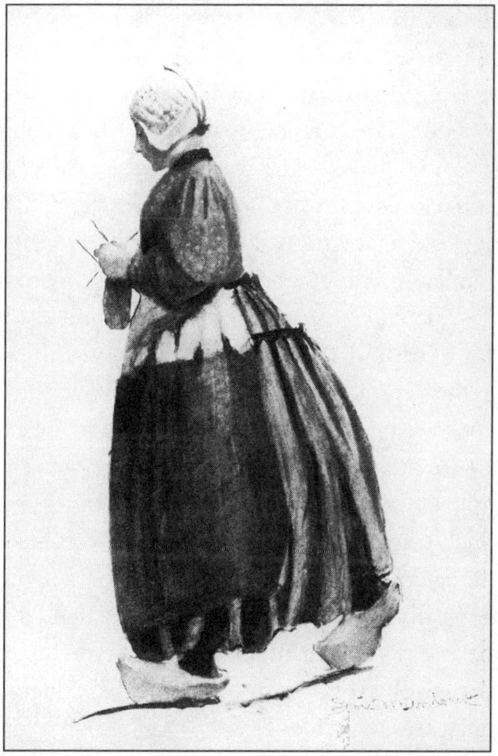

FIG. 18 *Edwin Austin Abbey's illustration of Volendam women seeing their fishermen off at dawn appeared in* Harper's New Monthly Magazine *in 1883. As one of the earliest widely published images of Volendam, it helped attract other artists to the town.*

FIG. 19 *The Dutch woman's habit of knitting whenever her hands were not otherwise occupied inspired Iris Andrews' picture,* Always Knitting.

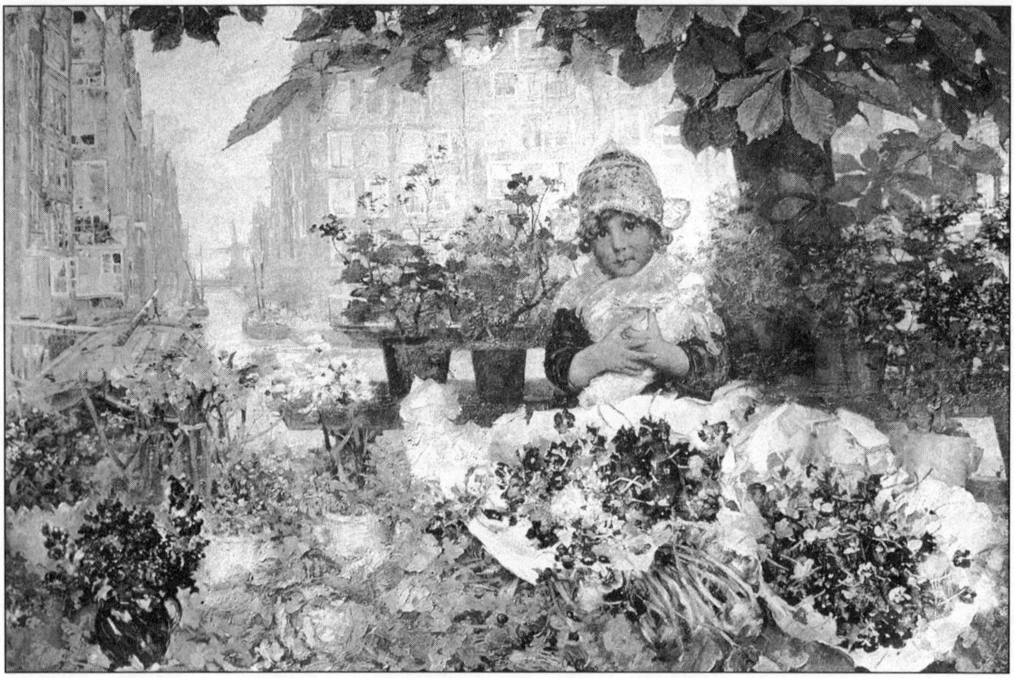

FIG. 20 *Orrin Peck's charmingly picturesque painting of a little Volendam girl in a flower market,* Stiefmutterchen, *typifies the tourist view of Holland. Images of this type appeared frequently on souvenir postcards.*

type of the happy Volendamer lazing away the day in idle talk or light household tasks.

Orrin Peck captured the American tourist image of Holland at its most charmingly picturesque in *Stiefmutterchen* (FIG. 20). He posed a little girl in her winged lace cap amidst an abundance of cut and potted flowers. A tree branch arches over her head, completing the bower setting. Past its leaves one sees city canals walled by tall brick canal houses, typical Dutch canalboats, and in the distance a single windmill silhouetted against the sky. Peck's subject gazes wide-eyed at the viewer while clutching her doll to her chest, a picture of sweet innocence. The calculated cuteness (however unlikely it may have been to see a four-year-old Volendamer seated alone in the middle of an Amsterdam flower market) combined with all the visual cues Americans expected of a Dutch picture—tulips, lace cap, canal, and windmill—to guarantee audience satisfaction. Peck and his colleagues, Raphael Beck of Buffalo and John Rettig of Cincinnati, painted fishermen smoking, children knitting, lovers skating, flower-girls, and milkmaids to supply the market for souvenir pictures produced by a rapidly growing tourist trade in Volendam after 1900.

One of the most striking qualities about Volendam, its color, caused the artist–illustrators to dub it the Magenta Village. According to Edward Penfield:

With partly closed eyes, looking down the broad pathway, magenta was overwhelming. It showed on the red tiles of the tiny houses, on the shirts of the men, it peeped up from the brick pavement, and a soft haze near the horizon scintillated its colors. The blue and black in the girls' costumes and the greenish-blue gables served only to accentuate the color and made it more pleasing.[22]

Penfield employed broad washes of magenta in his drawing of a Volendam man at leisure (FIG. 21c). Among the Dutch art colonies where Americans congregated, an emphasis on drawing; flat local color; clear, concise composition; and commercial purpose (all evident in Penfield's picture) is unique to Volendam. Volendam contained all the ingredients for popular success in an age when world travel, exotica, and picturesqueness were the rage. Its subjects appealed to the masses, and posters, prints, inexpensive watercolors, illustrated articles, and picture books supplied the popular demand as expensive oil paintings could not. Through the efforts of illustrators, Volendam appeared so widely in books, posters, magazines, and advertisements that it became synonymous with the Netherlands for many Americans.

After 1900, as young Volendamers abandoned the costume and customs of their elders and moved to the cities, the old-fashioned picturesqueness upon which artists depended became harder to find. As an aid to his artist trade, Spaander redecorated a room in the hotel to create an "Old Volendam" setting that would serve as a studio for the genre painters (FIG. 22). Furnished with delftware, lace curtains, old Dutch cabinets, and a tiled fireplace, it ensured the

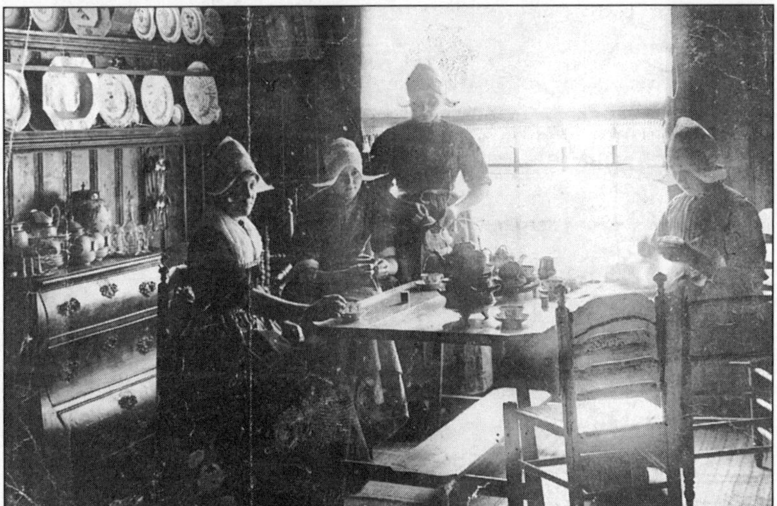

FIG. 22 *Many Salon paintings by artists of all nationalities were produced in this "Old Volendam" room at the Hotel Spaander using local models.*

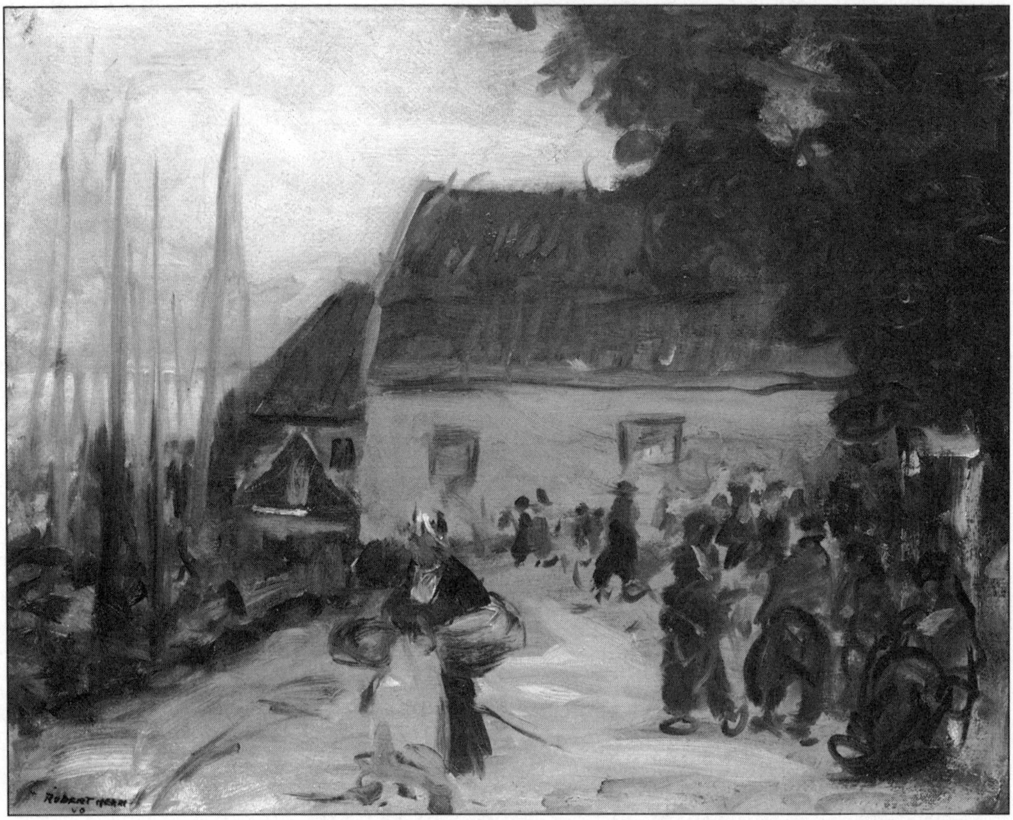

FIG. 23 *Using* ala prima *techniques and more attention to paint quality than subject matter, Robert Henri modernized the traditional vision of Volendam. He worked in Volendam in 1907 and perhaps briefly in 1910 when he painted* Volendam Street Scene.

continuation of traditional genre subjects. While the resulting paintings looked the same as earlier pictures, they were actually staged by Volendamers posing for the stereotypes earlier artists had established.

In the twentieth century, a few artists painted Volendam in a more modern style, notably Robert Henri, Jane Peterson, Alice Schille, Leopold Seyffert, and Abraham Walkowitz. Their appearance marked the end of this colony's most productive era for the Americans, because their stylistic goals conflicted with the traditional subjects and values on which the town had built its reputation. Henri included figures in his *Volendam Street Scene* (FIG. 23) but the costume can barely be distinguished and the sketchy quality of the buildings give them a generic appearance. The quaintness and "Dutchness" that Americans had come to expect is lost in the artist's attention to paint quality.

INFLUENCE OF THE OLD MASTERS AND THE DUTCH REPUBLIC

Just as American artists' often superficial contact with the Dutch population and their preoccupation with novel costumes and customs influenced the art they produced, so did the preconceptions of Holland they brought from the United States. Those preconceptions came from their understanding of Dutch history, from travel literature, and from paintings and illustrations of Holland.

While American artists no longer came to Holland only to see the old Dutch masters, the images created by earlier artists continued to condition their responses to the Netherlands. To some extent, the increasing preoccupation of American artists with the Netherlands at the end of the century resulted from studying the Dutch life represented in seventeenth-century art and comparing it to the life they saw on their travels. To all appearances, Ruysdael's trees still shaded the road; Rembrandt's mills still turned in the wind; farmers and millers went about their business in the time-honored ways. To foreign eyes, neither the landscape nor the people seemed to have changed in the two hundred and fifty years since the great paintings of Holland were produced. Naturally artists looked to the same models that had produced the greatest era of Dutch art to inspire their own efforts.

The question remains why artists on the Grand Tour in the 1880s began to see their surroundings as potential for a new art while previous generations of visiting artists had more often been content to let the subject rest with the old masters. The example of the Hague School artists, whose modern interpretation of Holland was inspired by the old masters, may bear some responsibility. And the increasing availability of old master paintings in the United States freed traveling artists from the necessity of spending every possible moment in Holland in the galleries. However, the main reason for Holland's new appeal arose from changes occurring elsewhere in the world, and nowhere more rapidly than in the United States. Outward manifestations of modernization such as skyscrapers, smokestacks, telegraph wires, and slums, caused the pastoral simplicity of rural Holland to assume new connotations of picturesqueness by contrast. Some American painters felt that such accoutrements of modern life as threshing machines and cotton gins made the pastoral American landscape unpaintable. Rampant urbanization and industrialization in the United States and in the art centers of England and France rendered the art material they sought still more scarce. For them, Holland became a last bastion of old-fashioned picturesque subjects, already stamped with the Golden Age seal of approval. "That Holland has entirely escaped the commonplace utilitarian spirit of our own times is too much to expect," declared the painter George Hitchcock, "but to this wind-swept, half-submerged corner of the earth it has been last to come."[23]

Not only did the urban industrial revolution in the United States and Europe highlight Holland's picturesque appearance, but it suggested the imminent demise of the old Dutch life, lending urgency to the artists' quest. American artists were already accustomed to preserving in paint those aspects of North America threatened with extinction (the Indian and the wilderness landscape, for example) and, together with European artists, they painted the Old World peasant in the same spirit. An anonymous reviewer for the *Toledo Daily Blade* newspaper explained why local Ohio painter Wilder Darling spent so much time in Holland:

> Holland, like the rest of the world, is gradually changing, and much of the old and picturesque is passing away. The old stone floors are being supplanted by wooden ones and the great fire places are falling into disuse through the introduction of crude and inartistic cast-iron stoves. However, Laren has been lightly touched by the hand of time, and while there have been some changes to conform with modern times, they are in the main but trivial, and consequently it is an ideal spot for the artist. Some day Laren, too, will be lashed in the whirl of modern progress, and so it is that Mr. Darling is anxious to use every one of the precious moments before the great change comes. He has been in Laren now for eight years.[24]

Love of the old Dutch masters helped elicit this romantic response to contemporary Dutch peasant life. American artists sought out small rural villages like Volendam and Laren partly because they looked most like the image of Holland found in the old paintings and described by Motley. Laren fulfilled preconceptions of what Dutch people and their land should look like much better than The Hague or Amsterdam where one found modern hotels, steamships, and city trams scattered amongst the old buildings and canals.

LAREN

Situated near the southern tip of the Zuider Zee on poor land at the base of North Holland, Laren housed a substantial colony of artists among its farmers and shepherds. Describing it for readers of *Century Magazine* in 1893, the American painter Henry Ward Ranger wrote, "It is in itself one of the most insignificant hamlets of Holland—nothing, in fact, but a succession of thatch-roofed cottages strung along a few intersecting roads and lanes, and surrounded by waste lands—now each season finds it full of artists from all parts of the earth, and the desolation of Laren contributes materially to the luxury of the art-loving world."[25] The many paintings produced in and around Laren by Dutch, American, and other artists bear out Ranger's observation. William Henry Howe painted there frequently, producing such pictures as *Landscape with Sheep* (Memorial Art Gallery, University of Rochester) and his masterpiece, *Early Start for Market* (FIG. 24). *Early Start for Market* amazed American viewers with its impression of lifelike authenticity. On this huge canvas, Howe painted four cows determinedly marching straight at the viewer down a rain-slicked mud road from a meadow

FIG. 24 *William Henry Howe won accolades for his 1888 Salon painting* Early Start for Market.

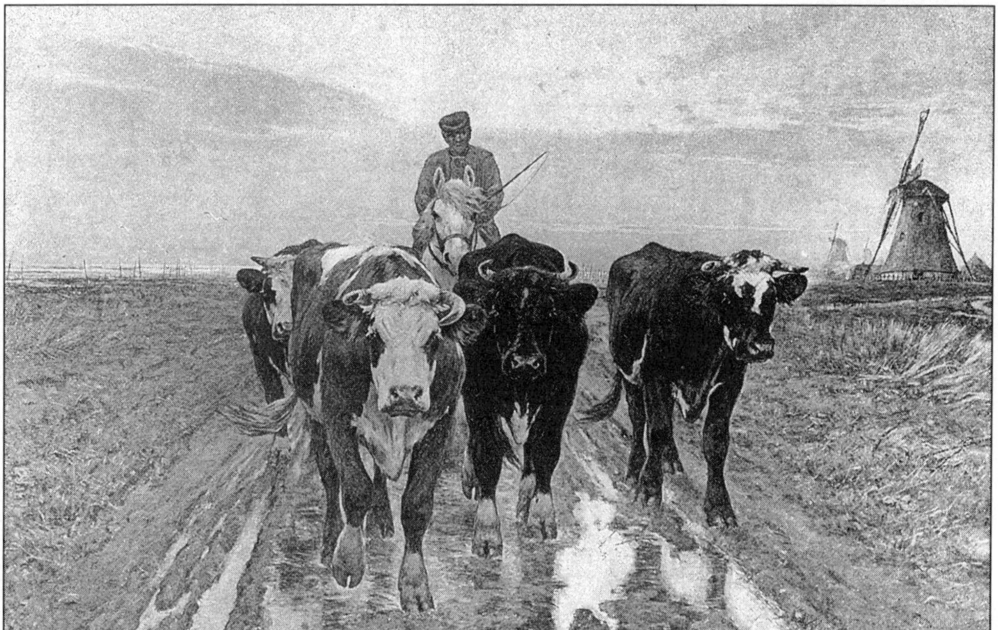

beside the Zuider Zee seen in the distance. Viewers remarked upon the uneasy feeling, when standing before the canvas, that one should move aside to let the beasts pass. By choosing a frontal perspective and severely foreshortening the cattle and the horse and rider driving them, Howe conveyed a feeling of immediacy that was apparently completely convincing. *An Early Start for Market* won at least four gold medals in international expositions.

Perhaps even more than daring composition and technical skill, *An Early Start for Market* demonstrated a premodern agrarian appeal. As an agricultural town with common pastures, the rights to which were inherited from generation to generation among local farmers, Laren proved attractive to cattle painters like Howe, who sympathized with the old-fashioned traditions portrayed by the seventeenth-century Dutchmen who specialized in animal painting. The old world method of raising cattle in small numbers and driving them a short distance to a local market contrasted with the mass production methods of the American beef industry. The huge herds raised on the western plains and shipped by rail to feedlots in the Midwest before being sent to Chicago's stockyards had made many American men rich. But the American method lacked the charm of the Dutch tradition where an owner might know each animal by name and personality.

Bovine subjects became fashionable in the United States after 1870 due, in part, to the growing popularity of old Dutch animal paintings by Albert Cuyp, Paulus Potter, and others. Americans who made their fortunes on cattle gladly decorated their homes with pictures of the source of their success, while others enjoyed pastoral scenes for their picturesque qualities. Nostalgia also played a role in the fashion for animal pictures, for the agricultural basis of many western economies appeared to be giving way to a new industrial order. Before the bottom fell out of the cow picture market around 1900, Howe could hardly keep up with the demand for his pictures.

Holland's green meadows, crisscrossed with ditches and dotted with windmills, provided a most picturesque setting for the familiar black and white cattle. Known as Holsteins in the United States and Friesians in Europe, the black and white Holstein-Friesian breed originated in Holland. It was valued throughout Europe and America for its high milk production. Early Dutch colonists first brought these cows to North America and American farmers continued to send to the Netherlands for their stock. The largest numbers of Holstein-Friesians arrived between 1850 and 1887, establishing the herds that still dominate dairy farming in parts of the United States today. Many rural American viewers of cattle paintings would have understood the fitness of the Dutch setting for black and white cows, beyond mere picturesqueness.

Most of Howe's Laren cow paintings are heavily imbued with the message of nostalgia for a premodern agricultural era. Three cows lying in the foreground of Howe's moonlit pasture scene, *Evening at Laren* (FIG. 25c), face the viewer while others dispose themselves in the distance. Low-key colors in a close range of values simulate the moment of twilight when the ability to distinguish colors fades. The subdued colors and flat, smooth texture of the paint surface enhance the mood of utter calm. Howe painted this view of contented cows as a nostalgic reminder of the values associated with the rural past. The cow, reputedly placid and gentle and known to be a source of wholesome dairy and meat products, symbolized the virtues of an agrarian life, which seemed increasingly to represent the antithesis of the hectic speed, questionable ethics, and constant change of modern urban life. Even a mathematics professor from New York recognized the symbolic significance of Dutch Holstein cows when he commented: "their magnificent race of cattle which has no rival in Europe for fecundity and beauty . . . are to be seen everywhere; they are reflected in all the canals, and dot with points of black and white, the immense fields that stretch on every side, giving an air of peace and comfort to every place, and exciting in the spectator's heart a sentiment of arcadian gentleness and patriarchal serenity."[26]

Howe gave an example of one of his favorite motifs—a single animal lying in the corner of a stable or pasture with a broken wall or crumbling fence in the background—to the local Laren innkeeper Jan Hamdorff in 1890 (FIG. 26c). After hanging many years over the mantel in Hamdorff's hotel, the painting now decorates Laren's town hall. The ruined architecture, like the twilight setting of *Evening at Laren*, symbolized the passing of the old agrarian order of society.

In addition to dairy cattle, sheep provided a vital part of Laren's economy. The Dutch Hague School artist Anton Mauve had made this subject his own, and although he died in 1888, his paintings of sheep on the Laren heath continued to attract animal painters to the region. The versatile American painter Charles Paul Gruppe's picture of sheep crossing a bridge provides an excellent example (FIG. 27c). Gruppe often repeated this compositional device, sometimes with a herd of cows.

Sheep provided the wool for carding, spinning, and weaving that kept much of Laren's population busy throughout the year. In her watercolor painting *The Breadwinner* (FIG. 28c), artist-teacher Emma Lampert of Rochester, New York, posed a woman spinning thread from wool yarn by the dim light of a window. The crude interior and the cabbages scattered on the floor testify to the poverty of life in this region. Lampert told a newspaper reporter that Jozef Israëls inspired the theme, and both the mood and palette do suggest the older artist. However, she painted it in 1891 during her first long summer in Holland while under the spell of her teacher, Jacob S. H. Kever, and it is equally indebted to his technical instruction. Accepted to the Paris Salon in 1892, *The Breadwinner* gained a place on the line (at eye level) near the central picture, an ideal location. It later won acclaim at the New York Water Color Club, received a medal and diploma at the World's Columbian Exposition in Chicago, and returned to Paris for the International Exposition of 1900. The subject portrayed the premodern, traditional method of making cloth.

Despite its strong community emphasis on tradition, Laren provided a livelihood for numerous professional female artists. In addition to Emma Lampert, Marcia Woodbury of Boston, Amy Cross of Milwaukee, and Isabel Edgar of New York discovered that the support of compatriots and of Dutch female artists resident in Laren, including Arina Hugenholz and Wally Moes, provided a nurturing atmosphere for women in the arts.

HATTEM–NUNSPEET

The Towns of Hattem and Nunspeet, located on the other side of the Zuider Zee from Volendam and Laren in the heart of the Noord Veluwe (northern badlands) also attracted a small group of American animal and genre painters. Henry Bisbing, a Philadelphia engraver who had studied with the renowned animal painter J. H. L. de Haas in Belgium, was the principal animal specialist of the group. He normally worked in Hattem only during the summers, making Neuilly, France his winter quarters. Like Howe's paintings, Bisbing's reflect his admiration for the preservation of seventeenth-century traditions in Dutch agriculture. *In the Meadow* (FIG. 29c), exhibited in the 1889 Paris Salon and purchased by the Philadelphia art critic Riter Fitzgerald for the Pennsylvania Academy of the Fine Arts, provides an excellent example of the kind of work Bisbing did in and near Hattem. In the foreground stand two black and white cows grazing on the flat meadow while their milkmaid attendant peers into the distance at a similarly clad woman tending two more cows. The use of milkmaids was a practice considered quaint and old-time by Americans. It recalled the presence of farmers and herders in seventeenth-century animal paintings by Paulus Potter.

Not all animal painters were men. Matilda Browne came to Hattem in 1890 in order to study with Henry Bisbing. She purchased livestock at the local cattle market and set to work painting studies. A painting of a recalcitrant calf, *The Unwilling Model* (location unknown), became her entry for the World's Columbian Exposition in Chicago three years later where it won an honorable mention and found a purchaser. When she returned to the United States she made a career of painting cows and sheep, often working in Old Lyme, Connecticut with other veterans of the Holland sketching grounds such as Howe and Ranger.

The best known of Hattem's American artists, Walter MacEwen, specialized in genre scenes. The *Judgement of Paris* (Tennessee Wesleyan College, Athens, TN) depicts a contemporary Dutch man and three women as the handsome Greek cattle herder Paris and the Greek goddesses Hera, Aphrodite, and Athena. According to the myth, Zeus chose Paris to be the judge in a beauty contest between the three goddesses, with a golden apple as the prize. MacEwen departed from the artistic tradition when he chose to present his Hattem goddesses fully clothed. He may have found classical nudity incompatible with his image of modest Dutch peasant women. However, in his choice of a Hattem man (possibly a cattle herder) to model for the figure of Paris, he made reference to one of the principal occupations of the region. In another painting, *Returning From Work* (FIG. 30c), MacEwen depicted laborers who may be returning from the peat bogs that served as fuel and provided the region with another important source of income. Hard labor produced a subsistence-level living for many of the people in this area.

It was, in part, the simplicity and poverty of Dutch peasant life, often described as honest and Godly, that attracted artists to Hattem and Laren, rather than to the sketching grounds in Zeeland and Friesland where lace, gold, and silver costumes and immense, well-furnished farmhouses belied the usual image of the poor European peasant. The clergyman and historian William Elliot Griffis visited Nunspeet as a tourist and later described a local Dutch cottage where he found Amy Cross, an artist from Milwaukee, at work.

> The living-room is probably twelve feet square. In one corner, where the mother sits, her face prematurely wrinkled, and every wrinkle a furrow of experience telling of a sorrow, is the spinning-wheel, on which she is at work even while she talks, making yarn and getting it ready for hose. Back of her, against the wall, is a little wooden case, in which are a few spoons and other eating utensils. In the middle of one wall and against it is a fireplace, where are crackling a few embers over which hangs the kettle, and, farther up, a hole rather than a chimney. The table on which the humble meals are set is in the middle of the room . . . .
>
> *The details of the little home reappear in the picture. The moment chosen is when, since the cottagers have no oven in which to bake their bread, the loaf has come home from the bakers. With eager eye the boy, having been trusted to weigh the ultimate product of yeast, flour, and caloric, scrutinizes the scales.*[27]

Cross exhibited this painting, entitled *Weighing the Bread* (location unknown), at the National Academy of Design in 1897.

Bisbing, Browne, MacEwen, and Cross certainly worked in this area between 1880 and 1914, yet much research is still needed before a clear picture of the colony at Hattem emerges, if indeed it can be called a colony. No records of these artists have been found in the town archives and only one mention of them has surfaced in Holland. An 1896 Dutch guidebook to Hattem states that "year after year a society of American painters of excellent reputation make their home here for some months and have derived from this region the subjects of the art work that is awarded gold medals in foreign countries."[28]

While Laren, Hattem, and Nunspeet attracted animal painters, landscapists, and figure painters with a nostalgic interest in the old Dutch traditions, the North Sea shore provided material for like-minded marine painters. The earliest American artists on the North Sea coast were marine painters who came, like their European counterparts, because of the great tradition of marine painting established by the Dutch during the seventeenth century. In that era of prosperity, Dutch artists had recorded maritime battles, commercial activity in the ports and harbors, coastal fishing fleets and individual ship's portraits. They had developed and refined the general seascape subject in which they devoted two-thirds of the canvas to Holland's atmospheric skies and dotted the water below with small ships and figures. Such scenes by the Ruysdaels, Jan van de Cappelle, and Willem van de Velde II were admired and emulated in the United States to the point that, according to an American critic of 1895, "almost all painters believed that it requires a Dutch rigged craft or at least an old fishing schooner to look well on canvas."[29] Although a strong market existed for American coastal views, the aesthetic set by Dutch art enticed a steady stream of marine artists to Holland in the last quarter of the nineteenth century.

KATWIJK

The art produced in Katwijk is characteristic of the activities of American painters on the North Sea, although Scheveningen (FIG. 31c), Noordwijk and Zandvoort also attracted artists. Stephen Salisbury Tuckerman probably began painting along the Dutch coast about 1876. His work on clipper ships in the East India trade as a young man undoubtedly affected his choice of specialization. After studying art with William Morris Hunt, and in England, he became the head of the New England School of Design in Boston and lived for a time in artist Fitz Hugh Lane's Gloucester house where he painted the New England coast. But he deserted Gloucester to make Holland his second home for over ten years, becoming a member of the national Dutch artist society Pulchri Studio in 1882. He spent the summers of 1883, 1884, 1885, and 1887 in Katwijk and sent the products of his brush back to New England. Each year the annual exhibition of Boston's Paint and Clay Club featured more of his paintings of Dutch fishermen's cottages, sail makers, herring boats, and net menders. Local patrons paid from $75 to $600 each to decorate their homes with his pictures.

In the spring of 1886 Tuckerman held a one-person exhibition called "Pictures From Holland" at the Tremont Street Studio Building in Boston. His many paintings of old-fashioned wooden fishing schooners breaking through stormy waves find their closest source in the work of Willem van de Cappelle the Younger, and sold readily in Boston where the old masters were particularly admired. Tuckerman's untitled view of a Dutch fishing vessel plowing through the sea (FIG. 32c) is characteristic of his brown-toned old-master look.

Dutch Coast (FIG. 33c) by William Stanley Haseltine is one of the most beautiful examples of the influence of old Dutch painting on late-nineteenth-century American artists. In this scene of herring ships riding the waves into shore, Haseltine used rich color glazes and a highly varnished surface to approximate the look of the old masters. The sky occupies two-thirds of the canvas and his attention to cloud formations and the light breaking through a grey day creates a luminous effect. The horizontal format and reduction of ships and people to staffage also evoke old Netherlandish seascapes.

Scenes such as these by Tuckerman and Haseltine advertised the North Sea coast to other marine painters, most of whom came from New York City and the Boston–Gloucester area. A Boston cleric traveling in Holland noted that America had no coast like the North Sea Coast, "even Marblehead and Gloucester at their quaintest are not so odd and old-time as the fishermen's quarters there."[30] Apparently many artists agreed with him for, among others, George Elmer Browne, Augustus Waldeck Buhler, William Partridge Burpee, Carleton Theodore Chapman, Walter Lofthouse Dean, Melbourne H. Hardwick, George and Martha Harvey, William Edward Norton, Stephen Salisbury Tuckerman, and Charles Herbert Woodbury regularly alternated between New England and North Sea coasts in the paintings they produced for the American market.

Photographers also journeyed to the coast of Holland and their work helped promote the picturesque qualities of this sketching ground. Most famous of these was Alfred Stieglitz, who set up his camera on the sands of Katwijk in 1894. His photograph *Watching for the Return* (FIG. 34) depicts a group of Katwijkers waiting on the beach in front of the church for the town's fishing fleet to return. Stieglitz attempted to capture the character of the people whom he described as "immense in stature, hardy, brave beyond belief, stoical from long habit, seeing brother, father, son, and husband leave on their perilous fishing trips far out in the North Sea, not knowing when or whether at all they will return, welcoming them with a simple handshake, no embrace, no tender kiss for the returning hero for hero he is."[31] Stieglitz exhibited his photographs in the United States and throughout Europe. He also used them to illustrate an article about the artistic merits of Katwijk. Similar compositions can be seen in the oil and watercolor paintings of Stieglitz's compatriots over the next two decades.

Of all the subjects on the beach, the process of getting the fishing fleet in and out of the water received the most attention from photographers and painters alike. It seemed to be exactly the same labor intensive method used centuries earlier. Lacking harbors, the North Sea fishermen used broad flat-bottomed boats that could be run up on the beach. Getting them in and out of the water required

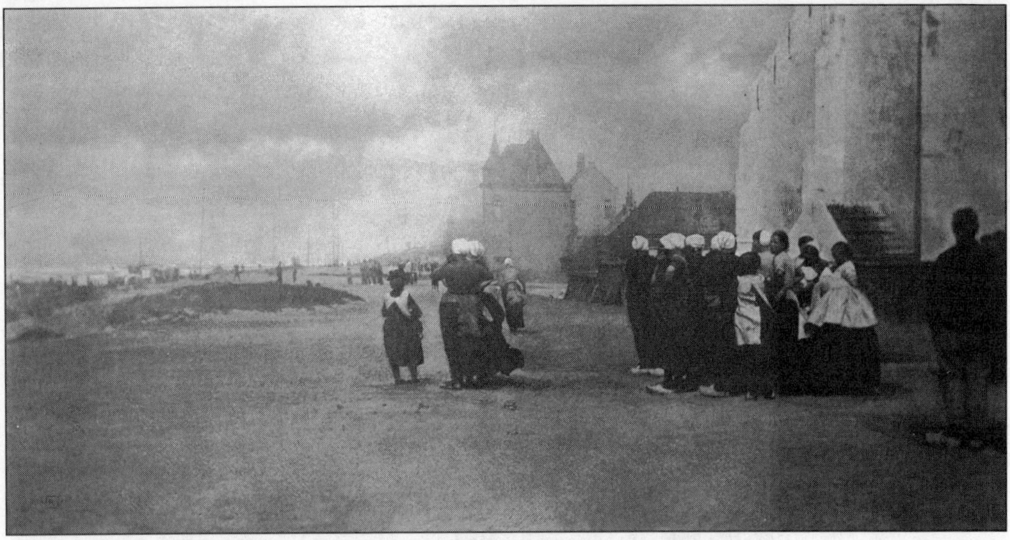

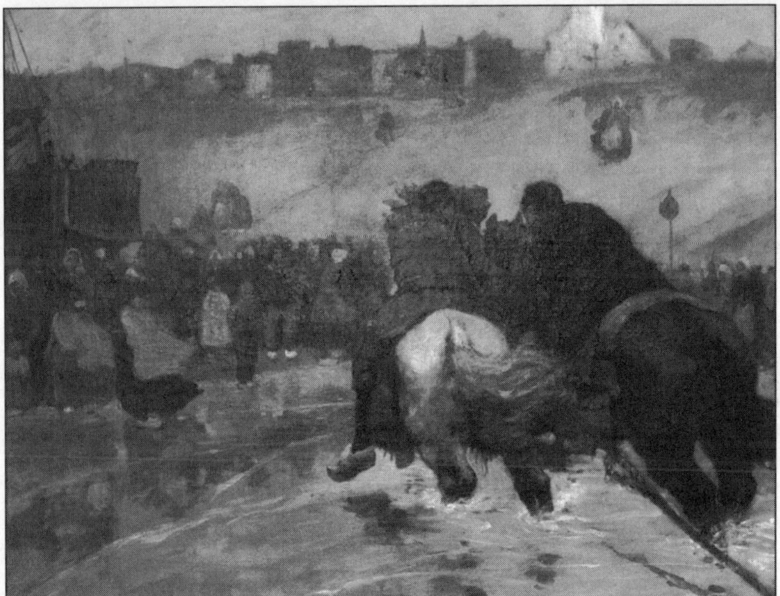

FIG. 34 *Although the New York photographer Alfred Stieglitz complained that blowing sand, an absence of natural light in the houses, and lack of running water made both photographing and developing difficult in Katwijk, he produced several award winning photographs there, including this carbon print called* Watching for the Return.

FIG. 35 *Reversing the usual point of view, Paul King painted* Hauling in the Anchor Line *from the sea rather than the land.*

teams of horses, log rollers, efficient use of the tides, and the efforts of the villagers. Paul Bernard King (1867–1947), an artist from Buffalo, New York, depicted the process from the perspective of the sailors on shipboard in his oil painting, *Hauling in the Anchor Line* (FIG. 35). The powerful hindquarters of the two horses moving through the sea to the waiting crowd of villagers on shore dominate the picture. At the very top of the painting the houses and church of

Katwijk are visible on the dunes. The unusual choice of viewpoint won the artist the Samuel T. Shaw purchase prize as well as the First Inness Prize when he exhibited *Hauling in the Anchor Line* at the Salmagundi Club in 1906. King had worked in Katwijk during the summers of 1905 and 1906, exhibiting his Katwijk scenes in Buffalo, New York City, Boston, Philadelphia, and Springfield, Massachusetts.

William Edward Norton captured another stage of the process in *A Moment's Rest* (FIG. 36c). Horses and men stop to smoke and rest from their labors with the beached ship's bow lying a few feet from the water. The solid figures and relaxed poses emanate an air of stability and dependability that reflects a common American characterization of Dutchmen. The photographer William Carlin testified that "independence, such a strong characteristic of the Hollander, is especially developed in the Katwijker."[32] Of course, independence was also a trait that most Americans admired and ascribed equally to themselves.

While the work of Tuckerman and Haseltine reflects seventeenth-century Dutch influence, these paintings by Norton and King establish that new approaches to North Sea subjects emerged in the late nineteenth century. With larger scale figures and more emphasis on the beach than on the sea, these turn-of-the-century marine paintings focused on the human element. Still, they chose to see only the human element that satisfied their expectations. The majority of Americans in Katwijk chose to portray a rosy view of an easy open-air lifestyle. Crowds of people stand about idly talking or watching the sea, women knit or mend nets outdoors, shell fishers wade in the shallows, but the sweat and strain of hauling the ships up the sand or unloading heavy cargos, and the messy task of gutting the fish are noticeably absent from the foreign painters' canvases. So, too, are shipwrecks and funerals, although Dutch artists did not hesitate to treat these common themes. While Katwijk had a tourist industry whose effluence littered the beach in the form of large wicker chairs, hotels, well-dressed cosmopolitans, and horse-drawn bathing machines, American artists remained blind to all but the old-fashioned local residents. Not only their love of the old master aesthetic, but also romantic nostalgia for the loss of the old ways and the contentment American city dwellers derived from believing that people still lived simply somewhere in the world motivated the artists' selective vision and their patrons' enthusiastic endorsement.

Between them, the artists summering in Katwijk (and a few who wintered there) captured every mood of the North Sea. Paintings such as Tuckerman's *Herring Boat coming to shore in a gale*, *Bad Weather*, and *Storm-horsemen going out for cable line* reaffirmed the age-old battle between humans and nature, reminding viewers of the untamable nature of the sea, even as Frederick Jackson Turner declared the last American frontier closed. The land of the United States might be conquered from coast to coast, but these pictures suggested that the sea would never submit to human control. It would continue to nurture the pioneering spirit so dear to Americans. No better subject could be found for this message than the Netherlands coast where the sea constantly threatened to sweep all the refinements of civilization before it. Paintings of crashing waves evoked the sublime fragility of that balance the Dutch had attained between the ocean and the pumped-out land they inhabited. Lest viewers miss the import of Dutch fishing subjects, the catalogue for the 1893 Boston South End Free Art Exhibition included this explanation for one of Tuckerman's paintings: "The Dutch are a nation of sailors, and though the sea has been their enemy invading their flat country and obliging them to build great dikes of stone to keep it from covering their land, yet the sea has been their friend too, and by their commerce they have grown rich and strong." American viewers appear to have appreciated this dichotomy between the sublime threat of the sea and its abundant provision of livelihood no less than they admired the strength and courage of the Dutch people.

Carleton Chapman pursued a different branch of marine painting, specializing in naval history, battle scenes, ships portraits, and commercial harbor scenes. Chapman studied ship models at the marine museum in Rotterdam, and from his sketches painted *The East Indiaman*, one of his early successes. He followed this with a variety of historical scenes, including the famous Flying Dutchman. Chapman painted fishing vessels in Katwijk in 1886, but became better known for his New York harbor scenes. Extensive sheltered harbors, navigation on the Hudson River as far inland as Albany, and the extension of inland access by means of the Erie canal from Albany to Buffalo and the Great Lakes had made New York the busiest port for foreign trade in North America. As such, New York harbor provided endless subjects for the artist, and its history as an early Dutch port into which Dutch residents of the Hudson Valley sailed their produce, suggested a logical connection with the Dutch tradition of marine painting. Rotterdam, likewise, may have attracted Chapman for its busy shipyards and docks.

While the original motivation for spending longer periods in the Netherlands was to remake Golden Age Dutch art and to record a passing era, for a few artists, prolonged contact with the Netherlands inspired new kinds of art. Although he admitted that "Holland to-day attracts more largely those painters who follow in the footsteps of the great Dutchmen," George Hitchcock averred that "a really sympathetic observer, a deeper and more subtle interpreter of this wonderful country and its interesting people, has an almost untrodden field before him."[33] Hitchcock considered himself a deeper and more subtle interpreter of the country than were the old masters, and he devoted thirty years to painting it with a modern vision. The emergence of the Egmond School of American painting, of which Hitchcock was a founder, marked a distinctive new phase of the picturesque, a colorful sunlit view of Holland.

In addition to the Egmond School, many individual artists such as Robert W. Grafton abandoned the old master aesthetic. The catalogue for a 1917–1918 exhibition and sale of Grafton's work at Thurber Art Galleries in Chicago described his Dutch interiors as being "painted in a true American style that makes them more interesting to those who have built or live in the modern home of today." The writer pronounced Grafton's color "more pleasant than the old brown and black envelopement [sic] of the Dutch painters." American artists like Grafton attempted to create a distinctly American view of the Netherlands, one appropriate for the decoration of American homes.

EGMOND

In this cluster of three villages on the North sea coast where Jacob van Ruysdael had frequently painted in the seventeenth century, two American artists, Julius Garibaldi (Gari) Melchers and George Hitchcock, founded an American school of art. Egmond aan Zee, a cluster of red-roofed houses huddled amidst the dunes on the edge of the sea (FIG. 37), provided good seascapes for marine painters and beach scenes for the genre artist interested in commercial fishing, shipping, and peasant life. A short distance inland, Egmond aan den Hoef provided landscapists with dune scenes and later with flower fields, while genre painters found slightly wealthier models, goat herders, farmers, and a beautiful little chapel. South of the Hoef,

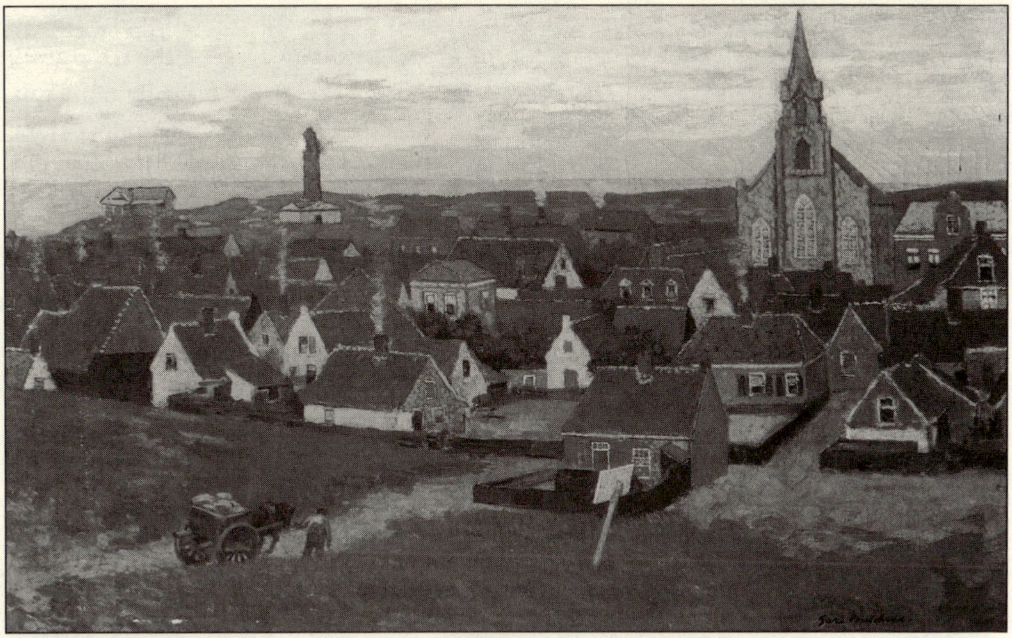

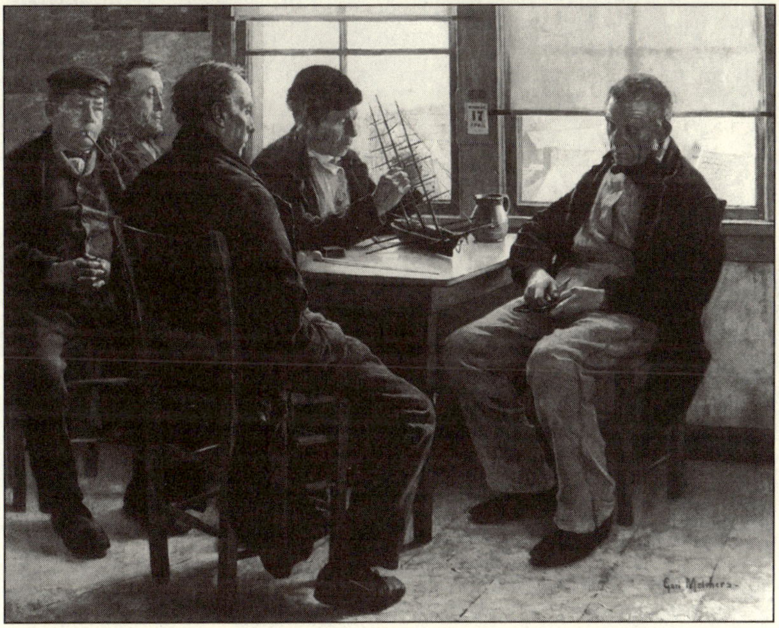

FIG. 37 *Gari Melchers recorded the features of the North Holland town in which he helped found an American art colony, Egmond aan Zee.*

FIG. 38 *The early efforts of the Egmond artists focused on the sea and the local fishing industry. Gari Melchers painted* The Pilots *in 1886.*

Egmond Binnen afforded an interesting setting in the church where Melchers painted *The Sermon* (National Museum of American Art), although most art activity centered on the other two Egmonds.

The colony began in the early 1880s in Egmond aan Zee. Here Melchers painted sea captains smoking and talking in a local inn (FIG. 38). The carefully observed details of the setting and dark tonalities recall his recent student years in Düsseldorf. Critics complimented Melchers for his ability to tell a story and the naturalism of his characters' gestures. While Melchers painted the Egmond folk on land, Hitchcock focused on the sea. He painted Egmond's fishing boats as they sailed out from the beach, in a style reminiscent of Hendrik Willem Mesdag's compositions (with whom he had studied briefly), but in darker tones, Hitchcock experienced some success when the Empress of Austria purchased one of his marine views. At about the same time, Gari Melchers's painting *The Sermon* received an honorable mention at the Paris Salon and he began to attract some critical attention.

Both men experimented with the grey tones of the Hague School during the 1880s. Then in 1886 Hitchcock painted a woman cutting flowers in a flower bed that combined the purer colors of the impressionists in unusual and daring combinations. *Tulip Culture* (private collection) won acclaim at the Paris Salon and went on to earn the artist awards in several other exhibitions. This successful venture convinced him to experiment more with color and he embarked on a series of paintings of colorful bulb fields and costumed figures. At about the same time, Hitchcock moved inland to a manor house near Egmond aan den Hoef, where agriculture provided the inhabitants' livelihood, rather than the sea.

Meanwhile, Melchers also experimented with stronger color compositions in paintings. Throughout the 1890s, Melchers and Hitchcock became bolder in their combinations of color. Inspired by the formal composition of Botticelli's *Madonna* at the Louvre, Hitchcock developed a subject type in which an elaborately costumed woman stands in full or partial sunlight against a backdrop of flowering branches or a hedge bordering a field of flowers. *In Brabant* (FIG. 39c) illustrates this development in his art. As his paintings won awards throughout Europe, this became the subject for which Egmond would be best known—costumed figures in brightly colored landscapes.

During the 1890s, art students came to Egmond in increasing numbers to work with Hitchcock. Karl Anderson, Alice Blair Ring, and Letta Crapo Smith are just a few of the students who spent their summers learning to paint Egmond's landscape and peasants. They painted the windmill and meadows, local women in their gardens, and interiors. Even when George Hitchcock's marriage broke up and he left Egmond with one of his students, never to return, former students continued to come to Holland each year for their summer

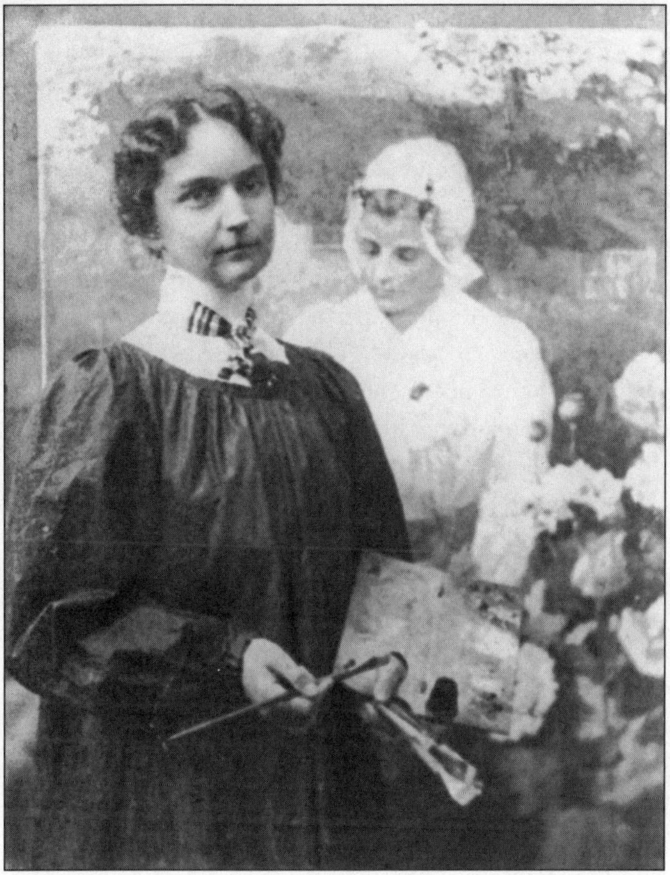

FIG. 40 *George Hitchcock's student, Alice Blair Ring, stands before one of her Egmond paintings in this turn-of-the-century photograph. Ring's painting reminds one strongly of a painting by James Jebusa Shannon showing George Hitchcock kneeling among poppies, now in the Telfair Academy of Fine Arts, Savannah, Georgia.*

work. A photograph of Alice Ring (FIG. 40) with her now lost painting of an Egmond woman against a flowered landscape reveals Hitchcock's influence in subject and composition. Although the majority of the students' Egmond paintings have disappeared into private collections, contemporary reviews of them consistently praised the bright color combinations and sophisticated handling of light and shadow. This legacy of a colorful, sunlit interpretation of the Netherlands is the Egmond School's primary contribution to American art.

James Jebusa Shannon, an American-born expatriate to London, is one of the few artists who also took note of Egmond's growing reputation as a beach resort. His painting *On the Dunes* (FIG. 41c) pictures his wife and daughter in cosmopolitan finery relaxing near the ocean. Egmond aan Zee had formed a tourist association to develop the town's potential as a bathing resort and several local people built hotels and restaurants after 1900 to encourage vacationers to come there. George Hitchcock had sketched a woman on the beach earlier, but the shift in the art colony's center from Egmond aan Zee to Egmond aan den Hoef was probably an attempt to avoid such evidence of modernization in their work.

Melchers married and purchased a house in Egmond aan den Hoef around 1903. Thereafter, he painted bright genre scenes in heavy impasto, as well as more subdued Vermeeresque interiors. His wife, former Egmond art student Corinne Mackall, became his favorite model. The late Egmond period focused on interiors, of which Melchers's *Penelope* (FIG. 42c) is an excellent example. Corinne sat for the figure of Penelope—possibly an allusion to the classical legend of Jason's wife, who used her needlework to ward off suitors until Jason returned from his search for the golden fleece—while their Dutch maid served as the other model for the picture. The interior portrayed is the parlor of Schuylenberg, Hitchcock's former Egmond residence. Following Vermeer's example, Melchers employed a window to light the scene from the side and created a mood of tranquil domesticity. Typical of his late Egmond pictures, and perhaps following Shannon's lead, *Penelope* divulges no hint of its Dutch setting, but takes on a cosmopolitan air. Other Egmond artists of this time also painted Vermeeresque interiors, but continued to clothe their figures in traditional North Holland costume and to place Dutch objects such as warming teapots, delft plates, and Dutch tiles in the pictures.

DUTCH COLONIES AS SUMMER SCHOOLS

Most of the art colonies, like Egmond, functioned as summer schools. Young American artists living or studying in Paris often brought classes of less experienced art students to the Dutch colonies for summer work. Arletta Lothrop led the Art Students League of Buffalo to Volendam in 1902 for a planned two-week sketch trip, made more memorable by a boiler explosion on their steamship from which they barely escaped. John Vanderpoel encouraged his students from the Art Institute in Chicago to spend a summer in Rijsoord. Alexander Robinson held classes in Volendam and in 1896 William Merritt Chase planned a winter class in Holland. Although that did not work out, he later took groups of students to Zandvoort.

An advertisement in the February *Brush and Pencil* for Chase's

1903 summer travel course describes three kinds of experience available to students: life study, copy work in the museums, and study of contemporary Dutch art.

> William Merritt Chase announces that next summer he will take a limited number of pupils to Holland. The class will be located near Haarlem. In addition to working from the landscape and model out of doors, one of the features of the trip will be the study of the old Dutch masters, special attention being paid to the works of Frans Hals. Excursions will be made to Amsterdam, The Hague and other neighboring places of interest.

The excursions to Amsterdam and The Hague provided the opportunity for students to meet the Hague School artists. Chase took his classes to the studios of Israëls and Mesdag where he reported enthusiastic receptions. The marine painter, Harry Chase, also visited Israëls and sketched the famous artist at work (FIG. 43). Israëls eventually became weary of the steady stream of American art students and politely told one of them that the United States would never develop a good national art if they did not stop imitating the Dutch and start painting their own country.[34] But in general, the warm welcome Holland and its artists extended to foreigners encouraged American artists' continued sojourns.

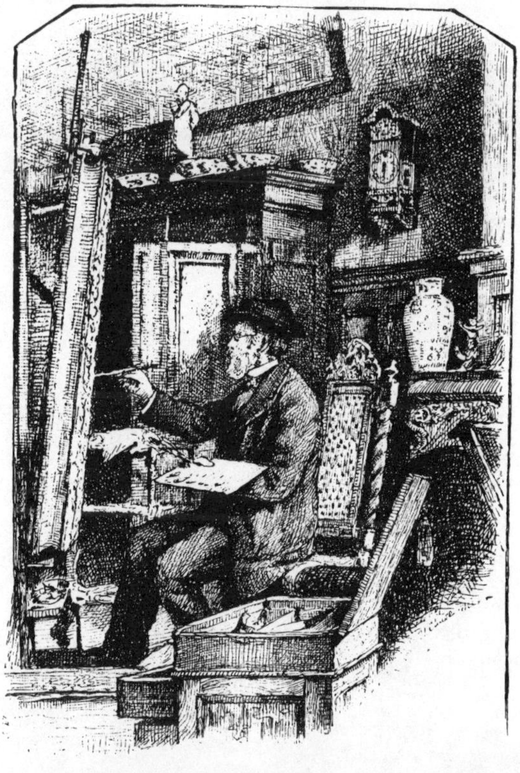

FIG. 43 *The American artist Harry Chase made this drawing of Jozef Israëls for the article "Dutch Painters at Home" that appeared in* Century Magazine *in 1889.*

Some art students went to Holland especially to work with the Dutch artists. Henry Ward Ranger recalled:

> My first sight of the works of Israel [sic], Maris, Bosboom, and Mauve gave me the same thrill which I had received from my first acquaintance with the Barbizon painters; and I wanted to know them also. . . . So I went to Holland, as you might say, with my hat in my hand and love and admiration in my heart. I had the pleasure of meeting all and knowing some of the masters intimately; and I have always remembered their kindness.

Ranger went on to describe evenings in the company of the Dutch artists at the hotel in Laren, as well as numerous private talks with Mauve and Israëls on art techniques and philosophy. Their ideas and methods reinforced Ranger's own, and in this supportive environment he found his style:

> One charming thing I remember of the Dutch painters was their universal simplicity. One seemed to feel, no matter how great they were, that they still considered themselves students. They were ever ready and willing to help and advise any youngling who was in earnest. I am very much indebted to them for the technical suggestions and illuminating remarks I heard during their conversation. There was none of that pose of: "Look up to me! I'm a master!"

Ranger's remarks carry an underlying assumption about the democratic nature of Dutch people that he shared with other Americans.[35]

RIJSOORD

While all the colonies attracted students, none was so exclusively a students' colony as Rijsoord. The half dozen or so artists who came to sketch and learn to compose pictures each summer were almost all students or amateurs, learning from one another. Even when Professor John Vanderpoel was in residence from the Art Institute of Chicago he appears not to have taught any classes or given regular criticisms. Although Vanderpoel spent numerous summers in Rijsoord, where four of his siblings had been born, the colony had no permanent artist resident until Wilhelmina Hawley settled there in 1901 and she stopped painting professionally within a few years. Consequently no distinctive Rijsoord style ever emerged. On the other hand, many artists who later developed successful careers will be found to have produced pictures and sketchbooks as students in Rijsoord. The town provided a relaxed environment for independent study.

Situated not far from Dordrecht along the banks of the slow moving Waal River, Rijsoord consisted of a single main street that crossed the river in the middle of town, two churches, a windmill, flax sheds, and a few shops. In the nineteenth century most of its inhabitants farmed or worked in the local flax industry, laboring from dawn to dusk six days a week, and going to church three times on Sunday. The women wore a traditional costume of a shoulder-length gauze veil and a tight-waisted, full-skirted dress. The inhabitants formed the primary subjects for the art students.

The American students' headquarters sat on the edge of the river in the center of town (FIG. 44). Alternately known as the Hotel Warendorp and the Rijsoordsch Koffiehuis, the building not only provided a living/dining room, public bar, and bed chambers, but also contained a large second floor studio where the artists hung their work and held critiques, and a broad second story balcony overhanging the river from which they fished. The proprietress took a keen interest in her guests, even allowing them to use her laundry wringer for a press to make monotypes. Although Americans seem to have dominated the small Rijsoord colony, occasionally others shared the town. When husband and wife artists Mary and Ernest Peixotto stayed there they reported that a professor from Carlsruhe and his students also occupied the Hotel Warendorp. Both groups

FIG. 44 *Every art colony had its center and in Rijsoord the Hotel Warendorp became the artists' headquarters.*

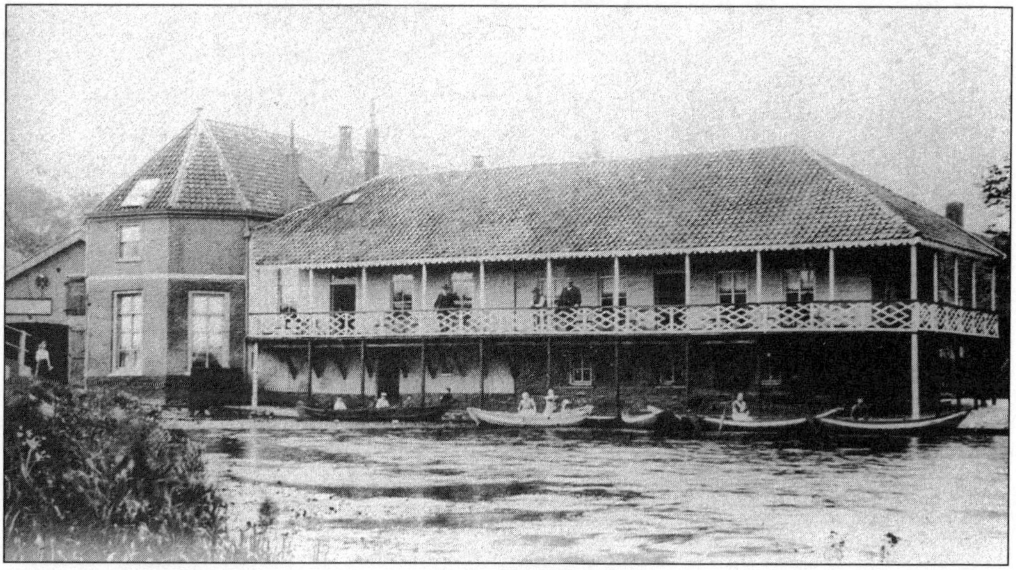

used the common studio and took pleasure in arguing over the comparative merits of the high key impressionistic style of some of the Americans, and the dark traditional style of the Germans.

Wilhelmina Douglas Hawley (1860–1958) moved from New York to Paris in 1892 with fellow artist Nannie Homans to study at the Academie Julian. A few days after their arrival in Paris the two women traveled north through Belgium to Rijsoord. This began a lifelong association for Hawley who returned to Rijsoord in 1894, and every year after 1897. In December of 1901 she married a local farmer eight years her junior, Bastiaan de Koning. Because Wilhelmina Douglas Hawley de Koning spent the rest of her life in this small Dutch town and most of her paintings stayed in the Netherlands, her work is virtually unknown in the United States today.

Hawley specialized in watercolor, which she taught in her "Special Course in Water Color and Pastel for Ladies" at the Academie Colarossi in Paris in the late 1890s. She also taught watercolor painting in Rijsoord. Some of her students gave her a handmade booklet entitled "A Kluster of Herr de Konings Klass '03" (private collection). The booklet contains photographs of her students Maria Thompson Daviess of Nashville, Edna Vosburgh of Denver, and Kathryn E. Fisher of New York City dressed up in Rijsoord costumes and assuming typical genre painting poses as "A Hearty Hollandish House-Vrouw," "A Simple Simpering Simpleton" and "A Wishy Washy Washer Woman," respectively. Daviess explained her motivation in traveling to Rijsoord:

> I had come to Rijsord [sic] to paint under Mevrouw Wilhelmina Dekoning, because I felt that the broad wash of her water colors, which I had seen in places of honor at the Salon des Beaux Arts in Paris in the spring, would be good to keep me from niggling my miniatures. And they did.[36]

That summer Daviess painted a miniature on ivory of a Rijsoord woman and her baby. When the baby died, the mother finished the pose holding her sister's baby, and the piece had so much pathos and sentimental value for the artist that she kept it by her bedside for many years. Daviess later made a good living in Nashville painting miniatures based on photographs that she took herself, but she is best remembered for her novels of southern life.

The most popular subjects for paintings in Rijsoord included women carrying water from the river on shoulder yokes, men and

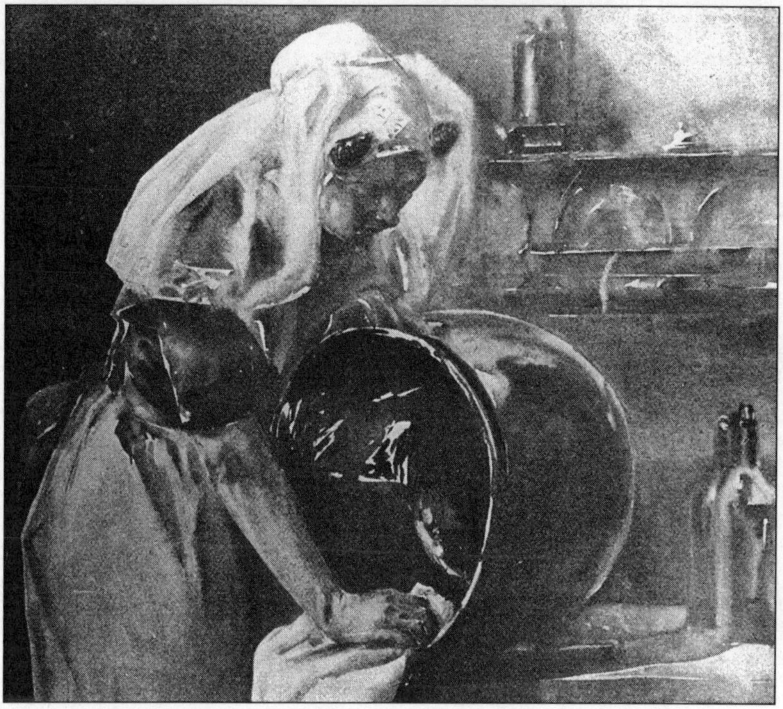

FIG. 45 *Wilhelmina Douglas Hawley entered* Scouring *in an exhibition in Canada where it drew favorable attention.*

women working with the flax, mothers caring for their children, and farm and river landscapes. Hawley painted all of these. *Scouring* (FIG. 45) typifies the figure subjects for which she was best known, and one of the popular themes among art students in Rijsoord. When shown in the Ontario Society of Artists exhibition at the turn of the century, Hawley's watercolor of a woman in traditional Rijsoord headdress scouring a large kettle with a cloth excited praise for the "virile" drawing and transparent quality of the color.[37]

Saturday was cleaning day in Rijsoord. According to accounts written by American artists there, every Saturday the inhabitants dragged the furniture out of their houses, which they then washed inside and out. While the houses dried, the furniture and kitchen-ware were cleaned and polished in the street. Wrote the sister of one of the artists: "Such cleanliness, even the most immaculate American housewife never dreamed of . . . Everything shines, I get so tired of my own mug reflected in everything, and long for a little dirt to make me feel at home."[38] The subject of a Hollander cleaning old brass pots appealed to Americans as characteristically Dutch, for it reinforced the popular notion of a Dutch virtue they particularly admired. The popularity of this oft-painted subject among artists rested in the challenge it provided to paint reflections in brass and copper as well as reflected metallic light on the polisher and her surroundings. Often, as in Hawley's *Scouring*, the subject is depicted gazing at herself in a gleaming surface. In these paintings and those of Rijsoord's student population, the themes of the premodern idyll and the stereotyped happy Hollander reappear.

THE LEGACY OF THE DUTCH COLONIES

The Dutch colony experience had a lasting effect through the activities of several American artists who eventually left Holland to found artist colonies in the United States. After finding his metier among the dunes and fisherfolk of Zandvoort, near Haarlem, Charles Webster Hawthorne established a studio and school in Provincetown on Cape Cod. The sandy beaches and close-knit fishing community recalled his environment in Zandvoort, although the Provincetown fisherfolk who became his primary subjects after 1899 came of Portuguese rather than Dutch stock. It should be noted that Hawthorne had already exhibited a preference for coastal subjects before going to Holland and had spent time at Chase's summer school in Shinnecock, but the period in Zandvoort, which completed his art training, certainly had an equal effect on his choice of Provincetown.

Hawthorne spent the summer of 1898 in Haarlem and Zandvoort and exhibited his Dutch work in New York that fall. According to a reviewer, Hawthorne painted the old Dutch couple (FIG. 46) in the Old Men's Almshouse of Zandvoort where Frans Hals used to paint. Although the cropped composition is purely late nineteenth century, the brush work reflects something of the excitement Hawthorne experienced upon first seeing Hals's handling of paint: "When I came here and saw the Hals I was so overpowered with the brush work I couldn't see anything else." Fearing that he would become enslaved to the brush work, Hawthorne began painting with a palette knife and developed his own style of portraiture.[39]

The experience of painting Dutch peasants and the impression Frans Hals made on him stayed with Hawthorne when he returned to the United States and set up his own school the next year. This is clearly evident in such pictures as *Cleaning Fish* (1899, Town of Provincetown) and *Laborers Drinking* (1903, unlocated), but continues to surface even as late as about 1921 when he painted *Three Women of Provincetown* (FIG. 47). This painting is in the tradition of seventeenth-century Dutch portraits of the regentesses of charitable

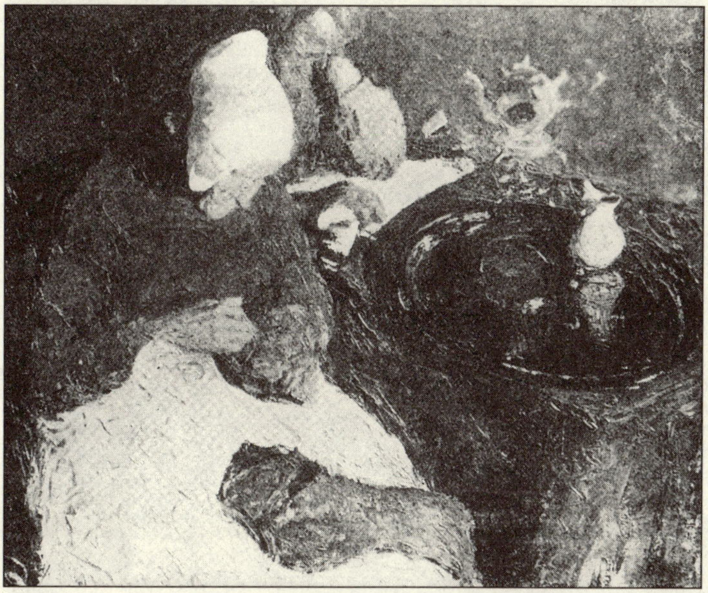

FIG. 46 *Charles Webster Hawthorne's heavy application of paint with a palette knife appears clearly in this reproduction of one of the pictures he painted in Zandvoort in 1898.*

FIG. 47 *The careful composition of the hands, detailed rendering of facial topography, and contrast of light skin against dark clothes and background in Charles Webster Hawthorne's* Three Women of Provincetown *recall the concerns of Frans Hals. Like Hals, Hawthorne painted a companion piece,* Selectmen of Provincetown *(1921, Art Institute of Chicago).*

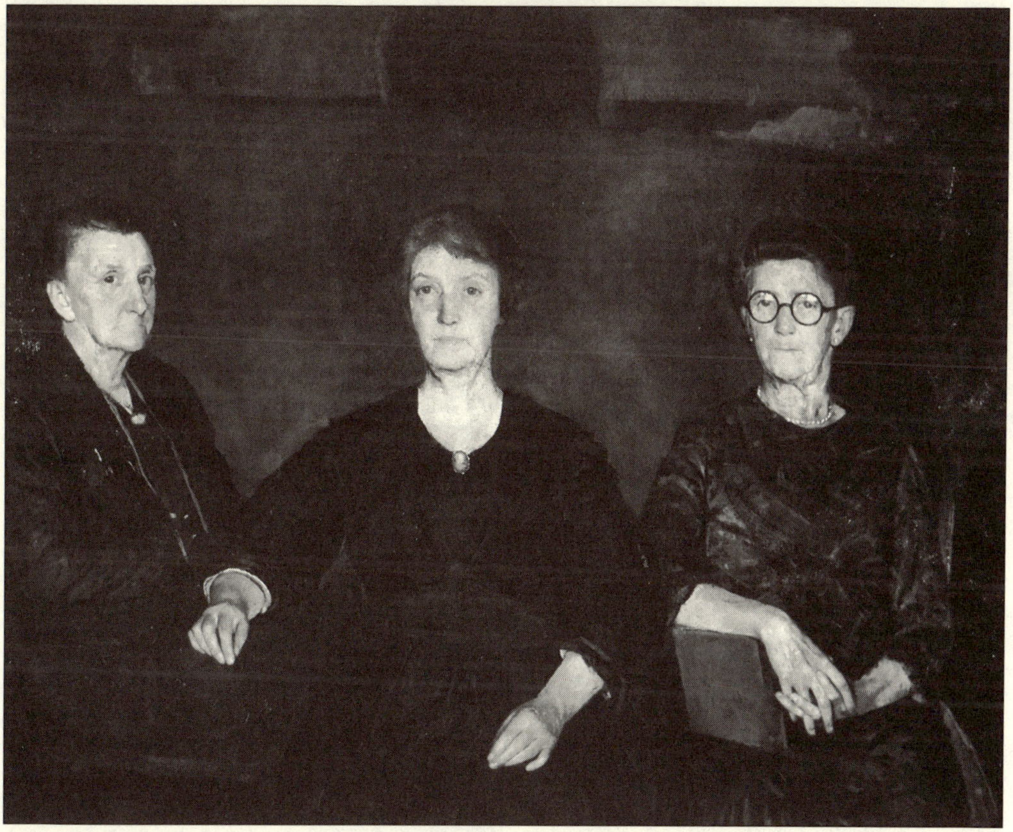

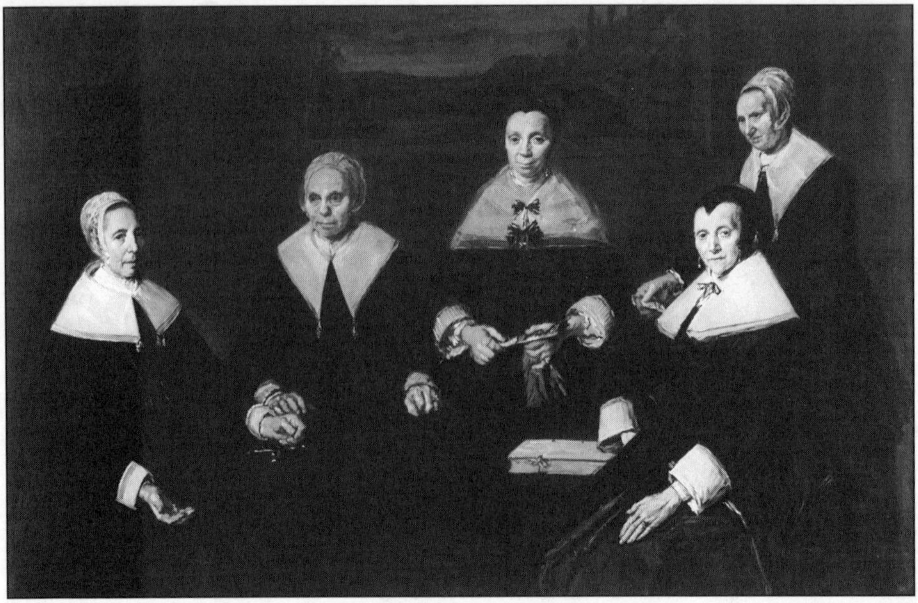

FIG. 48
Regentesses of the Old Men's Almshous *by Frans Hals provided inspiration for many American artists visiting Haarlem, including both Charles Webster Hawthorne, and his teacher, William Merritt Chase, whose copy of the painting Hawthorne may have known before he saw the original.*

institutions, and most closely resembles *Regentesses of the Old Men's Almshouse* (FIG. 48) by Frans Hals. Hawthorne had written about the Hals painting as soon as he saw it in Haarlem: "What pleased me most in the whole gallery was the 4 old ladies, you must know the reproduction, sitting around a table. He was over 80 years old when he painted it. To me it is the finest in the gallery. I came home and did a head the like of which I never did before. It is the first time that I have felt an influence on my work."[40] Although he mentions four ladies where there are five, he must be referring to the very popular *Regentesses*. Hawthorne painted the women of Provincetown with the same dark palette as Hals. Dressed in black, the fair tones of the women's heads and hands stand out against the darker background. Although their heads are arranged on one level, the variety of poses and carefully arranged hands give the composition the kind of interest of which Hals was a master. The summer in Holland served to synthesize Hawthorne's past learning and experiences and launched him on his very successful career as a painter and teacher in Provincetown.

It may be worth noting that E. Ambrose Webster and George Elmer Browne also started art schools in Provincetown, contributing to the growth of the artist colony there. Webster went to Cape Cod following several years of work in Egmond where he had absorbed the principles of *plein air* painting from George Hitchcock. Browne traveled frequently in the Netherlands beginning about 1901. He worked along the coast, painting beach scenes in Scheveningen and

Katwijk, and also painted inland shipping, landscapes, and city views. He did not establish his summer art school in Provincetown until 1915, although he had painted there earlier.

Charles and Marcia Woodbury painted in the Netherlands each year from 1890 through 1895, moving between Laren, Katwijk, and Volendam. After the birth of their son, however, they looked for a summer sketching site closer to home and found it in Ogunquit, Maine. Here they established a school and soon had a new summer colony. New England fishermen and children replaced the Dutch peasants in Marcia's paintings, while Charles continued to paint the breaking waves of the Atlantic that had become his forte. Although they did return to their lengthy Dutch sojourns when their son turned seven, Ogunquit remained their primary residence.

Henry Ward Ranger and William Henry Howe helped start the colony at Old Lyme, Connecticut around 1900. Its rural setting with green meadows and grazing cattle may have reminded them of the Dutch and French countrysides that inspired so many of their earlier pastoral paintings. These artists knew one another in Laren where they had gone in search of the new Barbizon style of the Hague School artists. Howe brought a bit of Holland to Old Lyme by decorating a door panel in Florence Griswold's house with a Dutch beach scene showing three characteristic flat-bottom fishing boats anchored in the surf under a stormy sky. The Griswold house served as the gathering place for the colony's artists.

The summer artist colonies in Provincetown, Ogunquit, and Old Lyme were patterned on their European counterparts and offered the same informal atmosphere of shared learning and *plein air* exercise. Their similarity to art colonies in France has been frequently noted—Old Lyme is called the American Barbizon—but the influence of the Dutch experience on the development of American art colonies at this time was equally strong.

All the American artist colonies in the Netherlands survived until about 1913 when political tensions in Europe discouraged artists in the United States from going abroad and convinced many expatriates in Holland to return home. The war years found only a few American artists in the Netherlands, notably those who had married Dutch citizens, and the colonies did not revive after World War I. Modern art had moved so far from the concerns of the erstwhile colonies that artists had little motivation to resettle in remote parts of Europe. World War I signaled an end to the life in Holland that hundreds of American artists had enjoyed for three decades.

THREE

Rewriting American History

IN 1903 THE *Ladies' Home Journal* PROCLAIMED HOLLAND the new Motherland of the United States, and the source of Americans' political and cultural roots. According to the *Journal*'s editor, Edward Bok, enlightened historians now recognized that:

> . . . the men who founded New York were not Englishmen, but largely Hollanders: that the Puritans who settled Plymouth had lived twelve years in Holland: that the Puritans who settled elsewhere in Massachusetts had all their lives been exposed to a Dutch influence: that New Jersey, as well as New York, was settled by the Dutch West India Company: that Connecticut was given life by Thomas Hooker, who came from a long residence in Holland: that Roger Williams, who founded Rhode Island, was a Dutch scholar: and that William Penn, the founder of Pennsylvania, came of a Dutch mother.[41]

These evidences of a Dutch heritage among the founding fathers and mothers of the United States provided the bedrock upon which some late-nineteenth-century historians built an argument for the country's essential Dutchness.

Because of the founders' Dutch heritage, explained Bok, they had looked to Holland for the ideals and institutions to make the new nation. The "four vital institutions" that he believed came directly from Holland included free public education, freedom of religious choice, freedom of the press, and the secret ballot. By attributing such integral aspects of American identity as personal freedoms and equal opportunity to the Dutch, he challenged Americans to rethink their relationship with the Netherlands. Bok believed that these and other evidences of the essential Dutchness of American character and culture were emerging in American consciousness and would soon lead to the repudiation of England as "the motherland of America" and the rightful elevation of the Netherlands to that title.

A decade of historical research and revisionist theory preceded Bok's revelation. In fact, he lifted whole segments of his essay straight out of the seminal argument for Dutch influence, an 1892 publication by the historian Douglas Campbell. Campbell's work and that of his adherents was, in turn, based on the writings of the older American historian, John Lothrop Motley.

JOHN LOTHROP MOTLEY

Motley's most famous books, *The Rise of the Dutch Republic* (1855), and *History of the United Netherlands* (1867), continued to provide Americans with their most basic understanding of Dutch history in the late nineteenth century. While Motley's stated purpose was to arrive through facts at the "truth" of Dutch historical events in the sixteenth and seventeenth centuries, his romantic style caused him to describe the emergence of a free Dutch nation as a thrilling drama in which the good Netherlanders fought the evil Spaniards and won. Questioning the significance of historical events for his own time, Motley wrote:

> Was it necessary that many generations should wade through this blood in order to acquire for their descendants the blessings of civil and religious freedom? Was it necessary that an Alva should ravage a peaceful nation with sword and flame—that desolation should be spread over a happy land, in order that the pure and heroic character of a William of Orange should stand forth more conspicuously, like an antique statue of spotless marble against a stormy sky?[42]

Motley's presentation of Spain in the guise of black evil threw the Dutch into relief as pure and heroic. His reference to William of Orange as a classical statue related the foremost hero of his story to what nineteenth-century Europeans and Americans considered the noblest periods of human history, ancient Greece and Rome. Motley tended to attribute this exemplary character to the Dutch people as a whole. He praised the citizens of Leyden, Naarden, and Alkmaar for their courage and heroism in persevering to the point of starvation through sieges by Spanish troops. He applauded the independence and spirit of self-sacrifice that led William the Silent to order the dikes cut and hundreds of hard-won acres of polder flooded so the Dutch could sail to the relief of their compatriots. Motley's dramatic, exclamatory prose alone might have guaranteed a good audience, but it was his sympathetic treatment of the subject that caused his histories of the Netherlands to become standard leisure reading in the United States.

Throughout *The Rise of the Dutch Republic*, Motley spoke from a distinctly American perspective. After outlining the history of Holland from Roman times to the fifteenth century, he concluded, "in this rapid sketch of the course and development of the Netherland nation during sixteen centuries, we have seen it ever marked by one prevailing characteristic, one master passion—the love of liberty, the instinct of self-government."[43] The rest of the book might have been written with a view to proving this characterization. Motley's stirring descriptions of one-sided battles in which small groups of brave Netherlanders defied the greater strength of disciplined Spanish troops had, for American readers, their obvious counterpart in the battles of the Revolutionary War. There too, common citizens had rebelled against an absentee monarch, fought a war for independence, and forged a new nation. Again and again Motley cited independence, courage, tolerance, and love of freedom as traits that characterized the Dutch people. By emphasizing the very traits that most Americans would have used to describe their own national character in his description of a struggle that paralleled the Revolutionary War, he won the sympathy and admiration of his American audience for the Netherlands.

In his four-volume *History of the United Netherlands*, Motley recounted the story of Holland's growing commercial interests and the Dutch Republic's spectacular rise to wealth and a position of world power. Although he made only brief mention of the United States in his prefaces and conclusions, he made it clear that he considered the history of the Dutch Republic of great importance to Americans, not only in providing a model for resistance to foreign despotism, but also in the rewards that seemed to follow naturally upon the adoption of policies of tolerance, equality, and freedom. He specifically cited "the political institutions bequeathed by the United States of the seventeenth century . . . vastly improved, both in theory and practice, by the United States of the nineteenth."[44] These hints that Americans owed fundamental principles to the earlier Dutch Republic, and that they were on the same course toward world power, set the stage for parallels to be drawn between the rise of the Dutch Republic in the sixteenth century, and the rise of the American Republic in the eighteenth. From this stage, revisionist historians built a new theory of American history in which Holland played the central role.

DOUGLAS CAMPBELL

The opening round in the battle to recognize Dutch influence in the founding of the United States and the formation of American character was fired in 1892 by Douglas Campbell, a lawyer whose interest in the history of jurisprudence in colonial New York had led him to the broader topic of his two-volume treatise, *The Puritan in Holland, England and America: An Introduction to American History*. Campbell's choice of title, particularly the order in which he placed the countries, gives the reader a preview of his perspective. He positioned the Dutch as first in significance throughout his discussions of American history.

Although Campbell's title suggests a relatively narrow subject matter, he did not limit himself to the study of a religious sect. By defining Puritans broadly as a class of Dutch and English reformers, he gave himself room to discuss the whole history of Holland, English relations with Holland, and finally the migration of people and ideas to North America. His real mission, as he revealed in his preface, was to prove that Holland, through the persons of the Puritans, exerted the seminal influence in the making of the United States.

Campbell left his readers in no doubt about the importance of his theory, stating in his preface:

> If I was correct in my hypothesis as to the debt which America owes to Holland—a debt incurred not only through New York, but also through the Pilgrims and Puritans of New England, and, as I afterwards discovered, through the Quakers of Pennsylvania—then our American history would occupy a different position from that usually accorded to it. Instead of standing alone as a phenomenon, to be studied by itself, or as a continuation of the record of

> Englishmen, to be studied on narrow insular lines, it would fill a much broader field, reaching back to Continental Europe, linking itself to the old civilization of the Romans, and forming more distinctly a part of that modern history which has been said to begin with the call of Abraham.

Here was a way to give the United States a unified and heroic history that extended back to antiquity, without recourse to the theory that it was a transplanted England.

To effect his ends, Campbell searched the historical records of old England, the old Dutch republic, and their colonies in North America for evidence of those institutions that later became distinguishing features of American identity. He used this material to pursue three lines of argument. First, he attempted to demonstrate that New Netherland had such American institutions as a system for recording deeds and mortgages, free public education, the principle of religious freedom, and the right of petition, and that New England did not. Second, he attempted to prove that those American institutions that did exist in New England actually came from Holland by way of English settlers who had taken refuge in Holland or who had been trained by Dutch immigrants in England before coming to America. Third, he stated that such things as the written ballot, prison reform, freedom of the press, religious liberty, and charitable institutions all came into existence in North America before they appeared in England, and thus could not have derived from England. Putting these three arguments together, Campbell concluded that most everything American had come from the Netherlands, either directly through Dutch settlers, or indirectly through Holland's influence on the British during the sixteenth and early seventeenth centuries.

An analysis of the accuracy of Campbell's and his followers' arguments is beyond the scope of this study. My purpose is to clarify their position and to show how their interpretation spread from a small group of historians to a fairly broad base of public acceptance. The fact that many Americans came to believe, for however short a time, that their roots were firmly planted in sixteenth- and seventeenth-century Holland provided the theoretical basis for their forays into Dutch culture.

In a chapter entitled "The Netherland Republic and the United States," Campbell set forth the ways in which he believed Dutch institutions entered colonial America. These are worth quoting because they are the arguments that contemporaries most often repeated, apparently having had the greatest force with his audience. Campbell reminded readers that in New York and New Jersey, which were settled by the Dutch, "Dutch laws and institutions reigned supreme for more than half a century." The first settlers of Plymouth Colony "also came directly from Holland, and, as Palfrey has pointed out, all that was best in the new additions for several years came from the same country." Most of the settlers of the Massachusetts Bay Colony came from the southern and eastern counties of England "in which a hundred thousand Netherland refugees had taken up their residence half a century before, and which always had the most intimate relations with the Dutch Republic." In Providence, Rhode Island, Campbell reported, Roger Williams "put into full operation the principles of religious and civil liberty which he had learned from the Dutch Anabaptists." Connecticut was created by "a little detachment from Plymouth, carrying Dutch ideas—some of its members having doubtless lived in Holland," and by the Englishmen, John Davenport and Thomas Hooker, who had lived in exile in Holland for three years. Connecticut Colony also had a written constitution, the first, according to Campbell, since the Union of Utrecht.[45]

Coming at last to "the most southern point to which Dutch influence upon the early settlers of America can be traced, and...the limit of the colonies whose institutions, except that of slavery, have affected the American Commonwealth," Campbell cited the founding of Pennsylvania and Delaware by William Penn. "Penn's mother was a Dutch woman from Rotterdam, and . . . . His peculiar religious ideas, as we have already seen, were derived from his mother's country. He travelled extensively in Holland, and spoke the language so well that he preached to the Dutch Quakers in their native tongue." Penn joined Algernon Sidney, "who was perfectly familiar with the institutions of the Netherland Republic, and on most intimate terms with its leading statesmen," to write the law code and constitution for Pennsylvania.[46]

Campbell followed this recital of Dutch contacts with still more institutions that he said the United States adopted from Holland. They ranged from the concept of a district attorney, to the use of one vote per state within the Senate. Of these arguments, the most persuasive among his contemporaries were probably those that Edward Bok chose to paraphrase: "Take the two documents upon which the whole fabric of the establishment and maintenance of America rests—the Declaration of Independence and the Federal Constitution of the United States—and one, the Declaration, is based almost entirely upon the Declaration of Independence of the United Republic of the Netherlands; while all through the Constitution its salient points are based upon, and some literally copied from, the Dutch Constitution."[47] No two written documents symbolized the character of the United States better than the Declaration of Independence and the Constitution. By giving them a Dutch genesis, Campbell sealed his argument.

Anticipating a poor reception of his thesis from traditional historians, Campbell attempted to smooth his path by explaining why earlier historians had missed the all-important Dutch connection. He concluded that previous histories had all been written from a British point of view by British historians who wanted to claim credit for American successes or by New Englanders who attributed everything not obviously British to native genius. An impartial audience, he contended, would see the justice of his theory.

Campbell's book started a sharp debate among scholars that slowly spread to a general audience through articles in popular magazines. Reviewing the book in *Lippincott's Monthly Magazine* five years after its publication, Sydney Fisher exclaimed:

> It was an unexpected, stunning blow, a clap of thunder out of a clear sky. Two large, handsome volumes, written in an attractive, even brilliant manner, informing us in sharp, sarcastic sentences, with an immense array of facts, that our most cherished liberties and customs were neither English nor native, but Dutch, were so dazing that no one at first knew what to say, and we have scarcely yet mustered courage enough to frame a reply.[48]

Fisher hit upon the two aspects of the book that caused historians the greatest consternation. It was too radical for scholars to swallow without a great deal more debate and proof, but so persuasively argued that the general public might easily accept it.

The strongest criticisms leveled at Campbell concerned his reliance on secondary sources and his penchant for accepting primacy as proof of origin without showing evidence of actual influence. Fisher expressed annoyance and unwilling admiration in equal parts for Campbell's ability to convince without showing proof. According to Fisher, Campbell was a master of suggestion and insinuation who gave general information in such a way that "an untrained mind can hardly resist the impression that America was thoroughly Dutch in origin." Campbell's lack of Dutch language sources also cast his scholarship into doubt. One of his strongest detractors, Henry Bourne, was particularly offended that "in proving this ambitious thesis, he depends largely upon a vilification of almost all English institutions, both present and past," and accused Campbell's Scottish heritage of prejudicing his scholarship. Even scholars who responded positively to the general thesis expressed reservations. At least one, while refraining from an outright endorsement of Campbell's claims, attempted to strengthen them by adding two new sources that "even Mr. Campbell, indefatigable and comprehensive as he was in his claims for the little republic, did not recognize."[49]

In spite of, or perhaps because of, the criticism and controversy, Campbell's revolutionary interpretation of American history found a wide audience. The first edition of *The Puritan in Holland, England and America*, which appeared in January, 1892, was quickly followed by a second, corrected edition in August and a third edition in December. Although the size of each printing is unknown, the advent of three editions in one year suggests a wider readership than author and publishers originally anticipated.

WILLIAM ELLIOT GRIFFIS

Campbell wrote primarily for scholars, and as the reviews above demonstrate, he was not entirely successful in convincing them. It took another author, William Elliot Griffis, to popularize Campbell's historical arguments. An enthusiastic historian with no Dutch ancestry, Griffis proved himself an indefatigable worker in the cause of the new history. He wrote eight books and dozens of pamphlets and articles, gave innumerable lectures and sermons, and organized clubs around the country to study Dutch influence and erect commemorative plaques in the Netherlands. His interest arose from research on the history of Schenectady, New York, where he served a Dutch Reformed church for nine years.

The practiced eloquence and polished oratory that Griffis developed as a dominie in the Reformed Protestant Church helped him bring his message to the public. Unlike Campbell, he did not cite sources or load his argument with facts and figures. Instead he simply stated as fact many of the conclusions that he and Campbell had arrived at almost simultaneously. In fact his first publication, a forty-page transcript of a lecture he delivered before the Boston

Congregational Club entitled *The Influence of the Netherlands in the Making of the English Commonwealth and the American Republic*, preceded Campbell's book by four months. This lecture did not have the impact on historical thinking that Campbell's book would because Griffis wrote it for a select religious audience and much of it explored the Dutch origins of Congregationalism. However, it provides an early example of Griffis's method of dealing with the issue of Dutch influence.

Like Campbell, with whom Griffis was in close correspondence, Griffis believed that Holland was the center of learning, arts, and civilization in the sixteenth century, while England remained barbaric and feudal. As Spanish oppression drove the Hollanders out, many took their skills and beliefs to England where, Griffis asserted, they were each required by law to train one English apprentice. Griffis attributed the subsequent development of English agriculture, painting, banking, and theology, as well as their industrial revolution, to that influx of Dutch refugees. He then enumerated the Dutch ideas that these English people, their compatriots who took refuge in Holland, and the Dutch colonists brought to North America: religious toleration, free presses, free schools, registered lands, local self-government, written ballots, the jurisprudence system, a republic of united states, and a written constitution. Griffis simply listed influences, but alerted his listeners to Campbell's forthcoming book which he said would document and develop the ideas he had set forth.

While Campbell wrote on a scholarly level, Griffis often employed a high school vocabulary and rudimentary syntax that made his writing accessible to a larger audience. For example, he chose to translate the name of the old Dutch republic (called by others the United Netherlands or the United Provinces) as the United States of the Netherlands in order to subtly reinforce his message of Dutch affinity with the United States of America. Sometimes he referred to both countries simply as the United States. In like manner, Griffis gave his principal book on Dutch influence the unpretentious title, *Brave Little Holland and What She Taught Us* (1894). *Brave Little Holland* reached a broader, more diverse audience than Campbell's two tomes and became one of Griffis's most popular works.

Despite his choice of expression, Griffis claimed the status of a scholar. He made numerous trips to the Netherlands to study Dutch documents and frequently worked in American archives. As a member of the American Historical Association, he attended Dutch conferences, and the Netherlandish Society of Letters in Leyden also elected him to membership, honors he rarely failed to mention in his writings. Griffis also lacked Campbell's fanaticism on the subject of Dutch influence versus British and thereby avoided the accusations of partisanship to which Campbell fell subject. Griffis happily credited the British with a positive influence on the development of American politics and culture and even dedicated *The Pilgrims in their Three Homes: England, Holland and America* (notice the change in word order from Campbell's similarly titled book) to his English ancestors and "mighty England." He presented the Dutch influence as an addition, not a replacement, of previous history. Griffis's moderation and his lack of pedantry, as much as his frequently repeated credentials and absence of Dutch blood helped to convince the general reader of his authority.

Like Campbell, Griffis pointed out that the Dutch Republic was a major economic power and one of the only alternatives to monarchy at work in the world in which the founding fathers prepared to create the United States of America. He concluded that they used this model. "From the Dutch system they borrowed the idea of a written Constitution, a Senate, or States-General, the Hague or District of Columbia, the Supreme Court (with vast improvements), . . . and many of the details of the Dutch state and national systems."[50] But Griffis improved on Campbell for the general audience because he supported such statements with quotes from famous Americans, including Benjamin Franklin, James Madison, George Washington, and John Adams, rather than with complex comparisons of the Dutch and American systems.

> In love of liberty and bravery in the defense of it, she has been our great example.
>
> —Benjamin Franklin

> The originals of the two republics are so much alike that a page from one seems a transcript from the other.
>
> —John Adams

These easy-to-remember quotes became standard fare in the subsequent debates over Dutch influence.

In addition to simplicity of expression and omission of documentation, Griffis personalized the Dutch-American connection to make it relevant and believable to the average American. His historical arguments were strewn with references to the present.

He contended that the most common American family names were "purely Dutch," having been altered in English from Pickard to Packard, Bruyn to Brown, DeWitt to Dwight, Kuyper to Cooper, and so on. He claimed that Hollanders invented many familiar aspects of American life besides names: the English language came from Frisian, American coinage from the Dutch daalder and cents, the liberty bell from Dutch town bells, the use of stars and stripes in red, white, and blue from the flags of the Beggars of the Sea and the Dutch Republic, and flowering bulbs—including a new variety called Abraham Lincoln—from Dutch cultivation and breeding. The modern plough, bricks and glazed tiles, the game of golf, the word "cookie," waffles, oil painting and wood-engraving, telescopes, microscopes, thermometers, the pendulum clock, the compass, glass hothouses, underclothing, starch, driving on the right hand side of the road, the standard gauge for wheeled vehicles, the song Yankee Doodle, Thanksgiving Day, and a host of other things Griffis also attributed to Holland. While the general public might not follow Campbell's abstruse arguments of primacy or remember historical details, everyone knew the American flag and Thanksgiving Day. By explaining such familiar American customs and objects in terms of Dutch precedent, Griffis went a long way toward convincing his audience of the importance of Holland in American history.[51]

Griffis also appealed to the experiences and observations of American travelers to argue that contemporary Americans felt more comfortable in Holland than in England. In 1899, Griffis published *The American in Holland*, a travel book based on his five voyages in the Netherlands. As he led his reader through the eleven provinces he lost no opportunity to point out the parallels between Dutch and American history and the similarities of Dutch and American customs. This proved particularly easy to do in travel articles and books, as the following passage about Utrecht demonstrates:

> Well might every patriotic American uncover at the mention of this Dutch city's name, for here was the first seat of federal government in Northern Europe. At Utrecht the 'Liberty Bell' first rang out. Here men talked of 'the Father of his Country,' the 'Declaration of Independence,' the 'Written Constitution,' 'Freedom of speech and conscience for all men,' and 'The supremacy of the National Government over secession.' Here it was declared that 'the Union must and shall be preserved.' . . . So uninformed are we Americans of our real origin that thousands of us think of these phrases as American: that we coined them: that they are our own! And yet,

> over there in the Dutch city of Utrecht, were they born nearly two hundred years before our Republic was born, and carried over here by our forefathers.[52]

Without recourse to the facts of history, by simply repeating patriotic phrases familiar to every American, Griffis suggested America's debt to Holland. By these various means, Griffis's writings first made revisionist history widely accessible to average Americans.

THE DUTCH INTERPRETATION DISSEMINATED

Many other authors followed with new compilations of information from Motley, Campbell, and Griffis, reinforced by their own reasons for believing in the Dutch essence of the United States. Edward Bok's essay "The Mother of America" not only cited political influences, but pointed out the advances in commerce and merchandising, medicine, international law, publishing, education, and music that seventeenth-century Holland gave as a legacy to the United States and the world.

Tiemen de Vries, professor of Dutch institutions at the University of Chicago, published eight lectures in his book *Dutch History, Art and Literature for Americans* (1912). The first lecture explained the influence of Holland on America in much the same terms used by Campbell and Griffis. To this he added a succinct discussion of the parallels in Dutch and American history, intended to convince the hearer of Dutch influence on the United States without actually showing any point of contact. According to De Vries, the histories of the old Dutch republic and of the United States could be described in ten identical, sequential stages: (1) A period of separate independent colonies/provinces, (2) Suppression by the foreign sovereign ending in revolution, (3) Declaration of Independence/Act of Abjuration, (4) Act of Confederation/Union of Utrecht, (5) War of Independence led by the father of the country, (6) A critical period, (7) Growth of the Republic and balance of two parties, (8) Conflict of two parties ending in a civil war, (9) Continuation of the two parties to the present time, (10) Democratic, Republican, religious, and social spirit. Three years later another Dutch-American, H. A. Torchiana, produced a slender volume entitled *Holland, The Birthplace of American Political, Civic and Religious Liberty*. Torchiana also followed Campbell's and Griffis's strategy of stressing the differences between the United

States and England and the similarities between the United States and Holland in a comparison of political institutions and customs in the sixteenth and seventeenth centuries. His condensation of their arguments produced an easily absorbed statement of the theory of Dutch influence.

The multiplying resources on Dutch-American historical relations could not pass unnoticed, and began to enter casually into patriotic discourse. Addressing a crowd on Forefather's Day, David Gregg said, "I notice in the very start that there are new claims being made to-day on behalf of the Dutch. American history is being rewritten; new research is being made to find the origin of our civil institutions." After stating that historians had ignored Holland's influence on America because of their strong English bias, Gregg explained that the Dutch actually helped build the United States "by hewing and shaping and filling and inspiring the English Pilgrims and Puritans" and "by the colony of the New Netherlands which they established upon our shores, and by the influence which it exerted in sister colonies."[53] Such generalizations of the Dutch influence became fairly routine and could be accepted without necessitating the total abandonment of previously held beliefs about American history.

Once the historical relationship between Holland and the United States was established, seemingly any aspect of American life could be attributed to Dutch influence. For instance, Edward Bok included the following passage in his 1903 editorial:

> We speak of the American woman to-day as a type apart from the women of all other nations, and I am inclined to think that sometimes, in our forgetfulness of the world's history, we are apt to think of her as of our own creation. But we need only to read a few chapters of Dutch history to see whence she came.

Bok was referring to the relative freedom enjoyed by American women and he was not alone in believing they got it from the example of Dutch women. J. A. Metz, an author for *The World To-day*, declared that the Netherlands deserved the honor of hosting the International Woman Suffrage Alliance in 1909 because few other nations could claim the achievements Holland had made in equal education, suffrage, children's rights, and equal pay for equal work. Bok put it bluntly:

> The direct influence of the emancipation of woman as a sex—whether we regard the question from the original source of the laws

> relating to a married woman, her equal education with men, or her absolute sovereignty in the home—came from the Netherlands.

American women may have shared this perception, for Elizabeth Champney reported that, after Paris, more female art students went to Holland for training than to any other European Country and she attributed this in part to "the excellence of the academies, in which women have an equal footing with the men."[54] In reality only one American woman, Amy Cross, and a handful of men enrolled in Dutch art academies, but it is true that women went to Holland to work with more experienced compatriots like Emma Lampert and Wilhelmina Hawley and perhaps with Dutch women such as Wally Moes or Arina Hugenholz. In any case, the fact that Americans found it possible to ascribe to foreign influence anything they prided themselves on as much as the unique "American Girl" suggests the extent to which a new understanding of Holland had pervaded American culture.

Perhaps more influential and successful than any other medium in selling the Dutch interpretation of American history were the Chautauqua Literary and Scientific Circles (CLSC), which devoted their 1908–1909 curriculum to a study of the Netherlands. As the continuing education branch of the popular summer education movement known as Chautauqua, the CLSC offered correspondence classes during the winter for adults who organized themselves into study groups in their home towns throughout the United States. *The Chautauquan*, the official CLSC publication, provided required readings and study guides. In 1908, *The Chautauquan* carried a series of articles called "A Reading Journey in the Hollow-Land" by the artist-illustrator George Wharton Edwards, and a separate series on Dutch art. Edwards had read and thoroughly absorbed the work of Campbell, whose ideas he skillfully inserted into his travel description of Holland. The extent to which this course of readings followed the new history can be gathered from a representative sampling of the review questions provided by the magazine. Some review questions for "A Reading Journey" included: "How did early Dutch history compare with that of England?" "In what ways have the Dutch people proved their genius?" and "How do Dutchman and American seem to resemble each other?"

The Chautauquan supplemented the essays in its pages with suggestions for specific readings in other books and magazines, including *Brave Little Holland* by Griffis, several popular Dutch travel books, maps, current events in newspapers, and articles on

Dutch artists in *International Studio* and *Century Magazine*. Even a series of articles published by George H. Boughton in *Harper's Magazine* twenty-five years earlier, "Artist's Strolls in Holland," resurfaced as recommended reading. The Chautauqua course used both word and image to present Holland to its learners, emphasizing Dutch art and the new history.

To help students assimilate this diverse information, the magazine provided a series of activities for each week of the month. In the weekly roll call, members of local circles took turns contributing answers to specific questions. One week they had to list "national characteristics of the Hollander." Another time the roll call required identification of famous paintings or contribution of current news items relating to Holland. Other weekly activities included papers and oral reports researched by individuals and presented to their groups. *The Chautauquan* suggested topics such as the work of Motley as historian of the Netherlands, the Pilgrims in Amsterdam, the position of women in Holland, characteristics of the States General, the Dutch army and navy of today, Hugo Grotius, and the Dutch East India Company. In this manner, small reading circles and individuals throughout the country were led through a study of the geography, history, literature, art, social customs, politics, and current events of the Netherlands, with frequent reference to its relevance for the United States. The Chautauqua program produced an audience well prepared to accept the veracity of historians' claims for Holland.

The Dutch theory of American history shocked many hearers at first acquaintance, but it had a natural correlate in the germ theory, an argument set forth by historian Herbert Baxter Adams of Johns Hopkins University. Baxter saw the foundation of American civilization in Germany and traced its journeys through England to America, using the imagery of germs, seeds, roots, and branches. Griffis and some of the other proponents of Dutch origin, while denying German primacy, nevertheless appropriated the terminology of germ theory. Griffis wrote, "To my mind it is more than probable that our American Congregationalism was borrowed, in germ, at least, from these Dutch refugees in England," and more broadly, "The seeds of that spirit were implanted in the Netherlands in the breasts of the earliest makers of this country and have flowered broadcast to their development with a faithfulness to their Dutch originals in many cases nothing short of amazing."[55] Of course, the nearness of German and Dutch cultures makes the parallel between these theories even more striking. In a broader sense, they could both be described as part of the concept of

Manifest Destiny, which saw the flow of civilization from east to west as a God-given mandate. So even though the notion of American institutions originating in Holland struck many Americans as improbable at first, its position beside the germ theory under the umbrella of Manifest Destiny lent it credibility.

HISTORY OF NEW NETHERLAND

The general arguments presented by Campbell, popularized by Griffis, and solidified by *The Chautauquan* and other journals were particularized in the many new histories that appeared on very specific areas related to the Dutch–American question. One of these areas of research was the history of New Netherland and its impact on later developments in New York and New Jersey (FIG. 49c). The contemporary scholar Paul Huey has noted that archeological interest in seventeenth-century New York sites began to increase in the 1880s, and reached a peak as construction sites between 1900 and 1920 revealed more old Dutch artifacts.[56] A review of the literature on colonial New York from 1800 to 1920 shows a similar awakening of interest in the 1880s, but particularly in the 1890s after Campbell's work appeared.

One of the main authorities on colonial American history, John Fiske, published a two-volume history of the Dutch and Quaker colonies in 1899. Cognizant of the long tradition of interpreting American history solely in terms of its English colonists, and of the recent reaction to that tradition in the appearance of ethnic studies, Fiske chose a middle road between the two. While valuing the work of historical societies and special interest groups, he pointed out their excess of enthusiasm as a common flaw, citing Campbell's work as an example of this problem. He included a whole chapter on the Dutch influence on England, carefully correcting those aspects of the revisionist theory with which he disagreed and embracing those that found his favor. Accordingly, he enlarged upon Griffis's discussion of the translation of Dutch names into English, concluding that "there is thus strong ground for the assertion of Mr. Griffis, that many Americans who boast of their 'unmixed English stock' are descended from Dutch or Flemish ancestors who first saw England in the Duke of Alva's time."[57] On the other hand, Fiske denied the revisionists' assertion that only the Dutch and Quakers paid the Indians for their land and noted that the patroon system in New Netherland lacked any semblance of democracy.

On either side of Fiske may be found interpretations of New Netherland history leaning strongly to the Dutch or to the English side. The ubiquitous William Elliot Griffis in his *Story of New Netherland*, predictably, took the former position. One of Griffis's goals was to challenge the effects of Washington Irving's *A History of New-York by Diedrich Knickerbocker*. Irving's fictional satire was the best known discussion of the colonial Dutch published before 1880, and many people apparently accepted its bias as fact. Griffis recounted Irving's characterization of the Dutch people as lazy dreamers and stupid humorists in order to refute it with his own glowing appraisal: "They stood for pure family life, for the Church and the school, and for farming, the true source of all legitimate national wealth of land-dwellers, for they were, most of them, either skilled workmen or tillers of the soil."[58] Most of his book reasserts the theory that the Dutch contributed largely to forming American character.

On the other side of Fiske's moderate position stands Maud Goodwin. Far from repudiating Irving, Goodwin appears to have accepted Irving's tales as true American myths, indicative of the credulity of the Dutch people: "We may find it hard to reconcile the reputation of the Dutch as a phlegmatic and unimaginative people with the fact that they and their children endowed the Hudson with more glamour, more of the supernatural and of elfin lore than haunts any other waterway in America....tales were told of phantom ships, of ghosts walking on the cliffs of the Highlands." She even quoted Diedrich Knickerbocker to describe the true life of colonial New Amsterdamers.[59]

Historians approached the subject of English versus Dutch influence in early New York from their separate perspectives. Goodwin explained the changes that took place after England conquered New Netherland as great benefits to the Dutch colonists. This steady progress met a temporary setback, in her view, when the Dutch reclaimed the territory. Opposed to this British perspective is Griffis's Dutch bias. He believed that the Dutch colonists had maintained most of their culture even after England gained control. "Happily for the future of the United States, Dutch republican ideas remained. In politics everything was nominally English, but social and church life and democratic ideas were Dutch."[60]

Well before the advent of Campbell's revisionist history, historical and genealogical societies with special interest in Dutch ancestry had promoted the study of New Netherland history. They had already advanced colonial Dutch contributions to the United States and they continued to speak for Dutch-American interests throughout this period. The City History Club of New York worked to spread the message of America's debt to the Dutch. Mrs. Robert Abbe founded the City History Club in 1896 out of her conviction that New York was being overrun by "hundreds of thousands of illiterate Hungarians, Italians, Slavs, Jews, Turks, Armenians, Greeks, and Bohemians—the rag-tag and bobtail of the earth, most of whom have never heard of history, do not know what it is, and herd in the tenements like rabbits in a warren."[61] The growing fear that the established American culture would be overwhelmed by the cultures of new immigrants from southern and eastern Europe increased interest in Holland's contributions to the forming of the nation on the part of Americans of the old stock. The new history reinforced the idea that essential aspects of American identity originated in western Europe. Mrs. Abbe believed that the diverse new elements she abhorred could become Americanized if they learned the Dutch history of the United States. The club's many publications included the *Half-Moon Papers* and the *New Amsterdam Year Book*, which provided a forum for articles on old Dutch families, customs, and architecture in New York.

The Holland Society of New York, established in 1885 for male descendants of colonial Dutch settlers, had as its purpose the collection and preservation of information respecting early Dutch history in North America. In addition, it published speeches from its annual banquets and summaries of its yearly activities. The Holland Society shared the City Club's concern that the basic character of the United States was in danger of being debased by thousands of German, Irish, and Italian immigrants. In 1890 Theodore Roosevelt addressed the Holland Society, of which he was a prominent member, with these words:

> [Early Dutch colonists] possessed the faculty of becoming good American citizens, completely Americanized in heart and mind, paying no heed to things European, but pressing all their energies into the service of the mighty Republican Commonwealth of which they had become a part. The history of our Dutch ancestors, and of the part they have played in America, . . . has a direct bearing upon one of the great questions of the present day, the assimilation of the masses of our foreign-born fellow-citizens. The thoroughness with which the Hollander has become Americanized . . . makes him invaluable as an object-lesson to some of the races who have followed him to America at an interval of about two centuries.[62]

This view assumed that American and Dutch culture and character were closely allied. It articulated a need for all non-Dutch immigrants to embrace the Dutchness of America. The City History Club went so far as to form history classes for immigrant children in which the participants played roles as Dutch colonists in order to learn American history and inculcate patriotism.

While other regions took up the Netherlands as a novelty, residents of New York City, Albany, Rochester, and other old Dutch communities in the east had a deeper stake in the national focus on Holland. By digging into local history and family genealogies, people in these cities added materially to the growing knowledge of a Dutch-American connection. To give just one more example, in 1897 Helen Lincklaen Fairchild published the eighteenth-century journals of her ancestor John Lincklaen. He had traveled through Pennsylvania, upstate New York, and Vermont as an agent of the Holland Land Company, inspecting land for possible purchase by the Netherlands investors who formed the Company. Fairchild's investigation of her ancestor's activities provided the context for his journals and chronicled the purchase of over one million acres of land from the Iroquois by the Holland Land Company. Such research into areas of strong Dutch influence made that influence more visible. But even in Boston, where colonial Dutch influence was minimal, historical societies got into the act. In 1896 the Old South Club invited Griffis to lecture on Motley's history of the Dutch Republic and published a translation of the "Dutch Declaration of Independence."

Many publications for the promotion of Dutch-American history and relations were founded in this period. One of the most significant, *The New Amsterdam Gazette* edited by Morris Coster, began publication in July, 1883, as a ten-cent weekly. Coster explained in this first issue the *Gazette*'s purpose to recall "to the New Yorkers of to-day the early founders of their city, by acquainting them with the current history of Holland." The *Gazette* reported not only on current events in Dutch and American affairs, but also followed the progress of Dutch immigrant communities throughout the United States. Many of these communities began their own newspapers, either in the Dutch language or bilingual Dutch and English. To name but a few, Paterson, New Jersey produced *De Telegraaf* (1880–1921) and *Het Oosten* (1904–1940); Pella, Iowa published *Pella's Weekblad* (1861–1942); Holland, Michigan produced *De Hope* (1865–1933) and *De Grondwet* (1860–1938); Orange City, Iowa

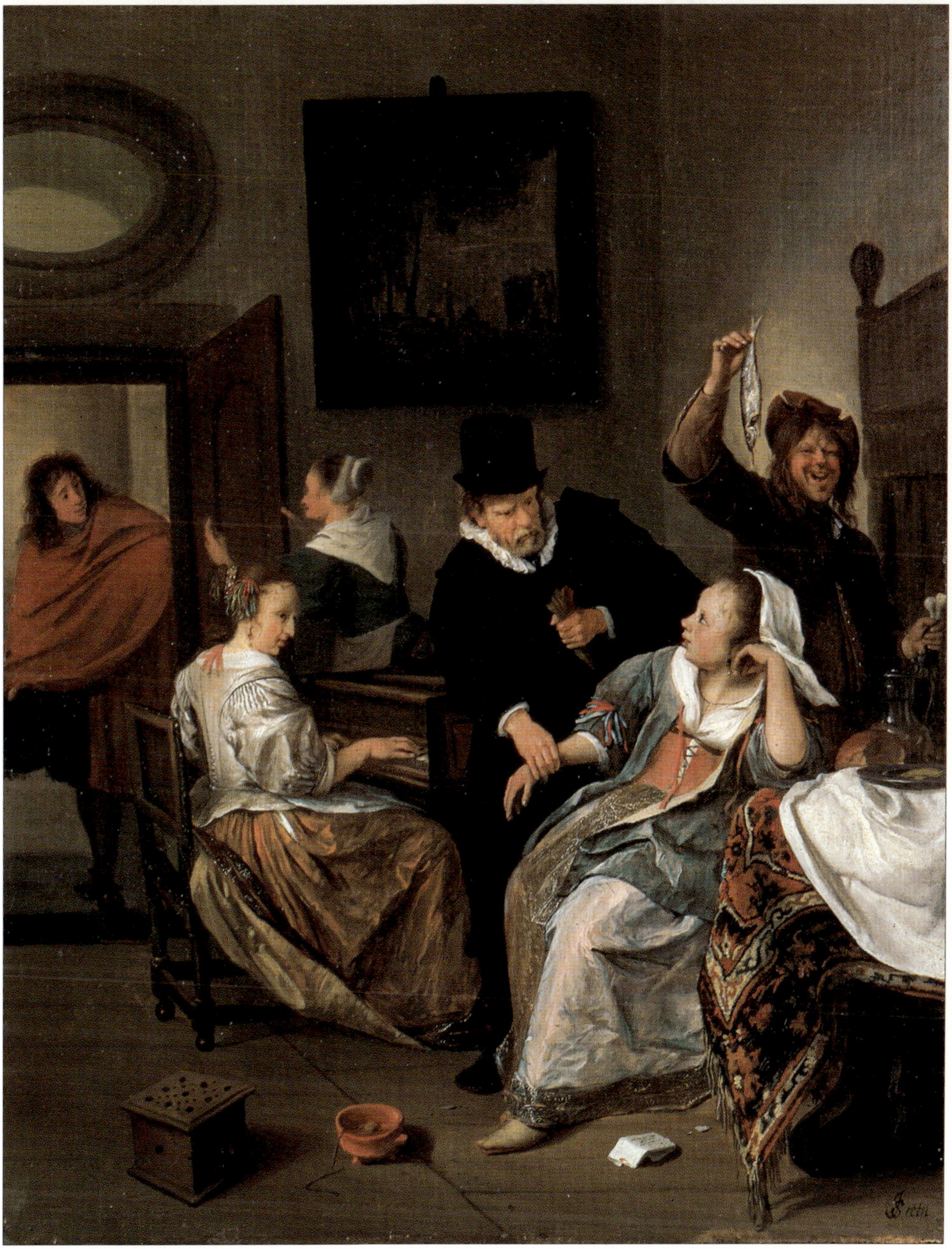

FIG. 1 *Philadelphia collector John Graver Johnson bought* The Doctor's Visit *by Jan Steen in 1899 to supplement his growing collection of old Dutch masters.*

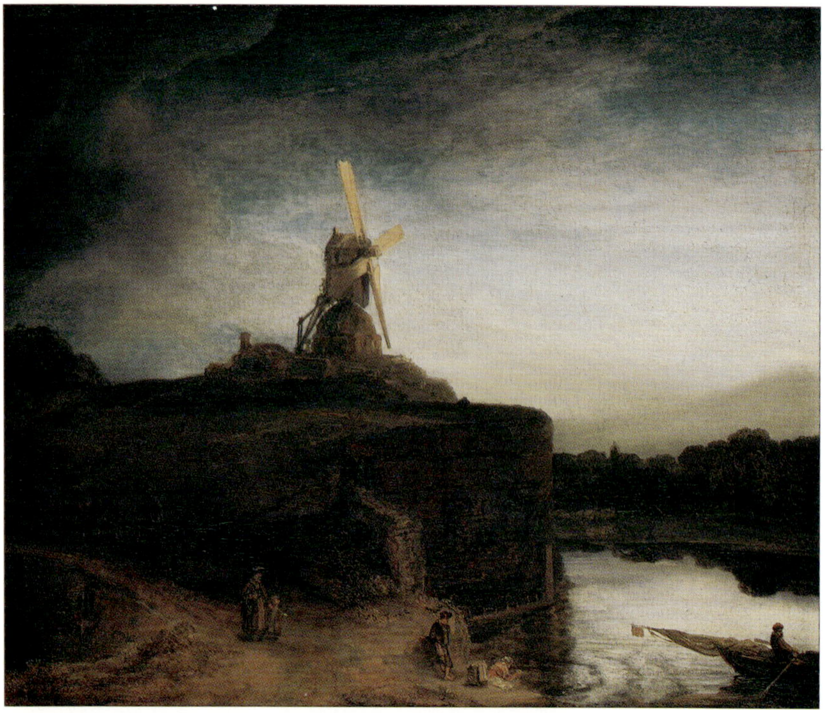

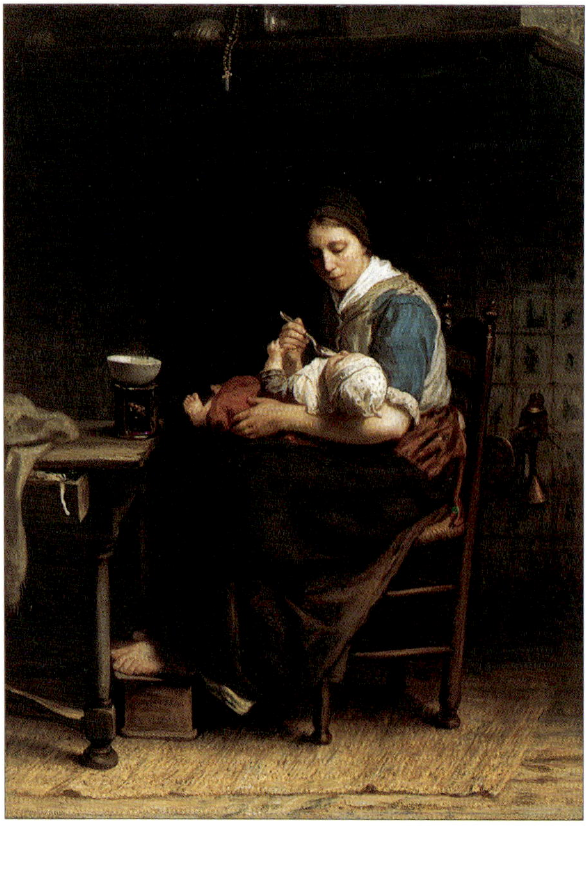

FIG. 2 *Peter Widener purchased* The Mill *from Lansdowne for a record £100,000 in 1911. He later gave it, with his collection, to the National Gallery of Art in Washington, D.C., where it is still considered an outstanding example of Rembrandt's work. Scholars continue to debate the attribution.*

FIG. 4 *Mrs. Harry N. Torrey purchased* The Cottage Madonna *by Jozef Israëls in 1902 and later gave it to the Detroit Institute of Arts. Israëls was the best known contemporary Dutch artist in turn-of-the-century America.*

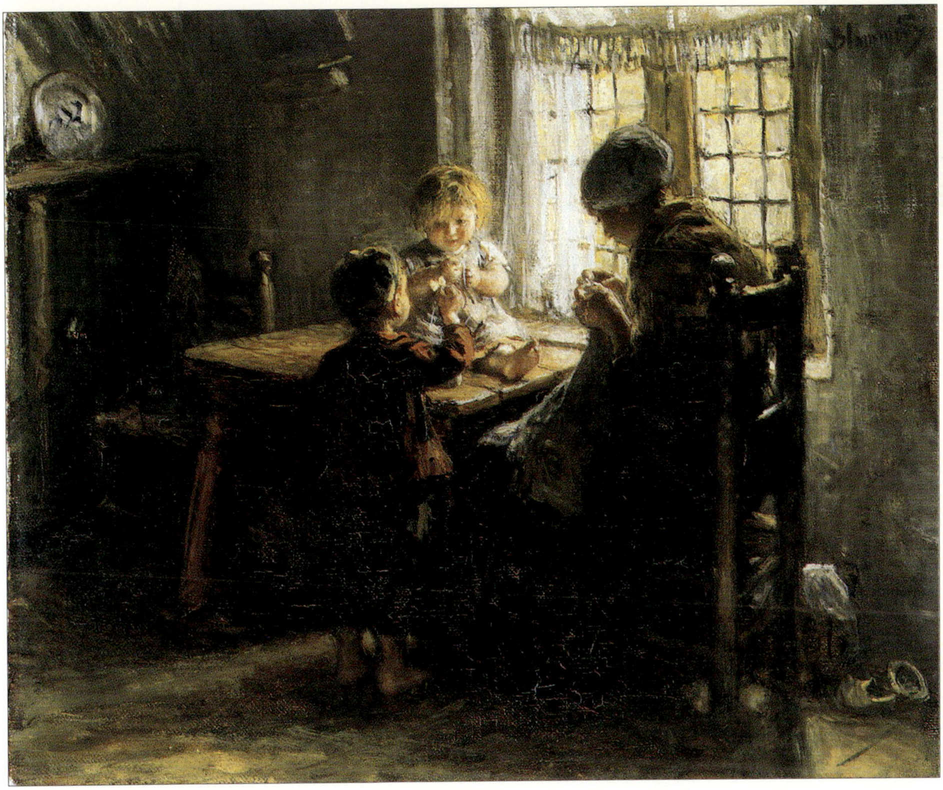

FIG. 5 *Knoedler and Company of New York, one of the major American dealers in Dutch pictures, helped George Eastman acquire paintings by Rembrandt and Hals, as well as numerous examples by artists of The Hague School, including* The Butterfly *by Bernardus Johannes Blommers. Eastman gave* The Butterfly, *with part of his collection, to the Memorial Gallery of the University of Rochester.*

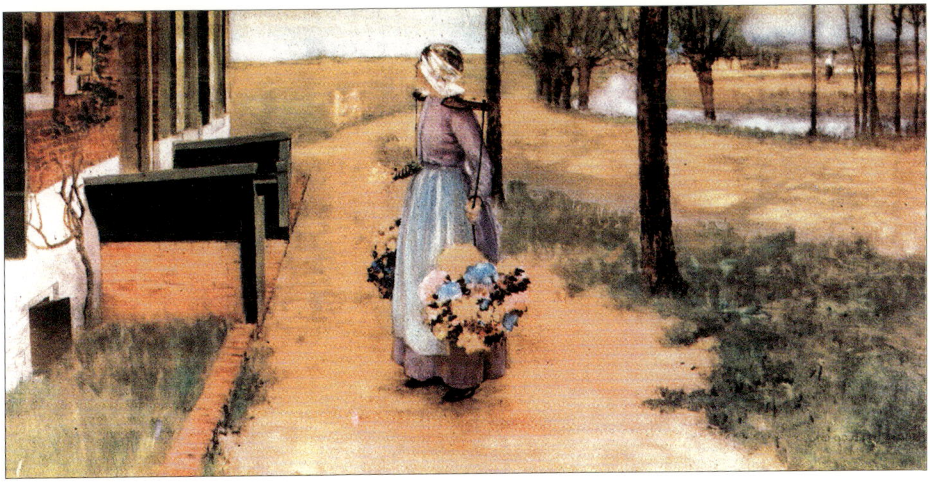

FIG. 10 *The popularity of George Hitchcock's painting,* Flower Girl in Holland, *is indicated by the many fine art reproductions of it that were available around the turn of the century. Prints like this hung on many people's walls, while the original oil graced the collection of Chicago hotelier Potter Palmer.*

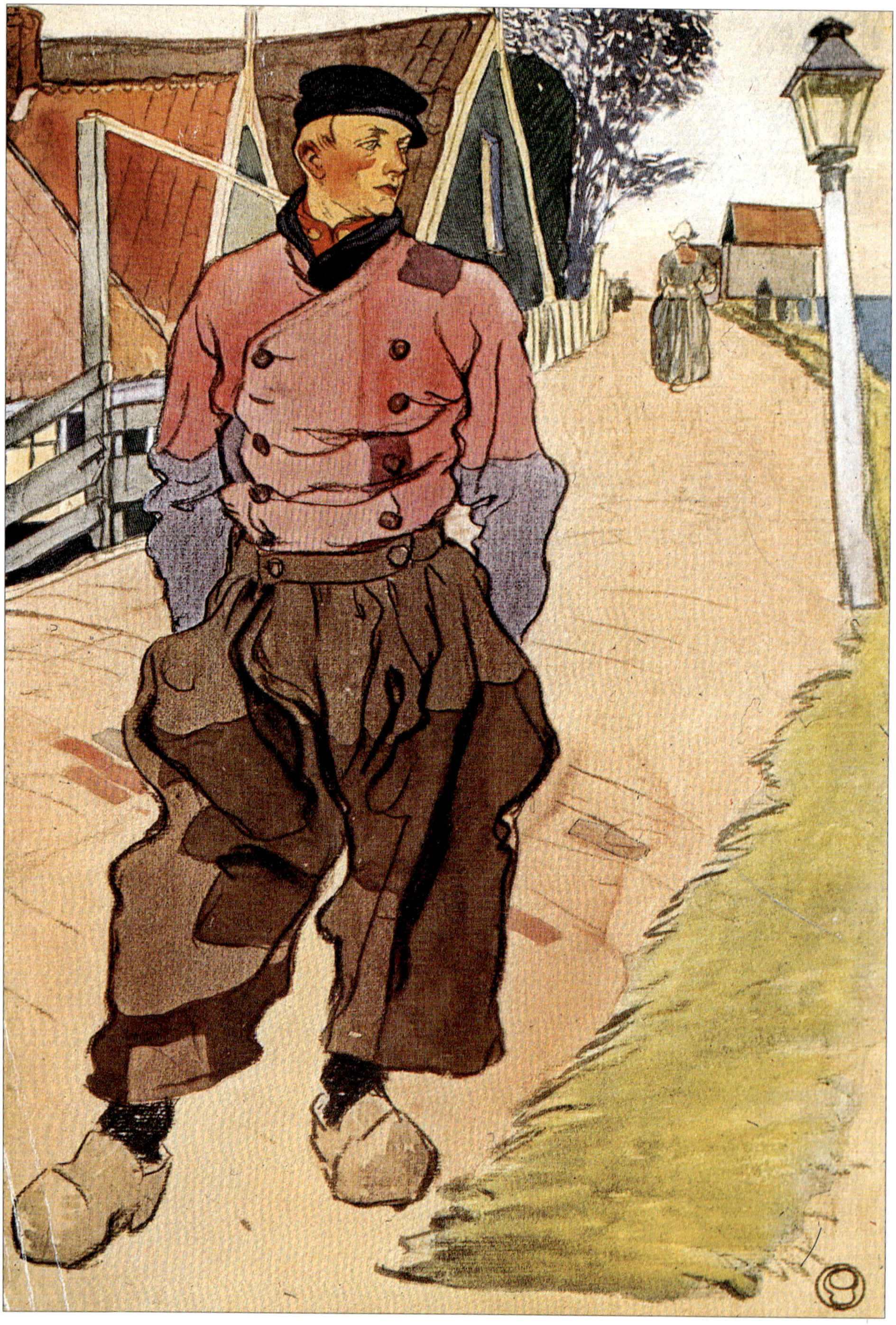

FIG. 21 *Edward Penfield entitled this image "Magenta was Overwhelming" and used it as an illustration of the harmonious coloration that many artists considered typically Dutch.*

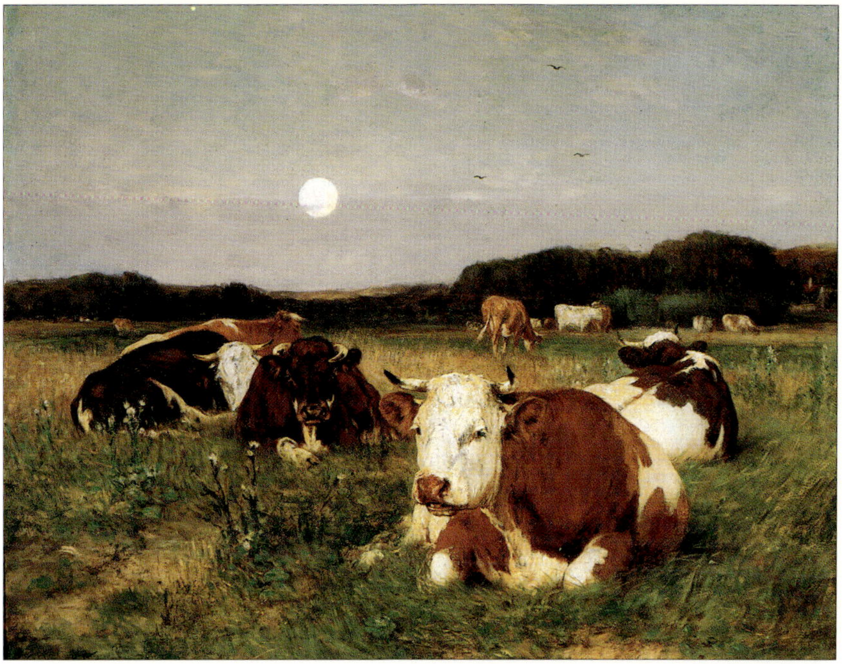

FIG. 25 *Bucolic cattle scenes like* Evening at Laren *by William Henry Howe evoked the peaceful mood of a preindustrial agrarian order.*

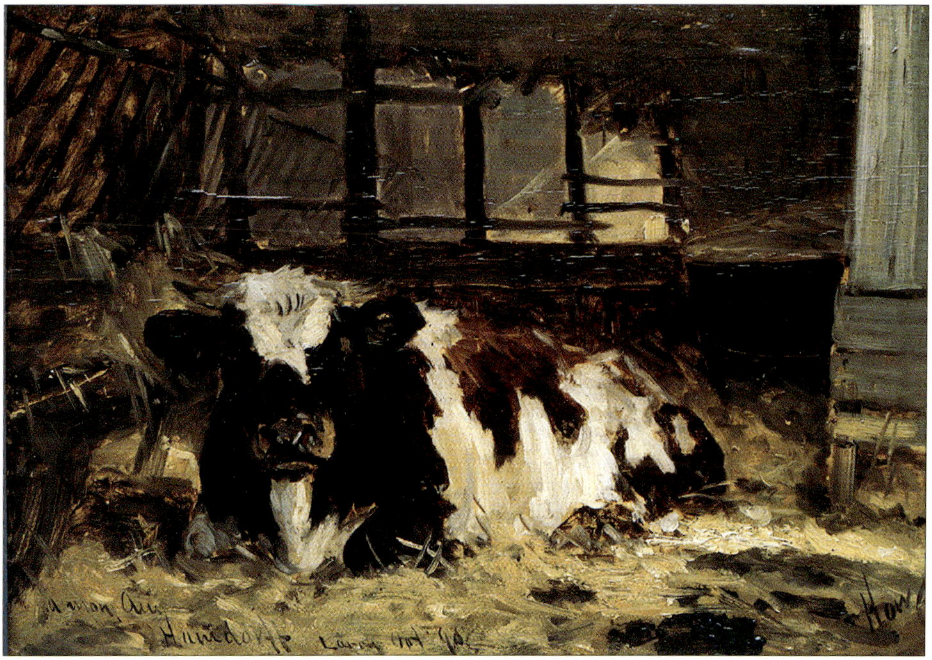

FIG. 26 *A gift to the owner of the artists' hotel in Laren, this painting by William Henry Howe hung for many years in the Hotel Hamdorff.*

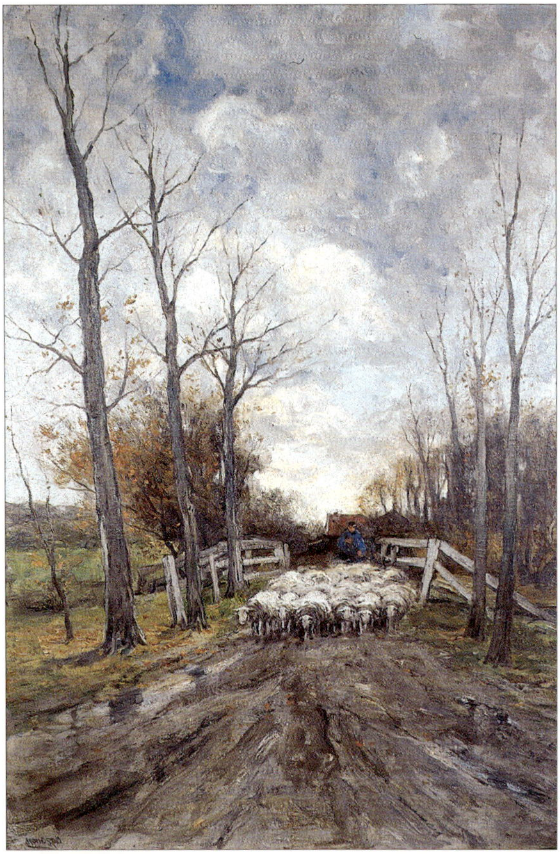

FIG. 27 *Charles Paul Gruppe summered in Laren for several years painting landscapes, animals, genre scenes, village views and this Anton Mauve-inspired picture of a shepherd herding his flock.*

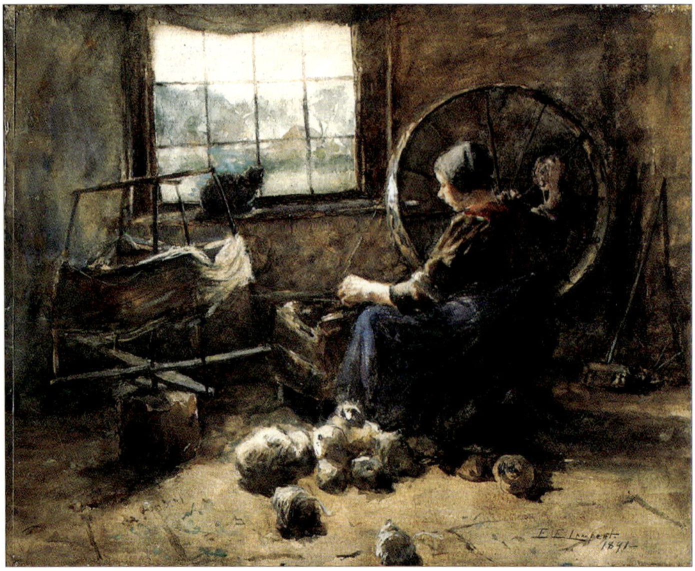

FIG. 28 *Emma Lampert was one of a group of American women who studied watercolor painting with the modern Dutch masters. Her painting* The Breadwinner *depicts a Laren woman spinning wool.*

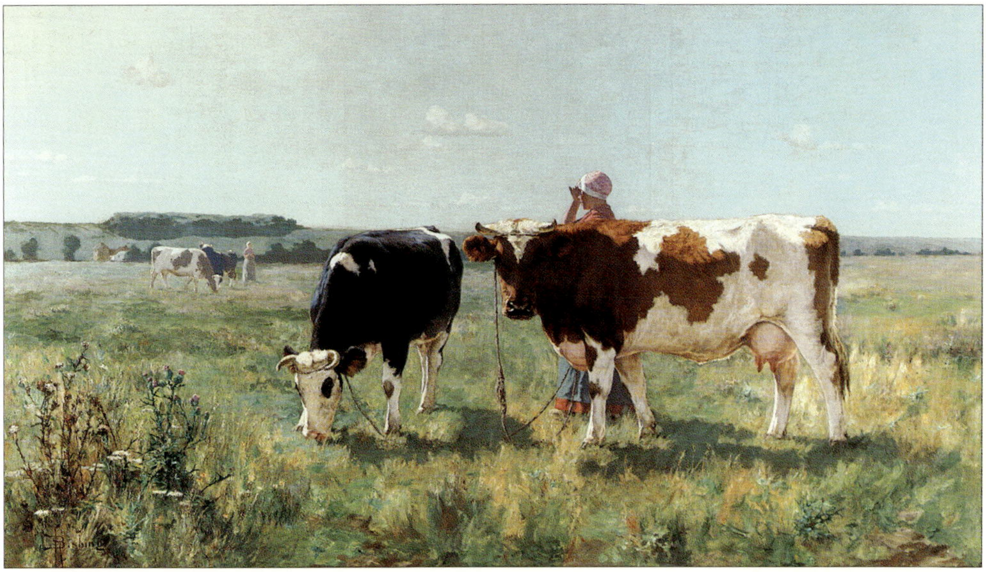

FIG. 29 *Like Laren, the colony at Hattem was known for its cattle paintings. Henry Bisbing included a young woman wearing the everyday patterned headdress of the Hattem-Nunspeet region in his painting* In the Meadow *of 1888.*

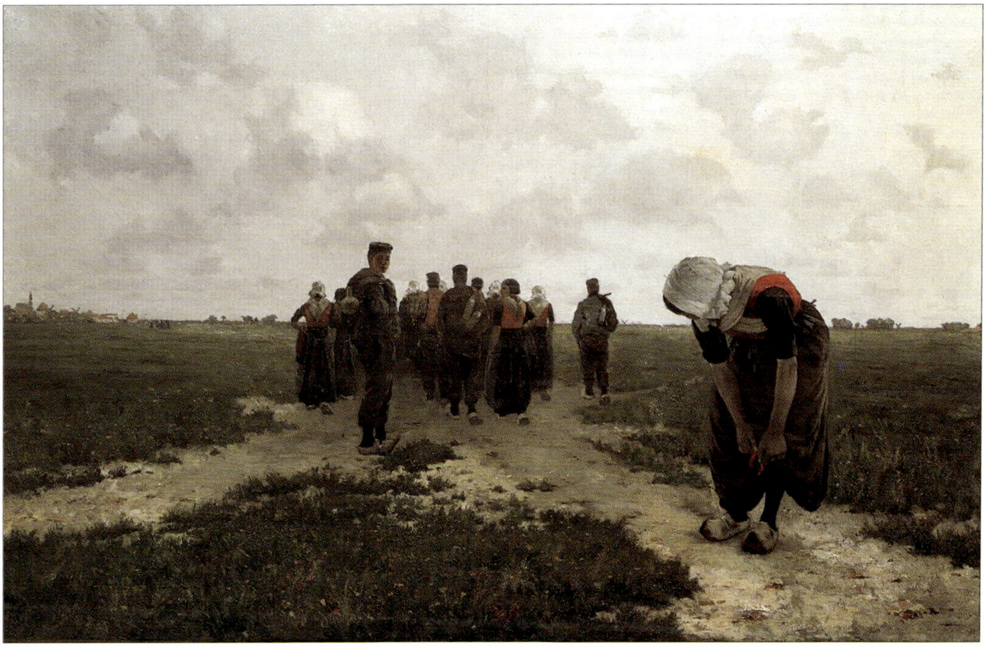

FIG. 30 *The people of the Hattem-Nunspeet area provided peasant models in keeping with the well-established French peasant tradition. Walter MacEwen painted these impoverished workers crossing the fields in* Returning From Work.

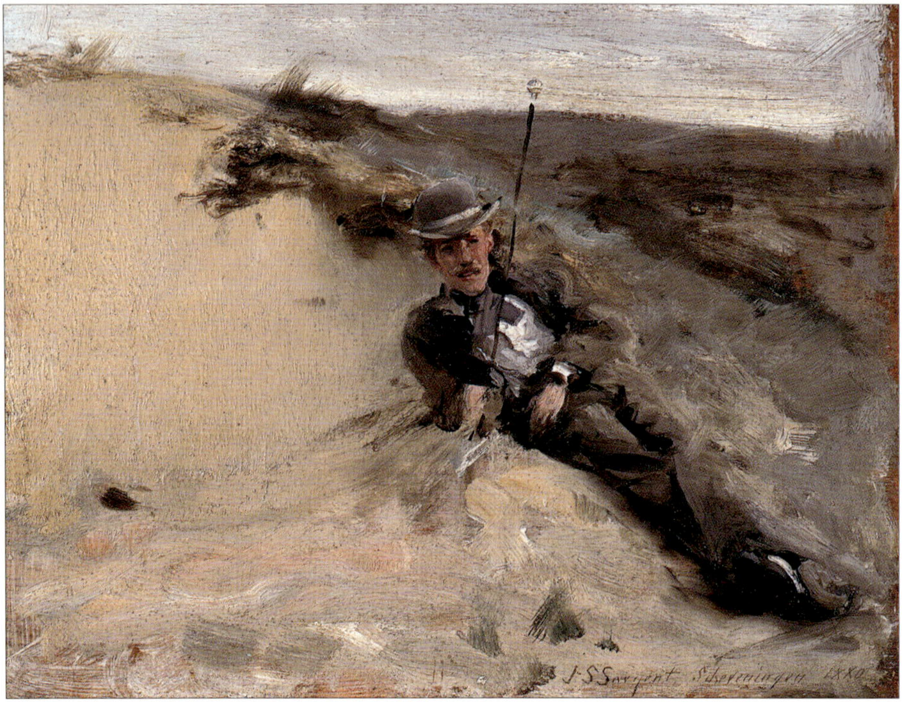

FIG. 31 *On a short trip through the Netherlands in 1880, John Singer Sargent paused on the beach at Scheveningen to paint this picture of his cousin, the artist Ralph Curtis. Reclining against a sand dune in leisurely unconcern, Curtis looks the typical American tourist enjoying one of the most popular watering spots in Holland.*

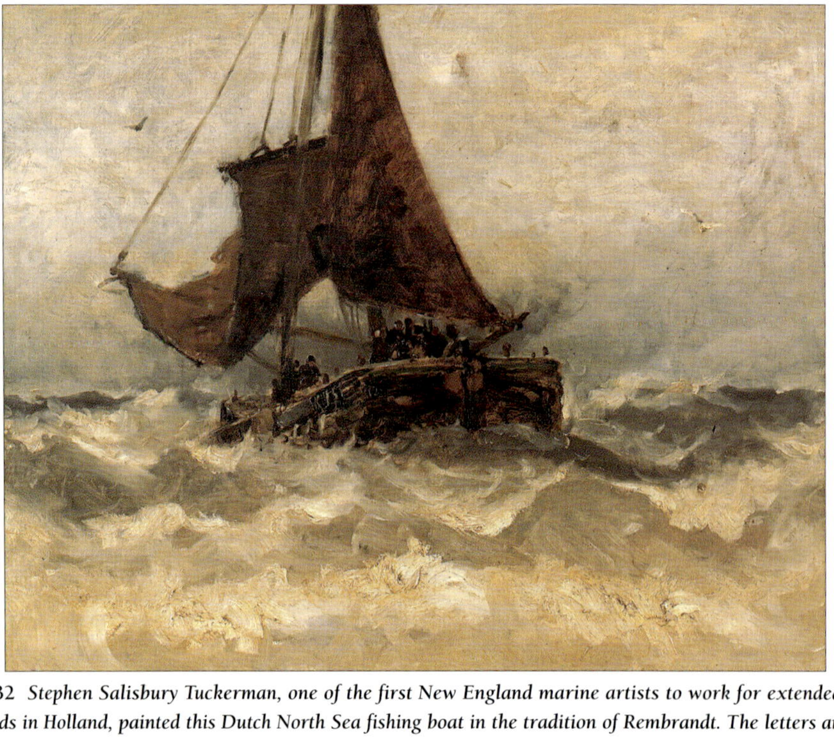

FIG. 32 *Stephen Salisbury Tuckerman, one of the first New England marine artists to work for extended periods in Holland, painted this Dutch North Sea fishing boat in the tradition of Rembrandt. The letters and numbers painted on the sides and sails of such boats indicated from which town's fishing fleet they came.*

distributed the *Volksvriend* (1874–1951); and Grand Rapids, Michigan had *De Standaard* (1875–1918). Most of these papers targeted Dutch-Americans and provided community, national, and church news. As immigrant communities matured, they felt the need to preserve their histories through books, pamphlets, and newspaper articles. This research filtered out into the greater American community as it was published in English and as non-Dutch students entered the colleges established in Dutch communities.

An example of the impact of Dutch-founded colleges brings us back to William Griffis. Born and raised within an English community in Philadelphia, Griffis first became aware of Dutch-American culture when he attended Rutgers, a college established in New Jersey in 1766 by Dutch settlers. His friendships with Dutch-American boys there opened his eyes and piqued his interest to what would become one of his avocations—the study of Dutch influence in the history of the United States. Other Dutch-founded colleges that undoubtedly exposed young Americans to Dutch-American culture included Union (1795) in Schenectady; Central (1853) in Pella; Hope (1862) in Holland; Calvin (1876) in Grand Rapids; and Northwestern (1882) in Orange City. Some of these institutions would later play a key role in preserving and distributing knowledge about the history of the Dutch in North America.

PILGRIM HISTORY

Another area of even more specialized research emerged in church history. Campbell had touched on it in his study of the Puritans, but historians pursuing the histories of Congregationalism, the Dutch Reformed Church, the Brownists, the Anabaptists, Quakers, and Separatists went into greater detail. Both Campbell and Griffis accepted the Dutch origin of religious toleration as a basic part of their thesis. As early as 1888, G. H. Emerson had set forth the key arguments in his article, "What Protestant Liberty Owes to the Dutch." Emerson told his readers that "it would be base ingratitude not to pay Old England the tribute of profound praise, for the service she has rendered both religious and constitutional liberty is very great. None the less the heroes of the heroes were not Englishmen: *they were Dutchmen*."[63]

Historians interested in Pilgrim history had long recognized that a group of English Separatists sought refuge from King James I in the Netherlands, where they remained for twelve years. When their leaders realized that the younger generation was merging with the Dutch people, these Pilgrims determined to preserve their identity by moving to North America. They purchased a ship, the Speedwell, and made plans to rendezvous with another group of Pilgrims in England who would be sailing on the Mayflower. When the Speedwell proved unseaworthy, the ships turned back to the coast and as many Pilgrims as possible crowded on the Mayflower, so that only the one ship coming from England was recorded in the popular history of America. These basic facts were well known to enthusiasts of Pilgrim history, who had, as early as 1820, formed the Pilgrim Society at Plymouth, Massachusetts to research and commemorate the Pilgrim Fathers. But most Americans in the middle of the nineteenth century remained unaware of the Dutch period in Pilgrim history. Children learned in school merely that a group of English people sailed on the Mayflower and founded Plymouth colony in 1621. By the end of the century, perhaps due to the general emphasis on Dutch contributions to American history, the relatively short period the Pilgrims had spent in Holland began to loom larger in American interpretations of Pilgrim history (FIG. 50).

Historians reviewed William Bradford's first-hand account of the Plymouth colony for evidence of the Dutch period. This source divulged that while in England, the Pilgrims determined "to goe into the low countries where there was freedom of religion for all men," and that after they had established themselves in North

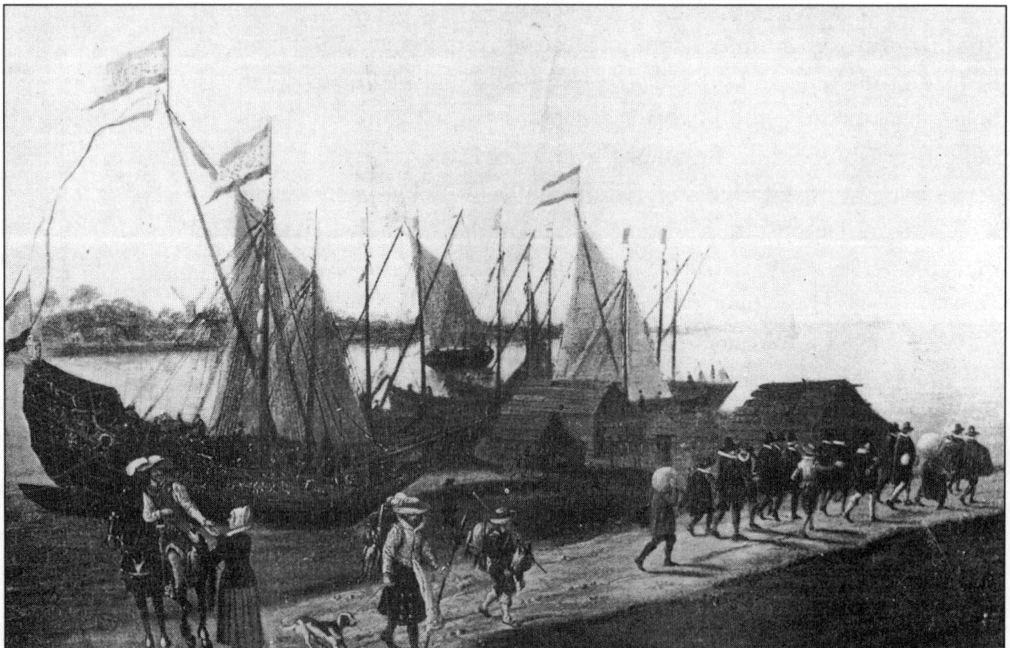

FIG. 50 Departure of the Pilgrims from Delfshaven, ***once owned by the Anglo-American painter George Henry Boughton, and believed by him to have been painted in 1620 by Albert Cuyp, became a standard illustration in Pilgrim histories around 1900.***

America they wrote to their Dutch neighbors in New Netherland concerning a proposed alliance between the two colonies:

> Yet are many of us tied by the good and courteous entreaty which we have found in your country, having lived there many years, with freedom and good content, as many of our friends do this day; for which we are bound to be thankful, and our children after us, and shall never forget the same.[64]

As American historians journeyed to Holland to search for records of the Pilgrims in Dutch archives, new information emerged and joined the Bradford quotes to become part of the revisionist theories of American history. Researchers found evidence that the Pilgrims had originally planned to make their American home in New Netherland and only abandoned the idea when they failed to obtain promises of military protection from the Dutch government. They discovered the locations of the Pilgrim's homes in Amsterdam and Leyden, and revealed the histories of prominent figures there, including John Robinson, Elder Brewster, William Bradford, and Miles Standish.

The new information about the Dutch period in Pilgrim history, combined with Motley's enthusiastic descriptions of the Holland they lived in, caused some historians to view it as paramount. Writing in 1907, Frederick A. Noble stated:

> Without the experience of those testing years in Holland they would not have been fitted for the 'great and honorable actions' of the subsequent years in America . . . They were stronger, they were wiser, they were in every way better for their sojourn and intercourse with the Dutch. From the inception of the movement at Scrooby to the consummation of it at Plymouth, the providence of God is nowhere and in nothing more marked than in leading the advocates of a free church and founders of a free state through a land whose people had illustrated the loftiest heroism and made every sacrifice demanded of them in order to rid their country of ecclesiastical and civil tyranny.[65]

William Elliot Griffis agreed. In his preface to J. De Hoop Scheffer's *History of Free Churchmen*, he diminished the supposedly English character of the Pilgrims by explaining that the group comprised at least eight nationalities and concluded that "It was Robinson's church company, which sailed in the Speedwell (and not the Mayflower party, "shuffled in" as Bradford tells us) which proved to be the soul and the most influential, effective and finally victorious element in the initial founding of our six Eastern states."[66]

One of the best known nineteenth-century writers on the Pilgrims, Morton Dexter, maintained that the Pilgrims introduced Dutch laws, constitutional principles, pet phrases, and political party names to America. When Senator George F. Hoar of Massachusetts addressed a gathering in Plymouth, he attributed the Pilgrims' supposed love of civil and religious freedom, their municipal republican government, and the impetus for the Revolutionary War to the Pilgrims' experience in Holland. Members of the Pilgrim Society and other New Englanders who had assembled to celebrate the 275th anniversary of the Pilgrims' landing comprised Hoar's audience. With political savvy, Hoar also insisted that the Pilgrims remained essentially English despite all their Dutch influence. As politicians, ministers, teachers, and scholars spread the Dutch interpretation of Pilgrim history, they bolstered the larger body of revisionist history.

These specialized histories of New Netherland and the Pilgrims augmented the ideas of general Dutch influence, first presented in comprehensive form by Douglas Campbell. While not always accepted in its entirety, no historian after 1900 could afford to ignore the Dutch theory of American origin. In his *History of the United States of America*, Henry William Elson devoted five pages to refuting and clarifying the assertion that American institutions derive more from Dutch than from English sources. He reiterated Campbell's claims for Dutch primacy in various liberties and admitted that Dutch influence on both English and American colonists must have contributed to the making of the United States.

While the Dutch interpretation of American history never entirely replaced the English version, many people did accept that their roots as Americans, regardless of personal genealogy, were to be found in the old Dutch Republic. Many agreed with Howard Ellis that "our American people possess the true spirit of the Dutch nation."[67] This view of national character reinforced the general trend toward Holland Mania and transformed the study of Holland, the collecting of Dutch artifacts, and the ownership of Dutch paintings into acts of patriotism. Ideas of Dutch influence infiltrated standard history texts, such as Elson's, as well as children's books, advertising, and many other areas of American life. By 1914 Americans had erected thirteen memorials in Holland to their own historical roots there.[68] Most importantly, this notion of Holland as an essential part of American history altered concepts of American identity and methods of portraying it.

FOUR

Images of Nederland, Old and New

IT WILL BE APPARENT TO THE READER BY NOW THAT THE CHARACTER of Holland Mania depended upon a profound confusion of time. Old Dutch master paintings of seventeenth-century Holland complemented Motley's written descriptions of the sixteenth- and early-seventeenth-century Dutch Republic to provide the basis of many nineteenth-century Americans' understanding of Holland. At the same time, contemporary travel literature and revisionist history conspired to convince people that Holland remained essentially the same in the nineteenth century as it had been in the seventeenth. Historian Douglas Campbell complicated matters further by stating that "if an American of the present generation could go back to the Dutch Republic of two centuries and a half ago, he would find himself in a familiar land, because he would be among a people of the nineteenth century."[69] Campbell considered the ideas of seventeenth-century Holland essentially modern, as they correlated so well with ideas he saw operating in the United States. Revisionist historians intermixed arguments of historic contact and arguments of contemporary affinity with dizzying speed as they attempted to prove that the most cherished qualities of American identity originated in Holland. It is not surprising that many Americans began to associate colonial America with nineteenth-century Holland and nineteenth-century America with the seventeenth-century Dutch Republic, or that the importance of Holland for many tourists was its role in American history—which they now believed they could readily see in the land and people around them as they traveled through the Netherlands.

The same confusion of seventeenth-century time with nineteenth-century time is evident in contemporary paintings and prints. A decade before the new historical interpretations of America's Dutch roots began to appear, the work of American artists in Holland reflected many of the ideas that historians would crystallize into a theory of American identity. In search of the picturesque, they settled in the countryside to paint peasants, windmills, and flower fields. Although contemporary, these subjects had the appearance of an earlier era. Windmills reminded American viewers of Rembrandt's Holland. Tulip fields conjured visions of tulip mania, when seventeenth-century merchants made and lost fortunes speculating on flower bulbs. People in the remoter regions wore dress reminiscent of an earlier age. Inspired by these similarities, many of the American artists in Holland produced history paintings of Old and New Netherland as well as the contemporary views of Holland already discussed.

NEW AMSTERDAM

George Henry Boughton and Edwin Austin Abbey made their sketching trips through Holland in the summers of 1880 and 1881 to acquire sketches and notes for a series of travel articles in *Harper's New Monthly Magazine*. Both men doubled the benefits of the Dutch excursion by making drawings and paintings of New Netherland in addition to the illustrations of contemporary Holland that *Harper's* had commissioned.

The results of the sketching trip were not published in *Harper's Magazine* until 1883, but already in January of 1882 Abbey had made use of his sketches to create "authentic" illustrations for Charles Gray's poem "New Amsterdam, 1655." Abbey's letters reveal that he conscientiously pursued veracity in his history pictures. He used sketches from his recent trip to make his New Amsterdam pieces authentically Dutch, a practice he could only have undertaken if he believed the Dutch had changed little in over two hundred years. His pursuit of accuracy led Abbey to abandon Gray's text whenever it contradicted his personal knowledge of contemporary Dutch practice. Gray clearly described Katrina with "bosom whiter than the snow" and "cap of quilted calico." But Abbey, just returned from the Netherlands, knew that rural Dutch women covered their chests and he had seen no quilted caps, so he drew Katrina with her bosom discreetly covered, wearing a simple white linen cap (FIG. 51). Both alterations made his image of this colonial woman consistent with nineteenth-century Dutch custom. The rest of the dress is also clearly based on the costumes Abbey recently had seen worn by women in Holland. Although the poem made no mention of knitting, Abbey portrayed his Katrina with knitting needles, an image consistent with the contemporary stereotype of Dutch women as inveterate knitters.

Abbey's drawing of the battery (FIG. 52), which does not correlate with any part of Gray's poem but was intended to give a general idea of New Amsterdam in 1655, needed even less modification to transform it from a picture of two Volendam women knitting in 1880 to a picture of New Amsterdam colonists in 1655. They wear the wooden shoes and complete costume of a nineteenth-century Volendamer, while the little boy at their side and the men in the background wear clothing more appropriate to a seventeenth-century painting. Abbey added hills and a bay to convey the idea of the American shore, but otherwise the center section of this drawing might have come straight out of his Dutch sketchbook. Such combinations

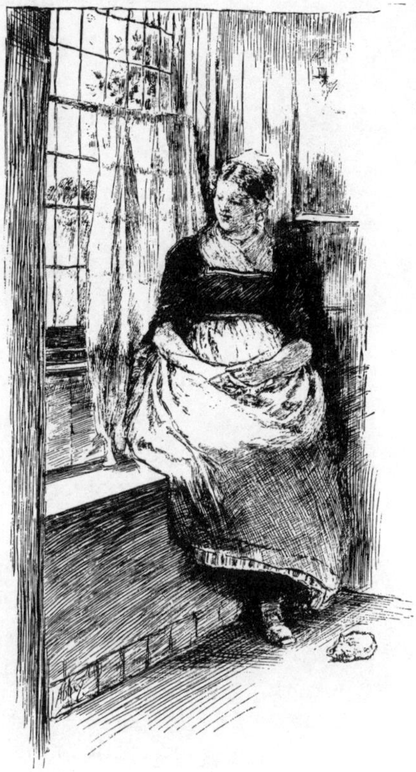

FIG. 51 *Edwin Austin Abbey drew* Katrina *to illustrate Charles Gray's poem "New Amsterdam, 1655."*

FIG. 52 *Edwin Austin Abbey based this illustration of colonial New Amsterdam,* The Battery, *on his recent sketches from Holland.*

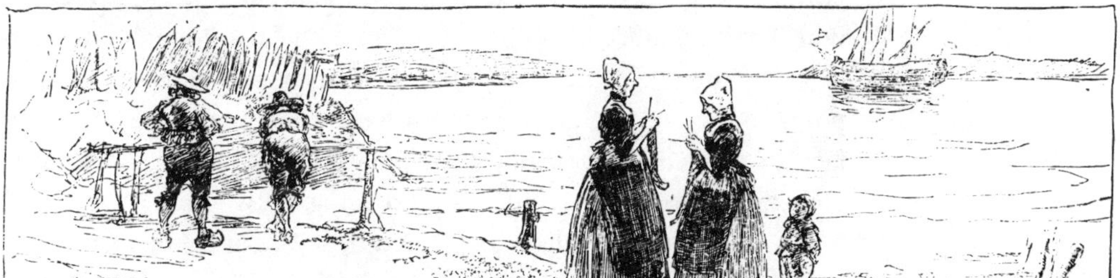

of source materials served to establish ties between contemporary and historic Holland and America in the eyes of American viewers. The combination of nineteenth-century Volendam clothing with seventeenth-century habiliments may have helped convince tourists who saw such illustrations before going to Holland that what they were seeing on Dutch women in Volendam were dresses unchanged from the days of New Amsterdam. In that way, history paintings helped establish the expectation that Holland had remained the same for centuries and increased the sensation of traveling back into American history for tourists.

In December of 1882, Abbey contributed three more drawings of New Amsterdam for a special *Harper's Christmas* by the members of the Tile Club. Others contributing scenes of New Amsterdam included George Boughton, William Merritt Chase, F. Hopkinson Smith, and Julian Alden Weir, all of whom had recently worked in the Netherlands.

While Abbey made effective use of his Dutch sketches in illustrations of historic New Amsterdam, Boughton became much better known as a painter of colonial America. Boughton painted both New England and New Netherland and often entangled them. Henry James accurately described the situation when he wrote about Boughton in 1889: "This pictorial element in which he moves is made up of diverse delicate things, and there would be a roughness in attempting to unravel the tapestry. There is old English, and old American, and old Dutch in it, and a friendly, unexpected new Dutch too—an ingredient of New Amsterdam—a strain of Knickerbocker and of Washington Irving."[70] The mix of English and Dutch can be seen by comparing Boughton's illustration of Katrina (FIG. 53) with the one by Abbey, just discussed. While Abbey used the plain dress of a Volendam woman, with the broad outlines characteristic of multiple skirts and good health, as the basis of his illustration, Boughton put his Katrina in the short dress, stockings, pointed corseted bodice, and lace fichu and cuffs of English tradition. The only touch of Holland is found in the cap. Boughton painted many pictures of Dutch and English women in which the models, poses, and costumes are quite indistinguishable from one another. In fact he painted most, if not all, of his colonial Dutch and historic Holland scenes in his London studio using British models.

It is not only the elision of Dutch, English, and American components that distinguishes Boughton's history paintings. Like Abbey, he found the contemporary to be compatible with images of two centuries or more previous. By combining seventeenth-century

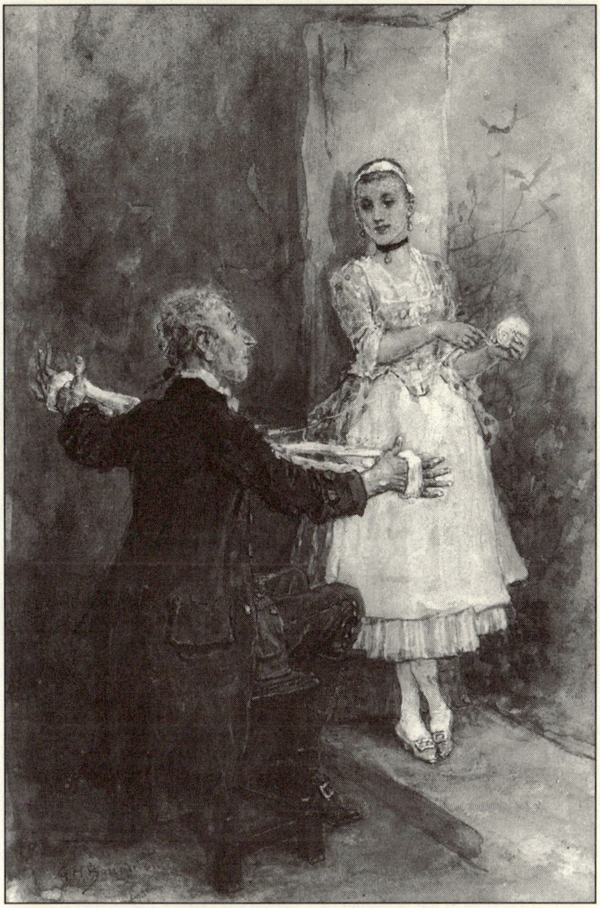

FIG. 53 *In 1895, George Henry Boughton exhibited thirty-one of his watercolor illustrations for Washington Irving's* Rip Van Winkle *and the* Legend of Sleepy Hollow *at the Avery gallery in New York. This one of Ichabod Crane and Katrina Van Tassel was probably among them. © Collection of the New-York Historical Society.*

FIG. 54 *George Henry Boughton became the preeminent painter of colonial America. Less concerned than Abbey with accuracy, he drew freely from Dutch, English, and American sources and from literature and his own imagination.* The Edict of William the Testy, *formerly in the Metropolitan Museum of Art collection, illustrates an episode in Washington Irving's* History of New York *by Diedrich Knickerbocker.*

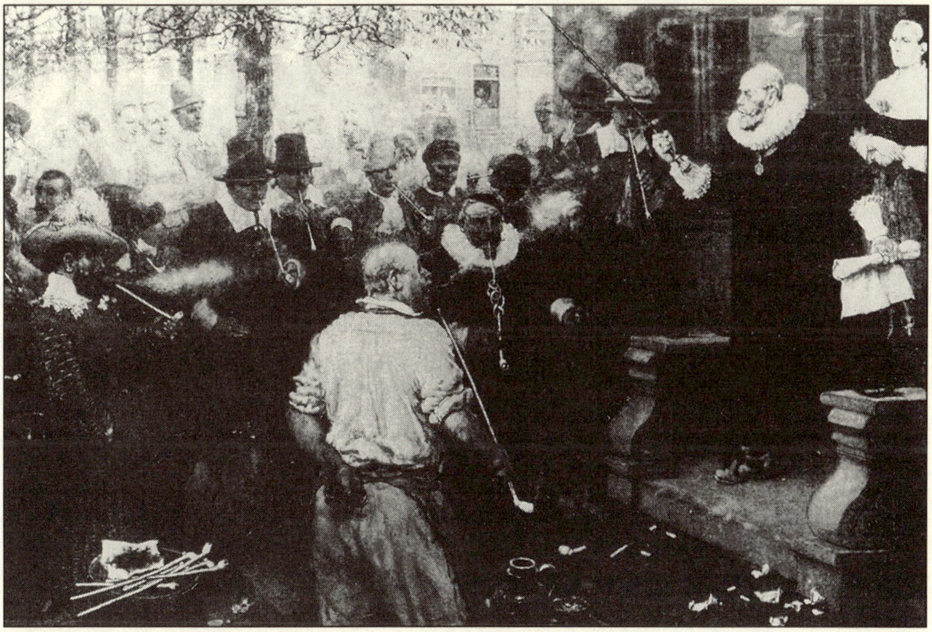

images with nineteenth-century images, Boughton created the impression of a historic connection between Holland and the United States in his pictures. The revisionist historian William Griffis, an admirer of Boughton's colonial Dutch paintings of the 1880s and early 1890s, pointed out that "in studying his Knickerbocker pictures, one can easily see that he has drawn his faces and figures of magistrates from the classic canvases of Rembrandt, Hals, Van der Helst, etc., while those of the young women and men in the humbler walks of life are reproductions of his own sketches from life in the Holland of to-day."[71]

Revisionists found plenty of material in Boughton's art to inspire them. Boughton's painting, *The Edict of William the Testy* (FIG. 54), illustrates an incident described in the Knickerbocker history of New York as the burghers of New Amsterdam protesting against Governor Stuyvesant's decree forbidding tobacco smoking by gathering in front of his house and smoking furiously. *The Chautauquan* used this painting in its year-long study of Holland, commenting: "Our relation to Holland seems very close when we look upon the Dutch garb of these New World residents and realize that while Wilhelm Kieft was governing Manhattan Island from 1634 to 1647, Spain and Holland were fighting to the death, and Rembrandt was painting his immortal masterpieces."[72] For this writer, the painting signified a bond in time and circumstance between colonial New York, Motley's old Dutch Republic, and the art of the old Dutch masters—three of the key ingredients underpinning Holland Mania.

Many other artists took up the theme of colonial New York. Some, like Francis Millet (*Antony Van Corlaer, the Trumpeter*), Charles Xavier Harris (*Surrender of Niew Amsterdam in 1664* and *Rysingh Outwitting Van Puffenberg at Newcastle, Delaware 1656*), Maurice Fromkes (*The First Mayor of New Amsterdam*) and Thore de Thulstrup (*The Trumpeter of Amsterdam*) painted scenes from Washington Irving. Others, such as Edward Penfield (*Winter Days in New Amsterdam*), created generic views of life in New Netherland. Some followed Boughton's lead and mixed British with Dutch character, but most relied more on their own travels in the Netherlands for sources.

Not surprisingly, many paintings of New Netherland were commissioned as decorations for buildings in New York and New Jersey. To give just two examples, Abbey had the opportunity to use all his experience with illustrations of Holland in a mural painting, *A Game of Bowls*, for the Amsterdam Hotel in 1897 and Francis Newton painted a twenty-six foot long decoration for the trial room of the new police headquarters in Manhattan, *The Rattle Watch of New Amsterdam* (1908). It depicted the island's first police force, established by Peter Stuyvesant in 1650.

All of these paintings, together with numerous illustrations of other colonial Dutch history in America (FIG. 55c), are part of the Colonial Revival inspired by the country's centennial. Colonial Revival paintings provided a neutral zone where the demands of both sides of the issue of a national art form could be met. Demands by art critics for the return from Europe of American expatriates and the creation of a national art form based on native subject matter increased sharply at the end of the nineteenth century. By that time, it was standard procedure for American artists to study in Europe, join American art colonies abroad, and establish their reputations by exhibiting in the Paris Salons. Paintings by American artists still commanded significantly lower prices from American collectors than from their European counterparts and American artists found the environment in European art circles more enlightened and supportive. But living in Europe at a time when *plein air* painting dominated the scene meant many artists painted European subjects in styles indistinguishable from continental styles. American critics hoping for a national art found that situation intolerable. The increasingly close popular association between modern Holland and colonial America, however, made it possible for artists to live in Holland and paint pictures that viewers perceived as American. Artists also found they could live in England and produce history pictures of the English colonies, and some worked in both countries. George Henry Boughton is a good example of the expatriate Colonial Revival specialist. One of the most successful artists to focus on contemporary Holland as a source for historic American pictures was Walter MacEwen.

Like Abbey and Boughton, MacEwen used the same Dutch source materials to paint pictures of New Amsterdam, the old Dutch Republic, and modern Dutch peasants. Often these subjects can be distinguished from one another only by their titles. *Stad Herberg, Nieuw Amsterdam (New York), 1690* (FIG. 56c) portrays MacEwen's vision of the interior of the town hall tavern in colonial New York. Since the old town hall no longer existed and details of its interior were unknown, he drew upon his experiences in Holland to invent the setting. Consequently, it matched the settings he used for *The Ghost Story* (FIG. 57c) and other pictures of contemporary Holland.

The men in *Stad Herberg* wear clothing based on old paintings. They are not the caricatures of Irving's imagination (although MacEwen made other paintings based on Irving literature), but sober burghers as MacEwen saw his Dutch models and imagined their ancestors might have lived. The single serving woman wears exactly the same costume as three of the figures in *The Ghost Story*. One painting portrays Dutch America in 1650, the other Holland in 1887, yet they depict virtually the same costumes and setting. MacEwen also painted numerous pictures of the old Dutch Republic. *Dutch Courtship* (FIG. 58) portrays three women in the same Volendam dresses from *Stad Herberg* and *The Ghost Story* and a variety of nineteenth-century Dutch coifs entertaining a man in the rich dress of the seventeenth-century courtier. The use of the same source materials for all of these paintings strengthened the visual relationship between Holland and America, the past and the present.

Even more obviously seventeenth century is MacEwen's Vermeer series. Paintings like *The Secretary* (FIG. 59), which shows a man and woman seated at a table, a map on the wall behind them, and a window to the left, can be recognized as depicting seventeenth-century Holland because they follow a formula based on the work of seventeenth-century artist Johannes Vermeer. Even the satin dress and fur-trimmed jacket are motifs straight out of Vermeer and other little Dutch masters. In at least two examples, MacEwen modernized this old master look by altering the pose. *A Girl Looking in a Mirror* (FIG. 60) shows a favorite motif of MacEwen's, a girl standing near a wall gazing at herself in a mirror. She wears the fur-trimmed jacket of other pictures in the series, but in this case it drops down her back exposing one bare shoulder and creating an alluring effect of dishabille never seen in the little Dutch masters. She has apparently already removed the fitted jacket top of her dress, which rests on a chair beside her, and the skimpy underclothing revealed as she pulls the loose over-jacket back on appears to be in the nineteenth-century fashion.

These few examples from an enormously productive career typify the ease with which MacEwen moved between Dutch and American, seventeenth- and nineteenth-century motifs. Because the titles often offered the only indication of place and time, much of what he painted in Holland could be interpreted visually as Dutch or American. A Vermeeresque picture like *The Secretary* could remind the viewer of the fact that the Dutch and Pilgrims settled North America at the same time that this couple worked in Holland.

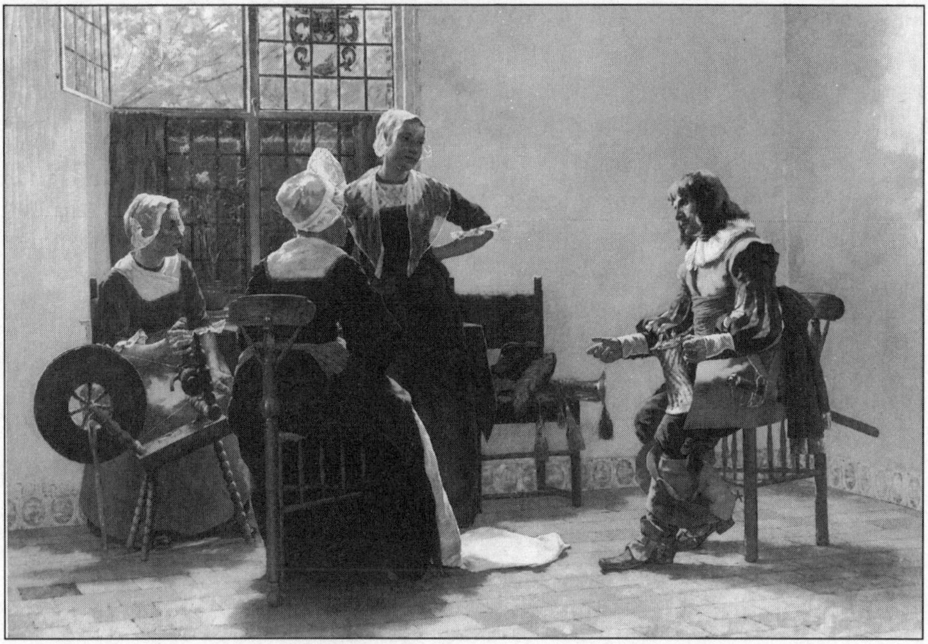

FIG. 58 *Walter MacEwen painted numerous versions of* Dutch Courtship, *representing seventeenth-century life in Holland.*

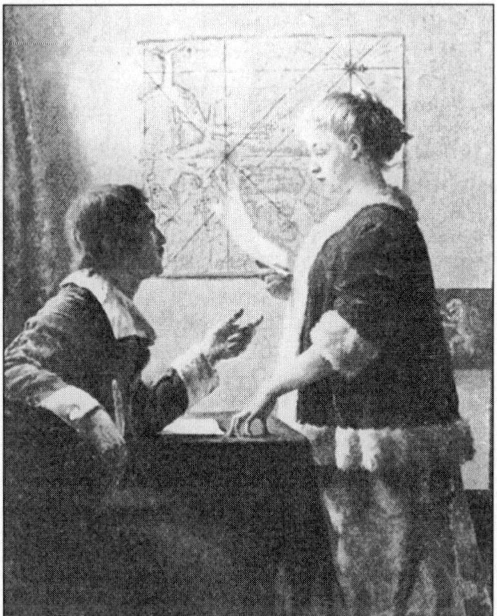

FIG. 59 *Walter MacEwen produced a whole series of Vermeeresque genre scenes, including* The Secretary.

FIG. 60 *A few paintings in Walter MacEwen's Vermeer series, including* A Girl Looking in a Mirror, *present a modern appearance.*

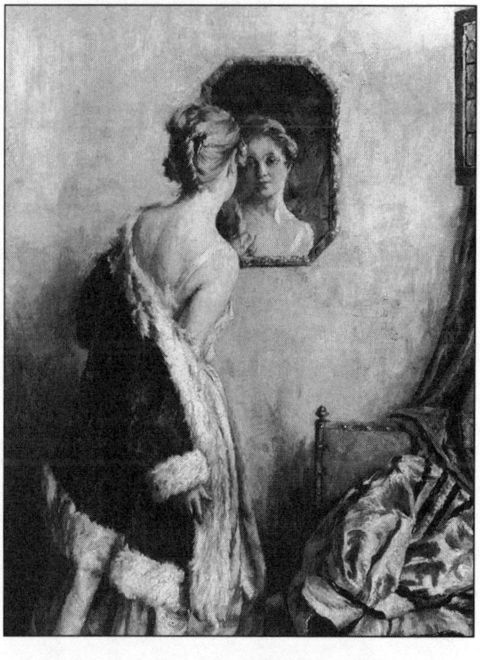

MacEwen's Dutch paintings, when taken as a body, visualize the theory of America's Dutch origins that would soon emerge.

In 1890 Walter MacEwen exhibited *Stad Herberg* and *A Dutch Courting* together in Chicago. They bore numbers 112 and 113 in Room XIV, suggesting a side-by-side placement, and they were joined by other images of both old and new Netherland by the same artist. These paintings appeared together again in a Denver show two years later. In fact, it was MacEwen's usual practice to mix images of historic Holland, the American colonies, and contemporary Holland in his exhibition entries. By so doing, he made the connection between the United States and a Dutch motherland visible.[73] By using contemporary Dutch dress for the female figures in both, he also drew the more subtle inference of continuity in the two countries. He seemed to be saying that Americans should be interested in Holland as a motherland where traces of the earlier era could still be seen. After the publication of Campbell's work and the public emergence of the debate over Holland's contributions to the United States, MacEwen's paintings confirmed for viewers that late nineteenth-century America was tied to Holland through colonial contact and that the ties were still visible in modern Holland. This message allowed him to spend his summers in his Dutch studio without being condemned by American critics or abandoned by American collectors interested in a national art form.

The example of Walter MacEwen proves that it did not require colonial subjects to convey nationalistic messages through Dutch subject pictures. American artists in Holland often painted pictures situated at the intersection of Dutch and American history, character and interests. A closer look at four examples will reveal some of the subtleties of nationalistic sentiment expressed through Dutch pictures.

CHARLES FREDERICK ULRICH, *THE VILLAGE PRINT SHOP*

The Village Print Shop (FIG. 61c), an oil painting on wood panel about twenty-two inches square by Charles Frederick Ulrich, has often been used by scholars to illustrate the representation of American technology and labor in nineteenth-century art. That interpretation is neither incorrect, nor entirely accurate. Ulrich actually painted the picture in Haarlem, Holland, during a five-month stay from May through October of 1884. In November, the

New Amsterdam Gazette reported that Ulrich had returned to New York from Haarlem with several paintings, including one that, "finished on the spot, is a scene in a 'Village Printing Office—Haarlem, Holland,' with two men at work on the hand-press, and a boy drinking at a table in the near foreground."[74] One month later Ulrich exhibited *The Village Printing Shop, Haarlem, Holland* in the inaugural exhibition of the American Art Association's new galleries. There can be little doubt that this picture and the one now titled *The Village Print Shop* in the Terra Museum are one and the same. With the shortening of the title, the Dutch origins and content of the painting were forgotten.

Ulrich signed this painting twice, once in red in the lower right corner and less visibly in perspective on the wood panels of a cupboard or counter at the right. Although a printer's shop offers many opportunities for the inclusion of the printed word and the Dutch language would seem a natural clue to the location of the subject in Holland, his signatures are the only words that appear in the painting. There are no internal clues to the fact that this print shop is located in Haarlem. The figures wear generic modern work clothes, exactly like those depicted in photographs of nineteenth-century Haarlem print shops—and also just like the clothes worn by American printers. The furnishings, if in any way distinct from American print works, would not be detected as Dutch by most American viewers. In short, the picture looks, as a reviewer of the December exhibition commented, "extremely American."[75] Yet the title in the exhibition catalogue informed gallery patrons that this was a Dutch scene. I believe that Ulrich purposely created a uninational image, equally American and Dutch, in order to comment upon America's Dutch heritage. There are two issues involved here.

First, a lengthy and inconclusive battle was fought during the nineteenth century over the invention of movable type. Haarlem claimed that a local printer, Laurens Coster, was responsible for the innovation that revolutionized printing, while the city of Mentz put forth similar claims for the German printer, Johann Gutenberg. Many authors poured out passionate defenses of their favorite, working with scant evidence on either side. In 1871 Antonius Van Der Linde's arguments for the supremacy of Gutenberg's claim were translated into English and a few years later a New York publication also treated the Coster claims as a legend based on civic pride. But in the early 1880s J. H. Hessels, who had translated and endorsed Linde, reversed his opinion. He published a vindication of the

Dutch claims and the battle raged quietly on. Residents of Haarlem, never in any doubt of the true cause, had been holding an annual Coster Jubilee since 1823, which Ulrich may have attended in 1884. Haarlem had also marked Coster's house with a plaque and erected a statue of him in the church square. William Griffis pointed out the statue and repeated Coster's story in several of his publications, even directing readers to the park where he said that Coster cut his wooden type.

George Wharton Edwards and other American artist–authors in Holland also noted Haarlem's claims, whether they endorsed them or not. "It is stated and claimed that Coster of Haarlem invented wooden type, and that the first newspaper printed in Europe appeared in the Dutch language," reported Edwards.[76] Two popular travel writers, Baedeker and De Amicis, proclaimed the Dutch claims invalid but they, too, discussed them in relation to Haarlem. Ulrich could certainly have expected that viewers reading the title of his painting, *The Village Printing Shop, Haarlem, Holland*, would be reminded of the debate and of the significance of this technological invention for world communication. In spite of its modern appearance, it would have evoked visions of that first Haarlem print shop. Certainly one of the underlying meanings of the painting was to refer to the possibility that the Dutch gave the world printing presses of movable type. It might also have brought to mind, in its American appearance, the perceived talent for invention and technological progress ascribed to the seventeenth-century Dutch and to the nineteenth-century American, forging yet another bond between the two nations.

Second, the painting suggests the theme of freedom of the press. In his article claiming Holland as the true Mother of America, Edward Bok wrote of the "four vital institutions upon which America rests . . . free education; our freedom of religious worship; our freedom of the press; and our freedom of suffrage . . . all of these four institutions came to America directly from Holland."[77] Although Bok wrote those words after Ulrich had finished his painting, they expressed a sentiment that had arisen much earlier. The idea that the Dutch were the most tolerant, enlightened, freedom loving people in sixteenth-century Europe had been well instilled by Motley, and the Dutch origins of religious toleration and freedom of speech were two of the most readily accepted ideas of the many claims that the revisionists eventually put forth. In an article about the Pilgrim press in Holland, Griffis explained that the Dutch government's protection of the Pilgrims' right to print during the seventeenth century, even in the face of English entreaties and threats, inspired a love of free speech in the Pilgrims. He said that the Pilgrims brought the concept of freedom of the press to North America and their descendants incorporated it into the United States.[78] This argument made the importance of the supposed early Dutch toleration of free speech specific to Americans. More than simply a view of modern labor, Ulrich's painting invoked a patriotic American principle, freedom of the press, and connected it to a Dutch heritage.

Although the largest painting that Ulrich made in Haarlem that summer was a genre scene of a girl blowing bubbles for her friends in the playroom of the city orphanage called *The Waifs* (location unknown), there is evidence that the printing theme most occupied him. Besides the painting just discussed, he produced a study for it showing the boy counting papers rather than drinking, and a third picture, *Dutch Typesetter*, that he apparently sent to the 1884 Paris Salon. The report of Ulrich's summer work in the *New Amsterdam Gazette* described *Dutch Typesetter* as a single figure standing at his type case near a partly curtained window through which housetops were visible. With three of his four pictures that summer painted on the theme of printing in Holland, it seems he had a message to communicate—about a Dutch heritage of technological inventiveness, printed communication, and freedom of the press.

CHARLES YARDLEY TURNER, *OLD DUTCH WOMAN READING HER BIBLE*

Old Dutch Woman Reading her Bible (FIG. 62), painted in Holland by Charles Yardley Turner, illustrates another of Bok's four vital institutions—freedom of religious choice. Most viewers today would interpret this painting of a woman seated before a bookstand reading a huge old Bible as a nineteenth-century facsimile of earlier Dutch genre paintings. With its chiaroscuro, old-fashioned costume, and subdued mood, it exhibits strong Rembrandtesque qualities. But viewers in Turner's time understood it to be an illustration of the belief that Holland had, during the sixteenth century, preserved the principle of religious toleration for the world. In his essay "What Protestant Liberty Owes to the Dutch," G. H. Emerson explained that Philip II of Spain had made the destruction of Protestant liberty a vocation, relentlessly pursuing the Inquisition to stamp out all

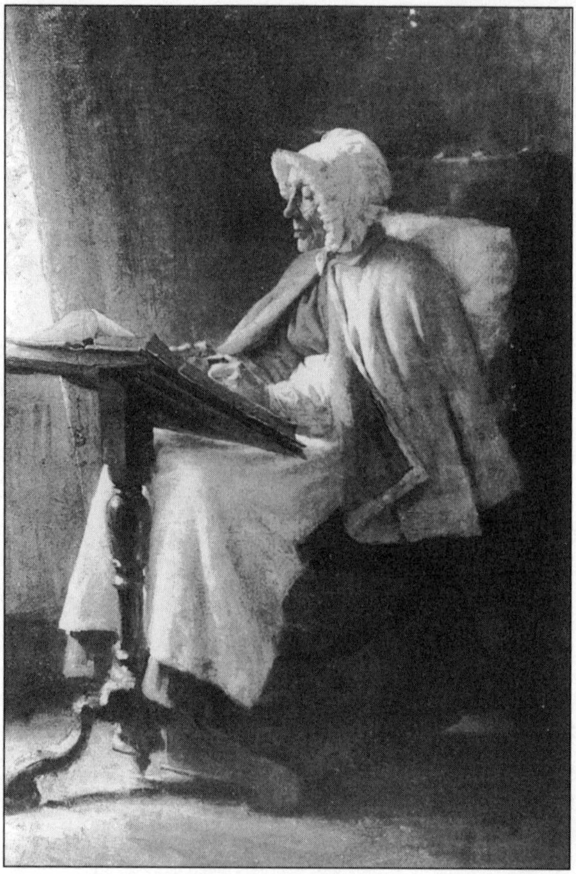

FIG. 62 *Charles Yardley Turner exhibited* Old Dutch Woman Reading her Bible *at the first annual banquet of the Holland Society of New York in 1886, together with the Bible that it depicts. The Bible was printed in Amsterdam in 1643.*

opposition to Roman Catholicism. But Philip was foiled by the fierce Dutch love of tolerance, according to Emerson, and the Dutch settlers of New York and New Jersey, the Pilgrims from Holland who settled Plymouth, and Roger Williams who championed separation of state and religion in Rhode Island, transferred that liberty to North America.[79]

In 1886 the newly formed Holland Society of New York held its first annual banquet. The decorations included copies of old Dutch master paintings by American artists, as well as numerous scenes of contemporary Holland painted by Americans working abroad. Among them were a Rembrandt copy by Turner and his *Old Dutch Woman Reading her Bible*. One of the speakers at the banquet, Chauncey M. DePew, referred to Turner's work in this way:

> Gentlemen, what heart here has not thrilled this evening at that beautiful painting by Mr. Turner, the 'Old Dutch Woman Reading her Bible!' How many a gray head have knelt years ago at such a

> knee! The influence of Dutch women such as that has molded the fate of religious liberty in this whole world![80]

It may seem only natural that a descendant of an early Dutch colonist, speaking to a gathering of Dutch New Yorkers, would emphasize the message that Holland gave religious liberty to Europe and America, but others also embraced this reading of the image. Speaking on Forefathers Day some years later, David Gregg said:

> I call upon you to-night to honor the civil fathers of America. Hold on to their intense trust in God and to their reverent spirit toward God. . . . Let Turner's painting, "The Old Dutch Grandmother Reading her Bible," be translated into life in every American home. . . . The world to-day needs America, as America once needed Holland.[81]

In Gregg's interpretation, the United States not only inherited religious toleration from the Netherlands, but also inherited its position in relation to the world as preserver and evangelist for liberty. Turner's painting stood for the responsibility to preserve freedom that Americans inherited from the Dutch along with the principle of religious toleration.

Turner's painting also occupies a position in relation to the large number of images produced in the last quarter of the nineteenth century depicting European peasants reading Bibles, going to church, saying rosaries, praying in the fields, and participating in community religious rites. Popular in both Europe and America since the time of the Barbizon School, the majority of such subjects depicted the elaborate rituals of Roman Catholicism in France and Italy, with a few examples of Russian and eastern European Orthodox ceremonies. Alternatively, Holland and Germany offered many opportunities for the depiction of Protestant peasants in their less elaborate ceremonies. Like their Catholic counterparts, these images suggested to viewers that peasants enjoyed a closer relationship to God than urban dwellers by virtue of their close communion with nature and the lack of artificial civilized veneer. They were believed to be naturally direct, honest, and pure. But the Dutch subjects were also seen as closer to the predominantly Protestant United States than were French subjects. Gari Melchers, for example, was conscious of the differences when he painted *The Communion* (Cornell University) to show the simple community meal of the Dutch Reformed Church and *Easter Sunday* (Toledo Museum of Art, Ohio), which he intentionally set in the first North Holland Church built for a protestant faith and not simply converted from a Catholic church. An inventory of Melchers's library reveals that he owned a copy of Campbell's revisionist history, *The Puritan in Holland, England and America.* Melchers certainly understood the historical and cultural relationships between the United States, where he had lived the first twenty years of his life, and Holland, where he spent much of the next thirty years. In stressing a Protestant Holland and referring to events in Holland's past, Melchers suggested ideas similar to those conveyed by Turner's work. Turner's *Old Dutch Woman Reading her Bible* can be seen as the parent of Melchers's and other American artists' Dutch religious peasant scenes.

WALTER MacEWEN, *MAKING THE FLAG*

Although Walter MacEwen's painting, *Making the Flag*, is currently unlocated, a detailed description of it from a 1924 American Art Galleries sale catalogues suggests it as an excellent illustration of another parallel between the histories of the United States and the Netherlands.

> A Dutch family of moderate means is portrayed in a room of precise neatness, before a great window of small panes of glass whose lower coruses [sic] are screened by black curtains, the light being admitted above them. On the outside one sees the walls of a mansion. Within the room, at a table across the window, is seated at left an old woman who is observed in profile to right, sewing on a Dutch flag. Next to her a young matron standing and pouring wine is seen *profil perdu*, and at the right end of the table sits the grandfather, painting the gilt top for the flag pole. At his knee his little grandchild, holding her doll.

This description immediately calls to mind, for American viewers, the legend of Betsy Ross who was popularly supposed to have sewn the first flag for the United States.

Many claims were made in the 1880s for the Dutch origins of the American flag. Walter MacEwen did not picture the Betsy Ross legend in *Making the Flag*, but its Dutch prototype. The Dutch Republic had had a flag of red or orange, white, and blue stripes, and the Beggars of the Sea, a small Dutch fleet that fought Spain in the sixteenth century, flew a flag with the five-pointed star on it. These design elements were said to have signified the patriotism of the Dutch in their struggle for independence from a foreign monarch and their championing of religious, personal, and political liberties.

Authors in the late nineteenth century suggested that the American patriots not only adopted the Dutch institutions, but modified the Dutch symbols of those institutions for their own use in the American flag. Therefore, a painting of a middle-class Dutch woman sewing a red, white, and blue flag at home while her husband painted the gilt top naturally suggested the origins of the Betsy Ross legend and of the American flag.

MacEwen increased this suggestion of a colonial American connection by depicting a three-generation family that includes grandparents, young mother, and child. Late-nineteenth-century Americans often considered the colonial period to be their grandparents' generation and in fact Betsy Ross had only died in 1836, about fifty years before MacEwen painted this picture. The presence of the grandparents helps direct the viewers' thoughts back into history. In addition, the painting carries the message of family values and of the family as the basic unit of Dutch and American social fabrics.

ELIZABETH NOURSE, *ON THE DYKE AT VOLENDAM*

The nineteenth-century American historian Frederick Jackson Turner promoted the thesis that the land, specifically contact with the wilderness at the frontier, transformed Europeans into Americans. This idea of the land as a causative agent in forming national character was also one of the most common explanations given for the origins of Dutch character. The peculiar topography of the Netherlands, much of it below sea level and only maintained by constant repair of dikes and pumping stations, attracted much attention from foreigners. Dutch topography was one of the first things to enter almost every travelogue and historical discussion of the Netherlands. Their ingenuity (in pumping out lakes and sea to create more land), their courage (to live with the constant threat of inundation), their tenacity, cleanliness, and phlegmatic disposition were all attributed to the necessities of the landscape. The wife of an American painter in the Netherlands wrote, for example:

> The Hollanders were early educated into the practice of patience and determination, through a stern conflict with the sea. . . . They had to win and they now are obliged to hold against the ocean the very earth on which they tread. . . . The transformation has meant toil, self-denial, suffering; in a word, the exercise of all that hero-

> ism, intelligence, and industry which an inhospitable country tends to stimulate and develop.[82]

According to Turner, Americans developed many of the same traits because of their contact with the inhospitable elements of an untamed wilderness and hostile Indians. The parallel between the situations for the old Dutch republic and the new American republic would have been obvious to any who considered it. A Dutch writer expressed it thus:

> The Americans have achieved their present greatness in the same way that Holland earlier won hers. As we had to fight the water, they had to fight the vast prairies with their native Indians. Every acre of ground had to be captured. . . . Thus Americans are, like us, self-made men.[83]

Elizabeth Nourse created a pictorial representation of this notion in her painting, *On the Dyke at Volendam* (FIG. 63). A group of Dutch women stand on Volendam's dike at the edge of the Zuider Zee, in defiance of the wind and spray that billow their clothes and graphically represent the forces of nature against which the Dutch people had fought for centuries. Nourse composed the scene with the women standing so close together that their forms merge in a solid bulwark against the elements of nature. The impassive expressions on their faces as well as the monumentality of their figures suggest the solidity and stability of Dutch character, often described in the nineteenth century as phlegmatic. Nourse's similar composition featuring a French peasant on a sand dune, *Fisher Girl of Picardy* (National Museum of American Art), carries some of the same connotations of hardy peasant stock. The Dutch women in *On the Dyke at Volendam* look out to sea, presumably waiting for the fishing fleet and their men to return, a reminder that the sea also provided a living for many.

Similarly, the German-born naturalized American artist Eugene Mulertt posed an old woman of Katwijk against the sea to reveal the effects of a lifetime spent in a coastal village where the sea provided everyone's livelihood (FIG. 64). In the simplicity of his composition, consisting only of a straight profile against a pure seascape, Mulertt presented his subject as a woman who had not been conquered by the ocean, but whose craggy features and stern, indomitable character were unalterably tied to it. Mulertt repeated in the figure the same rough paint textures he employed in the sea, reinforcing the unity of the Dutch woman and her environment. Her weather-beaten, impassive, yet serene features portray Dutch endurance and fortitude.

Such American interpretations of the Dutch people in their landscape served to repeat the parallels between Dutch and American national character. For this reason, at least one Dutch art critic considered Americans better qualified than other foreigners to paint the Netherlands: "[Charles Paul] Gruppe loves Holland and sees it as possibly only a Hollander or a Dutch-disposed American can see it."[84]

Boughton, Abbey, MacEwen, Ulrich, Turner, and Nourse exemplify the late-nineteenth-century expatriate American's ability to make Dutch subjects relevant and meaningful to an American audience. While the paintings of contemporary Holland may show little surface affinity with the United States, the context in which they were created and viewed transformed them into symbols of American values, institutions, and history. The temporal confusion in which the artists and their audience participated equalized scenes of contemporary Holland, of historic Holland, and of colonial Dutch America, facilitating the interpretation of any one of them as American history.

FIG. 63 *Elizabeth Nourse frequently exhibited* On the Dyke at Volendam, *one of her most important paintings from Holland. A collector in Washington, D.C. eventually purchased it.*

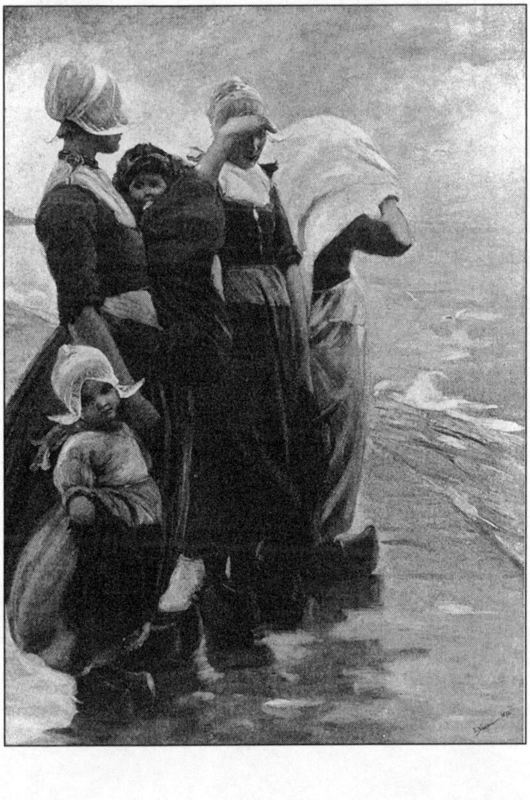

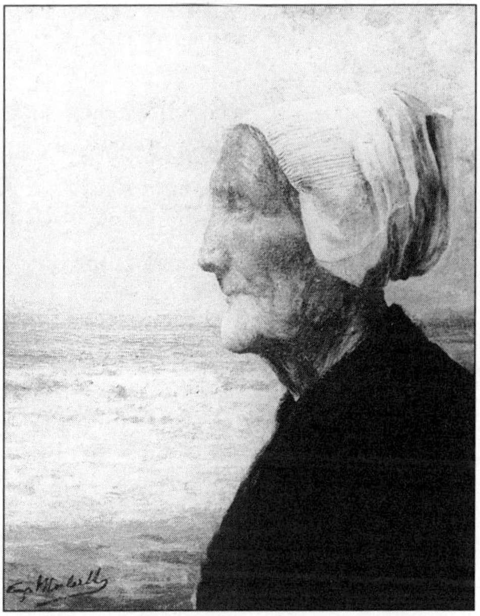

FIG. 64 *Eugene Mulertt, who spent the last sixteen years of his life in Katwijk, painted many genre scenes and portraits like this one of an old woman standing by the sea.*

FIVE

Tourism and Travel Literature

TOURISM PLAYED A VITAL ROLE IN THE DEVELOPMENT AND spread of Holland Mania. Increased travel to Holland supported the growing American art market for Dutch images, and the spread of Dutch images in American art and advertising stimulated the tourist trade, forming a mutually beneficial cycle. First-hand experience of Holland also reinforced the new historical view that American civilization descended from the Dutch. A body of literature developed in response to Dutch-American tourism in which three approaches dominated: the artistic tour, the historic tour, and the mythic "windmills and wooden shoes" tour. These three perspectives reflect the preconceptions American tourists brought with them.

THE VOYAGE

Transoceanic travel increased steadily in the second half of the nineteenth century as ships became faster, safer, less expensive, and more comfortable. However, tourist travel to the Netherlands remained negligible until the 1880s when, with the growth of American interest in Holland, travelers began to look to this small country as a vacation spot. The establishment of the Dutch steamship company, De Nederlandsch-Amerikaansche Stoomvaart Maatschappij, also supported increased travel to Holland at this time. With accommodations for 396 passengers, the small steamer

Rotterdam made the company's maiden voyage in October, 1872 to establish regular passenger service between Rotterdam and New York. The company slowly expanded, building and buying larger and faster vessels. By 1882 it had a fleet of passenger ships and the crossing time had been cut from sixteen to nine days.

This line became the principal means of direct tourist travel between the United States and Holland, with ports in Baltimore (1880s), Boston, Hoboken (FIG. 65), New York, Rotterdam, and Amsterdam (1883–1893). Although much of its passenger trade derived from Hollanders emigrating to North America, regional offices in Chicago, Boston, St. Louis, San Francisco, Minneapolis, and New Orleans helped promote Holland as a vacation spot for Americans. Round-trip second-class fare cost only $90, well within the means of the more affluent members of the ever-growing middle class. As a further aid to advertising itself in the United States, in 1896 De Nederlandsch-Amerikaansche Stoomvaart Maatschappij officially changed its name to Holland-America Line—which is virtually the same in Dutch—Holland-Amerika Lijn (FIG. 66c). Ten years later it was carrying more than 30,000 people annually from American ports to Europe, and it was only one of several companies engaged in this trade.

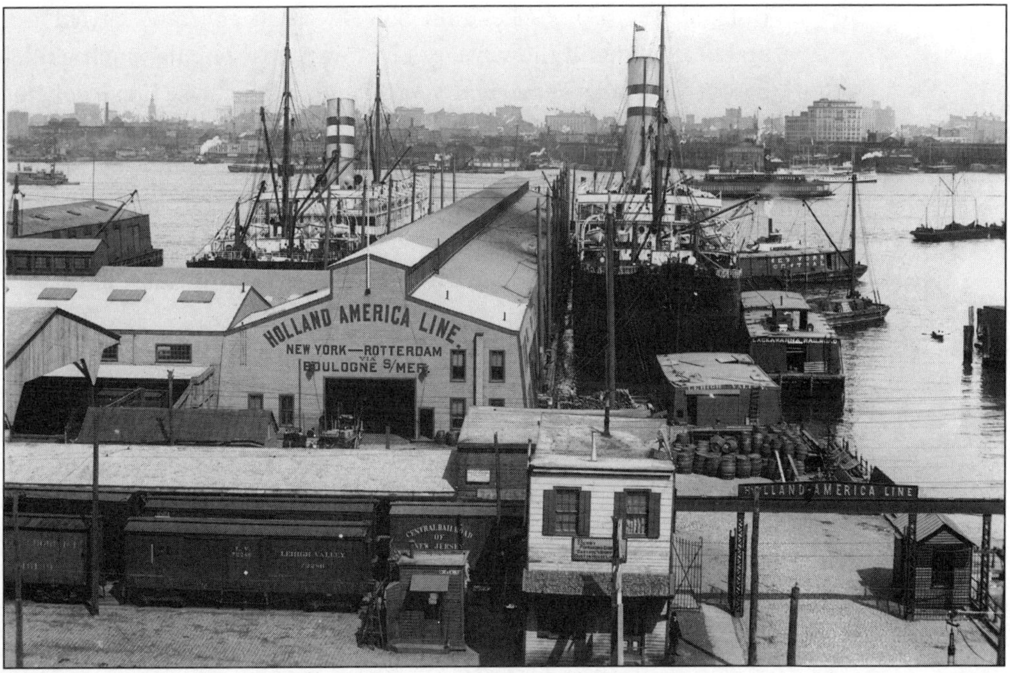

FIG. 65
The Holland-America line maintained an office in Hoboken from which passengers sailed to Rotterdam.

The Red Star Line also ferried many American tourists and businessmen back and forth to Holland. Founded in 1873, it sailed between Philadelphia and Antwerp under the Belgian flag. Antwerp provided a convenient port for tourists bound for the Netherlands and the fares on this line were somewhat lower than those of the Holland-America Line. The Red Star Line was subsumed in 1884 by the Pennsylvania Railroad's American Line and after various mergers and name changes, again became the American Line in 1893, sailing under the United States flag. By this time it had added weekly express service between New York and Antwerp to its fortnightly Philadelphia service. In addition to a six- to seven-day express voyage on luxury liners, the Red Star Line, as it was still commonly called, provided an eight-day first-class passenger service on large freighters with comfortable staterooms for only $60 to $75. The Netherlands Royal Mail and the German Bernstein Line both advertised service between Rotterdam and New York at the turn of the century. Alternatively, passengers could take the Cunard, Dominion, or White Star Lines to England and then make their way across the channel to Holland.

GUIDEBOOKS

As the number of Americans traveling through the Netherlands increased, so did the amount of travel literature published about Holland (FIG. 67). Pocket guidebooks were meant to be carried as a practical guide on the voyage. The three most popular such guidebooks—Baedeker's *Belgium and Holland*, Murray's *Handbook for Travellers in Holland and Belgium*, and Ward, Lock & Company's *Handbook to Holland*—provided maps and factual information on topography, climate, means of internal travel, hotels, and currency. They gave a short synopsis of Dutch history and an overview of Dutch art. The bulk of each guidebook described things to do and see in Holland, city by city.

By emphasizing certain cities and sights over others, the guidebooks helped shape the tourist's experience of the Netherlands. The Talbert party, for example, recalled that "we had spoken of going north a few miles to the village of Bloemendaal . . . but as our guidebook promised nothing better than the ruins of the old Brederode chateau, we cut it out of our program and headed south toward Leiden."[85] Guidebooks routed visitors through the largest cities and directed them toward museums, government buildings and churches. Art museums often received special attention with printed floor plans, lists of principal pictures with their locations, and even photographs of some of the not-to-be-missed paintings. Tourists were also directed to a select few rural villages where they were supposed to experience the flavor of traditional Dutch life.

TRAVEL ACCOUNTS

Travel accounts, each of which recorded an individual's personal experience of Holland, proved more popular for leisure reading than the guidebooks full of timetables and statistics. Tourists read travel accounts to provide preparatory information and as mementos of their vacations. Teachers used them in geography classes and others read them for entertainment. Armchair travelers relied upon them for their total experience of the Netherlands.

In the 1880s the two travel books read most widely among Americans were written by an Italian and a Frenchman, although British travel books also found a market in the United States. Beginning in the 1890s many more books were written from an American perspective, a reflection of the growing recognition that the American viewpoint varied from those of Holland's nearer neighbors. A look at both the foreign and the American accounts of travel in the Netherlands at the turn of the century will provide an idea of the values that eventually shaped a uniquely American attitude toward the Dutch and guided American travelers' experiences of the Netherlands.

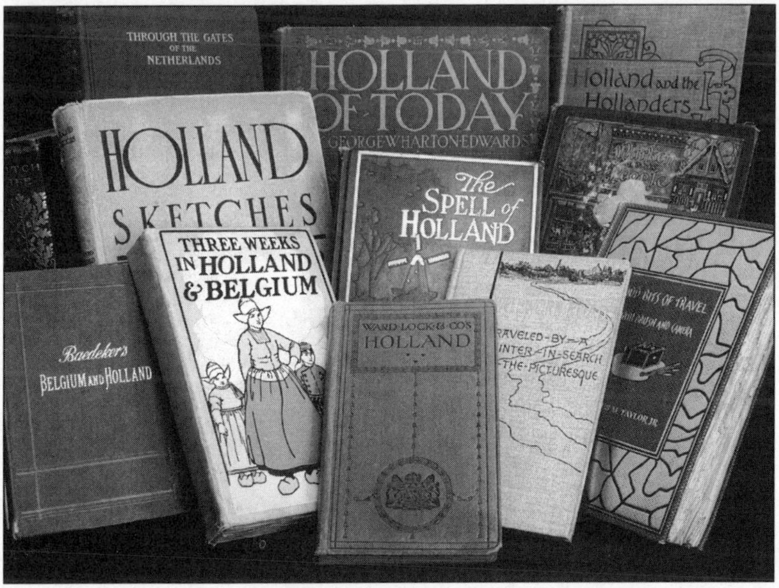

FIG. 67 *An abundance of pocket guides and travel accounts aided Americans in acquiring a quaintly old-fashioned view of the Netherlands.*

Writing in 1874, Henry Havard described the "dead cities" of the Zuider Zee in *La Hollande Pittoresque, Voyage aux Villes Mortes du Zuiderzee*. An English language edition came out in London the next year, making it more accessible to American readers. In the nineteenth century most Americans of the class that could afford to travel in Europe had a good working knowledge of French and German, but English language editions were easier to acquire and reached more people. Whether read in French or English, Havard's romantic descriptions of the unknown North Holland villages that had declined from their earlier glory helped to popularize Volendam, Marken, Hoorn, Edam, and Zwolle among tourists. He wrote amusing anecdotes about the people he met and the history of the towns and illustrated them with a few drawings by himself and his two artist companions. An American couple later explained the extension of their Holland tour by noting: "This trip about the Zuyder Zee was to enable us to visit those 'Dead Cities,' about which M. Havard had written so entertainingly."[86]

More widely read in the United States than Havard was the work of Edmondo De Amicis. He first published *Holland and Its People* in his native Italian, but it was quickly translated into French and English. De Amicis took his readers on a tour of the major cities of Rotterdam, The Hague, Haarlem, and Amsterdam; the historic cities of Delft, Arnhem, and Leyden; a few of the smaller North Holland towns; and the provinces of Zeeland, Friesland, and Groningen. He helped reinforce the pattern of American travel established by guidebooks, which centered on the large cities and moved to the outlying regions as time permitted. He also solidified some common impressions of Holland by starting his book with lengthy explanations of Holland's topography and relations with the sea, then describing the city sights in terms of seventeenth-century history and finally discussing Dutch art at length.

Some of De Amicis's observations have a distinctly Italian flavor. A devout Roman Catholic, he found the cathedral at Rotterdam—the first Protestant church he had ever entered—ugly and bare. Dutch people seemed cold and unemotional to his Latin temperament, though he took care to explain that beneath their impassive facades lived kind people. To De Amicis, Dutch food was more plentiful than tasty and he regretted the lack of inexpensive table wines and bread at meals. Perhaps the strongest indication of the author's Italian point of view comes out in his discussions of Dutch art. Accustomed to Italian Renaissance madonnas and Southern

Baroque biblical, mythological, and historical subjects, De Amicis found it hard to appreciate what he considered the "ugly and trivial subjects" of Dutch art, its emphasis on realism, and its lack of emotion. He concluded that the Dutch people were "more conservative than creative."[87]

Such opinions, while apparently interesting to American readers (who bought many editions of the book), did not catch on. The predominantly Protestant experience of many Americans predisposed them to take a positive view of religion in the Netherlands. Most American travelers found the Dutch love of fine coffee and the availability of fresh milk to be of greater significance than the lack of wine since fine wines were notably absent from American cuisine as well. Likewise, the lack of an art tradition in the United States to compare with Holland's, and the popularity of Dutch art among American collectors, ensured that American tourists received Holland's art more positively than had De Amicis. However, many of De Amicis's other observations struck a responsive chord among his American readers. He characterized the Dutch people as patient, calm, courageous, sensible, independent, and liberty loving—assessments that American tourists and travel writers echoed.

An inexpensive popular edition of De Amicis's *Holland and Its People* by the New York publisher G. P. Putnam's Sons went through five printings in its first two years, 1880–1882. To temper De Amicis's Italian slant, Putnam's edition included notes to the American audience. For example, to De Amicis's observation that the Dutch closed shutters on their houses to indicate the degree of relationship with a deceased person, was added the observation that Philadelphians had practiced the same observance until recently. Rather than use analogies between Dutch and Italian cities, Putnam's edition compared Amsterdam to New York and The Hague to Washington, D.C.

The Knickerbocker Press also released an American edition of *Holland and Its People* in 1885. In a limited printing of 600 copies called the Zuyder Zee Edition, the publisher intermingled prints after paintings by Rembrandt, Teniers, Potter, and Ruysdael with contemporary etchings by the New York artists Robert Swain Gifford (FIG. 68), Charles A. Vanderhoof, Samuel Colman, Joseph Pennell, and Charles Adams Platt to add an American touch to De Amicis's text. Both seventeenth-century Dutch and nineteenth-century American illustrations emphasized the ancient character of the land and the people.

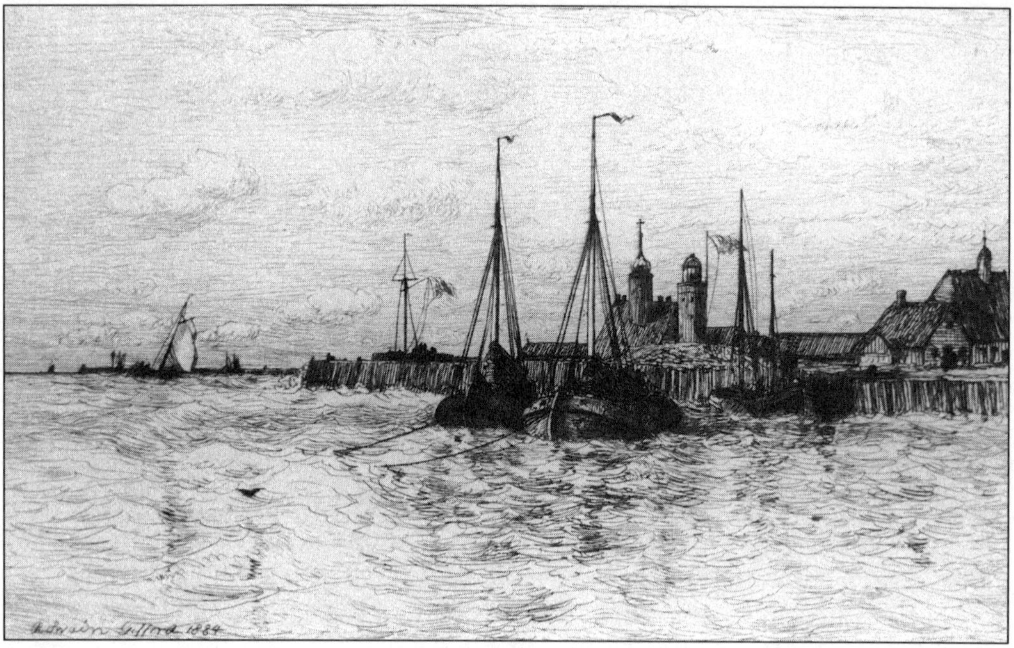

FIG. 68 *The addition of etchings by American artists, such as Swain Gifford's* Harlingen, *lent an American note to Edmondo De Amicis's popular Italian travel account,* Holland and its People.

Although American publishers altered these early French and Italian accounts to suit American tastes, they usually published British accounts verbatim. The British author David S. Meldrum wrote several books about Holland that were distributed in the United States or published in American editions. While British writers revealed admiration for the Netherlands many also voiced criticisms, and Meldrum was no exception. He found the landscape melancholy, declaring, "upon many spectators the reduplication of these horizontal lines has a saddening and a depressing effect . . . indeed, it is difficult for a stranger to live a week in the low countries without suffering from a depression of spirit."[88] He repeatedly described the Dutch boer, or farmer, as lazy, addicted to gin and too stubborn to change his methods from those of his grandfather. Meldrum thought class barriers in Holland were more rigid and confining than those in British society. Comparing Dutch servants, shopkeepers, and farmers to their British counterparts, he found the latter unquestionably superior.

The slightly derogatory tone of many British-authored books on Holland reached its apogee in the writing of Augustus Hare, who seemed hard pressed to find any redeeming features at all. Hare thought Rotterdam "the most odious place we ever were in—immense, filthy, and not very picturesque." He did not like Gouda any better: "expensive as we found every hotel in Holland, we were nowhere so outrageously cheated as here." Of the popular tourist spot, Scheveningen, Hare warned, "the flat monotonous shore would soon pall upon one." The famous St. Bavo church in Haarlem was "bare and hideous" and he could discover nothing of interest in Broek. While he considered the Helder landscape "bare and desolate in the extreme," capped only by the "grey, monotonous, desolate district of the Drenthe," even the clipped trees confirmed his belief that "in artificial Holland every work of Nature is artificialized." Although Hare had good things to say about the Dutch people, he moderated his praise with hints that they were unintelligent, inhospitable, and greedy, concluding, "Every man seemed to be systematically smoking away the few wits he possessed."[89]

In his tendency to temper every positive comment with a negative one, Hare revealed a typically British attitude toward Holland. In part this mild antipathy was due to a long history of competition and conflict between the two countries. In part it may be attributed to a conflicting aesthetic. For example, the British author–artist team of Mahaffy and Rogers echoed Hare's attitude toward the Dutch landscape:

> So perfectly have they subdued their mother earth, that they tyrannise [sic] over her laws, and warp her intentions after the most capricious designs. . . . A more perfect piece of artificial gardening could hardly be imagined, but artificial it is, in the strict sense of being opposed to what is natural, and therefore wanting in regularity and precision.[90]

Simply put, the Dutch cultivation of nature countered a British predilection for the romantic landscape epitomized by eighteenth-century English landscape gardening.

By the 1890s American publishers began producing many more American accounts of travel in Holland. These diverged from the European accounts in several ways, reflecting Americans' interpretation of the old masters and Motley's romantic histories of Holland as well as revisionist interpretations of Dutch and American history. In general, American accounts put a more positive light on Holland.

In contrast to the British view, most American accounts failed to see anything but beauty in the Dutch landscape (FIG. 69). A typical description called it "a landscape of which one can never tire." With regard to clipped trees, Margaret Preston considered that "nothing is so trimly dealt with as to interfere with a certain sense of natural freedom, which to an American eye is delightful." The repose of Holland's horizontal lines, far from inducing boredom, recommended itself as an antidote to the restless pace of modern American life. Turn-of-the-century physicians had noted a marked rise in nervousness among Americans which they diagnosed in the worst cases as neurasthenia, or nervous exhaustion. Known as "the American disease," neurasthenia was thought to result from the pressures of modern industrial society and doctors frequently recommended travel as a means of removing the patient from the stress of daily life. William Griffis noted the recuperative benefits of Dutch landscape when he explained, "the country in general induces a spirit of quiet restfulness, so grateful to the overwrought American."[91]

FIG. 69 *While British travel writers often found the Dutch landscape boringly flat, American writers emphasized its picturesqueness. The vertical format and romantic lighting of illustrations like Thomas Moran's "On the Way to Delft" supported textual assertions of Holland's unique beauty.*

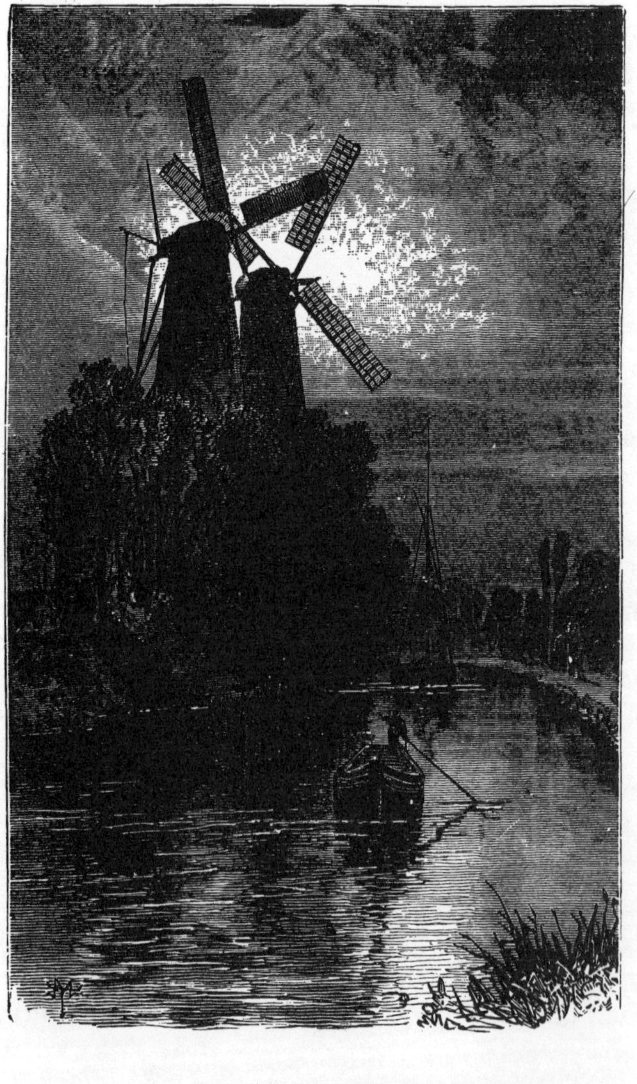

While Meldrum and Hare, and even De Amicis, had mixed feelings toward their Dutch hosts, American travel writers waxed enthusiastic over the character of the people. Fairly typical is this assessment by Charles Taylor, written in 1900:

> The natives of Holland are kind and peaceable in disposition, and fair in their dealings with one another. They are personally very attractive on account of the natural simplicity of their everyday lives, and the high principle of honor and morality upon which they conduct their business transactions.[92]

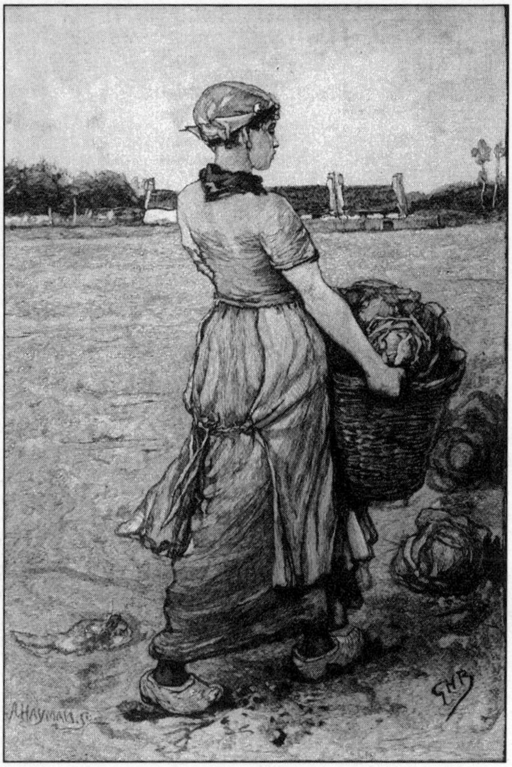

FIG. 70
George Boughton, and other American travelers, admired the hardworking Dutch women. Boughton made numerous illustrations like this one of a woman harvesting cabbages.

Louise Robinson's similar evaluation reveals the roots of this bias in preconceptions about Dutch history and landscape. She wrote home from the Netherlands:

> Our admiration of the Dutch, always great, is much increased by this trip through the country. When one sees the obstacles they had to contend against in making their land habitable—old ocean itself, for one—and the victory they have achieved, it seems more wonderful even than their conquering the tyranny of Spain. They are an industrious, persevering, and honest people.[93]

Typically, this view considers the people to have gained their character from the nature of the landscape.

Where several British authors discovered sloth and laziness in the Dutch working class, Americans more often perceived honest industry (FIG. 70). A traveler from Kansas wrote:

> The numbers of women doing all sorts of work are very large. It seems a pity they cannot be told of the great demand there is in America for their labor. They are the best of help—faithful, honest, industrious, and apt to learn. . . . Hundreds of them could get double their present wages in Kansas, and live much easier lives.[94]

Although some British authors deplored Holland's class stratification, American observers invariably discovered a completely democratic spirit. They pointed out that in the Netherlands, as in the United States, the common man could rise to positions of power within the government. A traveler from Ohio asserted, "They are perfectly democratic in their ways and when their Queen comes to visit them they shake hands with her just as we would shake hands with the president."[95] In like manner visitors frequently noted that all men were addressed as *mijnheer* (mister) even if they held noble titles. This lack of pretension among the Dutch people confirmed Americans' belief in their democratic spirit.

American viewers had perceived the same spirit of democracy in Holland's seventeenth-century art and in Motley's explanations of Dutch history. In spite of the changes wrought by the intervening centuries, tourists came to Holland expecting to see democratic and republican values at work. Revisionist history heightened their expectations by suggesting that Americans would find the basis of their own form of government in Holland. Tourists fulfilled their expectations by focusing on the Queen's handshake and ignoring her position as monarch. As one man explained:

> I very well understand that Holland is a constitutional monarchy, . . . yet I am glad to know that in this solid old kingdom, the birthplace of religious toleration, every man is eligible to every office except that of King. . . . There is a twang of incipient democracy about that fact.[96]

Americans made concessions for a form of government they normally repudiated, in part because rulers of the Netherlands descended from William the Silent, whom Motley had immortalized for the American reader as a Dutch George Washington. When Wilhelmina gained the throne in 1898, several writers implied that she ruled as the people's representative by popular acclaim. In other words, while conceding that a monarchy existed in the Netherlands, American travelers chose to represent it as an inherited presidency in which the monarch ruled by the consent of the governed.

The shift from the popularity of French, Italian, and British travel books about Holland to books authored by American travelers corresponded to three trends: the expanding market in Dutch and Dutch–American art, the development of revisionist history, and the increase in American tourism. As American travel books proliferated, they incorporated one or more of these trends as their foci.

THE ARTISTIC TOUR

Visual images, both past and present, helped to shape the American tourist's perspective on Holland. The travel writer Grace Ellery Channing explained:

> There are of course many ways of seeing a country . . . I believe that the artist's way is the only way. At any rate the artist's way is a particularly good way to see Holland, which is mainly an artist's country.[97]

Publishers apparently agreed with her, for they produced many travel books written and illustrated by artists. George Boughton's *Sketching Rambles in Holland* (1885), Hopkinson Smith's *Well-Worn Roads Traveled By a Painter in Search of the Picturesque* (1886), Charles Taylor's *Odd Bits of Travel with Brush and Camera* (1900), Edward Penfield's *Holland Sketches* (1907), and George Wharton Edwards's *Holland of Today* (1909) and *Marken and Its People* (1912) are just a few of the travel books presented from an artist's point of view.

One of the first artist's travelogues appeared in seven installments on the pages of *Harper's New Monthly Magazine* in 1883 and 1884. Harper's had sent George Henry Boughton, an English-born American artist then living in London, and Edwin Austin Abbey, a New York illustrator recently arrived in London, to travel through the Netherlands during the summers of 1880 and 1881. They were to make sketches that would accompany a writer's commentary. When the writer failed to appear, Boughton took over the task of providing a text. His writing style was often caustic, but his enthusiasm for the Netherlands came through and strongly influenced both tourists and artists. In fact, the series proved so popular that Harper's reissued it as a book, *Sketching Rambles in Holland.* It appeared simultaneously in the United States and England and rapidly went into a second printing. When Ward, Lock & Company published the sixth edition of their *Handbook to Holland* around 1912, Boughton and Abbey's *Sketching Rambles in Holland* still topped the list of suggested reading material on the Netherlands.

"We did not refer to Murray or Baedecker [sic], uselessly bulging out our coat pockets," wrote Boughton, "what we were simple enough to enjoy most of all, those excellent guides took no note of." In abandoning the guidebooks to follow their artist's eye, Boughton and Abbey helped establish one of the most popular methods of seeing Holland. Using artist's parlance, Boughton described the sights and sounds of the Netherlands:

> *As we moved from foreground to foreground, so to speak, how splendidly it would "compose" with the masses of quaint gables and red roofs; then with tops of trees golden with autumnal colors; . . . Threading in and out the ever-moving kaleidoscope of form and color, as spots of high light, were the white caps of the women-folk.*

By casting his description in such terms, Boughton brought to his readers' minds the numerous paintings and prints that constituted many Americans' primary assumptions about Holland.[98]

According to Boughton and other artist–authors, the people of Holland had an innate sense of the artistic. They painted their houses and boats many colors, wore coordinating shades of clothing, ornamented every utensil, and preserved the artistic heritage of the past. Explaining why so many landscape artists wanted to work there, the painter George Hitchcock wrote: "Holland is the most harmonious of all countries, either in sun or shadow. It is never crude; it is always a picture, atmospherically, as it stands, without change or thought of change." As a figure painter Hitchcock also thought that Dutch costume revealed the innately artistic qualities of a people who "seemed to clothe itself with a view to being painted." Dutch architecture made an equally good impression: "One cannot but admire these beautiful examples of brick-work, the lines and colors of which have been so deftly softened by time: nothing jars, nothing is out of harmony; a perfect adjustment of space and proportion, and withal, so cosily homelike," explained Edward Penfield, art editor for Harper's periodicals.[99]

The art critic Theodore Child also urged tourists to experience the Netherlands from an artistic point of view. He considered color and light to be the country's greatest assets, noting that "the cottages are deep red, the meadows deep green, the sky gray-blue, capable of changing almost at any moment into the most curious shades of black-gray and burnished copper." Such writing heightened the casual tourists' awareness of the aesthetic qualities of their surroundings. It suggested that one should look at the land and people exactly as one looked at paintings in a gallery. Indeed, William van Allen described Holland as "God's own breeze-swept galleries" filled with "ever-changing pictures of His painting."[100]

Most art-travel books and articles were illustrated with drawings, prints, or photographs by American artists. Soon tourists began to describe their Dutch travels in terms of the illustrations and paintings they had seen before departure (FIG. 71c). Writing about the Dutchmen in North Holland, Elbert Baldwin said:

> There are not a few veterans standing about, clad in blue shirts and long trousers, men on the order of those made familiar in pictures by Herkomer, Gari Melchers, and others. One old man is holding up a little child, whose golden, curly head contrasts well with his white locks, and a great brown sail looms up behind. Stop! I have seen just that bit of genre in some gallery. Did an artist once tell the old chap to stand just thus—I wonder if one really did?[101]

There is in this description such a complete association between the tourist's experience of Holland and his experience of paintings of Holland that they become inseparable.

The emphasis on an artistic interpretation of the Dutch tour also found expression in the large number of tourists who sketched as they traveled. Amateurs, students, and dilettantes tried their hand at making pictures of their European experience. Ward, Lock & Company even included a section of sketching tips in their *Handbook to Holland.* This explained where to go for each type of subject and color, the best time of day to sketch (4 to 6 P.M.), and the best seasons (summer, fall, and spring).

The most significant factor in the common decision to experience Holland from the artist's point of view, however, was the widespread knowledge of and admiration for seventeenth-century Dutch paintings (FIG. 72). As Child noted, "through seeing specimens of

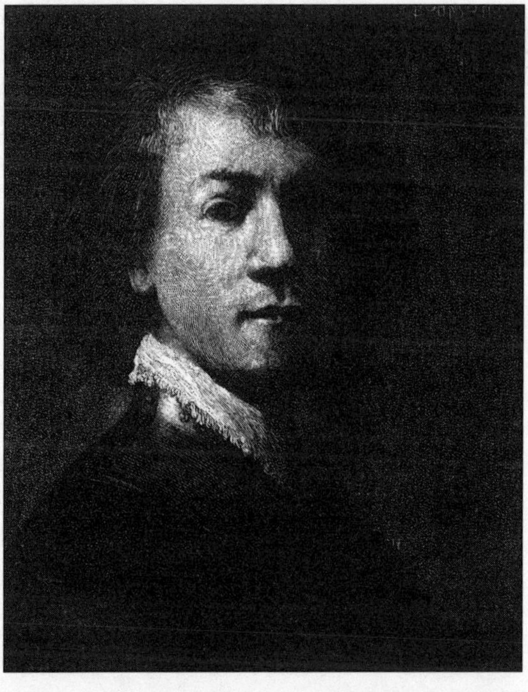

FIG. 72 *While Boughton wrote enthusiastically about the haunting quality of Rembrandt's* Portrait of Burgomaster Six, *most Americans knew it, and other Dutch masterpieces, only through black and white illustrations like this one published in* Harper's Magazine. *Consequently, the opportunity to visit art galleries was a much desired benefit of travel in the Netherlands.*

this painting in the museums of the world one becomes so familiar with every detail of Dutch life and landscape that when one does visit the country and sees the real thing one is tempted to remark, naively, 'How like a Dutch picture!'" This was precisely how many travelers did describe the Netherlands for their friends and relatives back home. Eva Madden thought the Dutch women she met "seemed like Rembrandt portraits stepped out of the Moritzhuis [sic] or Ryks Gallery picture-frames to entertain me." Margaret Preston agreed that the "antiquely dressed women, with their frilled caps, and the flaxen-haired children, with their short red petticoats and puffy knickerbockers, all look as if they had just stepped out of Teniers's or Ruysdael's pictures."[102]

In effect, Americans thought of going to Holland as entering an elaborate *tableau vivant*, a popular form of entertainment in which each participant assumed the dress and pose of a figure from a famous work of art in order to create a "living picture." Charles Howell said he liked Scheveningen because "here one sees in actual life the fascinating things he has marveled over in the canvases of Teniers, Jan Steen, and Gerard Dou."[103]

Given the emphasis travel literature placed on Dutch art and the tendency of common tourists to describe Holland as a living painting, travelers' reactions to seeing the real paintings are sometimes ironic. Tourists dutifully visited Paulus Potter's *The Young Bull* (FIG. 73c) but its fame often puzzled them. De Amicis had considered the bull worthy "to be placed in the Vatican beside the *Transfiguration* by Rafael"—high praise, indeed, from an Italian who usually found Dutch art wanting. Not only did Potter's painting receive favorable notice in the guidebooks, but it was also widely reproduced in the United States as a masterpiece and the Cincinnati Museum Association owned an oil copy of it. Its reputation notwithstanding, American tourists found little to love in this painting. "Potter's bull is doubtless a thing of beauty," wrote one, "for artists generally extol it; but to my mind its failure in portions, the ewe-neck, and the unnatural twist of the head back toward the shoulders, take away much of the claim of fidelity made for it, and the type of bull painted is of the poorest sort of 'scrub.'" A self-described "ordinary observer," not feeling adequate to the task of making an aesthetic judgment, noted that Potter could have chosen a better subject than a "scrubby eight-months-old bull calf that would not be permitted to invade the Panhandle of Texas." This evaluation of the model's worth as livestock typifies the average American tourist's practical perspective on art matters. Another viewer, equally unwilling to tackle a critique of the painting's artistic merits, stuck to a discussion of monetary value: "It is said to be worth $25,000—a large price to give for a bull, and yet I have known some of our American cattle fanciers to pay that much for a cow."[104]

Despite occasional bewilderment or disappointment in the face of museum art, old Dutch master paintings continued to guide tourists' impressions of the Netherlands. Author Sarah Orne Jewett described the landscape as "the Holland that Ruysdael painted," while Charles Taylor asserted that "every bend in the road shows a fresh picture such as Vermeer alone of masters might have hoped to paint." Travelers of less refined knowledge likened Holland to "a picture from a Dutch plate," or "Delft tiles come to life." By describing the present sites of Holland in terms of famous pictures from two centuries previous, writers ensured that their audience would form a clear mental picture, but they also reinforced the notion that the Netherlands was old-fashioned and unchanging. "It is claimed by Americans that if in England one sees the present century, to visit the United States is to take a peep into the next century. Equally, to see Holland is to take a peep into the last century," explained one guidebook.[105]

The voyage to Holland was a form of time travel for turn-of-the-century tourists. Knowing Rembrandt, Ruysdael, Hals, and others through reproductions, Americans went to the Netherlands to see the original paintings, expecting also to see the unchanged living models. Small variations in costume and environment between the seventeenth-century image and the nineteenth-century reality were easily overlooked. The cities themselves facilitated this view of Holland, for most contained an old quarter dating back to the middle ages (FIGS. 74c, 75). Travelers had only to seek out these parts to feel themselves in a previous age. For lodgings, meals, and shopping, of course, the comfort of the newer sections was welcomed, but for the experience of what they referred to as "real" Holland, only scenes that matched the images in old Dutch paintings would do.

The Holland-America Line played up the notion of Holland as the original model of an old master canvas by publishing *A Journey Through Old Holland*, a travel book with a Rip Van Winkle twist and profuse illustrations of old Dutch paintings. The book's author, J.J. De Gelder, adopted the premise that the narrator fell asleep and in his dreams toured the Holland of the old masters with a seventeenth-century Dutch-American colonist. Although the narrator

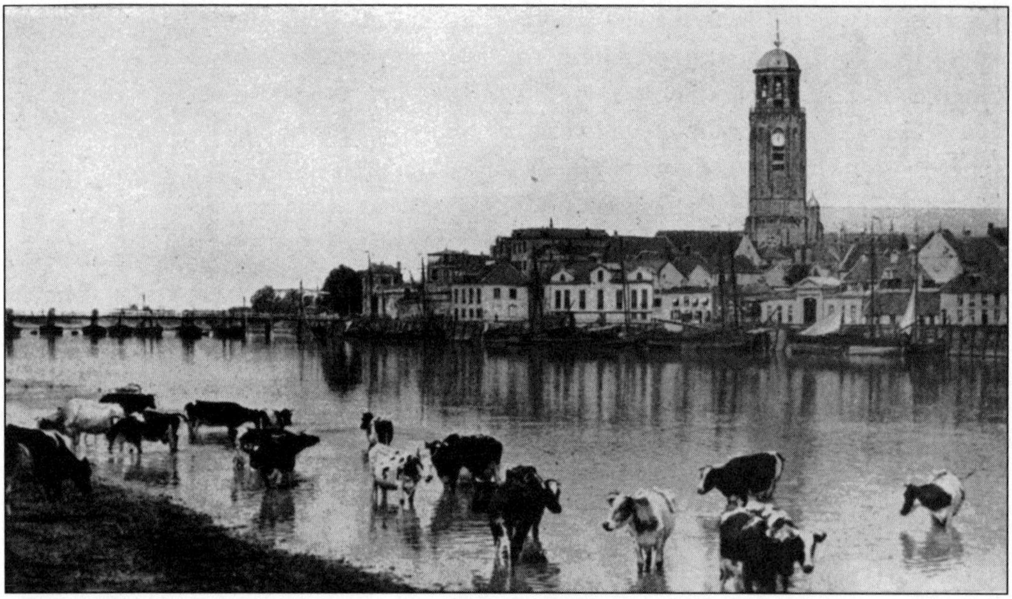

FIG. 75 *A photograph of Deventer published in Ward, Lock & Company's* Handbook to Holland *stressed the old time character of the city by filling the foreground with cows.*

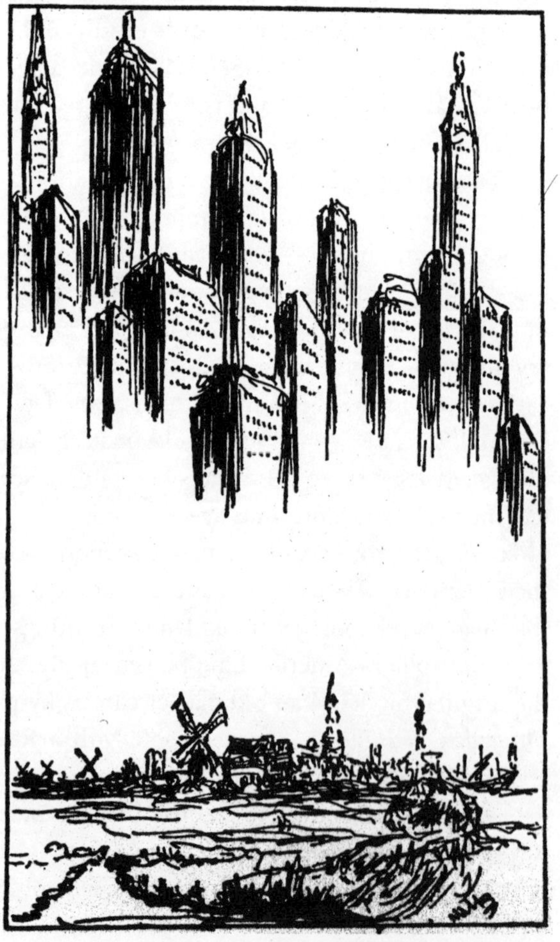

FIG. 76 *Historical ties between the United States and Holland increased American tourists' interest in some sights over others. This travel book illustration called* Old and New Amsterdam *stressed the colonial Dutch-American connection.*

woke up at the end of the tour to discover it was all a dream, the impression left with the reader was that one need only board a Holland-America steamer to experience the same kind of time travel.

Holland's success among American tourists and travel writers owed much to its national art and to its continued artistic appearance. Harper publishers made an abortive attempt to create a Scandinavian equivalent for Boughton's popular *Sketching Rambles in Holland* by sending Edwin Abbey, Swain Gifford, and Frank Millet to sketch in Denmark, Norway, and Sweden. According to Abbey the venture failed because these countries lacked an art tradition comparable to that of the Netherlands, and had not retained the picturesque aspect of an earlier age.[106]

THE HISTORICAL TOUR

Just as paintings and illustrations prepared American travelers for their experience of Holland, so did written histories. Most travel book authors referred regularly to Dutch histories by John Lothrop Motley and even the guidebooks threw in tidbits of Dutch history at strategic junctures. After the appearance of Campbell's *The Puritan in Holland, England and America* and Griffis's numerous books on the relation of Dutch and American history, references to history in travel books often acquired a nationalistic flavor (FIG. 76).

New researches on Pilgrim history and the more general knowledge of the Pilgrim's sojourn in Holland increased American interest in those places where the Pilgrims were said to have lived. American travel books rarely failed to point out the Brownist's alley in Amsterdam or John Robinson's house in Leyden. "Every good American will want to go to Leyden," explained Albert Osborne, "not because there is any special charm in the quiet old town, but because of the influence the former life of the place had in determining the form of many of our American institutions." He went on to recount the history of the Pilgrims in Holland and the long list of American features that "clearly derived their inspiration from Dutch sources."[107]

In the early 1880s no one knew exactly where in Delfshaven the Pilgrims had spent their last hours or from which wharf they had sailed for America. Horace Scudder, writing a children's book in 1882 based on his own trip to Holland, caused his literary heroes to walk the whole length of the Delfshaven waterfront to be sure they had seen the point of embarkation. Ten years later so many

American tourists were searching for the spot that authorities in Delfshaven renamed one of their quays Pelgrim Kade (Pilgrim Quay). The church where legend decreed the Pilgrims spent their last night in prayer received enough visits from these latter-day pilgrims that a visitors book and a framed print depicting the Pilgrims holding their first worship meeting in North America in 1621 were installed in the vestibule (FIG. 77).[108]

Most historians and travel book writers agreed that the parts of Amsterdam, Leyden, and Delfshaven once occupied by the Pilgrims had changed little since that time and that Americans could see their own living history in the architecture and costumes of these places (FIG. 78). Standing before the cathedral at Utrecht, the American cleric William Harman van Allen mused that it must have looked almost the same 300 years earlier when his ancestor sailed from Utrecht in the *Gilded Beaver* to settle in Beverwijk, now Albany. Perhaps the most famous American descendant of a Dutch family at that time, President Theodore Roosevelt, included Delft in his brief tour of Holland. According to the Dutch journalist M.J. Brusse who wrote a book about Roosevelt's tour, Delft was the city from which the former president's ancestor Claes Maartensz van Roosevelt had come to North America, and old Delft had changed little since then. There Roosevelt paid homage at the tomb of William the Silent. In Haarlem, Brusse reported, Roosevelt was delighted to learn that Van Rooseveldstraat was named after a fifteenth-century Haarlem Burgomaster killed in a Spanish siege. For travelers who found their names inscribed in historic Holland, it was easy to imagine a direct family connection with the places they visited.

The historical tour held particular appeal for groups such as the Holland Society of New York, which made an excursion to the Netherlands in 1888. The *New York Herald* sent a correspondent along to report back to other New Yorkers and Sheldon Viele published a book about the experience two years later. Composed entirely of men whose Dutch ancestors colonized North America, the Holland Society hoped to solidify relations with New York's parentland and to visit sites of historic interest for New Netherland. Because of the nature of the organization it was more of a diplomatic journey than that experienced by most Americans. Dutch diplomats and crowds met them in Rotterdam and Amsterdam and the American ambassador, himself a member of the Holland Society, entertained them. Similarly, a group of Congregationalists journeyed to England and Holland in 1896 to visit sites of interest to

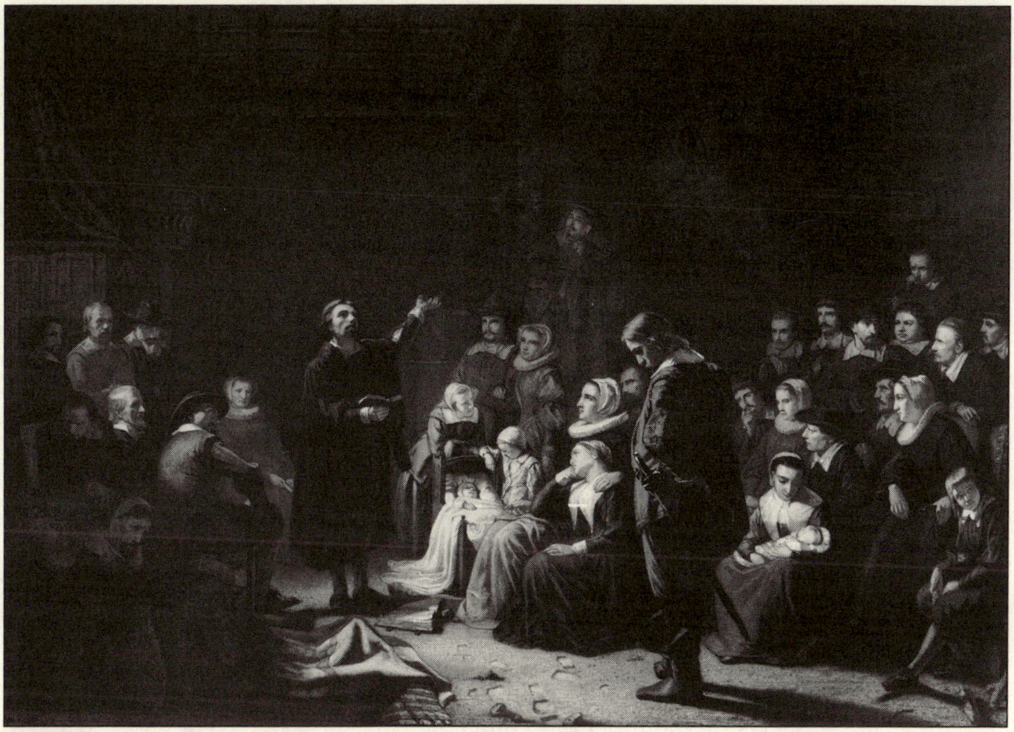

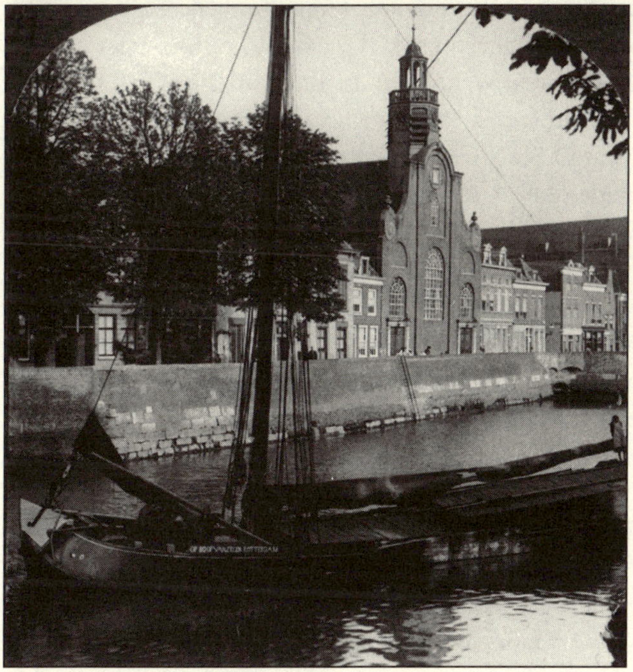

FIG. 77 *The Philadelphia expatriate to Holland, John George Schwartze, painted* Pilgrim Fathers Holding their First Meeting for Public Worship *in 1858. The painting was lost during the Civil War when the ship carrying it to the United States sank, but the image was preserved in fifty prints by August Allebe. One of them hung in the vestibule of the so-called Pilgrim Fathers Church in Delfshaven at the turn of the century. Schwartze's daughter Therese posed for the figure of the girl by the cradle and later became, in historian William Griffis's opinion, Holland's best woman painter.*

FIG. 78 *Many American tourists made their own pilgrimages to the sites where the Pilgrims were believed to have spent their last hours before traveling to America. Those unable to go to Delfshaven could enjoy stereoview photographs of such scenes as the* Church where the Pilgrim Fathers Prayed before Embarking for America *right in their own parlors.*

Congregational Church history. During their eight days in the Netherlands they made the complete tour from Rotterdam to The Hague to Amsterdam, by way of Haarlem. They, too, published an account of their travels that focused on those sites of specific historic interest to Americans. Bringing art and history together, one member of the party suggested that the Pilgrims might have seen the young Rembrandt while they all lived in Leyden.

William Griffis's travel book, *The American in Holland*, provides an outstanding example of the historical tour. In each place he traveled, Griffis recounted some anecdote of Dutch or American history, frequently connecting the two. For example, he wrote that the town of Werkhoven was the home of the famous Dutch family Van Braams, and added that a member of that family had been George Washington's military instructor and comrade-in-arms. Like other travelers, Griffis also found personal historic connections, even though his ancestors did not derive from Holland. Griffis, who had lived for several years in Schenectady, New York, saw reminders of that town's Dutch heritage in several towns that he visited. In Beverwijk he discovered a church bell cast at the same eighteenth-century foundry as a church bell in Schenectady. The zigzag patterns in Veenwoude's brick houses reminded him of Schenectady's masonry. A baker's shop in Hoogeven evoked memories of the sugar cookies given to children who went door to door on New Year's Day in Schenectady, an old Dutch custom whose passing the author regretted. Griffis went to Bloemendaal, near Haarlem, because he wanted to see the namesake of Bloomingdale, New York. He traveled to Breukelen, near Utrecht, in order to see the place from which he believed the original settlers of Brooklyn, New York had come.

Increased awareness of New York's Dutch history meant that New Yorkers with no personal Dutch ancestry were apt to tour Holland with New Amsterdam in mind. Travel writer Ernest Talbert was born and raised in Brooklyn, New York. Although he took leave to doubt that this place ever carried the Dutch name Breukelen (preferring the authority of old English surveys that called it Brooklands), he did grant that Brooklyn was more typically Dutch than Harlem or Bloomingdale. Reversing the usual formula of declaring a Dutch town in Holland unchanged through the centuries, Talbert declared that Brooklyn, New York in 1913 preserved "the serene, unchanging atmosphere Americans admire so greatly in Holland, though they decry it at home," adding as proof, "only a few years ago, admirers of Holland might have seen an old Dutch farmhouse standing on Fulton

Street opposite Arlington Place, in the very center of Brooklyn; in fact, it is there today, though lost to sight behind a modern store-front." Talbert's reflections on Brooklyn's Dutch heritage emerged from a trip to Utrecht, which reminded the traveler of New Utrecht on Long Island beyond the Flatbush area of Brooklyn.[109]

Still more striking evidence of the non-Dutch-American tourist's willingness to claim a Dutch birthright is the speech that F. Hopkinson Smith said he gave to persuade a crowd in Amsterdam to let him paint a picture on a busy market quay:

> I reviewed the history of old Amsterdam and its traditions; its reputation for hospitality; its powerful colonies scattered over the world; its love for art and artists. Then I passed to the greatest of all its possessions—the New Amsterdam of the New World, my own city, . . . I had come three thousand miles to carry home to their children in the New World some sketches of the grand old city they loved so well, . . . I would appeal to them as brothers to decide whether these streets of Amsterdam were not always open to her descendants, and whether I was not entitled to use them at all times by virtue of my very birthright.[110]

Since the Anglo-American Smith's only claim to Dutch blood came through his marriage to a Dutch-American woman, the birthright to which he referred was the right of all New Yorkers, regardless of ancestry, to claim Holland as the founder of their city. Personal ties such as these, based on knowledge of Holland's history and its intersection with American history, made the historical tour a popular one among many travelers.

THE MYTHIC "WINDMILLS AND WOODEN SHOES" IMAGE

Calling his travel book *Windmills and Wooden Shoes*, Blair Jaekel opined: "Probably the majority of travelers go to the Netherlands, not for art, nor for scenery, nor even for history, but for windmills and wooden shoes (to epitomize the characteristics of the country and its peoples)."[111] Most American travel book authors promoted a consensus image of Holland as a pastoral Eden inhabited by healthy cows; sturdy, honest people wearing wooden shoes; and picturesque windmills, dikes, and canals (FIG. 79c). This utopian idyll resulted quite naturally from the habit of viewing Holland through the rose colored lenses of art and history.

Many people started their tour of Holland at Rotterdam, port of the Holland-America steamship line. Baedeker considered the docks and harbor some of Rotterdam's principal attractions, mentioning specifically a coal tip, electric cranes, floating docks, and petroleum tanks. Because of its cosmopolitan and industrial character, Rotterdam failed to satisfy what most Americans sought in Holland and they seldom stayed there long. Some travel book writers played down Rotterdam's industry in an attempt to make the city conform to American ideals of Dutchness. In his book, *Holland as Seen by an American*, James Gore included three photographs of Rotterdam. One shows a medieval city gate, another a row of windmills, and in the third the photographer carefully positioned an old city mill to obscure the modern factory behind it. Such selective vision is very typical of the way most Americans looked at Holland.

Travel book writers agreed that the characteristic "windmills and wooden shoes" image was most easily found in rural areas. Edward Penfield recommended the remote island of Marken, "for it takes you out into the country, away from modern influences, and lands you in an atmosphere of unadulterated Dutchness." "It must be understood that neither Amsterdam, Rotterdam nor The Hague

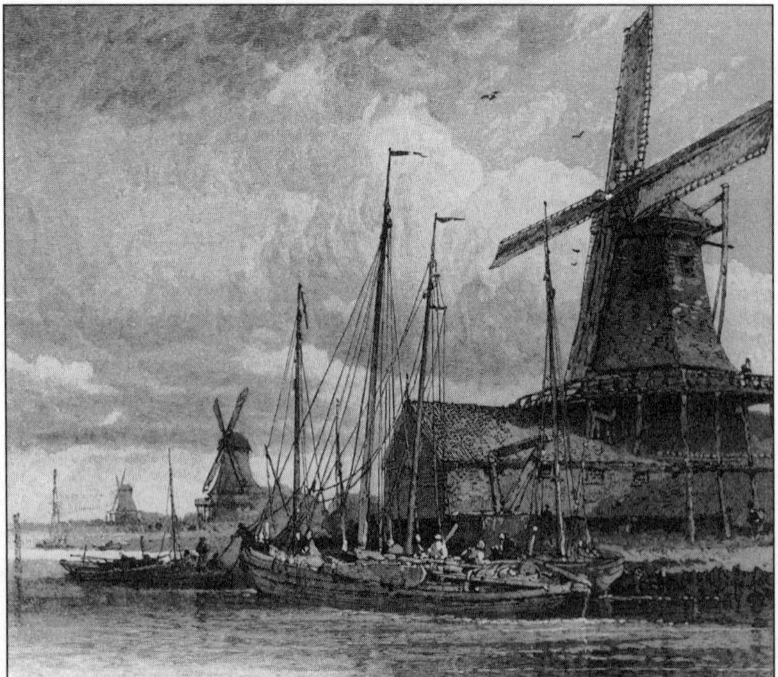

FIG. 80 *For tourists seeking their childhood dream of Holland, Zaandam with its rows of mills usually gave satisfaction.*

gives the concrete characteristic idea of the Netherlands," agreed George Wharton Edwards. "For real character one should go into the interior and seek the smaller towns, wherein he will find something of the air of the seventeenth or eighteenth century. These are really Dutch, and here one finds quiet, cleanliness, and the comparatively unaltered quality of ancient customs." The notion that Marken was more Dutch than Amsterdam by virtue of its closer resemblance to the seventeenth century suggests both the invisibility of modern Holland for Americans whose interest in the country was ruled by history, and the extent to which old master paintings controlled the American view of the Netherlands. Old fashioned windmills and costumes represented the only Holland that many travelers wanted to experience (FIG. 80).[112]

Travel authors urged methods of transportation that capitalized on the picture postcard aspects of rural Holland. Art critic Theodore Child recommended canalboats as a means of escaping from the modern Dutch city:

> The canalboat is the real vehicle from which to see Holland, and you will get a truer and more complete impression of the dykes, polders, canals, and windmills, from an afternoon's journey on a *trekschuit* or a *stoomboot* than from days of travelling from town to town in a railway car.[113]

Similarly, several authors recommended touring the countryside by bicycle. Holland's roads were level, tree-shaded, paved with brick, and in excellent condition. Rental and repair shops were easy to find and the railroads allowed passengers to carry bikes on the trains for a minimal charge. Baedeker provided an extensive biking itinerary that circled Holland. Less adventuresome cyclists could join one of the Portland, Maine-based F.A. Elwell's personally conducted European bicycle tours. They included at least one week in Holland, hitting all the sites of the typical Dutch tour. Elwell also published a handbook for the League of American Wheelmen, to facilitate cyclists planning their own trips abroad, in which Holland came highly recommended as a cyclist's country. The advantages of seeing Holland by bike included a relaxing pace, opportunities to come into closer contact with the Dutch people, and the conviction that the back country roads and tiny towns through which one rode were more Dutch than the cities most tourists frequented.

Of course, not everyone preferred an old-fashioned Holland. Soon after the turn of the century the automobile introduced a new way to tour Europe and a more modern image of old world countries. When the Woods described their adventures through the Netherlands in 1910 their vision was as modern as their conveyance:

> The distances in Holland from city to city are never long, and with a motor-car one can pass from town to town in quick succession. . . . The people whom one sees are quite ordinary-looking men and women. They dress in very much the same fashion as do the English or French or Germans. Their everyday clothes are not the baggy trousers, the wide skirts, the blue caps and the white coifs so often seen in pictures of Holland life.[114]

The Woods' ability to discern a modern side of the country placed them in the minority. Most travelers were willing to go out of their way to see baggy trousers and white coifs.

As motor touring became more popular, Holland accommodated modernity by establishing car rental agencies, touring clubs, information offices, and hotel garages. A few years after the Woods published their trip, Ernest Talbert insisted that "the 'only' way for the general public to see Europe is in hired motorcars." Talbert pointed out that motor travel had formerly belonged to the very wealthy who shipped their automobiles and chauffeurs to Holland, but argued that now, in 1913, most people could afford to hire a car and drive themselves. However, he advocated this modern mode of travel as a means of seeing things off the beaten tourist track, of finding the still untouched, old-fashioned Holland.

The Bostonian William Harman van Allen, who began and ended every European tour in the province of Zeeland, recommended Veere as a place where Americans could avoid others of their kind:

> A few artists frequent it, since Boughton discovered it thirty years ago; now and then a Frenchman who has read Henri Havard's *Heart of Holland*, finds his way here. But the 'tripper' is happily absent; the Cook's tourist knows it not; the loud-voiced, hurrying, money-getting Philistine who makes one blush for his native land finds nothing to draw him here.[115]

In fact, the artists made much of Veere, and so, too, did many tourists who made lengthy enough stays in the Netherlands to venture there after first seeing Amsterdam and The Hague. The town hall furnished a superb example of old Dutch architecture—the ancient tower at the mouth of the harbor offered a romantic place to stay overnight and the abandoned air of the town invited peaceful walks through its tree shaded brick lanes.

To experience the stereotypical "windmills and wooden shoes" Holland, many tourists spent a few hours in Veere, Broek, Delft, Edam, Marken, Volendam, or Zaandam. The fame of Broek, a dairy town with a well-established reputation as the cleanest place in the world, attracted many. Each visitor in turn reported their inability to discern any greater cleanliness in Broek than existed in every other spotless Dutch town, thereby reasserting cleanliness as one of the dominant traits of national character. Despite disavowals of uniqueness, tourists continued to travel to Broek to inspect the clean streets and exclaim over a model farm where the family lived in one parlor and cows in another. Clean white muslin curtains hung at all the windows and only the furniture and floor covering indicated which half was which. As the source of delftware, Delft provided another popular excursion for those in pursuit of a stereotype. A variety of antique shops attracted travelers in addition to the city's picturesque pottery, architecture, and history. Edam, home of Edam cheese and a weekly cheese market, provided a chance to study the traditional costumes of North Holland.

Day trips from Amsterdam to Marken and Volendam eventually became the favorite tourist excursions in Holland (FIG. 81). Artists had discovered in Marken a place that preserved a complete national

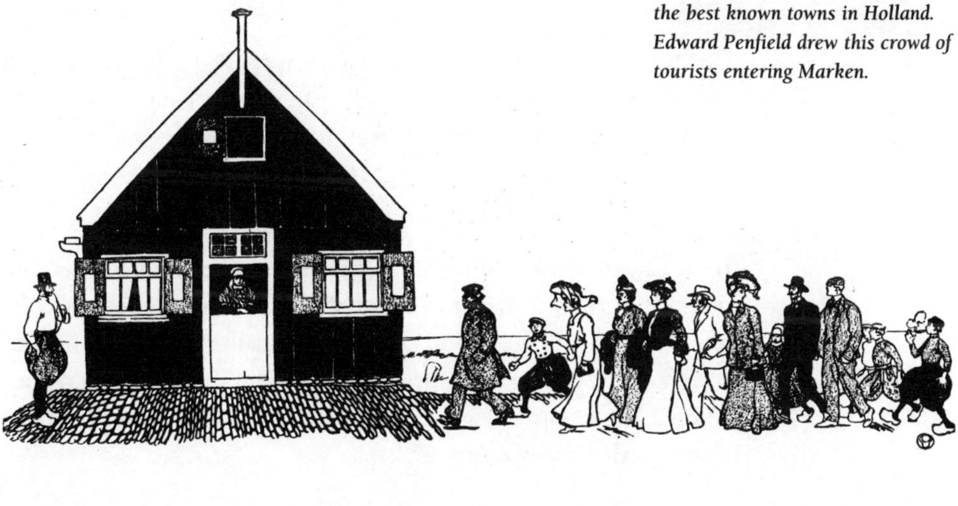

FIG. 81 *Marken and Volendam, perhaps the most atypical of Dutch villages, became the most popular tour destinations and, ironically, the best known towns in Holland. Edward Penfield drew this crowd of tourists entering Marken.*

dress for both sexes. As time went on and the work of the artists helped advertise it, passenger service to the island became a regular thing and package tours brought many more tourists to Marken. Reports of hostility toward visitors, usually secondhand, became numerous. In 1900, when Marken had become a well-known stop for Amsterdam tours, visitors continued to represent the Marken people as completely isolated from the outside world and shy of foreigners. Some naively attributed attempts on the part of natives to avoid having their pictures taken to a primitive belief that their souls would be captured. So often did tourists report that they had to get the skipper, a Markenite who spoke some foreign languages, to help them make the Marken people cooperate, that one cannot but suspect collusion on the part of the islanders to milk the gullible tourists.

Within a short time Marken had made concessions to tourism. The widow Marretje Thijssen Teerhuis opened her home as a showplace to anyone willing to pay a fee, thus earning a small income and protecting her neighbors from the curiosity of visitors. It also resulted in making nearly every painting and illustration of a Marken interior from this time period look alike (FIG. 82). Another Markenite opened a small hotel for the more adventuresome traveler around 1898. Few accounts mention its existence, however, as most people were content to absorb the Marken experience in an afternoon. They usually came on Sunday, when the fishing fleet was in and the islanders dressed in their Sunday best, and left at the end of the day.

Over time, contact with tourists brought changes that disappointed many Americans looking for the "true atmosphere of Dutchness" they had been led to expect there. One disillusioned traveler reported:

> Marken is another place that has been spoiled into self-consciousness by too much attention. Old customs and costumes are retained on this tiny island, but you feel that their preservation is a matter of revenue and not reverence. The children beg for pennies, and the women clamor for positions in front of the camera.[116]

Ironically, too many tourists in any spot always spoiled the atmosphere of authentic Dutchness for visitors. Once a place had been discovered, published, and admired, it came under suspicion of being fabricated for the tourists. Broek, Marken, and Volendam all suffered from tourists' apprehensions that they were being taken in by artificial show places.

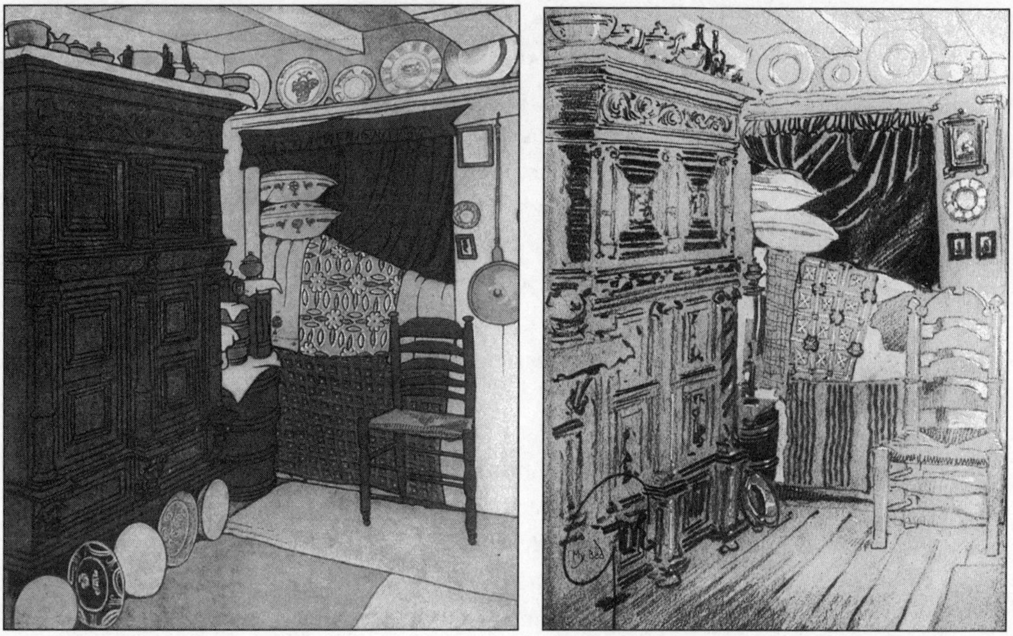

FIG. 82 *Edward Penfield's illustration of* A Marken Interior *(left) and George Wharton Edwards's illustration* Wall Bed in Which I Slept *(right) portray Marretje Teerhuis's home, the only house regularly open to artists. Although they titled their pictures differently, most illustrators and photographers who pictured a Marken interior at this time showed exactly the same scene, emphasizing the characteristic Dutch bed, chest, and plates.*

Like Marken, Volendam retained a complete traditional costume for each sex. Consisting of a lace cap with wings turned back from the cheeks, tight bodice with three-quarter length sleeves, multiple skirts, and a particolored apron for the women, and billowing ankle-length pants, double breasted shirts, and fur caps for the men, this costume provided much of the flavor of Volendam. Travel accounts frequently described the experience of buying wooden shoes or complete suits of clothing (FIG. 83c). The purchase of these items was part of the ritual of experiencing a foreign culture. It was not enough to see Hollanders in their costumes; tourists wanted to walk in wooden shoes and to return home and model the native costume for the entertainment of their friends. Wearing Dutch costume, however briefly, enhanced the sensation of participating in a grand *tableau vivant*. Their surroundings already seemed like a living old master painting and by donning the appropriate costume, travelers could imagine themselves having walked through a Rembrandt painting into the Holland of the Pilgrims.

Of the many accounts of costume buying, Charles Taylor's tale poignantly reveals the single-mindedness with which some American tourists pursued this activity. When Taylor found that the only available suit of clothes in Volendam was a discarded boy's outfit he described as fit only for a ragman, he set about convincing the boy's father to make the child wear the rags so that Taylor could have the boy's good suit. Although the child had already refused to sell his clothing to Taylor, the father compelled him to sell and Taylor gave him a metaphorical pat on the head, "The evidence of good will on the part of the parent, and the obedience of the son charm me even more than the possession of the coveted garments. The boy is a noble lad." The incident was not yet over, however, for as he was about to leave, Taylor discovered that the boy also owned a set of the silver coin buttons traditional in this town. "In general they are cherished as treasures beyond price: these worn by the boy are exceedingly rare, and are more than a hundred years old, having belonged to his great-grandfather," exulted Taylor who promptly bought the silver buttons. This reduced the boy to tears, which Taylor took as further proof of the value of his find. "For this final test of obedience I thank him heartily, and bestow upon him a liberal reward for the sacrifice, together with much praise." The whole incident may have been a product of the author's imagination, but the acquisitive attitude was typical.[117]

Volendamers soon began making costumes to sell to tourists. The tables had certainly turned in Talbert's 1913 account of costume buying:

> Crowds of villagers followed us, children begging for cents while young girls and women offered articles for sale; . . . Scoffy bought a child's cap from a girl who pressed her wares on him . . . he was stopped by a bevy of pretty girls and, since nothing short of violence could have liberated him, he purchased one of the very ordinary lace caps the girls sell at a price worthy of the fine ones which they wear.[118]

Although it became increasingly difficult to find, Americans clung to their image of a backward, premodern Holland (FIG. 84). Writers inadvertently contributed to this mythical image of Holland when they sought explanations for things foreign to their understanding. Traveling for such brief periods, they naturally misunderstood some of what they saw. Burton Stevenson informed his readers that the Dutch commonly referred to the automobile as a *snelpaardeloos-zoonderspoorwegpitroolrijtung*. John Higinbotham concluded that no one in Enkhuizen spoke English and that Dutch cattle lived solely on pasturage because he did not happen to meet any English speakers in Enkhuizen or see grain fields during his three weeks in the Netherlands. Eva Madden divulged the interesting news, gleaned

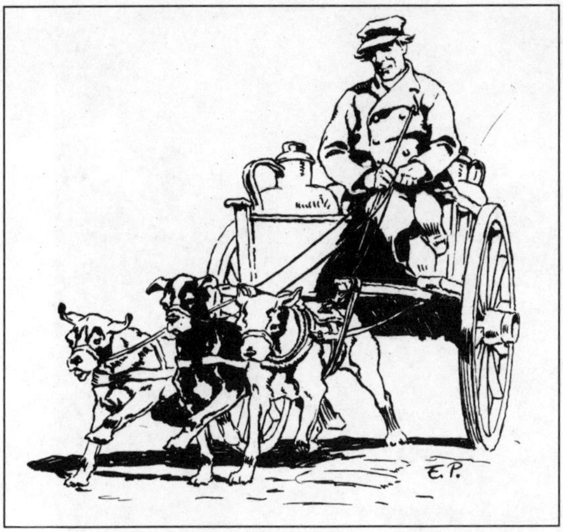

FIG. 84 *Descriptions and illustrations of Dutch dog carts and the animals bred to pull them appeared in some travel accounts. Edward Penfield made this drawing and defended the practice that some other American writers considered cruel.*

during one week in Holland, that Dutch women had contracted no marriage engagements for two years because the winters had not been severe enough to freeze the canals, where most engagements took place. Other startling revelations concerning the supposed betrothal and funeral customs of the Dutch people compounded the American mythology about Holland.

Even the most enthusiastic seekers after the picturesque ideal recognized drawbacks in their idyll (FIG. 85). The traditional Dutch bed in a cupboard attracted much admiration for its "Dutchness," but most travelers suspected that inadequate ventilation rendered them unhealthy. A few daringly slept in them, but most were content just to say they had seen one. Many travelers believed that the Dutch people's love of cleanliness failed to extend to their persons. For some tourists inconvenient bathing arrangements in the hotels confirmed the suspicion that the Dutch were not as concerned with personal hygiene as were Americans. Writers who enjoyed a good smoke and appreciated the opportunity to buy two cigars for a penny rejoiced in the Dutchmen's love of fine tobacco, but even confirmed smokers disapproved of six- and seven-year-old children smoking. Numerous travelers complained of the attitude rural inhabitants exhibited toward them, from the begging of little children to the crowding of curious adults around them. Charles

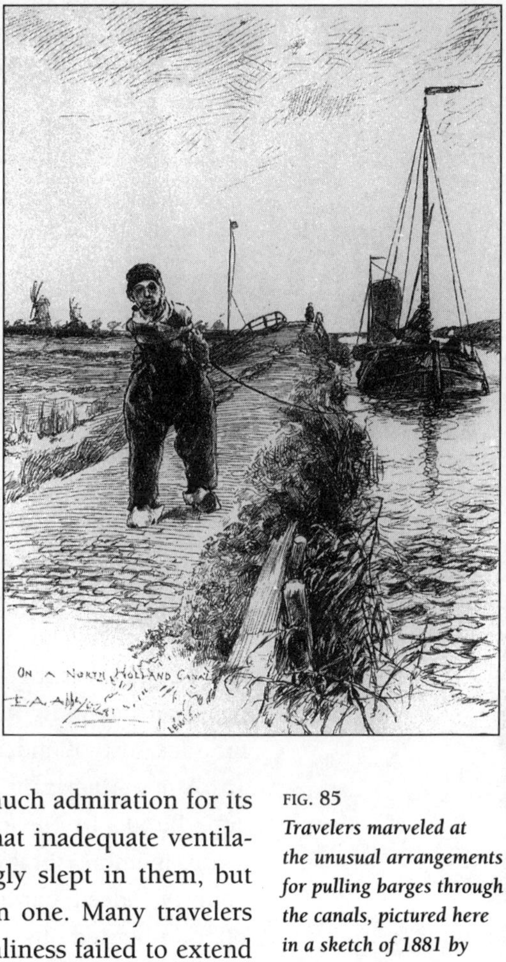

FIG. 85
Travelers marveled at the unusual arrangements for pulling barges through the canals, pictured here in a sketch of 1881 by Edwin Austin Abbey. Charles Taylor condemned the "pitiable sight of two young girls, harnessed like mules," and another writer reported with disgust that he had seen a cow and a woman harnessed together.

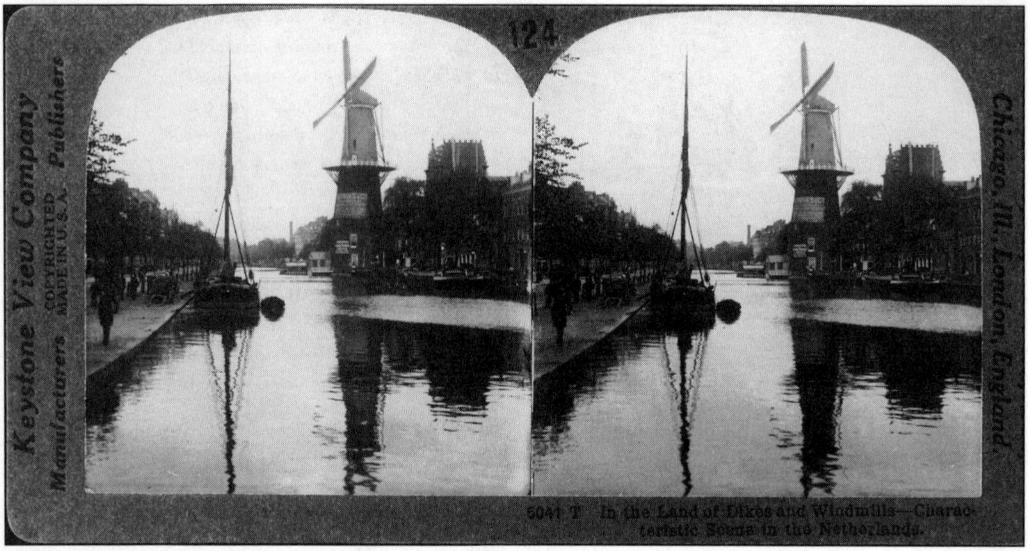

FIG. 86 *Popular stereoview cards, like this one called "In the Land of Dikes and Windmills," brought Holland to three-dimensional life when viewed through a stereoscope. Such scenes highlighted some of those traits Americans most wanted to see in images of Holland.*

Taylor claimed he had to hire the town crier to convince villagers that the American visitors did not wish to be followed everywhere by crowds of curious Dutchmen. The hut in Zaandam where Peter the Great spent a week learning shipbuilding disappointed nearly everyone who mentioned it. A small unassuming house covered with the graffiti of previous visitors, tourists complained that it could not even be photographed because the Russian authorities had built a protective brick shelter around it. The numerous guides who met incoming boats, hoping to take tourists to see Peter's hut for a fee, also offended many visitors.

A few Americans considered a visit to the Netherlands entirely superfluous. In *The European Tour*, Grant Allen declared: "Belgium, again, is immeasurably more important than Holland, which latter country, indeed, hardly calls for a visit on any ground save that of its often rather tedious paintings."[119] However, Allen's voice is decidedly in the minority. Most American travel book authors agreed with the consensus image of Holland as a land of windmills and wooden shoes (FIG. 86).

By 1910 evidence had filtered back to the United States that the American view of the Netherlands disturbed Hollanders. The Dutchman M.J. Brusse wrote a travel book for American consumption in which he protested: "The export-pictures and the absurd picture postcards, which are sold to you by hundreds and thousands have perhaps given you the impression that we are, properly speaking, a sort of anachronistic anecdote in old fashioned Marken hats . . . But really however alluring this picture, of old-Holland may seem to you, it does in point of fact not correspond with the reality."[120] Nevertheless, Brusse's book was illustrated entirely with the same stereotypical views that American books used. Published by the Holland-America Line, its purpose was to attract American tourists to the Netherlands, and the proven means for doing so was with the wooden shoe image.

Another Dutch writer convinced George Wharton Edwards to add a postscript to the revised edition of *Holland of Today* protesting the mythical image (FIG. 87c). A brief excerpt from that letter reveals some of Americans' more common misconceptions, as well as the things that most bothered the Dutch about an image they had themselves done much to create:

> Tell your readers that all Dutchmen are not Volendam or Marken fishermen . . . That the horizon is not always bounded by hundreds of red, white and blue whirling windmills. That there are other flowers besides tulips . . . That there are certainly other means of travel in the Netherlands than man-towed or horse-drawn antique canal boats, and stage coaches . . . That, in short, the people of the Netherlands are entirely and fully 'up to date,' and desire to be so considered.[121]

Clearly the tourism that brought in welcome revenue was not an unmixed blessing. While it undoubtedly increased Americans' admiration and love for the Netherlands, it did not always increase their understanding. Instead, the tourist experience helped to confirm the old-fashioned "windmills and wooden shoes" stereotype of Holland that prevailed in the United States at the turn of the century. It also reinforced the seventeenth-century image of Holland in old Dutch master paintings and history books, while asserting the importance of that Holland in American history.

SIX

"An American Renaissance of Dutch Architecture"

TOURISM AND TRAVEL LITERATURE CONTRIBUTED TO AMERICAN familiarity with Dutch architecture, and a growing interest in colonial Dutch buildings emphasized the Dutch-American connection. By the 1890s, William Elliot Griffis would observe: "The American renaissance of Dutch architecture is very noticeable in this last decade of our century."[122] This "renaissance" of Dutch architecture took several forms, some based on Renaissance and Baroque buildings throughout northwestern Europe, and others based on colonial Dutch-American models.

Turn-of-the-century American architects and architectural critics rarely distinguished between building styles in the region occupied by the Netherlands, Belgium, Luxembourg, and northern France, labeling all of it Dutch or Flemish with equal ease. Occasionally the Dutch was associated with a middle-class or rural architecture while the Flemish called up a more polished urban image. For example, Harper's Publishing Company created their Dutch Room, to be used as a conference and reception room, in tribute to the Harper brothers' mother, who was of Dutch descent. When the architect J. Cleveland Cady chose the decor for the Dutch Room, *The American Architect and Building News* reported: "Mr. Cady selected the Flemish type as being more refined in many details and in the general treatment than the pure and simple boer Dutch."[123] Because of this notion that the Dutch built an architecture for the common people, forms based on rural farmhouses were more often called Dutch and those inspired by urban buildings of the Northern Renaissance were more likely to be termed Flemish. But again, there was no consistency and often no obvious reason for the labels used.

While so-called Dutch or Flemish architectural styles were popular and widespread in the United States at the end of the nineteenth century, they took their place alongside Italianate, Shingle Style, Queen Anne, late Gothic Revival, Swiss Chalet, French Chateauesque, Richardsonian Romanesque, and English-based versions of the Colonial Revival. Popular taste continued to be eclectic and architects and builders freely combined Dutch motifs with other styles for picturesque effect. The Dutch-Flemish influence, then, forms a small but significant strand in the architectural eclecticism of that era. After 1920, however, the specific house type now known as Dutch Colonial Revival became enormously popular.

DUTCH RENAISSANCE REVIVAL

Griffis made his remark about "the American renaissance of Dutch architecture" in a travel book while discussing the city of Haarlem. Haarlem's *Vleeshal* (FIG. 88), an early seventeenth-century butchers' guild hall and meat market, reminded him of a style of building that he noted was becoming popular in Manhattan under such common labels as "zebra" or "beefsteak" architecture, due to its alternating stripes of red brick and cream-colored stone, stucco, or terra cotta. The taste for urban buildings in decorative combinations of brick and stone, with crow-stepped or curved gables that appeared to be inspired by sixteenth- and seventeenth-century buildings in the Lowlands, emerged in the United States about 1880 and maintained a minor but distinctive presence into the twentieth century.

The Collegiate Church and School of New York (FIG. 89), built on West End Avenue in 1892 from a design by Robert W. Gibson, exemplifies the adaptation of Dutch Renaissance architecture in an American building. Gibson based the church's design on the Haarlem *Vleeshal*, which was considered a model of Dutch Renaissance architecture and the crowning achievement in the career of the famous master mason and Haarlem city architect Lieven de Key. Gibson adopted the general form of the *Vleeshal* with its rectangular block massing, steep stepped gables, and matching step-gabled dormers. The accentuation of red brick walls with contrasting terra cotta

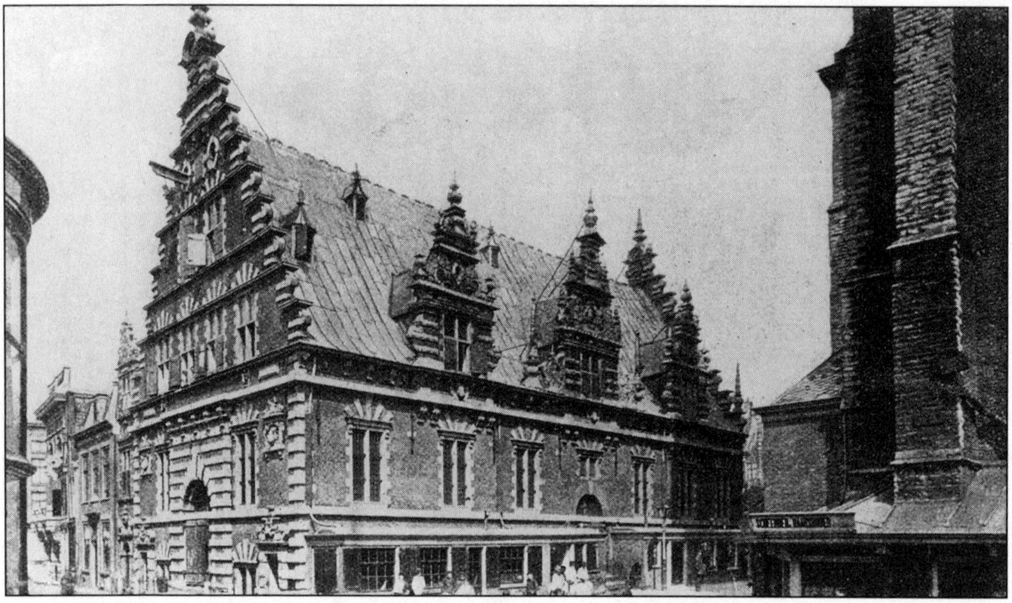

FIG. 88 *A landmark in Haarlem, Holland since 1603, Lieven de Key's Vleeshal provided the immediate inspiration for Robert Gibson's Collegiate Church and School* (FIG. 89).

quoins, belt courses, and voussoirs conveys a similar visual impression to the Dutch prototype, and specific details such as the front door treatment and the gable finials have been only slightly modified from the original. But Gibson toned down the elaborate ornamentation of the *Vleeshal* in his church, and replaced the multiple stories of variegated window openings in the *Vleeshal*'s facade with a single round window capped by a relief panel. Gibson undoubtedly considered an early-seventeenth-century Dutch building a particularly appropriate model for a Dutch Reformed church and school in a city founded by the Dutch. Griffis, a clergyman in Reformed and Congregational churches, certainly saw a fitness in the prototype, even if it necessitated a conversion from secular to sacred architecture. The Collegiate Church quickly became one of the most frequently cited examples of the successful incorporation of Holland's architecture into American buildings. The *Brick Builder*, a trade journal for masons and architects, pronounced it "picturesque enough to suit anyone, it is logical," and "homelike in character."[124]

Gibson's Collegiate Church was just one of many Netherlands inspired urban buildings that began to appear in New York City in the mid-1880s. Public schools, fire stations, rapid transit control houses, clubs, apartment buildings, a theater, and even a skyscraper carried the style, although rarely with such close modeling on a specific Dutch prototype as found in the Collegiate Church. The John Wolfe Building (FIG. 90), erected in 1895 from a design by Henry

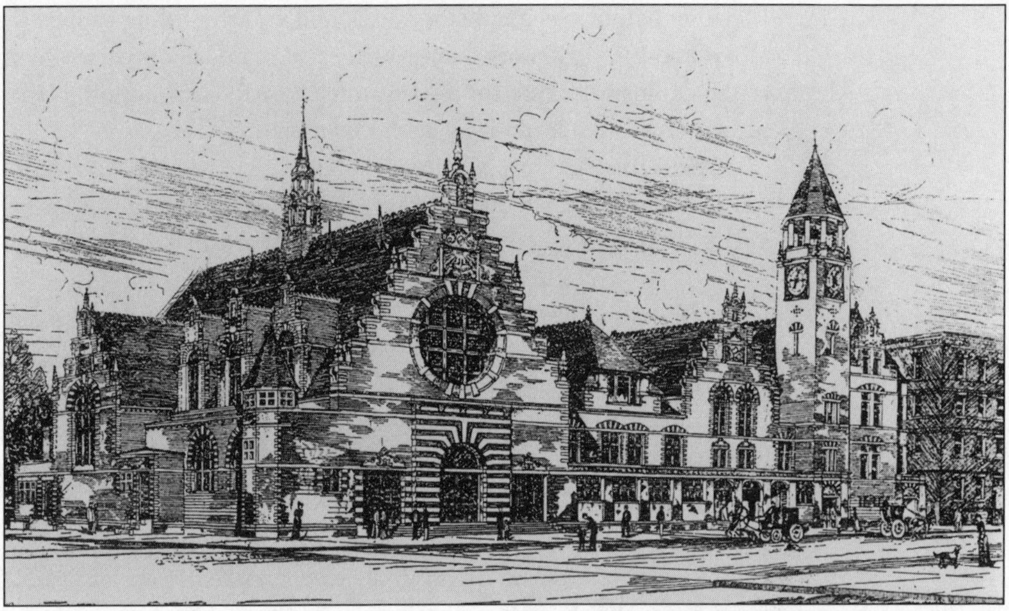

FIG. 89 *Robert W. Gibson's 1892 Collegiate Church and School on West End Avenue in New York City reflects the stepped gables, stone string courses, alternating brick and stone voussoirs, and steeply pitched roofs of Northern Renaissance architecture.*

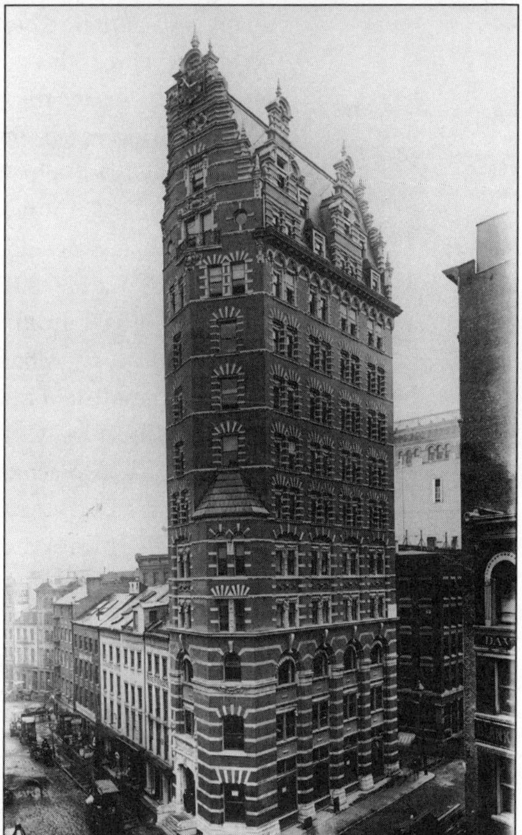

FIG. 90 *Henry J. Hardenbergh gave the John Wolfe Building a step-gabled roof and dormers. © Collection of the New-York Historical Society.*

J. Hardenbergh, was a ten-story brick and stone building capped by a two-and-one-half-story step-gabled roof and dormers. It was part of the extensive search for a style suited to tall office buildings that ultimately veered away from such historicizing.

The contemporary architect and author Robert A. M. Stern notes that the Dutch Renaissance Revival style emerged in New York's West End (the area west of Central Park between 59th and 110th streets) in 1885 when McKim, Mead and White built five variegated brick houses with crow-stepped gables on West End Avenue at 83rd Street. Other architects, including Frederick B. White, Robert W. Gibson, Clarence True, and Frank Miles Day, developed the theme in a series of buildings along West End Avenue that included several blocks of row houses.[125]

The city of Albany, begun by Dutch traders in 1624 as Fort Orange and reestablished by Governor Peter Stuyvesant of New Netherland in 1652 as Beverwyck, also experienced a revival of interest in Dutch architectural styles at the turn of the century. Albany still contained examples of Dutch style buildings dating to the late seventeenth and early eighteenth centuries, but the nineteenth century saw the destruction of more than a dozen historic structures. Increased public awareness of this loss of the city's heritage may have helped precipitate the return to a Dutch architectural vocabulary around 1890. In a recent guide to Albany's architecture, Diana Waite documents a dozen extant buildings erected between 1890 and 1917 that incorporate Dutch-Flemish styling, and many others from that period have disappeared during the twentieth century. Albany's Pruyn Library (FIG. 91), dedicated in 1901 and demolished in the 1960s, was a gem of Dutch Renaissance Revival architecture. Cities along the Hudson River between Albany and New York also acquired new "old Dutch" buildings at the turn of the century. Despite some recent alterations, the storybook Dutch quality of the Helen Davenport Building in Kingston, for instance, is quite evident.[126]

The style occurs, as well, in areas of the Midwest settled by nineteenth-century Dutch immigrants. Elizabeth Voorhees Hall, built as a women's dormitory for Hope College in Holland, Michigan, not only exhibits stepped gables and limestone detailing, but contrasting shades of brick laid in Dutch cross bond form a diamond pattern in the gable ends and dormers (FIG. 92). The main entrance assumes a form common to this style of architecture. Alternating courses and voussoirs of red brick and light limestone

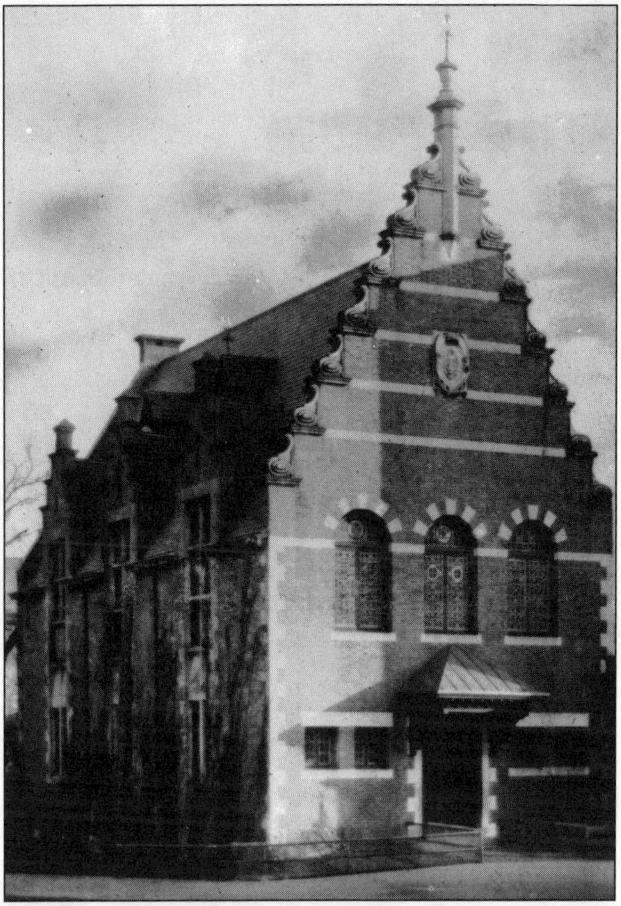

FIG. 91 *Albany's Pruyn Library took the form of seventeenth-century Dutch architecture seen in old prints of colonial Dutch-American towns. Local architect Marcus Reynolds designed several other Dutch Renaissance Revival buildings for his home town as well.*

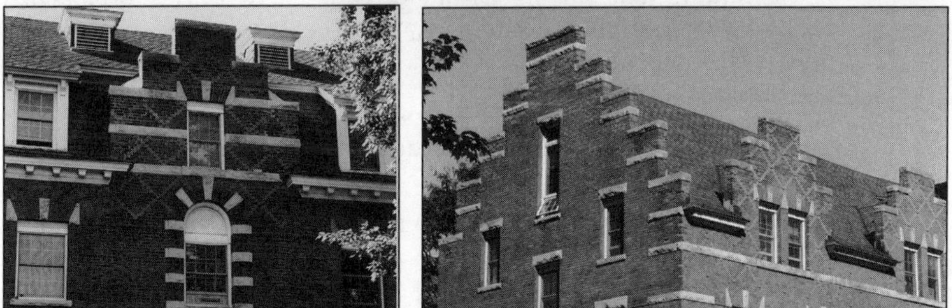

FIG. 92 *The entrance to Elizabeth Voorhees Hall, originally the women's dormitory at Hope College in Holland, Michigan, displays typical styling of the American Dutch Renaissance Revival. Patterned brick work, visible in the right-hand view of the back of the building, adds to the visual complexity of the design.*

form a round-arch entry in a square pavilion set slightly forward from the body of the building. Founded in 1866 by the Dutch Reformed Church, Hope College built earlier structures in Richardsonian Romanesque and Italianate styles. Not until 1907 was the Dutch-Renaissance-Revival Elizabeth Voorhees Hall constructed.

It is likely that the Dutch heritage of all these areas caused architects and patrons to desire a reflection of the Netherlands in their buildings. But the fact remains that variations on the stepped and curved gables of sixteenth- and seventeenth-century Holland and Flanders cropped up all around the country, wherever brick was in common use. In Chicago, Daniel Burnham and John Wellborn Root experimented with northern European details in domestic architecture of the 1880s. A variety of fanciful gables graced houses of essentially Romanesque, Queen Anne, and Art Nouveau character. Perhaps the best of these was the Edward A. Burdett House, with elaborate relief scroll ornamentation filling the crow-steps to form a straight-line gable and surrounding the circular window in the center of the brick gable end. Built in 1885–1886, it has since been demolished. The Rainier Club by Kirkland Cutter provides an example of the Dutch-Flemish type on the West Coast. This large brick building with steeply-pitched roof and multiple scrolled gables was erected in Seattle, Washington in 1904. In Atlanta, Georgia a highly eclectic corner building dating from 1891 combines a shingled square turret, tall chimneys, and an oriel window with its two brick ornamental stepped gables for a visually rich and complex facade with a hint of the Dutch Revival. The Finnish, Cornish, and Italian immigrants who settled Hancock, Michigan built their combination fire station and town hall of rusticated sandstone, but covered it with a very steeply pitched roof and crow-steps-over-scroll-curved gables pierced with a broad Romanesque Revival arch. Such examples suggest that the appeal of Netherlandish gables and decorative brickwork existed well beyond areas of Dutch settlement.[127]

The publication and national distribution of such designs in books like *The Complete House Builder*, published in Chicago about 1890, and *Palliser's New Cottage Homes and Details* of 1887 provided builders and their patrons with drawings for facades reminiscent of Amsterdam canal houses (FIG. 93). The imaginative variety of gables on Palliser's row houses reflects the diversity of an Amsterdam street. Many of Palliser's row houses and duplexes carry dates and inscriptions in the gables in typical Dutch fashion. But American row houses, unlike

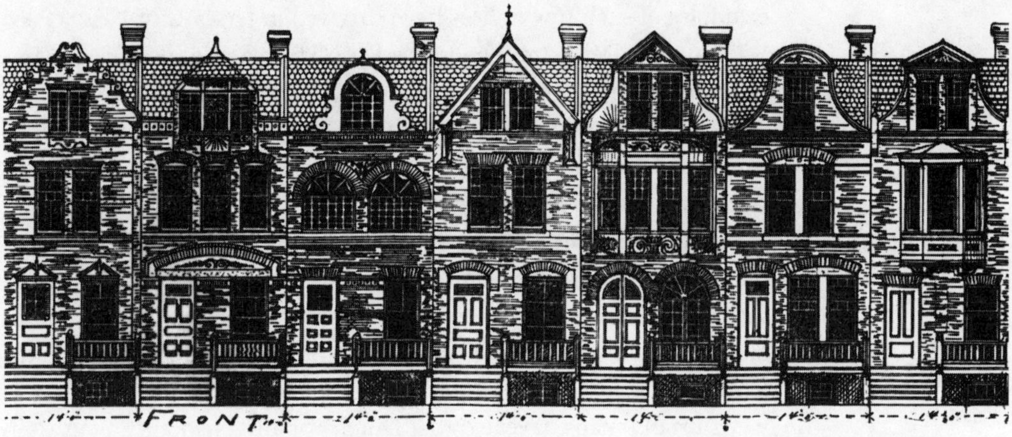

FIG. 93 *Palliser designed these urban row houses in 1882 and 1883 with a variety of gables reminiscent of Dutch canal houses.*

Amsterdam canal houses, usually had a pitched-roof surface running parallel to the street. This was interrupted by a large dormer to create the impression of a gable end. These false gables usually concealed a full story behind them. Large windows, often having many small panes of glass, marked the facades of both Dutch and American designs.

These American plan-book row houses with their Dutch gables adhere to the type that nineteenth-century architectural critic Mariana Griswold van Rensselaer labeled the Dutch high stoop. She considered this form the most lasting legacy of colonial Dutch–American architecture to New York City. The steep stairs leading from the sidewalk up to a small porch giving entry to the parlor level contrasted with the English basement type in which the entrance stood at street level and people traversed an interior staircase to the parlor above. Van Rensselaer remarked in 1886 that even in Boston the Dutch high stoop was beginning to outpace the English basement type.[128]

It should be noted that neither the New York architectural firm of Palliser, Palliser & Company nor the anonymous author of *The Complete House Builder* made any claims for the Dutch inspiration of their lavishly gabled, high stoop designs. In fact, Palliser specifically denied European influence, calling its designs "American Homes of today, not, however, of any well defined style of Architecture, except what may be termed our National style, for it would be folly for us . . . to undertake to transplant to this new country any foreign style which was perfected centuries ago."[129] Palliser's eclectic designs combine aspects of Queen Anne, Tudor, Elizabethan, Jacobean, Ruskinian Gothic, and Romanesque with urban Dutch styles. The originality of their multiform nature might have been considered uniquely American, but the underlying Netherlandish quality of the gables is inescapable. A few examples of such row houses have survived in Jersey City, New Jersey; Wilmington, Delaware; Lancaster, Pennsylvania and elsewhere. Most have disappeared through urban development.

The proliferation of old Dutch and Flemish architectural styles in American cities at the turn of the century was related to increasing interest in the colonial Dutch roots of the United States. That is perhaps most apparent in Albany where new brick buildings with steeply pitched roofs and Dutch gables replaced disappearing eighteenth-century buildings of somewhat similar appearance. The complete absence of such examples from the early Dutch period in New York City was felt by many to be a great loss. Old prints, as well as inserts of town views on old maps, revealed that Dutch colonists had once built step-gabled brick warehouses and public buildings in New Amsterdam. The general lack of surviving historic examples may have turned late-nineteenth-century architects' attention to northern Europe.

In the absence of the originals, books such as an American translation of Felix Narjoux's *Notes and Sketches of an Architect Taken During a Journey in the Northwest of Europe* (1877) and *Old Houses in Holland* by Sydney R. Jones (1913) provided detailed illustrations of authentic seventeenth- and eighteenth-century architecture in the Netherlands. Paintings, prints, travel literature, posters, and postcards supplemented that limited source of information. Nevertheless, for people such as illustrator Edward Penfield, drawings and written descriptions failed to satisfy New York's need for tangible evidence of its Dutch heritage. Penfield's book *Holland Sketches* contained a plea for New Yorkers to buy one of Amsterdam's canal houses, cut it in sections, and transport it to the United States where it would provide an authentic model of a New Amsterdam structure (FIG. 94c). Penfield's willingness to import Dutch architecture in a patriotic cause is symptomatic of the extent to which many Americans understood and experienced Holland on their own terms.

William Rhoads has demonstrated that most colonial building styles came to be seen during the nineteenth century as something peculiarly American, separate from their European prototypes, and, for many, the only true basis of a national architecture. As a result, Rhoads explains, importations of French, Italian, and British styles were scorned. To a limited extent, this was true of colonial Dutch architecture as well. Yet belief in the distinctive American character of colonial Dutch architecture did not stop architects from admiring and adopting architectural styles directly from the Netherlands. Montgomery Schuyler wrote about the approximately three hundred

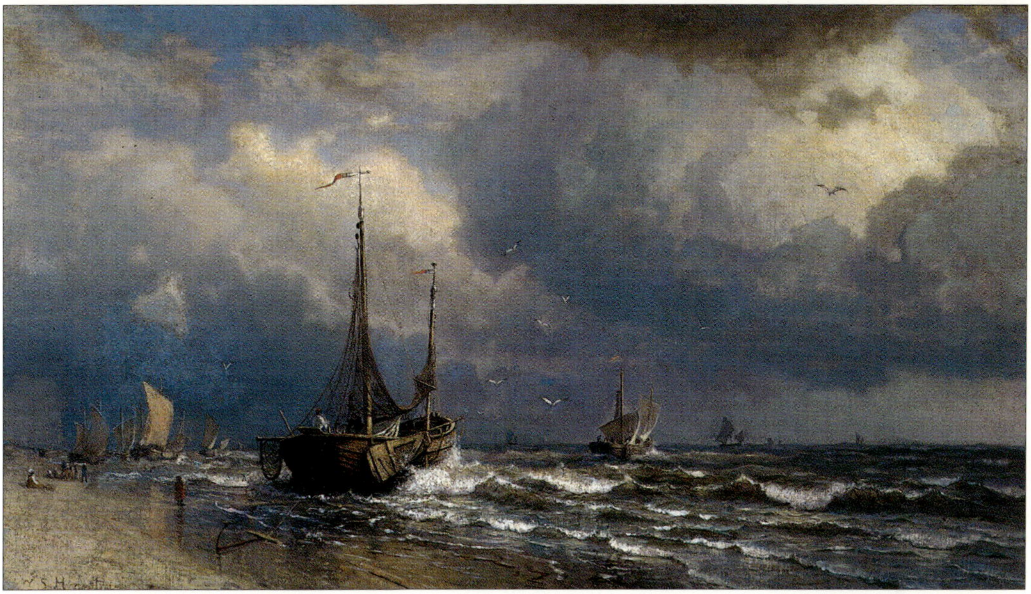

FIG. 33 Dutch Coast *by William Stanley Haseltine exploited the common belief that Dutch vessels were more picturesque than American ones.*

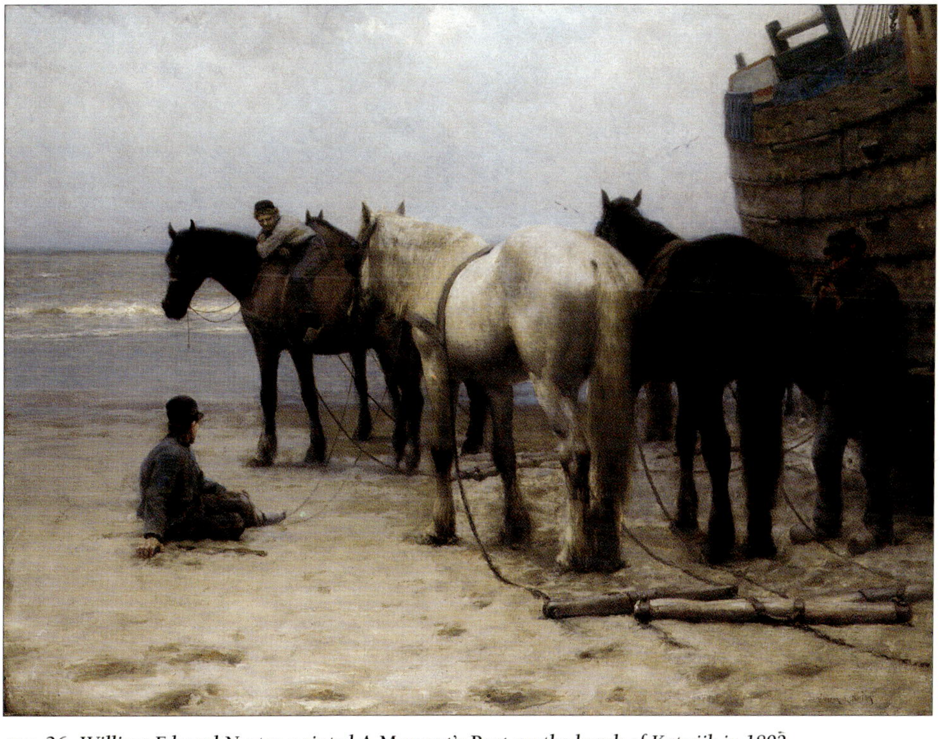

FIG. 36 *William Edward Norton painted* A Moment's Rest *on the beach of Katwijk in 1892.*

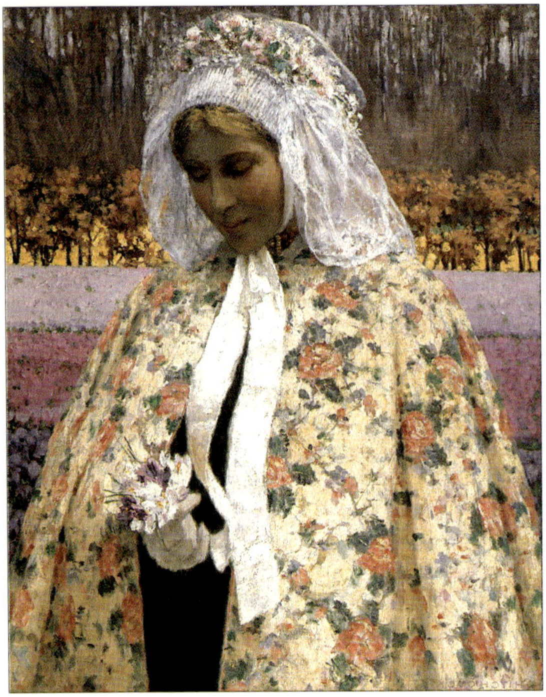

FIG. 39 *George Hitchcock collected headdresses from around the Netherlands for use in his costume pictures. The example worn by this model in In Brabant of 1895 is the characteristic* muts en poffer *of the province of North Brabant.*

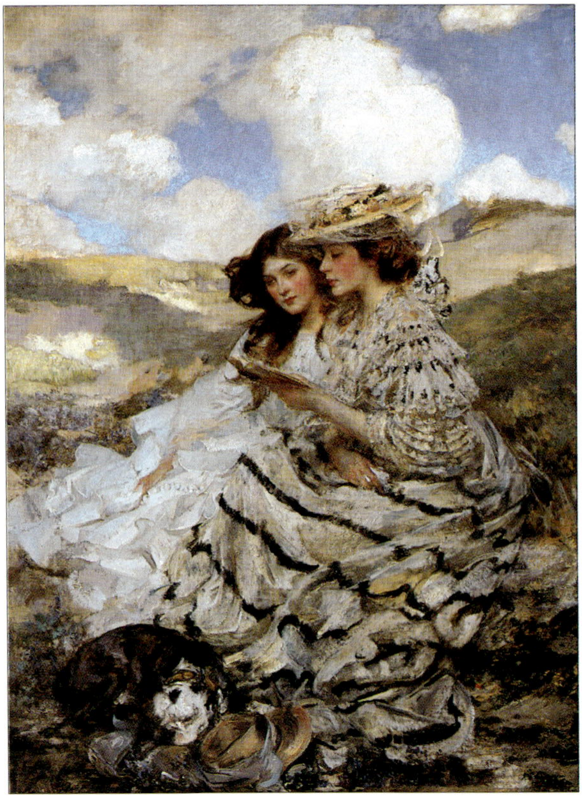

FIG. 41 *James Jebusa Shannon was one of the few Egmond artists to recognize the local tourist industry in his work. He portrayed his wife and daughter relaxing near the beach in their cosmopolitan finery for* On the Dunes.

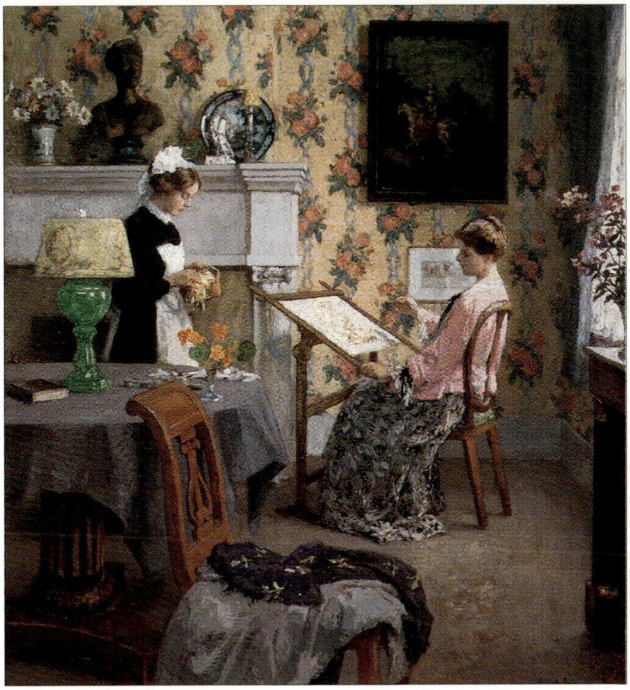

FIG. 42 *In its late period, the Egmond school turned to interior genre scenes like* Penelope, *1910, by Gari Melchers.*

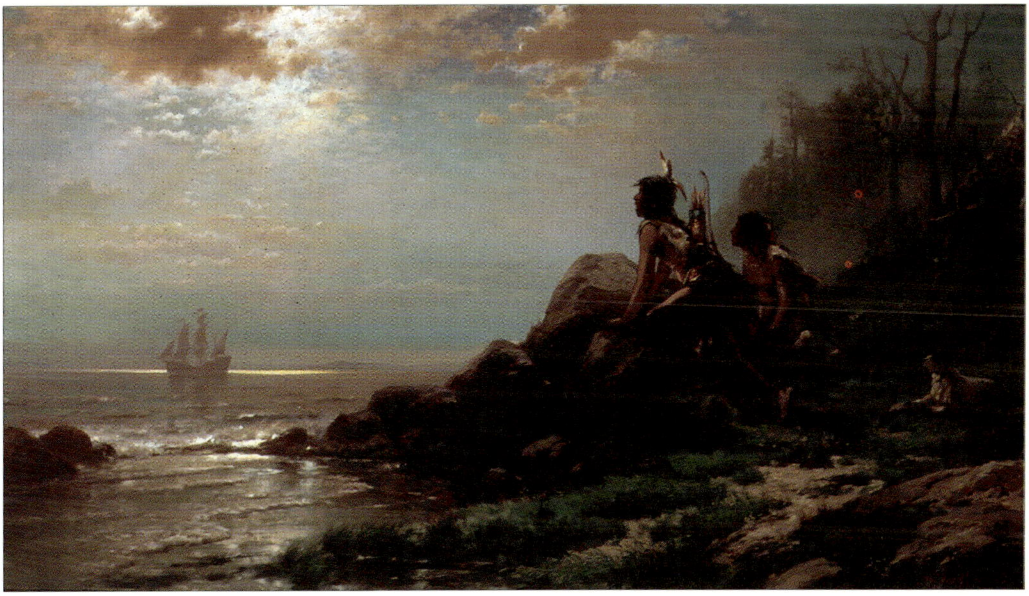

FIG. 49 *Edward Moran painted two versions of Hudson's ship, the Half Moon, entering the river named for him. The first, painted in 1892, is called* Henrik Hudson, Entering New York Harbor, September 11, 1609, *while the second version, shown here, is entitled* Henry Hudson Entering New York Bay, September 3, 1609. *Americans often gave Englishman Henry Hudson the Dutch appellation Henrik, either in recognition of the fact that the Dutch financed his voyage, or from the common misconception that he was Dutch.*

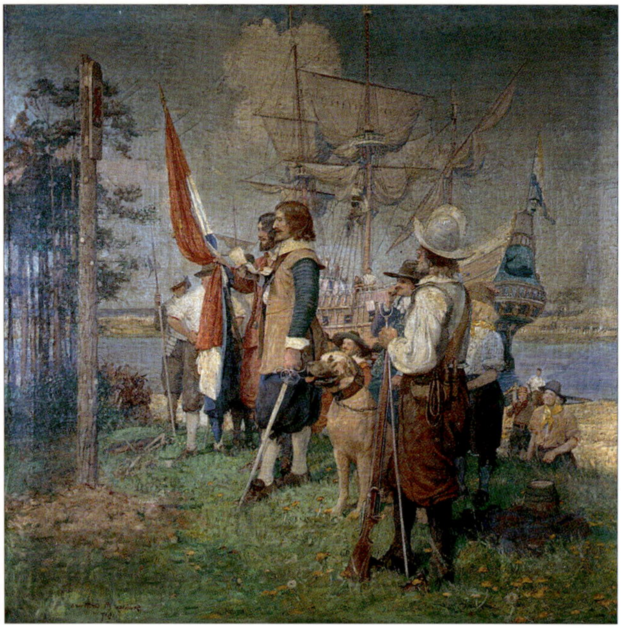

FIG. 55 *Interest in America's colonial Dutch heritage inspired a wide variety of history paintings such as* Landing of the DeVries Colony at Swaanendael, Lewes, Delaware, 1631 *by Stanley Arthurs. Although the colony survived less than a year, it provided the statutory basis upon which Delaware won its independence against British claims that it was part of Maryland.*

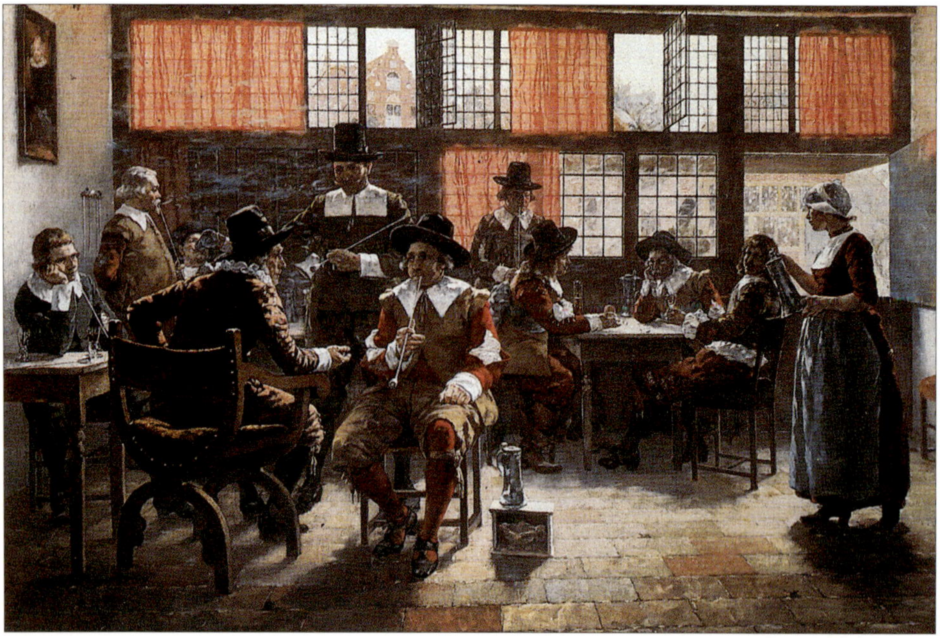

FIG. 56 *Walter MacEwen painted this genre scene representing the New Amsterdam town hall-city tavern as it might have looked in 1650. He frequently exhibited it and received a medal for it at the Paris Universal Exposition in 1889.*

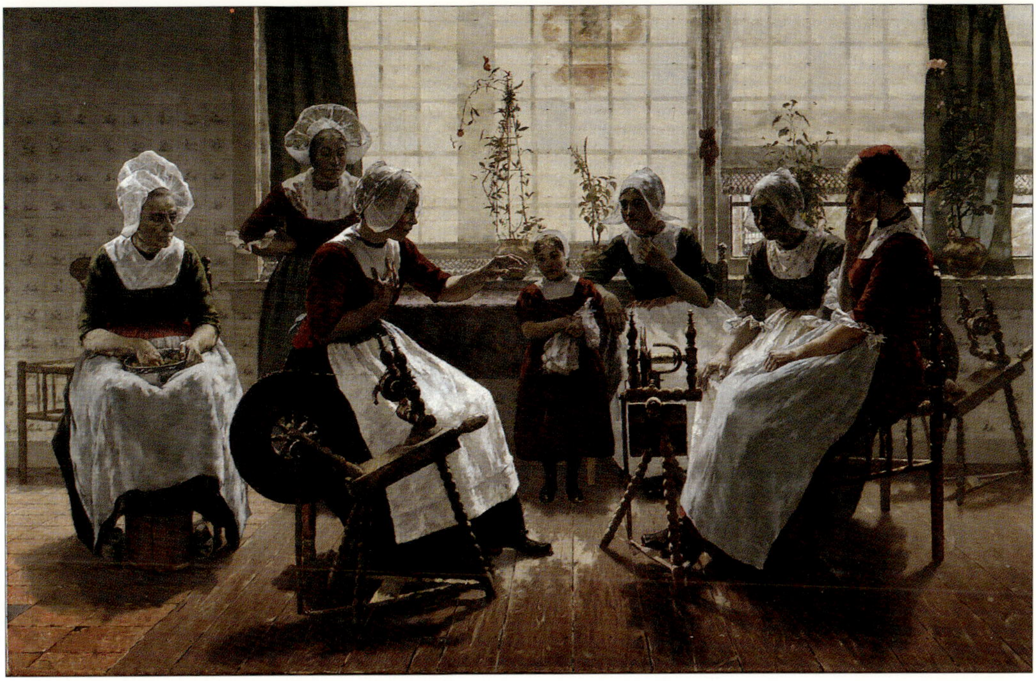

FIG. 57 *Although it depicts women in the costume of Volendam, Walter MacEwen painted* The Ghost Story *in his studio in Hattem.*

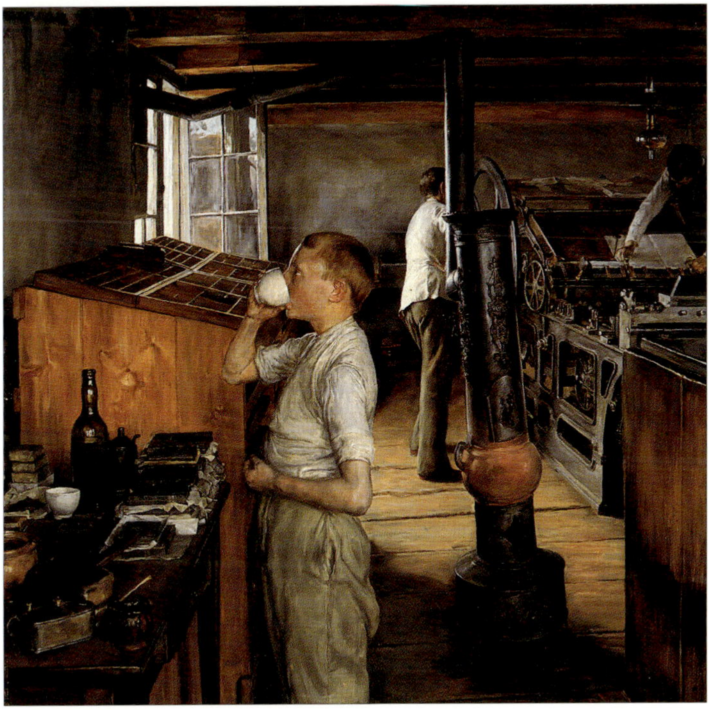

FIG. 61 *Charles Ulrich originally entitled this painting* The Village Printing Shop, Haarlem, Holland, *1884. He exhibited it at the American Art Association in 1884 and at the Inter-State Industrial Exposition of Chicago in 1888.*

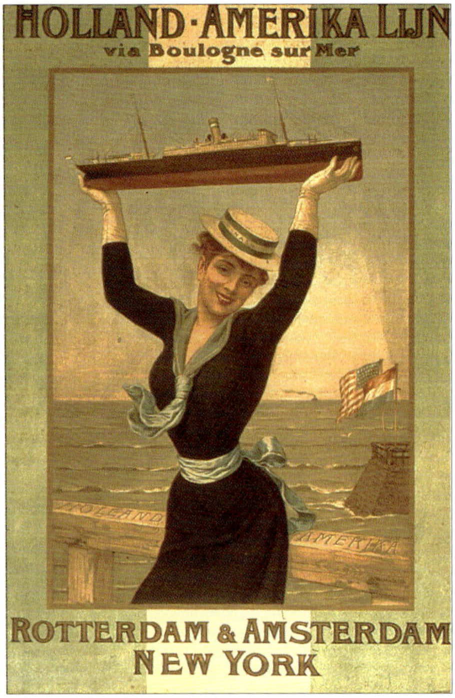

FIG. 66 *The Holland-America line used posters, picture postcards, bandanas and other memorabilia to advertise Holland as a vacation mecca.*

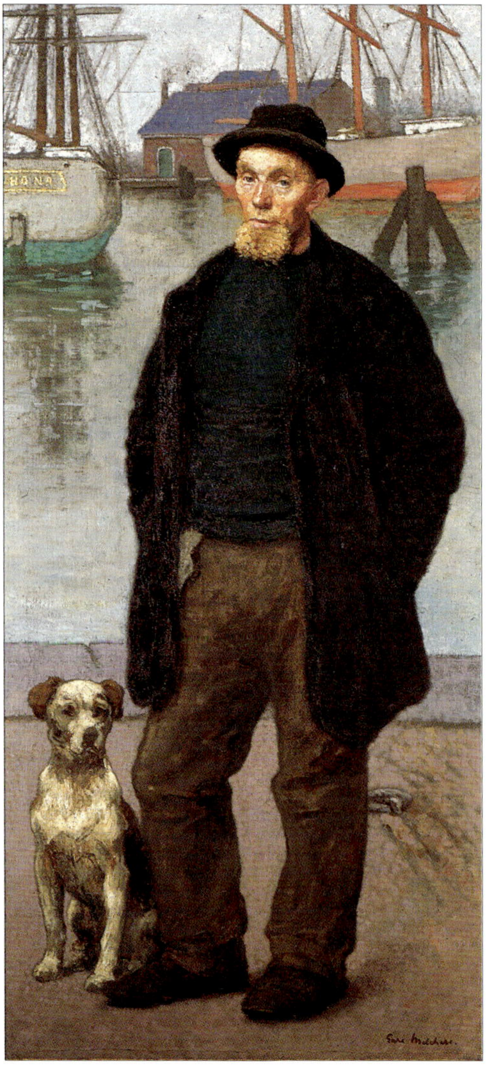

FIG. 71 *Paintings like* Sailor and his Dog, *by Gari Melchers, prepared tourists for what they would see in the Netherlands.*

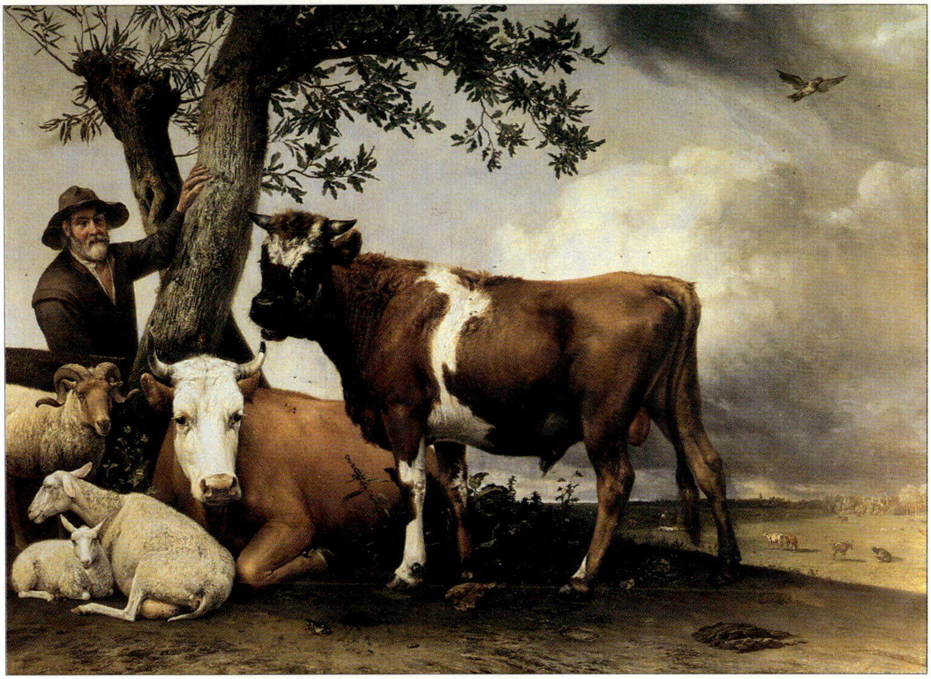

FIG. 73 *Most travellers took time to see Paulus Potter's famous painting* The Young Bull *at the Mauritshuis when they visited The Hague. It was reproduced in many travel books.*

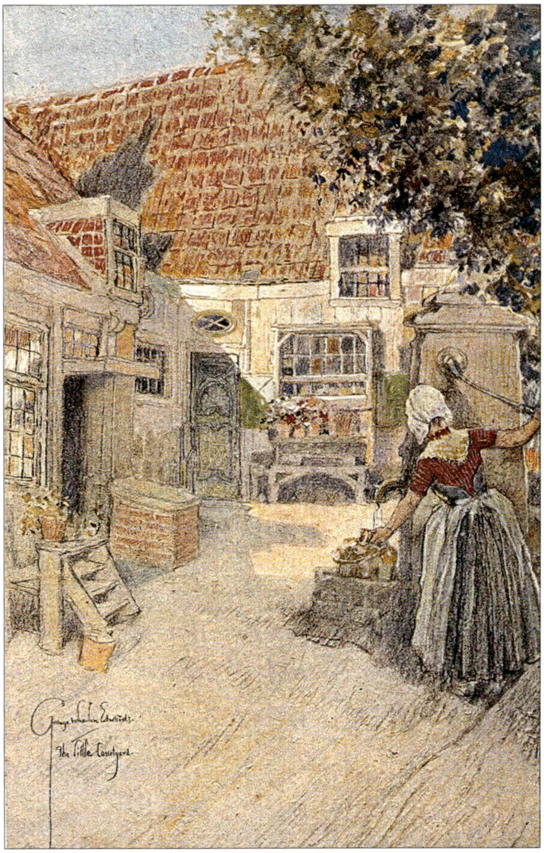

FIG. 74 *By focusing on the most old-fashioned corner of Amsterdam he could find, George Wharton Edwards succeeded in making Holland's largest commercial city look like a quaint seventeenth-century town in his illustration* Amsterdam—Little Courtyard.

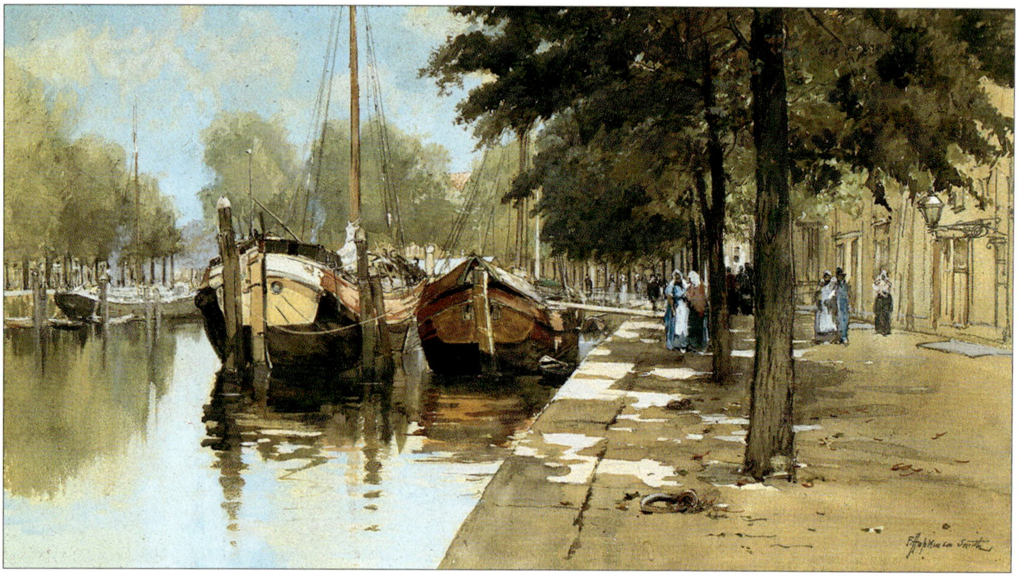

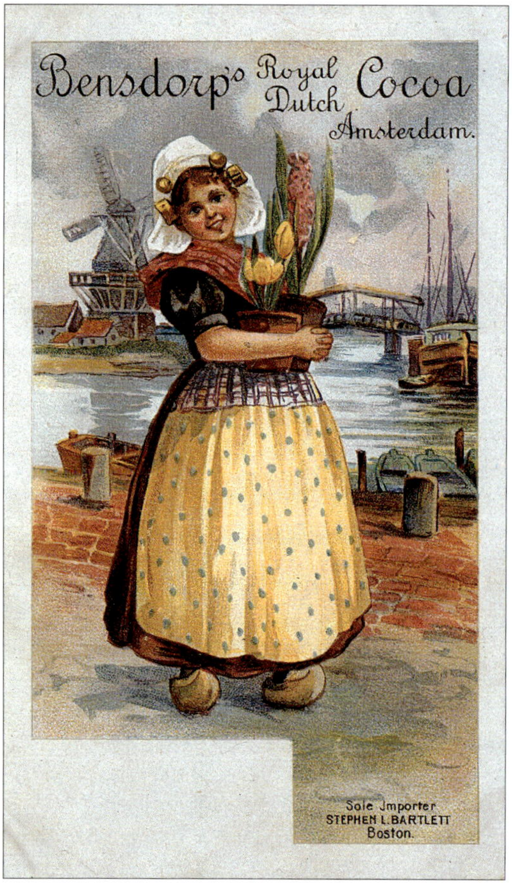

FIG. 79 *F. Hopkinson Smith painted this watercolor and used it to illustrate "drenched leaves quivering in dazzling sunlight" after a rainstorm in his favorite Dutch city, Dordrecht. Its characteristic tree-lined canals and canal boats illuminated the pages of his amusing account of life in Dordrecht, published in* Scribner's Magazine *in 1899.*

FIG. 83 *Travelers regularly bought wooden shoes to take home as souvenirs. Edward Penfield depicted the process in this illustration.*

buildings in New Amsterdam at the moment the British took over: "there is no evidence that the most pretentious of these fairly represented the state of architecture in Holland, where the Flemish Renaissance, to which a resort has been had within the past twenty years . . . was then in its most flourishing condition." Schuyler points out that New Amsterdam buildings were distinct in their simplicity from old Amsterdam buildings, but also notes that it was the more pretentious old Amsterdam style that architects revived in the 1880s. Perhaps Holland was so firmly tied to its glorious past and to Americans' colonial heritage in American consciousness that a traditional style of Dutch architecture could be seen as just as American as any colonial era building found in the United States. Thus Penfield demanded the importation of an Amsterdam canal house, discounting its two hundred or more years of historic and human associations in Dutch history in favor of the brief period in its history when it merely coexisted with Dutch colonists on the other side of the Atlantic Ocean. In the same spirit American architects modeled new buildings on old examples in Holland, and Palliser, Palliser and Company insisted on calling their improvisations on Dutch canal houses a purely American national style.[130]

Although it is easy, today, to see the inspiration for Griffis's American renaissance of Dutch architecture in nostalgia for a lost colonial Dutch–American architecture, this urban style was not generally considered colonial at the time. The terms that Schuyler and Griffis used to identify it, "Flemish Renaissance" and "American Renaissance of Dutch Architecture," reveal its more direct European inspiration. A quite different style that became even more popular was based on rural Dutch–American buildings of the colonial and federal periods. It emerged in the 1890's as "modern Dutch colonial" and is known today as Dutch Colonial Revival.

MODERN DUTCH COLONIAL

In 1876 the United States celebrated the centennial of its declaration of independence from England. The world's fair in Philadelphia marked the start of a period of research, publication, and societies devoted to colonial studies. The Philadelphia Centennial Exhibition included an old-time New England kitchen, crafts demonstrations, and other reminders of colonial material culture. The late-nineteenth-century American enthusiasm for the Netherlands must be attributed in part to the centennial-inspired examination of North America's colonial relationship with Holland. Scholars began serious research into the architecture of New Netherland as part of this broader emphasis on colonial roots.

In 1877 architect J. Cleveland Cady made a speech before the New York chapter of the American Institute of Architects in which he praised the old Dutch farmhouses of New Jersey for their simplicity, hospitality, broad horizontal massing, coziness, and common sense integration with their sites. Although Cady declared Washington Irving's caricature of the colonial Dutchman to be "not a whit exaggerated," he still concluded "that both outside and inside of their dwellings, the old Dutchmen can teach us much that is sensible and interesting." Cady's speech reached a broader professional audience through publication in the *American Architect and Building News*. What he admired in the low stone and clapboard farmhouses of New Netherland and vicinity were qualities that were becoming a standard part of the American stereotype of the Dutchman: lack of pretention, earth-bound practicality, love of home, picturesqueness. The Modern Dutch Colonial architecture that developed at the end of the nineteenth century, and surpassed in popularity the urban Dutch Renaissance Revival, catered to middle-class Americans of moderate means, whether they lived in the country, suburbs, or city. Its basis on a colonial American, as opposed to a European model, and the emphasis on its farmer-class roots and hospitable, unpretentious image may account for its broader appeal.[131]

As a non-British model, a few people also found the Modern Dutch Colonial a more appropriate visual symbol of American independence from England than the much more numerous English styles of Colonial Revival. Several writers saw it as a promising basis for the establishment of a national architecture, although it soon proved too unpretentious, unimpressive, and limited for such an ambition. Architects designed numerous small businesses and offices in the style and several large country estates used it. Of the latter, the house that architect Ernest Flagg designed for himself and his family on Staten Island called Stone Court is most notable. But the style's primary use was for modest country and suburban homes and in this niche its popularity proved lasting. Long after most other signs of a Dutch cultural vogue disappeared, well into the 1930s, Modern Dutch Colonial houses were still being built, often as tract homes.

The gambrel roof became the most common distinctive feature of Modern Dutch Colonial architecture. Denver architect Frederick J. Sterner designed such a house for the English-born manager of the Argo Smelter, Harold Pearce (FIG. 95). Completed in 1899, the Pearce-

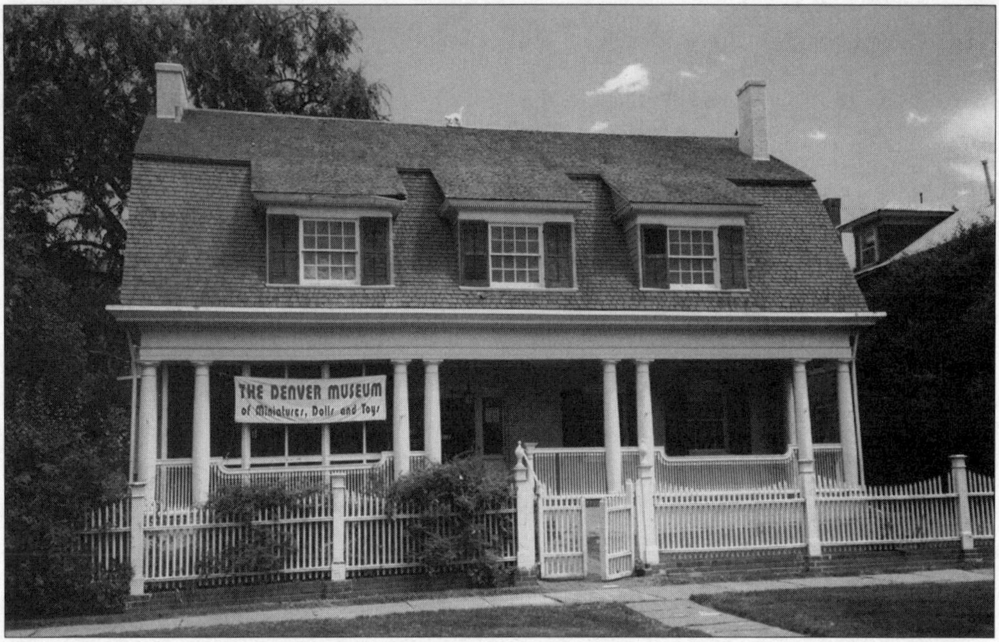

FIG. 95 *When it was built in 1899, the Pearce-McAllister House stood in the rural outskirts of Denver. Today it has been surrounded by an old residential neighborhood and contains a doll and toy museum.*

McAllister House features a gambrel roof with its characteristic short upper slope and longer, steeper-pitched lower slope. Like most Modern Dutch Colonial houses of this type, dormers pierce the roof to bring light, air, and headroom into the gambrel attic space. This efficient use of space allowed the attic to function comfortably as a second story without increasing the building's height and cost. The Pearce-McAllister House has three separate shed dormers that extend from the roof break with the same pitch as the upper slope, an especially common dormer type for Modern Dutch Colonial houses. By the second decade of the twentieth century, a continuous shed dormer often replaced the individual units, sometimes occupying so much of the roof that only a narrow strip remained at the ends to suggest the gambrel form. Although critics disparaged that arrangement, it became a common form in the 1920s. Most modern Dutch-style gambrel roofs stopped flush with the end walls, but occasionally, as in the Pearce-McAllister house, a narrow eave remained. Often the gambrel roof overhung the front wall of the house sufficiently to create a porch, in this case supported by painted wooden Doric columns. The cast-iron cat walking the roof's ridge provides an individual touch, and elegant interiors brought the price of this brick house to a substantial $15,000.

Although turn-of-the-century colonial revivalists considered the gambrel roof a sign of Dutchness, historians recognized that English colonists had built houses with gambrel roofs as well. Harold Eberlein, an early-twentieth-century expert on colonial architecture, explained that the English gambrel roof tended to have a longer upper slope than the Dutch and a shorter, steeper lower slope. He agreed with many other observers of the time that the Dutch version, which had included flared eaves beginning in the eighteenth century, produced a more aesthetically pleasing result. William Nelson Black championed the colonial buildings found in Hackensack, New Jersey as the best models for contemporary architecture. He enthused over the "graceful sweep of the roof as the line descends and curves upward into the projecting eaves . . . in the true spirit of thoroughly artistic design." Black opined that this roof form had unfortunately disappeared "as the English settlers with their cruder taste succeeded in forcing their straight and angular conceptions into the art of building."[132]

The origin of the gambrel roof and its primacy among Dutch or English settlers concerned some commentators. A writer in 1877 who focused on the architecture of colonial New England noted that the gambrel roof had become common there in the period from 1686 until 1737. Finding no comparable roof form in England, he admitted that he did not know where it originated, but speculated that it may have come directly from Holland to New England. His statement that "it could hardly be a fashion adopted from New York" reveals his New England bias to be as strong as Black's Dutch bias. Black believed that the gambrel roof originated in Holland and was conveyed to North America by the Dutch colonists. Still others, including Cady, considered it to be an American invention by Dutch colonists that was unknown in the Netherlands. Mariana van Rensselaer expressed what seems to have been the most common belief, although she was speaking of colonial architecture generally: "whether of Dutch or of English origin, a family likeness marks them all, for the English model itself had been influenced by Dutch ideas." Eberlein agreed, stating that the New England gambrel roof "was, in all probability, borrowed from the Dutch." Hence, architects incorporated the whole range of gambrel roofs into their Modern Dutch Colonial work and the gambrel roof became almost synonymous with Dutch colonial.[133]

The next most popular Dutch colonial roof form at the turn of the century may be seen in George B. Post and Sons design C-5 for the Eclipse Park Development in Beloit, Wisconsin (FIG. 96). This New York architectural firm designed Eclipse Park as a Colonial Revival village to house the engineers, clerks, and foremen of the Fairbanks Morse Company. By providing 350 inexpensive, well-designed, single-family homes, the Morse Company hoped to attract and retain a good

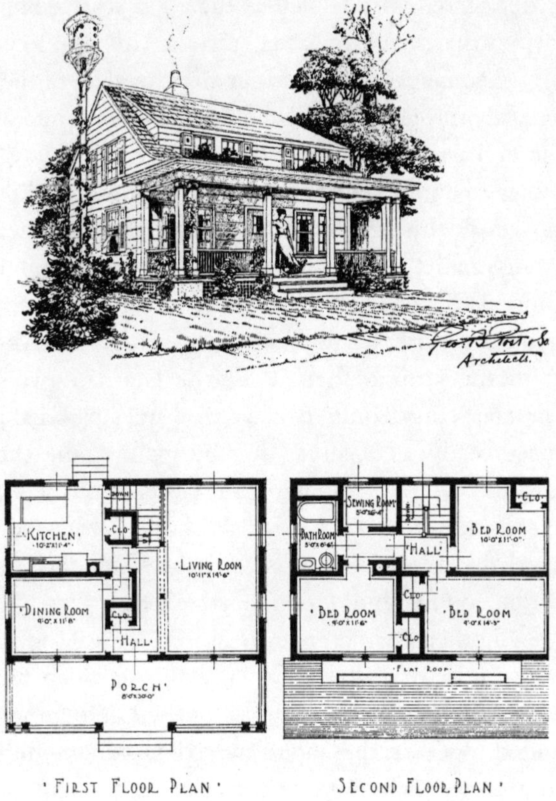

FIG. 96 *Some turn-of-the-century historians believed that Dutch colonists invented the American porch by gradually extending their roofs until they needed the support of posts. Model C-5 for the Eclipse Park Development in Beloit incorporates several Modern Dutch Colonial features.*

labor force. Post and Sons designed about forty variant styles based on Dutch and English colonial models, ranging in size from four to eight rooms. Model C-5 contains seven rooms under a straight gable roof that flares at the eaves to create a front porch. This roof type often extended in sweeping curves over both side walls and, as with the gambrel roof, dormers usually provided extra light and space.

Both of these roof–dormer combinations allowed relatively large houses to retain the appearance of humble, one-story dwellings. The roof lines draw the eye downward, often seeming to hug the ground. An architect who designed many houses in the Modern Dutch Colonial style, Aymar Embury, called this the "long, low house" and claimed that cultivated Americans preferred it to more pretentious homes. Another authority on the style explained further that "the man who is building in the country today has a penchant for the low, rambling type of house, possibly because he sees quite enough of high buildings in the city . . . and also because there is a certain charm of homeyness [sic] with low types of houses." These comments point to notions of domesticity and democracy that were readily associated with an established

Dutch stereotype, as well as the conservative appreciation for rural virtues that was associated with the Colonial Revival.[134]

In some houses the lower slope or flare of the roof continued in a narrow projection, called a Germantown hood or pent-roof, across the end walls. Charles Barton Keen, a Pennsylvania architect who designed a number of Modern Dutch Colonial houses and businesses, used this device in Wrangley Lodge near West Chester, Pennsylvania (FIG. 97). The roof with its low-pitched shed dormer conceals a story and a half. The lower roof flare and Germantown hood cover part of the first story walls to make the roof appear closer to the ground than it is. The Germantown hood also helped emphasize horizontal over vertical lines by breaking up the vertical space of the end gable, thereby maintaining the building's visual lowness. When Wrangley Lodge was published in 1905, its use of stone end walls and plaster side walls, protected by the flared roof overhang all around, was said to reflect the practice of "the old Dutch colonial builders of northern New Jersey."[135]

Another characteristic feature of the Modern Dutch Colonial house was the Dutch door (FIG. 98). Divided horizontally, the top and bottom sections could be opened and closed separately. When bolted together, the halves moved as a single unit. In their original rural usage, Dutch doors served to keep small children in and animals out while conducting more light and fresh air into the house. The late nineteenth century seems to have adopted them less for practical considerations than for their symbolic association with Dutchness. Charles Edward Hooper considered them "the principal legacy of the Dutch settlers." Most late-nineteenth-century home builders' books and manuals included an example or two along with the admonition that Dutch doors belonged on exterior walls only.[136]

Occasionally a Dutch door is the only Dutch feature on a house of a different character. For example, Charles P. Baldwin designed a large shingle style house at Forest Hill, New Jersey around 1891. When fellow architect A.W. Cobb published it in his book, *Suburban and Country Homes*, he featured a drawing of the Dutch door, the only detail given with the plans and elevations. Other Modern Dutch Colonial buildings had entrances consisting of a batten door carried on large brass hinges or the paneled door with a transom that had developed in the late colonial period.

Sometimes a Dutch stoop and benches accompanied the Dutch door. The stoop, or small porch placed before the front entrance, differed from the high Dutch stoop of New York City brownstones

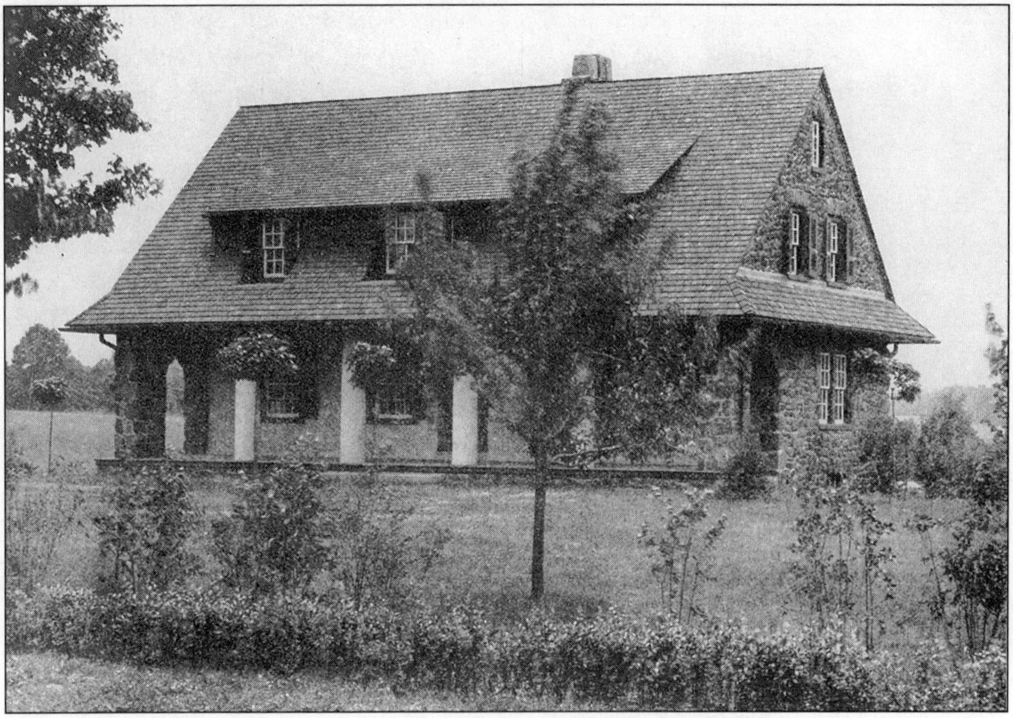

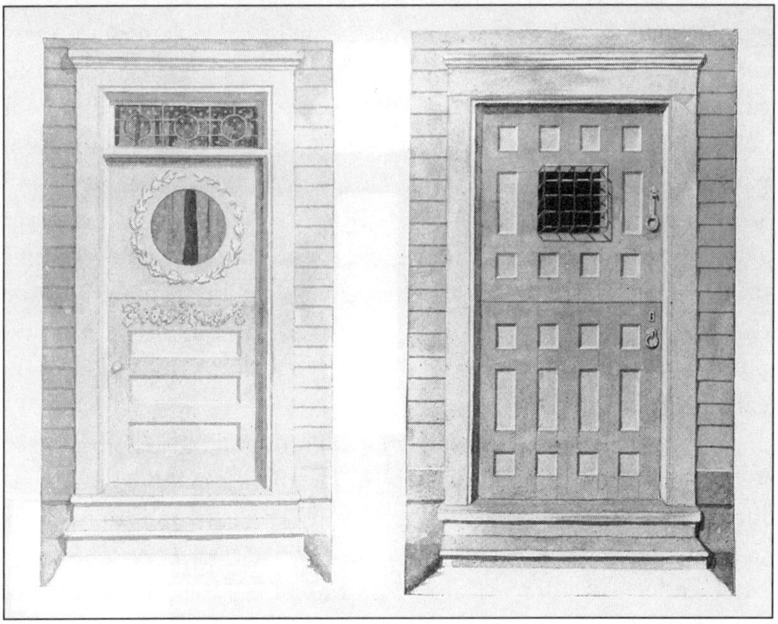

FIG. 97
Charles Barton Keen designed Wrangley Lodge with a Germantown hood and what was believed to be a colonial Dutch practice of extending the steep, pitched roof to protect the walls.

FIG. 98 *Home owners could select from a wide variety of Dutch door designs such as these from an 1898 publication. The form, not the style, gave them the Dutch name.*

in its lower height. Unlike the long porch incorporated under the overhanging eaves mentioned earlier, it was only wide enough to accommodate two facing high-backed wooden benches flanking the door. Sometimes a small projecting porch hood provided shelter from the elements. This can be seen in Post and Sons design C-8 for Eclipse Park (FIG. 99). This gambrel roof model with continuous shed dormer has a porch under the overhang on one side and a small stoop with hood on the other.

In at least one instance a house was identified as having Dutch windows, but this does not seem to have been a common term. Helen Churchill wrote in 1896 that one of the best features of the Long Island country residence designed by Lamb and Rich for Charles A. Rich was "an entrance hall with Dutch windows." Each window in the bank of five hall windows to which she referred consisted of two parts, a small horizontal band of six lights over a taller section of twelve lights. Large window areas, often composed of many panes of glass, characterized much architecture in the Netherlands and this group may have been considered Dutch for that reason. Occasionally, so-called Dutch houses in the United States featured fanciful leaded windows with rows of stained glass tulips across the tops. A good example of this can still be seen in South Denver.[137]

Regardless of the window type, shutters often appeared on Colonial Revival houses. The Dutch variety were usually solid wood panels painted green, cream or white. Sometimes cut-out stars, crescents, or tulips decorated the upper portion, a characteristic of old rural houses according to late-nineteenth-century authorities on colonial Dutch architecture. More rarely, louvered shutters took the place of solid panels.

Builders constructed Modern Dutch Colonial buildings from a variety of materials: stone, brick, wood, shingles, stucco, and plaster. Frequently, they combined several different materials, for example, brick end walls with plaster walls under an overhanging porch roof, or a first story of stone surmounted by a shingle gambrel roof.

A house published in the March 1909 number of *Harper's Bazar* as "a good example of the modern Dutch colonial architecture, modified to meet the demands of the present time" exemplifies many of the characteristics previously described above (FIG. 100). This large stone and shingle house featured a gambrel roof with a continuous shed dormer and a porch incorporated under the roof line. A divided Dutch door, painted green, and a fireplace faced with delft blue picture-tiles provided further Dutch accents. The estimated cost of construction, $8000, brought it within the price range of the upper-middle-income American.

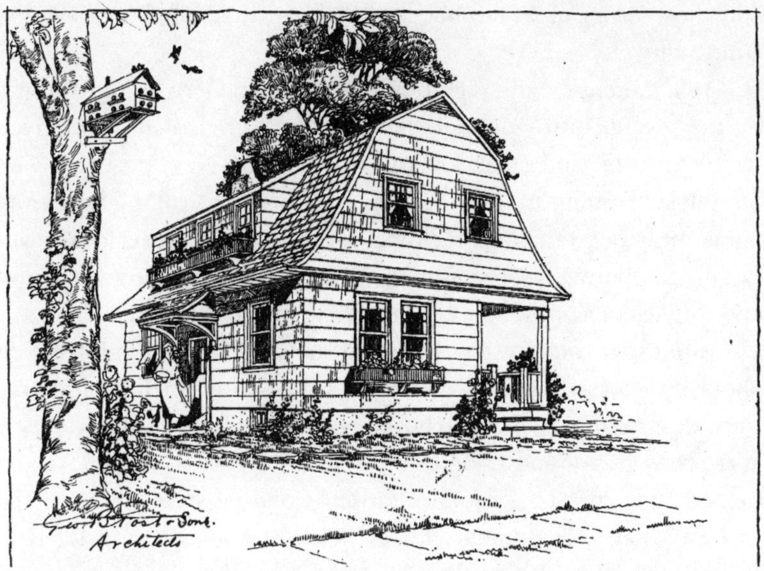

FIG. 99 *This is one of numerous Modern Dutch Colonial houses designed for workers in Beloit, Wisconsin by the New York architects George B. Post and Sons.*

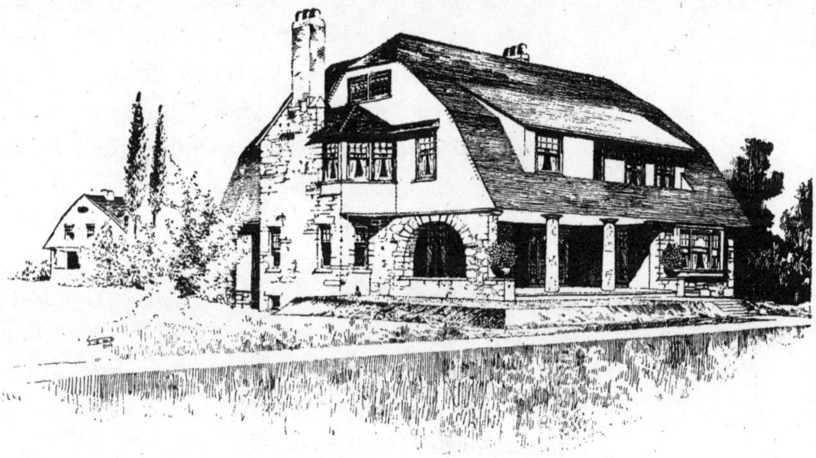

FIG. 100 Harper's Bazar *published the plans for this $8,000 Modern Dutch Colonial house in 1909. It is just one of many Dutch gambrel roof houses built at the turn of the century.*

Harper's considered it's Modern Dutch Colonial house suitable for any climate and geographic region in the United States, and similar houses did spring up all over the country between 1890 and 1940 when the second flowering of the Colonial Revival subsided. In their *Field Guide to American Houses*, Virginia and Lee McAlester estimate that about ten percent of all Colonial Revival houses built during that period were of the gambrel or cross gambrel types that became firmly associated with the concept of colonial Dutch architecture at the turn of the century. They reproduce examples from Kentucky, North and South Carolina, Ohio, Connecticut, Missouri, and the District of Columbia, and one can find this house type in almost any city.

To a limited extent, architects based the modern colonial house on the seventeenth- and eighteenth-century originals that survived in the Hudson and Delaware River Valleys, in New Jersey and on Long Island. Some architects in these areas visited colonial sites and made measured drawings for their own reference. Others, especially outside the region, relied more heavily on illustrations in books and articles to acquire knowledge of the colonial Dutch style.

Interest in old Dutch–American architecture and information about it increased steadily. A slowly growing movement to preserve the oldest examples of urban buildings and rural farmhouses of New York, New Jersey, and Long Island contributed to the literature and helped popularize the Modern Dutch Colonial style. Some of the earliest articles, beginning with Cleveland Cady's, previously cited, focused on New Jersey. Black's 1894 argument in favor of old Hackensack, New Jersey houses as the basis of modern architecture may be the most insistent of these, but numerous articles appeared in the 1890s and early 1900s describing and illustrating buildings like the Ackerman–Brinckerhoff House in Hackensack (FIG. 101). A one-story stone house with gambrel roof, its low sweeping lines (and those of similar buildings) gave an impulse to the modern work. Comparison of the Ackerman–Brinckerhoff House with Post and Sons Eclipse Park house design C-8 (FIG. 99) reveals essential similarities. The Eclipse Park house's roof lines echo those of the Ackerman–Brinckerhoff House with its short upper slope and long lower slope sweeping out over the supporting walls to form a protective porch roof. On the gable ends, the roof stops flush with the supporting walls. The Ackerman–Brinckerhoff House was one of the most often reproduced colonial Dutch houses, but many similar examples also appeared.

Surviving buildings in New York state also received attention from writers. An extensive review of the colonial buildings of Rensselaerwyck by Albany architect Marcus T. Reynolds appeared in 1895. In 1904 Perriton Maxwell published an essay on old Dutch homesteads of New York illustrated with pictures of eight standing houses in Flatbush, Long Island. These wood-frame, shingle-clad houses exhibited both types of Dutch roof, the gambrel and the gable with flared extended eaves. A monograph on the original farmhouses of New Netherland by Aymar Embury, and one by Lemuel Hoadley Fowler on forgotten farmhouses of Manhattan

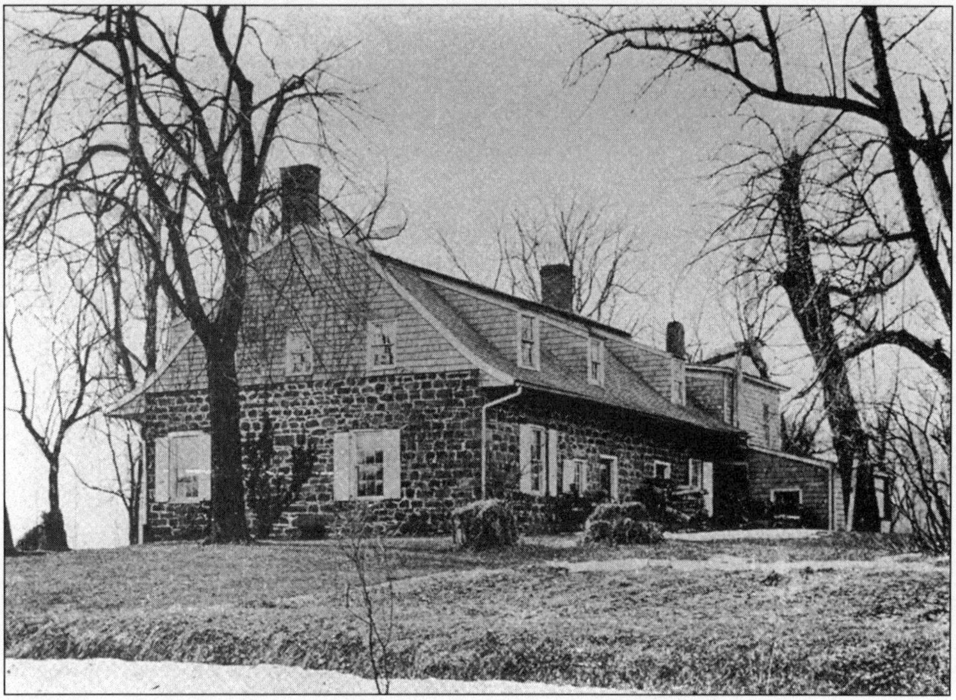

FIG. 101 *Turn-of-the-century architects interested in a modernized version of Dutch colonial buildings looked for inspiration to still-standing rural farmhouses like the Ackerman–Brinckerhoff house, built in 1704.*

Island, were well illustrated with photographs and details that turn-of-the-century builders might adapt to their own designs. Sponsored by lumber interests, these last two publications were part of a series intended to encourage the modern use of white pine by demonstrating its historic usage.

In 1913 Aymar Embury produced *The Dutch Colonial House*, the most thorough study of colonial Dutch buildings up to that time. He carefully documented the style with photographs of extant buildings, although he admitted that the purpose of his book on the colonial Dutch house was "to illustrate its applicability to modern construction." When Harold Eberlein published his classic study of colonial American architecture two years later, he chose to start with the architecture of the Dutch colonies which he, like Embury, saw as peculiarly suited to his own times:

> Of all the types of domestic architecture that have been either evolved or modified in America during the Colonial period, none more generally commends itself to the favourable consideration of the modern home builder than that which the Dutch settlers of Manhattan, North Jersey and Long Island worked out . . . in every instance, whether early or late, we find the omnipresent charm of domesticity, which in the long run is more valued by the majority

of people than a stately formality which sacrifices a measure of comfort to the exacting purity of proportion.

As this implies, Eberlein considered the Dutch style as the best model for American domestic architecture because he accepted the common characterization of Dutch people as unassuming, home-loving, and democratic. He contrasted the soft lines of Dutch gambrel roofs and the rambling, add-on character of colonial Dutch farmhouses with what he considered the more formal colonial English house with its rigid rectangularity and use of classical orders for door and window surrounds. A mail-order house catalog explained that "there is a hospitable 'homey' feeling about a Dutch Colonial home which has endeared it to countless persons."[138]

Embury, too, had interpreted Dutch architecture as a reflection of the Dutch people's natural domesticity and their supposed dislike of formality and pomp, traits he considered they shared with typical, middle-class Americans. Accordingly, Embury used the Dutch colonial style for small- and medium-sized rural houses for middle-class Americans. The titles of some of the books in which Modern Dutch Colonial designs appeared also bear out this emphasis on the middle and working class as the proper inhabitants of the style: *Inexpensive Homes of Individuality*, *Distinctive Homes of Moderate Cost*, and *Modern Houses for Little Money*. In this sense also, the Modern Dutch Colonial was loosely based on knowledge of surviving colonial buildings and their original inhabitants.

The modern version of the Dutch colonial style even returned to its agrarian roots upon occasion. Sometime before 1910, New York City architects Albro and Lindeberg designed a complex of Colonial Revival buildings at Foxhollow Farm in Rhinebeck, New York for Tracy Dows. The principal residence and the superintendent's cottage display the formal English Georgian style with classical details. Very slightly flared eaves over long porches in small wings on both buildings give the suggestion of the colonial Dutch tradition. A third building, the farm cottage, is a much more modest wood-frame one-story building with low sweeping roof lines extending over porches supported by simple wood posts. Stone chimneys on both gable ends carry out the colonial theme. The apparent class transition from the owner's mansion down to the farm laborer's cottage seems to be one from English sources to Dutch, formal to casual, classical to vernacular.[139]

In 1923, *Wallace's Farmer*, an Iowa agricultural journal, published plans by William Draper Brinckloe for "a Farm Home of the

Dutch-colonial type." Brinckloe's design was supposedly inspired by a picture of an early Dutch farmhouse in northern New Jersey. A hollow tile house with gable end chimneys, gambrel roof, shed dormers, and a full front porch under the eaves, this modern farmhouse incorporated a back entry and washroom for the use of the farmer. The writer pointed out that the gambrel roof reflected a common type of barn roof and had been loved by "Peter Stuyvesant and the rest of those practical old Dutchmen," making it the ideal image for a modern American farmhouse.[140]

In light of all the literature and interest in old colonial Dutch buildings, one of the remarkable qualities of Modern Dutch Colonial architecture was its lack of resemblance to the architecture of New Netherland. While some of it shared broad outlines with its colonial ancestry, much departed from that model in most other ways. Aymar Embury, an architect who strongly advocated the colonial Dutch style for modern domestic architecture, admitted: "I must confess that with a few exceptions, most of it, including my own work, shows little resemblance to the original style whose name it bears. The most we can claim for the modern work is that it is, to some extent at least, Dutch in spirit, and the sort of thing which the Dutch architects might have done had they happened to think of it."[141]

Even such admirers of the colonial Dutch gambrel roof as Embury and Eberlein recognized that it did not adapt well to modern uses. Its low pitch and long gentle slope created a dark, low ceiled attic space. Modern advocates of the style either raised the roof pitch to accommodate a full second story under the roof or they opened up the roof space with extensive use of dormers. These techniques can be seen in all the examples that have been discussed. As a result, modern houses were usually larger than true colonial buildings.

Modern Dutch Colonial homes could assume elaborate forms with up to three differently pitched roof slopes, bell shaped gambrels, parapets, heavy window ornamentation, roof moldings, and spacious porches that did not appear in the originals. Architects introduced bay windows, eyebrow dormers, set-back gables, continuous shed dormers, and cross gables. The low gambrel roofs of the late seventeenth century sometimes rose two full stories in their early twentieth-century reincarnation. An example published by the H.W. Johns Manufacturing Company in 1895 to promote their house paint demonstrates such effects (FIG. 102c). It roams far from the simplicity of its colonial predecessors in New Netherland, sacrificing the image of humble domesticity, democratic virtue, and earthbound practicality usually associated with rural colonial Dutch forms.

Modern colonial houses also diverged from their prototypes when it came to color. Experts declared that the Dutch colonists had painted the wood on their houses in strong colors like those in their homeland. Blues, reds, and greens had predominated, according to Harold Eberlein, but builders of the Colonial Revival house ignored such information in favor of subdued tones. Manufacturers of house paints commonly published booklets of house designs to promote their paints, such as the one by H.W. Johns. For the "colonial, Dutch, and other styles of houses on this order," Johns recommended either a grey, light yellow drab, or buff body color with white or cream trim. The Gordon-Van Tine Company of Davenport, Iowa, one of the first lumber outlets to go into the mail-order house business in 1910, included grey house paint for the body and white for the trim with their prefabricated colonial Dutch homes.

According to Embury, the only aspect of the colonial Dutch floor plan worth preserving was the placement of the kitchen in a separate one-story wing. The turn-of-the-century Dutch colonial style house contained spacious interiors and modernized room arrangements. Even in a comparatively modest home like Eclipse Park's C-5 (see FIG. 96), a special room for sewing, and varied room sizes reflecting their specific functions accommodated modern needs better than an exact colonial replica could have done. Embury considered two bathrooms to be a practical necessity and maids' rooms, butler's pantries, a study, and a reception room might all be added depending on the family's needs. Built-in closets replaced the Dutch kas or wardrobe, a piece of colonial furniture especially characteristic of New Netherland, but one that was not revived in the late-nineteenth-century trend for things Dutch. Interior design expert Mary Humphreys considered the wardrobe "a particularly worthless piece of furniture," superfluous in a well-designed modern house. Floor plans of Modern Dutch Colonial houses provided for the conveniences of modern life in ways that more faithful adherence to a colonial type could not.[142]

Embury reported that the old Dutch colonists had built with a complete freedom from tradition, and in a spirit of inventiveness and spontaneity that resulted in a wide variety of colonial homes. That observation may have helped legitimize the imaginative approach to the colonial that Embury and his contemporaries advocated. They rejected the notion of a revival or reproduction of the old style. By incorporating aspects of other styles with modified traits from colonial buildings, architects like Embury invented an entirely new form. For this reason they called it Modern Dutch Colonial and I have chosen to acknowledge their point of view, rather than employ the now well-established term Dutch Colonial Revival.

Convenience is only part of the reason for the departure of Modern Dutch Colonial from its origins. Despite scattered articles in the 1880s and 1890s, it was not until the 1910s that complete books appeared on the subject of colonial Dutch architecture and by then the modern version of it had been firmly established. The first thorough survey of old Dutch houses in the Hudson River Valley finally appeared in 1929 when Helen Reynold's work, sponsored by the Holland Society of New York, was published. At that time, the modern style had reached its peak and concrete information about the original buildings made no impact on it.

In addition to relatively sketchy knowledge in the formative years, scholars of colonial architecture debated how much influence the Dutch colonists had actually had over colonial architecture after the English took control of the former colony of New Netherland. Critic Montgomery Schuyler argued in 1895 that, with the exception of a continuing preference for Holland brick, a type slightly smaller than English brick, the dominant colonial style became British as soon as the British took political control from the Dutch. Historian Harold Eberlein, on the other hand, believed the Dutch style had not disappeared until much later. Therefore he considered that the colonial Dutch continued as a style distinct from others, exerting a continual influence on American architecture in the country's formative years. Eberlein cited the builders of Hurley, New York, a seventeenth-century Dutch town settled after the fall of New Netherland, to prove his point:

> To show their absolute fidelity to the traditional type of Dutch house, we may refer to the amazement created in the mind of a Dutch diplomat who, when taken to visit Hurley two or three years ago, declared that it was more Dutch than almost anything left in Holland . . . Old Hurley is just as Dutch as Dutch can be; Dutch in its people, Dutch in its houses, Dutch in its looks.[143]

Yet isolated pockets of rural seventeenth- and eighteenth-century Dutch stone architecture like Hurley had relatively little influence in the late-nineteenth-century development of a Modern Dutch Colonial style.

While some authorities argued over the relative influence of Dutch and English architectural forms after the fall of New Netherland, the Dutch or English derivation of the colonial gambrel roof, and the merits of the Dutch as opposed to the English colonial as a symbol of American independence from Great Britain, not all saw English and Dutch in opposition. Joseph Chandler made little distinction among colonial era buildings of different national origins in his book, *The Colonial House*. He believed the principal differences occurred along chronological, not ethnic, lines. Thus he described the colonial house as a single entity that went through three periods, occasionally noting traits originating with a single group of people, but blended with others. His originating point of view is New England. For example, Chandler considered the "first period" Pierce–Little House in Newbury, Massachusetts to be the "oldest example possible to illustrate" of a Dutch door and of the picturesque combination of brick and stone typical of Dutch colonial work.

Many turn-of-the-century architects shared Chandler's approach. Joy Wheeler Dow designed a house for his family that, in his own words, "is made up of Dutch and English farm-house motives" (FIG. 103). The steep gable roof with its "delicious sense of home and peace" extended straight down over the stone wall to create an overhang across the front, and flared out over the eaves on the back side in a long sweeping curve. The roof and its dormers, with their shaped false gables he described as Dutch, while an English garden provided privacy. The south gable, shown in the illustration, combined what he called an English grille gateway with a New Amsterdam style stone wall, chimney, anchor iron, and cellar entry. This comfortable mixture of influences may actually be more true to the spirit of colonial American architecture, which combined national influcnces with colonial invention.

Sometimes the Modern Dutch Colonial style was labeled as such and sometimes it was not. The house that *Harper's Bazar* considered a good example of Modern Dutch Colonial looks remarkably like designs labeled Craftsman houses by Arts and Crafts architects.[144] As I have pointed out elsewhere, the Arts and Crafts Movement shared values and ideals with advocates of Dutch and Dutch-American styles. Both were anti-modern in their appreciation of hand labor, natural time, and an aesthetic of individuality. Whether a particular building was called Dutch Colonial, Craftsman, American, Queen Anne, Colonial, or Shingle depended on its blend of traits and the perspectives of the owner, architect, and audience.

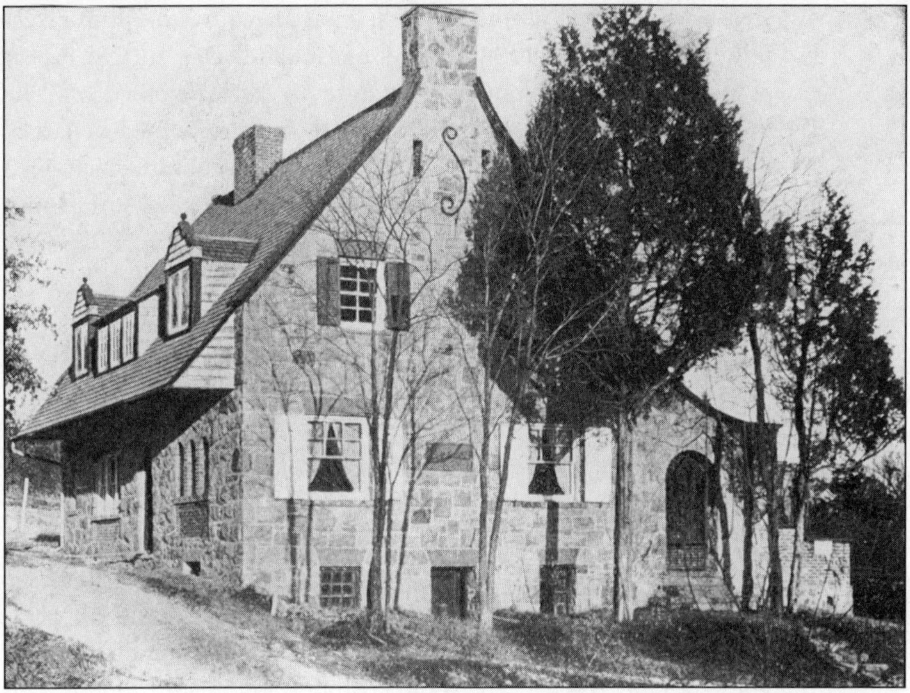

FIG. 103 *Joy Wheeler Dow designed his family home, Princessgate, from Dutch and English colonial farmhouse motifs. The steep roof with its short straight overhang is reminiscent of the colonial Old Dutch House at New Castle, Delaware.*

Sears Robuck named most of the house designs it sold by mail from 1908 on. In 1926 Sears advertised "a two-story quaint Dutch colonial home" called the Amhurst, and a house "designed to reflect the modern trend in Dutch colonial architecture" named Oak Park. Neither name suggests the Dutch style indicated in the descriptions. But in the same year, Dutch-sounding names marked other Sears models. The Van Dorn provided a "fine example of modern Dutch colonial architecture" and the Van Page combined "all of the important features that are of Dutch–American ancestry." All four were two-story side-gambrel-roof houses with continuous shed dormers, shutters, and small stoops. It is possible that the supposed Dutchness of the design became a better selling point over time, since Sears described its earliest gambrel roof types as colonial, and after 1920 gave half or more of them Dutch titles or descriptions. But it is equally possible that the style was so commonly understood as Dutch colonial in the early years of the century that advertisers felt it unnecessary to say so.

The turn-of-the-century version of colonial Dutch architecture bore no resemblance to architecture found in the Netherlands. Instead it emphasized what were supposed to be Dutch-American features in an imaginative variety of forms based only loosely on rural colonial Dutch architecture. Only in the association of the style with an ideal of middle-class, agrarian virtues did it intersect fully with the broader stereotype of Holland. One further aspect of Modern Dutch Colonial architecture deserves a closer look. The image of the Dutch windmill has already been examined as part of Americans' stereotype of Holland. The fact that old mills survived along the east coast allowed this familiar form to be absorbed into the Modern Dutch Colonial style.

WINDMILLS

Most of the colonists from various European countries built windmills. On Long Island, Dutch mills had been erected in the west, and English mills in the east. Experts might discern the different structural traits, but for most Americans windmills signified an old-fashioned picturesque ideal most often associated with Holland. The original Dutch mills of New York City had disappeared long before, but in the 1870s a variety of windmills in the vicinity were in their last years of operation. In the 1880s and 1890s many of these mills became vacation homes for city dwellers and summer studios for artists. Around 1913, the socialite Beatrice Claflin remodeled an old windmill on her father's estate in Southampton for her personal use as a furniture workshop and residence. Despite the area's English heritage, *Harper's Bazar* described Miss Claflin's mill as one of numerous "Dutch relics of the early settlers of this locality." Its picturesque exterior with wooden sails and the flowers and shrubs she planted disguised eclectic interiors.

An interest in the technical side of the windmill complemented the nostalgic reverence for its picturesque qualities. The Netherlands portion of the centennial world's fair in Philadelphia had provided visitors with up-to-date information about that country, together with some insights on Holland's colonial connection with the United States. A large exhibit on hydraulic engineering and land reclamation proved to be a popular attraction. The technical expertise and invention of the various pumps, locks, and watergates made by the Dutch struck a sympathetic chord with the American public who were proud of their own advances in agricultural and manufacturing technology and admired inventions, gadgets, and mechanical ingenuity in others. Drawings, relief maps, and models demonstrated how the Dutch had used three steam-pumping engines working around the clock for three-and-a-half years to drain 832,000,000 cubic meters of water from the Haarlem Lake to form farm land. Other displays explained the construction of dikes and dams, the great Lock William III at the

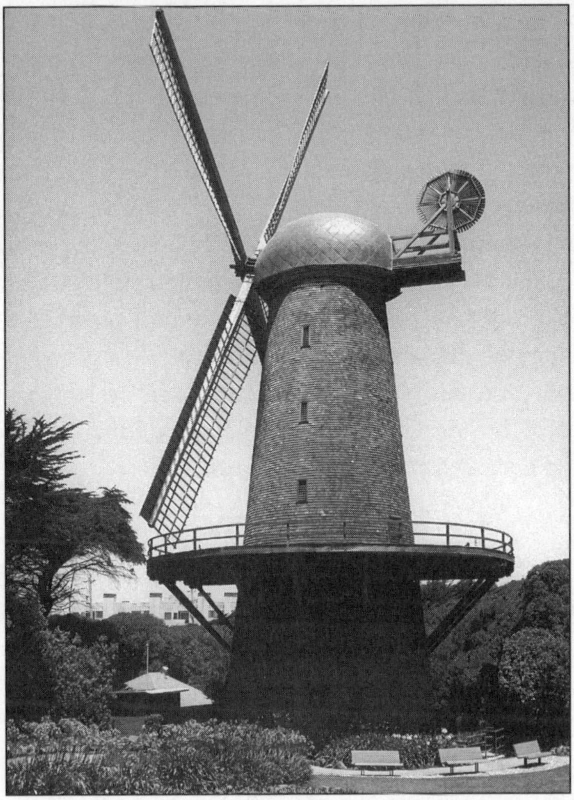

FIG. 104 *Rather than the utilitarian metal frame towers typical of American windmills throughout the west, San Francisco chose to build two Dutch windmills to irrigate Golden Gate Park. The North Mill, pictured here, was constructed in 1902.*

entrance of the North-Holland Canal, harbor works at Harlingen and Flushing, ongoing construction of two major canals and the projected draining of the Zuider Zee. Maps of North Holland in 1575 and 1875 provided a picture of the extent of change to Dutch topography wrought by hydraulic engineering over three centuries. The Netherlands exhibit at the 1893 World's Columbian Exposition in Chicago once again drew crowds to its land and water management display. In addition, manufacturers of American metal frame windmills erected their structures to compete against each other and against the Dutch mills in a great world's fair milling contest. For Americans such as Joseph Pennell, who included the windmill as a symbol of Dutch technology in his book about world work, the technical aspect of the windmill rendered it all the more interesting.

Citizens of Illinois and Iowa built or imported several Dutch windmills in the late nineteenth century to grind grain. In 1902, the city of San Francisco erected a full-size working Dutch mill to irrigate a large tract of land under development for a city park (FIG. 104). This irrigation system combined the picturesqueness of old-fashioned windmills with the technical ingenuity that had made the Dutch world leaders in hydraulic engineering. With the completion of a second windmill in 1905, San Francisco could pump 60,000 gallons of water per hour, more than enough to turn the California duneland into Golden Gate Park.

Windmill replicas also began to appear as restaurants in the early twentieth century. In 1916, August Anheuser Busch, the beer mogul, opened the Bevo Mill in St. Louis, a beer-garden style restaurant in an old-world building complete with a windmill. It looked more German than Dutch, but according to the Bevo Mill's advertising postcard, Busch and his architect spent a year in Holland studying examples before designing the St. Louis building. False windmills of this type were also occasionally built as homes.

OTHER DUTCH INFLUENCES

American architects completing their education often traveled through Europe on a grand tour, thereby gaining exposure to historic European styles, including those of the Netherlands. Some architects returned regularly throughout their careers, while for others it provided a one-time inspiration. Cass Gilbert made detailed pencil and watercolor drawings of towers throughout Europe. His rendering of the Gothic tower on the Cathedral at Utrecht (National Museum of American Art, Washington D.C.) exemplifies his careful observation of Dutch architecture. Gilbert established his reputation as an innovator in the development of an American architectural form, the skyscraper, and is best known for his neo-Gothic Woolworth Building. At the time that he drew the Utrecht tower, however, he was working on his first New York City skyscraper, the Broadway Chambers Building (completed in 1900 and later demolished). Like some other tall buildings of the time, including the John Wolfe Building, the Broadway Chambers exhibited the three-part organization of a classical column, but Gilbert distinguished the parts through the color of the materials: granite for the base, red brick for the fifteen-story shaft, and terra cotta for the four-story crown. There is no visual relationship between the Utrecht tower and Gilbert's skyscraper, but his study of European architecture, especially gothic church towers and Northern architects' use of contrasting materials for visual effect, contributed to his ability to achieve unique designs. A pencil sketch (Library of Congress) that Gilbert made on French hotel stationery in 1933 comparing towers at Utrecht and Venice with his Broadway Chambers building in New York also suggests that he thought about his work in relation to older European models.

While American architects in Holland acquired overt or subtle Dutch stylistic influences, Dutch builders and architects in the United States contributed from their experience. Kathryn Bishop Eckert, surveying the buildings of Michigan, maintains that Dutch influence exists throughout the western part of the Grand River Valley Region. She notes that the Netherlands-born Jan Hendrik Veneklasen opened the first of several brickyards in 1848 at Zeeland, Michigan. Using local red and yellow clays to produce a variety of colored bricks, Veneklasen provided patterns for laying the brick in decorative Dutch designs that appear on many buildings in the area (FIG. 105). From the middle of the nineteenth century through the early twentieth century, brick houses were erected around Zeeland

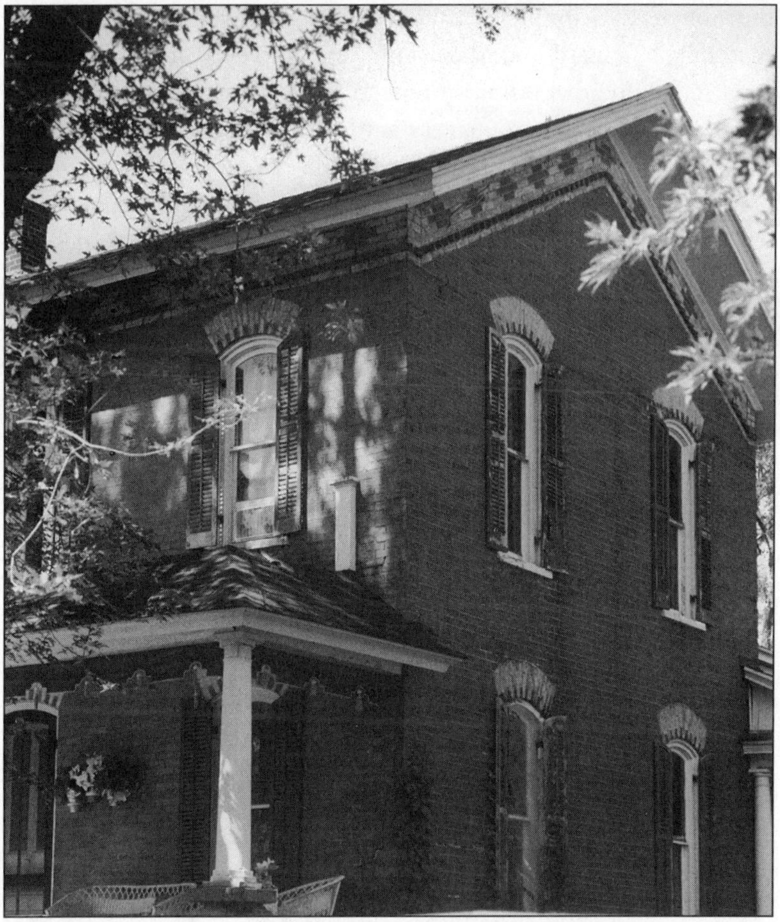

FIG. 105
Dutch immigrants and their descendants in rural western Michigan often fabricated their houses of brick made locally in the old Dutch tradition. The patterned band under the eaves is typical of this local style.

with patterned bands under the eaves and over doors and windows. Similar isolated Dutch styles may exist elsewhere; more research needs to be carried out. Designers, builders, and patrons of buildings whose forms seem Dutch must not only be identified, but their roots in the Netherlands and elsewhere must be investigated. What architectural styles did they know before emigrating to the United States? What training did they receive and where? Did they use the pattern books commonly available in the United States, or bring their own from Holland? Did they leave any written record of their design choices or attitudes toward architecture as an expression of ethnicity and national identity? How are the Veneklasen patterns related to similar images found in brick bungalows and other American houses throughout the country? All of these questions must be answered before the relationship between Dutch-American architectural styles and Dutch immigration can begin to be understood.[145]

It is also important to recognize that Americans of Dutch birth did not necessarily prefer Dutch architectural styles. Architectural historians Gebhard and Mansheim, who surveyed the buildings of Iowa, conclude that ethnic groups "almost instantly assumed whatever was the prevailing imagery and method of construction found in the architecture of their adopted land." When Dutch immigrants arrived in the Midwest at midcentury, they built their homes in a variety of styles reflecting popular local modes, as did their descendants near the end of the century. Arend Vander Veen, leaving Amsterdam to establish his medical practice in Grand Haven, Michigan, built a large Italianate house with characteristic square tower in 1870–1872. John Kleyn erected a simpler Italianate home in 1872–1873 for the first mayor of Holland, Michigan, the Dutch-born Isaac Cappon. John Voorhees settled in Pella, Iowa where he built a house described by Gebhard and Mansheim as a combination of French Second Empire and Italianate. A Christian Reformed Congregation (one of two major Dutch sects in the United States at the time) asked local builders Verbeek, Venema, Zalsma and Slenk of Holland, Michigan to erect a Neoclassical temple style church for them in 1856. A few years later another Reformed Church in the same town took shape as a Gothic Revival building. There was apparently no desire on the part of any of these Dutch immigrants to portray their ethnic heritage through architecture, not even when the building functioned as a symbol of a specifically Dutch religion.

Although much more research is needed on the influence of

Netherlandish architecture within the United States, available information seems to show no consistent correlation between Dutch ancestry and the application of a Dutch architectural style to a home or business at the turn of the century. The various styles of architecture described at the time as Dutch or Flemish appeared throughout the country, designed and built by people of nearly every ethnic background for owners of equally varied ancestry and interests. Areas of strong Dutch and Flemish influence, such as eastern New York State, New Jersey, and western Michigan, may have had a greater concentration of such styles—as most contemporary scholars believe—but no solid evidence has yet been compiled to either support or disprove the theory. For now, one can only say that while some Hollanders and their descendants may have chosen Dutch derived styles for sentimental reasons, many others preferred to build in the variety of styles popular in the United States at the turn of the century. At the same time, modern versions of Dutch Renaissance and colonial Dutch–American architecture were widely admired. These styles appeared throughout the country, built and occupied by Americans of every description, who may have chosen them for practicality and personal preference as much as for their associations with Holland in a period when Holland was in vogue.

SEVEN

The Spread of Holland Mania

BUILDINGS, TRAVEL POSTERS, BOOK ILLUSTRATIONS, paintings, souvenirs, and picture postcards spread the image of Holland across the United States. Although the Dutch interpretation of American identity never gained ascendancy over more traditional views, interest in Holland and in America's Dutch past had a visible impact on American culture at this time. Antique collecting, furniture, interior design, popular entertainments, women's fashions, literature, advertising, and product design all revealed the increased interest in the Netherlands.

ANTIQUES

Americans collected antique Dutch brass, silver, tiles, furniture, and costumes. Some who lived or traveled abroad, like Mr. and Mrs. George Hitchcock, rented wagons and spent days roaming the countryside searching for bargains from country farmers. The Hitchcocks' home was so full of such finds that a visitor declared they could not squeeze another thing in. In a painting by Gari Melchers, Henriette Hitchcock has displayed a delft horse and other objects from her collection while an old Dutch cupboard in the background reveals more of the treasures she and her husband collected on their antiquing forays in Holland (FIG. 106c). Others took advantage of serendipitous occasions. The young architect Charles Adams Platt reported that when he admired the tiles in a cobbler's shop where he had gone to buy wooden shoes, the owner chipped them out of the wall and sold them to him on the spot.[146]

The Hollanders' ready business acumen turned bargain hunting into a challenge as prices rose and supplies diminished or were suppressed. William Merritt Chase, an inveterate bric-a-brac hunter, reported back to his wife in New York from Haarlem where he was spending the summer with a class of his art students: "My pupils have about bought all that there is to be had in brass and copper here and the price has actually gone up since our arrival. I am getting some interesting things in furniture." Indeed, his letters chronicled his search for lace, jewelry, cloth, and other Dutch and Flemish accessories, as well as furniture. It was not necessary to travel abroad in order to acquire Dutch accessories for the home, but the experience of finding and bargaining for a treasure added to its sentimental value. "Delft ware is often imported to this country," noted one expert, "but the unique and interesting bits that one sees now and then which have been discovered in some little Dutch town by a traveller always seem to possess a greater value."[147]

Enthusiasm for antique Dutch silver reached its zenith in the United States during the first decades of the twentieth century. Many Americans collected old silver, gold, and brass through dealers at home and abroad. Mrs. Samuel P. Avery amassed a formidable collection of silver spoons, including about one hundred Dutch examples, which she gave to the Metropolitan Museum of Art in 1897. A year later the museum published a catalogue of the collection that provided a guide for other collectors.

For those who could not afford the real thing, Dutch firms made reproduction silverware to be sold in the tourist shops and for the British and American export trade. Soon reproduction Dutch silver was being manufactured in New Jersey as well. According to one connoisseur, even fake Dutch silver was better than the modern silver available in the United States: "For the householder, who cares not for authenticity, these objects of substitution and commerce are pretty, and generally of better design than those of the frankly modern silversmith." The open dislike of an aesthetic based on mass production that is expressed here undoubtedly motivated others to collect "quaint" Dutch silver. In addition to legitimate reproductions, silversmiths in Holland appear to have done a booming business in forged antique brandy bowls and American factories were accused of producing all sorts of scurrilous antiques for the trade. Explained Robert and Elizabeth Shackleton in a colorful, if inaccurate, illustration of the problem: "there are, for example, more veritable old Dutch chatelaine bag-clasps for sale in New York than all the ladies of Amsterdam ever possessed.[148]

Research on colonial American silver began in this same period and many Dutch-born and Dutch-descended early American smiths received scholarly attention for the first time. Churches in Albany, Tarrytown, and New York City owned seventeenth-century Holland-made beakers that had been used as models by colonial smiths and provided scholars with material for their research. In 1903 John Buck published a revision of his 1888 volume on early American silver and three years later the Boston Museum held one of the first exhibitions of colonial plate. In 1911 the National Society of Colonial Dames sponsored an exhibition of early New York and New Jersey silver at the Metropolitan Museum and published a catalogue. Such studies convinced scholars that Dutch influence on colonial styles and decorative motifs had lasted long after the Dutch lost political control of New Netherland to the British. This interpretation of material culture augmented the historical arguments for colonial Dutch influence in the formation of American culture, and contributed largely to American interest in the decorative arts of the Netherlands.

Esther Singleton wrote her illustrated history of Dutch and Flemish furniture for a British audience (who vied with Americans for Dutch antiques), but this book, together with her history of colonial American furniture, provided American collectors with a good guide to historic Dutch furniture and a patriotic reason to buy it. To describe Dutch interiors of the seventeenth century she relied on household inventories from Dutch families living in late-seventeenth-century New York, juxtaposed with genre paintings by the little masters of Golden Age Holland. The combination demonstrated a close association between the material culture of the Netherlands and that of colonial New York, and emphasized that the American collecting of old Dutch furniture carried nationalistic overtones. The inventories and paintings described quantities of carved furniture, pictures, linens, toys, and silver, suggesting the comfort and elegance of colonial Dutch life in North America.

Other writers advised potential collectors to study the furniture in such places as the Van Cortlandt Mansion in New York City before pursuing the old Dutch furniture readily available around

New York. According to the Shackletons, who built a career around hunting genuine antiques, southern states provided the best field for seekers after colonial era furniture from the Netherlands. They believed that the South had produced relatively little furniture of its own and must have imported it from England, Holland, and Flanders. Although few could afford to put real Dutch antique furniture in their homes, just as with silver, the taste for colonial era furniture inspired reproductions and, inevitably, forgeries.[149]

The journalist Eugene Field satirized the American desire for Dutch artifacts of the seventeenth century, a fad that he apparently considered to have gone to unfortunate lengths. In his poem, "In Amsterdam," Field described an enthusiast's search through an Amsterdam shop full of "wares quaint and curious, new and old" where he found "swords, teacups, helmets, platters, clocks, bright Dresden jars, dull Holland crocks." These are just the kinds of things that tourists brought home in abundance. In the poem, Field's enthusiast discovered an ancient oak bed that the shopkeeper told him had belonged to a king and was worth the steep price of 1000 guilders. Field, through the voice of the enthusiast, pondered the motivations that could make an American covet a Dutch king's bed:

> I thus discoursed within myself:
> "O happy Holland! where's the bliss
> That can approximate to this
> Possession of the rare antique
> Which maniacs hanker for and seek?
> My native land is full of stuff
> That's good, but is not old enough.
> Alas! it has no oaken beds
> Wherein have slumbered royal heads,
> No relic on whose face we see
> The proof of grand antiquity.

The need for an ancient and honorable national history had motivated historian Douglas Campbell to write the new Dutch interpretation of American origins and it sent people looking for the physical artifacts of that heritage. The romance of acquiring objects that some famous historical figure might have used or that Rembrandt or Vermeer might have painted added to the appeal.

Field's poem also poked fun at the gullible collector who discovered, just in time, a trademark on the coveted bed that revealed it as a patented antique made by "Birkey & Gay [sic], Grand Rapids, Michigan, U.S.A." The voice of the enlightened enthusiast concludes the poem:

> At present I'm not saying much
> About the simple, guileless Dutch;
> And as it were a loathsome spot
> I keep away from Kalverstraat,
> Determined when I want a bed
> In which hath slept a royal head
> I'll patronize no middleman,
> But deal direct with Michigan.

Grand Rapids had a large Dutch immigrant population and it developed a strong furniture industry in the late nineteenth century, shipping every imaginable style of furniture around the country. Berkey & Gay, a well-known manufacturer of reproduction French, English, Flemish, and Dutch antiques, produced a booklet in 1900, *The Old Feeling or The Past Revived*, that explains something of the appeal of Dutch antiques. According to Berkey & Gay, an old Dutch hall settle advertised in the booklet could infuse a sterile American entrance hall with the cozy home atmosphere associated with interiors in old Dutch master pictures. The visitor would feel welcomed and the cares wrought by a fast-paced modern lifestyle could be shed upon entering the hall occupied by such a settle. "The very sight of it broadens one's ideas, influences one's hospitality," exclaimed the copy writer, "You can feel the Old Dutch cordiality. It has 'welcome' emblazoned all over it. . . . Scrutinize every detail! Don't be in a hurry. For here is a piece of art, that represents the work of ages. . . . You can see the 'old masters' in every inch of this settle. . . . Consider the paneling of the back. Have you ever seen an oil painting with such a wonderful depth of light and shade. Yet this is only wood work." According to this text, by purchasing a Berkey & Gay old Dutch hall settle, one would acquire the equivalent of an old Dutch master painting and at the same time introduce the warmth and human connectedness that Americans feared their industrialized urban society was losing.

Berkey & Gay's use of two themes commonly associated with Holland, a master art tradition and an emphasis on the home, might be dismissed as so much advertising hype, but experts often agreed with Field's enthusiast that Americans should purchase modern reproductions of the Berkey & Gay sort in preference to actual

Dutch antiques. Their reasons varied from issues of quality and authenticity to price. Some noted that reproductions combined quality design with pristine condition. Others admired modern techniques of seasoning the wood and acquiring lustrous finishes. When architect Aymar Embury chose illustrations for a chapter on antique Dutch furniture in his book *The Dutch Colonial House*, he decided "to take the designs of two or three of the best modern manufacturers whose pieces can be bought by anyone, rather than to illustrate it with genuine antiques, for whose purchase one would have to compete with Mr. Morgan or the Metropolitan Museum of Art." He supplemented his illustrations of contemporary American-made Dutch and Flemish type beds, chairs, and desks with interior views of homes in the Netherlands, arguing that colonial era Dutch–American furniture had either been imported from the Netherlands or copied from such imports by colonial craftsmen. This argument became another justification for the modern reproduction of old Dutch furniture styles.[150]

OTHER DUTCH FURNITURE

In addition to replicas of Dutch antiques, American furniture makers used the adjective "Dutch" to describe a wide variety of objects. The Nelson Matter Furniture Company of Grand Rapids produced a "Dutch colonial chamber suite in circassian walnut" with massive low proportions, broad scrolls of carved wood, rich moldings, and blocky claw feet. Also in Grand Rapids, the Oriel Cabinet Company marketed a very different looking "Dutch Dining Room Suite" of lighter proportions with straight lines tapering toward the top and no ornament except leaded glass. A number of manufacturers throughout the country produced a still more severe design known as Dutch Mission furniture (FIG. 107). Its straight lines, wooden slats, lack of carved or molded ornament, and the visibility of its structural components marked it as Mission, a style originally inspired by furniture from Spanish missions in California. Thus, one could purchase an Olde Dutch Clock from C.A. Warner and Company of New York City or an Ithaca Dutch clock from Ithaca, New York and in both cases acquire a tall oak clock of the Mission style. This whole varied range of styles were marketed as Dutch, although they had relatively little in common with one another or with traditional furniture in the Netherlands.[151]

In some instances the reason for the terminology is clear. One

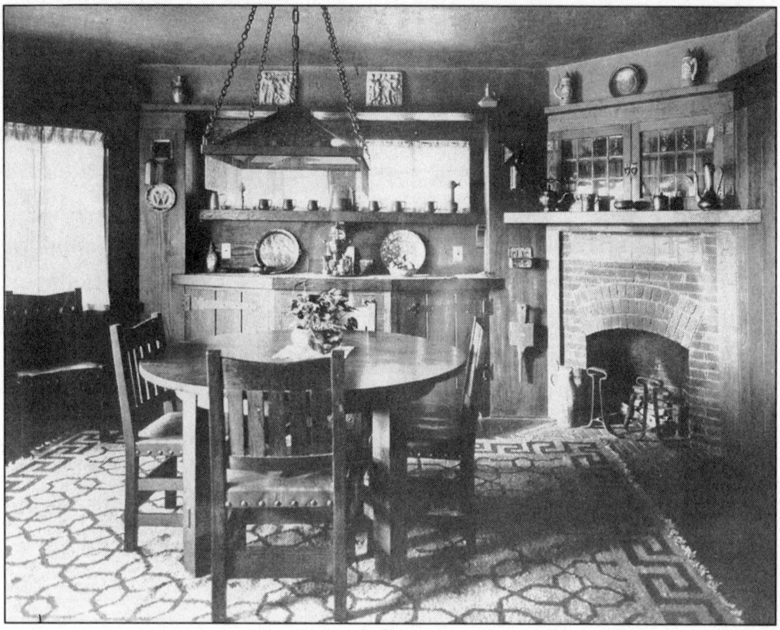

FIG. 107 *According to turn-of-the-century writer Alwyn Covell, "such a room is popularly called 'Dutch,' and the furniture, heavier than 'Cottage' furniture, is called by the same name." This was the dining room in Ernest Elmo Calkins' home "Upwey" in Elmsford, New York. It was designed by Bates and How with a built-in china cabinet and bookshelves.*

of the most popular furniture finishes of the time was called Flemish Oak because it approximated the dark color of old Flemish furniture. Utrecht velvet, named for the city in the Netherlands that originally produced it, became a favorite upholstery fabric for railroad cars in the United States. But often the reason for a Dutch descriptor is less evident. The weight and solidity of some Mission furniture made it "Dutch," Alwyn Covell explained in an essay on Mission furniture, while lighter appearing varieties were called Cottage. This application of the term may have originated with the visual weightiness of real Dutch antiques. As Berkey & Gay had noted about the old Dutch hall settle, "the massive, ponderous modeling gives stability of character." Whether based on real Dutch designs or not, that kind of solidity in furniture came to be associated with the Lowlands and with stability of moral character.[152]

The metaphoric weightiness of Dutch furniture may be more important than its real weight in understanding the trend for naming things Dutch. Americans' tendency to see Holland as a seventeenth-century survival and to associate that period with a mythical era of utopian ideals allowed them to use Dutch as a term designating old-fashioned values. Thoroughly modern in appearance, Mission furniture such as Warner's olde Dutch clock was "olde" by virtue of the old-fashioned, handcrafted methods of construction that were believed by many to hold greater moral value than machined objects. The American artist George Hitchcock had helped to establish such views about Dutch objects in the United States with articles like "The Picturesque Quality of Holland Interiors and Bric-a-Brac," published in *Scribner's Magazine* in 1889. He admired Dutch adherence to handcrafts, praising the humanity, sincerity, and beauty of their everyday objects, while reviling American machines and mass-produced tin wares as "soulless." Warner's olde Dutch clock was also "olde" because to call something new and Dutch was almost a contradiction in terms. In the American mind, if it was Dutch, it was old.[153]

Only one furniture manufacturer actually tried to justify calling Spanish Mission or British-inspired Arts and Crafts furniture "Dutch" by tracing them directly to Holland and Flanders. Charles P. Limbert moved to Grand Rapids from Chicago, another furniture center that produced replicas of Dutch furniture for the mail-order trade. After producing and retailing a variety of styles, Limbert brought out his "Holland Dutch Arts and Crafts furniture" (an insistently Dutch name) shortly after the turn of the century (FIG. 108c). In 1906 he moved the production end of the business to the city of Holland a few miles from Grand Rapids, because he felt the more rural setting and higher concentration of Dutch immigrants would produce superior furniture. Thereafter, Limbert published a magazine, *DeLimbert Boek*, and many furniture catalogues in which he explained that:

> In furniture making a pronounced Dutch influence can be seen in many of the Period styles. English styles, such as Elizabethan, Queen Anne and Tudor, as well as the French Louis XIV and XV periods, embodied more or less of Dutch ideas. Henry VIII brought to England famous Dutch artists and workmen to beautify his palaces. . . . Queen Anne and William and Mary furniture was of pronounced Dutch character due to the importation of skilled Dutch Craftsmen by William of Orange, who was himself a Dutch Stadholder.[154]

Essentially, Limbert has applied the broad outlines of Campbell's and Griffis's revisionist history to furniture history by showing the intermingling of English and Dutch history that brought Dutch influence to the United States via England. Like them, Limbert pretty much ignored any English influence on the Dutch during this period. Unlike those historians, he traced a more direct Dutch influence on American culture through Spain. According to Limbert:

> Spain, not being a manufacturing nation, depended largely upon the Holland Dutch importations...and in consequence, the Spanish missionaries and monks who settled on the western coast of America and established the missions of Mexico and California were familiar with styles of furniture made in the Netherlands, and patterned after them as well they could with the crude materials and inadequate tools they had at hand. From the fact that these crude imitations of the old Dutch designs were found in the Spanish missions originated the term "Mission" as applied to straight line furniture.

Limbert may have stood alone among manufacturers of furniture in seeing a direct line of design descent from Holland via England, France, and Spain to the United States, but he was joined in his opinion by some furniture historians at this period. In an issue of *The Mentor*, a publication that claimed to give the enquiring American mind all it needed to know on a given subject, Esther Singleton attributed the claw and ball foot to Holland as the country that imported it from China, and she considered the English period styles to have been formed largely through Dutch influence. Singleton also argued that the Pilgrims' cultural taste was shaped in Leyden, a notion familiar from revisionist historians. However, she understood that design influences in Europe had been intermingling for centuries and could not be entirely unentangled, so she coined the term Anglo-Dutch as a more accurate description of hybrid colonial furniture than Hepplewhite, Chippendale, and the rest.[155]

Even when the style of a piece of furniture bore no relation to Dutch or Flemish furniture, it was often advertised as being made by the descendants of Dutch craftsmen. The West Michigan Furniture Company, established in Grand Rapids in 1889, produced French and English period furniture, but its trademark of a Dutch woman standing before silhouetted windmills denoted the Dutch-American workmanship of every piece. As the firm's advertising copy boasted, "Its craftsmen are Holland descent in whom the pride of creative workmanship is traditional." Going a step farther, Limbert (every page of whose later catalogues carried the notice "the handiwork of Holland Dutch artists and craftsmen") attributed Grand Rapids's furniture success to its Dutch-American workers:

> To the Dutch the furniture industry of America owes much of its importance and success today. Not only for the examples of their

> famous cabinetmakers, but more especially for the skill, perseverance and fidelity of the Dutch workmen. In Grand Rapids the majority of workmen in all the factories making the better grades of furniture are Dutch.

American entrepreneurs such as Limbert, Warner, and Berkey & Gay built upon the solid reputation of the old Dutch craftsmen.

To a limited degree, American-made "Dutch" furniture also employed Dutch motifs. Limbert produced at least two lamp designs in which stained glass shades bore images of windmills and costumed figures. Some early Limbert desks and chairs had wood or copper inlays with Dutch scenes. House magazines of the era depict pieces of unknown manufacture that display tulip-shaped cutouts or inlaid tiles painted with Dutch motifs. But more often the Dutch label referred to a general character of solidity and structural integrity or to its production by American craftsmen of Dutch descent.

INTERIOR DECORATION

It should be noted that in the United States no direct correlation existed between Dutch architectural styles and Dutch interior decoration. The interiors of Modern Dutch Colonial and Dutch Renaissance Revival buildings were not necessarily given a Netherlandish treatment. On the other hand, Dutch interiors were very popular and appeared in buildings of every conceivable type. While decorators rarely applied a Hollandish motif to the interior of an entire building, individual Dutch rooms or accents abounded.

A single piece of Dutch furniture could become the key around which a room's decor revolved. In an essay on "House Decoration and Furnishing" published in a practical guide to the house and home of 1896, Mary Humphreys illustrated this concept by describing for her readers a bedroom in which a wrought iron, supposedly antique Dutch bed set the tone. Its high head and foot were filled with large, colorfully painted iron tulips. Old flowered chintz curtained the windows and formed a frieze above cream-red tinted walls, while old Dutch marquetry furniture completed the look.

Isolated Dutch accents were still more common than fully coordinated Dutch room interiors. At the turn of the century, the *Ladies' Home Journal* reported that "the desire for 'things Dutch' in the furnishing of American homes has grown with wonderful rapidity." Porcelain figurines and lace window panels, not to mention wooden shoes of all sizes, provided Dutch accessories for many interiors. Ladies' magazines gave instructions for sewing pillow covers and making magazine racks with Dutch motifs. Mary Humphreys noted a sizeable demand for amusing and grotesque decorative objects supplied by delft potteries. According to Humphreys, it was fashionable to group blue and white pots decorated with Dutch scenes along the order of Van Ostade interiors on a low table as a center of interest. Rookwood Pottery of Cincinnati also produced a line of wares decorated with seemingly old Dutch interiors and portraits in tones of brown and yellow. Humphreys identified this taste for humorous decorated delft conversation groups and the Rookwood Dutch vases as a "necessary reaction from the strain of modern life." To some extent, the placement of any Dutch accents, even lace and wooden shoes, in American homes could be called a reaction to the strain of modern life, for these were the accoutrements of a seventeenth-century image of Holland upheld by Americans against any evidence to the contrary. Such antimodernism fell far short of rejecting the modern conveniences provided by American technology, however. Many women threw themselves wholeheartedly into the study of modern domestic science, purchased the newest kitchen gadgetry, planned modern interior spaces with their architects, and discussed the latest improvements in domestic plumbing, but they also scattered comforting reminders of an earlier, supposedly less complicated era through their homes. A room might have a good example of antique furniture, or a few throw pillows stitched with windmills, or perhaps just the walls would allude to the fashion for Hollandish motifs.[156]

Many people hung pictures of Holland on their walls, sometimes allowing a large piece to become the visual focus of a room. Explaining the universal popularity of Dutch art, Ernest Talbert wrote in 1913: "What is there about the old Dutch paintings that makes them so interesting, so restful and satisfying to contemplate? They fit into any environment and yet never lose their individual atmosphere and charm." As Talbert intimated, democratic Dutch images seemed suited to every class of domestic setting. While wealthy connoisseurs placed old masters in their halls, the upper middle class hung old master copies and modern Dutch and American paintings on parlor and dining room walls. The lower middle class and a few working class people collected prints and reproductions from magazines. Experts decreed that a Ruysdael or Hobbema picture would coordinate with old furniture of any style period.[157]

Dutch pictures played a dual role in interior decoration. Not only did they place a little bit of Holland in many homes, but genre scenes illustrating Dutch interiors combined with the impressions tourists gained on their travels to provide ideas for designing Dutch rooms. As one authority explained to an audience eager to remodel their homes with a colonial era decor: "we have only to look at the interiors of Jan Steen, Terburg, Pieter de Hooch and other 'Little Masters' to learn how the rooms of the Dutch colonists were furnished." Pictures also suggested ideas for the treatment of fireplaces and walls, although the latter rarely resembled the originals in their American incarnations.[158]

Wallpaper and fabrics printed with Holland figures were available for curtains, upholstery, and wall coverings. The owners of the Ebenezer Devotion House in Brookline, Massachusetts hung an intricately patterned wallpaper of Dutch landscapes in octagonal lozenges alternating with stylized windmills in their front hall and stairs. Curator Stephen Jerome believes it may have been a colonial reproduction wallpaper, installed as part of a restoration project between 1900 to 1910.[159] Stenciling provided a less expensive way of attaining lasting wallpaper effects that was especially popular for borders. Paint sellers often included free stencils with each purchase of interior wall paint. In a 1914 advertisement for Alabastine wall tints in the *Woman's Home Companion*, three of the five stencils pictured were Dutch: two stylized tulip motifs and the ever-popular dancing Dutch couple. Based in Grand Rapids and New York City, Alabastine sold nationally.

While paint and wallpaper covered the other rooms of the house, Sanitas, a popular oilcloth wall covering printed to look like glazed tiles, decorated many a kitchen and bathroom (FIG. 109). Tile designs in blue and white or green and white became especially popular for bathrooms around 1910. A desire for hygienic surfaces arose from increased scientific knowledge of germs and led to the extensive use of washable surfaces such as ceramic tile, linoleum, and oil cloth. This concern for hygiene intersected with the long-standing reputation of the Dutch as an extraordinarily cleanliness-conscious people, so that Dutch and pseudo-Dutch designs were seen to provide a fitting decoration for such surfaces.

For the parlor and hall, family magazines published examples of Dutch mantels (FIG. 110) to provide guides for building or renovating fireplaces on a modest budget. These so-called Dutch fireplaces often bore little resemblance to anything found in the Netherlands.

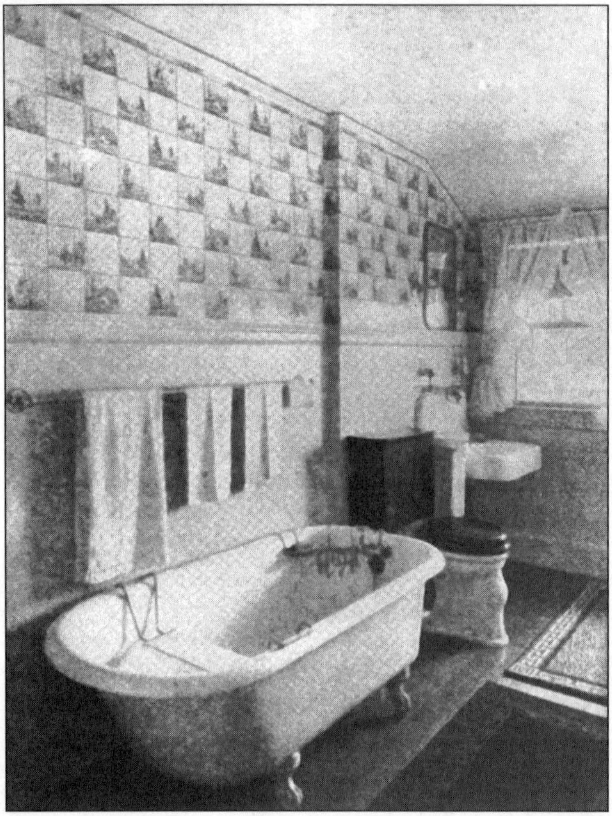

FIG. 109
Many decorators promoted the use of Dutch ceramic tiles or printed oilcloth wall coverings with Dutch designs for use in the modern, hygienic bathroom. This example illustrated Martha Cutler's essay on modern decoration in 1911.

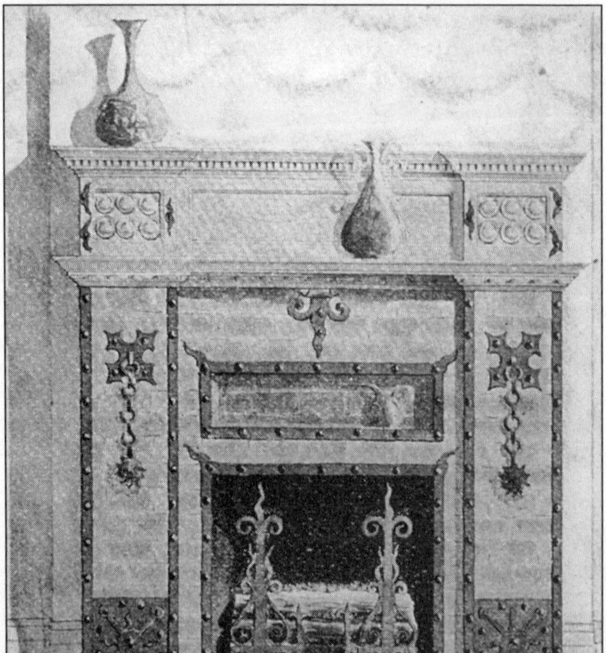

FIG. 110 *The* Ladies' Home Journal *called this "the Pure Dutch Mantel" when it was published in 1894.*

Aymar Embury advocated red brick as the proper facing for the colonial Dutch fireplace. He considered that the tiles facing fireplaces in Holland worked well for small peat fires, but that tile was too "stagey and artificial" to frame a big American wood fire.[160]

Embury's opinion notwithstanding, the Holland look became most fashionable for dining rooms, where a fireplace faced with solid blue or green tile took center stage in many middle-class homes (FIG. 111). While the inspiration for such fireplaces was often Dutch, the Arts and Crafts movement with its art pottery component and a new emphasis on architectural tile added impetus for much of this type of tile work. Healthier purses often leaned toward figured delft tiles, such as those incorporated into the 1897 Duncan Phillips mansion in Washington, D.C., producing a more unabashedly Dutch look. Architect Stanford White covered one entire wall of the dining room in his St. James, New York mansion with old Dutch tiles in blue and white. The wooden mantel shelf above the tiles served as a plate rack and held a ruffled shelf curtain in Dutch fashion, while an old iron fireback gave the wall visual focus.[161]

Several turn-of-the-century authorities on interior decoration recommended blue and white as the overall color scheme for the dining room. The popularity of delftware reinforced this trend. "There is something so quaint and decorative in Delft-ware, with its

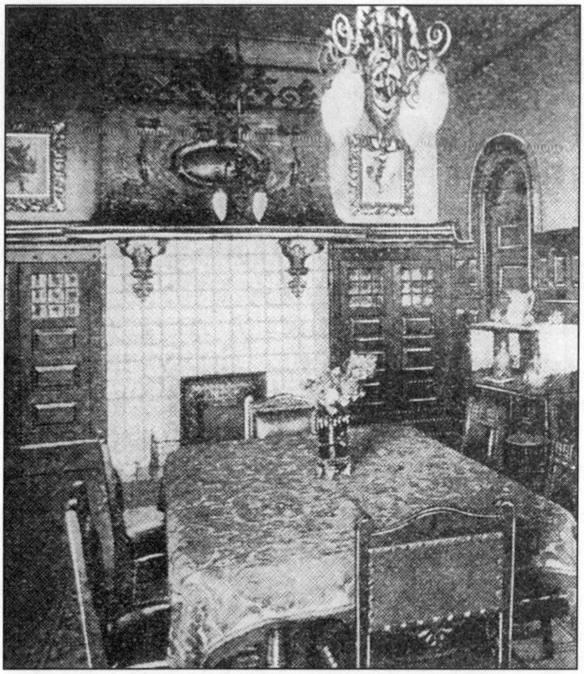

FIG. 111 *This New York dining room mantel published in the* Ladies' Home Journal *in 1899 demonstrates a closer relationship to Dutch sources than the so-called pure Dutch mantel. The seventeenth-century style chairs and carpet-covered table also evoke old Holland.*

water and windmills, odd trees and scenes, that it makes a never ending source of delight," remarked Celestine Cummings, one of the advocates of the Dutch dining room. Another, Julia Cowles, saw in delftware an allusion to the colonial period. "There are wares shown in the blue and white, both in china and porcelain, which look as though they had just stepped down from grandmother's corner cupboard, and which are veritable treasures, even though they are not heirlooms." This writer recommended walls papered in a white colonial pattern on delft blue ground with white woodwork and narrow shelves over the doors to show off the blue and white pottery in the dining room.[162]

A later, unrelated development in dining arrangements was the Dutch breakfast room, a small area in the kitchen containing a built-in table and benches. Windows, often with many small panes of glass, made these cheerful areas for multiple uses. According to design historians Jan Jennings and Herbert Gottfried, Dutch breakfast rooms began appearing in house plans by 1915.[163] Intended to provide a relaxed informal setting, they were particularly common in bungalows where they assumed the straight line form of Mission furniture. The name probably referred to the Dutch propensity for designing efficient interior spaces through the use of built-in furniture, however, Dutch breakfast rooms were more commonly known by less cumbersome titles, such as breakfast nook or dinette.

The desire to live in an environment similar to the quaint interiors seen in pictures of Dutch homes, both seventeenth century and contemporary, was an expression of identification with Holland and particularly with the seventeenth-century Dutch who colonized North America. By the turn of the century, many social clubs contained a Dutch room. The Grolier Club of New York, a society of authors, publishers and bookbinders, decorated their taproom in what they considered to be a rustic Dutch style. They hung on their wall the motto "Lust en Rust, Vriendschap en Gezelschap, Vrengde bij Vrede en buiten Zorg," meaning "Pleasure and Repose, Friendship and Sociability, Joy with Peace and without Care." Members of the Salmagundi Club, an organization of artists and intellectuals, created a unique Dutch tile fireplace in 1898 by painting the tiles with windmill landscapes, old-masterish heads and peasant genre scenes (FIG. 112). Charles Volkmar, the club potter, made the tiles and Alexander Theobald Van Laer used forty of them to paint the central Dutch landscape. George M. Reevs later painted a view of autumn in Holland on one of the smoking room

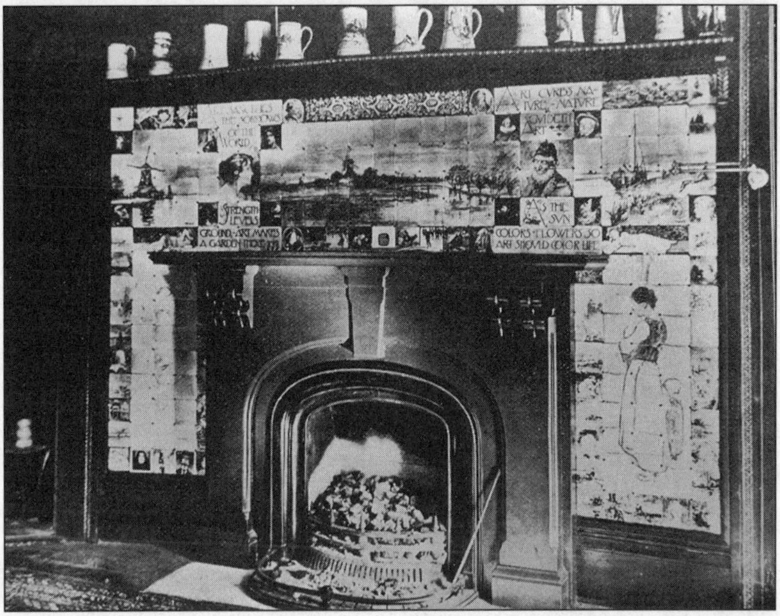

FIG. 112 *Members of the Salmagundi Club of New York painted tiles to create their Dutch fireplace in 1898. To raise money for their library, members also painted and auctioned drinking steins, many of which carried Dutch motifs and some of which grace the mantel in this photograph.*

doors. Every year the club held a fund-raising auction of drinking steins decorated by the members. The artists often used Dutch motifs and a few steins were retained to complete the clubhouse decorations. These clubs may have considered the Dutch decor especially appropriate due to their location in New York City, however this association of men's social space and activities with Dutch decor extended into many homes via the den. Kathleen Eagan Johnson has demonstrated that the den became another area of concentrated Dutch design.[164]

ENTERTAINMENT

As interiors took on a Dutch appearance, so did the social functions within them. Dutch tea parties, costume parties, dinners, and readings gained popularity. At one such dinner party, twenty-two people sat down at a table decorated with a canal of mirrors down the center and a miniature canal boat filled with fruit and candy at each place. The meal consisted of Dutch dishes and ale, followed by a smoking session for the men on imported long-stem clay pipes. For the Hudson-Fulton celebration in 1909, one popular national magazine recommended that American families decorate their Thanksgiving tables with wooden shoes in place of traditional pumpkin and turkey ornaments.[165]

Tableaux vivants, living pictures created to imitate famous paintings or statues by posing with simple costumes and props, were a popular entertainment and often took the form of Golden Age Dutch paintings. It was a simple matter to improvise a neck ruff over a black dress, but more elaborate costumes had also become popular for masked balls and banquets. Many tourists had returned with wooden shoes, lace caps, and Dutch trousers, so that fairly authentic living reproductions of Dutch paintings were often contrived. Contemporary paintings like George Hitchcock's *The Flower Girl* also provided models (FIG. 113).

Stereopticon lectures on Dutch art and life became commonplace, even in small towns, as returned travelers entertained their neighbors and artists went on the lecture circuit to promote their foreign work. John Ferguson Weir was not unique in offering a lecture on Holland in the time of Rembrandt, which he illustrated in part with lantern slides of his own paintings of the Netherlands. Such techniques emphasized the relationship of seventeenth-century Holland and nineteenth-century America and satisfied curiosity about old Dutch masters while promoting the work of contemporary American artists. Should a town fail to have a traveler in their midst, they could turn to published lectures like Ellerslie Wallace's "A Descriptive Reading on Holland Illustrated by Twelve Lantern Slides." With this aid, anyone could assume the role of the returned traveler. The advent of motion pictures such as Lyman H. Howe's "moving pictures of Quaint Holland" provided another vehicle for Dutch entertainments.[166]

A type of entertainment known as Dutch Dialect, on the other hand, actually caricatured Germans and had little to do with Holland Mania. The Vaudeville-style Dutch Dialect humorists wrote and recited in heavy pseudo-German accents, poems with titles such as " A Dutchman's Answer," "Dutch Maud Muller" and "Ein Deutsches Lied," about characters named Schneider, Pfeiffer, Strauss, and Schnitz. Dutch Dialect got its name through the mistranslation of Deutsch as Dutch. A verse by Charles G. Leland entitled "How to Learn Dutch" began each stanza with "Vill'st dou learn de Deutsche Sprache?" and then talked about sauerkraut, Sherman bier and the emperor of Germany. Occasionally a reference to Hans Brinker or another recognizable Holland motif appeared in Dutch Dialect, but it was primarily composed of German themes and language. Several collections of Dutch Dialect appeared in print between 1890 and 1920, including *Cooper's Dutch Dialect: Readings and Recitations* (1891) from which the above examples were extracted.

People participating in the Chautauqua Scientific and Literary Circle's year-long study of the Netherlands found many ways to translate their new knowledge into educational entertainments for their friends and communities. For example, the Des Moines Chautauqua Union reported that they "held a costume party in the late autumn, Dutch gowns being much in evidence while one of our well known artists, Mr. Charles Cumming, gave a stereopticon lecture on Dutch artists. These union meetings play a very important part in the life of our city." A circle of self-described "housekeepers, doing our own sewing and mothering our families" in Barre, Vermont, sponsored a Dutch Domestic Science afternoon. The Chautauqua societies encouraged such activities as a means of attracting new members, suggesting specifically the staging of Dutch *tableaux* after famous paintings, readings from the literature for the year, or an illustrated lecture on Holland. Such social and literary activities spread the influence of Chautauqua's Holland studies well beyond the immediate subscribers.[167]

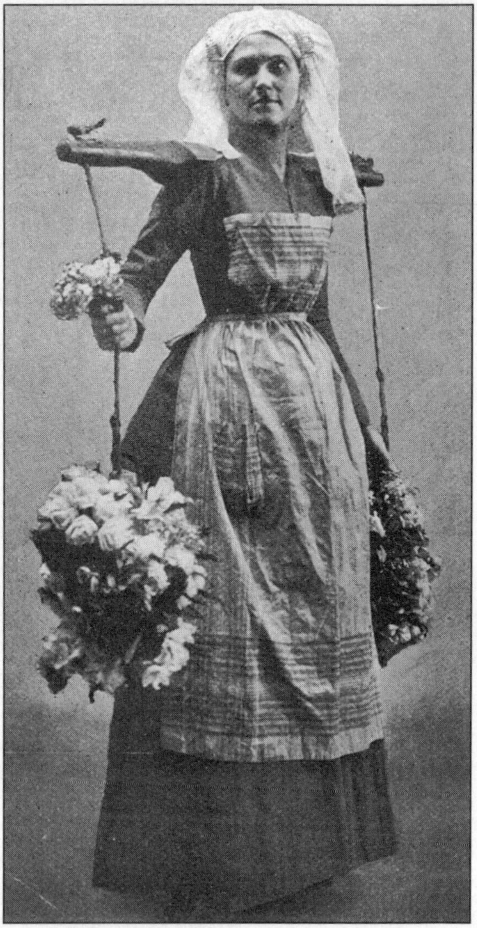

FIG. 113 *This photograph of a woman posing in* tableau vivant *manner as the principal figure in George Hitchcock's popular painting,* The Flower Girl, *was published in a turn-of-the-century magazine. The original painting is unlocated, but many old prints of it exist.*

Just as Chautauqua had declared 1908–1909 the year to study Holland, the *Woman's Home Companion* named Holland the theme for the 1913 club year. The *Companion* outlined Holland's history from the time of Julius Caesar and suggested readings from history books and novels as the basis for ten, twenty, or more meetings. "Clubs would do well to take a year of study on the last general topic [Dutch art] alone," noted the editor. "The history of the men of science and philosophy and the analysis of the work of the painters are enough to fill easily many programs." Dutch housekeeping, with its reputation for cleanliness and thrift, inspired numerous women's clubs to focus their meetings on this topic.[168]

For the more ambitious social club, *Harper's Bazar* recommended a full-scale Dutch kermis. Their American version of this traditional Dutch fair consisted of booths where club women could sell fruit, dolls in Dutch costume, Dutch bulbs and flowers, reproduction antique brass and imitation delft, as well as all kinds of Dutch candy and pastries. "The booths where the *poffertjes* are sold will be crowded if they are properly made," promised the article, and this booth should be called "the *poffertjes-kraam* [sic] to give it a characteristic unpronounceable Dutch atmosphere." The kermis workers were instructed to dress in full black skirts with blue gingham aprons, a V-necked black blouse with a little white lace in the neckline, a coral necklace, and a white lace cap. While conceding the difficulty of obtaining gold head ornaments in the United States, the author urged wooden shoes as a necessity. A large imitation Dutch windmill from which these Dutch maidens could serve milk and cheese and an exhibition of Dutch folk songs and dances completed the plans for the kermis. This Dutch kermis idea pre-dated all the Dutch festivals currently enacted in towns founded by Dutch immigrants, such as the tulip festival in Holland, Michigan. *Harper's Bazar* directed its suggestion, not toward Dutch-Americans, but toward any women's group around the country wanting to raise money at a time when Holland was in vogue.[169]

The institution of such celebrations, especially the *tableaux vivants* and costume balls, allowed Americans to playact at being the Dutch forebears of their country. They also perpetuated many of the stereotypes developed by artists and the tourist trade. Wooden shoes and lace caps, tulips, windmills, cheese, and art characterized Holland for most Americans.

FASHION

Dutch dress for women made its way from the occasional use of a costume in an entertainment to high fashion in the mid-1890s. In 1894, the *Ladies' Home Journal* reported that of all the season's new hats, "the shape which is most favored is that known as the Dutch cap, which fits the head quite closely, after the fashion of the velvet and bead hats worn by the pretty Dutch girls in some pictures."[170] The Dutch cap was decorated with a large stuffed bird or, more appropriately according to the editors, with bunches of velvet tulips (FIG. 114). It did not resemble traditional Dutch dress very closely, but as the fashion editor stated, was inspired by hats in paintings, such as the one reproduced here from a detail of a painting by the American artist Gari Melchers (FIG. 115). The combination of increased travel to Holland and wide-

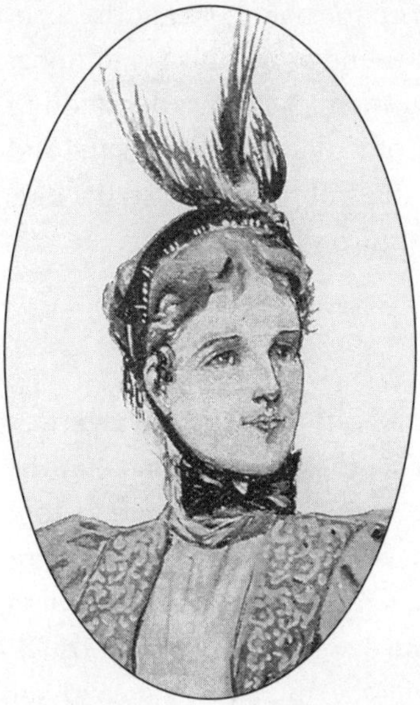

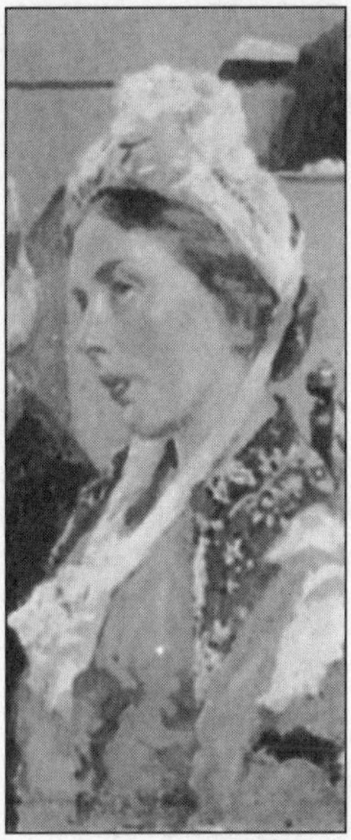

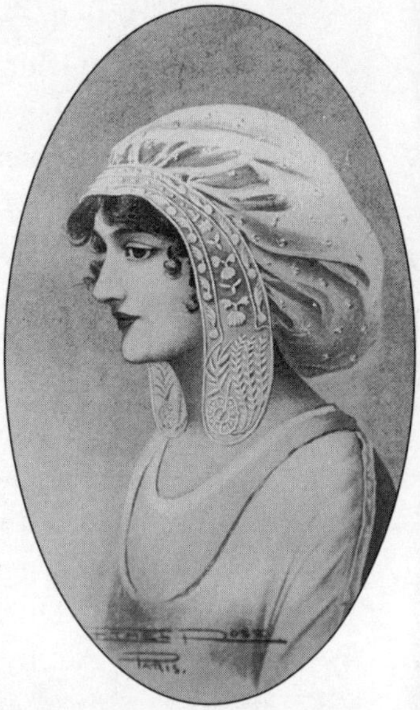

FIG. 114 *American women adopted hats like this "Dutch Bonnet" when they saw them illustrated in popular magazines. This one appeared in the* Ladies' Home Journal *in 1894.* FIG. 115 *The popularity of Dutch paintings and prints supported the fashion for Dutch hats in the United States. This detail from Gari Melchers's painting,* Easter Sunday, *reveals a hat similar to that in* FIG. 114.

FIG. 116 *This was one of several examples of Dutch boudoir caps advertised in* Harper's Bazar *and other popular magazines around 1912.*

FIG. 117 *Publicity photographs c.1911-13 show Irene Castle wearing authentic Dutch caps, but American entrepreneurs mass-produced their own versions of the lace cap.*

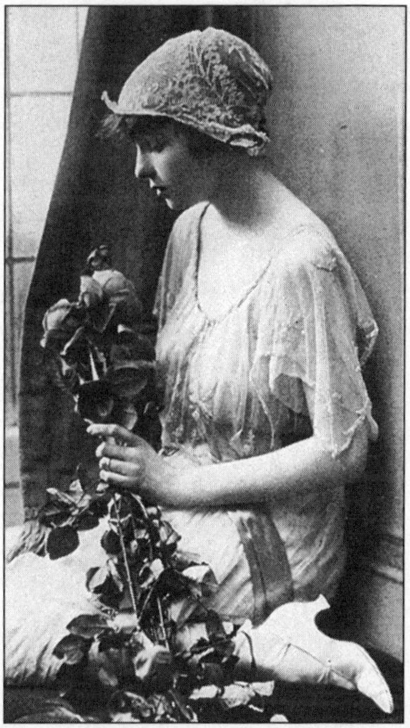

spread images of Dutch women wearing elaborate caps helped promote the fashion in the United States.

Around 1912, traditional Dutch lace caps became popular morning wear. Called boudoir caps, women often made them at home from bits of lace and net, although they were also available from exclusive design shops (FIG. 116). Women wore boudoir caps only at home, but soon the famous dance team, Vernon and Irene Castle, helped to popularize the public use of lace caps, and extended their use into the afternoon. When a friend brought Irene Castle an authentic Dutch cap from Rotterdam, she began wearing such caps for afternoon dancing and for numerous publicity photographs (FIG. 117). Other women quickly followed her lead. Castle fashion look-alikes appeared in several women's magazines in 1913. In a short time *Harper's Bazar* noted that "the little Dutch caps of lace which have been worn with the lingerie frocks this summer will be chic for the theatre this coming season." According to Irene Castle, even bathing caps and motor bonnets took the form of Dutch headdresses for a season. Thus one of the most traditional and picturesque aspects of Dutch dress entered American fashion to complement the increasing popularity of Dutch entertainments and interiors. It was a passing fad, but one that subtly expressed the new significance of Holland in American culture.[171]

LITERATURE

Dutch architecture, antiques, entertainments, fashion, and interiors expressed the prevailing enchantment with the Netherlands, at the same time spreading its influence. The revision of American history to suggest an ubiquitous Dutch heritage also fed that enchantment and increased curiosity about the Netherlands. In the early twentieth century, libraries across the country added special sections on Dutch literature and history to accommodate the increased demand for information. The University of Chicago hired a professor of Dutch Institutions in 1911 and soon after, Columbia University established the Queen Wilhelmina Lectureship in the Language and Literature of the Netherlands, which was later upgraded to a professorship.

A revival of interest in Washington Irving's fictitious histories and legends of Old Dutch New York occurred in the 1880s and early 1890s as part of the Colonial Revival. With the expiration of Irving's copyrights, new editions appeared for everyone. They ranged in price from a twelve cent paper copy of *The Legend of Sleepy Hollow* to a one hundred and fifty dollar, twenty-seven volume edition of Irving's complete works. Washington Irving's Sleepy Hollow stories also appealed to all ages. MacMillan published a children's edition of *Rip Van Winkle and Sleepy Hollow*, illustrated by George Boughton, that educators frequently recommended to parents and teachers.

Joseph Jefferson's famous theatrical interpretations of the sleepy old Dutchman added to the general interest in Irving's Dutch tales. Jefferson played Rip in cities throughout the country, from his introduction of the revised play in New York in 1866 until his death in 1905. Paintings, prints, and photographs of the actor in his most famous role spread his reputation, and that of Rip, even beyond his appearances (FIG. 118). For many nineteenth-century Americans, Joseph Jefferson *was* Rip Van Winkle. In addition, Dion Boucicault, whom Jefferson had enlisted to rewrite the play, published *Joseph Jefferson's Rip van Winkle: the text of the play*, from which home and local theatricals were produced.

Incidentally, the versatile Jefferson also painted landscapes, including a number of Dutch scenes, and he collected the work of the Hague School painters.

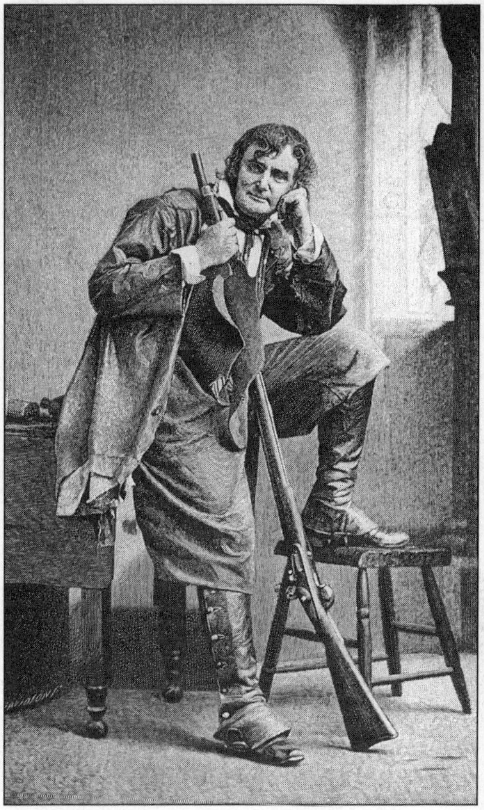

FIG. 118 *Joseph Jefferson played Rip Van Winkle to packed theaters across the country.*

Irving's satirical portrayals of early Dutch settlers in America are some of the least positive of all the American literature about the Dutch. Written as a humorous spoof on history, they nevertheless affected the perceptions many Americans had of Dutch influence in the formation of the United States. In his 1893 study of Washington Irving, Charles Dudley Warner pointed out that Irving's history of New York was a farce that had nothing in common with the character of the Dutch in either Holland or America, but he accepted that the error of treating it like history was already too firmly entrenched in American culture to be changed. The desire to correct Irving's image of Dutch Americans inspired some historians, artists, and writers at the turn of the century to promote the more positive characterization of the Dutch that dominated the period of Holland Mania.

At least one scholar, Tiemen de Vries, attempted to define a general Dutch influence on American literature in his book, *Holland's Influence on English Language and Literature*. Among other things, he argued that Irving borrowed the story of Rip Van Winkle from Erasmus. In reality, few works by Dutch authors had ever found their way into American translations. Even at the turn of the century, only Joost van den Vondel's *Lucifer* was readily available in English, although one could sometimes find poems by Jacob Cats and by Jacob Steendam, a seventeenth-century Dutch poet who had lived in New Netherland. The case for a Dutch influence in American literature proved too difficult for even such a devoted fan as Tiemen de Vries to argue with any success.

More recently, Celia Betsky has pointed out that fiction of the Colonial Revival period often stressed Old Dutch New York roots. Edith Wharton named the principals in *The House of Mirth* the Van Osburghs and the Van Alstynes and Henry James created Gustavus Vanderbank to suggest colonial Dutch families. In real life, recurring fears that foreign immigration would overwhelm American culture caused a backlash against immigrants that induced many non-Dutch immigrants to anglicize their names. Dutch names never suffered from such a stigma. On the contrary, with the reinterpretation of American history and character, Dutch ancestry enjoyed new prestige.[172]

GENEALOGY

Genealogy is a timeless passion. People have always been interested in tracing and recording their ancestry, whatever it might be. Nevertheless, at the turn of the century in the United States, Dutch ancestry carried a particular cachet. The enviable wealth and social position of the Vanderbilts and Roosevelts in the late nineteenth century undoubtedly contributed to the desirability of a line of Dutch ancestors at one's back, particularly for residents of New York. Thaddeus Vanderslice coined the term "pedigreemania" to describe the impulse that set him searching through family Bibles, cemeteries, and civil records to find the first Van der Sluys in America and motivated others on similar quests for Dutch ancestry. A victim of acute pedigreemania, Charles Conrad of Dexter, Michigan, determined that he and his family descended from an eighteenth-century Dutch King. He supposedly brought his claims to the people of the Netherlands in an open letter in a Dutch newspaper, reassuring them that the principles of "independence, liberty and . . . the will of the people" would continue to be upheld if and when the American heirs should choose to take the Dutch throne. Others chose to publish books about their families, such as May King Van Rensselaer's pictorially documented volume of 1888, *The Van Rensselaers of the Manor of Rensselaerswyck*.[173]

People lacking a pedigree, or the time to search for one, could take advantage of an advertisement that appeared in the New York papers for a time in 1899. Playing on the snob appeal of colonial Dutch lineage, a private firm in Holland offered for sale "authentic" oil portraits of seventeenth-century Dutch men and women to Americans wanting to establish a suitable ancestry.[174]

By 1914 the United States had at least fourteen Dutch societies, including the Holland Society of New York, founded in 1885, and the Netherlands Society of Philadelphia, established in 1892. Most existed for the preservation of colonial Dutch history and were composed of descendants of Pre-Revolutionary War Dutch families. The Holland Society limited membership to men who could prove direct descent in the male line from a Dutchman living in New

Netherland before 1675. Their female counterpart, the Society of Holland Dames, was founded ten years later and established a policy only a little less exclusive by admitting descendants in both the male and female lines. The Netherlands Society of Philadelphia accepted any man whose Dutch ancestors arrived in New Jersey, New York, Delaware, or Pennsylvania before 1776 and a Milwaukee group, Tot Nut van 'tAlgemeen, liberally welcomed all Hollanders and their descendants regardless of where they lived or when they arrived.

COMMERCE AND ADVERTISING

While America's Dutch connection held special interest for Dutch immigrants and their descendants, the fascination with the Netherlands was general. Manufacturers acknowledged the extent of Holland's appeal by giving new products Dutch names. When the G. H. Johnson Cigar Company joined five other small companies to form the Consolidated Cigar Corporation, they agreed to make Johnson's popular Dutch Masters cigar the flagship of the corporation and eventually promoted it to one of the top selling cigars in the country. Hollanders' reputation as connoisseurs of fine tobacco made "Dutch Masters" an appropriate name for a cigar. The use of Rembrandt's famous *Syndics of the Drapers Guild* to advertise and package the product suggested that the cigar was a masterpiece and the smoker a connoisseur. But it also reminded American smokers of Motley's Holland and their own colonial Dutch forebears.

Other products that adopted Dutch brand names and logos at the turn of the century included paints, cleansers, cocoa, a variety of foods, and flower bulbs. Advertisers built upon the popular nineteenth-century image of Holland to help sell their products to an American audience. For example, when twenty-five manufacturers of lead in the East and Midwest merged to form the National Lead Company in 1891, they needed a single brand name to give their product a national identity. Advertising manager O.C. Harn invented Dutch Boy to fill that role. He recognized that people associated painting with the Dutch—not just fine art painting, but the artistic use of paint to cover all sorts of surfaces, from boats and furniture to utensils and houses. Harn's Dutch Boy brand also tapped the sentimental preference shown by the general public for images of children. The visual symbol for Dutch Boy paint, a blond boy in baggy pants and cap, was created for the company in 1907 by the artist Lawrence Earle (see first image in FIG. 149). Earle hailed from the Dutch-American community of Grand Rapids, where he had received his first art training from the Dutch-born painter Marinus Hartung. Earle is supposed to have engaged a nine-year-old Irish neighbor as his model for the Dutch Boy, but he had no difficulty replicating the Dutch type already so familiar to Americans. Dutch Boy paints became a fast-selling, nationally recognized product.

The Netherlands exported Dutch bulbs and cocoa to the United States in large quantities. Most importers of flower bulbs depended on pictures of wooden shoes, windmills, and flower fields and on the Dutch reputation to sell their products. Stephen L. Bartlett, the Boston importer of Bensdorp's Royal Dutch Cocoa, published a series of picture postcards with costumed Dutch men and women to help advertise his product (FIG. 119c). Dutch cocoas provided so much competition that even the leading American company, W. Baker, began to refer to its Dutch rivals in advertisements (FIG. 120). Trying to turn the tables, Baker adopted the slogan, "unlike the Dutch process, no alkalies." This slogan was also consistent with Baker's policy of promoting its product on health issues, but within a decade Baker, too, would employ the image of a Dutch peasant woman to sell its cocoa.

Utopia yarn took advantage of the popular conception of Dutch women as skilled knitters and advertised with a series of pictures that showed Volendamers winding and knitting with Utopia yarn.

FIG. 120 *In the 1890's, Dutch companies used a variety of strategies, from Van Houten's appeal to patriotism with an Uncle Sam figure to Blookers' colonial image, in order to successfully market their cocoa in the United States. In response, the American manufacturer, W. Baker, developed the motto "Unlike the Dutch Process—No Alkalies."*

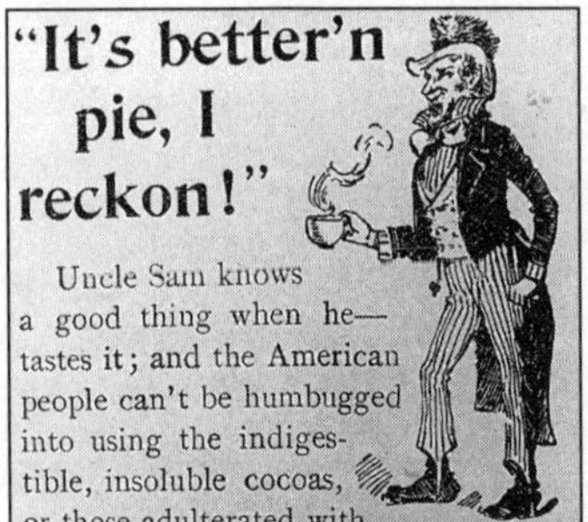

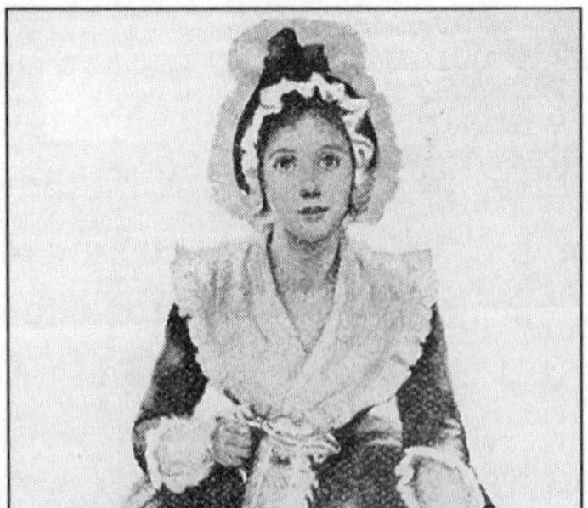

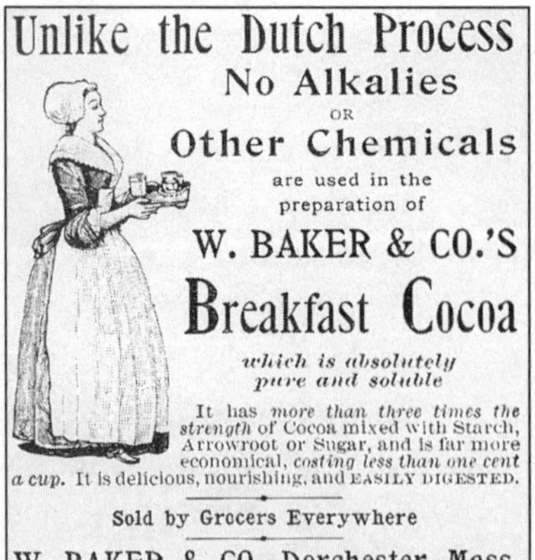

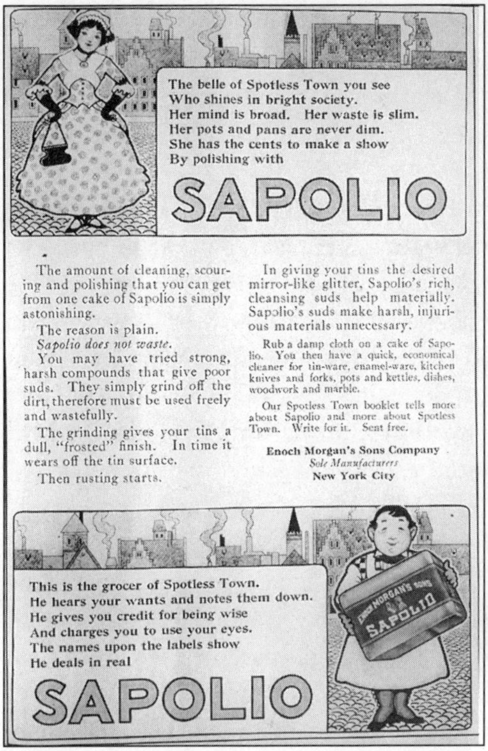

FIG. 121 *Because Americans believed in Dutch hygiene, advertisers found they could sell cleaning products simply by including some reference to Holland, such as the step-gabled brick houses that appeared in Sapolio ads.*

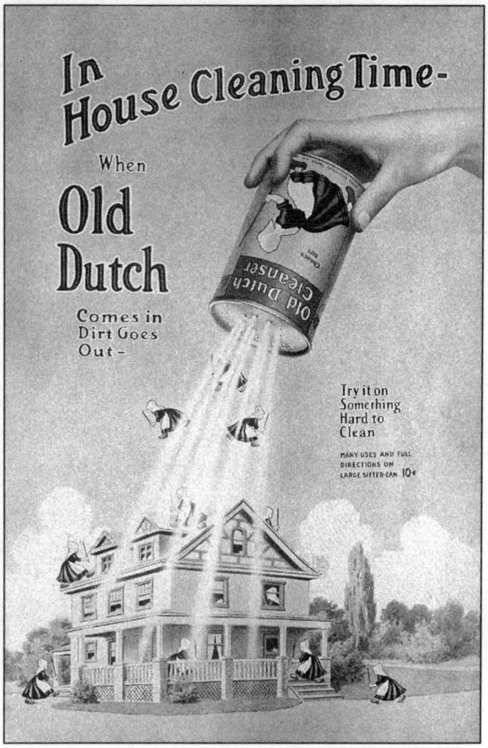

FIG. 122 *Old Dutch Cleanser moved rapidly to the top selling cleanser in the United States after it was introduced in 1905.*

Walk-Over shoes developed an advertising campaign featuring a pair of Dutch children in wooden shoes who admire Walk-Overs in shop windows and on the feet of American pedestrians.

Advertisers discovered that for certain types of products, such as cleaning agents, even a vague visual reference to Holland might improve sales. Sapolio soap ran a series of ads featuring Spotless Town (FIG. 121). A single row of Dutch gabled houses in the background was sufficient to draw associations with the legendary cleanliness of Holland and sell the soap. This marketing ploy was so successful that when the American author Theodore Dreiser needed an analogy to describe Haarlem's cleanliness, he likened it to "Spotless Town—the city of advertising fame." Still better known was Old Dutch cleanser with its trademark Dutch woman chasing dirt with a stick. First marketed in 1905, Old Dutch benefited from imaginative national advertising campaigns, such as one in which little Dutch housewives attack a big American house (FIG. 122).

By 1920, when psychologists George Hotchkiss and Richard Franken conducted a national test of brand advertising, they found Old Dutch to be the leading cleanser by a wide margin. Mentioned by 744 of the 1,024 subjects in their test, its nearest competitor received only 41 mentions.[175]

Some companies chose Dutch sounding brand names and visual logos to reflect the owner's ethnic heritage, rather than purely as a marketing strategy. In 1915 when Theodore Van de Kamp and his family established their potato chip stand in Los Angeles, the women designed Dutch costumes for the counter help. They soon added baked goods to their menu and a windmill logo became part of the packaging design. By 1921, Van de Kamp's Holland Dutch Bakers had opened the first of a chain of eighty bakeries housed in buildings made to look like windmills.

Other companies used Dutch imagery as part of a larger "foreign types" campaign. The Singer Manufacturing Company issued a large series of advertising postcards featuring costumed figures from around the world. One of the Netherlands cards depicted a couple from the Island of Marken, with the woman seated at a Singer sewing machine stitching designs for the intricate Marken costume. The advertising text noted that Singer had over twenty offices in Holland and sold thousands of machines there annually. Collectible postcards, calendars, business cards, and tiny drawing books with similar Dutch motifs are part of a host of advertising paraphernalia produced by a wide variety of American companies to promote their goods.

The imagery that worked for such national products as Dutch Masters cigars, Dutch Boy paints, and Old Dutch cleanser with their substantial advertising budgets, worked equally well for small local businesses with limited resources. For this market, printing companies offered generic trade cards with Dutch motifs. Enterprises as diverse as a butcher and a railroad chose to have their names printed on a business card with a picture of a floating wooden shoe on it. The Dutch emblem had little to do with their products, but apparently appealed to someone of authority in each company who assumed it would also appeal to their clients. Printers also produced picture postcards for business correspondence by independent salesmen and small businesses. One of the most popular was a pair of cards printed to look like blue and white delft tiles (FIG. 123c). One bore a picture of a Dutchman carrying baskets of bread, cheese, and poultry over the legend "We carry the best in the market." The other, depicting a female farm laborer, alleged "The best in the field." Any enterprising businessperson could write the appropriate information for his or her business in the blank space beneath the legend, or have the cards printed with a name and message.

The Dutch influence came to advertising late. Singer's use of Dutch figures to sell sewing machines is an early example, dating from 1892, and part of a much broader strategy. Most uses of specifically Dutch imagery in advertising appeared after the turn of the century and some continued to be employed through the 1920s and 1930s. Because marketers relied so heavily on public recognition of a motif, it was not until the mythic image of Holland had become very broad based and firmly entrenched in public consciousness that national advertisers ventured to employ it.

Manufacturers of greeting cards and souvenir picture postcards also commonly offered a Dutch series for collectors (FIG. 124c). During the heyday of postcard collecting, from 1890 to 1920, many of these series featured a caricature Dutch boy and girl, representing the lowest common denominator of the picturesque image. The clothing bore only a general resemblance to Dutch dress and the figures were recognized as Dutch mainly by their wooden shoes, lace caps, and windmill settings. This motif was so common that picture postcard collectors and dealers today typically use "Dutch kids" as a category heading. The accent on the written greeting for many Dutch kids postcards was of the Dutch Dialect type, a parody of German. Other Dutch kids postals were of higher artistic merit and all served an array of purposes, from birthday greetings and valentines to Thanksgiving, Christmas, Easter, or New Year's wishes.

The widespread distribution of such advertising and collectible images after 1900 compounded the effects of Holland Mania. Images of Holland, often old-fashioned ones reminiscent of the colonial period and therefore of the country's Dutch heritage, slowly permeated many aspects of popular culture in the United States.

EIGHT

Cincinnati, a Case Study

In seeking information about turn-of-the-century Dutch influence in American culture, one logically turns to towns and cities in New York and New Jersey that were founded by Dutch colonists or to areas such as western Michigan that were settled by Dutch immigrants in the nineteenth century. However, it is the widespread appearance of Dutch themes and motifs in non-Dutch localities that certifies the breadth and depth of America's love affair with the Netherlands. In that regard, Cincinnati, a city that developed a connection with the Netherlands during the 1880s and manifested a full-fledged mania for it after the turn of the century, provides an excellent case study.

Cincinnati was founded around 1790 by westward bound pioneers of mostly English and German extraction. German immigrants rapidly expanded the city's population in the first half of the nineteenth century and a substantial Irish community developed at the same time. While the occasional Dutch immigrant may have stopped in Cincinnati, the city never acquired a significant population of Dutch-Americans. The Ohio River and the Miami and Erie Canal provided transportation and water for the development of breweries, stockyards, and industries including leather goods, metal works, and railroad car manufacturing. As its industrial base grew and wealth accumulated, civic leaders began to support the arts, hoping to make their city both the manufacturing and the cultural center of the Midwest. The city built the Music Hall in 1878 as a performance center and staged annual arts festivals and huge operas and theatrical extravaganzas. The Conservatory of Music, McMicken School of Design, Cincinnati Art Museum, and numerous other institutes, academies, and clubs helped to foster the fine arts.

THE EIGHTIES

As in other American cities, it was the local artists who introduced Holland to Cincinnati's notice. In the early 1880s a number of painters, including William Jacob Baer, Robert Frederick Blum, Martha Scudder, and John Henry Twachtman, went to the Netherlands in the summertime to sketch. Twachtman, Blum, and Baer were born within a city block of one another in 1853, 1857, and 1860 respectively. Scudder was born in the suburb of Avondale in 1861. Blum and Baer attended the same public school, swam together in the canal as boys and studied art at the McMicken School of Design, forming a lifelong friendship. About 1880 they both went to Europe to continue their art education. After making brief independent journeys in the Netherlands they spent the summer of 1884 with New York artists William Merritt Chase and Charles Frederick Ulrich in Haarlem and the nearby fishing village of Zandvoort. Here they studied paintings by Haarlem's most famous old master, Frans Hals, and sketched retired fishermen, orphans, and beach scenes.

While Baer painted Zandvoort's interiors and fisherfolk, Chase painted a picture of Blum and a young woman sitting in the garden of the house where Chase had rented a room (FIG. 125c). A fellow New York painter, Hopkinson Smith, later recalled visiting Chase briefly at this address in a long row of whitewashed houses in the Zandvoort dunes as Chase was just beginning the painting. According to Smith the young woman in the hammock, also a visitor to the town, lodged next door.[176] The painting, which is now called *Sunlight and Shadow*, was completed by November when a New York paper reported:

> The principal canvas which Mr. William M. Chase brought back from Zandvoort, in Holland, is a large work called "The End of the Honeymoon"—a couple by a late breakfast table in the garden of one of the fishermen's houses, where visitors lodge—he moody, and toying with a cup of tea, while the "Gil Blas" has dropped at his side, and she swinging idly in a hammock, with one-half of her face seen over the side, and a coquettish look in her eye.[177]

This is the kind of narrative painting that invites the viewer to unravel the story, as this writer has done, but it is also a picture of a Cincinnati artist in Holland—one of the first of a host of Cincinnatians to spend the summer months this way.

Besides serving as Chase's model, Blum painted some of his own pictures in this same spot (FIG. 126c). He stayed in the area for almost a year, producing many pastel paintings on brown paper, drawings, watercolors, and a few oils. One of the oils that he sent to New York with Ulrich when the latter returned in October was an interior genre scene of a woman in a pale purple dress knitting at the table, with a view through an open door to another woman hanging out clothes. Another small oil painting by Blum of a Zandvoort girl knitting in a dark interior is now in the Cincinnati Art Museum. Blum experimented with media and techniques, especially pastel, and developed a mature style during this period in Holland. His pastel of a slaughtered ox in a Haarlem butcher shop (Sterling and Francine Clark Art Institute, Williamstown, Massachusetts) was completed soon before he left the Haarlem-Zandvoort area. The subject of this work was inspired by Rembrandt's painting of the same, but it reveals the rapid application and heavy medium typical of Frans Hals's technique. Blum's pastels received considerable notice when they were shown at the Second Exhibition of the Painters in Pastel a few years later in New York. They included sketches of bright flower beds against gray skies, narrow streets of red-tiled roofs, sleepy canals and brown dunescapes.[178]

Appearing in the same exhibition with Blum's Zandvoort pastels were three Dutch scenes by John Twachtman: *In Holland*, composed of blue, black, grey, and white pastel on gray paper; a windmill in a quiet mood; and another picture of a windmill on a low dune with a pool and reeds in the foreground. A few years older than the others, Twachtman had also studied at McMicken and preceded Baer and Blum to Munich where he spent several years at the Royal Academy. Around 1880 he and a fellow member of the Cincinnati Etching Club, Martha Scudder, learned printmaking at the club. After Scudder and Twachtman married in 1881, they made a trip through Europe with the brothers Julian Alden Weir and John Ferguson Weir. They took etching plates on their walks and boat trips in the country around Dordrecht so they could sketch directly on the plates. The result of this venture was a series of etchings by John and Martha Twachtman of the windmills, canals, and riverboats of South Holland (FIG. 127). They returned to the Netherlands in the summer of 1885, twice visiting the Frans Hals pictures in Haarlem and enlarging their own repertoire of Dutch images. John Twachtman painted several large tonal canvases of windmills, probably from the sketches made in Holland. One of these, *Windmills*, achieved considerable success in American exhibitions and was placed in the Smith College art collection (FIG. 128).

How much of an impact the Dutch images by these four artists may have had in Cincinnati is an open question. The Twachtmans returned to Cincinnati after their initial work in Holland and undoubtedly exhibited their paintings, drawings, and etchings locally, but after only a

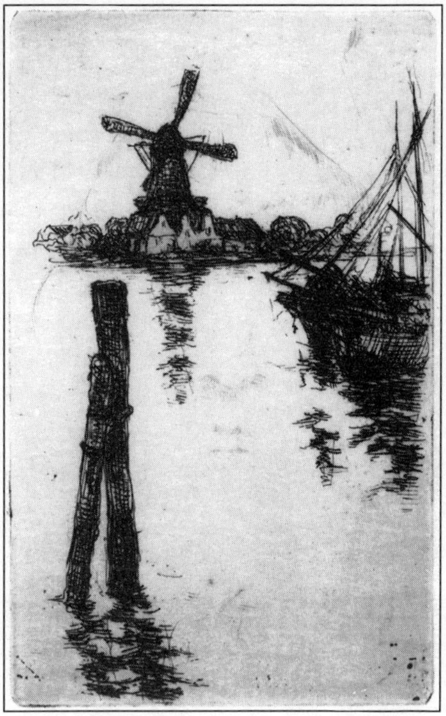

FIG. 127 *Martha Scudder Twachtman spent part of her honeymoon in the Dutch countryside making etchings like* A View of the Meuse.

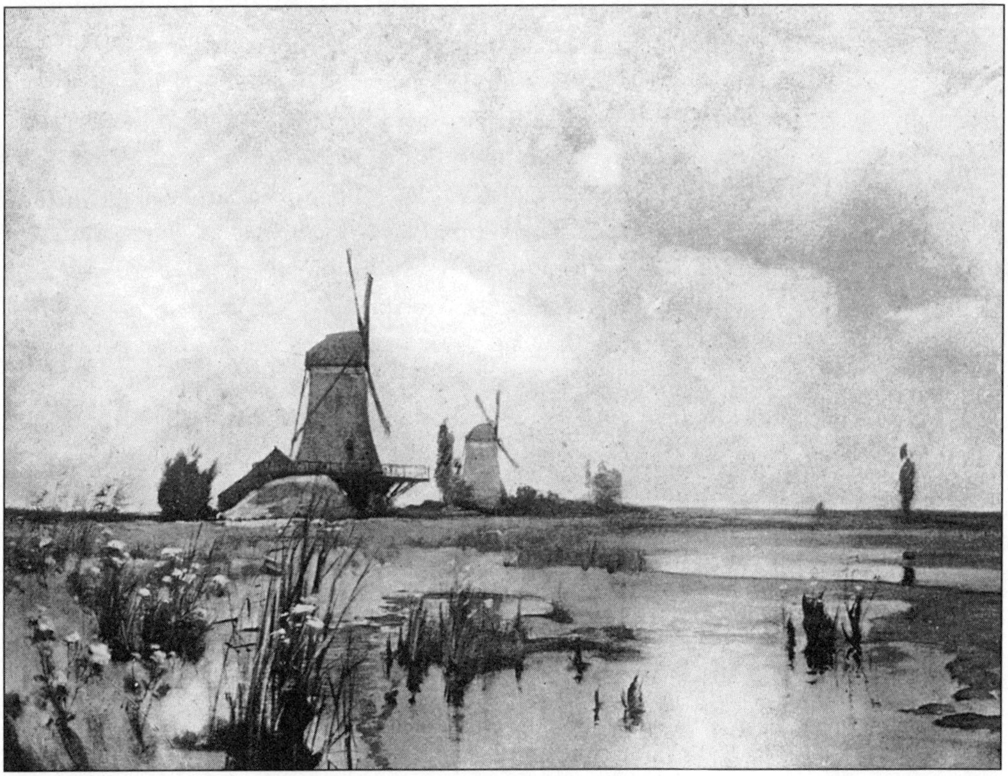

FIG. 128 *John Henry Twachtman painted several Dutch landscapes, including the now unlocated* Windmills.

year they moved to Paris and later settled in Connecticut. Blum and Baer chose to establish studios in New York City and abroad. However, the artists' families remained in Cincinnati and may have retained some of their Dutch work. In 1905 the Cincinnati Art Museum held a retrospective exhibition of Blum's work, including at least fourteen examples from Holland, and his sister gave the museum many of his works at that time. Martha Twachtman exhibited three etchings of Holland in the Ohio Valley Centennial exhibition, held in Cincinnati in 1888, and the same year fine art publisher C. Klackner of New York reproduced at least two of John Twachtman's Dutch etchings. As photogravures, *Holland Dykes* and *Boats on the Maas* received broader distribution and recognition than the dozen or so prints pulled from his plates by the artist.

Possibly inspired by the example of Baer, Blum, and the Twachtmans, Lewis Henry Meakin chose to work in the Netherlands at this time. Like them, Meakin had no Dutch ancestry in his immediate background. In fact, he was born in England and emigrated to North America with his family as a child. He, too, studied art in Munich and made his first journey to the Dutch province of Zeeland while a student. There he produced etchings, including a view of Vlissingen that he exhibited in Boston in 1885. Five years later Meakin spent a summer in the coastal town of Katwijk aan Zee, not far from Zandvoort. His large oil painting, *Holland* (private collection) reveals Dutchmen working in the fields before a distant town with several windmills in the background. The broken brushwork and colorful autumn palette attest to a strong impressionist influence, quite removed from the Munich style. As an instructor at the Cincinnati Art Academy from 1886 until his death in 1917, and as the paintings curator for the Cincinnati Art Museum, Meakin exerted a more immediate influence over local art than did the others artists. He may have had something to do with the continuation of Cincinnati's artistic ties to the Netherlands. On various occasions he painted pictures in the provinces of North Holland, South Holland, and Zeeland.

As noted, all of the early Cincinnati artists who went to Holland, except Martha Scudder, had first studied in Munich. The German connection within Holland Mania was particularly strong in Cincinnati because of the city's German heritage. The Germans had long admired seventeenth-century Dutch art, as evidenced by the dark palette, glazes, heavy varnish, and chiaroscuro effects of the Munich School style. Journeys to Amsterdam, Haarlem, and The Hague to study the old Dutch masters were a well-established part of art education in the academies at Düsseldorf and Munich and provided some American students with their first exposure to the Netherlands. Frank Duveneck, who was considered Cincinnati's master painter by his contemporaries, attracted many of his fellow artists to Munich where he had studied in the 1870s and later taught. Duveneck's *Woman with Forget-Me-Nots* (FIG. 129c) is a good example of the Dutch influence within the Munich style. Dressed in a black seventeenth-century costume, the subject is posed in a manner reminiscent of a Frans Hals portrait. In his study, *Unsuspected Genius, the Art and Life of Frank Duveneck*, Robert Neuhaus suggests that Rubens's *Portrait of Isabelle Brandt* provided the inspiration for Duveneck's painting. In either case, the refined brushwork, dark shadows of the background, and controlled use of light recall earlier Dutch art.

Duveneck may have been inspired to paint pictures like *Woman with Forget-Me-Nots* as much by the American art market as by his admiration for Netherlandish art. Old Dutch masters brought some of the highest prices on the art market and for those collectors who could not afford them or were afraid of being deceived with a forgery, paintings in the old Dutch style by contemporary Americans provided an economical alternative. This was the sentiment of Cincinnati businessman Allen Collier when he wrote to a local artist who specialized in Dutch scenes: "I have not the money to purchase a Rembrandt so don't worry about it, but I do want a few pictures in my home and offices painted by men who are my friends and in whom I have a personal interest."[179] Other Cincinnatians felt the same. In 1894 a group of citizens purchased by subscription a picture of a Dutch woman seated at a table in a dark interior by Edward Henry Potthast (FIG. 130). They donated it to the Cincinnati Art Museum for the benefit of the community. Potthast, who had been born in Cincinnati in 1857, went to Munich to study art around 1883. He painted several landscapes and interiors in Holland during the late 1880's and exhibited paintings entitled *Dutch Washerwoman*, *Souvenir of Holland*, *Katwyc-an-Zee* and *A Dutch Interior* between 1898 and 1912, suggesting his continued interest in the theme.

THE NINETIES

The end of the eighties marked a turning point in Cincinnati's relations with the Netherlands. Many more artists traveled to Holland during the next decade and through their activities Dutch influence began to spread into the social arena. Unlike the earlier group, most

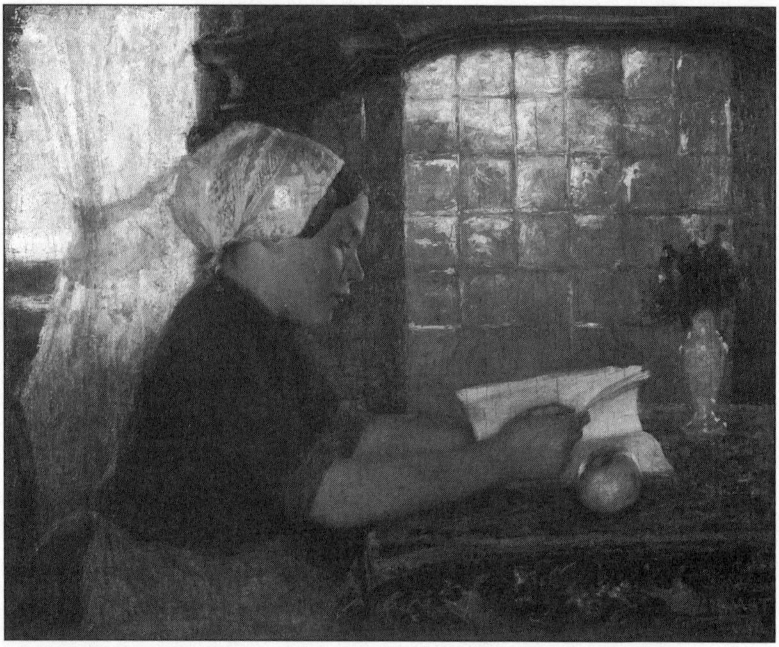

FIG. 130 *Although little is now known of Edward Henry Potthast's travels in Holland, the Cincinnati Art Museum owns two of his Dutch subjects, this 1890 painting,* A Dutch Interior, *and* A Milkmaid with Her Cow.

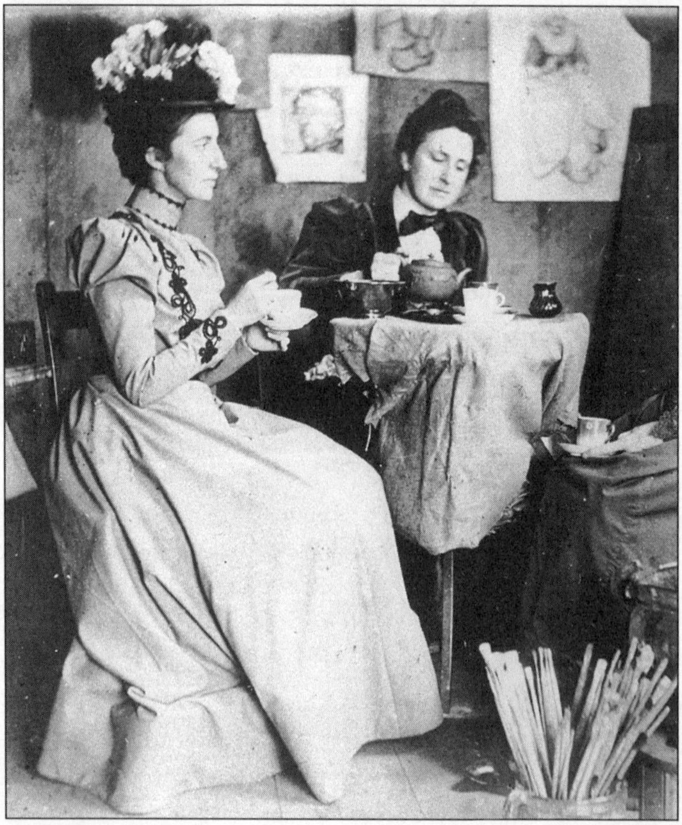

FIG. 131 *This photograph was identified by Leendert Spaander as an image of Henrietta Wachman in her Volendam studio. Wachman spent more time in Volendam than Elizabeth Nourse and was better known to the residents, but the woman pouring tea bears a striking resemblance to Nourse.*

of these artists were women. They ignored the North Sea coast and the southwest part of the country where most of their predecessors had worked, in favor of Volendam, a unique village on the Zuider Zee. It was the women artists of the 1890s who introduced Dutch costume and customs to Cincinnati society, and it was their art that established Volendam motifs as a theme in Cincinnati interiors.

In 1892 Elizabeth Nourse and her sister Louise, together with fellow Cincinnati artist Henrietta Wachman and her sister Laura, journeyed to the small old fishing town (FIG. 131). Volendam had already established a reputation as an international artists' colony and pictures of the town were to be seen every year in the Paris Salons and in scattered European and American exhibitions. Nourse and Wachman had undoubtedly encountered examples and heard stories of this extremely picturesque spot while living in Paris, and determined to go there and try it out. They secured two houses, one on the dike where the Nourses slept and they all ate, and one on the dunes where Elizabeth and Henrietta painted. They hired someone to build them a platform outside their studio window so they could work in the comfort of the interior while their models stood in the light and breeze in order to maximize the naturalism of their paintings. Elizabeth Nourse produced two major salon paintings here, *On the Dyke at Volendam* (see FIG. 63) and *In the Church at Volendam* (FIG. 132c), along with several lesser paintings and many genre studies and heads.

Nourse's *In the Church at Volendam* provides a good example of the image that Cincinnatians soon identified as typically Dutch. Six girls and one boy, ranging in age from about four to twelve, sit quietly in church pews with their attention focused on an unseen priest or on their prayer books. Most distinctive to Cincinnati viewers were the girls' lace hats and straw bonnets. Volendam's children were a favorite subject because they dressed exactly like their parents, causing them to look like miniature adults. Female artists seem to have been especially attracted to the children, invariably commenting on their clothing. Nourse's description, written to her twin sister Adelaide in Cincinnati, is typical:

> With the exception of Russia I have never been in a country where a costume is so general—everybody wears it here—even the tiny new born baby wears a lace cap like the mother and the darling little boys swagger around in wide breeches just like their daddies.[180]

Volendam girls wore white lace wing caps over close-fitting black caps that completely covered their hair. The multiple skirts and tight bodices that disguised their mothers' figures, perfectly suited the children's immature bodies. Boys wore wide baggy breeches fastened with two large buttons of silver, gold, or brass and a double-breasted shirt.

By the time the Nourses left Volendam, they had become extremely attached to the children who posed for Elizabeth and for whom, in her spare time, she had made many sets of doll clothes:

> We will be sorry to leave these lovely and good people here whom we love dearly, above all my dear little Dutch babies. . . . They are wonderfully kindhearted and so thoughtful and the children are angels. . . . The children all went to the boat and threw kisses and waved their hands until we were out of sight.[181]

For *In the Church at Volendam* Nourse provided her "angels" with a setting in the Catholic church. Although Volendam had a Reformed church, this was one of the unusual Dutch towns where the Catholic church was the more popular and much the larger. Nourse, herself a devout Catholic, may have felt drawn to this town (as she did to several French peasant communities) for the primitive simplicity of the faith and the pageantry of the rituals. She chose to paint the children of Volendam during a quiet moment as they sat listening in the pews. The innocence of the children, symbolized by large eyes and cherubic facial expressions, betokens pure spiritual faith and is probably intended to evoke the words of Jesus, "See that you do not despise one of these little ones; for I tell you that in heaven their angels always behold the face of my Father who is in heaven," and "unless you turn and become like children you will never enter the kingdom of heaven." (Matthew 18:10, 3).

The work of another Cincinnati artist, Euphemia Bailey's *The Young Smoker* (FIG. 133), depicts a boy of six or seven years trying his first tobacco and emphasizes the sentimental message contained in most Volendam child pictures. Although the painting is lost, a drawing of it published in the *Commercial Gazette*, November 12, 1893, reveals that her subject not only wears clothes to look like his father, but Bailey has shown him trying to act like an adult as he puffs out his chest and takes his first drag of tobacco. The sweet, chubby features cause the incongruous act of smoking to appear charming. Public response when it was exhibited in Cincinnati may have been the same as that elicited by Caroline Lord's painting of a little Dutch girl. "It was amusing to see people standing before the canvas, smiling back at the child," wrote an observer.[182] The reaction of the Cincinnati audience to Dutch child paintings usually paralleled that of the artists to their models.

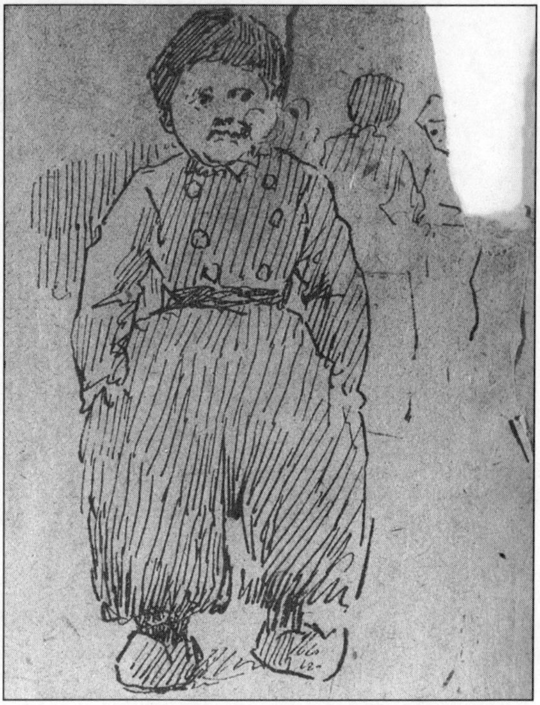

FIG. 133 *Although American tourists often faulted the Dutch for excessive smoking in public and were dismayed at the young age of Dutch smokers, Euphemia Bailey romanticized the image in her painting,* The Young Smoker, *seen here in an old newspaper rendering.*

Although Nourse chose to make her permanent home in Paris, her art, too, was well known in Cincinnati where many of her patrons resided. In 1893 she exhibited her European pictures at the Cincinnati Art Museum, including twenty-seven from Holland. The first two listed in the catalogue were her two Volendam salon pictures, offered for sale at $700 for *On the Dyke* and $800 for *In the Church at Volendam.* Most of the Dutch oil sketches ranged in price from $25 to $50, making them more affordable for the Cincinnatians who came to see her exhibition. She also showed consideration for her hometown by lowering the price of *On the Dyke* for the Queen City Club's consideration. When the Club decided against the purchase, she raised the price again.

From time to time in later years Nourse returned to the Dutch peasant subject. In 1895 she painted a picture of a Volendam woman sitting near a window sewing while her daughter looked over her shoulder to learn the technique. Mrs. Daniel B. Meacham purchased *The Sewing Lesson* for her Cincinnati home. It provided the type of tranquil domesticity that made such scenes acceptable as decorations in Victorian America. The theme of an older generation passing handicraft skills down to their children was strongly associated in American minds with the European peasant and a pre-industrial way of life. It was not at all unusual to find such agrarian scenes proliferating in the homes of rapidly industrializing cities like Cincinnati.

In addition to Wachman and Nourse, Caroline A. Lord apparently also worked in Volendam in the summer of 1892. Lord gave a drawing of a little girl to her Volendam landlord, Leendert Spaander, and exhibited two Volendam landscapes and a portrait the following spring. The Nourses, Wachmans, and Lord represented a small Cincinnati contingent in the busy Volendam art colony. They walked the narrow streets, met for coffee in the local hotel, watched the town's fishing fleet come and go from the harbor, and chatted with the local women and children. For one summer they did their best to fit into the remote Dutch village life while maintaining their American habits, and at the end of that time their paintings and drawings brought Volendam to life for their friends and neighbors in Cincinnati.

The Woman's Art Club of Cincinnati became an important agent in spreading Dutch influence from the art world to society at large. Local artists established the Woman's Art Club in 1892 because they were excluded from the Art Club, formed a few years earlier by the city's male artists. The women met monthly in members' studios, contributed studies of a predetermined theme for criticism, held annual fall and spring exhibitions, and sponsored social activities. At a meeting in her Covington, Kentucky home, Euphemia Bailey described her sketching trip through the Netherlands by canal boat with fellow member Christine Bredin. Another time the members put on a series of *tableaux vivants* by dressing up young society girls to look like the figures in paintings. Mary Stem, the debutante daughter of the president of an auto repair company, appeared in a black dress and white ruff as a Frans Hals painting. Still other meetings were devoted to lectures on Rembrandt, the contemporary Dutch painter Jozef Israëls, and the Golden Age of Dutch painting. Throughout the 1890s and later, members of the Woman's Art Club found their way to Holland or created Dutch pictures at home. The painters Euphemia Bailey, Christine Bredin, Alice and Jeannette Guysi, Atha Haydock, Eudora Hereford, Ysabel Kaplan, Caroline Lord, Emma Mendenhall, Dixie Selden, Mary Sheerer, Harriette Strafer, and Henrietta Wilson all submitted Dutch pictures to the club exhibitions.

By 1899 the club's exhibition was attracting between two thousand and twenty-five hundred visitors. Puzzled writers attributed this success to the social status of the artists, rather than to the art. For example, Caroline Lord, who sold the first picture from a Woman's Art Club exhibition, was the daughter of state senator Henry C. Lord. She lived in her parents' mansion in Riverside, a suburb four miles from Cincinnati on the Indianapolis, Cincinnati and Lafayette Railroad, of which her father was president. The names of Dixie Selden, the Wachman family, and Emma Mendenhall were also inscribed in Cincinnati's Blue Book, and the Guysi family owned a two-acre estate in Avondale, impressive enough to be mentioned in a contemporary guide book. "Perchance, it is the popularity of the women which is the reason for the tremendous crush of yesterday, and the day previous," wrote one critic. "Society honored the pictures, but also paid a willing homage to the club's members, who made the event one of much distinct social pleasure as they always do," noted another.[183] For reviewers of the exhibitions, who devoted almost as much space to reporting which women were present and who served tea at the opening as they did to critiques of the art, the social function served to legitimize the women's professional activities. For the artists, the social aspects of their meetings and exhibitions may have been a means of proving their femininity in the face of doubts that their serious artistic intentions may have raised.

Typically, Henrietta Wilson's eight North Holland paintings in the 1899 exhibition received effusive and uncritical praise in a local newspaper:

> They are unqualifiedly and unreservedly good. It would be difficult to single out from this...stunning series of watercolors any one especially deserving over its mates. They are all good. The foreign influence is manifest in every one of them. Miss Wilson would do well to paint some more of these things.[184]

In fact, Wilson occupied an important place in the art life of Cincinnati. As an instructor at the McMicken School—later the Cincinnati Art Academy—she became a role model and mentor for other women in the arts and she worked to improve art education and the lot of art teachers in the city. Wilson, together with Mary Spencer, first called upon the women of Cincinnati to form the Woman's Art Club, and she served as its president for several years.

A newspaper critique of another entry, Christine Bredin's painting *The Volendam Woman*, provides some information about the pictures she made in Holland and reveals some of the qualities Cincinnatians admired in them:

> The homely character of the good plain mother and the child, a chip of the old block, so entirely in keeping with the surroundings and all that they suggest, of the homely abode by the sea, the honest calling of the fisher husband and father, the shrinking a little from the gaze of some stranger, which makes one feel that a certain refinement and delicacy is not unknown in their humble lives, while their solid look of health and independent air inform one that the sons and daughters of luxury are not called upon to commiserate their lot.[185]

It is the moral worth of the subject—the sterling character of the Dutch people described in this short paragraph as good, plain, honest, refined, healthy, and independent—which the reviewer chose to praise rather than the manner in which the picture was painted. However, Bredin was generally considered one of the most advanced of Cincinnati's women artists, having studied with Carl

Marr in Munich and with Colarossi and Courtois in Paris before returning to teach in Cincinnati, and she received some of the highest prices for her work. A few years later she moved to New York City to try her fortune in a larger market. Whether the enforced social role proved a help or a hinderance to the artists depended on their individual ambitions, but it certainly played a part in transferring Dutch life from the canvas to real life in Cincinnati.

The nineteenth-century belief that women were by nature the guardians of culture played no small part in bringing the arts to the attention of society dames, and these women were the primary patrons of the Woman's Art Club. The movement to establish an art museum in Cincinnati had begun in 1877 when women of influence in the city formed the Woman's Art Museum Association. Many of the same people became involved in the Woman's Art Club activities. A spirit of sisterhood prevailed in this era when the male world was still largely closed to them. Among other things it took the form of moral and financial support for fellow Cincinnati women who painted, carved, and modeled in clay. In addition, social advantages accrued to women who became art patrons. They were publicly seen to be fulfilling the prescribed feminine role of cultural sponsor and gained favorable notice for it. When Miss Jessie Kennedy purchased Henrietta Wilson's painting of a fisherman's wife, *Volendam Vischvrouw* (FIG. 134), a local paper praised her choice as the cleverest of Wilson's Dutch subjects and congratulated her purchase.

While patronage for the Woman's Art Club came primarily from the upper echelons of local society, the pictures were within the means of many others. Mostly drawings, watercolors, and oil studies, they were offered for sale at the annual exhibitions for prices ranging from seven to fifty dollars. The average price started very low in the first exhibition and gradually rose to about twenty dollars in the late 1890s. Mrs. A. G. Corre, wife of a prominent hotelier, bought a painting by Christine Bredin of a little Dutch girl peeling apples for fifty dollars. Miss Van Voast, debutante daughter of a local colonel, owned a picture of Marken fishing boats by Henrietta Wilson and Miss Prague, member of a Cincinnati tobacco family, loaned *Zaandam Windmills*, by the same artist, to an exhibition in 1899.

EXPRESSIONS OF HOLLAND MANIA

Perhaps because the main patrons of this art were women and because the home was nineteenth-century woman's domain, it was

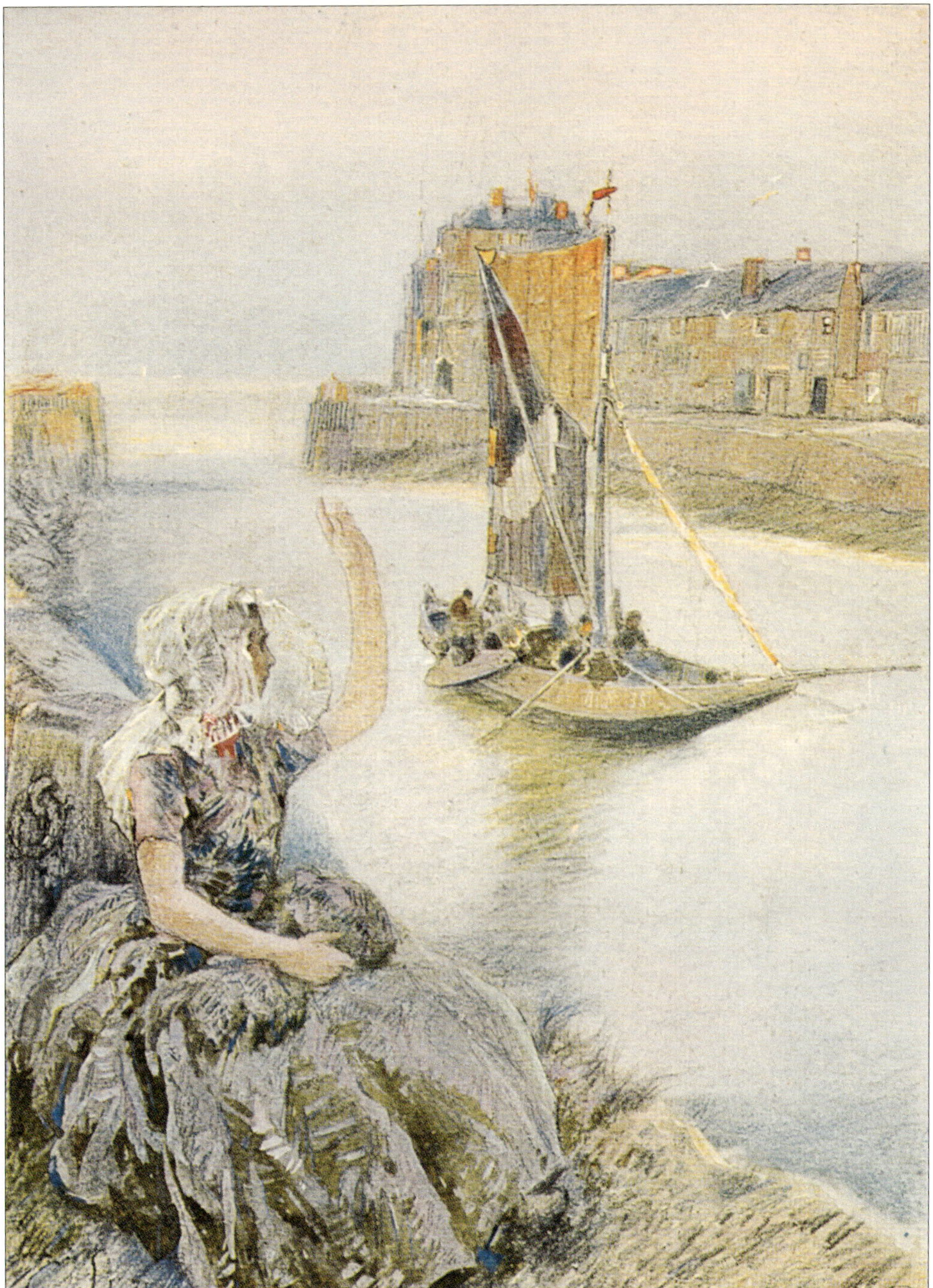

FIG. 87 *Although he called his travel book* Holland of Today, *George Wharton Edwards joined other writers and illustrators in emphasizing the old-fashioned costumes and leisurely rural life of Holland's yesterdays.*

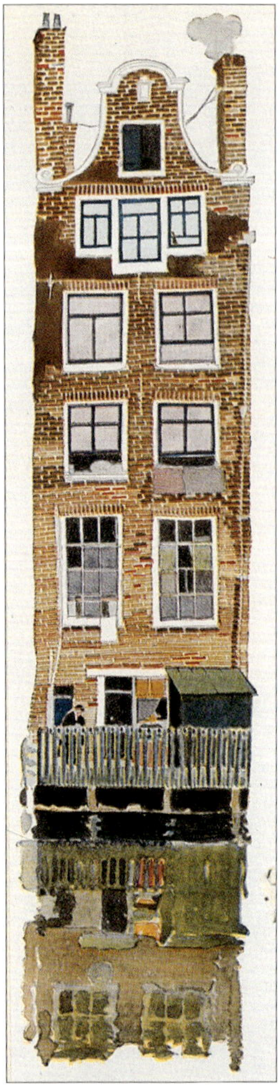

FIG. 94 *Edward Penfield proposed cutting down a canal house in Holland, like the one he drew to illustrate his book* Holland Sketches *(1907), and shipping it to New York to give that city an "authentic" example of its early architecture.*

FIG. 102 *H. W. Johns Manufacturing Company of New York published this Modern Dutch Colonial house in 1895 to promote their house paint and shingle stain.*

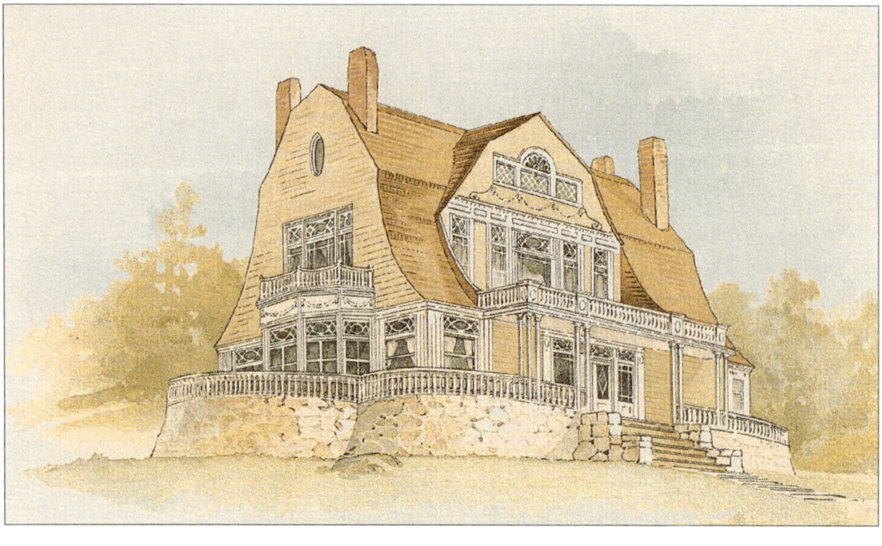

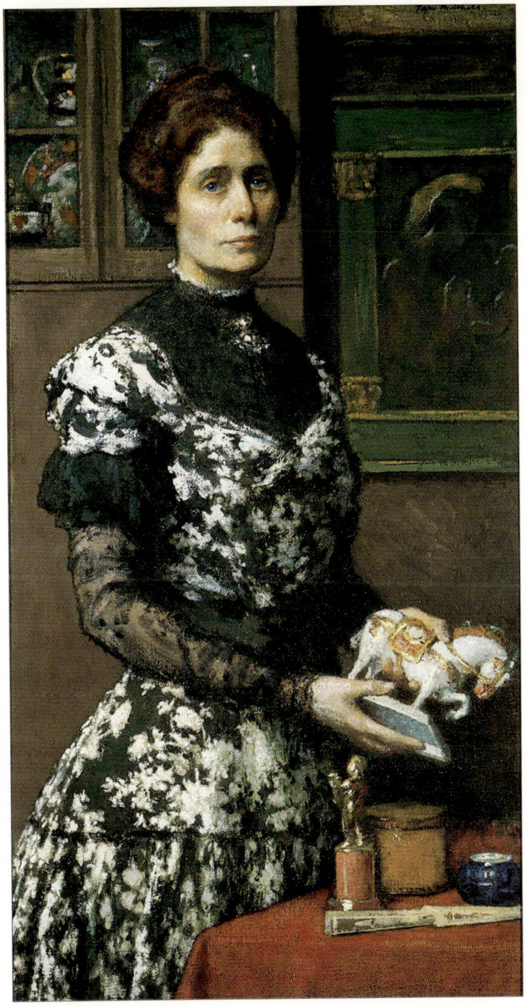

FIG. 106 *Gari Melchers painted two versions of* The Delft Horse *showing Henrietta Hitchcock with part of her collection of Dutch antiques.*

FIG. 108 *Charles P. Limbert prided himself on his Holland Dutch Arts and Crafts Furniture, produced by Dutch-American workers in Holland, Michigan. This library from a Limbert sales catalog features the company's "Flanders" line.*

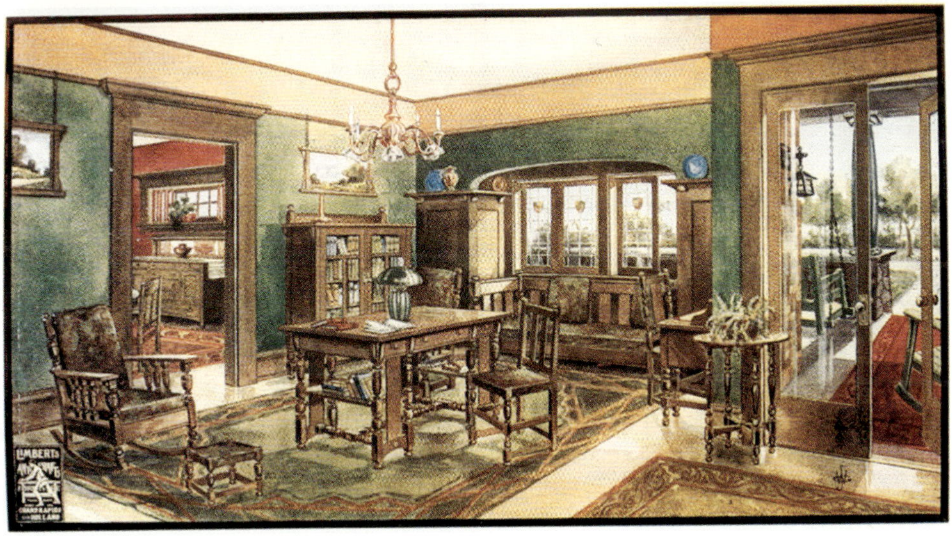

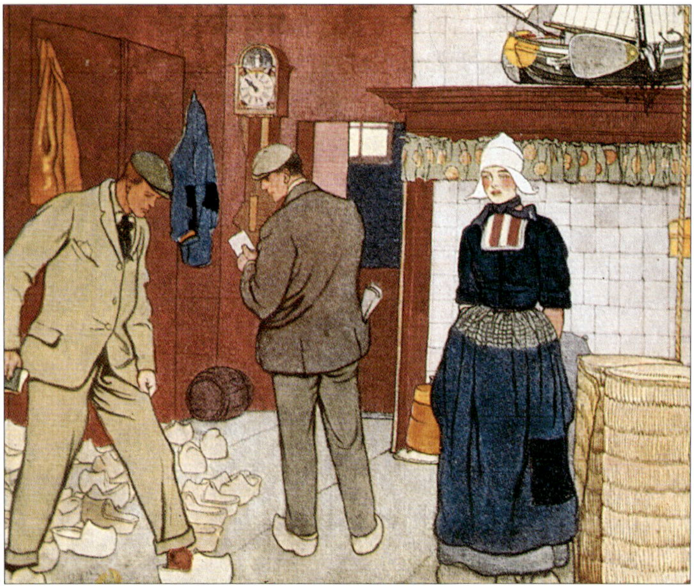

FIG. 119 *Stephen L. Bartlett, a Boston importer, called upon all the cliches of windmills, tulips and wooden shoes to sell Bensdorp's cocoa.*

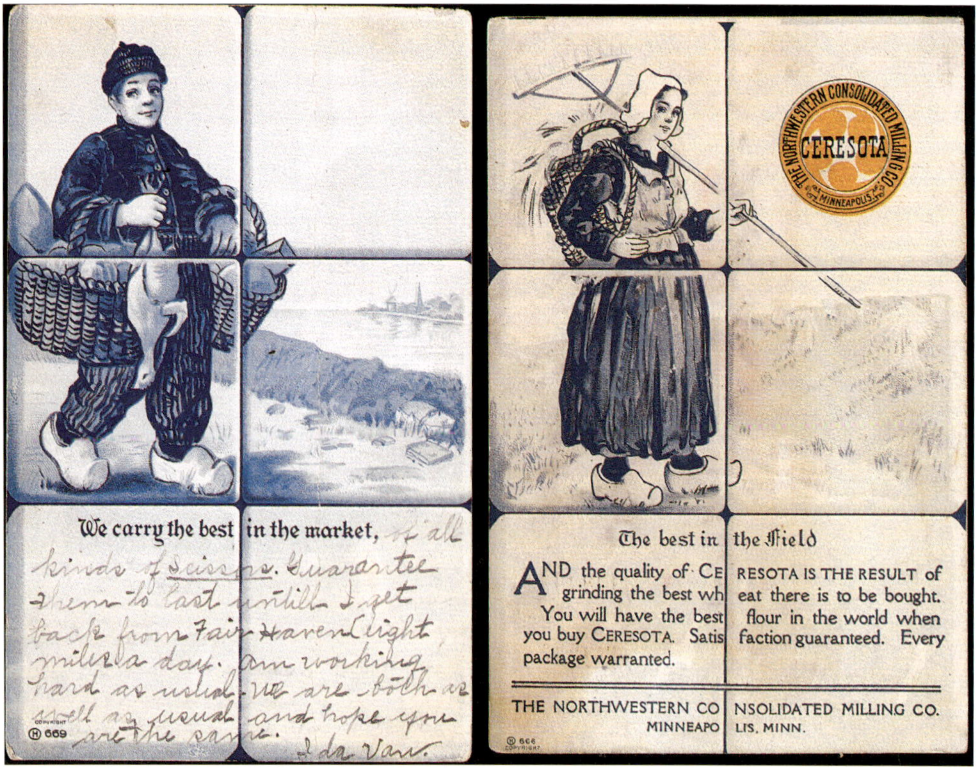

FIG. 123 *Sales people and small business owners used these Dutch tile postcards to promote items from scissors and cigars to flour.*

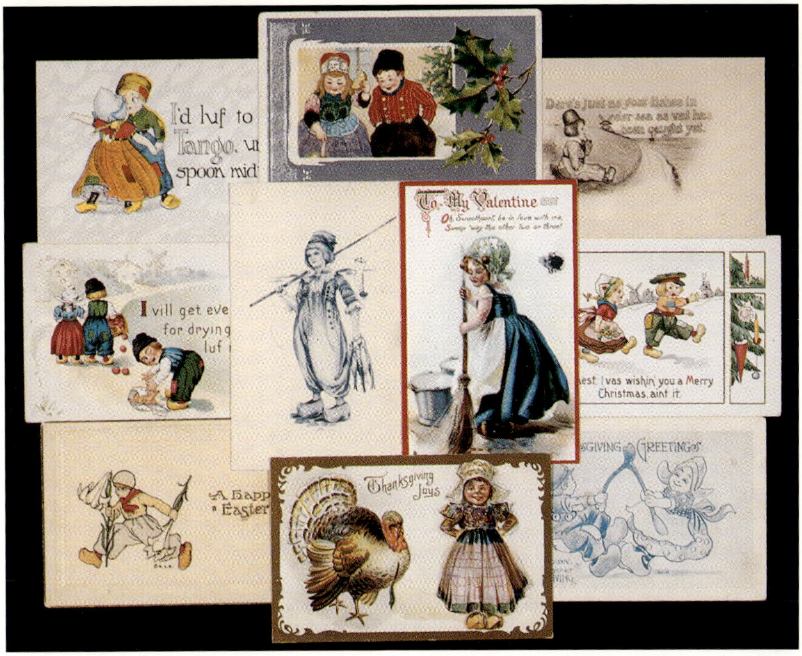

FIG. 124 *Images of Dutch kids made popular postal greeting cards for birthdays, holidays, and everyday.*

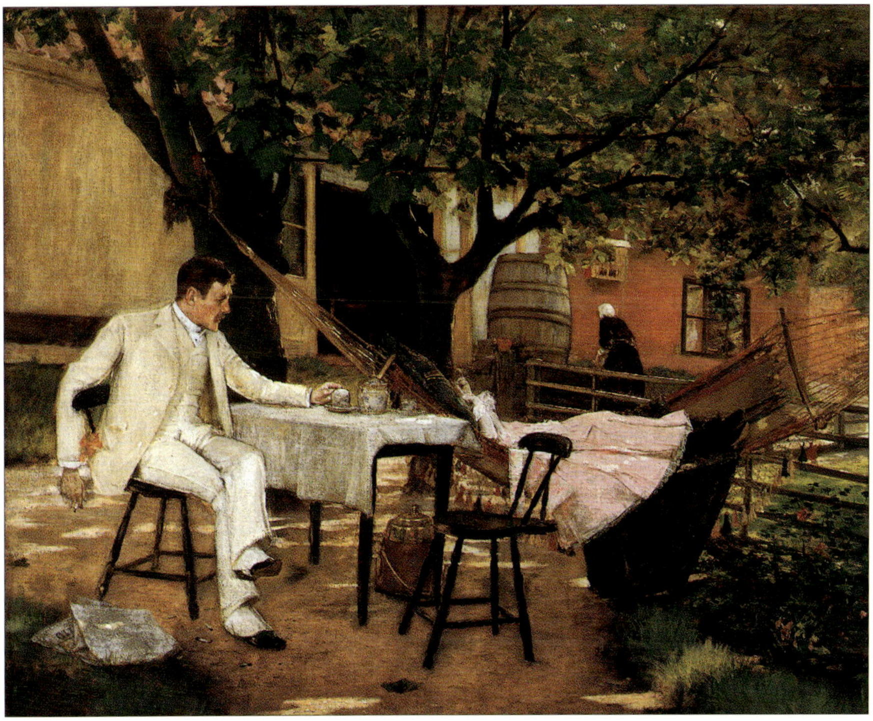

FIG. 125 *Cincinnati artist Robert Blum posed at the breakfast table in Zaandam for this painting by William Merritt Chase called* Sunlight and Shadow.

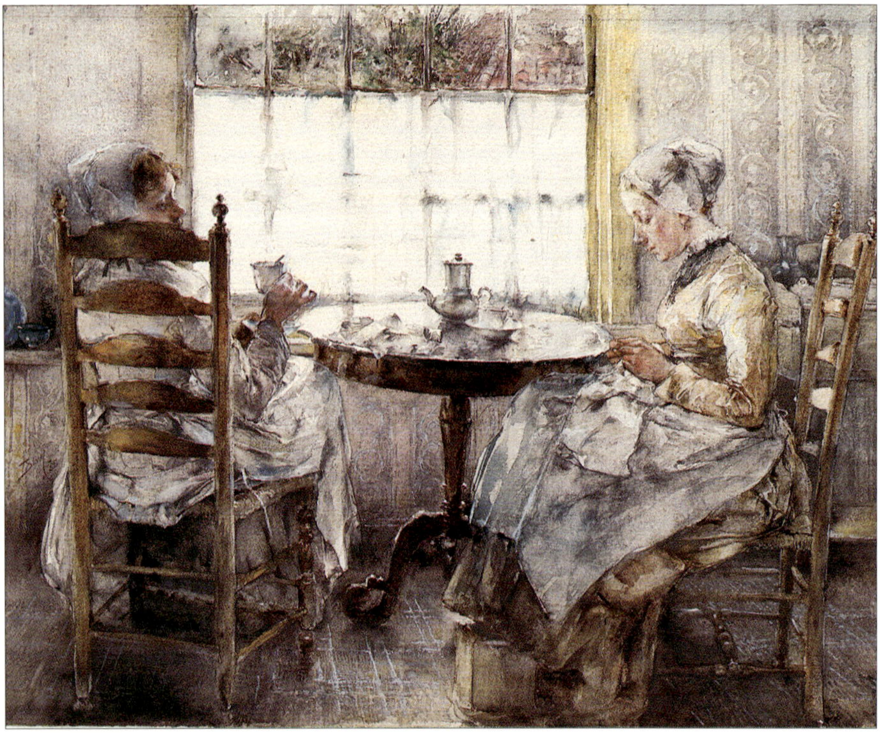

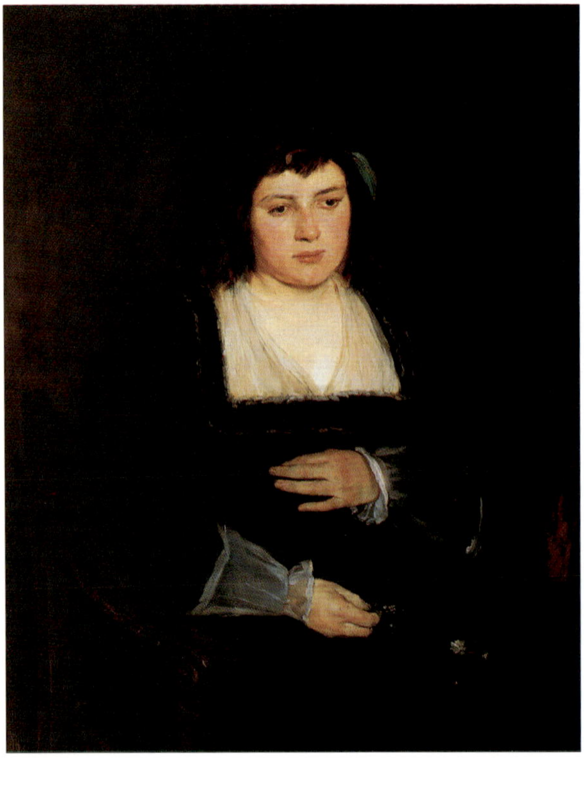

FIG. 126 *Dutch women knitting, feeding their babies or drinking tea with their feet on warming boxes became a favorite motif of American artists in Holland. Robert Blum painted* Two Dutch Girls Having Coffee *in Zandvoort in 1885.*

FIG. 129 *Frank Duveneck, dean of the Cincinnati artists, studied the work of the old Dutch masters whose influence is clearly evident in* Woman with Forget-Me-Nots.

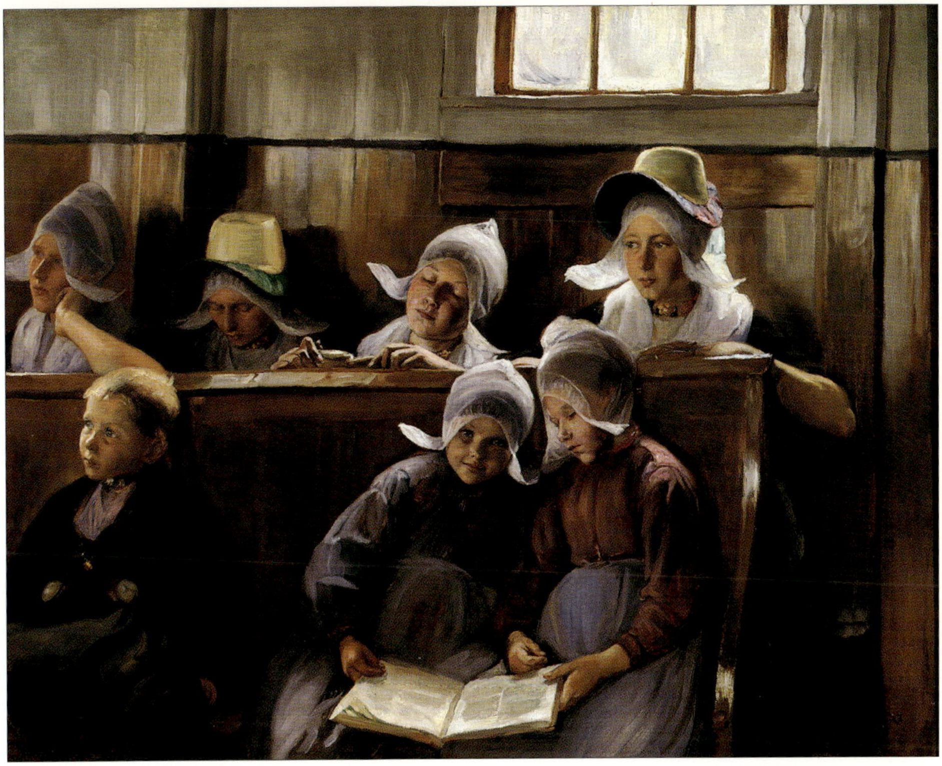

FIG. 132 *Elizabeth Nourse sold her painting,* In the Church at Volendam, *for $1000, but before it was delivered the new owner decided it was too large for the house and traded it for two smaller pictures.*

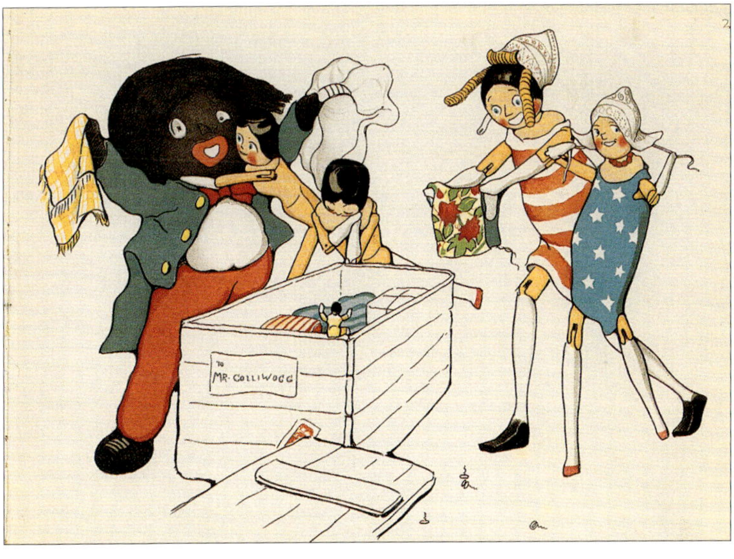

FIG. 141 *Some authors and illustrators combined Dutch and American ideas. The mother-daughter team of Bertha and Florence Upton caused their wooden doll characters to exchange American flag costumes for traditional Dutch clothes in their book* The Golliwogg in Holland, *1904.*

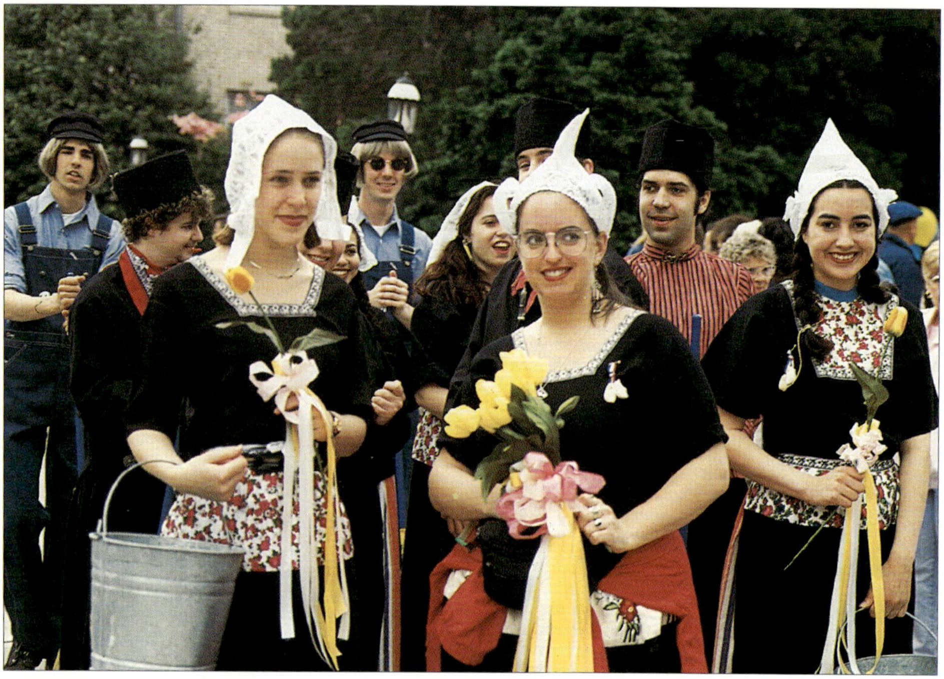

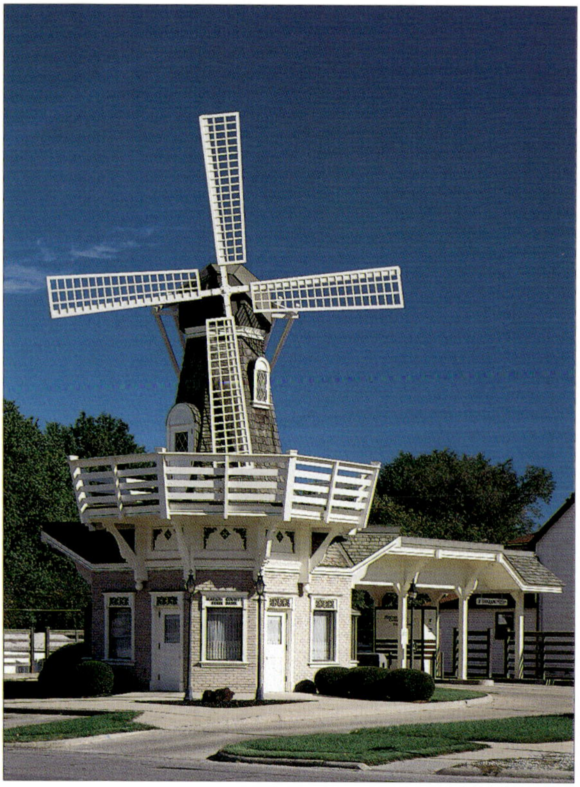

FIG. 147 *Annual Dutch festivals, like this one sponsored by Hofstra University on Long Island, help keep the Holland Mania image of the Dutch alive.*

FIG. 148 *Pella has capitalized on its Dutch heritage by remodeling and building new structures, like this drive-up bank, in a wide variety of Dutch and pseudo-Dutch styles.*

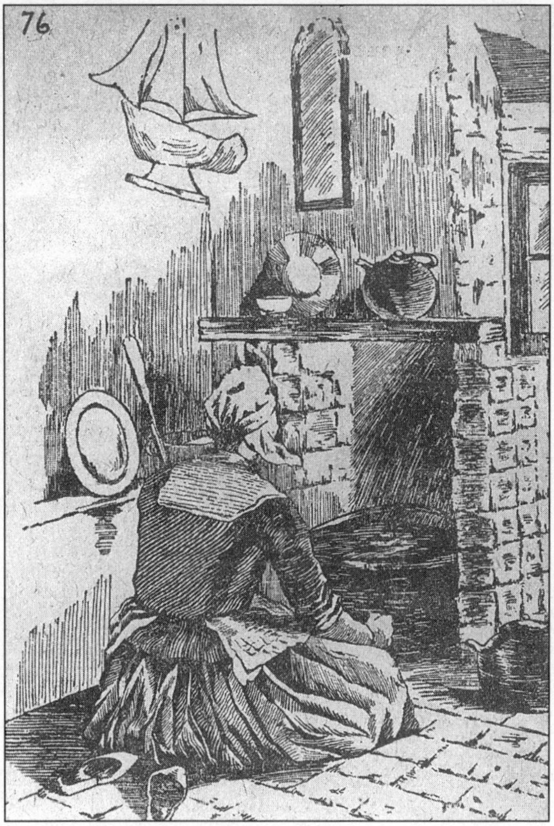

FIG. 134 *Henrietta Wilson pleased Cincinnati with her many paintings of life in Volendam. This drawing was published in a local newspaper to illustrate her painting* Volendam Vischvrouw (Volendam Fisherman's Wife).

not long before the Dutch motifs pictured in the artists' work began to have an effect on interior decoration in Cincinnati Society. Nourse had painted several views of Dutch house interiors, usually inhabited by a woman sewing or a couple seated by the hearth. These interiors disclosed some of the unique features of Dutch home life such as the beds built into the walls, huge open hearths with tile backs, narrow mantel shelves, and collections of delft plate decorating the walls. Henrietta Wilson's *Volendam Vischvrouw* depicted a costumed woman seated on the floor before the hearth in the subject's small house. A ship model hanging from the rafters indicated her husband's occupation while the various kitchen utensils surrounding her identified her tasks in the home. The wealth of details describing foreign housekeeping in Nourse's and Wilson's paintings attracted a female audience. "One constantly sees something new to study," wrote one Cincinnatian, "from the pretty tiles to the housewife peeling onions, the rows of jars, the plants, etc., and in fancy one can almost hear the kettle sing."[186] By 1900 the quantity of paintings of Holland being hung in Cincinnati's homes, and the attention paid to interior genre scenes with their "pretty tiles . . . the rows of jars, the plants, etc." had begun to establish a vogue for the Dutch motif in interior decoration. Nourse supplied Helen Rawson with a design for a ceramic plate depicting a Dutch milkmaid. Many women in Cincinnati were beginning to experiment with the decoration of ceramic wares and some of the blue and white china that began to appear in homes may have been produced locally. Although traditional Dutch design influence was not particularly evident in the art pottery movement, Cincinnati's Rookwood Pottery produced some wares decorated with old-master-style Dutch portraits in golden brown tones.

While most people settled for a few souvenirs, blue and white china and pictures of windmills or peasants, Simon Hubig ordered an entire frieze for the dining room of his Academy Avenue home. About eighteen inches high, it encircled the room above the windows and the oak paneled wainscoting. In panoramic fashion, the mural by local artist John Rettig described a day in the life of Volendam, from the boats leaving the harbor at dawn, to villagers gossiping on the dike in the afternoon, and cows grazing outside the town in the evening. The figures represented real people whom the artist knew in Volendam.

John and May Rettig went considerably further in decorating their own home in the Dutch manner. They brought home enough furniture, tiles, and housewares from their trips in the Netherlands to furnish an entire room (FIG. 135). Among other things, it contained an old delft tile fireplace from Veere, a cupboard bed, a turf pot and brass bedwarmer from Dordrecht, a Zaandam tobacco box, ships' models from Hoorn, an Edam ginger jar, tea cups, silver spoons, and costumes from Goes, Middleburg, Scheveningen, and Volendam. This Dutch room served Rettig as a studio and became the setting of many of the paintings that would decorate his neighbors' homes. Naturally, with such a hodge podge of items, the paintings might have lacked cohesion and authenticity to a Dutch eye, but they appear to have satisfied Cincinnati buyers who knew that the individual details were authentic. As Holland Mania gained momentum, the Dutch room also became a focal point for Cincinnati social events, thereby familiarizing more people with Dutch decor.

At least one man used Dutch subject paintings to help decorate his place of business. Theodore Foucar owned a saloon on Walnut Street and acquired a collection of paintings by local artists Frank Duveneck, Henry Sharp, Henry Farny, and John Rettig to help set the tone of his establishment. By offering a free lunch of beef, ham, caviar, and other delicacies with the purchase of a five-cent glass of beer, he attracted a lunchtime clientele of downtown businessmen. For many years Foucar's Cafe was one of the most stylish restaurants in town, attracting the patronage of Cincinnati's social elite. It was decorated in marble and wood paneling with brass fixtures and the paintings gave it a final touch of class. He paid between $40 and $500 for each of his three Dutch Rettigs. With the advent of prohibition, Foucar closed his business, gave one painting to the Cincinnati Art Museum, and used the rest to decorate his home.

Some of the city's social events also took on a Dutch flavor at this time. In 1897 seventy men attended a New Netherland Christmas Dinner, an event that occupied the city papers' social

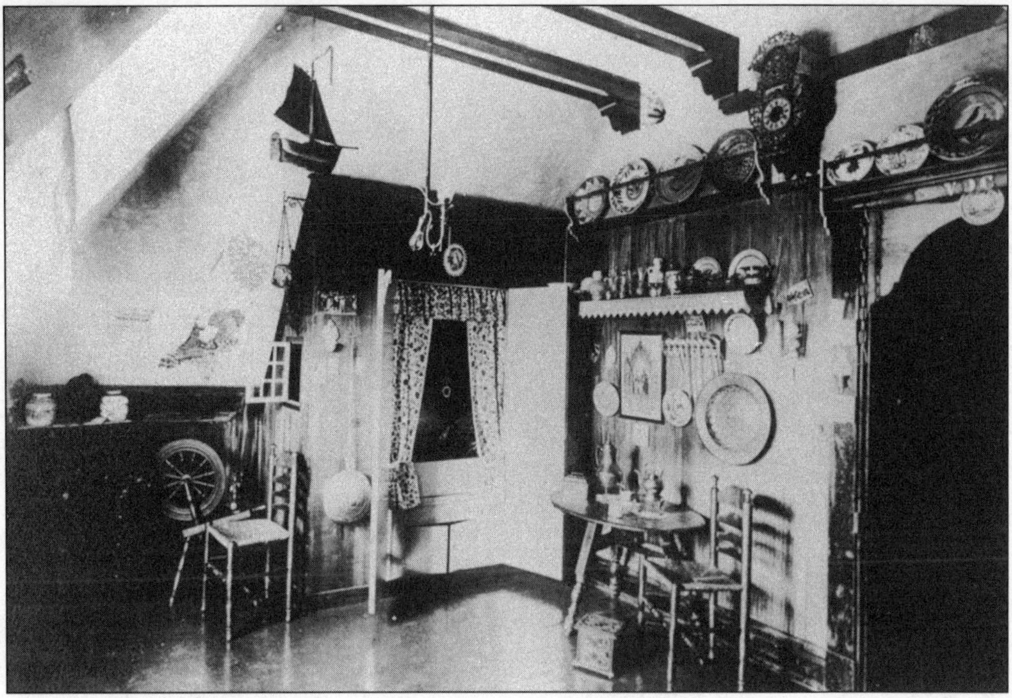

FIG. 135 *John and May Rettig assembled a Dutch room in their Kemper Lane home. They sent this postcard of it to Mrs. Spaander in 1908. After John's death in 1932, the whole room was removed to the Holland Museum in Holland, Michigan.*

pages for a month preceding it and continued to excite conversation long after. According to one source, the men chose the Dutch theme "as being most picturesque, not only on account of the costumes in vogue at that time, but because history at that period was going through with some of its most sensational chapters."[187] All the guests dressed in costumes of the era from 1620 to 1700. Some came as wealthy Dutch burghers, and others imitated trumpeters, pirates, and Indians. Rudolph Wurlitzer won accolades as a Dutch peasant girl while Charles Webber donned wooden shoes and peasant dress to impersonate a Dutch farmer. Many of the men chose Dutch names for the evening. Presiding over the meal in the guise of Peter Stuyvesant, complete with fake wooden leg, sat the photographer Leon Van Loo. A great favorite in Cincinnati, his Belgian ancestry as much as his affectionate nickname "Burgomaster" earned him the role of the Governor General of New Netherland. The evening entertainment consisted of an original play wherein Stuyvesant, the Dutch farmer, Rip Van Winkle, and a crew of pirates from the mock ship Black Dutchman, played starring roles. Parts of "authentic" New Amsterdam documents were read, toasts proposed, and the whole published in the paper for the entertainment of those not in attendance.

A few years later the MacDowell Society of Cincinnati put on another play with a cast of characters including Rip Van Winkle, Rembrandt—Captain of the Night Watch, Pieter de Hoogh—Drummer, and Jan Steen—first shooter. The contents of the play are difficult to reconstruct but the cast certainly suggests a Dutch theme with artistic inspiration.

In the late 1880s, iron manufacturer James Albert Green and Dr. Le Boutillier collaborated on an illustrated lecture called "Irving and the Hudson." While Green described the Tarrytown–Sleepyhollow area and recounted some of Washington Irving's Dutch tales, Le Boutillier showed dissolving stereopticon views from the men's travels through the Hudson Valley. Green explained that Irving had made his home, Sunnyside, thoroughly Dutch and had sent Diedrich Knickerbocker into retirement there to write his history of the Dutch in America. The stereoviews gave their Cincinnati audience a look at the original settings for the tales of Mynheer Van Tassel and his daughter Katrina, Ichabod Crane, Rip Van Winkle, and other favorite characters. Other public lectures in Cincinnati at the turn of the century included talks on the art of the Netherlands and life in Holland. The public library sponsored a lecture for the Children of the Republic, a young persons organization, about the children of Holland.

Many of Cincinnati's business elite traveled with their families to the Netherlands for vacations. Amsterdam and The Hague found favor, but because of their previous exposure to Volendam through art exhibitions and lectures, most Cincinnatians described Volendam as the primary attraction. Some were lucky enough to be guided through the town by Cincinnati artists residing there. They were introduced to the hotel keeper Leendert Spaander, his wife Aaltje, and their nine children, and to some of the residents whose portraits decorated many a Cincinnati home (FIG. 136). They saw the harbor with its fishing fleet, took the canal boat to Edam to visit a cheese market, and sailed to the island of Marken.

Tourism and art proved mutually supportive. The steady stream of Cincinnati tourists encouraged artists to produce more paintings of Volendam, and their travels induced Cincinnati's citizens to buy them for souvenirs. James Albert Green, the news reporter and city editor who went into the iron and steel business and is best known for his tireless work to establish a public library in Cincinnati, visited Volendam's Hotel Spaander in June or July of 1906. At an art sale in Cincinnati the following spring he bought a painting of the dike on which the hotel is located. Paul Schulze wrote to the creator of his painting of Volendamer

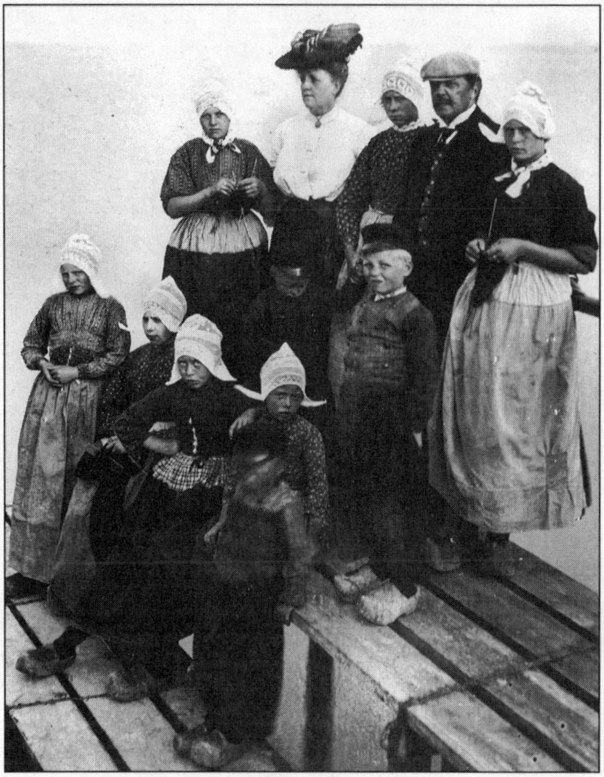

FIG. 136 *May and John Rettig (top row), who had no children of their own, became quite attached to his Volendam models. They took the children on outings and threw parties for them.*

Jan van Ompie: "I assure you that it will always be a pleasant reminder of our visit to your studio."[188] In 1930, one of the last years he was there, artist John Rettig reported that he had 81 visitors from Cincinnati. Reviewing one of Rettig's exhibitions, Cherry Greve noted: "If one has ever been to Volendam he will revel in this exhibition as I did; without that good fortune one can get a real idea of the place from these paintings, for they can truly be called Volendam."[189]

Both art and travel aroused Cincinnati's curiosity about life in Volendam. The city newspapers published letters from travelers abroad and carried pictures and descriptions of individual Volendamers. Thus, residents of the Queen City learned that the men of Volendam feted Christmas with a barrel of Wiedemann beer from the Cincinnati/Newport brewer. They knew that Geertje Boosman had begun supporting her family at age six by posing for artists and that seven-year-old Bregje wanted to move to Cincinnati and experience for herself all the things she had heard about from tourists. Under the headline "Cincinnati Girls Donned Dutch Attire in Holland," appeared a story about two young women who put on Dutch costumes while staying in Volendam and fooled some newly arrived American college men into thinking they were Dutch—until their silk stockings gave them away.

It was only a short step from playing dress up in Volendam to recreating Dutch life in Cincinnati. After her trip to Holland, Isabel Neff had her cooking class at Woodward High School prepare a Dutch tea for the community, served by students in full Dutch costume. The students put on a play while Neff gave a talk on cooking schools in Holland and May Rettig entertained the guests with a description of Dutch markets. After 1900 debutante events picked up the Dutch theme with a vengeance. The mothers of Ethel Graydon and Roberta Dohrmann honored their junior debutante daughters at a Dutch tea party where Miss Graydon wore a traditional costume and headdress of South Holland and Miss Dohrmann appeared in the elaborate Volendam attire (FIG. 137). Both girls carried wooden Dutch dolls and guests received blue and white china figurines of a Dutch girl and boy as party favors. The event took place in Rettig's Dutch Room at Kemper Lane, a room that also hosted social events for the Norwood Literary Club, Cincinnati Crafters, and the Household Department of the University Club. In addition, Dutch dress became a favorite at the Riding Club's annual masque ride and ball for debutantes and their escorts. In 1908 Ethel Graydon won first place for another Holland costume, an outfit she had purchased on the island of Marken during a trip to Holland, and she was not the only "Dutch peasant" in the contest. Such "dressing up" was confined to the women, however, as their escorts wore contemporary evening clothes.

After 1900 the artist John Rettig and his wife May were often to be found at the center of Cincinnati's Dutch affairs. They had discovered Volendam in 1903 and for a time thereafter spent at least six months of each year living in Spaander's hotel. John rented space for a studio in the attic of a fish warehouse (FIG. 138). While he painted, May entertained his child models, importing a chest of toys and clothes from Cincinnati each year for that purpose. She also attended weddings and funerals and chatted with the village women. On Rettig's birthday she distributed pastries to all his models and the couple often took their Dutch friends and models on picnics and canal excursions. Each incident received full coverage with pictures in the Cincinnati press. The Rettigs' attitude toward their hosts was unintentionally patronizing, but Cincinnati writers liked to describe the Rettigs as living the life of the Volendamers and fitting right in. When John Rettig wore wooden shoes on the winter streets of Cincinnati it was hailed as another instance of his complete conversion to Dutch custom.

Each winter the Rettigs returned to the United States, stopping in New York City for a few weeks to exhibit the season's products and then returning to Cincinnati, where the Dutch exhibition became an annual institution. Rettig's Dutch exhibition was described by one writer as the art event of the year. May served tea and helped her husband regale their visitors with stories of each of the models and settings in the pictures. Many were simply sketches tacked unstretched to the wall. He displayed a few in simple frames and one or two of his best pieces were treated with a more formal

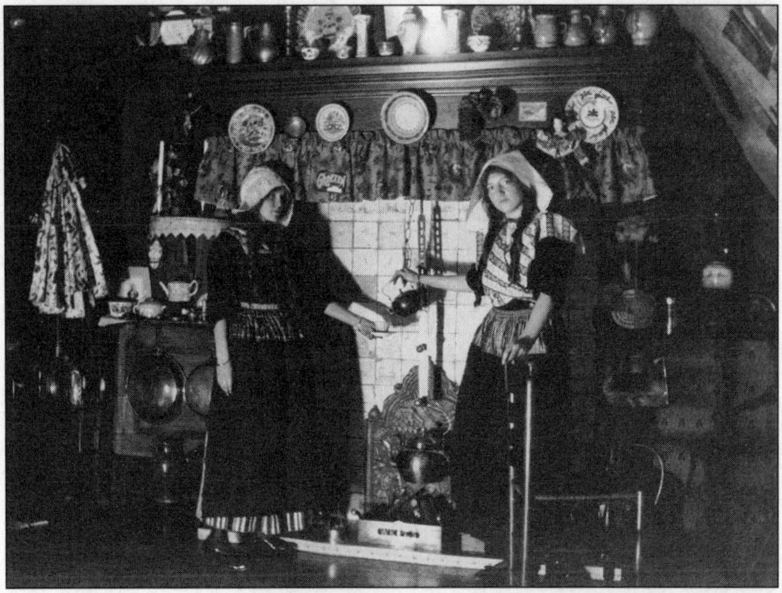

FIG. 137 *The Dutch look became so popular that young socialites Helen Graydon and Roberta Dohrmann wore complete Dutch costumes for a debutante party in their honor.*

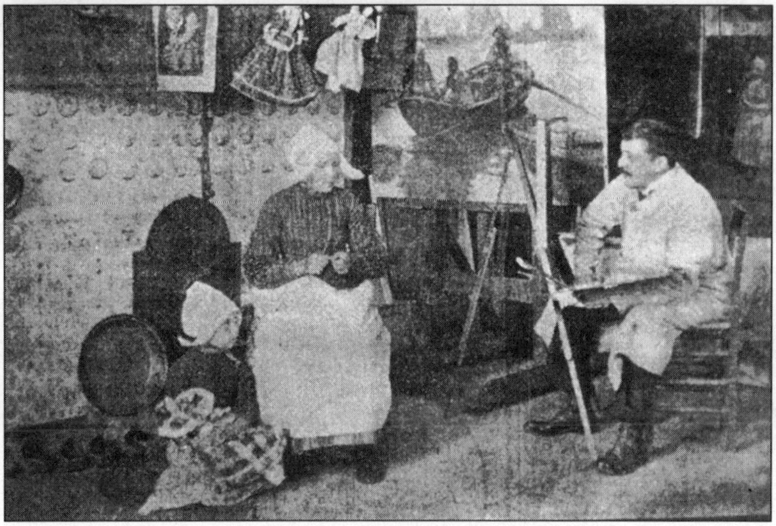

FIG. 138 *The* Cincinnati Times-Star *published this photograph of John Rettig painting in his Volendam warehouse studio around 1906.*

presentation. Rettig kept a list of his patrons and acquaintances and sent out invitations each year. His social standing ensured an adequate number of likely buyers and he did very well with this marketing technique. For the rest of his stay in Cincinnati he would finish paintings or start new ones from his sketches and participate in the city's social and art life. After five trips to Volendam he considered moving there permanently but apparently decided it would be more convenient to bring Holland to Cincinnati. It was at that time that he created the Dutch room. After 1908 he stayed in

Cincinnati and painted in his Dutch room using local models dressed in the costumes he had purchased or relying on memory and sketches. He finally returned to Holland in 1925 and 1929.

Rettig followed the precedent of earlier artists in his choice of subjects. Many depicted children playing with toys. Others showed the harbor, streets, and dike of the town. He painted the kermis—an annual lenten festival, women washing clothes in the harbor, fishermen smoking on the quay, and their wives visiting in the streets. He also painted many interiors in which one or two costumed figures sip tea, knit, or enjoy a smoke. Many of his paintings are simply portraits of his favorite models, people like Heinje Tol and Arisje Koning who became familiar to Cincinnati society because their visages appeared year after year on the walls of the city's galleries and found resting places in homes in Avondale, Mt. Auburn, and other upper middle-class neighborhoods. Not only Rettig, but also Anthony Biester, George Debereiner, Edward Potthast, and F. Carl Smith painted and exhibited such pictures in the early twentieth century.

Through endless repetition, the image of the Volendamer gained recognition as *the* Holland type. In actuality, Volendam dress was never representative of the Netherlands, or even of a province. Only the relatively few people who actually lived in and around the town of Volendam ever wore it and it was just one of numerous distinctive costumes that survived in the Netherlands at the end of the century. Artists, illustrators, and advertisers portrayed it so often, however, that it became a symbol of the entire country. Through their proliferation of the image, Cincinnati artists contributed to the American conception of the Dutchman as an anachronistic, wooden-shod, pipe smoking seaman, and his wife as a quaintly clad knitter.

Advertisers did their part to spread the Volendam image (FIG. 139). The Potter Shoe Company and Alms and Doepke promoted their Red Cross shoe among Cincinnati women by showing a picture of a Volendam woman wearing *klompen* and asking "Did YOU ever walk in wooden shoes?" The ad copy compared ordinary shoes to wooden shoes in order to emphasize the comfort of their brand's flexible leather, but the effectiveness of the marketing ploy resided in the proven appeal of the Volendam image. The Baldwin Piano Company and Cincinnati Art Club used Volendam scenes on their calendars, United Playing Card Company purchased an image of Volendam boats—presumably for the back of their playing cards, and John Rettig designed a winter scene of the Volendam harbor for the ice rink at the Zoo. So ubiquitous was the decorative costume of Volendam that when one

Cincinnati tourist finally laid eyes on real Volendamers he could only think to describe them as looking "just like the pictures of the Hollanders on the wall-paper borders."[190]

PATRONAGE

Who were the people in Cincinnati who absorbed the wealth of Dutch images being produced? The role of society women in supporting the efforts of female artists has already been discussed, but only accounts for a portion of the total. Noting the remarkable range of prices paid for Dutch oil paintings, one would suspect that homes from the working class to the upper class housed them. The range of prices, though, is misleading. Investigation of each sale of a Dutch painting by John Rettig, for example, whose work brought from five dollars to twelve hundred dollars, reveals a client of substantial income. The only painting by Rettig definitely in the hands of a working-class citizen during the artist's lifetime was a still life Rettig donated to a local festival. Adam Voelker wrote to inform the artist that he had won the picture and admired it the more because he could not have afforded it. He confided, "Dear Sir you may rest assured that your fine painting will be more appreciated in the home of a workingman than in many a home of the rich."[191] Dutch images generally entered working class homes by way of prints, magazine illustrations, printed fabrics, and wallpapers.

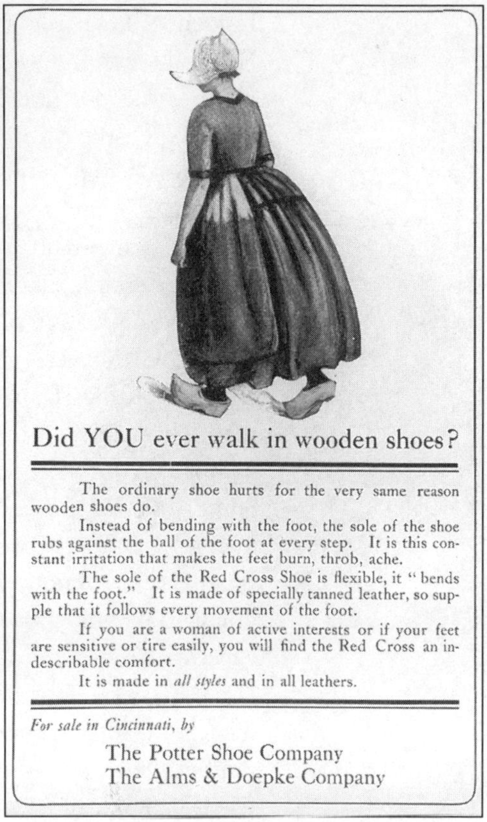

FIG. 139 *The Volendam figure became so common in Cincinnati that she even helped to sell shoes.*

A few Dutch paintings by Cincinnati artists did become part of local millionaires' collections. Learner Blackman Harrison's estate was valued at five million dollars when he died a few years after he and his wife purchased one of Nourse's Dutch figure paintings. Louis J. Hauck inherited the John Hauck Brewing Company from his father and also became involved in banking, railroads, and real estate. He built a mansion on "Millionaire's Row" not far from the brewery and purchased paintings by local artists to decorate it, including *The Net Maker of Volendam* by John Rettig. Hauck's sister Emilie married Charles H. Heine, a financier and grocery tycoon, and lived in a stone residence down the street from her brother. She also purchased a Holland scene from Rettig. But some of the best and most expensive pictures did not find buyers in Cincinnati at all. John Rettig's two most expensive paintings entered New York collections and neither of Nourse's important Volendam salon paintings found a home in Cincinnati. The majority of the Dutch paintings produced by resident Cincinnati artists were purchased in the local market by upper-middle-class professionals, businessmen, and their wives.

An examination of John Rettig's sales records for the period from 1900 to 1915 reveals that at least thirty-five Cincinnatians purchased Dutch paintings from him. Three-quarters of them were businessmen, the majority of whom owned or were presidents of their own companies. Another twelve percent were lawyers and/or politicians. Some, like Edmund H. Lunken, inherited their wealth and their business. Others struggled up from obscurity to make a place for themselves. Simon Hubig is a typical collector of Dutch images—one who remained firmly in the middle class in spite of his business success. He was born to German immigrants in the working class community of Newport, Kentucky. His father, a rolling-mill worker, died soon after Simon's birth in 1860. He went to work in his mother's bakery business while still a child and by age fifteen had reached the position of foreman. Having learned the business thoroughly, in 1891 Simon Hubig opened his own bakery in Price Hill, Cincinnati. The lower slopes of Price Hill housed factories, shops, and stockyards while the upper slopes were mainly populated by middle-income families. Many of the inhabitants were Irish and German Catholic workers who commuted to the city on the electric streetcars. Hubig made his home on Purcell Avenue near his bake shop. He rapidly expanded his business and moved it into a new brick plant on West Fifth Street. By 1910 he was said to have the largest bakery in the United States, producing about thirty thousand pies daily. Hubig specialized in honey fruit pies and originated the idea of selling pies in a variety of sizes, including a small one for schoolchildren's lunches that proved extremely popular. He patented specially designed bags and crates that enabled him to ship pies all over the country. In addition to his pie business he owned the Domestic-Science Baking Company for the automated production of bread and became a director of the Cosmopolitan Bank of Cincinnati.

Simon Hubig bought his first two Rettig's in 1907, a harbor scene and a large oil panel called *At the Rudder*. He paid $100 and $125, respectively, very typical prices for Rettig's Dutch oil paintings. Hubig purchased the pictures to decorate the new home he had built at 1055 Academy Avenue. Part of a subdivision of about twenty acres developed in the 1890s and named for the Sisters of Charity Academy that had owned it, it was a step up from his previous domicile but was still in the Price Hill neighborhood. No matter how wealthy he became, Hubig continued to identify with his working-class roots, rubbing shoulders with working neighbors and managing the daily operations of his bakery himself.

Apparently satisfied with his first purchases, the next year Hubig commissioned Rettig to paint a twenty-panel mural of Volendam for his dining room. Hubig was not Dutch by ancestry, nor is there a record of his traveling in Holland, though he may have done so. His acquisition of $2,675 worth of Dutch subject paintings, including the full-scale panorama of Volendam, are clear indications of his predilection for Holland motifs in the decoration of his home. He continued to buy individual Dutch paintings at intervals even after he moved his home and business headquarters to Texas. In 1924 he apparently beat another buyer to *The Young Mother*, a picture of a Volendam woman sewing by a cradle. Congratulating Rettig on his "splendid creations," Hubig assured the artist that the picture was hanging in the parlor and was feeling at home. He expressed sympathy for the disappointed buyer and invited her to come see it at any time.[192] Hubig also collected a few Rettigs done on other subjects and bought pictures by other American painters, many of them from Cincinnati. By 1909 a local newspaper described his as the most interesting private collection of paintings in the city. According to this account, Hubig intended to build a gallery onto his house to be opened to the public, but nothing seems to have come of this. He did give a large Rettig painting, an allegory of history, to Price Hill for their new high school building, but there is little other evidence of activity as an art benefactor. The intention of making a public collection and the gift of a painting to the community set him apart somewhat from other middle-class patrons. But Hubig's use of paintings to decorate his home, his exclusive interest in American art, and his support of local artists whom he knew personally are all typical of the middle-class buyer.

One of Hubig's neighbors on Price Hill, Perrin P. Hunter, also wanted to support the arts locally. Understanding the appeal of Dutch subjects in Cincinnati, Hunter not only helped Rettig finance his first trips abroad, but in 1906 he wrote to the artist in Volendam to suggest another means of helping him get ahead. He proposed that

Rettig paint any subject of his choice in Holland, bring it back to Cincinnati, and place it in his annual exhibition so it would be reviewed in the local papers. Then Hunter would have it framed, quietly pay the artist $100, and submit it to the art committee of the Queen City Club. In that manner it would be placed in one of the city's most popular and exclusive clubs where it might gain Rettig new clients. The first part of the plan was apparently carried out, and Hunter bought *Gossipers* the next year for $100. As the Queen City Club has no record of the painting, however, Hunter may have kept it in his own collection. Housed on the second floor of the American Carriage Company, of which Hunter was proprietor and president, his "Metropolitan Collection of Pictures and Curios" also included paintings of Dordrecht, a medieval Dutch city in South Holland.[193]

Many of John Rettig's patrons wrote to him to express their pleasure in his Dutch paintings. The letter writers followed a formula in which they first described where in their homes they had hung the picture and then reported that all their friends admired it. A note from John Graydon, treasurer of the Macdonald Kiley shoe manufacturing company, concerning a painting of a little Volendam boy typifies the formula: "I am enclosing blank check signed. Fill in with the amount you would have charged any outsider for that picture. It looks dandy in the dining room, and everybody admires it."[194] Rettig charged him fifty dollars. This consistent response suggests two things. First, Dutch paintings were purchased as decorations for the home, not (with the exceptions already noted) as part of an art collection to be viewed by the public or donated to an institution, nor as a financial investment. Their exact location in the home was important as it signified the esteem in which the painting was held; places of honor included the dining room and the overmantel in the parlor. William Bainbridge, a New York shipper and framer, reported to Rettig that he had been called in to hang paintings for Mrs. Ehret, one of Rettig's most important New York patrons. Bainbridge noted that Mrs. Ehret was pleased with the hanging of *Cleaning Day* over the sideboard in her dining room.[195] Cincinnati railroad manufacturer Horace Males assured Rettig that he had given *On the Dyke* a place that would please the artist, and another owner informed Rettig that she had tried her painting on all four walls to find the best place for it.[196] Second, a painting's success was determined by the admiration of the owner's circle of friends. The paintings were usually meant to enhance the owner's standing among his or her own social group, and they succeeded to the degree that friends and relatives admired the patron's choice. This may also provide a clue to the continued popularity of Dutch scenes. Once a few members of a social set took it up, others not wishing to be left behind followed suit.

John Rettig often made judicious gifts of his paintings. Herbert Corey, the Cincinnati *Times Star*'s New York correspondent, received *A Dutch Grandfather* in 1906 after he had given Rettig's Dutch exhibition a favorable review, and he continued to notice Rettig's annual shows thereafter. Apparently overwhelmed by the importance of the painting, which he said brought tears to his wife's eyes whenever she looked at it, he wrote to thank the artist. Corey conferred the highest praise on Rettig by noting that his wife had reorganized their entire flat around the painting.[197] On other occasions Rettig used a gift to reanimate a patron who had not made a purchase for a few years, or to sweeten the price of a painting for a hesitant buyer. He also gave a Dutch landscape to Clara Ann Rich Devereux, the acknowledged arbiter of Cincinnati society. Devereux wrote the social column for a local paper, served as a clearing house for the city's social calendar, and edited the Blue Book. Her goodwill must have been valuable for securing invitations and meeting prospective patrons.

For the most part, Rettig's patrons had little experience of art and lacked confidence in their aesthetic judgment. They based their choices, instead, on a set of criteria that included personal acquaintance with the artist, knowledge of the subject, and fashionability. None of Rettig's Cincinnati patrons appears to have been of Dutch descent, so their appreciation of Holland art was not motivated by ancestry. However, Josephine Woodward may have expressed another reason for the Dutch fad when she thanked Rettig for his gift of a small painting of the Monnikendam mill. Remarking that she was glad it depicted a windmill, she added: "It may be I've a invisible temperament that makes me take to them."[198] This kind of "invisible temperament" toward a particular motif has caused collecting fads in our own time for images of pigs and cows. Windmills appear to have had this same compulsive appeal for some people at the turn of the century. For example, Margaret Woodbury Strong's early twentieth-century collection of art and kitsch in Rochester, New York includes innumerable windmills in watercolor, oil, and ceramic.

The expanding market for Dutch images in Cincinnati supported the activities of many local artists between 1880 and 1930. The Holland pictures in turn spurred residents' fascination with the Netherlands, affecting tourism, advertising, interior decoration, and social events.

Conclusion

THE CURRENTS OF THOUGHT AND EVENTS SURROUNDING the widespread Dutch cultural influence that began around 1880 and spread to many areas of American life in the following four decades are complex. Once it started, every new manifestation in art, entertainment, interior design, history, fashion, and architecture encouraged it to grow, but a broader political and cultural atmosphere also nourished it. Some aspects of this context have already been mentioned. Advanced transportation and communication technologies, for instance, coupled with the emergence of a leisure class of Americans who had the means to travel and to collect, facilitated the rise of Holland Mania. Improved printing and photographic methods permitted mass distribution of popular images, especially advertising, posters, postcards, stereographs, and inexpensive reproductions of paintings. The Colonial Revival, inspired by the country's centennial celebrations and reinforced by the 1893 World's Columbian Exposition in Chicago, contributed to an atmosphere in which the past accomplishments of the Netherlands, its relationships with the North American colonies and with a developing United States, and the present state of Holland mattered to Americans. Other aspects of the atmosphere that produced or supported the fashion for Holland include children's literature, Dutch immigration, the Boer War, President Theodore Roosevelt, and the Hague Peace Conferences. Not until this atmosphere disappeared did Holland fade to the back of

American consciousness once more. From the 1920s to the present, American attitudes toward the Netherlands have remained fairly consistent with the idyllic stereotype developed at the turn of the century, but beliefs about (and awareness of) the contributions Holland made to the formation of an American culture have altered considerably.

JUVENILE LITERATURE

Adults may have been peculiarly susceptible to Holland's appeal because of attitudes formed in childhood. Juvenile literature combined text and image to produce the idyllic picture that many people would pursue as adults. As one man put it: "Ever since the blessed day when tiny tots are able to see and read they are fed on a type of juvenile literature in which wooden-shoed kiddies, windmills, dikes and tulip lands are supposed to convey a true picture of all that is the Netherlands."[199] Publishers supplied Dutch stories for all ages, from preschool picture books like *Hans and Little Hilda*, to primary readers such as *Ned and Nan in Holland*, to history books and stories for secondary school children. Such books established general ideas about the Netherlands that often carried over, unexamined, into adulthood, forming the basis of perceptions and responses in business relations, politics, and travel.

Because nineteenth-century schoolchildren learned their lessons by rote, the short maxims they memorized often remained firmly imbedded in their minds as adults. Eva Madden recorded her first impressions of the Netherlands when she traveled there as an adult: "Over and over I kept repeating, as if in my geography class at school, 'Holland is noted for windmills, dikes, and the cleanliness of its people.'"[200] During her stay she found countless proofs of the accuracy of her school lesson. She described Dutch women polishing kettles and beating rugs, exclaimed over the amount of foot wiping expected of a visitor and admired the view of windmills from her hostess's veranda. Although there were plenty of railroad stations, factories, and cosmopolitan hotels to see when she made her journey in 1909, Madden had been conditioned from childhood to look for windmills and the cleanliness of the people.

Some people actively searched out those aspects of the Netherlands and its people that would confirm the preconceptions formed from childhood reading. One writer advised fellow tourists to visit Volendam because it seemed to him "much more typical of

Holland of the story books than Amsterdam or The Hague." Florence Albrecht confirmed that opinion of Volendam, noting, "Here are those veritable Dutchman's breeches of your childish imaginings, but bigger broader, baggier than ever wildest fancy painted them." Tourists in Volendam and Marken tended to describe the small houses with their efficiently furnished interiors as doll houses. The smallness of Holland and everything in it, by American standards, probably contributed to tourists' association of the Netherlands with the idyllic place they had learned about in their storybooks as children. A consciousness shaped by the vast spaces of the North American continent perceived these Dutch towns as miniature playlands. Another visitor to Holland, Charles Howell, enthused over Scheveningen: "quaint little children like sturdy Dutch toys escape from the press and clatter off home, with an air of vast responsibility, hugging in both arms a brown loaf of bread a yard long. How it recalls the bright pages of 'Hans Brinker.'"[201]

Mary Mapes Dodge's tale, *Hans Brinker or the Silver Skates*, remained one of the most popular children's books through the turn of the century. First published in 1865, *Hans Brinker* appeared in many new editions between 1880 and 1910 as a generation of Americans who had grown up with the story purchased it for their children (FIG. 140). In *Hans Brinker*, Dodge created a work of pure fiction. She had not visited Holland when she wrote it and relied on a variety of published sources about Dutch life, literature, and art for her information. She also mined the memories of a Dutch-born couple living in the United States, and mentioned all these sources in her preface. Indeed, she used her preface to convince the young reader of the accuracy of her portrayal, explaining, "careful descriptions of Dutch life and customs have been given in the narrative, and many of the incidents are drawn directly from life. Even the wonderful experiences of Raff Brinker are founded strictly upon fact." Having set the stage for her readers to believe the impressions of Holland and its people conveyed in her story, Dodge went on to characterize the Netherlands:

> There is not a braver, more heroic race than its quiet, passive-looking inhabitants. Few nations have equalled it in important discoveries and inventions; none has excelled it in commerce, navigation, learning and science, or set as noble examples in the promotion of education and public charities; and none, in proportion to its extent, has expended more money and labor upon public works.

Throughout the book, Dodge held up the Dutch people as everything good and admirable by American standards. The ultimate illustration of Dutch national character appeared in her story of the little Dutch boy who stuck his finger in a leaking dike and stayed there all night until help came to save his village. Lest anyone miss the point, Dodge assured her readers that every Dutch boy and girl knew this *true* story and explained, "that little boy represents the spirit of the whole country. Not a leak can show itself anywhere, either in its politics, honor, or public safety, that a million fingers are not ready to stop it, at any cost." The fanciful tale of a finger in the dike, which was repeated by other authors of juvenile literature, undoubtedly went some distance toward establishing in young American minds a belief in the courage, independence and trustworthiness of the Dutch.[202]

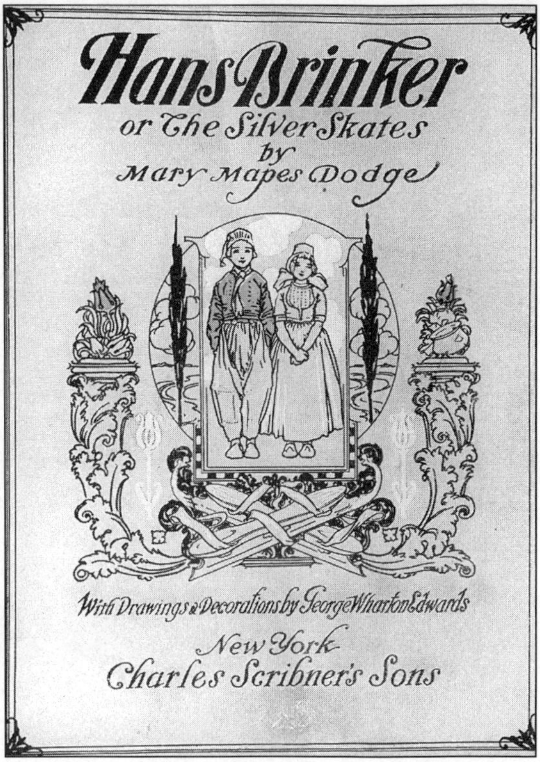

FIG. 140 **Hans Brinker or the Silver Skates** *provided many Americans with their earliest images of Holland. Mary Mapes Dodge's text, and illustrations by a succession of artists at the turn of the century, conspired to suggest that the Dutch still wore national costumes, skated all winter, and relied on wind-powered mills to keep their land dry.*

Schoolchildren in the United States learned the history of Holland through fact and fiction. Most stories of Dutch history focused on the sixteenth-century struggle for independence. Both history books and general stories about Holland emphasized those aspects of Dutch history that touched upon American history (FIG. 141c). In *The Bodley Grandchildren and their Journey in Holland* the grandchildren's parents explain the reason for their journey to Holland:

> The children are American children, and their first interest is in this country. But they never can be the best Americans until they know something about Europe, especially about those countries in Europe which have had so much to do with American history. They have read and studied the history of the United States so much that I am very sure if we were traveling in Spain, or Holland, or England, they would be all the while noticing places which were connected with the early discoverers or with the colonists.[203]

Horace Scudder set the scene for this exploration of America's Dutch ancestry by making his principal characters two sets of siblings who married, the Boston Bodleys of English descent and the New York Van Wycks of Dutch descent. Their subsequent journey with their children is a series of discoveries of the Dutch origins of American things as disparate as the pronunciation of the word mattress and the arrangement of rooms in a typical home. They go to Leyden to see where the Pilgrims lived and discuss John Adams and early diplomatic relations with the United States.

Adults may also have made a subconscious connection between the storybook image of Holland absorbed during their own childhood and the towns they visited in order to experience the childhood of the United States via colonial-era Holland. In other words, to some extent adults saw nineteenth-century Holland through a childish lens as a throwback to the era of America's childhood. These kinds of historical associations, like the connection between Volendam's smallness and childhood toys, helped shape American perceptions of the Netherlands as a loveable, familiar, unthreatening place of "windmills and wooden shoes."

Many children's books about Holland, especially after 1900, belonged to series used in the primary grades to introduce American children to the people and cultures of other countries. *Our Little Dutch Cousin* by Blanche McManus accompanied at least thirty-four other Little Cousin books by various authors. Inspired by the success of her first schoolbook, *The Dutch Twins* (FIG. 142), Lucy Fitch Perkins wrote twenty-four more books about twins of various nationalities and historic periods. Graded for school use, there were actually two Dutch twin books, a primer to teach first graders to read and a third grade edition. Other series included Bertha Upton's Golliwog books, Horace Scudder's Bodley books, the Peeps at Many Lands series, The World's Story, and the Little Journeys series. All these books promoted a simple picture of Holland as a waterlogged land of wooden shoes, herring, cabbages, canals, windmills, dikes, cheese, cupboard beds, and tulips. The Dutch children in them clean windows and scrub doorsteps, attend church, work in the vegetable or flower garden, see the queen, make and sell butter or cheese, skate on the frozen canals, and go to a kermis.

There is some evidence that children's literature presented an increasingly stereotyped image of the Netherlands as time passed. For example, national costume in early books, such as *The Bodley Grandchildren*, often reflected the true wealth of variety and detail in native Dutch dress. But after 1900 most children's books about Holland were illustrated with fanciful variations on the costume of Volendam. This might reflect the rapid conversion of rural Hollanders to cosmopolitan urban dress near the end of the century, except in isolated areas and in places like Volendam where tourism encouraged the retention of native dress. But the fact remains that authors and illustrators believed traditional costumes were essential for a portrayal of real Dutchness, even if the majority of Dutch people no longer wore them. The more common contemporary Dutch dress does not appear in children's literature at all. The ubiquity of the Volendam costume in juvenile literature would account for Albrecht's comment, when she visited Volendam as an adult, that here were the *real* Dutchman's breeches of her childhood imaginings.

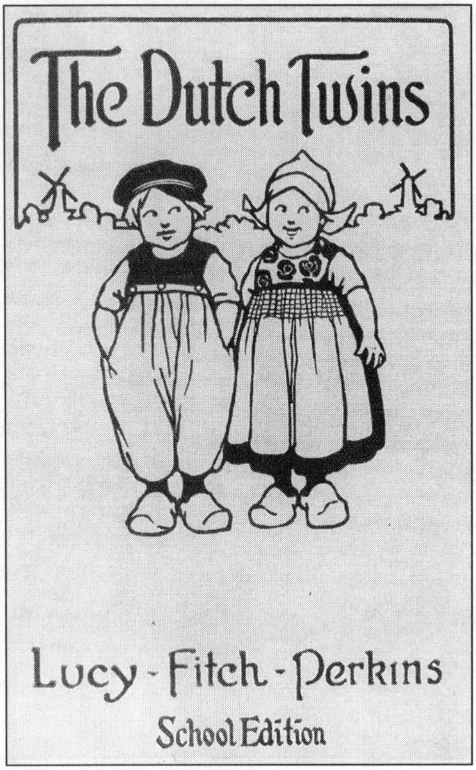

FIG. 142 *Elementary schools used books like* The Dutch Twins *by Lucy Fitch Perkins to teach reading and geography. After 1900, many children's books settled on the costume of Volendam as most characteristic of the Netherlands and the repetition of this type ensured its recognition in the United States as Dutch.*

Not only the costume, but also the environment and technology of the Netherlands was more frequently misrepresented in children's literature after 1900. *Rollo in Holland*, published in 1857, had presented the Netherlands as a place of active commerce and industry crisscrossed with modern railways and possessed of fascinating modern waterworks. When Scudder wrote *The Bodley Grandchildren* in 1883 he pointed out that windmills had added steam engines and chimney stacks for use when the wind was not blowing. Early twentieth-century books usually fail to mention railroads, commerce, or industry. They describe windmills as quaint and old-fashioned, and ignore the fact that gas and electricity actually powered many. In *Nixie Bunny in Faraway Lands*, written in 1917, the traveling bunny Molly asks, "What makes the windmills go round?" and is told simply, "The wind makes the arms go round and round." The observation was not untrue, but it fed the general misconception that Holland lacked technological development. Perhaps Holland Mania helped create a market for the stereotypes that fill the later books. Certainly American perceptions of the Netherlands were increasingly out of step with reality. By the time Joseph Sindelar wrote *Nixie Bunny*, Holland seemed so strange and exotic that he included it with Africa, Japan, China, and "Eskimo Land" as a faraway place of wonderment.

Newspaperman and author Eugene Field wrote numerous Dutch poems, including two lullabies, "Sleep, little tulip, sleep!" and the popular "Dutch Lullaby" of 1889, which begins:

Wynken Blynken and Nod one night
Sailed off in a wooden shoe—
Sailed on a river of crystal light,
Into a sea of dew.

The Chicago artist Mabel Landrum Torrey created a statue of Wynken, Blynken and Nod (FIG. 143), which Denver's Mayor Spear saw in a Chicago art exhibition. Knowing that Torrey was a native of Colorado, he commissioned the replica that stands in Denver's Washington Park.[204] Such fantasies fit right in with the supposedly true picture of Holland presented in children's literature.

Child culture in the United States helped to produce Holland Mania by preparing the first generation of artists, tourists, and historians, born around 1860, to receive Holland in a very positive frame of mind in their adult years. Such books as *Hans Brinker* and school activities in which children built Dutch villages and windmills may have encouraged them to seek out the Netherlands in their adult years and certainly encouraged the perpetuation of

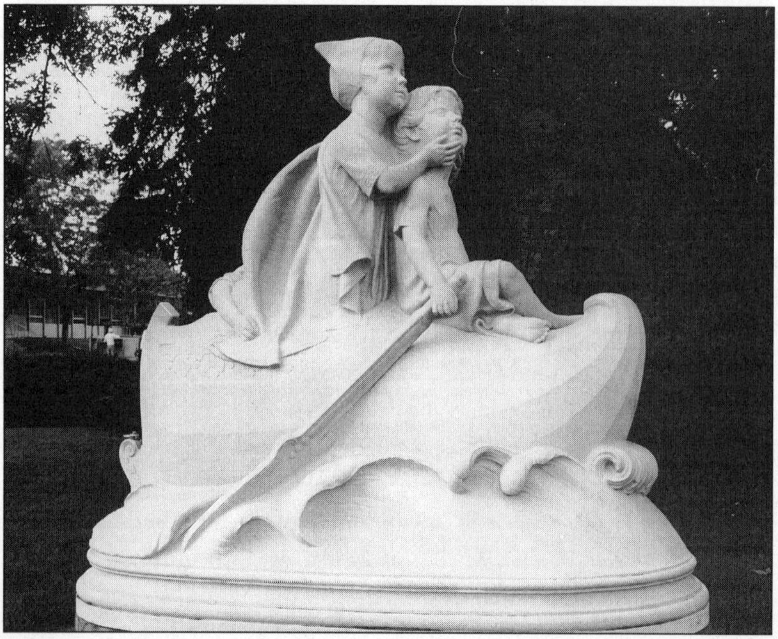

FIG. 143 *Eugene Field's "Dutch Lullaby" inspired Mabel Landrum Torrey's 1918 sculpture of Wynken, Blynken and Nod sailing in their wooden shoe.*

Dutch stereotypes. Throughout the last quarter of the nineteenth century and the beginning of the twentieth century, quantities of literature about Holland prepared succeeding generations of children to participate in the enthusiasm for the Netherlands.

DUTCH IMMIGRANTS

The presence of Dutch immigrants in the United States in the second half of the nineteenth century also helped to establish some Americans' attitudes toward Holland and to reinforce the impact of Holland Mania. Although the total number of Dutch immigrants during the nineteenth century remained low in comparison to the large incoming populations of Irish, Italians, Germans, and Scandinavians, significant numbers of Dutch people settled in Michigan, Iowa, Illinois, Ohio, Wisconsin, Pennsylvania, New Jersey, and New York. The first large influx occurred in the 1840s when Domine Van Raalte established Holland, Michigan; Father Theodore van den Broek led settlers to Little Chute and Hollandtown in Wisconsin; and Reverend H.P. Scholte founded Pella, Iowa. Other towns named after the Dutch provinces or cities from which the settlers originated sprang up around these. In western Michigan alone may be found Overisel, Vriesland, Zeeland, Graafschap, Watervliet, Kinderhook, New Holland, and De Wit.

Hollanders continued to immigrate through the rest of the century with a peak of 10,000 new arrivals in 1882. A second peak occurred in the period from 1911 to 1915 when 31,000 immigrants arrived. They started their own businesses, Dutch Reformed churches, newspapers, and colleges, all of which helped them maintain strong ethnic traditions. The Holland-California Land Company and Maxwell Land Grant Company actively recruited colonists from the Netherlands to establish new communities in Colorado, New Mexico, and California during the last quarter of the nineteenth century. Doctors in the Netherlands also sent many tuberculosis patients to live in Maxwell City, New Mexico for the beneficial effects of the dry climate. Immigrants who joined Dutch settlements in the East and Midwest often migrated westward to establish new communities. This was the case in Denver, for example, where Dutch immigrants and their descendants from Maxwell City and Grand Rapids began a Dutch neighborhood from around 1910 to 1920. Dutch towns also appeared in Massachusetts, Kentucky, Kansas, Nebraska, Montana, Minnesota, and the Dakotas. Americans throughout the country were exposed to Holland through these small transplanted Dutch communities.

The collective American opinion on nineteenth-century Dutch immigrants was extremely positive. They were considered quiet, honest, diligent people and were even described as modern pilgrim fathers. Their ethnic appearance—light skin, blond hair, and blue eyes—helped them blend into dominant Anglo-American society. Because they usually moved to rural areas they avoided the suspicion and slurs cast upon other ethnic groups who congregated in urban ghettos. Dutch people rarely competed for the domestic positions and menial jobs that occupied so many newly arrived immigrants, and so they escaped both the resentment of working-class Americans and the disparagement of the middle and upper classes. The conduct of nineteenth-century Dutch immigrants—their courage and independence in forming their own communities, their love of the land, success in business and sober manner—confirmed Americans in their belief that Dutch character was only marginally different from American. When the Chicago, Milwaukee, and St. Paul Railroad expanded westward into North Dakota it named two new stations The Hague and Zeeland, hoping to entice Dutch immigrants to settle there. The *New Amsterdam Gazette* took pride in announcing on August 31, 1889 that the wealthiest man in South Dakota was one William Van Eps, a first generation Dutch-American who worked his way up from printer's apprentice to bank president and owner of mills, mines, and real estate. Similarly, Edward Bok's rags to riches story, from Dutch-speaking immigrant child to editor of one of America's largest circulating monthly magazines and friend of presidents, was well known. The ease with which the Dutch accomplished Americanization endeared them to their compatriots.

Throughout the period, immigrants provided an important point of contact between Americans and Holland. Their presence in the United States further disseminated knowledge of Holland, while their conduct may have reinforced the character attributed to the Dutch by historians, tourists, connoisseurs and popular culture.

BOER WAR

Several current events also served to put the Netherlands and its connection to United States history in the news. Between 1899 and 1902 the Dutch South African republics of Transvaal and the Orange Free State, joined by Dutch Boers and other sympathetic colonists in the British colonies, fought for complete independence from England. Major monthly magazines in the United States, including *Scribner's*, *Harper's*, and *Century*, carried feature articles arguing the merits of each side. American citizens avidly followed the outcome of each battle in the newspapers and magazines, while photo companies, including the American Stereoscopic Company, Griffith and Griffith, Standard Scenic Company, Underwood and Underwood, and Keystone, sold thousands of stereographs of the war as seen from both sides of the battlefield.

American interest and sympathy rested primarily with the Dutch, in spite of the fact that British writers had greater access to American publications. In the first two months of the war, E. E. Easton claimed he was the only foreign correspondent behind Dutch lines and because the British controlled all the telegraph lines and mail it was nearly impossible to get out an uncensored report. British sympathizers faced no such difficulties. They attempted to counter the American predisposition toward Holland by stating that the Boers in South Africa were totally unlike the Dutch and spoke a debased language incomprehensible to real Dutch people. They commonly depicted Boers as ignorant oafs centuries behind the times, one writer going so far as to say that up-country Boers still believed the earth was flat. George Lacy characterized the Boers as unwashed, shifty-eyed, blood-thirsty, immoral, immodest, uneducated, overbearing, inhospitable, dishonest, unpatriotic, quarrelsome to the last degree, and absolutely callous to suffering.[205]

Boer sympathizers countered this strong rhetoric with equally impassioned claims on their side. Some thought of the war as a reenactment of the American Revolution. This view recognized that the Dutch had colonized Africa in the seventeenth century soon after they settled in North America. Descendants of the Boer colonists had moved north out of Cape Colony to escape British colonial rule and establish free republics in the 1820s and 1830s, but continued to find themselves under the long arm of English policies. Now they were fighting the British for their independence, as the Americans had before them. According to this perspective, untrained but determined colonists fought without proper arms or provisions against regular British troops and their native allies, just as the Americans had done. While the British fought in traditional formations and trenches and launched charges against an often unseen enemy, the Boers worked independently with their own hunting guns, shooting from whatever cover they could construct or find. This interpretation of the Boer War as a counterpart of the American War for Independence engaged American sympathy for the Dutch–African side.

Numerous comparisons were made between the South African veldt and the American frontier, and the pioneer character of the inhabitants of both. "The Dutch Boers handle the rifle and ride on horses from childhood," explained William Griffis. "Thus far their dauntless spirit, sure aim, and intense patriotism have enabled them to resist British aggression." Writers who saw the Boers as latter-day American patriots reenacting the Revolutionary War, were lavish in their praise of the national characteristics of the Boers. Descriptions of some of the early battles in which 400 to 600 Boers defeated 2000 to 3000 British soldiers also sounded like Motley's descriptions of heroic battles in the Dutch war against Spain. Senator Hoar of Massachusetts said of "the farmers of the little Dutch republics of South Africa, in whose veins flowed the blood of the men who three centuries ago stood on the walls of Haarlem and Leyden. . . . There has been no more heroic struggle than theirs since Thermopylae, and none in a holier cause."[206]

Public opinion held especially firm for the Dutch side among Dutch-Americans. A town in South Dakota voted to rename itself Joubert, after the Boer general who led Dutch forces to victory in the opening campaigns of the war. Some Americans of Dutch descent went to South Africa as volunteers and others raised funds and made speeches to garner public support for the Boer effort. In 1902 American artists working in Holland contributed paintings and funds to the Union Pro-Boer's Scheveningen art exhibition benefiting Boer widows and orphans.[207]

Many non-Dutch Americans, perhaps swept along by Holland Mania, were also predisposed in favor of the Boer cause. Estimates of the time placed as many as nine out of every ten Americans in favor of the Boers, usually on moral and nationalistic grounds. According to historian Richard Mulanax, Americans of Irish and German descent comprised the largest, most vocal pro-Boer group in the United States. Motivated by anti-British sentiment as well as concern for the Boers, they volunteered for service in South Africa and agitated for pro-Boer government policies in the United States. Nevertheless, official U.S. policy remained neutral, and in a practical sense, often favored the British. This occurred despite the fact that in 1900 Americans elected a Dutch-American to the second highest office in the country and he became President the next year after the assassination of President William McKinley.[208]

President Theodore Roosevelt confided to his sister, Anna Roosevelt Cowles: "The South African business makes me really sad. I have a genuine admiration for the Boers; but the downfall of the British Empire, I should regard as a calamity to the race, and especially to this country." Roosevelt acknowledged the Dutch Boer War–American Revolutionary War analogy, and sympathized with the Dutch, but he believed that American interests rested solidly with Great Britain. He refused to allow a sentimental view of early Dutch–American history to sway him, arguing from a position of race pride and imperialism: "I think it would be a great deal better if all the white people of South Africa spoke English, and if my Dutch kinsfolk over there grew to accept English as their language just as my people and I here have done, they would be a great deal better off." Ultimately, as Mulanax has shown, pro-Boer popular sentiment in the United States went no farther than an academic or moral stance. Self-interest dictated an officially neutral, and unofficially pro-British foreign policy.[209]

Because of the war more information about everyday life in Dutch South Africa entered the American consciousness. Ladies' magazines published articles describing life among Boer women and girls (FIG. 144). According to these sources, Dutch women of the Transvaal presented "an ideal picture of womanhood," equally familiar with rifle and Bible. The town girl "differs little from the American town girl except that she uses the Dutch dialect." Mrs. Kruger, the president's wife, was admired for her domesticity, social position, and democratic ideals.[210]

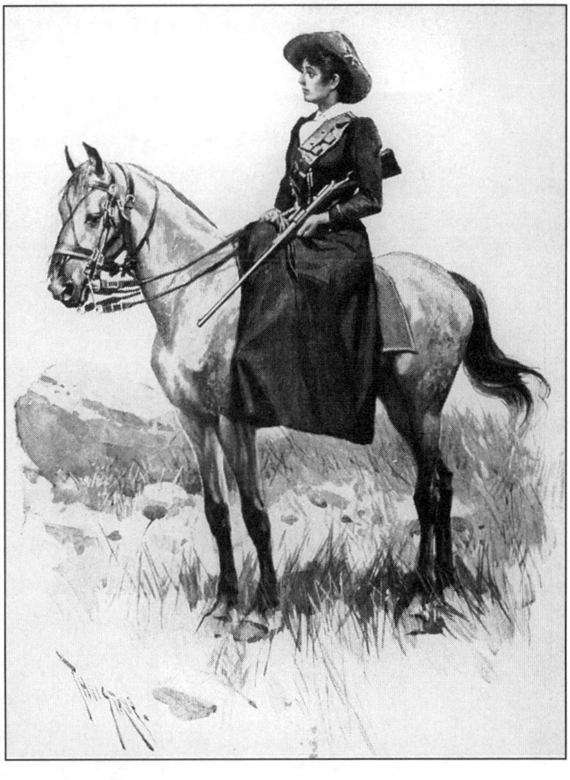

FIG. 144 *Thore de Thulstrup's illustration of a "Transvaal Commandant's wife who fought beside her husband at the Tugela" illustrated an article about the Boer War in* Harper's New Monthly Magazine, *July 1900.*

Even after the war drew to a close it remained in the American consciousness. A South African circus owner and promoter, Frank Fillis, brought six hundred British, Dutch, and native troops as well as 250 horses and quantities of artillery to the United States to reenact three of the most famous

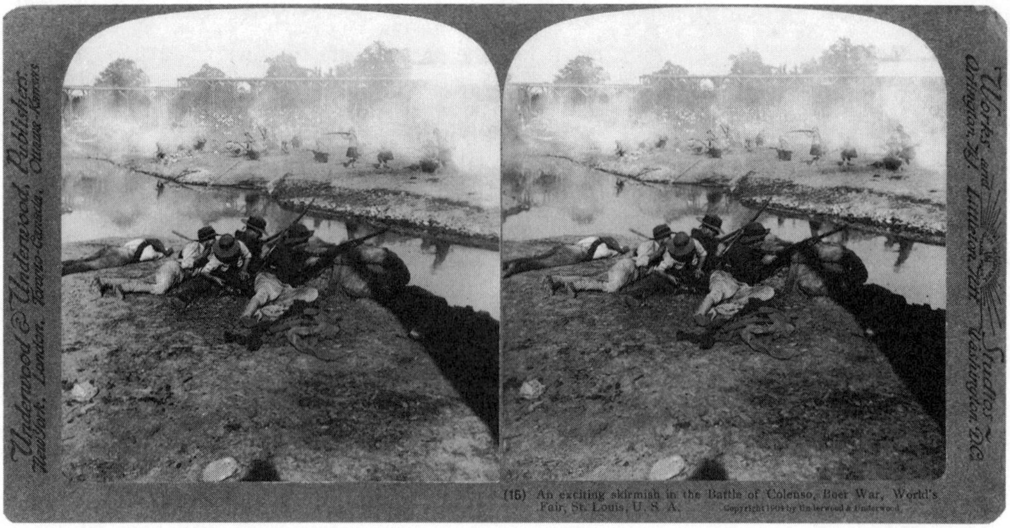

FIG. 145 *A close look through the gunsmoke will reveal grandstands packed with spectators at this reenactment of a Boer War battle at the World's Fair in St. Louis in 1904.*

battles from the Boer War (FIG. 145). The cast included many veterans of the war, most notably General Viljoen, Commandants Van Dam and Mare, and Cornet Van Glass, whose feats were well known to their American audiences. In a postwar spirit of fairness, the exhibition battles divided the victories between British and Dutch. Cincinnati artist John Rettig painted a huge backdrop for the show and with the help of gunpowder and fireworks, this spectacular drama drew thousands of spectators to three performances a day at the 1904 World's Fair in St. Louis. When the fair closed, Fillis took the show on the road to Kansas City and Chicago where headlines read, "Boer War Draws Cheering Crowd." According to local reports, more than a thousand people were turned away from the opening performance in Chicago.[211]

THEODORE ROOSEVELT

Another event that served to underscore Dutch-American ties was the accession of America's second president of Dutch descent to office in 1901 and his election to a second term of office in 1904. Theodore Roosevelt represented the eighth generation of Roosevelts in America, the first having come from Delft to New Amsterdam early in the seventeenth century. Members of his family had held important positions in state and national politics, and Robert B. Roosevelt was the United States Ambassador to the Netherlands from 1888 to 1890. The family actively participated in the Holland

Society and they preserved the Dutch family Bible and other colonial relics of the first Roosevelts in America. The general feeling of goodwill toward the Dutch and awareness of Holland's contribution to colonial America may have subtly aided Roosevelt's campaigns, and the election of this popular president certainly did not hinder the momentum of Holland Mania.

Although political expediency at various times caused Roosevelt to claim a variety of ethnic ties, he was sincerely attached to his Dutch identity. In 1909 while hunting in Africa, Roosevelt tried out a Dutch lullaby that his grandparents had taught him on some of the Boers, with whom he felt an affinity. "It was interesting to meet these men whose ancestors had gone to the Cape about the time that mine went to America two centuries and a half previously," he wrote, "and to find that the descendants of two streams of emigrants still crooned to their children some at least of the same nursery songs."[212] On a journey through the Netherlands two years later, Roosevelt recited the same Dutch lullaby as proof of his continuing Dutch heritage.

As president, Roosevelt served as a symbol of America's broader Dutch heritage. He spoke both personally and for the nation when he told the Dutch people, "I come from a great free Republic to the home of my forefathers, of whom it may be said, that they were among the very first, to establish freedom as we now understand the word."[213]

During Roosevelt's second term of office, the Netherlands bolstered its positive position in the American public eye by hosting a world peace conference. At the turn of the century, world leaders hoped to achieve a lasting accord among the principal nations of the world. The Hague played an important role in that endeavor by sponsoring the first Hague Peace Conference in 1899 with 26 countries in attendance, and the second in 1907 with almost twice that number. Although these efforts ultimately failed, Americans gave credit to the Dutch for promoting peace and viewed Holland's role in the talks as one more example in their long history of upholding the principles of tolerance and freedom. "There is a peculiar fitness," wrote one man, "in the fact that the scene of these events so pregnant for the peace and welfare of the world is the land of Erasmus, . . . and of Grotius, . . . the little land which first powerfully illustrated to the modern world the virtue of those principles of federation and political cooperation which the nations represented at The Hague now seek to apply to international affairs." Even Roosevelt, who considered most world peace conferences to have had a detrimental effect, exempted the Hague Conferences from his general condemnation.[214]

Holland's effort so impressed Pittsburgh steel magnate Andrew Carnegie that he donated one and a half million dollars to build a permanent Peace Palace in The Hague. Hermann Rosse, the decorator of the Peace Palace, also produced the mural that ornamented the Netherlands Pavilion at the Panama-Pacific International Exposition in San Francisco in 1915. Called *The Arts of Peace*, the mural depicted an allegorical figure of Holland holding an image of peace above her head and surrounded by the industries, crafts, motherhood, and child's play.

All of these factors created an atmosphere in which Holland appeared to many people to be the best option for a reconstructed American past. Some Americans wanted an alternative to their British heritage that would emphasize liberty, democracy, republican virtues, bourgeois values, and a distinctive culture. Art, politics, history, literature, popular culture, and personal experience combined to convince a significant segment of the American population that Holland offered just such an image. More and more people embraced a national Dutch identity after the turn of the century and the trend continued to grow until political and social conditions again altered the atmosphere.

THE END OF HOLLAND MANIA

When Edward Bok discussed the appearance of Holland Mania in his editorial of 1903, he also predicted its future:

> Some are inclined to think that this interest in the people of the Netherlands, and in Dutch things generally, is a passing fad. But others who study things more closely lean to the belief that it is based on something more intelligent and permanent: that it rests on a national awakening born of an inherent influence and blood kinship that has too long been lost sight of.[215]

Bok was destined to be disappointed. The Dutch experience in America, which began with a flood of pictures and travel accounts in the 1880s, gained momentum with the rewriting of American history in the 1890s and culminated in a widespread cultural influence in the early twentieth century, could not sustain itself after World War I.

Artists and tourists returned to the United States in 1913 and 1914 as it became clear that the unrest in central Europe would overtake the Netherlands. Although many continued to paint Dutch subjects and read and write travel books, the war years necessitated a break in physical contact with Holland and turned attention from the picturesque Dutch past to contemporary political events and the uncertain future.

At the same time, the taste for quaint Dutch images, both verbal and pictorial, reached saturation point. An excerpt from Marjorie Bowen's *The Netherlands Display'd*, published in 1927, will serve to demonstrate the new attitude:

> [Dutch towns] are odd and pretty enough, and must at one time have been really peculiar and delightful, but suffer now from considerable over-exploitation on the part of painters, photographers and tourist agencies.
>
> There is really very little left to be said about them save that they are very bright and clean and far too obviously picturesque, and look a great deal too much like the pretty wooden toys made in their likeness.
>
> The inhabitants are, of course, serious and hard-working fisher and peasant folk, but they have somehow lost their air of reality through no fault of their own.
>
> They are not to blame if they look more like a railway poster or a souvenir postcard than human beings, and it is only wonderful that the steady stream of tourists has not spoilt them more.[216]

As Bowen was aware, the effects of tourism and mass marketing eventually caused changes in Holland and in the way Americans viewed the Dutch. While art had once imitated the originals, the originals were now thought to be imitating art. This produced a situation unacceptable to Americans who sought the "real" Holland.

The Dutch interpretation of American history went the way of art and travel. In 1945 when Bernard Vlekke, a Professor of the History of the Netherlands, wrote about Dutch-American relations, he began by explaining:

> About half a century ago there was a tendency among historians to see a close connection between the growth of the American Republic and its conception of freedom and the Dutch traditions of the sixteenth and seventeenth centuries. It was also pointed out that the organization of the United States as a federative republic showed some similarity to that of the Dutch Republic. However, there never existed more than a similarity, and a very superficial

one at that. The Netherlands did not contribute to the political and ideological structure of the American Republic.[217]

By the time Vlekke wrote this, most historians were barely aware of the existence of a theory of dominant Dutch influence. Only specific studies of New Netherland or Dutch immigration touched on the question of what Holland gave to the United States.

Holland Mania died a quiet death in the 1920s. Paintings, prints, and photographs of the Netherlands were stored away in attics and museum basements. Costumes and souvenirs gathered dust and history reverted to the theory of a heritage dominated by England. But the brief period in which the United States saw itself through a Dutch lens can provide insight into Americans' continuing efforts to establish their place in history and to construct a national image on the basis of ethnic heritage.

AFTER 1920

Although the intensive interest in things Dutch that I have termed Holland Mania faded around 1920, Dutch influence in American art and culture continued on a less visible level. Most of the popular ideas about Holland and its people remained unchanged in essence, but these perceptions rarely surfaced in American consciousness. For a brief period in the 1960s and 1970s, a youthful generation associated Amsterdam with readily available mind-altering drugs and sex, quite a change from earlier stereotypes! But in general, Holland's quiet demeanor in the world news (from an American perspective) and in U.S. affairs, did nothing to disturb post-Holland-Mania attitudes.

Since 1920, there has been one period of distinct Dutch influence in American and world art, De Stijl. The rectilinear geometric organization, primary colors, and clarity of design that characterize the modernistic De Stijl had a profound impact on architecture and graphic design. Some of this influence came by way of the Bauhaus where the Dutch De Stijl leader Theo van Doesburg's influence was strong. Painter Piet Mondrian's presence in the United States as a refugee from war-torn Europe also inspired some painters and designers to explore De Stijl principles. And the rich cross-fertilization between Dutch and American architecture, noted by Robert Olpin in his discussion of Hendrik Petrus Berlage and Frank Lloyd Wright for the encyclopedia *Dutch Art*, contributed to the development of the International Style. Dutch designers Paul Schuitema and Piet Zwart have attracted notice from American historians of graphic design for their adaptations of De Stijl principles and innovative use of typography as a medium of pure design. Print media, generally, has benefited from the talents of such typographers as Jan van Krimpen of Gouda who developed the popular Lutetia typeface for the Haarlem printer Enschedé in the 1920s. He followed that with other new and successful typefaces. Hendrik Werkman's creative use of old wooden type and hand inked and printed shapes with their resulting irregularities inspired designers who emphasized the art over the craft of graphic design. A 1987 exhibition of Dutch posters from the period of 1890 to 1940 at the Krannert Art Museum in Illinois testifies to the power of graphic design in the Netherlands. Postwar Dutch design has continued to influence commercial graphic art, especially public signage.

Individual Dutch artists over the past eighty years have occasionally made an impact in the United States. For example, M.C. Escher's graphic optical illusions have intrigued Americans since the fifties and Willem DeKooning's contributions to Abstract Expressionism are well known. Contemporary Dutch artists also maintain a presence in the U.S. art scene as individuals. Some, such as Coosje van Bruggen, who collaborates with Claes Oldenburg on large public sculptures, have acquired fairly high visibility. But Americans do not, and could not, identify these artists with a national Dutch school of art the way that the little Dutch masters or The Hague School became recognizably Dutch to an aware American public at the turn of the century. With the exception of De Stijl, Dutch art has made little impact on American public consciousness since the 1920s.

Although the collecting of old Dutch paintings dropped off sharply after 1915, the art historical evaluation and popularity of seventeenth-century Dutch art remained consistently high. The past decade has found art institutions in the Netherlands and the United States collaborating on a number of major exhibitions focused on the old Dutch masters. A 1989–1990 exhibition of paintings by Frans Hals at the National Gallery of Art in Washington, D.C., the Royal Academy in London, and at the Frans Halsmuseum in Haarlem reconsidered attributions and the historical context of the Haarlem painter. The next year, the Fine Arts Museums of San Francisco and the Mauritshuis sponsored an exhibition of Great Dutch Paintings from America. Another show, shared by the

Worcester Art Museum in Massachusetts and the Frans Halsmuseum in 1993, introduced the work of Hals's contemporary, Judith Leyster, to a broader audience. Several exhibits have featured Rembrandt's paintings and prints, with a focus on the international effort to determine proper attributions for the huge body of work claiming to be from Rembrandt's hand. Public fascination with this process brought crowds to the Metropolitan Museum's 1995–1996 exhibition "Rembrandt/Not Rembrandt." The same year witnessed the first (and many people believe it will be the only) assemblage of most of Vermeer's very limited number of oil paintings in a show organized by the Mauritshuis and the National Gallery of Art. These exhibitions involved years of preparation and scholarly study and sparked numerous new publications.

Yet the results of this appreciation for Golden Age art are different today than they were one hundred years ago. American artists do not flock to Holland to study Dutch art or to paint the contemporary scene. If anything, Dutch artists are more inclined to come to New York. Since 1920 American art, which in the era of Modernism showed little interest in representation of any sort, has rarely incorporated Dutch imagery. The Postmodern artist, well-trained in the history of art, may refer to past masters as Mark Tansey did when he based his 1981 painting, *Innocent Eye Test* (FIG. 146) on Paulus Potter's *The Young Bull* (see FIG. 73c). But the purpose and results of contemporary borrowing from Dutch art differ from those at the turn of the century. In Tansey's painting, a cow stands in an art museum gazing at Potter's painting while museum officials wait expectantly for her verdict. A bespectacled art expert standing in front of the painting obscures Potter's farmer, who is headless and nearly formless in Tansey's copy. Unlike his turn-of-the-century predecessors, Tansey's purpose seems to have little to do with recreating the effects of the old masters. He seems more interested in the relationships between art object and audience and in the questions of value and objectivity raised by the notion of an "innocent eye." Given the practical evaluations of Potter's picture by the American "innocents abroad" quoted in Chapter Five, and Tansey's substitution of the art expert for the farmer, not to mention his placement of a cow before the painting as the ultimate judge of its realism, questions of expertise and authority resonate all through the picture. *Innocent Eye Test* is part of the Postmodern fascination with theories of the gaze and the deconstructive idea that there is no fixed meaning in art; all depends on context and perspective. Dutch

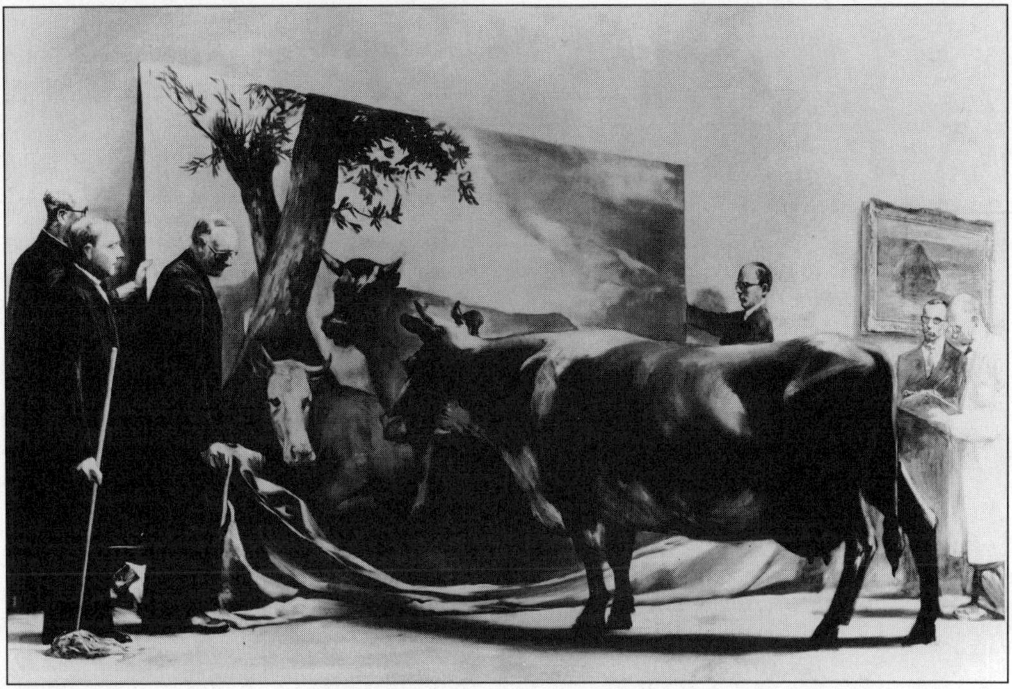

FIG. 146 *The New York artist Mark Tansey placed Paulus Potter's* The Young Bull (FIG. 73) *at the center of his 1981 oil painting,* Innocent Eye Test. *It recalls the humble, practical opinions of Potter's work expressed by turn-of-the-century American tourists.*

art, past and present, continues to play a role in American art, although it is a different and, arguably, less prominent role than that at the turn of this century.

If the popularity of Simon Schama's book about Golden Age Dutch culture, *The Embarrassment of Riches* (1987) is any indication, the American public is still intrigued by the romance of sixteenth- and seventeenth-century Holland. Nevertheless, most Americans today would be hard pressed to retell the events of history in the Netherlands beyond the broadest of generalizations. Similarly, colonial Dutch history in North America often expresses itself for the average American only in a vague awareness that the Dutch founded New York. While historians remember the Pilgrims' sojourn in Holland and many details of colonial Dutch-American historical relations, they no longer consider these to have been particularly significant in establishing the character of American culture. Colonial Dutch studies have turned to questions of ethnicity, race, and multiculturalism, as have so many areas of academic inquiry. The discovery of the African burial ground in New York City added impetus to this line of study, which was rarely touched at the turn of the century. David Gregg was one of the few people, then, to write about the contributions of women and African Americans as founders of the United States.

On the other hand, historians continue to produce excellent studies of Dutch–American relations, such as Jan Willem Schulte Nordholt's *The Dutch Republic and American Independence* (1982), David Steven Cohen's *The Dutch-American Farm* (1992), and Augustus J. Veenendaal's *Slow Train to Paradise: How Dutch Investment Helped Build American Railroads* (1996), to name just a few. While the present state of scholarship is encouraging, its impact on American culture at large is negligible.

Attempts to preserve Dutch-American history by residents of regions with a historic Dutch connection, whether themselves of Dutch ancestry or not, are ongoing. In Hurley, New York, owners of historic stone houses make heroic efforts to preserve their buildings while living in them. In other towns, Dutch colonial and revival buildings have become house museums. Still others have been dismantled and incorporated into museums. In 1952 the Brooklyn Museum acquired a house built in Flatlands in the seventeenth century by the Hollander Jan Martense Schenck. The museum eventually installed its two rooms as part of a display of historic interiors. Upon acquiring the eighteenth-century house of Schenck's grandson, Nicholas, the Brooklyn Museum added four rooms and a stair hall to their display. Both efforts to preserve a part of Brooklyn's Dutch architectural heritage were documented by books in an effort to encourage preservation of the remaining fourteen or so old Dutch farmhouses in the area. These are just a few examples of the many efforts to preserve America's Dutch heritage in the regions where it was strongest.

Some of the Dutch American heritage associations founded at the turn of the century remain active in this endeavor. The Holland Society of New York maintains its offices in its old building on East 58th Street and continues to publish historical data. In the 1920s and 1930s it undertook a major survey of extant Dutch buildings in the middle Atlantic states that resulted in two well-illustrated volumes. The Netherland Club of New York, founded in 1903 for people of Dutch birth or ancestry, still has about 400 members and the Daughters of the Society of Holland Dames is also still in existence. The Holland Purchase Historical Society, established in Batavia, New York in 1894, continues to preserve and publicize regional history by maintaining the Holland Land Office Museum. Some other groups, especially those formed to aid immigrants, have died out. As early as 1921, the president of the Netherlands Society of Philadelphia warned members at the annual meeting, "Our members are gradually growing less, and unless some of these young men and some of these old men get their sons and sons-in-law in here I am afraid the Society will sometime die out."[218] Although it never attracted a very large membership, the Society was still active in 1969.

As interest waned or functions became obsolete, some groups merged for survival. The present Netherland-America Foundation, which oversees educational exchanges, resulted from the 1921 merger of the Dutch American West–Indian Foundation with the Netherlands–American Community Association. In 1971 it absorbed the Netherland Benevolent Society of New York, which had been founded in 1908 as an aid association for Netherlanders and people of Dutch descent. Even as some of the original societies reshaped themselves, new groups emerged. Descendants of the original settlers of Albany created the Dutch Settlers Society of Albany in 1924. The Society maintained historical and genealogical records and today it also supports an annual tulip festival.

While Dutch societies of the 1880–1920 period tended to be located in New York, New Jersey, and Pennsylvania, most of those founded since 1920 have headquarters in the Midwest and West. This reflects the coming of age of the nineteenth-century immigrant population which settled primarily in Michigan, Illinois, Iowa, and Wisconsin and has reached the stage of wanting to preserve its heritage. These later organizations are also commonly of a more academic nature than were their predecessors. The Holland Historical Trust was established in 1937 to preserve the history of Holland, Michigan and maintains a Dutch–American history museum. From 1963 through 1994 it joined four Dutch-founded colleges and seminaries in the state to provide a resource for scholars as the Dutch–American Historical Commission. Calvin College began assembling the Dutch Immigrant Letter Collection in 1961, one of several important archives for Dutch immigrant studies. In Iowa, Northwestern College established the Association for the Advancement of Dutch–American Studies in 1979. This, too, is an academic venture intended to promote knowledge of Dutch-American history and culture. Farther west, the Dutch Family Heritage Society has gathered and disseminated information on Dutch–American history and genealogy in Utah since 1987. The Netherlands–American Society of the Rockies opens its arms to anyone interested in Holland or Dutch-American relations. More specialized societies exist for people interested in Dutch breeds of cattle, horses, and rabbits, and since 1975 the American Society for Netherlands Philately has promoted the study of postage stamps issued by the Netherlands and its Dutch colonies.

Individual families have also formed societies. The Association of Blauvelt Descendants organized in 1926, for instance, and the Peter Alrichs Foundation for descendants of a seventeenth-century landowner in New Castle, Delaware, organized as recently as 1987. Numerous families have published their genealogies, among them the Van Deventers (1943), Vandeveers of North Carolina, Kentucky, and Indiana (1960), Van Schaicks (1982) and Van Voorhees (1984). All of these groups, and others like them, continue to play a role in preserving and disseminating knowledge of Dutch influence in the United States.

It is also worth noting that although small in quantity and isolated in terms of geographic impact, Dutch immigration continues. For residents of Stephenville, Texas, for instance, the Dutch have become a noticeable presence in the last twelve years. A number of dairy farmers in search of affordable land and less restrictive government policies have left the Netherlands to establish themselves here.

Across the country, Dutch-American communities preserve the memory of their ethnic heritage with festivals. Holland, Michigan began celebrating Tulip Time in 1929, followed by Pella, Iowa in 1935, Orange City, Iowa in 1941, and Albany, New York in 1949. Lynden, in the state of Washington, holds two Dutch festivals, Holland Days in the spring and Sinterklaas in December. An annual Dutch festival on Long Island has been sponsored since 1984 by Hofstra University in honor of the area's early Dutch settlement (FIG. 147c). Denver's Dutch festival is staged by Bethesda Hospital, the institutional descendant of a turn-of-the-century sanatorium established by Dutch-American sufferers of tuberculosis. Other Dutch festivals have provided community events and tourist attractions in Little Chute, Wisconsin; South Holland, Illinois; Edgerton, Minnesota; Nederland, Texas; and Corsica, South Dakota, to name a few. The festivals are an invention of the twentieth century. They have roots in the isolated kermis entertainments of the turn of the century; not in any historical celebration or holiday imported from Holland.

Most of these annual tourist festivals emphasize the "windmills and wooden shoes" image. Participants usually don traditional costumes and wooden shoes for an opening parade, frequently preceded by a ceremonial street scrubbing. Food stands provide such traditional Dutch pastries as poffertjes (tiny, light pancakes) and olie bollen (deep fried dough balls). A street market selling imported Dutch foods, flower bulbs, wooden shoes, and ceramic souvenirs is fairly standard. Some festivals include an arts and crafts show. Others have Dutch dancing, singing, and storytelling. A windmill of one sort or another usually provides some background scenery. All of these celebrations remind us of Dutch-Americans' continuing allegiance to their roots. They do so by means of a stereotyped image familiar from the turn of the century that may still express the most prominent American attitude toward Holland and its culture today.

The relatively static image portrayed through Dutch festivals does not reflect the changes experienced by Dutch-American communities. One of the earliest of these was loss of the Dutch language. Emphasis on Americanization during and after World War I, combined with the natural process of assimilation for succeeding generations of descendants, caused much of the Dutch-language press to die out in the 1920s and 1930s. Philip Webber's book *Pella Dutch* provides a fascinating study of one of the last areas in the United States where a spoken form of Dutch was still in use.

There can be no doubt that the consciously chosen and carefully orchestrated image of the Dutch festival satisfies a dual purpose: affirmation of ethnic pride and economic development. A non-Dutch resident of Holland, Michigan first conceived the idea of a Dutch festival there, and Holland's Irish mayor strongly promoted it. Dutch joined non-Dutch in creating a unified civic image through the symbolism of Dutch-American culture. Holland, Michigan imported tulips for its earliest festivals, but after World War II, during which period the festival had been suspended, area farmers began cultivating tulips and developed a large commercial bulb business, for which the festival serves as an advertisement. Festivals in some towns raise funds for targeted community projects, while tourism remains a primary focus for the larger festivals.

In an effort to exploit the Dutch theme for economic development, towns like Orange City and Pella, Iowa have literally rebuilt themselves. The transformation is most dramatic in Pella where, until about 1965, the two- and three-story flat-roofed buildings facing the town square looked like any other Midwest town. Then two local businesses, Pohlmann's Insurance and Paardekooper's, remodeled with Dutch motifs. In January 1966, H.S. Kuyper, grandson of the Dutch-born founder of Pella's largest business, the Rolscreen Corporation, announced that the company would provide

$400 of assistance to each business willing to remodel their premises in a Dutch style. The conversion of the town's business district followed as brick veneers, painted shutters, tiled roofs and a variety of Dutch gables transformed the old facades. Plans are moving forward to add a canal in the middle of town. Since the 1950s, false windmills have served as an information booth in Pella's city park, an office building, and a phone booth in Orange City, and as banks in both places (FIG. 148c). In 1930 Michigan Bell Telephone completed its office building for the city of Holland in a Netherlands inspired style of concrete, brick, and tile, capped by stepped gables. Twentieth-century half-timbered buildings with small panes of window glass convey a European flavor in several Dutch-American towns and citizens vie with city governments in planting tulip beds to enhance the impression of Dutchness.

While festivals foster the rather superficial "windmill and wooden shoes" image in Dutch-American communities, exporting it to a somewhat broader audience through tourism, even this limited awareness of a Dutch-American connection is restricted to a few geographic areas. There is no longer a broader national consciousness of the Netherlands or of Dutch-American history. Architects designing for non-Dutch regions or non-Dutch Americans, rarely choose a Netherlandish motif, despite the propensity of Postmodernism to appropriate from history at will. Historical references to colonial Dutch buildings occasionally appear in the Postmodern work of architects in traditionally Dutch regions. New Jersey architect Robert Bennett, for example, and New York architect Robert A.M. Stern, both of whom are steeped in the architectural traditions of the region, have referenced Dutch-American farmhouses in their work. Residents in other parts of the country may live in a suburban Dutch Colonial Revival house without knowing it, so little awareness remains.

Advertising firms, marketing departments, and development offices rarely recommend Dutch names or logos when introducing new products to the American public. A few of the products marketed nationally at the turn of the century do remain on the market. Dutch Boy paint has used variations on Earle's 1907 design through the years, and in 1987 revived the original image as part of an advertising campaign to reposition Dutch Boy in the market (FIG. 149). Its long-term recognition factor made this a viable strategy. But Dutch Boy is one of the few national brands still using Dutch imagery in its marketing and it makes no attempt to play up its Dutch traits in current advertising copy. Van de Kamps switched from bakery products to frozen fish and dropped its windmill logo. Old Dutch cleanser and Dutch Masters cigars eventually lost their high visibility.

Most products with Dutch brand names or logos today are produced in Dutch-American ethnic communities or by people of Dutch descent. In the past decades, for instance, the Holland-American Wafer Company of Grand Rapids has produced Dutch Treat candy and Dutch Twins snack food. Dutch Boy yeast comes from Holland, Michigan and the Old Dutch Mustard Company manufactures condiments in Great Neck, New York. A few enterprises deal with ethnic products. Until recently Holland Honey Cake Company of Holland, Michigan marketed a traditional Dutch ginger-flavored breakfast cake. Other products seem unrelated to their brand names. The Vandermolen Corporation makes Windmill brand lawn equipment and Old Dutch International sells its kitchen ware under the name of Leyden. These examples indicate the continuing presence of Dutch-Americans in American commerce, rather than a widespread attraction to things Dutch on the part of the average consumer.

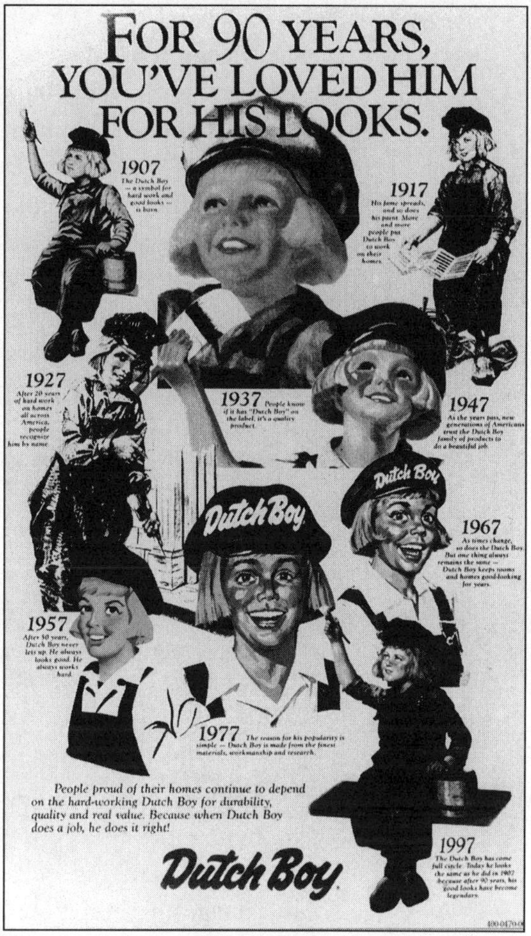

FIG. 149 *Lawrence Earle's image for Dutch Boy paints has gone through many variations since he created it in 1907. The original reappeared on its 80th birthday and is still in use in 1997. This is one of the only products invested with Dutch name and image at the turn of the century that still flourishes in the United States.*

Since 1903 the Netherlands has maintained a Chamber of Commerce in the United States to promote economic development (the United States did not open its Chamber of Commerce in the Netherlands until 1961). As early as 1912, the Royal Dutch Shell/Shell Group entered the American market, forming the Shell Union Oil Corporation ten years later. Since 1985 Shell Oil Company has been wholly owned by The Hague-based Royal Dutch Shell/Shell Group. This may be one of the most pointed examples of Dutch economic interest in United States commerce, but it is certainly not unique. Several companies, like Amsterdam-based

Heineken beer and Philips electronics have held strong positions in their respective American markets during the twentieth century. In addition, the Dutch banks ABN Amro and International Nederlanden Groep are strongly involved in U.S. banking and financial services. Although the Dutch are major foreign investors in the United States, their presence generally goes unnoticed by the American public. This contrasts with the often controversial Japanese presence. Perhaps Americans are unable to see beyond the stereotypes that solidified at the turn of the century, and are perpetuated by local Dutch festivals, to recognize the Dutch as sophisticated financiers and businessmen. That image still attaches to the seventeenth-century Netherlands but has yet to become visible to most Americans as part of the character of the Netherlands in the twentieth century.

All of this suggests that as the intense Dutch bias of Holland Mania died out, and the national awareness of the Netherlands and its impact on U.S. history faded, isolated pockets of strong Dutch interest emerged. These pockets center on communities founded by immigrants from the Netherlands. Rather than non-Dutch Americans suggesting that the basic institutions that produce American character came from the Netherlands, as happened when Holland was in fashion, these contemporary Dutch-Americans promote cities like Pella and Holland as little oases of Holland in America. Their very isolation intensifies the stereotypical nature of the image they promote, an image virtually unchanged from the turn-of-the-century tourist stereotype. If the land of windmills and wooden shoes was an American playland one hundred years ago, these towns have taken a role as Dutch vacation spots today. Meanwhile, the real presence of Netherlands influence in the United States today seems almost invisible and the lament that ended a number of travel books around 1910—that Americans view the Netherlands through an out-of-date and childish lens—may still apply.

APPENDIX

DOCUMENTATION OF AMERICAN ARTISTS' ACTIVITIES IN HOLLAND FROM DUTCH ARCHIVES

This appendix, compiled from archival sources in the Netherlands, is intended to aid the art collector, dealer, historian and researcher in documenting individual artists' presence in the Netherlands. Each entry begins with the name and address given by the artist in the first archival source listed. If information was changed or added in subsequent visits or sources, the changes are listed in the appropriate place. Otherwise, the information continued to be used by the artist and it is not repeated in the entry. Most visitor books depended on the signer to write down the date. Where no date appeared with a signature I have provided an approximate date in brackets based on the position of the signature relative to dated signatures. Other information that I deemed useful, such as traveling companions, is also included in brackets. All unbracketed information was provided by the artist in the archival source.

Archival sources are indicated in small caps as follows: RIJKSMUSEUM COPY PERMITS—record of permits to copy art in the Rijksmuseum, Amsterdam, now in the State Archives of North Holland, Haarlem; HALSMUSEUM—visitor books of the Municipal Museum of Haarlem (renamed the Frans Halsmuseum in 1913), now in the Municipal Archives of Haarlem; HOTEL FRITZ VELDHUIZEN, VOLENDAM—guest register, private collection; HOTEL SPAANDER, VOLENDAM—guest registers, excluding volume one which was not available, property of Hotel Spaander; DORDRECHTS SOCIETEIT AMICITIAE—record book of introductions, now in Dordrecht Municipal Archives; DORDRECHT MUSEUM—visitor books, now in Dordrecht Municipal Archives; ARTI ET AMICITIAE—membership records of this national fine art association which maintains its own archive, Amsterdam; ACADEMY OF FINE ARTS, THE HAGUE—student enrollment records, Municipal Archives of The Hague; HAAGSE KUNSTKRING—membership records of this artist society established in 1891, Municipal Archives of The Hague; PULCHRI STUDIO—membership records of this national fine art association which maintains its own archive, The Hague; EGMOND BAD BODE—a weekly summer newspaper that listed visitors to the town, Egmond Municipal Archives. Most of these sources involved signatures, some of which were nearly illegible or contained mistakes. This was particularly true in the case of the Rijksmuseum copy permits, because information from the applications that artists filled out was transferred to record books by Dutch scribes who had to decipher the unfamiliar names and handwriting. The reader should be aware that spellings of names vary according to the recorder's transcription of the original and my ability to decipher the recorder's signatures. Occasionally, too, artists spelled their names more than one way, as is the case with Walter MacEwen or McEwen.

It was not always possible to determine whether a signature belonged to an artist or someone else with the same name. When in doubt, I have chosen to err on the side of inclusion. I also included a few art critics and historians, as well as everyone who identified him or herself as an artist in the archives, even if they are unknown today. Since visitors were not required to sign museum books, this may only represent a fraction of those artists actually visiting the museums. Similarly, volumes of guest registers and newspapers were incomplete.

Abbey, Edwin A., London, at HALSMUSEUM 7 Oct 1880. At DORDRECHT MUSEUM, New York City [with George Boughton, Sept or Oct 1880].

Aiken, May, Boston, RIJKSMUSEUM COPY PERMITS 17 Nov 1909 and 8 Dec 1909, oil, Rembrandt *Elizabeth Bas*. At HALSMUSEUM 27 Nov 1909.

Alexander, J.W., artist, New York USA, at DORDRECHT MUSEUM [July 1884].

Anderson, Karl J., New York USA, at HALSMUSEUM 2/3 July 1901. In EGMOND BAD BODE, [no address], 15 Aug 1901, staying at the Hotel Belvedere.

Andrews, Iris M., Ohio USA, at HOTEL SPAANDER, VOLENDAM [late Aug or early Sept 1903].

Ayers, Ch. H.A., New Haven, RIJKSMUSEUM COPY PERMITS 2 July 1913, oil, Fr Hals *Nicolaes Hasselaer*; 20 Aug 1913, oil, Hals *De Nar*.

Bacon, Chas R., New York, at HALSMUSEUM 9 June 1890.

Bacon, Julia, Boston USA, at HOTEL SPAANDER, VOLENDAM [apparently with M.R. Sturgis, Spring 1900].

Bailey, Euphemia, Kentucky USA, at HALSMUSEUM 10 Oct 1890 [with Henriette Wachman and Christine S. Bredin].

Bain, Harriet F., Kenosha Wisconsin, at HALSMUSEUM 18 July 1889 and 18 Aug 1891.

Ball, Alice W., America, in EGMOND BAD BODE, 3 Au 1903, 17 Aug 1903, 3 Sept 1903.

Barlow, W. [Myron?], Paris, RIJKSMUSEUM COPY PERMIT 17 May 1898, oil, studies of various paintings.

Barlow, Myron, Paris, at HALSMUSEUM 14/15 April 1898, 24/25 Oct 1898, 23/27 Oct 1903; Etaples France, 26/27 July 1905, 16 Aug 1906; Paris, 11 Dec 1907.

Barone, Antonio, New York, at HALSMUSEUM 17 Sept 1910. At HOTEL SPAANDER, VOLENDAM [spelled Antonie Baroni here] 9/21-10/4/10.

Barrie, Alice H., America, in EGMOND BAD BODE, 3 Aug 1903, 17 Aug 1903, 3 Sept 1903.

Barthold, Manuel, Paris et New York USA, at HOTEL SPAANDER, VOLENDAM [Sept or Oct 1906].

Bartle, Miss Sara N., Washington City DC, at HOTEL SPAANDER, VOLENDAM [July or August 1899].

Beaux, Miss Cecilia, Philadelphia, at HALSMUSEUM 27 July 1900. At HOTEL SPAANDER, VOLENDAM [with Anne Blake, Aug 1900].

Beckington, Alice, Des Moines USA, at HALSMUSEUM 3 Sept 1885. At DORDRECHT MUSEUM Sept 1885.

Beckwith, Carroll, New York, at HALSMUSEUM 4 Aug 1887.

Bedford, H.E., New York, NY USA, at HALSMUSEUM [probably with Gari Melchers, between 3 & 15 June 1883].

Benoni, Irwin, San Francisco, RIJKSMUSEUM COPY PERMIT 17 May 1878, oil, Fr Hals.

Biddle, George, Philadelphia, at HOTEL SPAANDER, VOLENDAM [with Sydney Biddle, June or July 1906].

Bittinger, Charles, Paris, RIJKSMUSEUM COPY PERMITS 24 Aug 1904, oil, Vermeer *Woman Reading a Letter*; 17 Sept 1906, oil, some porcelains. At HALSMUSEUM, Washington DC USA, 11 Sept 1902; Paris France, 5 Sept 1904 and 26 Sept 1906.

Black, Norman I., Boston USA, at HALSMUSEUM 22 June 1908.

Blake, Miss Anne D., Boston, at HALSMUSEUM 29/30 June 1904. At HOTEL SPAANDER, VOLENDAM [with Cecilia Beaux, Aug 1900].

Blashfield, E.H., New York City USA, at HALSMUSEUM 27 July 1900.

Blum, Paris, at HALSMUSEUM 1 Aug 1883.

Blumenschein, E.L., New York, at HOTEL SPAANDER, VOLENDAM, "The Big four on wheels through Holland July 1900" [with S.W. Farrar of Melrose, MA, F.A. Gendrot of Boston and S. Walden of Paris].

Bogert, George H., New York, RIJKSMUSEUM COPY PERMIT 6 June 1899, oil, J. Maris *City View*. At HALSMUSEUM 2 July 1898 and 28 Sept 1899.

Boggs, F.M., Paris, at HALSMUSEUM 25 Sept 1886. At HOTEL SPAANDER, VOLENDAM, Frank Boggs [July 1907]. At DORDRECHT MUSEUM, artist, New York [1883].

Borgord, Martin, Laren, RIJKSMUSEUM COPY PERMITS 4 Dec 1903, oil, Hals *De Nar*; 12 Dec 1903, oil, Hals *The Merry Drinker*; Pittsburgh, 13 Dec 1904, oil, Rembrandt *The Jewish Bride*. At HALSMUSEUM, Pittsburgh USA, 5/7 July 1902, 10/19 Dec 1902, 15/16 Oct 1903; Paris, 9 May 1910.

Boughton, George H., London, at HALSMUSEUM 7 Oct 1880, [4-5 Oct 1881]. At DORDRECHT MUSEUM [with Edwin Abbey, Sept or Oct 1880].

Bredin, Christine S., USA, at HALSMUSEUM 10 Oct 1890 [with Euphemia Bailey and Henriette Wachman].

Brevoort, James R., New York, at HALSMUSEUM 18 July 1894.

Bridgman, F.A., [no address given] at HALSMUSEUM 16/17 June 1902.

Browne, G.E., New York, RIJKSMUSEUM COPY PERMIT 1 June 1901, oil, Fr. Hals *The Merry Drinker*. At HALSMUSEUM, Geo Elmer Browne, New York City, 3/4 Aug 1905.

Buehler, Lytton, Gettysburg Pa USA, at HALSMUSEUM 14 Aug 1908 [apparently with Annie T. Lang].

Burleigh, C.C., Philadelphia, RIJKSMUSEUM COPY PERMIT 12 June 1882, oil, Rembrandt.

Burnside, Cameron, Paris France, at HALSMUSEUM 3 Aug 1908, 2 Oct 1908 [apparently with Myron Barlow], 4 May 1911 "artiste peintre" [with wife all three times].

Burnside, Mrs Cameron, Paris, at HALSMUSEUM 3 Aug 1908, 2 Oct 1908 [apparently with Myron Barlow], 4 May 1911 "artiste peintre" [with husband all three times].

Butler, Miss Mary, Philadelphia, at HALSMUSEUM 30 June 1910 [with Elizabeth R. Butler]. At HOTEL SPAANDER, VOLENDAM [with Elizabeth Butler, June 1910].

Bye, A.E., Philadelphia, RIJKSMUSEUM COPY PERMIT 21 Dec 1910, oil, Anon. *Portrait of a Man* [now attributed to Joos van Cleve].

Caffin, Charles H. [art historian], New York, at HALSMUSEUM 13 June 1908.

Calder, Ralph, Philadelphia USA, at HALSMUSEUM 29 Aug 1908 [with Gerald Holmes & Roy Bassette].

Cassatt, Miss, Paris, at HALSMUSEUM 14/16 June 1902.

Cauldwell, Leslie G., New York City, at HALSMUSEUM [July 1884].

Champney, J. Wells, New York, RIJKSMUSEUM COPY PERMIT 26 Aug 1893, pastel, J.F.A. Tischbein *Portrait of Frederika Louisa Wilhelmina*. At HALSMUSEUM 22 Aug 1892.

Chase, H., St. Louis USA, at HALSMUSEUM 2 Aug 1878, 20 May 1879.

Chase, J. Eastman, Boston, at HALSMUSEUM [July 1883].

Chase, Prof. W., New York, RIJKSMUSEUM COPY PERMIT 21 Aug 1903, fragment of Hals *The Company of Captain Reynier Reael*. At HALSMUSEUM, Chase, Wm M., 29 Aug 1878, [July 1883], [17-24 June 1884], 18 Aug 1885, 5 Sept 1885, 1/2 July 1903.

Clarke, Thos S., Pittsburg Pa USA, at HALSMUSEUM [9-12 July 1884]. At DORDRECHT MUSEUM, painter [with Louis S. Clarke, masher, July 1884].

Claus, W.A.G. [J.?], Boston, RIJKSMUSEUM COPY PERMIT 15 July 1892, oil, Rubens *Portrait of Anna Maria*.

Clephane, Lewis, Washington D.C., at HOTEL SPAANDER, VOLENDAM [Aug or Sept 1911].

Coate, Harry W., New York, RIJKSMUSEUM COPY PERMIT 18 Sept 1903, oil, Hals *The Merry Drinker*.

Closson, W.B., Boston, at HALSMUSEUM [2 Sept 1882].

Cochrane, Miss. J.G., America, in EGMOND BAD BODE, 3 Aug 1903, 17 Aug 1903, 3 Sept 1903.

Cole, A.P., New York, RIJKSMUSEUM COPY PERMIT 25 Aug 1892, oil, Vermeer *Woman Reading a Letter*.

Cole, J. Foxcroft, Boston, at HALSMUSEUM 29 Sept 1887, 14 June 1890.

Cole, Timothy, New York, RIJKSMUSEUM COPY PERMITS 18 June 1892, engraving, mid section of Rembrandt's *Nightwatch*; 10 Aug 1892, engraving, Hals *De Nar*; 4 Sept 1893 [?], various examples; 31 Aug 1892, engraving, Gerard Dou *The Night School*; 28 Nov 1892, etching, Jan Steen *St. Nicolaas*.

Congdon, Adairene, Paris 83^{lei} rue N D des

Champs, at HOTEL SPAANDER, VOLENDAM [with husband Thomas, June or July 1906].
Congdon, Thos R., New York, at HALSMUSEUM 27/29 Sept 1902. At HOTEL SPAANDER, VOLENDAM, Paris 83lei rue N D des Champs [with wife Adairene, June or July 1906].
Cook, Miss B., America, RIJKSMUSEUM COPY PERMIT 24 July 1903, studies of some paintings.
Cooper, Emma L. see Lampert, Emma E.
Cope, Caleb, honorary member of ARTI ET AMICITIAE, AMSTERDAM, 1863.
Corner, Mr. Thomas Cromwell [no address given], RIJKSMUSEUM COPY PERMIT 9 Oct 1901, oil, Rembrandt *The Syndics*. At HALSMUSEUM, Thos C., Baltimore USA, 22 Nov 1888, 5 June 1890, 18 Sept 1901.
Cortissoz, Royal [art historian and critic], New York, at HALSMUSEUM 18 April 1891.
Corwin, C.A., Newburg NY USA, at HALSMUSEUM [with Duveneck and Theo. Wores, June 1881].
Couse, E. Irving, NY, at HOTEL SPAANDER, VOLENDAM [with Kibbey W. and Virginia W. Couse, July 1900].
Cox, Kenyon, New York, at HALSMUSEUM 12 Sept 1889.
Cranmer, Miss Frances, Washington, RIJKSMUSEUM COPY PERMITS 7 Sept 1911, oil, Fr Hals *Nicolaes Hasselaer*; 25 Sept 1911, oil, Vermeer *Kitchen Maid*.
Crawford, Theron C., New York, RIJKSMUSEUM COPY PERMIT 2 Feb 1904, drawings, various subjects.
Cross, Miss Amy, New York USA, at HALSMUSEUM 15 July 1890 and 4/5 April 1894; Miss. Cross, 29 June 1907. Attended ACADEMY OF FINE ARTS, THE HAGUE, winter 1889-1890, summer 1890, winter 1892-1893. Member of PULCHRI STUDIO, THE HAGUE, 1893-97.
Cross, Anson R., Boston, at HALSMUSEUM 17 July 1890.
Cucuel, Edward, Munich & San Francisco, at HALSMUSEUM 21 May 1908.
Cutler, Carl G., Newton Mass USA, at HALSMUSEUM 3/4 June 1901. In EGMOND BAD BODE, C.J. [sic] Cutler, America, 1 July 1897, 15 July 1897, 1 Sept 1897; Carl C. [sic] Cutler, 15 Aug 1901, 7 Sept 1901, staying at the Hotel Belvedere.
Dahlgreen, Charles W., Chicago, RIJKSMUSEUM COPY PERMITS 14 Oct 1909, oil, Frans Hals *De Nar*; 20 Oct 1909, oil, Rembrandt *Nightwatch*. At HALSMUSEUM 29 Nov 1909.
Davey, Randall V., East Orange NJ, at HALSMUSEUM 17 June 1910, 2 July 1910.
Dean, W.L., Boston USA, at HALSMUSEUM [July 1883].
Debereiner, George, Cincinnati O, at HOTEL SPAANDER, VOLENDAM July 14 to Nov 10 1904 [Though dated 1904, this signature is located in the middle of Nov 1903 signatures].
Denby, Edwin H., Philadelphia, RIJKSMUSEUM COPY PERMIT 7 Sept 1896, sketches of the museum building interior.
Descombes, Emilie D., Boston USA, at HALSMUSEUM 12/19 Nov 1895.
Dessar, Louis Paul, New York, at HALSMUSEUM 28 Aug 1899.
Devoll, F. Usher, Providence RI USA, at HALSMUSEUM 11 June 1907.
Dey, H.E., America, in EGMOND BAD BODE, 19 Aug 1896, 1 June 1897.
Dickinson, Sidney, Boston, at HALSMUSEUM [8 July 1884].
Dieleman, Fr., New York, RIJKSMUSEUM COPY PERMIT, 1 Aug 1899, oil, D.A.C. Artz *At Grandmother's House*. At HALSMUSEUM, Frederick, 7 July 1899 [with Marion L. Dielman].
Dillaye, Blanche, Phila USA, at HALSMUSEUM 28/29 June 1899. At DORDRECHT MUSEUM, artist, [with E.L. Peirce, July 1884].
Dirks, Rudolph, N.Y. City, at HOTEL SPAANDER, VOLENDAM [with Mrs. H Dirks, between March and June 1913].
Dobson, Geo H. Jr., painter, U.S. of America, at DORDRECHT MUSEUM [with C.Y. Turner, 1880, probably June], [Sept 1880].
Donaldson, Fred N., Philadelphia, RIJKSMUSEUM COPY PERMIT 30 June 1911, oil, Vermeer *Woman Reading a Letter*.
Donoho, G. Rugor, artist, Washington D.C. USA, at DORDRECHT MUSEUM [with Charles Vanderhest, Sept 1880].
Duveneck, [no first name], Covington KY USA, at HALSMUSEUM [with C.A. Corwin and Theo. Wores, June 1881]; Frank, 17 July 1909.
Eaton, Chas Warren, [illeg.], at HALSMUSEUM 8 Sept 1886, New York 13/14 Sept 1905.
Edgar, Miss Isabel R., New York, RIJKSMUSEUM COPY PERMITS 26 Aug 1891, oil, P.L.J.F. Sadee *Naleren*; 22 Sept 1891, watercolor, Sadee *Return from the Fish Auction*.
Ehninger, John W., New York, at HALSMUSEUM 17 July 1888.
Eilshemius, L.W.[?], New York, at HALSMUSEUM 26 Aug 1887.
Elmendorf, D.L., New York, RIJKSMUSEUM COPY PERMIT 20 June 1905, photographs, various paintings. At

HALSMUSEUM, Dwight L., 12 July 1894, 14 May 1908.

Elmendorf, Stella, New York, RIJKSMUSEUM COPY PERMIT 18 June 1910, oil, H. W. Mesdag *Calm Sea*.

Elwell, painter, Boston, Introduction to DORDRECHTS SOCIETEIT AMICITIAE (Societeit de Harmonie) 7/8 Sept 1901, valid 14 days, sponsor [illegible].

Esté, Miss Florence, Philadelphia, at HALSMUSEUM 18 May 1888 and 19 April 1911.

Ewer, Mr R.C., Riverside Drive 456 New York City, at HOTEL FRITZ VELDHUIZEN, VOLENDAM, [first signature in guest register, c.1900]; later visit gave address as St. Helena Nafa Co. California [date unknown]. At HOTEL SPAANDER, VOLENDAM, Raymond C., 7/12/09.

Fairchild, Lucia, Boston, at HALSMUSEUM 3 June 1891 [with Lilla Cabot Perry].

Falcott, Allin Butler, Hartford (America), RIJKSMUSEUM COPY PERMIT 29 April 1890, oil, Rembrandt, fragments from *The Syndics*.

Faubaulas [?], F.P., Boston, RIJKSMUSEUM COPY PERMIT 18 Jan 1905, oil, Vermeer, *Woman Reading a Letter*.

Fauley, Albert C., Columbus Ohio, at HALSMUSEUM 27 July 1903. At HOTEL SPAANDER, VOLENDAM [with wife, June or July 1903].

Ferris, Edith, Paris, at HALSMUSEUM 7/17 March 1900, 24/26 June 1902, 19 July 1908.

Feudel, Arthur, New York City, at HALSMUSEUM 13/17 March 1903 and 16/18 May 1903; Katwijk Rijn, 19 Jan 1907 and 16 Nov 1910. Member of ARTI ET AMICITIAE, AMSTERDAM, 1906.

Flagg, Charles N., New York USA, at HALSMUSEUM 13 June 1880.

Fliermans, C.L. Jr., The Hague, RIJKSMUSEUM COPY PERMITS 28 Feb 1899, oil, Maria Vos *Still life*, Miss H. Ronner-Knip *Three Against One*, P. v.d. Velden *Double Blank*; 29 Mar 1899, oil, G.J. van Soeren *Homesick*; 15 April 1899, Chicago, oil, Hobbema *Windmills*. At HALSMUSEUM, New York, 19 April 1906.

Florian, Walter, Amsterdam temporarily, RIJKSMUSEUM COPY PERMIT 4 Dec 1902, oil, Vermeer *Woman Reading a Letter*.

Foley, Dorothea, Paris, at HALSMUSEUM 10 Sept 1902.

Foote, Mary, New Haven USA, at HOTEL SPAANDER, VOLENDAM [August 1899].

Forbes, Miss Elizabeth, Philadelphia, RIJKSMUSEUM COPY PERMIT 27 Aug 1912, oil, Vermeer *Kitchen Maid*.

Fox, Charles L., painter, Paris, at DORDRECHT MUSEUM [1885], 3/9 '85 [with Rotterdam painter Deickmann].

Fox, J., artist, Paris, Introduction to Dordrechts Societeit Amicitiae (Societeit de Harmonie) 22 June 1885, valid 14 days, sponsor [illegible]. [This may also be Charles Lewis Fox, who worked in Dordrecht for about a year and held an exhibition at the Dordrecht Museum in August 1886 before leaving.]

France, J.L., New York USA, at HALSMUSEUM 3 July 1888.

Freer, Miss [Cora?], Chicago USA, at HALSMUSEUM 25/26 June 1895.

Freer, Frederick W., New York, at HALSMUSEUM [July 1883].

Fromkes, M., New York, RIJKSMUSEUM COPY PERMITS 2 June 1899, oil, Rembrandt *Elizabeth Bas* and 14 July 1899, oil, Fr Hals *De Nar*. At HALSMUSEUM, Maurice, 2 June 1899, 2/4 Nov 1904, 16 July 1910, 20 Sept 1910.

Fromuth, Chas A.[?], Philadelphia, at HALSMUSEUM 13 Sept 1889.

Fuller, Lucia see Fairchild, Lucia Fuller.

Gamble, Roy C., Paris, at HALSMUSEUM 9 July 1910.

Garber, Daniel, Philadelphia, at HALSMUSEUM 10/12 Oct 1905 [with wife].

Gauley, Robert D., Boston, RIJKSMUSEUM COPY PERMITS 25 Aug 1898, sketch of Hals *De Nar*; 3 Sept 1898, [spelled Gauly this time], fragment of Fr Hals *The Company of Captain Reynier Reael*. At HALSMUSEUM, 10 Aug 1898 and 23 Aug 1898; Robert David, New York City USA, 16 Aug 1902, 13/18 Nov 1902, 13/17 March 1903.

Gay, Walter, Paris, RIJKSMUSEUM COPY PERMIT 15 November 1880, oil, Rembrandt.

Gendrot, Felix A., Boston, at HALSMUSEUM 20 Aug 1910 [with Almira B. Fenns-Gendrot]. At HOTEL SPAANDER, VOLENDAM [with Sidney D. Farrar of Melrose, before July 25, 1900], "The big four on wheels through Holland July 1900" [with E.L. Blumenschein of New York, S.W. Farrar of Melrose and S. Walden of Paris].

Gilbert, Cass, USA, at HALSMUSEUM 11/18 Dec 1897.

Gilchrist, W.W., Philadelphia, RIJKSMUSEUM COPY PERMIT 22 Nov 1900, oil, Fr Hals *De Nar*. At HALSMUSEUM, W. Wallace Jr., 4/6 Oct 1900. At HOTEL SPAANDER, VOLENDAM, W. W. Jr. [with Lucretia Gilchrist and Helen Niles, July or Aug 1903].

Gill, Miss Rosalie, New York, at HALSMUSEUM [17-24 June 1884], 6 Mar 1886 [with Emily Slade and Caroline Gridley].

Gottwald, F.C., Cleveland Ohio, at HALSMU-

SEUM 6/7 Aug 1903. At HOTEL SPAANDER, VOLENDAM May-Aug 1903 [with wife].

Grafton, Mr and Mrs Robert W., Fine Arts Bldg. Chicago, at HOTEL SPAANDER, VOLENDAM [between Sept 8 and 16, 1908].

Greacen [?], Edmund, New York, RIJKSMUSEUM COPY PERMIT 3 July 1906, oil, Frans Hals *Married Couple, full length*.

Grafton, Robert W., Chicago Ill, at HALSMUSEUM 27 Oct 1908.

Green, Frank Russell, New York City, at HOTEL SPAANDER, VOLENDAM [with wife and Miss Dorothy Green, July or August 1899].

Griffin, Walter, Portland Maine, at HALSMUSEUM 9 May 1910 [with William H. Singer].

Gruppe, C.P., Katwijk a Zee, at HALSMUSEUM 13/15 June 1899. Charles Paul Gruppe, member of ARTI ET AMICITIAE, AMSTERDAM, 1900. Attended ACADEMY OF FINE ARTS, THE HAGUE, winter 1890-91. Member of HAAGSE KUNSTKRING, 1898-1904. Member of PULCHRI STUDIO, THE HAGUE, 1898-1923.

Guild, Katherine E., Boston USA, at HALSMUSEUM 9 Nov 1894.

Gutmann, Bernhard & Bertha, NY, NY, at HOTEL SPAANDER, VOLENDAM [1908].

Hackubin, Miss Florence, Baltimore, RIJKSMUSEUM COPY PERMIT 5 Aug 1914, oil M J v Miereveld *J Cats*.

Hale, E.D., Boston, RIJKSMUSEUM COPY PERMIT 4 June 1881 [exact date uncertain, between 4 June & 1 Aug], oil, various Rembrandts [with H. M. Knowlton]. At HALSMUSEUM [5-6] July 1881.

Hale, Robert, Paris, RIJKSMUSEUM COPY PERMIT 30 Aug 1902, oil, Rembrandt *Mythological Performance*.

Hall, Fr. G., Boston, RIJKSMUSEUM COPY PERMIT 11 Aug 1906, oil, N. Maes *Woman Spinning* [calling card of Frederick Garrison Hall, with "Hotel Het Water van Friesland, Beurstraat 19" pencilled in below the printed name, is inserted in record book here].

Hall, Geo Henry, New York, at HALSMUSEUM 1 July 1889, 24 July 1901.

Hall, Harvey W., Boston, RIJKSMUSEUM COPY PERMIT 15 May 1903, oil, Rembrandt *Portrait of a Woman*.

Hardwick, Melbourne H., Boston USA, at HALSMUSEUM 18 July 1910. At HOTEL SPAANDER, VOLENDAM, Gloucester, Mass., [Aug or Sept 1910].

Harrison, Mr L. Birge, Plymouth Mass USA, at HALSMUSEUM 15 Aug 1902.

Haskell, William H., America, in EGMOND BAD BODE, 15 Aug 1901, 7 Sept 1901, staying at the Hotel Belvedere.

Hawley, Margaret F., Washington DC, at HOTEL SPAANDER, VOLENDAM [about 7 August 1899].

Hawley, Wilhelmina D., New York, at HALSMUSEUM 23 Aug 1892, 9 Aug 1894.

Healy, G.P.A., Paris, RIJKSMUSEUM COPY PERMIT 23 Sept 1885, oil, Rembrandt.

Hecht, Victor D., Amsterdam, RIJKSMUSEUM COPY PERMITS 1 July 1909, oil, Hals *De Nar*; 5 July 1909, oil, Hals *Nicolaes Hasselaer*; 6 July 1909, oil, Hals *The Merry Drinker*; 10 July 1909, oil, Hals *The Company of Captain Reynier Reael*. At HALSMUSEUM, New York City, 13 July 1909 and 20 June 1911.

Henderson, Wm P., Boston, RIJKSMUSEUM COPY PERMIT 5 Nov 1902, oil, Hals *The Merry Drinker*.

Henri, Robert, NY City USA, at HALSMUSEUM 28 June 1907, 17 June 1910, 2 July 1910. At HOTEL SPAANDER, VOLENDAM [between July 2 and 7, 1907].

Herdle, G.L., Rochester NY, at HALSMUSEUM 13/15 June 1899.

Hergesheimer, Miss Ella S., Allentown Pa USA, at HOTEL SPAANDER, VOLENDAM [with Alice Schille, Sept or Oct 1903].

Herrmann, F.S., New York, at HALSMUSEUM 7 July 1888, 16 July 1895.

Higgins, Eugene, St Louis MO USA, at HALSMUSEUM 21 July 1904.

Hilliard, W.H., Boston USA, at DORDRECHT MUSEUM Sept 1st 1885 [with Walter Lansil].

Hills, Laura Coombs, Boston USA, at HALSMUSEUM 20 July 1908.

Hitchcock, George, USA, at HALSMUSEUM [2-19 Sept 1880], [20] May 1881, [6 May 1884]; Egmond aan Zee, 4 July 1887 and 29 Aug 1887; Egmond a/Hoef, 26 June 1901 and 31 Mar 1903; Providence R.I., 28/29 June 1904. In EGMOND BAD BODE, America, 1 July 1897, 15 July 1897, 1 Sept 1897.

Hoa-LeBlanc, E.M., New Orleans La USA, at HALSMUSEUM 23/26 July 1904.

Holland, F. Raymond, Pittsburg, at HOTEL SPAANDER, VOLENDAM [1908].

Homans, Nannie, Springfield MA, at HALSMUSEUM 23 Aug 1892. In EGMOND BAD BODE, Miss N. Homans, America, 3 Aug 1903, 17 Aug 1903, 3 Sept 1903.

Hopkins, Pery [sic] R., America, in EGMOND BAD BODE, 15 Aug 1901, 7 Sept 1901, staying at the Hotel Belvedere.

Horton, William S., New York, at HALSMUSEUM 22/23 June 1894.

Howland, Alfred C., N Y City, at HOTEL SPAANDER, VOLENDAM Sept. 2, 1900.

Hubbard, Miss M.W., New York, at HOTEL SPAANDER, VOLENDAM Aug '09. In EGMOND BAD BODE, Miss Mary W. Hubbard, 1 June 1897, 1 July 1897, 15 July 1897, 1 Sept 1897.

Hunt, Leigh, New York City, at HALSMUSEUM 7 Aug 1908.

Hutchens, F.T., New York, RIJKSMUSEUM COPY PERMIT 28 Dec 1907, oil, Fr. Hals, *De Nar*. At HALSMUSEUM Frank T., Canandaique NY USA, 27 July 1897, 8 Aug 1907; New York 11 Nov 1907.

Huurkes, Joseph, New York, RIJKSMUSEUM COPY PERMIT 27 Aug 1903, sketches of some paintings.

Inness, George, New York, at HALSMUSEUM 16 July 1894.

Ives, Chauncey, Brooklyn NY, at HALSMUSEUM [April 1886].

Ives, Halsy C., St Louis, at HALSMUSEUM 25 Aug 1891.

James, William, Jr., Boston, RIJKSMUSEUM COPY PERMIT 11 Aug 1906, oil, Vermeer *Woman Reading a Letter* [calling card of William James, Jr., with "Hotel Het Water van Friesland, Beurstraat 19" pencilled in below printed name, is inserted in record book here].

Jarrow, H.K., Pennsylvania, RIJKSMUSEUM COPY PERMIT 22 July 1913, oil, Frans Hals *Maritje Voogt*.

Jay, Miss., England, in EGMOND BAD BODE, 3 Aug 1903, 17 Aug 1903, 3 Sept 1903.

Jones, Miss Jessie B., America, in EGMOND BAD BODE, 3 Aug 1903, 17 Aug 1903, 3 Sept 1903.

Kaula, Lee Lufkin, Amsterdam, RIJKSMUSEUM COPY PERMIT 2 June 1903, oil, Hals *De Nar*. At HALSMUSEUM, Kaula, Mrs. Wm. J., Boston, 2/3 June 1903 [with William J. Kaula]. [see also Lufkin, Lee]

Kaula, Wm. J., Boston, Mass USA, at HALSMUSEUM 2/3 June 1903 [with Lee Lufkin Kaula].

Keffer, Francis, Des Moines Iowa, at HALSMUSEUM 11 Sept 1908.

Keith, W. Castle, USA, at HALSMUSEUM 8 Aug 1907. At HOTEL SPAANDER, VOLENDAM Castle Keith, Syracuse N.Y. [with his aunt Miss Ellen Lee, Aug or Sept 1910].

Kellogg, A.D., artist, Chicago USA, at DORDRECHT MUSEUM [with K.S. Kellogg and G.E. Kellogg, July 1888].

King, Charles B., Detroit USA, at HALSMUSEUM 30 Aug 1907 [with wife].

King, Paul, New York, at HALSMUSEUM 10 Aug 1905.

Klumpke, Miss Anna E., Boston, at HALSMUSEUM 29 Aug 1895.

Klumpky, Miss E., Boston, RIJKSMUSEUM COPY PERMIT 2 Sept 1895, oil, studies of various paintings.

Knight, Aston, artist, Paris, Introduction to DORDRECHTS SOCIETEIT AMICITIAE (Societeit de Harmonie) 1 Jan. 1899, valid 14 days, sponsor Notnij[?].

Knowlton, H.M., Boston America, RIJKSMUSEUM COPY PERMIT 4 June 1881 [exact date uncertain. between 4 June & 1 Aug], oil, various Rembrandts [with E.D. Hale]. At HALSMUSEUM [5-6] July 1881.

Koopman, Aug. B., USA, at HALSMUSEUM 13 May 1892; Etaples France, 16 Aug 1906.

Kronberg, Louis, Paris, RIJKSMUSEUM COPY PERMITS 19 May 1896, oil, Hals *De Nar*; 15 June 1896, oil, studies of various paintings. At HALSMUSEUM 22 May 1896.

Kruseman van Elten, H.D., member of ARTI ET AMICITIAE, AMSTERDAM, 1855.

Kurtz, Charles M, [art critic], New York, at HALSMUSEUM 25 Aug 1891.

Lamb, Chas R., New York, at HALSMUSEUM 11 June 1885 [with Frederick S. Lamb].

Lamb, Fred S., New York, at HALSMUSEUM 11 June 1885 [with Charles R. Lamb].

Lambert, Mr John, Philadelphia, RIJKSMUSEUM COPY PERMIT 21 Sept 1904, oil, Hals *De Nar*. At HALSMUSEUM 22 Sept 1904.

Lampert, Emma E., Rochester NY, at HALSMUSEUM 20 Aug 1891.

Landis, Benj. F., Lancaster Pennsylvania, RIJKSMUSEUM COPY PERMITS 22 April 1893, oil, Rembrandt *Nightwatch*; 31 March 1898, oil J. Neuhuys *Courting*; 14 April 1898, oil, D.A.C. Artz *At Grandmother's House*; 29 April 1898, oil, P.J.C. Gabriel *In the Month of July*; 13 May 1898, oil, Rembrandt *Elizabeth Bas*; 3 June 1898, oil, D.A.C. Artz *At Grandmother's House*; 8 July 1898, oil, Rembrandt *The Syndics*; 24 Sept 1898, oil, N. Maes *Woman Spinning*; 3 Oct 1898, oil, N. Maes *Prayer Without End*; 26 April 1899, oil, Rembrandt *The Syndics*; 20 Feb 1901, oil, N. Maes *Prayer Without End*; 11 June 1901, oil, N. Maes *Prayer Without End*; 5 Aug 1901, oil, N. Maes *Prayer Without End*; 5 Oct 1901, oil, J. Ruysdael *River Scene Wijk bij Duurstede*; 24 June 1902, oil, N. Maes *Prayer Without End*; 23 Aug 1902, oil, Hals *De Nar*; 2 Dec 1902, oil, Rembrandt *Elizabeth Bas*; 17 Feb 1903, oil, N. Maes *Prayer Without End*; 18 April 1903, oil, Hals *De Nar*; 4 June 1903, oil, D.A.C. Artz *At Grandmother's House*; 28 July 1903, oil, N. Maes *Prayer Without End*; 11 Sept 1903, oil, D.A.C. Artz *At Grandmother's House*; 21 Oct 1903, oil, Rembrandt *Nightwatch*; 7 July 1908, Amsterdam temporarily, oil, Hals *The Merry Drinker*; 21 July 1908, America, oil, Hals *De Nar*; 8 Sept 1908, oil, C. Lelienbergh *Dead Birds*; 15 Sept 1908, Amsterdam, oil, Rembrandt *Elizabeth Bas*; 13 Oct 1908, oil, J Steen *After the Drinking Party* [now known as *The Drunken Couple*]; 25 Nov 1908, oil, Hals *The Merry Drinker*; 26 Jan 1909, oil, Rembrandt *Elizabeth Bas*; 26 Mar 1909, oil, Hals *The Merry Drinker*; 19 April 1909, pastel, J.F.A. Tischbein *Portrait of Frederika Louisa Wilhelmina*; 14 June 1909, oil, Maes, *Woman Spinning*; 2 July 1909, oil, Vermeer *Woman Reading a Letter*; 3 Aug 1909, oil, Vermeer *Kitchen Maid*; 17 Aug 1909, oil, Maes *Woman Spinning*; 6 Sept 1909, oil, P. de Hooch *Mother's Duty*; 17 Nov 1909, oil, Vermeer *Kitchen Maid*; 19 Feb 1910, oil, C. Troost *Anatomy Lesson of Prof. W Roell*; 5 April 1910, oil, Joh v Neck *Anatomy Lesson of Prof Fr. Ruysch*; 26 April 1910, oil, M de Hondecoeter *Menagerie*; 1 June 1910, oil, M de Hondecoeter *The Contemplative Magpie*; 22 Aug 1910, oil, Hondecoeter *Farmstead*; 22 Nov 1910, oil, C. Lelienbergh *Dead Birds*; 30 Nov 1910, oil, Vermeer *Kitchen Maid*; 12 Jan 1911, oil fragment of Cornelius Troost *Inspectors of the Collegium Medicum*; 6 March 1911, oil, P. de Hooch *Interior*; 21 April 1911, oil, Vermeer *Woman Reading a Letter*; 30 Oct 1911, oil, Hals *The Merry Drinker*; 26 Nov 1911, oil, Vermeer *Woman Reading a Letter*; 6 Dec 1911, oil, Vermeer *Kitchen Maid*; 1 Feb 1912, oil, Hals *The Merry Drinker*; 2 Mar 1912, oil, Vermeer *Woman Reading a Letter*; 21 May 1912, oil, N. Maes *Prayer Without End*; 13 June 1912, oil, A. Cuyp *Birds Fighting* [now anonymous]; 30 July 1912, oil, P. de Hooch *The Pantry*; 20 Nov 1912, oil, Rembrandt *The Syndics*; 27 Jan 1913, oil, Rembrandt *The Syndics*; 25 Mar 1913, oil, J. Jordaens *A Satyr*; 11 June 1913, oil, J. Jordaens *A Satyr*. At HALSMUSEUM, USA, 27 Dec 1910; Amsterdam, 4 Oct 1911.

Lang, Annie Traquair, Philadelphia, at HALSMUSEUM 14 Aug 1908, New York 24 June 1912.

Lansil, Walter F., Boston USA, at DORDRECHT MUSEUM 1 Sept 1885 [with William Henry Hilliard].

Lauter, Miss Flora, New York, RIJKSMUSEUM COPY PERMIT 18 June 1910, oil, Frans Hals *Maritje Voogt*. At HALSMUSEUM, Indianapolis, 15 June 1910 and 12 Sept 1910.

Leavitt, G.A., Washington, RIJKSMUSEUM COPY PERMIT 17 June 1913, sketches of W. Roelofs [*Landscape in the Neighborhood of The Hague*] and J. J. v.d. Sande Bakhuizen [*Landscape in Drenthe*].

Leavitt, William Hover, Boston, RIJKSMUSEUM COPY PERMIT 12 Aug 1892, oil, Hals *The Merry Drinker*. At HALSMUSEUM 28/30 Oct 1897.

Lesshafft, Franz, painter, Philadelphia, at HALSMUSEUM 4 July 1910 [with S.J. Lesshafft].

Lesshafft, S.J. Popa, paintress, Philadelphia, at HALSMUSEUM 4 July 1910 [with Franz Lesshafft].

Lewis, John T., honorary member of ARTI ET AMICITIAE, AMSTERDAM, 1863.

Lloyd, Mary Lowell, Philadelphia, RIJKSMUSEUM COPY PERMIT 30 June 1913, oil, Vermeer *Woman Reading a Letter*.

Lockwood, R.W., Wilton CT, at HALSMUSEUM 26 July 1889.

Loeb, Louis, New York City, at HALSMUSEUM 4/16 June 1904.

Loring, F. Wm., Boston, at HALSMUSEUM 5 June 1888.

Lufkin, Lee, Lima Ohio USA, at HALSMUSEUM 23 Sept 1896. [see also Kaula, Lee Lufkin].

MacCord, George H., 294 Gates Ave., Brooklyn NY, at HOTEL SPAANDER, VOLENDAM [July 1900].

Magill, Beatrice, Swarthmore Penna USA, at HALSMUSEUM 28/29 July 1899. At HOTEL SPAANDER, VOLENDAM, Philadelphia [August 1899].

Mathews, Arthur F., artist, California USA, at DORDRECHT MUSEUM [1887].

Maury, C.F., St Louis Mo USA, at HALSMUSEUM 28 Aug 1900.

Maynard, Guy T., Chicago, at HALSMUSEUM 18 Aug 1887.

McChesney, Clara, New York USA, at HALSMUSEUM 3 Oct 1891, Clara T. [no address] 27 Sept 1898.

McEwen, Katharine, Detroit, at HALSMUSEUM 7 July 1903. At HOTEL SPAANDER, VOLENDAM [with Louise Murphy of Detroit in 1903, probably August].

McEwen, Walter, Munich, at HALSMUSEUM 13 Aug 1878; Chicago, 18 Aug 1885, 28 Oct 1885, 7 Oct 1886; Paris, France, 8/11 July 1904.

McKay, E. Murray, New York City USA, at HALSMUSEUM 28/29 June 1904; Laren (N.H.), 16/17 Nov 1905.

Melchers, J. Gari, Detroit Mich USA, at HALSMUSEUM [probably with Henry E. Bedford, between 3 & 15 June 1883], 21 Aug 1885; Paris France, 2 Jan 1886, 5 June 1886, 24 Dec 1886, 10 Aug 1897, 23 Sept 1897; Detroit, 28/29 June 1904; Egmond, 21 July 1904; Egmond aan Hoef, 2 Oct 1909, 29 Sept 1911. In EGMOND BAD BODE, Detroit, 1 July 1897, 15 July 1897, 1 Sept 1897; Paris, 15 Aug 1901, 7 Sept 1901, staying at the Hotel Belvedere; America, 1 Aug 1902, 10 Sept 1902, staying at the Drie Egmonden.

Mendenhall, Miss Emma, Cincinnati USA, at HOTEL SPAANDER, VOLENDAM [probably June 1903].

Meyvis, Aime L., Katwijk a Rhyn, at HALSMUSEUM 19 Jan 1907. Aime Leon Meyvis, member of ARTI ET AMICITIAE, AMSTERDAM, 1909.

Millar, A.T., New York, at HALSMUSEUM 21 Sept 1895; Addison T., 18 Aug 1902.

Miller, Charles H., New York USA, at HALSMUSEUM 3 Aug 1879.

Miller, Oscar, Bristol Ferry, R.I., at HOTEL SPAANDER, VOLENDAM [Aug or Sept 1910].

Miller, Wm. B., New York City, at HALSMUSEUM 16/18 May 1903.

Millet, F.D., New York, at HALSMUSEUM 6 July 1889.

Monte, Louis S.[?], Springfield Mass, at HALSMUSEUM 19 Aug 1909. At HOTEL SPAANDER, VOLENDAM Louis G. Monte, Formerly Directly [sic] of Art Classes for Robert Henri and Wm. M. Chase Aug. 19, 1909.

Morgan, Alexander C., NYC, at HOTEL SPAANDER, VOLENDAM [with wife, July or August 1899].

Mowbray, H. Siddons, New York, at HALSMUSEUM 21 Sept 1894.

Mulertt, Carel Eugene, member of ARTI ET AMICITIAE, AMSTERDAM, 1906.

Munsell, Albert H., Boston, at HALSMUSEUM 9 June 1888.

Muntz, Laura A., at HALSMUSEUM 9 Aug 1894.

Mura, Frank, attended the ACADEMY OF FINE ARTS, THE HAGUE, winter 1889-90. Member of PULCHRI STUDIO, THE HAGUE, 1888-1891.

Murphy, Hermann D., Boston USA, at HALSMUSEUM 30 Sept 1892.

Murphy, J. Francis, New York, at HALSMUSEUM 30 Oct 1886.

Nardus, L., New York, at HALSMUSEUM 23/24 Aug 1897, 10/12 Aug 1901.

Niles, Helen J., Toledo, at HALSMUSEUM 4 July 1910; America, 13 July 1910. At HOTEL SPAANDER, VOLENDAM [with Helen Kibbey of NY, July or Aug 1903], Helene James [with W.W. and Lucretia Gilchrist, Aug or Sept 1903], Helene J. [may be with Robert Henri, between July 2 and 7, 1907], Helen [Aug 1910].

Noble, Thomas S., Cincinnati Ohio, at HALSMUSEUM 17 May 1894.

Nollen, G.N., Pella America, at HALSMUSEUM 2 Aug 1888.

Norcross, Eleanor, Massachusetts, at HALSMUSEUM [27 July 1883].

Nordell, Carl J., Boston Mass, at HALSMUSEUM 25 Aug 1909.

Norton, W.E., USA, at HALSMUSEUM 10 July 1888.

Ochtman, Leonard, NY America, at HALSMUSEUM 8 Sept 1886.

Olney, L.F., New York, RIJKSMUSEUM COPY PERMITS 1 March 1887, drawing, de Faenars Testas; 16 March 1887, oil, Rembrandt *Elizabeth Bas*; 3 May 1887, oil, Rembrandt *Elizabeth Bas*; 13 May 1887, oil, Mauve *Herder with Sheep*.

Ostertag, Blanche A., St Louis USA, at HALSMUSEUM 9 Nov 1894.

Pach, Walter, New York, RIJKSMUSEUM COPY PERMIT 17 Sept 1906, oil, Hals *De Nar*. At HALSMUSEUM 29/30 July 1904, 31 July/1 Aug 1904, 16/17 Sept 1904, 23/25 Sept 1905, 24 Aug 1906, 2 Oct 1906, 22 Feb 1908, 21 Aug 1912.

Page, Walter G., artist, Boston USA, at DORDRECHT MUSEUM [1887].

Palmer, Walter L., America, at HALSMUSEUM 5 Sept 1885.

Parker, Edgar, Boston, at HALSMUSEUM [July 1883].

Parker, Emma A., Providence RI, at HALSMUSEUM 25 Aug 1909.

Parker, Lawton S., Paris, at HALSMUSEUM 8 July 1903.

Parkhurst, Thomas Shrewsbury, Toledo, Ohio, RIJKSMUSEUM COPY PERMIT 24 July 1913, oil, studies after Anton Mauve and Weissenbruch.

Parshall, De Witt, New York, RIJKSMUSEUM COPY PERMIT 8 Sept 1897, oil, Frans Hals *De Nar*. At HALSMUSEUM 6/7 Sept 1897.

Parsons, Miss Antoinette de Forest, New York, at HALSMUSEUM 29/30 June 1897, 19/20 June 1902, 6/7 Oct 1902. At HOTEL SPAANDER, VOLENDAM [may be with Lois M Hicks, NYC, in May or June 1902].

Patterson, Margaret Jordan, Boston, at HOTEL SPAANDER, VOLENDAM [July 1899].

Pattison, James William, USA, at HALSMUSEUM 24 July 1893; Chicago Art Institute 8/9 Sept 1905.

Paul, W.H. Jr, Philadelphia, RIJKSMUSEUM COPY PERMIT 12 Oct 1904, oil, Vermeer *The Love Letter*.

Paxton, Wm. M., Boston USA, at HALSMUSEUM 12 Sept 1907.

Pearce, Edgar L., Pennsylvania Academy, student, RIJKSMUSEUM COPY PERMIT 16 July 1908, oil, Frans Hals *Geertrujt van Erp*.

Pearson, Jos. T. Jr., Philadelphia, at HALSMUSEUM 4/6 Oct 1900, 20/21 May 1901.

Peck, Mrs J., America, RIJKSMUSEUM COPY PERMITS 12 May 1910, oil, J. A. van Ravesteyn *Dignade Both*; 17 May 1910, Miss J., Bussum, drawing, J. Verspronck *Portrait of an Old Man*.

Peck, Mr Orrin, Munich, at HALSMUSEUM 7 Oct 1898.

Peirce, E.L., artist, Philadelphia USA, at DORDRECHT MUSEUM [with Blanche Dillaye, July 1884].

Peixotto, Ernest, New York, at HOTEL SPAANDER, VOLENDAM [July 1906].

Penfield, Edward, New York, at HOTEL SPAANDER, VOLENDAM [before April 16, 1900].

Pepper, Charles H., USA, at HALSMUSEUM 29 Aug 1895. In EGMOND BAD BODE, America, 15 July 1897, 1 Sept 1897 [with wife and child].

Perry, Lila Cabot, Boston, at HALSMUSEUM 3 June 1891 [with Lucia Fairchild], 28 Aug 1906.

Peters, C.R., USA, at HALSMUSEUM 31 May 1888, 10 July 1888. At DORDRECHT MUSEUM, artist [1888].

Piper, Miss. Adeline, America, in EGMOND BAD BODE, 3 Aug 1903, 17 Aug 1903, 3 Sept 1903.

Platt, Charles A., New York, at HALSMUSEUM 30 Aug 1888.

Poore, Henry V., Kansas City M., at HALSMUSEUM 5 Aug 1910.

Post, Miss M.A., Philadelphia, RIJKSMUSEUM COPY PERMIT 12 Oct 1901, oil, Fr Hals *De Nar*. At HALSMUSEUM, May Audubon, 24/25 Aug 1901. At HOTEL SPAANDER, VOLENDAM [soon after Sept 25, 1901]; Oct 29th 1901; [signature immediately follows that of George Debereiner, probably Nov 1903]; 4446 Sansom St., Philadelphia [Oct 1906]; [Oct 1910].

Prang, Louis, Boston, at HALSMUSEUM 6 Aug 1887 and 16 June 1900.

Preyer, David C. [art historian], New York, at HALSMUSEUM 6/7 Aug 1903.

Raditz, Lazar, Pennsylvania Academy, student, RIJKSMUSEUM COPY PERMITS 16 July 1908, oil, Frans Hals & P. Codde *The Company of Captain Reynier Reael* [with Nina Ward & Edgar Pearce]; 19 April 1912, Philadelphia, oil, Rembrandt *The Syndics*; 1 May 1912, oil, Fr Hals *Married Couple, full length*. At HALSMUSEUM, Philadelphia Pa, 6 Aug 1907; Pa Academy of Fine Arts, 11 July 1908.

Ramsey, Chas. F., Phila USA, at HALSMUSEUM 1 Aug 1899.

Rawson, Miss F.H., Cincinnati, at HALSMUSEUM 18 Oct 1888.

Reaser, W.A., Paris, at HALSMUSEUM 12 July 1889; Wilbur Aaron Reaser, San Francisco, 8/10 Aug 1896.

Redenberg [?], H., Philadelphia, [may be Henry R. Rittenberg] RIJKSMUSEUM COPY PERMIT 31 Dec 1900, oil, Hals *De Nar*.

Redmond, John J., at HALSMUSEUM 5 Sept 1895.

Reid, Robert, New York, at HALSMUSEUM 21 June 1889.

Rettig, John, Cincinnati Ohio, at HALSMUSEUM 8 July 1903 and 27 Sept 1906. At HOTEL SPAANDER, VOLENDAM Aug to Nov 1905 [news clipping is pasted in the register from *Commercial Tribune* Cincinnati, Nov. 1 1908 "Mrs. John Rettig, Leader in the Cincinnati Social World], May 26th 1906 [with wife May Rettig], [with wife May Rettig, Nov 1907].

Rheinlander, Miss E.E., America, RIJKSMUSEUM COPY PERMIT 1 Aug 1903, studies of some paintings.

Richards, William T., Philadelphia USA, at HALSMUSEUM 20 Oct 1891.

Richardson, Miss Clara V., Philadelphia, at HOTEL SPAANDER, VOLENDAM 7-13-09, [August 1909].

Richardson, F.H., Boston, at HALSMUSEUM 18 Sept 1889.

Ring, Miss A.B., Egmond/Hoef, Oberlin, at HALSMUSEUM 28 June 1907.

Ring, Paul, New York, [possibly Paul King] RIJKSMUSEUM COPY PERMIT 10 Aug 1905, oil, J. H. Maris *City View*.

Rittenberg, Henry R., Philadelphia, At HALSMUSEUM 4 Sept 1912. [see also Harry Rittenburg, H. Redenberg and H.R. Rutenberg].

Rittenburg, Harry R., Philadelphia, at HALSMUSEUM 4/6 Oct 1900. [see also Henry R. Rittenberg]

Ritter, L., [no address given], at HALSMUSEUM 10 June 1880.

Robins, S., Boston, at HALSMUSEUM 29/30 June 1900. At HOTEL SPAANDER, VOLENDAM, Miss Susan [with Martha Silsbee, July or Aug 1900]; Miss Susan P.B. [with Martha Silsbee, July 1901].

Robinson, Alexander, [no address given], class of 13 persons, at HALSMUSEUM 5 Aug 1911. At HOTEL SPAANDER, VOLENDAM, Bruges Belgium [1905]; Boston [late 1910 and/or early 1911].

Robinson, Will S., Boston, at HALSMUSEUM 17 July 1890.

Rolshoven, Jul., Detroit Mich USA, at HALSMUSEUM [Aug 1884].

Ross, Denman W., Cambridge Mass USA, at HALSMUSEUM [after 25 Aug'81], [April 1886].

Rotch, Arthur, Boston USA, at HALSMUSEUM 28 Aug 1879.

Rutenberg [?], H. R., Philadelphia, [may be Henry R. Rittenberg] RIJKSMUSEUM COPY PERMIT 29 Nov 1900, oil, Fr Hals *Portrait of a Man*.

Sargent, John S., London, RIJKSMUSEUM COPY PERMIT 11 April 1901, watercolor, A.v. Dyke *Mary Magdalene*.

Sartain, Miss Harriet, at HALSMUSEUM 4/16 June 1904.

Sartain, John, honorary member of ARTI ET AMICITIAE, AMSTERDAM, 1863.

Schaus, William [art dealer], New York, at HALSMUSEUM 11 Aug 1888.

Schille, Miss Alice, Columbus Ohio, at HOTEL SPAANDER, VOLENDAM [with Mrs. J.W. Dorbers, 1908].

Schilling, Alexander, [illeg.], at HALSMUSEUM 13 Oct 1910. painter, 's Gravenhage, At DORDRECHT MUSEUM [late 1880].

Schmauss, P., New York, RIJKSMUSEUM COPY PERMIT 29 Jan 1884, Fr. Hals.

Sellers, Mary, Pittsburg, at HOTEL SPAANDER, VOLENDAM [Sept 1908], [April 1911].

Seyffert, L.G., Philadelphia, at HALSMUSEUM 29 Aug 1910. At HOTEL SPAANDER, VOLENDAM [with Mrs. L.G. Seyffert, late 1912].

Shannon, J.J., at HALSMUSEUM 17 Oct 1908. In EGMOND BAD BODE, London, 7 Sept 1901, staying at the Hotel Welgelegen.

Sharp, J.H., Cincinnati, at HALSMUSEUM 7 Oct 1889.

Shields, Thos. W., artist, America, at DORDRECHT MUSEUM [after July 8, 1880].

Shirlaw, Walter, New York, at HALSMUSEUM [after 15 Aug'81].

Siebert, Ed S., New York, at HALSMUSEUM April 1893.

Silsbee, M., Boston USA, at HALSMUSEUM 29/30 June 1900. At HOTEL SPAANDER, VOLENDAM, Miss M. [with Susan Robins, July or August 1900], [with Susan Robins, July 1901].

Singart, Rudolph S., New York City, at HALSMUSEUM 19 July 1909.

Singer, W.H. Jr., Pittsburgh Pa USA, at HALSMUSEUM 15/16 Oct 1903; Paris, 9 May 1910.

Slade, Emily, New York, at HALSMUSEUM 6 March 1886 [with Rosalie Gill & Caroline Gridley]; Misses Slade, 2 Aug 1888.

Smith, F. Carl, Washington DC, at HALSMUSEUM 24 Sept 1903. At HOTEL SPAANDER, VOLENDAM Sept 1903, [Oct 1907], [1908].

Smith, F.E., Munich, RIJKSMUSEUM COPY PERMITS 3 Sept 1889, oil, Hals *De Nar*; 10 Sept 1889, New York, oil sketches of Rembrandt.

Smith, F. Hopkinson, New York, at HALSMUSEUM 4 July 1884. Introduction to DORDRECHTS SOCIETEIT AMICITIAE (Societeit de Harmonie) Aug. 1894, valid 2 days, sponsor [illegible]. At DORDRECHT MUSEUM, artist, July 25, 1884 [with Geo. G. De Witt Jr., lawyer].

Smith, Joseph L., Boston, at HALSMUSEUM [April 1886].

Smith, Miss. L. Crapo, America, in EGMOND BAD BODE, 1 Aug 1902, 10 Sept 1902, staying at Kraakman studio building; Miss A. [sic] C. Smith, New York, 15 August 1911, staying at the Charlotte.

Snell, Henry B, New York City, at HOTEL SPAANDER, VOLENDAM 8/23/09.

Snow, E. Taylor, Phila Pa USA, at HALSMUSEUM 25 July 1903.

Speicher, Eugene, New York, RIJKSMUSEUM COPY PERMIT 27 June 1910, oil, Vermeer *Kitchen Maid*. At HALSMUSEUM 25 June 1910. At HOTEL SPAANDER, VOLENDAM, Eugene E., 7/1910 [with wife].

Squire, M.H., New York USA, at HALSMUSEUM 12/13 April 1904.

St. John, J. Allen, New York USA, at HALSMUSEUM 5 June 1907.

Steenks, Mr Gerard, New York, at HALSMUSEUM 10 June 1890. Attended the ACADEMY OF FINE ARTS, THE HAGUE, 1881-1884 [Dutch born, he first moved to the U.S. in 1884 at age 18].

Steinberger, S., New York, RIJKSMUSEUM COPY PERMITS 13 June 1889, oil, A. Mauve *Sheep in the Dunes*; 22 June 1889, oil, v.d. Sande Bakhuizen *Evening Landscape*.

Stephens, Anson T., New York, RIJKSMUSEUM COPY PERMIT 6 April 1887, oil, Rembrandt *Elizabeth Bas*.

Stephens, Mrs., New York, RIJKSMUSEUM COPY PERMIT 6 April 1887, oil, Hals *De Nar*.

Stevens, Thomas W., Chicago Ill USA, at HALSMUSEUM 26 July 1906.

Stevenson, Gordon, Chicago, at HOTEL SPAANDER, VOLENDAM [summer 1912]; Art Institute Chicago, c\o Dr. Frans Roes 18 Bazarstraat, Den Haag [late 1912 or early 1913].

Stieglitz, Alfred, New York, at HALSMUSEUM 16 Aug 1894.

Sturgeon, Ruth, Sterling Kansas, at HOTEL SPAANDER, VOLENDAM [July 1909].

Sturgis, M.R., Boston USA, at HOTEL SPAANDER, VOLENDAM [apparently with Julia Bacon, spring 1900]

Swift, Ivan, Michigan USA, Chicago Society of Artists, at HOTEL SPAANDER, VOLENDAM [late 1904 or early 1905, before March 6].

Taggart, Lucy M., Indianapolis USA, at HOTEL SPAANDER, VOLENDAM [with Nora Taggart, May 1906].

Talcott, Allen Butler, Hartford CT, at HALSMUSEUM 1 May 1890.

Teasdel, Mary, Salt Lake City Utah, at HOTEL SPAANDER, VOLENDAM, [June or July 1906].

Thayer, A.H., Scarborough NY USA, at HALSMUSEUM 1 Nov 1898.

Thomas, S. Seymour, Paris, at HALSMUSEUM 15 Sept 1894.

Thomason, F.Q., New York City, at HALSMUSEUM 11 Sept 1902.

Thompson, John E., Laren, at HALSMUSEUM 14 Nov 1908, 15 Feb 1909.

Thompson, Leslie P., Boston, RIJKSMUSEUM COPY PERMITS 4 Oct 1905, oil, Vermeer *Woman Reading a Letter*; 31 Oct 1905, oil, Vermeer *The Love Letter*.

Timmons, Ed., Chicago, RIJKSMUSEUM COPY PERMIT 3 Feb 1909, oil, Frans Hals *The Merry Drinker*.

Townsley, Channel, Great Bend Kansas, at HALSMUSEUM 3 Oct 1891; C.P. Townsley, Jr., New York, 1/2 July 1903.

Truesdell, G.S., Chicago, at HALSMUSEUM 12/14 Aug 1893.

Tryon, D.W., artist, U.S. of America, at DORDRECHT MUSEUM [with Arthur G Bell, artist, London in 1880].

Tuckermann, S. Salisbury, Boston, at HALSMUSEUM 8 July 1884, 16 Aug 1901. Member of PULCHRI STUDIO, THE HAGUE, 1882-89.

Turner, C.Y., New York USA, at HALSMUSEUM 20 Sept 1880. painter, At DORDRECHT MUSEUM [1880].

Twachtman, J.H., Cincinnati USA, at HALSMUSEUM 1 Aug 1881, 11 June 1885, America 5 Sept 1885.

Twachtman, Mrs J.H., Cincinnati USA, at HALSMUSEUM 1 Aug 1881.

Ullman, Eugene P., New York, at HALSMUSEUM 14 Oct 1898, 9 June 1902, 15 July 1903.

Ulrich, Charles F., New York, at HALSMUSEUM [May 1884].

Upjohn, Mrs J. Anna, New York, RIJKSMUSEUM COPY PERMITS 8 Aug 1910, oil, Fr Hals *Geertrujl van Erp*; 1 Sept 1910, oil, Fr Hals *Maritje Voogt*.

Upton, Miss A.L., New York USA, at HALSMUSEUM 17/20 May 1901.

Upton, Ethelwyn B., New York City, at HALSMUSEUM 11 Sept 1902.

Upton, Florence K., New York City, at HALSMUSEUM 26 Aug 1898, 17/20 May 1901, 11 Sept 1902, 2 July 1907. At HOTEL SPAANDER, VOLENDAM [with Ethelwyn B. Upton and Lettie E. Carlin of NYC, Sept 1902], Paris\New York [Sept or Oct 1903]. In EGMOND BAD BODE, America, 1 Aug 1902, 10 Sept 1902, staying at Pension Winkel; 3 Aug 1903, 17 Aug 1903, 3 Sept 1903, staying at the Hotel Welgelegen.

Vail, Eugene, USA, at HALSMUSEUM 27/31 Oct 1896.

Valentine, Miss. J.H., America, in EGMOND BAD BODE, 17 Aug 1903, 3 Sept 1903 [with Emily Valentine].

Vanderhest, Chas, artist, New York USA, at DORDRECHT MUSEUM [with Rugor Donoho, Sept 1880].

Vanderpoel, John H., artist, Chicago USA, at DORDRECHT MUSEUM [1887].

Van der Veer, Miss Mary, Amsterdam temporarily, USA, RIJKSMUSEUM COPY PERMIT 5 Aug 1901, oil, Fr Hals *The Merry Drinker*. At HOTEL SPAANDER, VOLENDAM, Amsterdam NY, USA [may be with Ada M. Kenyon of Buffalo NY, late July 1902]; Philadelphia [Autumn 1904].

Van der Weyden, Harry, Montreuil-sur-Mer, at HALSMUSEUM 8 Aug 1910.

Van Helden, Miss. Caroline West, Philadelphia, RIJKSMUSEUM COPY PERMIT 4 July 1905, oil, P. Moreelse *The Princess*.

Van Ingen, Henry, Poughkeepsie NY, at HALSMUSEUM 23 Aug 1890.

Van Laer, A.T., Jacksonville Ill, at HALSMUSEUM 9 Aug 1884.

Vinton, Frederick P., Boston USA, at HALSMUSEUM 3/4 Aug 1900.

Vos, Hubert, member of ARTI ET AMICITIAE, AMSTERDAM, c.1901. Member of HAAGSE KUNSTKRING, 1891.

Voss, Miss Lily, New York, RIJKSMUSEUM COPY PERMITS 23 July 1904, oil, D. Bailly *Portrait of a Young Man*; 2 Aug 1904, oil, Hals *Portrait of John Barclay*.

Wachman, Henriette, Cincinnati OH, at HALSMUSEUM 10 Oct 1890 [with Laura Wachman, Euphemia Bailey, and Christine S. Bredin].

Wales, Miss S.M.L., Boston, at HALSMUSEUM 27 Aug 1887.

Walker, Ferd G., Indiana USA, at HOTEL SPAANDER, VOLENDAM [1903].

Wapler, Louis, New York, RIJKSMUSEUM COPY PERMITS 17 May 1899, oil, W v d Velde *Still Water*; 31 May 1899, oil, Frans Hals *De Nar*.

Ward, Edgar M., New York USA, at HALSMUSEUM 6 Jan 1885.

Ward, Miss. Nina B., Pennsylvania Academy, student, RIJKSMUSEUM COPY PERMIT 16 July 1908, oil, A. van Dyck

Joh Bapt Franck. At HALSMUSEUM 11 July 1908; Philadelphia, 27 July 1908.

Ward, Phillipps, New York City, at HALSMUSEUM 10 Sept 1902 [may be Reginald P. Ward].

Ward, Reginald P., New York City, at HALSMUSEUM 14/15 Aug 1900 [may be Phillipps Ward].

Washburn, C., Haarlem, RIJKSMUSEUM COPY PERMITS 17 June 1896, oil, Hals *The Merry Drinker*; 15 July 1896, oil, fragment of Rembrandt *The Syndics*. At HALSMUSEUM, Cadwallader Washburn, Minneapolis, USA, 26 May 1896.

Washburn, Jessie M., Los Angeles, at HALSMUSEUM 10 June 1909. At HOTEL SPAANDER, VOLENDAM, Miss. Jessie M., artist [June or July 1909].

Webster, E. Ambrose, America, in EGMOND BAD BODE, 15 July 1897, 1 Sept 1897.

Weeks, John A., Boston, RIJKSMUSEUM COPY PERMIT 12 Sept 1907, drawings.

Weir, J. Alden, New York City, at HALSMUSEUM [before 9 Aug '81]. Introduction to DORDRECHTS SOCIETEIT AMICITIAE (Societeit de Harmonie), artist, New York, 18 July 1881, valid 16 days, sponsor J.C.J. Deventer.

Weir, John F., New Haven Conn, at HALSMUSEUM [before 9 Aug '81]. Introduction to DORDRECHTS SOCIETEIT AMICITIAE (Societeit de Harmonie), Prof. John F. Weir, director of the School of Fine Arts, Yale University, New Haven, 18 July 1881, valid 14 days, sponsor J.C.J. Deventer.

Whistler, J. McNeill, London, at HALSMUSEUM 1 Dec 1882.

White, C. Scott, Boston, at HALSMUSEUM 23/24 Sept 1901. Introduction to DORDRECHTS SOCIETEIT AMICITIAE (Societeit de Harmonie) Aug. 1904, valid 30 days, sponsor E. Noonen.

White, Joseph E., New York, Introduction to DORDRECHTS SOCIETEIT AMICITIAE (Societeit de Harmonie) July 1890, sponsor H. de Mandt.

Wigand, Mr. and Mrs Ol, NY, at HOTEL SPAANDER, VOLENDAM [with Elenor and Robert Wijand between Nov 1901 and May 1902].

Wiles, Irving R., New York, at HALSMUSEUM 5/6 Aug 1904.

Willard, Miss. Geneva, Art Institute-Chicago, at HALSMUSEUM 15 Aug 1902.

Williams, Miss. M. Frances, New York, RIJKSMUSEUM COPY PERMIT 22 July 1907, Frans Hals *De Nar*.

Wolff, Gustave, Buiksloot, RIJKSMUSEUM COPY PERMITS 13 Jan 1909, oil, J. H. Maris *Harbor View*; 16 Jan 1909, oil, J. H. Maris *River View*. At HALSMUSEUM, Gustav [no address] 10 July 1908.

Wood, Frank, Boston, at HALSMUSEUM 5 July 1910.

Wood, James L., Philadelphia, at HALSMUSEUM 9/10 Aug 1897.

Woodbury, Charles Herbert, Boston, at HALSMUSEUM 11 Aug 1890 [with Marcia Oakes Woodbury]. At HOTEL SPAANDER, VOLENDAM [with wife Marcia and son David Oakes Woodbury between Sept 14 and 19, 1903], [with son David, Nov 1907], [June or July 1909].

Woodbury, Marcia Oakes, Boston, at HALSMUSEUM 11 Aug 1890 [with Charles H. Woodbury], 29 April 1907. At HOTEL SPAANDER, VOLENDAM [with husband Charles and son David between Sept 14 and 19, 1903].

Woodward, Anna, America, in EGMOND BAD BODE, 1 Sept 1897; 3 Aug 1903, 17 Aug 1903, 3 Sept 1903, staying at the Hotel Welgelegen.

Woodward, E., New Orleans La USA, at HALSMUSEUM 9 July 1894; Ellsworth Woodward, 13 Aug 1909.

Woodward, Mabel M., Providence, R.I., at HOTEL SPAANDER, VOLENDAM [with Minnie S. Woodward, summer 1912].

Wores, Theo., San Francisco Cal, at HALSMUSEUM [June 1881].

Wray, Mr. and Mrs. Henry Russel, Colorado Springs, at HOTEL SPAANDER, VOLENDAM [Aug or Sept 1899].

Yelland, R.D., San Francisco, RIJKSMUSEUM COPY PERMIT 19 Aug 1887, oil, L. Meyer *Redding op Zee*. At HALSMUSEUM 4 July 1887. At DORDRECHT MUSEUM, artist painter [1887].

NOTES

ONE: DUTCH ART IN AMERICA

1. Quoted in Aline B. Saarinen, *The Proud Possessors* (New York: Random House, 1958), p. 109.

2. Walter Liedtke, "Dutch Paintings in America: The Collectors and Their Ideals," in *Great Dutch Paintings from America*, (Zwolle: Waanders Publishers and the Mauritshuis, 1990), p. 31.

3. P. Haven Korn von Rysewyck, article in the *Nieuwe Rotterdamsche Courant* quoted in translation in *American Art News* 10 (18 May 1912), p. 5, col. 4.

4. Edwin Buijsen, "The Battle Against the Dollar: The Dutch Reaction to American Collecting in the Period from 1900 to 1914," in *Great Dutch Paintings from America* (Zwolle: Waanders Publishers and the Mauritshuis, 1990), pp. 65-69.

5. Montezuma [Montague Marks], "My Note Book," *Art Amateur* 22 (February 1890): 51.

6. Charles Caffin, *The Story of Dutch Painting* (New York: Century Co., 1909), p. 72. For a less traditional side of Caffin's philosophy, see Sandra Lee Underwood, *Charles H. Caffin, a Voice for Modernism, 1897-1918* (Ann Arbor, Michigan: UMI Research Press, 1983).

7. The three quotes in this paragraph, in order of appearance, are from *The Collector and Art Critic* 2 (15 February 1900): 137; Mrs. Charles P. Gruppe, "The Art of B. J. Blommers," *Brush and Pencil* 12 (September 1903): 419; and Burton E. Stevenson, *The Spell of Holland* (Boston: L. C. Page & Company, 1911), p. 182.

8. *The Collector and Art Critic* 2 (15 February 1900): 137.

9. Tiemen de Vries, *Dutch History Art and Literature for Americans* (Grand Rapids: Eerdmans-Seevensma Co., 1912), pp. 114-15.

10. George Breed Zug, "Dutch Art and Artists: The Painters of Domestic Scenes," *The Chautauquan* 53 (December 1908): 79.

11. William Elliot Griffis, *The American in Holland* (Boston and New York: Houghton Mifflin & Company, 1907), pp. 38-39.

12. Constance Rourke, *Charles Sheeler: Artist in the American Tradition* (New York: Harcourt, Brace and Company, 1938), p. 21.

13. Sir George Clausen, "Autobiographical Notes," *Artwork* 7 (Spring 1931): 19.

14. On the Kendall sale see unidentified newspaper clipping in William Schaus Papers, Archives of American Art, Smithsonian Institution.

15. Lillie Gill Derby, "Contemporary Dutch Painting," *The Southern Magazine* 5 (January 1895): 325.

16. "Impressions of America on a Dutch Impressionist," *New York Times Sunday Magazine*, 1 May 1904.

17. D. Croal Thomson, *The Brothers Maris (James-Matthew-William)* (London: Offices of *The Studio*, 1907): BMiii.

18. *The Chautauquan* 54 (May 1909): 467.

TWO: AMERICAN ARTISTS IN HOLLAND

19. Felix O. C. Darley, *Sketches Abroad with Pen and Pencil* (New York: Hurd and Houghton, 1869), p. 85.

20. Sheeler is quoted in Rourke, p. 21. For Albrecht quote see Florence Craig Albrecht, "Veere, An Artist's Paradise," *The Outlook* 91 (27 March 1909): 328.

21. Edwin Austin Abbey, letter to Charles Parsons, 6 November 1880, quoted in E. V. Lucas, *Edwin Austin Abbey, Royal Academician, The Record of his Life and Work*, vol. 1 (New York: Charles Scribner's Sons, 1921), pp. 107-108.

22. Edward Penfield, *Holland Sketches* (New York: Charles Scribner's Sons, 1907), p. 138.

23. George Hitchcock, "The Picturesque Quality of Holland. Interiors and Bric-A-Brac," *Scribner's Magazine* 5 (February 1889): 163. For a more thorough discussion of this attitude, see Annette Stott, "Dutch Utopia: Paintings by Antimodern American Artists of the Nineteenth Century," *Smithsonian Studies in American Art* 3 (Spring 1989): 47-61.

24. "Darling's Fine Pictures at the Art Museum," *Toledo Daily Blade*, 26 November 1903, p. 10, cols. 4 & 5.

25. Henry Ward Ranger, "Artist Life By the North Sea," *Century Magazine* (March 1893): 753.

26. James H. Gore, *Dutch Art as Seen by a Layman* (New York: Holland-America Line, 1902), p. 15.

27. Griffis, *American in Holland*, pp. 194-195.

28. *Wandelgids voor Hattem en Omstreken* (Zwolle: De Erven J.J. Tijl, 1896), p. 10. "jaar op jaar een gezelschap Amerikaansche schilders van uitmuntende reputatie zich voor eenige maanden hierheen begeeft en aan deze streek de onderwerpen heeft ontleend voor kunstwerken, die in het buitenland meermalen met goud zijn bekroond."

29. Roger Mahlstick, "Walter L. Dean," *Boston Sunday Journal*, 12 May 1895, clipping in Walter Dean file, Cape Ann Historical Association, Gloucester, Massachusetts.

30. William Harman van Allen, *Travel-Pictures* (Milwaukee: The Young Churchman Co., 1912), p. 19.

31. Alfred Stieglitz and Louis H. Schubart, "Two Artists' Haunts," *Photographic Times* (January 1895): 11.

32. William E. Carlin enhanced his description of the Katwijk fishermen's homes, costume, marriage customs, fish auctions, and farm life with his photos in "The Dutch Fisher Folk," *Outing Magazine* 38 (August 1901): 526-532. Quote is from p. 532.

33. George Hitchcock, "The Picturesque Quality of Holland. Figures and Costumes," *Scribner's Magazine* 10 (November 1891): 629. See also the very similar comments by F. Hopkinson Smith, "Between Showers in Dort," *Scribner's Magazine* 25 (May 1899): 587.

34. Frank M. Collins, "A Visit To Joseph Israëls By Two Young American Painters, Through Whom the Famous Hollander Gives Some Excellent Advice to Ambitious Art Students," *Art Amateur* 33 (October & November 1895), pp. 86+ and 115+.

35. Ralcy Husted Bell, *Art-Talks with Ranger* (New York & London: G.P.Putnam's Sons, 1914), pp. 42, 48.

36. Maria Thompson Daviess, *Seven Times Seven, An Autobiography* (New York: Dodd, Mead and Co., 1924), p. 173.

37. "Studio Talk-Canada," *International Studio* 8 (July 1899): 62.

38. Gertrude Kellogg, letter to her sister Peggy, Rijsoord, 29 June 1888, microfilm 4182:994, Alice Kellogg Tyler Papers, Archives of American Art, Smithsonian Institution, quoted with permission.

39. Frederick Benjamin, "C. W. Hawthorne, Painter," *Brush and Pencil* (August 1899): 255-256 described the painting of the old Dutch couple. Charles Hawthorne, letter to Ethel Marion Campbell, 24 August 1898, quoted in *The Paintings of Charles Hawthorne* (Storrs, CT: University of Connecticut Museum of Art, 1968), n.p., relates his reaction to Hals. See also *The Collector and Art Critic* 1 (1 August 1899): 85.

40. Charles Hawthorne, letter to Ethel Marion Campbell, 29 June 1898, quoted in *The Paintings of Charles Hawthorne*.

THREE: REWRITING AMERICAN HISTORY

41. Edward Bok, "The Mother of America," *Ladies' Home Journal* 20 (Oct 1903): 16.

42. John Lothrop Motley, *The Rise of the Dutch Republic*, vol. 2 (New York: A. L. Burt, n.d.), pp. 89-90.

43. Motley, *The Rise of Dutch the Republic*, vol. 2, p. 80.

44. John Lothrop Motley, *History of the United Netherlands: From the Death of William the Silent to the twelve years' truce—1609*, vol. 4 (New York: Harper & Brothers Publishers, 1898), p. 539.

45. Douglas Campbell, *The Puritan in Holland, England, and America, An Introduction to American History*, 3rd edition, vol. 2 (New York: Harper & Brothers, 1893), pp. 411-417.

46. Campbell, vol. 2, p. 419.

47. Bok, p. 16.

48. Sydney G. Fisher, "Are American Institutions of Dutch Origin?" *Lippincott's Monthly Magazine* 59 (January 1897): 79.

49. Quotes in this paragraph, in order of appearance, are from Fisher, p. 80; Henry Eldridge Bourne, "Book Notices: The Puritan in Holland, England and America," *Yale Review* 1 (February 1893): 437; Warren F. Kellogg, "Editor's Table," *New England Magazine* n.s. 15 (January 1897): 637.

50. William Elliot Griffis, *Brave Little Holland and What She Taught Us*, revised edition (Cambridge, MA: Riverside Press, 1931), p. 237.

51. William Elliot Griffis, "Why are We So Different From the English?" *Ladies' Home Journal* 27 (February 1910): 6.

52. Griffis, "Why are We So Different?" p. 6.

53. David Gregg, W.W. Goodrich, and Sidney H. Carney, Jr., *Thoughts for the Occasion: Makers of the American Republic, A Series of Patriotic Lectures* (New York: E. B. Treat & Co., 1905), pp. 113-125.

54. Elizabeth W. Champney, "Woman in Art" in *American Art and Artists* (Boston: American Art Company, 1895), p. 203.

55. The first quote by Griffis is from *The Influence of the Netherlands in the Making of the English Commonwealth and the American Republic* (Boston: DeWolfe, Fiske & Co., 1891), p. 15. The second is from Griffis, "Why are We So Different?" p. 6.

56. Paul R. Huey, "The Archeology of Colonial New Netherland" in *Colonial Dutch Studies*, Eric Nooter and Patricia Bonomi, eds. (New York: N.Y.U. Press, 1988), pp. 54-55.

57. Fiske, John, *The Dutch and Quaker Colonies in America* (Boston & New York: Houghton Mifflin and Co, 1899), vol. 1, p. 46.

58. William Elliot Griffis, *The Story of New Netherland, The Dutch in America* (Boston & New York: Houghton, Mifflin, 1909), p. 25.

59. Maud Wilder Goodwin, *Dutch and English on the Hudson, A Chronicle of Colonial New York* (New Haven: Yale University Press, 1921), pp. 120-121.

60. Griffis, *Story of New Netherland*, pp. 149-150.

61. "Women's Work for their Cities," *Harper's Bazar* 43 (August 1909): 766.

62. Theodore Roosevelt speech in *New Amsterdam Gazette* 6 (25 January 1890): 3.

63. G. H. Emerson, "What Protestant Liberty Owes to the Dutch," *Universalist Quarterly and General Review* 45 (July, 1888), p. 266.

64. Quotes from William Bradford, *History of Plymouth Plantation* in Griffis, *Influence of the Netherlands*, p. 29.

65. Frederick A. Noble, *The Pilgrims* (Boston: Pilgrim Press, 1907), p. 143.

66. J. De Hoop Scheffer, *History of the Free Churchmen called the Brownists, Pilgrim Fathers and Baptists in the Dutch Republic, 1581-1701*, William Elliot Griffis, ed. (Ithaca, NY: Andrus & Church, c. 1922), p. xix.

67. Howard Ellis, *New York Herald* 21 September 1890, quoted in *New Amsterdam Gazette* 6 (20 Sept to 31 October 1890): 11.

68. For a complete account of such tributes see William Elliot Griffis, "Thankful America," *The Outlook* 106 (10 January 1914): 88-90.

FOUR: IMAGES OF NEDERLAND, OLD AND NEW

69. Campbell, vol. 2, p. 358.

70. Henry James, "Our Artists in Europe," *Harper's New Monthly Magazine* 79 (June 1889): 61.

71. William Elliot Griffis, "George H. Boughton, the Painter of New England Puritanism." *New England Magazine* n.s. 15 (December 1896): 501.

72. "The Edict of William the Testy," *The Chautauquan* 54 (April 1909): 295.

73. Karen Zukowski noted this type of relationship in MacEwen's choice of *Stad Herberg* and two contemporary Dutch scenes for his Paris Exposition entries in *Paris 1889*, ed. Annette Blaugrund (New York: Abrams, 1989), p. 182.

74. Charles F. Ulrich," *New Amsterdam Gazette* 2 (10 Nov 1884), p. 10, col. 2.

75. Review of American Art Galleries exhibition, *Art Amateur* 12 (January 1885): 28.

76.George Wharton Edwards, *Holland of Today* (Philadelphia: Penn Publishing Company, 1919), p. 58.

77. Bok, p. 16.

78. William Elliot Griffis, "The Pilgrim Press in Leyden," *New England Magazine* (January 1899): 559-575.

79. Emerson, p. 269.

80. Chauncey M. DePew in *The First Annual Dinner of the Holland Society of New York* (New York: Holland Society, 1886), p. 27.

81. Gregg, Goodrich, and Carney, pp. 130-131.

82. Mrs. Charles P. Gruppe, pp. 415-416.

83. P.A.M. Boele van Hensbroek, "Ch. P. Gruppe," *Elsevier's Geïllustreerd Maandschrift* 14 (Nov 1904): 291-292. ". . . maar wijl de Amerikanen hunne thans zoo hoog staande positie veroverd hebben op dezelfde wijze als Holland vroeger de zijne won. Hadden wij het water te bevechten, zij bestreden hun uitgestrekte prairiën en derzelver inwoners. Iedere bunder gronds moest veroverd worden. En waar wij onzen 80-jarigen oorlog hadden, zij hadden ook hun *War of independence*; en zij verwonnen . . . als wij. Zoo zijn de Amerikanen—evenals wij—'self-made men.'"

84. Van Hensbroek, p. 292. "Gruppe, heeft Holland lief en hij ziet het zoals mogelijk alleen een Hollander en een Hollandsch-gezinde Amerikaan het zien kan."

FIVE: TOURISM AND TRAVEL LITERATURE

85. Ernest Talbert, *Old Countries Discovered Anew* (Boston: Dana Estes & Company, 1913), p. 53.

86. Stevenson, p. 246. Havard's second book, *The Heart of Holland*, published in New York in 1880, covered the other regions of the Netherlands.

87. Edmondo De Amicis, *Holland and Its People*, vol. 2 (New York: G. P. Putnam's Sons, 1882), p. 13.

88. David S. Meldrum, *Holland and the Hollanders* (New York: Dodd, Mead & Co, 1898), p. 17.

89. Augustus Hare, *Sketches in Holland and Scandinavia* (preface 1884; New York and London: Macmillan & Co and George Allen, 1902), pp. 17-20, 27, 43, 45, 55, 34-35. Hare offers other reasons for his dislike of Holland, such as lost luggage, in his six-volume autobiography, Augustus J.C. Hare, *Peculiar People: the Story of My Life, vol.5* (Chicago: Academy Chicago Publishers, 1995), pp. 363-365.

90. J. P. Mahaffy & J. E. Rogers, *Sketches From a Tour Through Holland and Germany* (London: Macmillan and Co, c.1889), pp. 18-19.

91. For quotes, see A. T. and B. R. Wood, *Ribbon Roads, A Motor Tour Abroad* (New York and London: G.P. Putnam's Sons, 1910), p. 116; Margaret J. Preston, *A Handful of Monographs, Continental and English* (New York: Anson D. F. Randolph & Co., 1886), p.73; and Griffis, *The American In Holland*, pp. 198-199.

92. Charles M. Taylor, *Odd Bits of Travel with Brush and Camera* (Philadelphia: George W. Jacobs & Co., 1900), p. 128.

93. Louise Robinson, *A Bundle of Letters From Over the Sea* (Boston: J.G. Cupples Co., 1890), p. 280.

94. S.O. Thacher, *What I saw in Europe* (Topeka: Kansas Publishing House, 1883), p. 121.

95. May Rettig, *Cincinnati Commercial Tribune*, 13 January 1907, in John Rettig Scrapbook, vol. 7, Mss fXR439, Cincinnati Historical Society, Cincinnati Museum Center.

96. George Colton, *A Maryland Editor Abroad* (Annapolis: printed, not published, 1881), p. 79.

97. Grace Ellery Channing, "Holland . . . Boston Transcript," *Current Literature: A Magazine of Contemporary Record* 33 (August 1902): 201.

98. George Henry Boughton, "Artist Strolls in Holland, Paper I," *Harper's New Monthly Magazine* 66 (January 1883): 169.

99. George Hitchcock, "The Picturesque Quality of Holland," *Scribner's Magazine* 2 (August 1887): 161, and 10 (November 1891): 622. The architecture quote is from Penfield, p. 69.

100. Theodore Child, *Summer Holidays, Travelling Notes in Europe* (New York: Harper and Brothers, 1889), p. 87. Van Allen, p. 25.

101. Elbert F. Baldwin, "A Day in North Holland," *The Outlook* 90 (24 October 1908), p. 421.

102. Child, p. 86; Eva Madden, "In the Land of Windmills," *Harper's Bazar* 43 (August 1909): 761; Preston, p. 72.

103. Charles Fish Howell, *Around the Clock in Europe, A Travel-Sequence* (Boston & New York: Houghton Mifflin Co., 1912), p. 147.

104. The first quote is from De Amicis, p. 72, followed by the comment on its "failure in proportions" by Thacher, p. 120. The "ordinary observer" who considered it "scrubby" was John U. Higinbotham, *Three Weeks in Holland and Belgium* (Chicago: Reilly & Britton Co., 1908), p. 38, and Colton discussed the monetary value, p. 81. For a review of this painting's international reputation through time, see J. Hoes, "'Het vee zoals het is en niet anders': De reputatie van Paulus Potter (1625-1654)," in *Meesterlijk Vee: Neederlandse Veeschilders 1600-1900*, 87-100 (Dordrecht: Dordrechts Museum, 1988).

Tourists' criticism of Potter's subject as a specimen of livestock may be explained by scholars' recent theory that Potter constructed it from studies of variously aged bulls. See Amy Walsh, Edwin Buijsen, and Ben Broos, *Paulus Potter: Paintings, Drawings, and Etchings* (Zwolle: Waanders Publishers, 1994), pp. 74-77.

105. Sarah Orne Jewett, "An Afternoon in Holland," *Atlantic Monthly* 50 (December 1882): 804. Taylor, p. 134. Albert Osborne made the comparison to a Dutch plate in *Finding the Worth While in Europe* (1913; New York: Robert M. McBride & Company, 1923 revised), p. 54, and Howell made the remark about Delft tiles in *Around the Clock*, p. 142. The final quote is from Ward, Lock, p. 9.

106. Lucas, pp. 121-123.

107. Osborne, pp. 58-59.

108. Horace E. Scudder, *The Bodley Grandchildren and their Journey in Holland* (Boston: Houghton, Mifflin and Company, 1883), pp. 179-180. Both the print and the visitors book have since disappeared, but Griffis described them in *The Pilgrims in Their Three Homes*, pp. 296, 298. See also Georgine Schwartze, letter to De Lakenhal, 27 August 1920, De Lakenhal correspondence #2258, Municipal Archives, Leiden, and "Therese Schwartze," *Elsevier's Geïllustreerd Maandschrift* 2 (1892), pp. 10-11.

109. Talbert, pp. 64-65.

110. F. Hopkinson Smith, *Well-Worn Roads in Spain, Holland & Italy: Traveled by a Painter in Search of the Picturesque* (Boston: Houghton Mifflin & Company, 1896), pp. 53-54.

111. Blair Jaekel, *Windmills and Wooden Shoes* (New York: McBride, Nast & Company, 1912), p. 4.

112. Penfield, pp. 94-97. Edwards, p. 42.

113. Child, p. 94.

114. Wood, pp. 116, 119.

115. Van Allen, p. 22. Cook's, headquartered in England, was one of the first package tour agencies of the nineteenth century.

116. Higinbotham, pp. 76-77.

117. Taylor, pp. 260-262.

118. Talbert, pp. 34, 37.

119. Grant Allen, *The European Tour* (1899; New York: Dodd, Mead & Co, 1909), p. 30.

120. M.J. Brusse, *With Roosevelt Through Holland* (Rotterdam: Holland-America Line, 1911), p. 7.

121. Edwards, pp. 280-283.

SIX: "AN AMERICAN RENAISSANCE OF DUTCH ARCHITECTURE"

122. Griffis, *The American in Holland*, pp. 37-38.

123. W., "Correspondence: The Dutch Room at Harper's Publishing House," *The American Architect and Building News*, 3 (12 January 1878): 14.

124. In addition to Griffis, see Montgomery Schuyler, "A History of Old Colonial Architecture," *The Architectural Record* 4 (March 1895): 313; "Collegiate Reformed Dutch Church," *Architecture and Building* 17 (29 October 1892): 217; "New New Amsterdam," *Harper's Weekly* 38 (21 April 1894): 369-370; and "Recent Brickwork in American Cities, New York," *Brickbuilder* 3 (June 1894). 106-108, quote is from 107.

125. For illustrations and an excellent discussion of this style in the West End, see Robert A.M. Stern, Gregory Gilmartin, and John Montague Massengale, *New York 1900: Metropolitan Architecture and Urbanism, 1890-1915* (New York: Rizzoli, 1983), pp. 360-367.

126. On early Dutch buildings and their destruction, see Paul R. Huey, "Early Albany: Buildings before 1790," pp. 21-58 in *Albany Architecture: A Guide to the City*, ed. Diana S. Waite (Albany: Mount Ida Press, 1993).

127. For illustrations, see *In Pursuit of Beauty: Americans and the Aesthetic Movement* (New York: Rizzoli, 1986), p. 364; Sally B. Woodbridge and Roger Montgomery, *A Guide to Architecture in Washington State* (Seattle and London: University of Washington Press, 1980), p. 124; Kathryn Bishop Eckert, *Buildings of Michigan* (New York & Oxford: Oxford University Press, 1993), p. 468; Isabelle Gournay, *AIA Guide to the Architecture of Georgia* (Athens: University of Georgia Press, 1993), p. 75.

128. Mrs. Schuyler van Rensselaer, "Recent Architecture in America V, City Dwellings," *Century Illustrated Monthly Magazine* 31 (February 1886): 549, 558, and (March 1886): 678.

129. *Palliser's New Cottage Homes and Details* (New York: Palliser, Palliser & Co., Architects, 1887), introduction. For more examples of Dutch influenced designs see plates 17 and 65.

130. William B. Rhoads, "The Colonial Revival and American Nationalism," *Society of Architectural Historians Journal* 35 (December 1976): 239-254. Schuyler, p. 313.

131. J. Cleveland Cady, "Some Features of the Dutch Farm-Houses of New Jersey," *The American Architect and Building News* 2 (15 December 1877): 401-402. Cady's article is discussed by Alan Gowans, *Images of American Living: Four Centuries of Architecture and Furniture as Cultural Expression* (Philadelphia: J.B. Lippincott, 1964), pp. 48-49 and by William B. Rhoads, *The Colonial Revival*, vol. 1 (New York and London: Garland Publishing, 1977), p. 116.

132. Harold Donaldson Eberlein, *The Architecture of Colonial America* (Boston: Little, Brown, and Company, 1915), pp. 26-27. William Nelson Black, "Colonial Building in New Jersey," *The Architectural Record* 3 (March 1894): 261.

133. Today, scholars more often reverse the turn-of-the-century belief, writing that the Dutch borrowed the gambrel roof from the English, but they usually offer no more supporting evidence for their supposition than did Rensselaer and Eberlein. For a more recent (and more thorough) consideration of the colonial gambrel, see David Steven Cohen, *The Dutch American Farm* (New York: New York University Press, 1992), 34-37. "Georgian Houses of New England," *The American Architect and Building News* 2 (20 October 1877): 338. Mariana van Rensselaer, "American Country Dwellings," *Century Magazine* 32 (May 1886): 4. Eberlein, p. 26.

134. Aymar Embury, *The Dutch Colonial House: Its Origin, Design, Modern Plan and Construction* (New York: McBride, Nast & Company, 1913), p. ii. *The Book of Little Houses* (New York: MacMillan, 1914), p. 60.

135. Henry H. Saylor, ed. *Distinctive Homes of Moderate Cost* (New York: McBride, Winston & Company, 1910), p. 127, originally published in 1905.

136. Charles Edward Hooper, *The Country House* (Garden City, NY: Doubleday, Page and Company, 1913), p. 87, first published in 1904. For examples of Dutch doors, see Clarence A. Martin, *Details of Building Construction* (Boston: Bates & Guild Co., 1899), plates 18 & 19 and William L. Price, *Model Houses for Little Money* (Philadelphia: Curtis Publishing Company, 1898), pp. 129 and 141.

137. Helen Churchill, "House Building," in *The House and Home, A Practical Book* vol. 2 (New York: Charles Scribner's Sons, 1896): p. 68.

138. Embury, p. ii. Eberlein, p. 37. Gordon-Van Tine Co., *117 House Designs of the Twenties* (1923; rpt. Mineola, NY: Dover Publications & The Atheneum of Philadelphia, 1992), p. 16.

139. Foxhollow Farm is well illustrated in Frank Miles Day, *American Homes of Today* (New York: Architectural Book Publishing Company, 1911), pp. 4-6. None of the buildings in this book is discussed in terms of style or sources, but the English and Dutch motifs are evident.

140. William Draper Brinckloe, "Making Plans for the Farm Home," *Wallace's Farmer* (12 January 1923), p. 39.

141. Embury, pp. 19-20.

142. Embury, pp. 61, 63. Mary Gay Humphreys, "House Decoration and Furnishing," in *The House and Home, A Practical Book*, vol. 2, Lyman Abbott, L.W. Betts, et. al. (New York: Charles Scribner's Sons, 1896), p. 149.

143. Eberlein, p. 17.

144. See, for example, "A Craftsman House" from the *Craftsman*, May 1903 on page 48 of Gustav Stickley, *What is Wrought in the Craftsman Workshops* (Syracuse: Mason Press, 1904).

145. David Gebhard and Gerald Mansheim, *Buildings of Iowa* (New York & Oxford: Oxford Univ Press, 1993), pp. 19, 210-211. Eckert, pp. 281-284.

SEVEN: THE SPREAD OF HOLLAND MANIA

146. Collecting by the Hitchcocks and the Shannons is discussed in Kitty Shannon's memoir, *For My Children* (London: Hutchinson & Co., n.d.), p. 19. Charles Adams Platt, letter to his family, 26 August 1883, private collection.

147. William Merritt Chase, letter to Minnie Gerson, 1903, quoted in Roof, p. 209. "Old Delft Ware," *Harper's Bazar* 45 (March 1911): 117.

148. The first quote is from Edwards, p. 276. Further discussion of forgeries can be found in M. H. Gans and Th. M. Duyvene de Wit-Klinkhamer, *Dutch Silver* (London: Faber and Faber, 1961), pp. 61-69, and in Robert and Elizabeth Shackleton, *The Quest of the Colonial* (New York: The Century Company, 1921), p. 392, from whence the last quote comes.

149. Shackleton, p. 184.

150. Embury, *Dutch Colonial House*, p. 97. On the quality issue, see Humphreys, pp. 175-176, and Shackleton, pp. 391-392.

151. For illustrations of these pieces, see *The Grand Rapids Furniture Record*: colonial chamber suite (November, 1909), 742; Dutch dining room suite (December 1903), 69; Warner's Dutch clocks (April 1903), 473; and *Good Housekeeping*, Ithaca clock (April 1906), advertising section, n.pag. The tall clock form, also known as a grandfather clock, was thought to have originated in the Netherlands, another reason for calling such clocks Dutch.

152. On fumed or Flemish oak, see "The Staining and Coloring of Cabinet Woods." *Good Furniture* 4 (March 1915): 383-384. On Utrecht velvet, see Katherine C. Grier, *Culture and Comfort: People, Parlors and Upholstery, 1850-1930* (Rochester, NY: Strong Museum, 1988), p. 306. Alwyn F. Covell, "The Real Place of Mission Furniture." *Good Furniture* 4 (March 1915): 358-366. Berkey & Gay Furniture Company, *The Old Feeling or The Past Revived,* (Grand Rapids: Berkey & Gay, 1900).

153.For more on antimodern symbolic content see Annette Stott, "Dutch Utopia: Paintings by Antimodern American Artists of the Nineteenth Century," *Smithsonian Studies in American Art* 3 (Spring 1989):47-61 and Kathleen Eagan Johnson, "From Frans Hals to Windmills: The Arts and Crafts Fascination with the Culture of the Low Countries," in *The Substance of Style: Perspectives on the American Arts and Crafts Movement*, ed. Bert Denker (Winterthur, Delaware: Henry Francis du Pont Winterthur Museum, 1996), 47-67.

154. This and the following Limbert quotes are from Charles P. Limbert Company, *Limbert's Holland Dutch Arts and Crafts Furniture*, book #117 (Grand Rapids, Michigan: Charles P. Limbert Company, n.d.), pp. 8-9. Variations on this theme appear in all the Limbert catalogs for this line.

155. Esther Singleton, "American Colonial Furniture," *The Mentor*, 2 (1 July 1914).

156. Bok, p. 16. Humphreys, p. 178. For examples of other art potters employing Dutch motifs, see Johnson, pp. 52-56.

157. Talbert, p. 26.

158. Singleton, "American Colonial Furniture," p. 5.

159. The wallpaper no longer exists, but is well illustrated in Nina Fletcher Little, *Country Arts in Early American Homes* (New York: Dutton, 1975), p. 21. Stephen Jerome, to Annette Stott, 11 July 1992.

160. Embury, p. 88.

161.The Phillips mansion is open as The Phillips Collection and the fireplace can be seen since a coat of paint was removed from the tiles during renovation. White's fireplace is illustrated in Barr Ferree, *American Estates and Gardens* (New York: Munn & Col, 1904), p. 144.

162. T. Celestine Cummings, "Artistic Interiors," *Artistic Home Ideas* 3 (January 1903): 3. Julia Cowles, *Artistic Home Furnishing for People of Moderate Means* (New York: F. M. Lupton, 1898), p. 94. See also pp. 29-30 and 95.

163. Jan Jennings and Herbert Gottfried, *American Vernacular Interior Architecture, 1870-1940* (New York: Van Nostrand Reinhold Co., 1988), pp. 204-205.

164. Johnson, p. 58.

165. The dinner was reported in the *New Amsterdam Gazette*, 1 (31 March 1884), p. 6 and the suggestions for Thanksgiving decorations are in "Our Girls," *Harper's Bazar* 43-2 (1909): n. pag. Kathleen Johnson identifies the Hudson-Fulton celebration as the impetus for interest in things Dutch, but it should be evident to the reader that the trend started three decades earlier. Hudson Fulton might rather be seen as a milestone or focal point for the Hudson Valley region.

166. Weir's lecture is fully described in the Art Student's League of Buffalo Scrapbook for 1901-1909, Buffalo and Erie County Public Library. Emma Lampert illustrated a lecture on Holland with slides of her own paintings, according to a newspaper clipping of 1896 in her scrapbook, Emma Lampert Cooper Archives, Rare Book and Manuscript Collection, University of Rochester Library. For other work cited in this paragraph, see the bibliography.

167. Notes from the Des Moines Chautauqua Union are from *The Chautauquan* 54 (April 1909): 307. The Vermont group's report was published in *The Chautauquan* 54 (May 1909): 472, 465.

168. "The Club Year—-Holland," *Woman's Home Companion* 39 (December 1912): 68.

169. Martha Cutler, "A Garden Fete," *Harper's Bazar* 43 (September 1909): 921-922.

170. "The Bonnets for the Autumn," *Ladies' Home Journal* (September 1894): 19.

171. The quote is from *Harper's Bazar* 48 (September 1913): 29. Irene Castle discussed her impact on fashion in several publications: Mr. and Mrs. Vernon Castle, *Modern Dancing* (1914; rpt. New York: De Capo Press, 1980), p. 147; Irene Castle, *Castles in the Air* (Garden City: Doubleday & Co., 1958), p. 115; Irene Castle, *My Husband* (New York: Scribner, 1919), p. 27.

172. Celia Betsky, "Inside the Past: the Interior and the Colonial Revival in American Art and Literature, 1860-1914," in Axelrod, ed. *The Colonial Revival in America* (New York: W. W. Norton, 1985), pp. 249-250.

173. Vanderslice speech in *The Twelfth Annual Banquet of the Netherlands Society of Philadelphia* (Philadelphia: Netherlands Society, 1903), pp. 53-57. The Conrad claims were reported in *New Amsterdam Gazette*, 5 September 1884, p. 5, col. 2.

174. The ad was considered a trick to defraud the public by *The Collector and Art Critic*, 1 (1 July 1899): 70.

175. Theodore Dreiser, *A Traveler at Forty* (New York: The Century Co., 1913), p. 503. George Burton Hotchkiss and Richard B. Franken, *The Leadership of Advertised Brands* (Garden City, NY: Doubleday, Page & Company for the Associated Advertising Clubs of the World, 1923), pp. 147, 60.

EIGHT: CINCINNATI, A CASE STUDY

176. *A Book of the Tile Club* (Boston & New York: Houghton Mifflin, 1886), pp. 67-68.

177. *New Amsterdam Gazette*, vol. 2, no. 4, p. 10, col. 2 (November 10, 1884).

178. *The New Amsterdam Gazette* regularly reported on the activities of Baer, Blum, and Chase. See for example, the descriptions of their Dutch paintings in vol.1, no.7 (31 January 1884), p.3, col.1; no.9, (31 March 1884), p.2, col.2; vol.2, no.3 (9 October 1884) p.2, col.2; no.4 (10 November 1884) p.10, col.2; vol.3, no.9 (30 April 1886), p.2, col.2; vol.5, no.5 (21 May-30 June 1888), p.7, col.3.

179. Allen Collier, letter to John Rettig, 2 December 1924, John Rettig Papers, Archives of American Art, Smithsonian Institution.

180. Elizabeth Nourse, letter to Addie Pitman, 2 July 1892, Elizabeth Nourse Papers, Mss fN933c, box 1, folder 3, Cincinnati Historical Society, Cincinnati Museum Center.

181. Elizabeth Nourse, letter to Addie Pitman, 9 October 1892, Elizabeth Nourse Papers, Mss fN933c, box 1, folder 3, Cincinnati Historical Society, Cincinnati Museum Center.

182. Unidentified exhibition review, [November 1893], Woman's Art Club Scrapbook, Mss fW872ac, box 18, Cincinnati Historical Society, Cincinnati Museum Center.

183. Quotes are from newspaper clippings in the Woman's Art Club Scrapbook, Mss fW872ac, box 18, Cincinnati Historical Society, Cincinnati Museum Center.

184. "Private View of Art," *Commercial Tribune*, 8 March 1899, Woman's Art Club Scrapbook, Mss fW872ac, box 18, Cincinnati Historical Society, Cincinnati Museum Center.

185. C. T. Webber, "When Lovely Woman Stoops to Paint," *Commercial Gazette*, 12 November 1893, Woman's Art Club Scrapbook, Mss fW872ac, box 18, Cincinnati Historical Society, Cincinnati Museum Center.

186. "Exhibit of the Woman's Art Club," *The Enquirer*, 9 March 1899, Woman's Art Club Scrapbook, Mss fW872ac, box 18, Cincinnati Historical Society, Cincinnati Museum Center.

187. "Presto! Wonderland Reviewed," *The Enquirer*, 30 December 1897, John Rettig Scrapbook, vol.6, Mss fXR439, Cincinnati Historical Society, Cincinnati Museum Center.

188. Paul Schulze, letter to John Rettig, 28 March 1912, John Rettig Papers, Archives of American Art, Smithsonian Institution.

189. Cherry Greve, unidentified exhibition review, microfilm 3614:1175, John Rettig Papers, Archives of American Art, Smithsonian Institution.

190. "James Albert Green Talks Entertainingly of the Distinguished Nebraskan Who is Receiving Great Attention Everywhere Abroad," *The Cincinnati Times-Star*, 12 July 1906, John Rettig Scrapbook, vol. 7, Mss fXR439, Cincinnati Historical Society, Cincinnati Museum Center.

191. Adam Voelker, letter to John Rettig, 11 June 1916, John Rettig Papers, Archives of American Art, Smithsonian Institution.

192. Simon Hubig, letter to John Rettig, 3 January 1924 [mistake for 1925?], John Rettig Papers, Archives of American Art, Smithsonian Institution.

193. Perrin P Hunter, letter to John Rettig, 2 October 1906, John Rettig Papers, Archives of American Art, Smithsonian Institution.

194. John Graydon, letter to John Rettig, 9 March 1906, John Rettig Papers, Archives of American Art, Smithsonian Institution.

195. William J. Bainbridge, letter to John Rettig, 21 December 1907, John Rettig Papers, Archives of American Art, Smithsonian Institution.

196. Horace W. Males, letter to John Rettig, 29 March 1917, in John Rettig Papers, Archives of American Art, Smithsonian Institution. C.A.R. Devereux, letter to John Rettig,

7 April 1906, in Langstroth, "Colorful World of John Rettig", scrapbook, vol. 2, Public Library of Cincinnati and Hamilton County.

197. Herbert Corey, letter to John Rettig, 16 February 1906, John Rettig Papers, Archives of American Art, Smithsonian Institution.

198. Josephine Woodward, letter to John Rettig, John Rettig Papers, Archives of American Art, Smithsonian Institution.

CONCLUSION

199. Hendrik de Leeuw, *Crossroads of the Zuider Zee* (Philadelphia & New York: J. B. Lippincott Co., 1938), p. 7.

200. Eva Madden, "In the Land of Windmills," *Harper's Bazar* 43 (August 1909): 761.

201. Quotes in this paragraph, in order of appearance, are from Osborne, p. 61; Florence Craig Albrecht, "Volendam, The Artist's Village," *Scribner's Magazine* 41 (March 1907): 328; and Howell, pp. 147-148.

202. The above quotes are from Mary Mapes Dodge, *Hans Brinker or the Silver Skates: A Story of Life in Holland* (New York: Charles Scribner's Sons, 1905) pp. vii, 17, 154-155.

203. Scudder, p. 29.

204. Of all the visual arts, sculpture was least affected by Dutch influence. During this period, Frank Edwin Elwell, a former student and studio mate of Daniel Chester French, created *Death of Strength* for the church yard at Edam in North Holland. He was said to be the first American sculptor to place a work in the Netherlands. American tourists sometimes visited Elwell's memorial statue of an angel standing over a lion, but it exhibited no obvious Dutch influence and would have looked equally at home almost anywhere in the western world.

205. E.E. Easton, "Inside the Boer Lines," *Harper's Monthly Magazine* 101 (June 1900): 3-18. The comment about up-country Boers was made by S.B., "The Boer and the White Flag," *Harper's Weekly* 43 (9 December 1899): 1245. George Lacy, "Some Boer Characteristics," *The North American Review* 170 (January 1900): 43-53.

206. Griffis, *Brave Little Holland*, p. 5. Senator Hoar, quoted in Edwin D. Mead, "The World's Debt to Holland in the Cause of Peace," *New England Magazine* 37 (Oct 1907): 234.

207. The name change of a town in South Dakota is recorded by Gerald F. DeJong, *The Dutch in America, 1609-1974* (Boston: G. K. Hall, 1975), p. 209. For a description of one Dutch-American community's reaction to the Boer War see Philip E. Webber, *Pella Dutch: The Portrait of a Language and its Use in One of Iowa's Ethnic Communities* (Ames: Iowa State Univ. Press, 1988), pp. 60-62.

208. Richard B. Mulanax, *The Boer War in American Politics and Diplomacy* (Lanham, MD: University Press of America, 1994).

209. Theodore Roosevelt, *Theodore Roosevelt Cyclopedia*, (New York: Roosevelt Memorial Association, 1941), p. 48.

210. See for example, Howard C. Hillegas, "The Boer Girl of South Africa," *Ladies' Home Journal* 17 (January 1900): 6, from which these quotes are taken, or S. Kruger, "Boer Women," *Harpers Bazar* 33 (20 January 1900): 46.

211. Various news clippings in John Rettig Scrapbook vol. 8, Cincinnati Historical Society.

212. Theodore Roosevelt, quoted in Frank Freidel, "The Dutchness of the Roosevelts" in *A Bilateral Bicentennial: A History of Dutch-American Relations, 1782-1982*, ed. J. W. Schulte Nordholt & Robert P. Swierenga (Amsterdam: Meulenhoff International, 1982), p. 151.

213. M. J. Brusse, *With Roosevelt Through Holland* (Rotterdam: Holland-America Line, 1911), p. 42.

214. Mead, p. 232. Roosevelt, *Roosevelt Cyclopedia*, p. 423.

215. Bok, p. 16.

216. Marjorie Bowen, *The Netherlands Display'd* (New York: Dodd, Mead & Co., 1927), p. 176.

217. Bernard H. M. Vlekke, *The Netherlands and the United States* (Boston: World Peace Foundation, 1945), p. 15.

218. Charles Van Dyke Joline, Toastmaster speech at 1921 meeting, in *Addresses Made at the Annual Meetings of the Netherlands Society of Philadelphia, 1913 to 1930* (Philadelphia: Netherlands Society of Philadelphia, [c.1930]), p. 270.

PHOTOGRAPHIC SOURCES AND CREDITS

FIG. 1. Jan Steen, *The Doctor's Visit*, oil on panel, 1663-1665, 18⅛ x 14½", Philadelphia Museum of Art: The John G. Johnson Collection.

FIG. 2. Rembrandt van Rijn, *The Mill*, oil, c.1650, 34½ x 41½", Widener Collection, © 1996, Board of Trustees, National Gallery of Art, Washington, DC.

FIG. 3. Jacob Ochtervelt, Dutch, 1634/35-1708/10, *The Musicians*, oil on canvas, 1671, 80.2 x 65.5 cm, Mr. and Mrs. Martin A. Ryerson Collection, 1933.1088. Photograph © 1993, The Art Institute of Chicago, All Rights.

FIG. 4. Jozef Israëls, Dutch, 1824-1911, *The Cottage Madonna*, paint on canvas, 1867, 53 x 39¼", Bequest of Nell Ford Torrey, Photograph © The Detroit Institute of Arts (59.117).

FIG. 5. Bernardus Johannes Blommers, *The Butterfly*, oil on canvas, 16 x 19" (73.155), Memorial Art Gallery of the University of Rochester: George Eastman Collection of the University of Rochester.

FIG. 6. Charles Herbert Woodbury, *Society of Painters in Water Color of Holland*, poster, 1895, Engel Collection, Rare Book and Manuscript Library, Columbia University.

FIG. 7. Thomas Eakins, *B.J. Blommers*, oil on canvas, 1904, 24 x 20", The Toledo Museum of Art; Gift of Florence Scott Libbey (37.16).

FIG. 8. William Merritt Chase in his Tenth Street Studio, NYC, with copies after Hals, Velazquez, and other Old Masters on the wall, c. 1895, albumen print, 4½ x 7⅝", The William Merritt Chase Archives, The Parrish Art Museum, Southampton, New York, Gift of Jackson Chase Storm (83.stm.41).

FIG. 9. "Edward Bok, editor of *The Ladies' Home Journal*, in his Philadelphia office," illustration, c.1910-1920, from *The Americanization of Edward Bok: An Autobiography* (1924).

FIG. 10. Morris & Bendien, *Flower Girl in Holland*, print, c.1900, after an oil painting by George Hitchcock of 1887 in the Art Institute of Chicago.

FIG. 11. Illustration of a Dutch costume from *The Art Amateur* (July 1887).

FIG. 12. Henry Ward Ranger, *A Wet Day in Amsterdam*, illustration based on his watercolor, from *The Art Amateur* (January 1888).

FIG. 13. Photograph of the Cleveland Institute of Art costume class, 1902, courtesy Cleveland Institute of Art Archives, Cleveland, Ohio, copy photography by Richard Sandy.

FIG. 14. Oscar Miller, *Dutch Milkmaid*, oil, no date, courtesy of August B. Miller. Photograph of model posing for *Dutch Milkmaid*, courtesy of August B. Miller.

FIG. 15. Rebekah Rogers, *A Dutch Girl*, from a reproduction in *International Studio* (March 1914), present location of painting unknown.

FIG. 16. Map of the Netherlands around 1900 showing the towns and cities most frequented by American artists.

FIG. 17. Raymond C. Ewer, "*To Spaander*," mixed media, 1909, collection of the Hotel Spaander, Volendam.

FIG. 18. Edwin Austin Abbey, *Fishermen's Wives*, illustration, 1880, from *Harper's New Monthly Magazine* (January 1883).

FIG. 19. Iris M. Andrews, *Always Knitting*, illustration, 1905, from *Century Magazine* (November 1905).

FIG. 20. Orrin Peck, *Stiefmutterchen*, oil, from a reproduction, courtesy Rijksbureau voor Kunsthistorische Documentatie, The Hague. Present location of painting is unknown.

FIG. 21. Edward Penfield, *Magenta was Overwhelming*, illustration, c. 1905, from *Holland Sketches* (1907).

FIG. 22. *"Oud Kamer" at Hotel Spaander*,

Volendam, photograph, 1908, author's collection, courtesy of Willem Wouters.

FIG. 23. Robert Henri, *Volendam Street Scene*, oil on canvas, 1910, 20⅛ x 24", Gift of Mr. and Mrs. Gerard C. Smith, © 1997 Board of Trustees, National Gallery of Art, Washington, D.C.

FIG. 24. William Henry Howe, *Early Start for Market*, from a reproduction in *Figaro-Salon* (1888), reproduced courtesy of the Trustees of the Boston Public Library. Present location of the painting is unknown; it was stolen from the gallery of the Grand Rapids Art Association in 1922.

FIG. 25. William Henry Howe, *Evening at Laren, the Meadows - Cattle*, oil on canvas, 1890, 33 x 42¼", Collection of the Union League Club of Chicago, photograph by Michael Tropea.

FIG. 26. William Henry Howe, *Cow in a Stall*, oil, 1890, Art collection of the municipality of Laren, Netherlands.

FIG. 27. Charles Paul Gruppe, *Sheep*, oil, from the private Collection of Oak Hill Country Club, Rochester, New York.

FIG. 28. Emma Lampert Cooper, *The Breadwinner*, watercolor, 1891, 20 x 24", Memorial Art Gallery of the University of Rochester; Gift of Colin Campbell Cooper.

FIG. 29.Henry Singlewood Bisbing, *In the Meadow*, oil on canvas, 1888, 79 x 138", courtesy of the Pennsylvania Academy of the Fine Arts, Philadelphia. Gift of Riter Fitzgerald in memory of his father, Colonel Thomas Fitzgerald (1891.1).

FIG. 30. Walter MacEwen, *Returning From Work*, oil, c. 1885, 47½ x 74¾", Collection of George Haigh, Cambridge Fine Arts.

FIG. 31. John Singer Sargent, *Portrait of Ralph Curtis on the Beach at Scheveningen*, oil on panel, 1880, 10½ x 13¹³⁄₁₆", Gift of the Walter Clay Hill and Family Foundation, Permanent Collection of the High Museum of Art, Atlanta, Georgia (73.3).

FIG. 32. Stephen Salisbury Tuckerman, untitled marine view, oil, 1885, 24 x 29", Cape Ann Historical Association, Gloucester, Massachusetts.

FIG. 33. William Stanley Haseltine, *Dutch Coast*, oil, 1883, 14 x 25", The Currier Gallery of Art, Manchester, New Hampshire, Gift of Helen Haseltine Plowden, 1953.1.

FIG. 34. Alfred Stieglitz, *Watching for the Return*, carbon enlargement photograph, 1894, Alfred Stieglitz Collection, © 1997 Board of Trustees, National Gallery of Art, Washington, D.C.

FIG. 35. Paul Bernard King, *Hauling in the Anchor Line*, oil on canvas, 1905, 25½ x 31½", private collection.

FIG. 36. William Edward Norton, *A Moment's Rest*, oil on canvas, 1892, 48½ x 64⅞", Gift of Dr. Morris F. Weiner, National Museum of American Art, Smithsonian Institution, Washington, D.C. (1966.109).

FIG. 37. Gari Melchers, *Egmond aan Zee*, oil on canvas, undated, 33 x 50¼" Belmont, The Gari Melchers Estate and Memorial Gallery, Mary Washington College, Fredericksburg, Virginia.

FIG. 38. Gari Melchers, *The Pilots*, oil, 1886, 67¾ x 83½", Charles and Emma Frye Art Museum, Seattle, Washington.

FIG. 39. George Hitchcock, *In Brabant*, oil, 1895, 30¼ x 24¼", courtesy of Vance Jordan Fine Art Inc., New York. This painting has frequently been confused with another of the same size and, as a result, is sometimes published as *The Bride*.

FIG. 40. Alice Blair Ring with one of her Egmond paintings (now unlocated), photograph, c. 1905, private collection.

FIG. 41. James Jebusa Shannon, *On the Dunes (Lady Shannon and Kitty)*, oil, c.1900-1910, 73⅜ x 56⅜", National Museum of American Art, Smithsonian Institution, Gift of John Gellatly.

FIG. 42. Gari Melchers, *Penelope*, oil on canvas, 1910, 54½ x 50⅞", Collection of the Corcoran Gallery of Art, Museum Purchase, Gallery Fund.

FIG. 43. Harry Chase, *Jozef Israëls in his Studio*, illustration from *Century Magazine* (March 1889).

FIG. 44. *Hotel Warendorp, Rijsoord*, postcard, 1908, author's collection, courtesy of Mr. Wols.

FIG. 45. Wilhelmina Douglas Hawley, *Scouring*, watercolor, from a reproduction in *International Studio* (July 1899), present location of painting unknown.

FIG. 46. Charles Webster Hawthorne, *Old Dutch Folk*, oil, 1898, from a reproduction in *Brush and Pencil* (August 1899), present location of painting unknown.

FIG. 47. Charles Webster Hawthorne, *Three Women of Provincetown*, oil on canvas, c. 1921, 48½ x 60", Amherst College, Gift of George D. Pratt, class of 1893.

FIG. 48. Frans Hals, *Regentesses of the Old Men's Almshouse*, oil, 1664, Frans Halsmuseum, Haarlem.

FIG. 49. Edward Moran, *Henry Hudson Entering New York Bay*, September 3, 1609, oil, 1897, 54 x 96", courtesy of the U.S. Naval Academy Museum.

FIG. 50. Anonymous, *Departure of the Pilgrims from Delfshaven*, oil, once owned by George H. Boughton, present location of painting unknown. Photograph courtesy Pilgrim Fathers Documentation Center, Leyden, by permission of the Municipal Archives of Rotterdam.

FIG. 51. Edwin Austin Abbey, *Katrina*, illustration from *Harper's Weekly* (January 1882).

FIG. 52. Edwin Austin Abbey, *The Battery*, illustration from *Harper's Weekly* (January 1882).

FIG. 53. George Henry Boughton,

Ichabod Crane and Katrina Van Tassel, watercolor, c.1893, 11½ x 7½", © Collection of The New-York Historical Society, New York City.

FIG. 54. George Henry Boughton, *The Edict of William the Testy*, oil, from a reproduction in *The Chautauquan* (April 1909), present location of painting unknown.

FIG. 55. Stanley M. Arthurs, *Landing of the DeVries Colony at Swaanendael, Lewes, Delaware, 1631*, oil, 1917, 82½ x 85½", Permanent Collection of the University of Delaware.

FIG. 56. Walter MacEwen, *Stad Herberg, Nieuw Amsterdam (New York) 1690*, oil, c. 1885-1889, 56 x 81", courtesy of Christies, New York.

FIG. 57. Walter MacEwen, *The Ghost Story*, oil, 1887, 47¾ x 75¼", The Cleveland Museum of Art, Gift of Mrs. Edward S. Harkness, 23.416.

FIG. 58. Walter MacEwen, *Dutch Courtship*, oil, 1886, 60 x 82", courtesy of William Doyle Galleries, New York.

FIG. 59. Walter MacEwen, *The Secretary*, oil, c.1905, from a reproduction in *International Studio* (July 1907), present location of painting unknown.

FIG. 60. Walter MacEwen, *A Girl Looking in a Mirror*, oil, 11⁷⁄₁₆ x 9¹⁄₁₆", Sterling and Francine Clark Art Institute, Williamstown, Massachusetts.

FIG. 61. Charles Frederick Ulrich (1858-1908), *The Village Print Shop*, oil on panel, 1884, 21¼ x 22¹⁵⁄₁₆", © Terra Foundation for the Arts, Daniel J. Terra Collection, 1992.137; Photograph courtesy of Terra Museum of American Art, Chicago.

FIG. 62. Charles Yardley Turner, *Old Dutch Woman Reading her Bible*, oil, 1880, from a reproduction in *The First Annual Dinner of the Holland Society* of New York (1886), present location of painting unknown.

FIG. 63. Elizabeth Nourse, *On the Dyke at Volendam*, oil, 1892, from a reproduction in *International Studio* (December 1905), present location of painting unknown.

FIG. 64. Eugene Mulertt, *Portrait of an Old Woman*, oil, c. 1904-1920, collection of the Stichting Hervormde Gast en Weeshuis, Katwijk, South Holland.

FIG. 65. Photograph of a ship at the Holland-America headquarters in Hoboken, from a glass plate negative of the Detroit Publishing Company, Division of Prints and Photographs, Library of Congress.

FIG. 66. Holland-America Line, poster, 1898, courtesy Holland America Line Westours Inc., Seattle, Washington.

FIG. 67. Dutch travel books, author's collection.

FIG. 68. Robert Swain Gifford, *Harlingen*, illustration, 1884, from the Zuyder Zee edition of Edmondo De Amicis's *Holland and Its People*.

FIG. 69. Thomas Moran, etcher, *On the Way to Delft*, 1894, frontispiece of William Elliot Griffis's *Brave Little Holland and What She Taught Us*.

FIG. 70. George Boughton, *Gathering Cabbages*, illustration from *Harper's New Monthly Magazine* (September 1884).

FIG. 71. Gari Melchers, *Sailor and His Dog*, oil, c.1895, 79 x 38½", Belmont, The Gari Melchers Estate and Memorial Gallery, Fredericksburg, Virginia.

FIG. 72. *Rembrandt's Portrait of Burgomaster Six*, reproduction by "T Johnson" for *Harper's New Monthly Magazine* (January 1883).

FIG. 73. Paulus Potter, *The Young Bull*, oil, 1647, Photograph © Mauritshuis, The Hague, inv. nr. 136.

FIG. 74. George Wharton Edwards, *Amsterdam—-Little Courtyard*, illustration from George Wharton Edwards, *Holland of Today* (1919).

FIG. 75. A photograph of *Deventer* from Ward, Lock & Company, *Handbook to Holland*, 6th edition (c. 1910).

FIG. 76. *Old and New Amsterdam*, illustration from Hendrik Willem Van Loon's travelogue, *An Indiscreet Itinerary* (1933), copyright 1933 by Harcourt Brace & Company and renewed 1961 by Gerald Willem Van Loon, reprinted by permission of the publisher.

FIG. 77. August Allebe, *Pilgrim Fathers Holding Their First Meeting For Public Worship*, colored print, 20 x 28", after the lost oil painting of 1858 by John George Schwartze, courtesy of the Pilgrim Society, Plymouth, Massachusetts.

FIG. 78. Keystone View Company, *Church where Pilgrim Fathers Prayed before Embarking for America, Delfthaven, Netherlands*, stereoview photograph, author's collection.

FIG. 79. Francis Hopkinson Smith, *Dutch Canal Scene, Dort*, pencil, watercolor and gouache on paper, c.1888, 12¼ x 23¼, courtesy of Vance Jordan Fine Art, Inc., New York.

FIG. 80. George Boughton or E. A. Abbey, *Zaandam Windmills*, illustration from *Harper's New Monthly Magazine* (February 1883).

FIG. 81. Edward Penfield, *Tourists at Marken*, illustration from *Scribner's Magazine* (January 1905).

FIG. 82. left: Edward Penfield, *A Marken Interior*, illustration from *Scribner's Magazine* (January 1905). right: George Wharton Edwards, *Wall Bed In Which I Slept*, illustration from *Marken and its People* (c. 1908).

FIG. 83. Edward Penfield, *Buying Wooden Shoes*, illustration from *Holland Sketches* (1907).

FIG. 84. Edward Penfield, *Man in a Dog*

Cart, Holland, pen and ink, Division of Prints and Photographs, Library of Congress.

FIG. 85 .Edwin Austin Abbey, *On a North Holland Canal*, 1881, illustration from *Harper's New Monthly Magazine* (April 1883).

FIG. 86. Keystone View Company, *In the Land of Dikes and Windmills—Characteristic Scene in the Netherlands*, stereoview photograph, author's collection.

FIG. 87. George Wharton Edwards, *Veere*, illustration from *Holland of Today* (1919).

FIG. 88. Lieven de Key, *Vleeshal*, 1603, Haarlem, Holland, from a reproduction in *The Architectural Record* (March 1895).

FIG. 89. Robert W. Gibson, *Collegiate Church and School of New York*, 1892, New York City, from a reproduction in *The Architectural Record* (March 1895).

FIG. 90. Henry J. Hardenbergh, *John Wolfe Building*, 1895, photographed in 1910, New York City, © Collection of the New-York Historical Society, New York City.

FIG. 91. Marcus Reynolds, *Pruyn Library*, 1901, Albany, New York. Postcard view from the McKinney Library, Albany Institute of History and Art.

FIG. 92. Samuel Mast, *Elizabeth Voorhees Hall*, 1907, Hope College, Holland, Michigan, author's photograph.

FIG. 93. Palliser, Palliser & Company, *Row Houses*, 1882-1883, from *Palliser's New Cottage Homes and Details* (1888), courtesy the Winterthur Library: Printed Book and Periodical Collection.

FIG. 94. Edward Penfield, *In the City of Amsterdam*, illustration from *Holland Sketches* (1907).

FIG. 95. Frederick J. Sterner, *Pearce-McAllister House*, 1899, Denver, Colorado, courtesy of the Colorado Historical Society.

FIG. 96. George B. Post and Sons, *Seven-Room House C-5*, c.1916-1917, for Eclipse Park Development, Beloit, Wisconsin, from a reproduction in *The Architectural Record* (March 1918).

FIG. 97. Charles Barton Keen, *Wrangley Lodge*, West Chester, Pennsylvania, from a reproduction in Henry H. Saylor, *Distinctive Homes of Moderate Cost* (1910), courtesy the Winterthur Library: Printed Book and Periodical Collection.

FIG. 98. Dutch doors, from William L. Price, *Model Houses for Little Money* (1898) courtesy the Winterthur Library: Printed Book and Periodical Collection.

99. George B. Post and Sons, *Six-Room Clapboard House C-8*, c.1916-1917, for Eclipse Park Development, Beloit, Wisconsin, from a reproduction in *The Architectural Record* (March 1918).

100. "A House for $8,000," illustration from *Harper's Bazar* (March 1909).

FIG. 101. *Ackerman-Brinckerhoff House*, 1704, Hackensack, New Jersey, from a reproduction in Harold Donaldson Eberlein, *The Architecture of Colonial America* (1915).

FIG. 102. H.W. Johns Manufacturing Company, *Design No. 1*, illustration from H.W. Johns, *Artistic House Painting* (1895), courtesy the Winterthur Library: Printed Book and Periodical Collection.

FIG. 103. Joy Wheeler Dow, *Princessgate*, c.1902, illustration from *The Book of a Hundred Houses* (1906), courtesy the Winterthur Library: Printed Book and Periodical Collection.

FIG. 104. *North Mill*, 1902, Golden Gate Park, San Francisco, photograph by John Fuller McGuigan, Jr.

FIG. 105. A typical late-nineteenth-century house near Zeeland, Michigan, author's photograph.

FIG. 106. Gari Melchers, *The Delft Horse*, oil, c. 1900, 44¼ x 22¾", Belmont, The Gari Melchers Estate and Memorial Gallery, Fredericksburg Virginia.

FIG. 107. Bates & How, *Dining Room of "Upwey,"* before 1905, Elmsford, New York, from a reproduction in *Good Furniture* (March 1915), courtesy the Winterthur Library: Printed Book and Periodical Collection.

FIG. 108. Charles P. Limbert, *A Library in Limbert's Holland Dutch Arts and Crafts "Flanders"* from Limbert's Holland Dutch Arts and Crafts Furniture catalogue #114, no date, courtesy the Winterthur Library: Printed Book and Periodical Collection.

FIG. 109. Photograph of a tiled bathroom from *Harper's Bazar* (September 1911).

FIG. 119. *"The Pure Dutch Mantel"* illustration from *Ladies' Home Journal* (September 1894).

FIG. 111. Photograph of a Dutch style mantel in a New York home, from *Ladies' Home Journal* (March 1899).

FIG. 112. Photograph of the Salmagundi Club fireplace from *House Beautiful* (November 1899).

FIG. 113. *"Tableau—'The Flower Girl'—After the Painting by George Hitchcock"* from the W.G. Ball Collection of Art Clippings, Fine Arts Department, Boston Public Library, reproduced courtesy of the Trustees of the Boston Public Library.

FIG. 114. "A Dutch Bonnet," from *Ladies' Home Journal* (September 1894).

FIG. 115. Julius Gari Melchers, *Easter Sunday* (detail), 1910-1911, oil, 52 x 56", Toledo Museum of Art; Gift of Florence Scott Libbey.

FIG. 116 ."Boudoir Cap in Dutch Style" from *Harper's Bazar* (February 1912).

FIG. 117. Photograph of Irene Castle in her Dutch lace cap, c.1912-1913, from Vernon and Irene Castle, *Modern Dancing* (1914).

FIG. 118. *Joseph Jefferson in the role of Rip Van Winkle*, illustration based on an engraving by H. Davidson after a photograph by Napoleon Sarony, reproduced from *The Autobiography of Joseph Jefferson* (1890).

FIG. 119. "Bensdorp's Royal Dutch Cocoa," postcard, 1898, author's collection.

FIG. 120. Advertisements for Van Houten's Cocoa, Blooker's Dutch Cocoa, and W. Baker & Co.'s Breakfast Cocoa, from various magazines, 1893 & 1894.

FIG. 121. Advertisement for Sapolio soap from *Woman's Home Companion* (April 1913).

FIG. 122. Advertisement for Old Dutch cleanser.

FIG. 123. "We carry the best in the market" postcard, postmarked Poultney, Vermont, 1906, and "The best in the field," postcard, postmarked St. Louis, Missouri, 1906, author's collection.

FIG. 124. Selection of "Dutch kids" postcards, dates range from 1900-1915, author's collection.

FIG. 125. William Merritt Chase, *Sunlight and Shadow*, oil, 1884, 65½ x 77¾", Joslyn Art Museum, Omaha, Nebraska; Joslyn's Friends of Art collection, February 13, 1932 (JAM 1932.4).

FIG. 126. Robert Frederick Blum, *Two Dutch Girls Having Coffee*, watercolor and gouache over pencil, 1885, 12½ x 16$\frac{1}{16}$", Sterling and Francine Clark Art Institute, Williamstown, Massachusetts.

FIG. 127. Martha Scudder Twachtman, *A View of the Meuse*, etching, 1881, 3¾ x 2⅜", Museum Purchase, courtesy of the Museum of Fine Arts, Boston.

FIG. 128. John Henry Twachtman, *Windmills*, oil, 1884, 38 x 51½", from a reproduction in *International Studio* (January 1921), present location of painting unknown.

FIG. 129. Frank Duveneck, *Woman with Forget-Me-Nots*, oil, c. 1876, 40 x 32¾", Cincinnati Art Museum, gift of the artist (1904.195).

FIG. 130. Edward Henry Potthast, *Dutch Interior*, oil, 1890, 19½ x 25½", Cincinnati Art Museum, gift of A. Howard Hinkle, Theodore Hallam, Frederick H. Alms, Ault & Wiburg, C. H. Krippendorf, F. A. Bradley, Bellamy Stover & Alexander McDonald (1894.9).

FIG. 131. Photograph believed to represent Henrietta Wachman in her Volendam studio, c. 1890- 1900, author's collection, courtesy Willem Wouters.

FIG. 132. Elizabeth Nourse, *In the Church at Volendam*, oil, 1892, courtesy of the Burke Museum of Natural History and Culture, Seattle, Washington; photography by "Susan Dirk/Under the Light".

FIG. 133. Euphemia Bailey, *The Young Smoker*, from a reproduction in the Women's Art Club Scrapbook, courtesy of the Cincinnati Historical Society, present location of painting unknown.

FIG. 134. Henrietta Wilson, *Volendam Vischvrouw*, from a reproduction in the Women's Art Club Scrapbook, courtesy of the Cincinnati Historical Society, present location of painting unknown.

FIG. 135. John Rettig, collector and arranger, *The Dutch Room at Kemper Lane*, Cincinnati, postcard, c. 1908, private collection.

FIG. 136. May and John Rettig with his Volendam models, photograph, courtesy of the Cincinnati Historical Society.

FIG. 137. Helen Graydon and Roberta Dohrmann wearing costumes in the Rettigs' Dutch Room, 1911, from a photograph in the John Rettig Scrapbook, vol. 7, courtesy of the Cincinnati Historical Society.

FIG. 138. John Rettig in his Volendam Studio, from a photograph published in the Cincinnati *Times-Star*, John Rettig Scrapbook, vol. 7, courtesy of the Cincinnati Historical Society.

FIG. 139. Advertisement for Potter Shoe Company that appeared in a catalog for the Cincinnati Women's Art Club exhibition (April 1906), photograph courtesy of the Cincinnati Historical Society.

FIG. 140. George Wharton Edwards, *Hans Brinker or the Silver Skates*, title page from edition illustrated by Edwards (1915).

FIG. 141. Florence Upton, illustration from *The Golliwogg in Holland*, text by Bertha Upton, (1904).

FIG. 142. Lucy Fitch Perkins, *The Dutch Twins*, book cover, 1911.

FIG. 143. Mabel Landrum Torrey, *Wynken, Blynken and Nod*, stone, 1918, Washington Park, Denver, author's photograph.

FIG. 144. Thore de Thulstrup, *A Transvaal Commandant's Wife Who Fought Beside Her Husband At The Tugela*, illustration from *Harper's Monthly Magazine* (July 1900).

FIG. 145. Underwood and Underwood, *An exciting skirmish in the Battle of Colenso, Boer War, World's Fair, St. Louis, U. S. A.*, stereoview photograph, 1904, Library of Congress.

FIG. 146. Mark Tansey, *Innocent Eye Test*, oil, 1981, 6'6" x 10', The Metropolitan Museum of Art, New York City, promised gift of Charles Cowles in honor of William S. Lieberman, 1988. (1988.183).

FIG. 147. The Dutch Festival on Long Island, 1994, photograph courtesy of Hofstra University.

FIG. 148. Marion County State Bank, Pella, Iowa, photographed in 1997 by Dale Van Donselaar.

FIG. 149. Advertisement for Dutch Boy Paints, 1997, courtesy of Sherwin-Williams Company.

BIBLIOGRAPHY

ONE: DUTCH ART IN AMERICA

Adams, Charlotte. "The Costume Class." *The Art Amateur* 17 (July 1887): 34.

Advertisements for "Masters in Art" and "Contemporary Dutch Art" fine art prints. *The Chautauquan* 52 (Oct 1908): 231 and 54 (April 1909): 295.

Advertisement for Palette Art Company, *International Studio* 26 (1905): xxvii.

"The Altman Collection." *Art and Progress* 6 (December 1914): 79-87.

"Artists and Their Work: The Taste for 'Old Masters'." *Munsey's Magazine* 12 (February 1895): 445-448.

Beaux, Cecilia. *Background with Figures*. Boston & New York: Houghton Mifflin Company, 1930.

Billings, C.K.G. *Fort Tryon Hall-The Residence of C. K. G. Billings, Esq., A Descriptive and Illustrated Catalogue Issued Privately by the Owner.* Washington Heights, NY: 1911.

"Blommers' Art Chat." *American Art News* 20 April 1912, p. 3, col. 4.

Bok, Edward W. *The Americanization of Edward Bok: the Autobiography of a Dutch Boy Fifty Years After*. New York: Charles Scribner's Sons, 1924.

Brimo, Rene. *L'Evolution du Gout aux Etats-Unis: d'Apres L'Histoire des Collections*. Paris: James Fortune, 1938.

Broos, Ben. "Catalogue." In *Great Dutch Paintings from America*, 122-491. Zwolle: Waanders Publishers for the Mauritshuis, 1990.

Buijsen, Edwin. "The Battle against the Dollar: The Dutch Reaction to American Collecting in the Period from 1900 to 1914." In *Great Dutch Paintings from America*, 60-78. Zwolle: Waanders Publishers for the Mauritshuis, 1990.

Cady, E.C. "The Art of Johannes Hendrick Weissenbruch." *Brush and Pencil* 12 (April 1903): 44-55.

Caffin, Charles H. *The Story of Dutch Painting*. New York: The Century Co., 1909.

Cary, Elizabeth Luther. "A Comment on Matthew Maris." *Art in America* 2 (1914): 134-147.

Catalogue of a Loan Collection of Paintings Owned by Citizens of Buffalo. Buffalo: Fine Arts Academy, 1907.

Champney, Elizabeth W. "Modern Dutch Painters." *Century Magazine* 56 (July 1898): 395-407.

Chase, Emma Eames. "Dutch Painters at Home." *Century Magazine* 15 (March 1889): 755-765.

Chu, Petra Ten-Doesschate. "Nineteenth-Century Visitors to the Frans Hals Museum." In *The Documented Image: Visions in Art History*, ed. Gabriel P. Weisberg and Laurinda S. Dixon, 123-128. Syracuse: Syracuse Univ Press, 1987.

Clausen, Sir George. "Autobiographical Notes." *Artwork* 7 (Spring 1931): 12-24.

Cleveland Institute of Art Scrapbook. Cleveland Institute of Art Archives, Cleveland, Ohio.

"The Collection of Mr. James G. Shepherd, Scranton Pennsylvania." *The Collector and Art Critic* 4 (January 1906): 78-82.

The Collector and Art Critic. 2 (15 February 1900): 137.

Constable, W.G. *Art Collecting in the United States of America: An Outline of a History*. London: Thomas Nelson and Sons, 1964.

Cooper, Emma Lampert Papers. Rare Book and Manuscript Collection, University of Rochester Library.

DERBY, LILLIE GILL. "Contemporary Dutch Painting." *The Southern Magazine* 5 (January 1895): 325-334.

Exhibition of the Works of Hendrik Willem Mesdag. Chicago: Art Institute, 1903.

First Annual Exhibition in the United States of the Society of Painters in Water Colors of Holland. exh. cat. New York: Boussod Valadon & Co., 1895.

GOETZ, THOMAS H. *Taine and the Fine Arts*. Madrid: S.A. Playor, 1973.

GORE, JAMES H. *Dutch Art as Seen by a Layman*. New York: Holland-America Line, 1902.

GRIFFIS, WILLIAM ELLIOT. *The American in Holland*. Boston and New York: Houghton Mifflin & Company, 1907.

———. *Belgium: the land of art; its history, legends, industry and modern expansion*. Boston: Houghton Mifflin Company, 1912.

GRUPPE, MRS. CHARLES P. "The Art of B. J. Blommers." *Brush and Pencil* 12 (September 1903): 415-427.

GRUYTER, JOSIAH DE. *De Haagse School*. 2 vols. Rotterdam: Lemniscaat, 1969.

GUNSAULUS, FRANK W. "An Appreciation of Josef Israëls." *Brush and Pencil* 13 (February 1904): 347-361.

HALTON, E.G. "Modern Dutch Pictures in the Staats Forbes Collection." *International Studio* 27 (December 1905): 107-118.

HAUENSTEIN, EUGENIE, compiler. Eugenie Hauenstein Scrapbook. vol. 1, Albright-Knox Art Gallery Library, Buffalo, NY.

HOLCOMB, GRANT. "The Forgotten Legacy of Jerome Myers (1867-1940): Painter of New York's Lower East Side." *American Art Journal* 9 (May 1977): 90.

HOLMAN, LOUIS A. "America's Rembrandts." *Century Magazine* 80 (October 1910): 881-887.

The Hudson-Fulton Celebration, Catalogue of an Exhibition. New York: Metropolitan Museum of Art, 1909.

"Impressions of America on a Dutch Impressionist." *New York Times Sunday Magazine*, 1 May 1904.

Johnson, John G. *Catalogue of a Collection of Paintings belonging to John G. Johnson*. Philadelphia: Allen, Lane & Scott, 1892.

———. *Sight-Seeing in Berlin and Holland Among Pictures*. Philadelphia: Allen, Lane & Scott, 1892.

Jowell, Frances Suzman. *Thoré-Bürger and the Art of the Past*. New York: Garland Publishing, Inc., 1977.

Kirkup, Mary A. "Israëls and the Dutch Painters." *The Midland Monthly* 9 (April 1898): 304-312.

KOENRAADS, JAN P. *Dutch Painters from the Heart of Holland in the Last Century*. Amsterdam: A.J.G. Strengholt N.V., 1969.

KURTZ, CHARLES M. *Illustrations from the Art Gallery, World's Columbian Exposition*. Philadelphia: G. Barrie, 1893.

LANIGAN, FRANCES E. "The Woman Who Paints Cats." *Ladies' Home Journal* (September 1895): 3.

LEVY, FLORENCE N., ed. "Private Galleries, Washington, D.C." In *American Art Annual*, 406-408. New York: Macmillan Co., 1898.

LIEDTKE, WALTER. "Dutch Paintings in America: The Collectors and Their Ideals." In *Great Dutch Paintings from America*, 14-59. Zwolle: Waanders Publishers for the Mauritshuis, 1990.

Loan Collection of Works of Josef Israëls and other Contemporary Dutch Painters. Chicago: Art Institute, 1904.

MacBeth Gallery Papers. Archives of American Art, Smithsonian Institution.

"Madame Ronner and her Cats." *Ladies' Home Journal* (November 1899): 5.

MARKS, MONTAGUE, ed. "Dutch Paintings." *Art Amateur* 29 (September 1893): 84-85.

———. using pen name Montezuma. "My Note Book." *Art Amateur* 22 (February 1890): 51-52.

Memorial Art Gallery of the University of Rochester. *The George Eastman Collection*. Rochester, NY: Memorial Art Gallery, 1979.

———. *A Rochester Retrospective: Painting and Sculpture (1880-1950)*. Rochester, NY: Memorial Art Gallery, 1980.

MILLER, LILLIAN B. *Patrons and Patriotism: the Encouragement of the Fine Arts in the United States, 1790-1860*. Chicago: University of Chicago Press, 1966.

"Modern Painters of Holland: Paul Josef Gabriel." *Art Amateur* 36 (June 1897): 128-129.

MONROE, LUCY. "Chicago Letter." *The Critic* 23 (14 October 1893): 243-244.

MORTON, FREDERICK W. "Josef Israëls's Art From an Analytical Viewpoint." *Brush and Pencil* 13 (February 1904): 333-346.

———. "The Art of Hendrik Willem Mesdag." *Brush and Pencil* 9 (February 1903): 321-335.

"Notes on the Art Exhibit of Holland." *Brush and Pencil* 15 (February 1905): 130-136.

PREYER, DAVID C. *The Art of the Netherland Galleries*. Boston: L. C. Page, 1908.

"Recent Chase Sale." *Amerian Art News* 10 (16 March 1912), p. 6, cols. 3-4.

RETTIG, JOHN. "The Source of Modern American Art," unpublished lecture in vol. 6, "The Colorful World of John Rettig." Theodore A. Langstroth, compiler. Cincinnati Public Library.

ROURKE, CONSTANCE. *Charles Sheeler: Artist in the American Tradition*. New York: Harcourt, Brace and Company, 1938.

ROYAL ACADEMY OF THE ARTS. *The Hague School: Dutch Masters of the 19th Century*. exh. cat. London: George Weidenfeld and Nicolson Ltd, 1983.

RUTTER, FRANK. "A Consideration of the Work of Anton Mauve." *International Studio* 33 (November 1907): 3-17.

RYN, BROES VAN. "The Art of Mrs. S. Mesdag Van Houten." *Brush and Pencil* 15 (February 1905): 121-130.

RYSEWYCK, P. Haven Korn von. Article in *Nieuwe Rotterdamsche Courant* quoted in translation in *American Art News* 10 (18 May 1912), p. 5, col. 4.

SAARINEN, ALINE B. *The Proud Possessors: the lives, times and tastes of some adventurous American art collectors*. New York: Random House, 1958.

Salon's Secretary. "Salon of the Dilettanti—X, The Dump of the Doleful Dutch." *Brush and Pencil* 18 (September 1906): 96-105.

SCHAUS, HERMANN AND WILLIAM Papers. Archives of American Art, Smithsonian Institution.

"Shepherd's Dutch Pictures." *American Art News* 10 (18 May 1912) p. 5, col. 4.

SLIVE, SEYMOUR. *Frans Hals*. London: Royal Academy of Arts, 1989.

STEVENSON, BURTON E. *The Spell of Holland*. Boston: L.C. Page & Company, 1911.

STOTT, ANNETTE. "The Holland Society and the Arts." *de Halve Maen* 69 (Summer 1996): 25-32.

SUTTON, PETER C. *A Guide to Dutch Art in America*. Grand Rapids, MI: Wm. B. Eerdmans, 1986.

———. "Jan Steen, Comedy and Admonition." *Bulletin of the Philadelphia Museum of Art* 78 (Winter 1982/Spring 1983): 1-43.

SWEENEY, J. GRAY. *Artists of Grand Rapids, 1840-1980*. exh. cat. Grand Rapids, MI: The Grand Rapids Art Museum and Grand Rapids Public Museum, 1981.

______, ed. *Artists of Michigan From The Nineteenth Century*. exh. cat. Muskegon, MI: Muskegon Museum of Art, 1987.

TAINE, HIPPOLYTE. *Lectures on Art*, 2nd series, John Durand, trans. New York: Henry Holt & Company, 1877.

———. *The Philosophy of Art: Art in the Netherlands*. New York: Holt & Williams, 1873.

THOMSON, D. CROAL. *The Brothers Maris (James–Matthew–William)*. London: Offices of *The Studio*, 1907.

TOWNSEND, J.B. "Modern Painters of Holland: H. W. Mesdag." *Art Amateur* 37 (August 1897): 26-27.

———. "Modern Painters of Holland: William Roelofs." *Art Amateur* 37 (July 1897): 4.

VALENTINER, WILHELM REINHOLD. *The Art of the Low Countries: Studies*. Translated by Mariana Griswold Van Rensselaer. Garden City, NY: Doubleday, Page & Co., 1914.

VETH, JAN. "Modern Dutch Art: The Work of Josef Israëls." *International Studio* 17 (October 1902): 239.

VRIES, TIEMEN DE. *Dutch History, Art and Literature for Americans*. Grand Rapids: Eerdmans-Sevensma Co., 1912.

WESLY, EMILE. "Carel Storm van 'sGravesande." *Elsevier's Geïllustreerd Maandschrift* (October 1892): 329-344.

WINKELMAN, BARNIE F. *John G. Johnson, Lawyer and Art Collector*. Philadelphia: University of Pennsylvania Press, 1942.

WILSON, FRANCIS. *Joseph Jefferson, Reminiscences of a Fellow Player*. New York: Charles Scribner's Sons, 1907, pp. 79-96.

World's Columbian Exposition Official Catalogue, Part X, Department K, Holland. Chicago: W.B. Gonkey Co., 1893.

ZILCKEN, PHILIP. *H. W. Mesdag, Painter of the North Sea*. London & Paris: Cassell and Co., 1896.

———. "Johannes Bosboom." *International Studio* 33 (February 1908): 257-268.

———. "The Late Jacob Maris." *International Studio* 9 (February 1900): 231-240.

ZUG, GEORGE BREED. "Dutch Art and Artists." *The Chautauquan* 52 (Sept 1908): 65-84, 133, (Oct 1908): 214-231, 305, (Nov 1908): 376-396, 460; 453 (Dec 1908): 60-79, 143, (Jan 1909): 230-248, 288-289, (Feb 1909): 366-389, 432; 54 (March 1909): 50-76, 149, (April 1909): 224-245, 303, (May 1909): 377-399, 466.

TWO: AMERICAN ARTISTS IN HOLLAND

GENERAL

AERTS, J. "Heeze, een Brabants Dorp in Beeld." *Heemkronyk* 7 (1968-69): 30.

ALBRECHT, FLORENCE CRAIG. "Veere, An Artist's Paradise." *The Outlook* 91 (27 March 1909): 725-737.

BELL, RALCY HUSTED. *Art-Talks with Ranger*. New York & London: G.P. Putnam's Sons, 1914.

BENJAMIN, FREDERICK. "C.W. Hawthorne, Painter." *Brush and Pencil*. (August 1899): 255-256.

BLAUGRUND, ANNETTE, ed.. *Paris 1889*. New York: Abrams, 1989.

BRADBURY, M.R. "An Art Student's Holiday Abroad, Part I—Holland." *Art Amateur* 24 (April 1891): 118-120.

CLUNY, ANTOINE DE. *Holland as Painted by Charles P. Gruppe*. Leyden: A. W. Sijthoff's Uitgevers-Maatschappij, n.d.

CHAMPNEY, ELIZABETH W. "Woman in Art." In *American Art and Artists*, 201-210. Boston: American Art Company, 1895.

"The Chase School of Art and the Art Students' League." *Art Amateur* 35 (October 1896): 91.

COLLINS, FRANK M. "A Visit To Joseph Israëls By Two Young American Painters, Through Whom the Famous Hollander Gives Some Excellent Advice to Ambitious Art Students." *Art Amateur* 33 (October & November 1895):86+;115+.

CORTISSOZ, ROYAL, Horatio Walker, et. al. *The Book of Alexander Shilling*. New York: Paisley Press, 1937.

DARLEY, FELIX O.C. *Sketches Abroad with Pen and Pencil*. New York: Hurd and Houghton, 1869.

GORE, JAMES H. *Dutch Art as Seen by a Layman*. New York: Holland-America Line, 1902.

HAAS, KAREL H. De. *Alexander Shilling In Memoriam*. Rotterdam: Offices of the *Rotterdam Courant*, 1937.

HEIJBROEK, J.F. "Holland vanaf het water; De bezoeken van James Abbott McNeil Whistler aan Nederland." *Bulletin van het Rijksmuseum* 36, No. 3 (1988): 225-256.

HITCHCOCK, GEORGE. "The Picturesque Quality of Holland." *Scribner's Magazine* 2 (August 1887): 160-168.

———. "The Picturesque Quality of Holland. Figures and Costumes." *Scribner's Magazine* 10 (November 1891): 621-629.

———. "The Picturesque Quality of Holland. Interiors and Bric-A-Brac." *Scribner's Magazine* 5 (February 1889): 162-171.

———. "Sandro Botticelli." *Scribner's Magazine* 4 (Dec 1888): 711-718.

LUCAS, E.V. *Edwin Austin Abbey, Royal Academician, The Record of his Life and Work*, 2 vols. New York: Charles Scribner's Sons, 1921.

MANSFIELD, HOWARD. *Whistler in Belgium and Holland*. New York: M. Knoedler & Company, 1935.

MILLER, OSCAR Archives. Private collection.

NEUHAUS, EUGEN. *The History and Ideals of American Art*. Palo Alto, Calif: Stanford Univ. Press, 1931.

OIRSCHOT, ANTON VAN, ed. *"Heeze" Een Heerlijkheid in Brabant*. Heeze, Netherlands: De Heerlijkheid Heeze-Leende, 1963.

The Paintings of Charles Hawthorne. Storrs: University of Connecticut Museum of Art, 1968.

PENFIELD, EDWARD. *Holland Sketches*. New York: Charles Scribner's Sons, 1907.

RANGER, H[ENRY] W[ARD]. "Mr. H. W. Ranger, On Sketching in Holland." *Art Amateur* 28 (April 1893): 132.

———. "Sketching Grounds in Holland and Normandy." *Art Amateur* 31 (June 1894): 5.

ROOF, KATHERINE METCALF. *The Life and Art of William Merritt Chase*. New York: Charles Scribner's Sons, 1917.

ROURKE, CONSTANCE. *Charles Sheeler, Artist in the American Tradition*. New York: Harcourt, Brace, 1938.

RYN, JAN VAN. "Charles P. Gruppe, Painter." *Brush and Pencil* 9 (January 1902): 210-219.

Selections from the Paintings of Charles P. Gruppe. Rochester, NY: The Alfred Herle Press, n.d.

SMITH, F. HOPKINSON. "Between Showers in Dort." *Scribner's Magazine* 25 (May 1899): 585-598.

———. *Forty Minutes Late and Other Stories*. New York: Charles Scribner's Sons, 1909.

STOTT, ANNETTE. "American Painters Who Worked in the Netherlands, 1880-1914." Ph.D. diss., Boston University, 1986.

———. "Dutch Utopia: Paintings by Antimodern American Artists of the Nineteenth Century." *Smithsonian Studies in American Art* 3 (Spring 1989): 47-61.

Tentoonstelling van Kunstwerken van Levende Meesters. Annual exhibition catalogs. Amsterdam-Rotterdam-The Hague, 1890-1910.

THURBER ART GALLERIES. *Robert W. Grafton*. exh. & sale cat. December 10, 1917–January 5, 1918. Chicago: Thurber Art Galleries, 1917.

Various artist files. Department of Foreign Art. Rijksbureau voor Kunsthistorische Documentatie, The Hague.

WEBER, BRUCE. "Robert Frederick Blum (1857-1903) and his Milieu," Ph.D. diss., City University of New York, 1985.

WEINBERG, BARBARA. *The Lure of Paris: 19th Century American Painters and Their French Teachers*. New York: Abbeville Press, 1991.

YOUNG, DOROTHY WEIR. *The Life and Letters of J. Alden Weir*. New York: DaCapo Press, 1971.

VOLENDAM

ALBRECHT, FLORENCE CRAIG. "Volendam, The Artists' Village." *Scribner's Magazine* 41 (March 1907): 327-338.

ANDREWS, IRIS M. "Three Dutch Types from Volendam." *Century Magazine* 71 (November 1905): 128-131.

BURKE, MARY ALICE HEEKIN. *Elizabeth Nourse, 1859-1938, A Salon Career*. exh. cat. Washington, D.C.: Smithsonian Institution Press, 1983.

KOLFSCHOTEN, TH. C.P.M. *Edam en Volendam*. Edam: F.A. Keizer & Van Straten, 1933.

LANGSTROTH, T[HEODORE] A[SHMEAD], compiler. "The Colorful World of John Rettig." 6 volumes of scrapbooks compiled in 1965. Cincinnati Public Library.

MIDDLETON, G.A.T. "On the Shores of the ZuiderZee." *The Magazine of Art* (January 1893): 64-69.

NOURSE, ELIZABETH Papers. Cincinnati Historical Society.

PENFIELD, EDWARD. "The Magenta Village." *Scribner's Magazine* 40 (July 1906): 25-33.

QUIGLEY, JANE. "Volendam as a Sketching Ground for Painters." *The International Studio* 29 (August 1906): 118-125.

REICHWEIN, GUSTA. *Vreemde Gasten: Kunstschilders in Volendam 1880-1914*. Enkhuisen: Rijksmuseum Zuiderzeemuseum, 1986.

RETTIG, JOHN Scrapbooks. 8 volumes. Cincinnati Historical Society.

SIMONS, K. *Hotel Spaander 100 Jaar*. Edam: Keizer & Van Straten, 1981.

TUSSENBROEK, OTTO VAN. "Volendam als 'Sketching Ground'." *Elsevier's Maandschrift* 51 (April 1916): 275-290.

VEURMAN, B.W.E. *Volendammer Schilderboek*. The Hague: Kruseman's uitgeversmaatschappij, 1977.

LAREN

CHAMPNEY, ELIZABETH W. "Modern Dutch Painters." *Century Magazine* 56 (July 1898): 395-407.

COOPER, EMMA LAMPERT PAPERS. Archives of American Art, Smithsonian Institution.

"Darling's Fine Pictures at the Art Museum." *Toledo Daily Blade* 26 November 1903, p. 10, cols. 4 & 5.

DE VRIES, R.W.P., JR. *William Henry Singer, Jr., N. A.: the man and the artist*. Bussum, Holland: F. G. Kroonder, n.d.

Gooi en Eemlander. newspaper archives, Hilversum, North Holland.

KNIGHT, DAME LAURA. "Holland." Chap. in *The Magic of a Line*. London: William Kimber & Co., 1965.

———. "Holland." Chap. in *Oil Paint and Grease Paint*. London: Nicholson and Watson, 1936.

KOEKKOEK, GERARD. *Larense Dorpspraat*. Zaltbommel: Europese Bibliotheek, 1983.

———. *"t'Laer"*. Laren: Comite Feestweek, 1973.

MOES, WALLY. "Donker Laren." *Elsevier's Geïllustreerd Maandschrift* (June 1912): 475-490.

RANGER, HENRY WARD. "Artist Life by the North Sea." *Century Magazine* 45 (March 1893): 753-759.

RUST, W.J. *De Gooische Dorpen*. Amsterdam: Uitgeverij de Forel N.V., 1970.

SINGER Memorial Foundation. *Museum Catalogus*. Laren: Singer Museum, 1963.

HATTEM-NUNSPEET

GRIFFIS, WILLIAM ELLIOT. "The American Artist in Holland." Chap. in *The American in Holland*. Boston and New York: Houghton Mifflin & Company, 1907.

SPOEL, D., GERRIT KOUWENHOVEN, and H. Schulte Nordholt. *Schilders van Hattem*. Hattem: Stichting Streekmuseum Hattem Voermanhuis.

Wandelgids voor Hattem en Omstreken. Zwolle: De Erven J.J. Tijl, 1896.

KATWIJK

CARLIN, WILLIAM E. "The Dutch Fisher Folk." *Outing* 38 (August, 1901): 526-532.

DOWNES, WILLIAM HOWE. "Charles Herbert Woodbury and his Work." *Brush and Pencil* 6 (April 1900): 1-12.

HUCHT, J. VAN DER. *Bibliografie en Iconografie van de Beide Katwijken en 't Zand*. Katwijk: Genootschap Oud Katwijk, 1969.

Katwijk in de Schilderkunst. Katwijk: Katwijks Museum en Genootschap "Oud Katwijk", 1995.

MAHLSTICK, ROGER. "Walter L. Dean." *Boston Sunday Journal*, 12 May 1895, clipping in Walter Dean file. Cape Ann Historical Association, Gloucester, Mass.

OUD KATWIJK. *Katwijkse Knip-Sels*. Katwijk: Oud Katwijk, 1974.

"S.S. Tuckerman," *Cape Anne Weekly Advertiser*, 28 May 1886.

Stieglitz, Alfred and Schubart, Louis H. "Two Artists' Haunts." *Photographic Times* (January 1895): 9-12.

EGMOND

"Beeldende Kunst to Egmond aan Zee." *In en Om Kennemerland* 1 January 1905.

BOIS, GUY PENE DU. "George Hitchcock, Painter of Holland." *Arts and Decoration* 3 (October 1913): 401-405.

DAVIS, NORMA S. *A Lark Ascends: Florence Kate Upton, Artist and Illustrator*. Metuchen, NJ: The Scarecrow Press, Inc., 1992.

"De Oudheidkenner." *In en Om Kennemerland*. 15 August 1904, Gemeentearchief, Alkmaar, North Holland.

DREISS, JOSEPH. *Gari Melchers: His Works in the Belmont Collection*. Charlottesville: University Press of Virginia, 1984.

"George Hitchcock." *Art Amateur* 22 (February 1890): 54-56.

LANNOY, KATHINKA AND BOB DENNEBOOM. *Derper-Hoever-Binder: Over geschiedenis en volksleven van De Drie Egmonden*. The Hague: Kruseman's Uitgeversmaatschappij, n.d.

LEWIS-HIND, HENRIETTE. *Gari Melchers, Painter*. New York: William Edwin Rudge, 1928.

LYTTELTON, EDITH. *Florence Upton, Painter*. London: Longmans, Green and Co, Ltd, 1926.

MELCHERS, GARI AND CORINNE PAPERS. Belmont, The Gari Melchers Estate and Memorial Art Gallery, Fredericksburg, Virginia.

MELTZER, CHARLES HENRY. "A Painter of Sunlight." *Hearst's Magazine* 22 (July 1912): 131-134.

MESMAN, GEORGE. "Julius Garibaldi Melchers (1860-1932)." Ph.D. diss., City University of New York, 1990.

RING, ALICE BLAIR PAPERS. private collection.

SHANNON, KITTY. *For My Children*. London: Hutchinson & Co., Ltd., 1933.

SMITH, JOSEPH COBURN. *Charles Hovey Pepper*. Portland, ME: Southworth Anthoensen Press, 1945.

STOTT, ANNETTE. "The Holland Years." In *Gari Melchers, A Retrospective Exhibition*, ed. Diane Lesko, 55-74. St. Petersburg, Florida: Museum of Fine Arts, 1990.

———. "Letta Crapo Smith." In *Artists of Michigan From the Nineteenth Century*, ed. J. Gray Sweeney, 95-106. Muskegon, MI: Muskegon Museum of Art, 1989.

RIJSOORD

DAVIESS, MARIA THOMPSON. *Seven Times Seven, An Autobiography*. New York: Dodd, Mead and Co., 1924.

GOOD, ELIZA LEYPOLD. "A Holland Art Village." *Catholic World* 70 (January 1900): 514-526.

HAWLEY, WILHELMINA DOUGLAS PAPERS. Private collection.

PEIXOTTO, MARY A. "A Summer in Sabots." *Scribner's Magazine* 29 (May, 1901): 608-616.

"Studio Talk-Canada." *International Studio*. 8 (July 1899): 62.

TYLER, ALICE KELLOGG PAPERS. Archives of American Art, Smithsonian Institution.

VANDERPOEL, JOHN H. PAPERS. John H. Vanderpoel Memorial Art Association, Beverly Hills, Chicago, Illinois.

THREE: REWRITING AMERICAN HISTORY

BLACKBURN, RODERICK H. AND RUTH PIWONKA. *Remembrance of Patria: Dutch Arts and Culture in Colonial America, 1609-1776*. Albany, NY: Albany Institute of History and Art, 1988.

BOK, EDWARD. "The Mother of America." *Ladies' Home Journal* 20 (October 1903): 16.

BOURNE, HENRY ELDRIDGE. "Book Notices. The Puritan in Holland, England and America." *Yale Review* 1 (February 1893): 434-443.

"Campbell's Puritan in Holland." *The Nation* 55 (25 August 1892): 147-148.

CAMPBELL, DOUGLAS. *The Puritan in Holland, England and America: An Introduction to American History*. 3rd edition. 2 vols. New York: Harper & Brothers Publishers, 1893.

CHAMPNEY, ELIZABETH W. "Woman in Art." In *American Art and Artists*. Boston: American Art Company, 1895.

DEXTER, MORTON. *The Story of the Pilgrims*. Boston & Chicago: Congregational Sunday School & Publishing Society, 1894.

The Dutch Declaration of Independence in 1581. Old South Leaflet #72. Boston: Old South Meeting House, 1896.

"Dutch Influence in America." *Atlantic Monthly* 70 (November 1892): 698-704.

EARLE, ALICE MORSE. *Colonial Days in Old New York*. 1896; rpt. Detroit: Singing Tree Press, 1968.

EDLER, FRIEDRICH M. *The Dutch Republic and the American Revolution*. Baltimore: Johns Hopkins Press, 1911.

ELSON, HENRY WILLIAM. *History of the United States of America*. vol. 1. New York: The Macmillan Company, 1904.

EMERSON, G.H. "What Protestant Liberty Owes to the Dutch." *Universalist Quarterly and General Review* 45 (July 1888): 261-278.

FAIRCHILD, HELEN LINCKLAEN. *Travels in the Years 1791 and 1792 in Pennsylvania, New York and Vermont: Journals of John Lincklaen, Agent of the Holland Land Company*. New York and London: Knickerbocker Press, 1897.

FISHER, SYDNEY G. "Are American Institutions of Dutch Origin?" *Lippincott's Monthly Magazine* 59 (January 1897): 79-93.

FISKE, JOHN. *The Dutch and Quaker Colonies in America*. 2 vols. Boston & New York: Houghton, Mifflin and Company, 1899.

"A Glimpse of an Old Dutch Town." *Harper's New Monthly Magazine* (1881): 524-539.

GOODWIN, MAUD WILDER. *Dutch and English on the Hudson: A Chronicle of Colonial New York*. New Haven: Yale Univ Press, 1921.

GOODWIN, MAUD WILDER, ALICE CARRINGTON ROYCE, AND RUTH PUTNAM, eds. *Historic New York*. The Half Moon Papers series 1—volume 1. 1897; rpt. Port Washington, N.Y: Ira J. Friedman, Inc., 1969.

GREGG, DAVID, W.W. GOODRICH, AND SIDNEY H. CARNEY, JR. *Thoughts for the Occasion: Makers of the American Republic, A Series of Patriotic Lectures*. New York: E.B. Treat & Co., 1905.

GRIFFIS, WILLIAM ELLIOT. *Arendt Van Curler, First Superintendent of Rensselaerwick, Founder of Schenectady and of the Dutch Policy of Peace with the Iriquois* [sic]. n.p.: n.p., 1886.

———. *Brave Little Holland, and What She Taught Us*. Boston & New York: Houghton Mifflin Co., 1894., and revised ed. Cambridge MA: Riverside Press, 1931.

———. "Dutch Influence in New England." *Harper's New Monthly Magazine* 88 (January 1894): 213-221.

———. *The Dutch of the Netherlands in the Making of America*. New York: Holland Society of New York, 1921.

———. *The Influence of the Netherlands in the Making of the English Commonwealth and the American Republic*. Boston: DeWolfe, Fiske & Co., 1891.

———. *The Pilgrim Fathers in Holland*. Rotterdam: Bredee, 1906.

———. "The Pilgrim Press in Leyden." *New England Magazine* (January 1899): 559-575.

———. *The Pilgrims in Their Three Homes: England, Holland, America*. revised edition. Boston & New York: Houghton Mifflin Company, 1914.

———. *The Romance of American Colonization*. 1898; rpt. New York: Research Reprints Inc, 1970.

———. *The Siege of Leyden*. Boston: D.C. Heath & Co., 1903.

———. *The Story of the Walloons: at home, in lands of exile and in America*. Boston & New York: Houghton Mifflin Company, 1923.

———. *The Story of New Netherland: The Dutch in America*. Boston & New York: Houghton Mifflin Company, 1909.

———. "Thankful America." *The Outlook* 106 (10 January 1914): 88-90.

———. *Two Hundredth Anniversary of the First Reformed Protestant Dutch Church of Schenectady, NY*. Schenectady: Daily and Weekly Union, 1880.

———. "Why are We So Different from the English?" *Ladies' Home Journal* 27 (February 1910): 6.

———. *Young People's History of the Pilgrims*. Boston & New York: Houghton Mifflin Co., 1920.

HANKS, CHARLES STEDMAN. *Our Plymouth Forefathers, the Real Founders of Our Republic*. Boston: Author's Publishing Association, [c.1907].

HEWETT, PROF. W.T. "The University of Leiden." *Harper's New Monthly Magazine* 62 (March 1881): 491-505.

HOLLAND SOCIETY OF NEW YORK. *First Annual Dinner of the Holland Society of New York*. New York: Holland Society, 1886.

———. *Yearbooks*. 1886-1914.

HURLBUT, JESSE LYMAN. *The Story of Chautauqua*. New York: G.P. Putnam's Sons, 1921.

JAMESON, J. FRANKLIN. *Narratives of New Netherland, 1609-1664*. New York: Charles Scribner's Sons, 1909.

KELLOGG, WARREN F. "Editor's Table." *New England Magazine* n.s. 15 (January 1897): 636-40.

METZ, J.A. "Woman's Work for Women in Holland." 48 *The World To-day* (February 1909): 218-219.

MOTLEY, JOHN LOTHROP. *History of the United Netherlands: From the Death of William the Silent to the Twelve Years' Truce-1609*. 4 vols. New York: Harper & Brothers Publishers, 1898.

———. *The Rise of the Dutch Republic: A History*. 3 vols. New York: Harper & Brothers Publishers, 1880.

———. *The Student's Motley: The Rise of the Dutch Republic, Condensed*. Introduction & notes by William Elliot Griffis. New York & London: Harper & Brothers Publishers, 1898.

NETHERLANDS SOCIETY OF PHILADELPHIA. *Addresses made at the Annual Meetings of the Netherlands Society of Philadelphia, 1913 to 1930.*

Philadelphia: Netherlands Society of Philadelphia, [c.1931].
NOBLE, FREDERICK A. *The Pilgrims*. Boston: The Pilgrim Press, 1907.
NOOTER, ERIC AND BONOMI, PATRICIA U., eds. *Colonial Dutch Studies: An Interdisciplinary Approach*. New York & London: New York Univ Press, 1988.
PILGRIM SOCIETY. *The Proceedings at the Celebration by the Pilgrim Society, at Plymouth, December 21, 1895 of the 275th Anniversary of the Landing of the Pilgrims*. Plymouth: Pilgrim Society and Avery & Doten, Printers, 1896.
PLOOIJ, D. *The Pilgrim Fathers From A Dutch Point Of View*. New York: New York Univ Press, 1932.
SCHEFFER, JACOB G. DE HOOP. *History of the Free Churchmen called the Brownists, Pilgrim Fathers and Baptists in the Dutch Republic 1581-1701*. Ithaca, NY: Andrus & Church, c.1921.
SCUDDER, HORACE E. *The Bodley Grandchildren and their Journey in Holland*. Boston: Houghton, Mifflin & Co., 1883.
SHEPARDSON, FRANCIS W. "Dutch Influence Upon America." *The Dial* 17 (1 August 1894): 61-62.
SINGLETON, ESTHER. *Dutch New York*. 1909; rpt. New York & London: Benjamin Blom, 1968.
TORCHIANA, H.A. VAN COENEN. *Holland The Birthplace of American Political, Civic and Religious Liberty, An Historical Essay*. 2nd edition. Chicago: James H. Rook Co., 1915.
VLEKKE, BERNARD H.M. *The Netherlands and the United States*. Boston: World Peace Foundation, 1945.
VRIES, TIEMEN DE. *Dutch History, Art and Literature for Americans*. Grand Rapids: Eerdmans-Seevensma Co., 1912.
"Women's Work for their Cities." *Harper's Bazar* 43 (August 1909): 766.
YOUNG, ALEXANDER. *History of the Netherlands (Holland and Belgium)*. Boston: Estes and Lauriat, 1884.

FOUR: IMAGES OF NEDERLAND, OLD AND NEW

AHRENS, KENT. "Robert Weir's Embarkation of the Pilgrims." *Capitol Studies* 1 (Fall 1973): 60-62.
AMERICAN ART GALLERIES. *Very Important and Highly Valuable Oil Paintings by Celebrated Foreign and American Masters*. sale catalog. New York: American Art Galleries, 1924.
BOK, EDWARD. "The Mother of America." *Ladies' Home Journal* 20 (October 1903): 16.
CAMPBELL, DOUGLAS. *The Puritan in Holland, England and America: An Introduction to American History*. 3rd edition. 2 vols. New York: Harper & Brothers Publishers, 1893.
"Charles F. Ulrich." *New Amsterdam Gazette* 2 (10 November 1884), p. 10, col. 2.
COOK, CLARENCE. "An English-American Artist." in *American Art and Artists*. Boston: American Art Company, 1895.
DEPEW, CHAUNCEY M. Speech in *The First Annual Dinner of the Holland Society of New York*. New York: Holland Society, 1886.
DOWNES, WILLIAM HOWE. "George H. Boughton, Illustrator of the Pilgrim Fathers." *Boston Evening Transcript* 15 January 1905, New York Public Library Collection, Archives of American Art, Smithsonian Institution.
"The Edict of William the Testy." *The Chautauquan* 54 (April 1909): 295.
EDWARDS, GEORGE WHARTON. *Holland of Today*. Philadelphia: Penn Publishing Company, 1919.
EMERSON, G.H. "What Protestant Liberty Owes to the Dutch," *Universalist Quarterly & General Review* 45 (July 1888): 261-278.
GRAY, CHARLES G. "New Amsterdam, 1655." Illustrated by Edwin Austin Abbey. *Harper's Weekly* 26 (7 January 1882): 8-10, 13.
GREGG, DAVID, W.W. Goodrich, and Sidney H. Carney, Jr. *Thoughts for the Occasion: Makers of the American Republic, A Series of Patriotic Lectures*. New York: E.B. Treat & Co., 1905.
GRIFFIS, WILLIAM ELLIOT. *The American Flag of Stripes and Stars: Mirror of the Nation's History*. Ithaca, NY: Andrus & Church, 1890.
———. "George H. Boughton, the Painter of New England Puritanism." *New England Magazine* n.s. 15 (December 1896): 481-501.
———. "The Pilgrim Press in Leyden." *New England Magazine* (January 1899): 559-575.
GRUPPE, MRS. CHARLES P. "The Art of B.J. Blommers." *Brush and Pencil* 12 (1903): 415-416.
JAMES, HENRY. "Our Artists in Europe." *Harper's New Monthly Magazine* 79 (June 1889): 50-66.
LUCAS, E. V. *Edwin Austin Abbey, Royal Academician, The Record of his Life and Work*. vol. 1. New York: Charles Scribner's Sons, 1921.
NOURSE, ELIZABETH PAPERS. Cincinnati Historical Society.

The Picture of the Embarkation of the Pilgrims from Delft-Haven in Holland; Painted by Robert U. Weir. New York: Boggs, 1843.

REVIEW OF AMERICAN ART GALLERIES exhibition. *Art Amateur* 12 (January 1885): 28.

ROBIE, VIRGINIA HUNTINGTON. "Studies of Art in American Art II: Knickerbocker Days." *Brush and Pencil* 7 (October 1900): 48-57.

VAN HENSBROEK, P.A.M. BOELE. "Ch. P. Gruppe." *Elsevier's Geïllustreerd Maandschrift* 14 (November 1904): 291-299.

FIVE: TOURISM AND TRAVEL LITERATURE

ALBRECHT, FLORENCE CRAIG. "The Cheese Markets of North Holland." *Scribner's Magazine* 41 (May 1907): 606-619.

———. "The Passing of Kermis." *The Outlook* 91 (23 January 1909): 180-189.

ALLEN, GRANT. *The European Tour*. 1899; New York: Dodd, Mead & Co., 1909.

ALLEN, WILLIAM HARMAN VAN. *Travel-Pictures*. Milwaukee: The Young Churchman Co., 1912.

AMICIS, EDMONDO DE. *Holland and Its People*. Zuyder Zee Edition. New York and London: G.P. Putnam's Sons, 1885.

———. *Holland*. 2 vols. Translated from 13th edition by Helen Zimmrn. Philadelphia: Porter & Coates, 1894.

BAEDEKER, KARL. *Belgium and Holland*. 15th edition. New York: Charles Scribner's Sons, 1910.

BALDWIN, ELBERT F. "A Day in North Holland." *The Outlook* 90 (24 October 1908): 417-423.

BOER, DR. M.G. DE. *The Holland-America Line, 1873-1923*. Rotterdam: Holland-America Line, 1923.

BOUGHTON, GEORGE H. "Artist Strolls in Holland." *Harper's New Monthly Magazine* 66 (January 1883): 164-180; (February 1883): 387-405; (March 1883): 520-539; (April 1883): 683-705; 69 (August 1884): 327-242; (September 1884) 523-536; (October 1884): 699-714.

———. *Sketching Rambles in Holland*. New York: Harper & Brothers, 1885.

BRUSSE, M.J. *With Roosevelt Through Holland*. Rotterdam: The Holland America Line, 1911.

CARLIN, WILLIAM E. "The Dutch Fisher Folk." *Outing* 38 (August 1901): 526-532.

CHANNING, GRACE ELLERY. "Holland . . . Grace Ellery Channing . . . Boston Transcript." *Current Literature* 33 (August 1902): 201.

CHATTERTON, E. KEBLE. *Through Holland in the Vivette*. Philadelphia and London: J.B. Lippincott Co. and Seeley, Service & Co., Ltd., 1913.

CHILD, THEODORE. *Summer Holidays: Travelling Notes in Europe*. New York: Harper and Brothers, 1889.

COLTON, GEORGE. *A Maryland Editor Abroad*. Annapolis: printed, not published, 1881.

CULLER, MRS. LUCY YEEND. *Europe Through a Woman's Eye*. Philadelphia: Lutheran Publication Society, 1883.

DAM, WALTER VAN. *Scenery from Holland*. Kalamazoo, MI: n.p., 1907.

DARLEY, FELIX O.C. *Sketches Abroad with Pen and Pencil*. New York: Hurd and Houghton, 1869.

DREISER, THEODORE. *A Traveler at Forty*. New York: Century Co., 1913.

DYER, FRANCES F. *The Book of the Pilgrimage: A Record of the Congregationalist's Pilgrimage to England and Holland*. Boston: W.L. Greene & Co, 1896.

EDWARDS, GEORGE WHARTON. *Holland of Today*. revised ed. Philadelphia: Penn Publishing Company, 1919.

———. *Marken and Its People*. New York: Moffat, Yard and Company, 1912.

———. "A Reading Journey in the Hollow-Land." *The Chautauquan* 52 (Sept 1908): 36-64, 132-133, (Oct 1908): 192-213, 304-305, (Nov 1908): 352-375, 459-460; 53 (Dec 1908): 38-59, 142-143, (Jan 1909): 201-229, 288, (Feb 1909): 339-365, 431; 54 (Mar 1909): 27-49, 149, (April 1909): 201-223, 302-303, (May 1909): 358-376, 466.

———. *Thumb-nail Sketches*. New York: Century Co, 1893.

———. "Winter Spirit in Holland." *Collier's Weekly* 44 (12 February 1910): 15-16.

ELSON, LOUIS C. *European Reminiscences, Musical and Otherwise*. 1891; Philadelphia: Theo. Presser Co., 1914.

ELWELL, F.A. *Cycling in Europe*. Boston: League of American Wheelmen, 1899.

EMMONS, MYRA. "Alone in Europe." *Harper's Bazar* 43 (April 1909): 401-403.

GARDINER, SARAH D. AND MARY P. QUINCY. *Pages in Azure and Gold, The Letters of Miss Gardiner and Miss Quincy*. New York: Society of Colonial Dames of America, 1915.

GELDER, JAN JACOB DE. *A Journey through Old Holland*. New York: Holland-America Line, 1913.

GORE, JAMES H. *Dutch Art as Seen by a Layman*. New York: Holland-America

Line, 1902.
———. *Holland as Seen by an American*. New York: Holland-America Line, 1903.
———. *Holland, the Home of Peace*. New York: Holland-America Line, 1913.
GREW, EDWIN S. *What to See in the Netherlands*. The Hague: Official Information Office for Tourists, c.1910-1915.
GRIFFIS, WILLIAM ELLIOT. *The American in Holland*. 1899; Boston and New York: Houghton Mifflin & Co., 1907.
HARE, AUGUSTUS J.C. *Sketches in Holland and Scandinavia*. c.1884; New York & London: Macmillan & Co. and George Allen, 1902.
HAVARD, HENRY. *The Dead Cities of the Zuyder Zee*. Translated by Annie Wood. London: R. Bentley & Son, 1876.
———. *The Heart of Holland*. New York: Harper & Brothers, 1880.
———. *Picturesque Holland, a journey in the provinces of Friesland, Groningen, Drenthe, Overijssel, Guelders and Limbourg*. London: Richard Bentley & Son, 1876.
HIGINBOTHAM, JOHN U. *Three Weeks in Holland and Belgium*. Chicago: Reilly & Britton Co., 1908.
HOUGH, P.M. *Dutch Life in Town and Country*. New York & London: G.P. Putnam's Sons, 1902.
HOWELL, CHARLES FISH. *Around the Clock in Europe, A Travel-Sequence*. Boston & New York: Houghton Mifflin Co., 1912.
HUNEKER, JAMES. *New Cosmopolis, A Book of Images*. 1915; New York: Charles Scribner's Sons, 1925.
JAEKEL, BLAIR. *Windmills and Wooden Shoes*. New York: McBride, Nast & Company, 1912.
JEWETT, SARAH ORNE. "An Afternoon in Holland." *Atlantic Monthly* 50 (December 1882): 798-804.
JOHNSON, JOHN G. *Sightseeing in Berlin and Holland Among Pictures*. Philadelphia: Philadelphia Press, 1892.
A Jolly Summer. New York: White, Stokes & Allen, 1883.
JUNGMAN, BEATRIX AND NICO. *Holland*. London: Adam & Charles Black, 1904.
LEEUW, HENDRIK DE. *Crossroads of the Zuider Zee*. Philadelphia & New York: J.B. Lippincott Co., 1938.
LOON, HENDRIK WILLEM VAN. *An Indiscreet Itinerary or How the Unconventional Traveler Should See Holland*. New York: Harcourt, Brace & Co., 1933.
LUCAS, E.V. *Edwin Austin Abbey, Royal Academician, The Record of his Life and Work*. vol. 1. New York: Charles Scribner's Sons, 1921.
MADDEN, EVA. "In the Land of Windmills." *Harper's Bazar* 43 (August 1909): 759-765.
MAGINNIS, ARTHUR J. *The Atlantic Ferry*. London & New York: Whittaker & Co, 1893.
MAHAFFY, J.P. AND ROGERS, J.E. *Sketches from a Tour Through Holland and Germany*. London & New York: Macmillan and Co., [c.1889].
MELDRUM, D.S. *Holland and the Hollanders*. New York: Dodd, Mead & Co., 1898.
MONKHOUSE, COSMO. "'Sketching Rambles in Holland' by G.H. Boughton." *The Academy* 26 (6 December 1884): 369-370.
MURRAY, JOHN. *A Handbook for Travellers in Holland and Belgium*. 21st edition. London: John Murray, 1889.
"Old and New Netherlands United." *New Amsterdam Gazette* 5 (Aug/Sept 1888): 12-14.
OSBORNE, ALBERT B. *Finding the Worth While in Europe*. 1913; New York: Robert M. McBride & Co, 1923.
PENFIELD, EDWARD. "Amsterdam Impressions: A Side-Street Isle of Marken." *Scribner's Magazine* 37 (January 1905): 45-53.
PENFIELD, EDWARD. *Holland Sketches*. New York: Charles Scribner's Sons, 1907.
PRESTON, MARGARET J. *A Handful of Monographs, Continental and English*. New York: Anson D.F. Randolph & Co., 1886.
PREYER, DAVID C. *The Art of the Netherland Galleries*. Boston: L.C. Page & Company, 1908.
RETTIG, MAY. *Cincinnati Commercial Tribune*, 13 January 1907, John Rettig Scrapbook vol. 7, Cincinnati Historical Society.
ROBINSON, ELIZABETH. "On the Banks of the Zuider Zee: A Visit to Marken." *Outing* 35 (February 1900): 475-81.
ROBINSON, LOUISE B. *A Bundle of Letters From Over the Sea*. Boston: J.G. Cupples Co., 1890.
ROWEN, HERBERT H. "American Travelers in Holland Through Two Centuries." In *A Bilateral Bicentennial*, Nordholt and Swierenga, eds., 227-250. Amsterdam: Meulenhoff Int., 1982.
SCUDDER, HORACE E. *The Bodley Grandchildren and their Journey in Holland*. Boston: Houghton, Mifflin & Co., 1883.
SINGLETON, ESTHER. *The Standard Galleries: Holland*. Chicago: A.C. McClurg & Co., 1908.
SMITH, EUGENE W. *Trans-Atlantic Passenger Ships, Past and Present*. Boston: George H. Dean Co., 1947.
SMITH, F. HOPKINSON. *Well Worn Roads of*

Spain, Holland & Italy: Traveled by a Painter in Search of the Picturesque. Boston: Houghton Mifflin & Co, 1887.

STEVENSON, BURTON E. *The Spell of Holland*. Boston: L.C. Page & Co., 1911.

STOKVIS, PIETER R.D. "Some American views of the Netherlands during the Nineteenth Century." *De Negentiende Eeuw* 6 (June 1982): 59-82.

TALBERT, ERNEST. *Old Countries Discovered Anew: A Motor Book for Everybody*. Boston: Dana Estes & Co., 1913.

TAYLOR, CHARLES M., JR. *Odd Bits of Travel with Brush and Camera*. Philadelphia: George W. Jacobs & Co., 1900.

TERRY, MILTON S. *Rambles in the Old World*. Cincinnati: Cranston & Curts, 1894.

THATCHER, S.O. *What I Saw in Europe*. Topeka: Kansas Publishing House, 1883.

TUYN, W.J. *Old Dutch Towns and Villages of the Zuider-Zee*. London: T. Fisher Unwin, 1901.

TYLER, DAVID BUDLONG. *Steam Conquers the Atlantic*. New York & London: D. Appleton-Century Co., 1939.

VERSTER, J.F.L. DE BALBIAN. *Holland America*. Amsterdam: Bernard Houthakker, 1921.

VIELE, SHELDON T. *A Glimpse of Holland in 1888*. New York: De Vinne Press, 1890.

WALKER, BENJAMIN. *Aboard and Abroad, Vacation Notes in Ten Letters, Originally Published in the Lowell Daily Courier*. Lowell, MA: Courier Press and Marden & Rowell, 1889.

WALLER, MARY E. *Through the Gates of the Netherlands*. Boston: Little Brown & Co., 1909.

WALTER, L. EDNA. *The Fascination of Holland*. London: Adam & Charles Black, 1912.

WARD, LOCK & CO. *Handbook to Holland*. 6th edition, revised and enlarged. London: Ward, Lock & Co., Ltd., c.1910.

WILLIAMS, LUCY LANGDON and MCLOUGHLIN, EMMA V. *A Too Short Vacation*. Philadelphia: J. B. Lippincott, 1892.

WOOD, A.T. and B.R. *Ribbon Roads: A Motor Tour Abroad*. New York: G. P. Putnam's Sons, 1910.

WOODS, KATHERINE. "When I was with the Dutch Last Summer." *Ladies' Home Journal* 31 (July 1914): 14.

SIX: "AN AMERICAN RENAISSANC OF DUTCH ARCHITECTURE"

Artistic House Painting. New York: H.W. Johns MFG Co., 1895.

AXELROD, ALAN, ed. *The Colonial Revival in America*. New York: W.W. Norton & Co. and Henry Francis Du Pont Winterthur Museum, 1985.

BAILEY, ROSALIE FELLOWS. *Pre-Revolutionary Dutch Houses and Families in Northern New Jersey and Southern New York*. New York: W. Morrow & Company and Holland Society of New York, 1936.

BLACK, WILLIAM NELSON. "Colonial Building in New Jersey." *Architectural Record* 3 (quarter ending March 31, 1894): 247-262.

The Book of Little Houses. New York: MacMillan Company, 1914.

BRINCKLOE, WILLIAM DRAPER. "Making Plans for the Farm Home: Suggestions for a Farm Home of the Dutch-Colonial Type." *Wallaces' Farmer* (12 January 1923): 39.

CHANDLER, JOSEPH EVERETT. *The Colonial House*. New York: Robert M. McBride & Company, 1916.

CADY, J. CLEVELAND. "Some Features of the Dutch Farm-Houses of New Jersey." *The American Architect and Building News* 2 (15 December 1877): 401.

COBB, A. W. *Suburban and Country Homes*. 1893; rpt. Rockville Centre, NY: Antiquity Reprints, 1984.

COHEN, DAVID STEVEN. *The Dutch-American Farm*. New York: New York University Press, 1992.

DAY, FRANK MILES. *American Country Houses of Today*. New York: Architectural Book Publishing Co., 1912.

DIETRICH, E.G. "A House for $8000." *Harper's Bazar* 43 (March 1909): 219-222.

DOW, JOY WHEELER. "Princessgate." In *The Book of a Hundred Houses*, 58-63. New York: Duffield & Company, 1906.

DUNN, SHIRLEY W. AND ALLISON P. BENNETT. *Dutch Architecture Near Albany: The Polgreen Photographs*. Fleischmanns, NY: Purple Mountain Press, 1996.

EBERLEIN, HAROLD DONALDSON. *The Architecture of Colonial America*. Boston: Little, Brown, and Company, 1915.

EBERLEIN, HAROLD DONALDSON AND CORTLANDT V.D. HUBBARD. *Historic Houses and Buildings of Delaware*. Dover, Delaware: Public Archives Commission, 1963.

ECKERT, KATHRYN BISHOP. *Buildings of Michigan*. New York & Oxford: Oxford Univ Press, 1993.

EMBURY, AYMAR. *An Architectural Monograph on Farm Houses of New Netherlands*. St. Paul: White Pine Bureau, 1915.

———. "Architecture in American

Country Homes." *The Mentor* vol. 3, 15 October 1915.

———. *The Dutch Colonial House: Its Origin, Design, Modern Plan and Construction*. New York: McBride, Nast & Company, 1913.

———. "Modern Adaptations of Dutch Colonial." *International Studio* 35 (August 1908): XLIX-LII.

FOWLER, LEMUEL HOADLEY. *Some Forgotten Farmhouses on Manhattan Island*. St. Paul: White Pine Bureau, 1923.

GEBHARD, DAVID AND GERALD MANSHEIM. *Buildings of Iowa*. New York & Oxford: Oxford Univ Press, 1993.

GILLESPIE, HARIET SISSON. "A Transformed Dutch Windmill." *House Beautiful* 59 (April 1926): 465-467.

GORDON-VAN TINE CO. *117 House Designs of the Twenties*. 1923; rpt. Mineola, New York: Dover and the Athenaeum of Philadelphia, 1992.

GOWANS, ALAN. *The Comfortable House: North American Suburban Archi-tecture, 1890-1930*. Cambridge: MIT Press, 1986.

———. *Images of American Living: Four Centuries of Architecture and Furniture as Cultural Expression*. Philadelphia: J.B. Lippincott Company, 1964.

GRIFFIS, WILLIAM ELLIOT. *The American in Holland*. Boston and New York: Houghton Mifflin & Company, 1907.

HEFNER, ROBERT J. *Windmills of Long Island*. New York and London: Society for the Preservation of Long Island Antiquities and W.W. Norton & Company, 1983.

HOFFMANN, DONALD. *The Architecture of John Wellborn Root*. Baltimore & London: Johns Hopkins University Press, 1973.

HOOPER, CHARLES EDWARD. *The Country House: A Practical Manual of the Planning and Construction of the American Country Home and its Surroundings*. Garden City, NY: Doubleday, Page and Company, 1913.

HUREWITZ, MICHAEL. "Built To Last: New York State's Extraordinary Stone Houses . . ." *Historic Preservation* 38 (July/August 1986): 49-53.

JOHNS, H.W. M'F'G CO. *Artistic House Painting*. New York: H.W. Johns M'F'G Co., 1895.

JONES, ROBERT A. *Cass Gilbert: Midwestern Architect in New York*. New York: Arno Press, 1982.

JONES, SYDNEY R. *Old Houses in Holland*. London & New York: "The Studio", 1913.

KENNEDY, WILLIAM. *O Albany!*. New York: Viking Press, 1983.

KING, MOSES. *King's Handbook of New York*. New York: Moses King, 1893.

"Little Miss Claflin who lived in a Mill." *Harper's Bazar* 48 (September 1913): 15.

MARTIN, CLARENCE A. *Details of Building Construction*. Boston: Bates & Guild Company, 1899.

MAXWELL, PERRITON. "Some Old Dutch Homesteads of New York." *House Beautiful* 7 (June, 1900): 411-416.

MCALESTER, VIRGINIA AND LEE. *A Field Guide to American Houses*. New York: Alfred A. Knopf, 1985.

MCCULLOUGH, DAVID W. *Brooklyn and How It Got that Way*. New York: Dial Press, 1983.

MORRISON, HUGH. *Early American Archi-tecture from the First Colonial Settlements to the National Period*. New York: Oxford University Press, 1952.

NARJOUX, FELIX. *Notes and Sketches of an Architect taken during a Journey in the Northwest of Europe*, trans. John Peto. Boston: James R. Osgood and Company, 1877.

NOEL, THOMAS J. AND BARBARA S. NORGREN. *Denver, The City Beautiful and its Architects, 1893-1941*. Denver: Historic Denver, 1987.

The Old Dutch Homesteads of Brooklyn. New York: Long Island Historical Society, 1984.

PALLISER, PALLISER & COMPANY. *Palliser's New Cottage Homes and Details*. New York: Palliser, Palliser & Co., 1887.

PENFIELD, EDWARD. *Holland Sketches*. New York: Charles Scribner's Sons, 1907.

PENNELL, JOSEPH. *Joseph Pennell's Pictures of the Wonder of Work* (Philadelphia & London: J.B. Lippincott Company, 1916).

PRICE, WILLIAM L. *Model Houses for Little Money*. Philadelphia: Curtis Publishing Company, 1898.

RENSSELAER, MARIANA GRISWOLD VAN. "American Country Dwellings I." *Century Magazine* 32 (May 1886): 3-19.

———. "Recent Architecture in America V. City Dwellings." *Century Magazine* 31 (February 1886): 548-558.

REYNOLDS, HELEN WILKINSON. *Dutch Houses in the Hudson Valley Before 1776*. 1929; rpt. New York: Dover, 1965.

REYNOLDS, MARCUS T. "The Colonial Buildings of Rensselaerwyck." *Architectural Record* 4 (June 1895): 415-438.

RHOADS, WILLIAM B. *The Colonial Revival*. 2 vols. New York: Garland, 1977.

———. "The Colonial Revival and American Nationalism." *Society of Architectural Historians Journal* 35

(December 1976): 239-254.

ROTH, RODRIS. "The New England, or 'Old Tyme,' Kitchen Exhibit at Nineteenth-Century Fairs." In *The Colonial Revival in America*, Alan Axelrod, ed., 159-183. New York: W.W. Norton & Co and Henry Francis Du Pont Winterthur Museum, 1985.

ROYAL COMMISSION OF THE NETHERLANDS. *Special Catalogue of the Netherland Section, International Exhibition, Philadelphia, 1876*. Amsterdam: C.G. Van Der Post, 1876.

SAYLOR, HENRY H. *Distinctive Homes of Moderate Cost* New York: McBride, Winston & Company, 1910. Originally published 1905 by The John Winston Company.

SCHUYLER, MONTGOMERY. "A History of Old Colonial Architecture." *Architectural Record* 4 (quarter ending 31 March 1895): 312-66.

SELIGMANN, CLAUS. "The Popular Colonial Revival House of the Early Twentieth Century, Some Morphological Observations." *Architectural Association Quarterly* 12 (1980): 44-51.

SHANK, WESLEY I., compiler. *Historic American Buildings Survey: The Iowa Catalog*. Iowa City: Univ of Iowa Press, 1979.

SNYDER-GRENIER, ELLEN M. *Brooklyn! An Illustrated History*. Philadelphia: Temple Univ Press, 1996.

STERN, ROBERT A.M., GREGORY GILMARTIN, AND JOHN MONTAGUE MASSENGALE. *New York 1900: Metropolitan Architecture and Urbanism 1890-1915*. New York: Rizzoli, 1983.

STEVENSON, KATHERINE COLE AND H. WARD JANDL. *Houses by Mail: A Guide to Houses from Sears, Roebuck and Company*. Washington DC: The Preservation Press, 1986.

TAURANAC, JOHN. *Essential New York: A Guide to the History and Architecture of Manhattan's Important Buildings, Parks, and Bridges*. New York: Holt, Rinehart and Winston, 1979.

UPTON, DELL. *America's Architectural Roots: Ethnic Groups That Built America*. Washington, DC: The Preservation Press, 1986.

VEILLER, LAWRENCE. "Industrial Housing Developments in America I: Beloit, Wis., Eclipse Park." *Architectural Record* 43 (March 1918): 231-256.

VELDHEER, J.G., AND FREDERICA HULSWIT, "Dutch Houses and Gardens," *House and Garden* 2 (October 1902): 501-509.

WAITE, DIANA S. *Albany Architecture: A Guide to the City*. Albany: Mount Ida Press, 1993.

WEISS, HARRY B. AND GRACE M. *The Early Windmills of New Jersey and Nearby States*. Trenton: New Jersey Agricultural Society, 1969.

YERBURY, F. R. *Old Domestic Architecture of Holland*. London: The Architectural Press, 1924.

SEVEN: THE SPREAD OF HOLLAND MANIA

ADAMS, J. HARRY. "The Mantel and the Fireplace." *Ladies' Home Journal* (September 1894): 3; (March 1899): 19.

"An American Exhibition in Amsterdam." *The Grand Rapids Furniture Record* (February 1902): 75.

Artistic Home Ideas. 3 vols. (January 1902-June 1903) bound as one book. Carthage, IL: Home Ideas Publishing Co., [c.1903].

Artistic Houses. 2 vols. New York: D. Appleton & Co., 1883 & 1884.

BERKEY & GAY FURNITURE COMPANY. *The Old Feeling or The Past Revived*. Grand Rapids: Berkey & Gay, 1900.

BETSKY, CELIA. "Inside the Past: The Interior and the Colonial Revival in American Art and Literature, 1860-1914." In *The Colonial Revival in America*, Alan Axelrod, ed., 241-277. New York: W.W. Norton & Co. and Henry Francis Du Pont Winterthur Museum, 1985.

BOK, EDWARD. "The Mother of America." *Ladies' Home Journal* 20 (October 1903): 16.

"Bonnets for the Autumn," *Ladies' Home Journal* (September 1894): 19.

BUCK, JOHN. *Old Plate, Its Makers and Marks*. New York: Gorham Manufacturing Company, 1903.

CARVER, SALLY S. *The American Postcard Guide to Tuck*. Brookline, Massachussetts: Carves Cards, 1976

CASTLE, IRENE. *Castles in the Air*. Garden City, NY: Doubleday, 1958.

———. *My Husband*. New York: DeCapo Press, 1979.

CASTLE, VERNON AND IRENE. *Modern Dancing*. New York and London: Harper & Brothers, 1914.

CHAQUIN, MLLE. "Un Peu de Tout." *Harper's Bazar* 48 (September 1913: 29.

The Chautauquan. monthly issues for 1909.

"The Club Year—Holland." *Woman's Home Companion* 39 (December 1912): 68.

Cooper's Dutch Dialect: Readings and Recitations. New York: Henry J. Wehman, 1891.

COVELL, ALWYN F. "The Real Place of Mission Furniture." *Good Furniture* 4 (March 1915): 358-366.

COWLES, JULIA DARROW. *Artistic Home Furnishing for People of Moderate Means*. New York: F.M. Lupton, 1898.

CUTLER, MARTHA. "A Garden Fete." *Harper's Bazar* 43 (September 1909): 921-922.

———. "The Modern Bathroom." *Harper's Bazar* 45 (September 1911): 425.

DARLING, SHARON. *Chicago Furniture: Art, Craft, and Industry, 1833-1983*. New York and London: Chicago Historical Society and W.W. Norton, 1984.

DEJONG, GERALD F. *The Dutch in America*. Boston: G.K. Hall, 1975.

DIETRICH, E.G.W. "A House For $8000." *Harper's Bazar* 43 (March 1909): 219-222.

DOW, J.W. "Successful Houses: Princess-gate. *House Beautiful*. 7 (February 1900): 135-139.

Dutch Dialect: Recitations, Readings and Jokes. Chicago: F.J. Drake and Company, 1902.

Dutch Jokes and Funny Yarns with Original Sketches by Hartley and King. Philadelphia: Royal Publishing Company, 1902.

EDWARDS, GEORGE WHARTON. *Holland of Today*. Philadelphia: Penn Publishing Company, 1919.

FERREE, BARR. *American Estates & Gardens*. New York: Munn & Co., 1904.

FIELD, EUGENE. "In Amsterdam." In *Second Book of Verses*. New York: Charles Scribner's Sons, 1896.

FREEMAN, DR. LARRY, ed. *"Wish You Were Here" A Centennial Guide to Postcard Collecting*. Watkins Glen, NY: Century House, Inc., 1976.

GANS, M.H. AND TH.M. DUYVENE DE WIT-KLINKHAMER. *Dutch Silver*. London: Faber and Faber, 1961.

GILLET, JOSEPH E. "Holland's Influence on English Language and Literature." *Modern Language Notes* 33 (March 1918): 175-177.

GRAY, STEPHEN, ed. *Charles P. Limbert Company, Cabinet Makers, Grand Rapids, Michigan*. New York: Turn of the Century Editions, 1990.

GRIFFIS, WILLIAM ELLIOT. *The American in Holland*. Boston and New York: Houghton Mifflin & Company, 1907.

HITCHCOCK, GEORGE. "The Picturesque Quality of Holland Interiors and Bric-a-Brac," *Scribner's Magazine* 5 (February 1889): 162-171.

HOTCHKISS, GEORGE BURTON AND RICHARD B. FRANKEN, *The Leadership of Advertised Brands*. Garden City, NY: Doubleday, Page & Company for the Associated Advertising Clubs of the World, 1923.

HUMPHREYS, MARY GAY. "House Decoration and Furnishing." In *The House and Home: A Practical Book*, vol. 2, Lyman Abbott, L.W. Betts, et. al., 103-178. New York: Charles Scribner's Sons, 1896.

ITHACA CLOCKS. Advertisement in *Good Housekeeping* (April, 1906): unpaginated advertising section.

JAY, ROBERT. *The Trade Card In Nineteenth-Century America*. Columbia: University of Missouri Press, 1987.

JEFFERSON, JOSEPH. *The Autobiography of Joseph Jefferson*. New York: Century, 1890.

JENNINGS, JAN AND HERBERT GOTTFRIED. *American Vernacular Interior Architecture, 1870-1940*. New York: Van Nostrand Reinhold Company, 1988.

JONES, E. ALFRED. *Old Silver of Europe and America from Early Times to the Nineteenth Century*. Philadelphia: J.B. Lippincott and Co., 1928.

JORGENSEN, JANICE, ed. *Encyclopedia of Consumer Brands*. 3 vols. Detroit: St. James Press, 1994.

KING, PAULINE. "Decorated Mugs at the New York Salmagundi Club." *House Beautiful* 6 (November 1899): 276-281.

KLAMKIN, MARIAN. *Picture Postcards* New York: Dodd, Mead & Company, 1974.

KNOWLES, W. PITCAIRN. *Dutch Pottery and Porcelain* New York: Charles Scribner's Sons, [1904].

LANE, ANNA EICHBERG KING. *Kitwyk Stories*. New York and London: John Lane, 1904.

LIMBERT, CHARLES P. & COMPANY. Advertisement for *DeLimbert Boek*. In *The Grand Rapids Furniture Record* (February 1914): 124.

———. *Limbert's Holland Dutch Arts and Crafts Furniture*. Book #117. Grand Rapids: Charles P. Limbert Company, n.d.

———. *Limbert's Holland Dutch Arts and Crafts Furniture*. Probably book #100. Grand Rapids: Charles P. Limbert Company, n.d. Copy in the Henry Francis Du Pont Winterthur Museum, Winterthur, Delaware.

"Lingerie and Negligees." *Harper's Bazar* 46 (March 1912): 134.

LOCKWOOD, LUKE VINCENT. *Colonial Furniture in America*. 2 vols. New York: Charles Scribner's Sons, 1913.

———. *Silver By New York Makers, Late 17th Century to 1900*. New York: Museum of the City of New York, 1937.

MAREK, DON. *Arts and Crafts Furniture Design: The Grand Rapids Contribution, 1895-1915*. Grand

Rapids: Grand Rapids Art Museum, 1987.

MAXWELL, PERRITON. "A Decorative Illustrator." in *American Art and Artists*. Boston: American Art Company, 1895.

MILLER, GEORGE AND DOROTHY. *Picture Postcards in the United States, 1893-1918*. New York: Clarkson N. Potter, Inc., 1976.

"Needlework: Dutch Embroidery." *Delineator* 66 (July 1905): 91-93.

NETHERLANDS SOCIETY OF PHILADELPHIA. *Twelfth Annual Banquet of the Netherlands Society of Philadelphia*. Philadelphia, 1903.

"Old Delft Ware." *Harper's Bazar* 45 (March 1911): 117.

"Our Girls." *Harper's Bazar* 43-2 (1909): bound in unpaginated advertising section.

ROOF, KATHERINE METCALF. *The Life and Art of William Merritt Chase*. New York: Charles Scribner's Sons, 1917.

SAYLOR, HENRY H. *Distinctive Homes of Moderate Cost* New York: McBride, Winston & Company, 1910. Originally published 1905 by The John Winston Company.

SALMAGUNDI CLUB PAPERS. Archives of American Art, Smithsonian Institution, Washington, D.C.

SHACKLETON, ROBERT AND ELIZABETH. "The Charm of the Antique." *Good Housekeeping* (February 1914): 263-268.

———. *The Quest of the Colonial*. 1907; New York: The Century Company, 1921.

SHANNON, KITTY. *For My Children*. London: Hutchinson & Co., n.d.

SHELTON, WILLIAM HENRY. *The Salmagundi Club, A History*. Boston & New York: Houghton, Mifflin Co., 1918.

———. "The Unique Art Sale of America." *Brush and Pencil* 15 (April 1905): 245-250.

SINGLETON, ESTHER. "American Colonial Furniture." *The Mentor* 2 (1 July 1914): 1-11.

———. *Dutch and Flemish Furniture*. London: Hodder and Stoughton, 1909.

———. *The Furniture of Our Forefathers*, part 4. New York: Doubleday, Page and Company, 1901.

"The Staining and Coloring of Cabinet Woods." *Good Furniture* 4 (March 1915): 383-384.

STONE, JOHN RICHARDS. "The Dutch Room of the Grolier Club." *House Beautiful* 2 (July 1897): 28-32.

TALBERT, ERNEST. *Old Countries Discovered Anew: A Motor Book for Everybody*. Boston: Dana Estes & Co., 1913.

VRIES, TIEMEN DE. *Dutch History, Art and Literature For Americans*. Grand Rapids, MI: Eerdmans-Sevensma Co., 1912.

———. *Holland's Influence on English Language and Literature*. Chicago: C. Grentzebach, 1916.

WALLACE, ELLERSLIE. *A Descriptive Reading on Holland illustrated by twelve lantern slides*. Philadelphia: William H. Rau, 1890.

WARNER, C.A., & COMPANY. Advertisement for Olde Dutch Clocks in *The Furniture Record* (April 1903): 473, & (May 1903):

WARNER, CHARLES DUDLEY. *The Work of Washington Irving*. New York: Harper and Brothers, 1893.

WILSON, FRANCIS. *Joseph Jefferson: Reminiscences of a Fellow Player*. New York: Charles Scribner's Sons, 1907.

WOOD, JANE. *The Collector's Guide to Post Cards*. Gas City, Indiana: L.-W. Promotions, 1984.

EIGHT: CINCINNATI, A CASE STUDY

ANDERSON, EMMA M. *Elizabeth Nourse, A Sketch*. Cincinnati: published privately, 1922.

A Book of the Tile Club. Boston & New York: Houghton Mifflin & Co., 1886.

CINCINNATI ART MUSEUM. *The Golden Age: Cincinnati Painters of the Nineteenth Century Represented in the Cincinnati Art Museum*. Cincinnati: Cincinnati Art Museum, 1979.

———. *"The Ladies, God Bless 'Em": The Women's Art Movement in Cincinnati in the Nineteenth Century*. Cincinnati: Cincinnati Art Museum, 1976.

"City Block Produced Three Great Artists Who Won World Fame." *The Cincinnati Times-Star*, 4 July 1929, p. 7, col. 3.

CLARK, ELIOT. "The Art of John Twachtman." *International Studio* 72 (January 1921): 76-86.

CUVIER PRESS CLUB. *Cincinnati, "The Queen City" Newspaper Reference Book*. Cincinnati: Cuvier Press Club, 1914.

DEVEREUX, CLARA ANN RICH AND MARION. *Mrs. Devereux's Blue Book of Cincinnati Society*. Cincinnati: James, Jennings & Graham, 1894-1899.

FOUCAR, THEODORE. obituary. *The Cincinnati Times-Star*, 6 November 1933.

GIGLIERANO, GEOFFREY J. AND DEBORAH A. OVERMEYER. *The Bicentennial Guide to Greater Cincinnati: a Portrait of 200 Years*. Cincinnati: The Cincinnati Historical Society, 1988.

GOSS, REV. CHARLES FREDERICK. *Cincinnati, the Queen City, 1788-1912*. 4 vols. Chicago & Cincinnati: S. J. Clarke

Publishing Co., 1912.
GREEN, JAMES ALBERT PAPERS. Cincinnati Historical Society.
GREVE, CHARLES. *Centennial History of Cincinnati and Representative Citizens*. vol. 2. Chicago: Biographical Publishing Co., 1904.
HURLEY, DANIEL. *Cincinnati, the Queen City*. Cincinnati: Cincinnati Historical Society, 1982.
KOLFSCHOTEN, TH. C.P.M. *Edam en Volendam*. Edam: F.A. Keizer & Van Straten, 1933.
LABREE, COL. BEN, ed. *Notable Men of Cincinnati at the Beginning of the Twentieth Century*. Louisville, KY: Geo. G. Fetter Co., 1903.
LANGSTROTH, T[HEODORE] A[SHMEAD], compiler. "The Colorful World of John Rettig." 6 volumes of scrapbooks compiled in 1965. Public Library of Cincinnati and Hamilton County.
LYNES, RUSSELL. *The Tastemakers: The Shaping of American Popular Taste*. 1955; rpt. New York: Dover Publications Inc., 1980.
MAXWELL, SIDNEY D. *The Suburbs of Cincinnati*. 1870; rpt. New York: Arno Press, 1974.
NEUHAUS, ROBERT. *Unsuspected Genius, the Art and Life of Frank Duveneck*. San Francisco: Bedford Press, 1987.
New Amsterdam Gazette. 1 (31 January 1884), p.3, col. 1; (31 March 1884), p. 2, col. 2; 2 (9 October 1884), p. 2, col. 2; (10 November 1884), p. 10, col. 2; 3 (30 April 1886)), p. 2, col. 2; 5 (21 May-30 June 1888), p. 7, col. 3.
NOURSE, ELIZABETH PAPERS. Cincinnati Historical Society.
"The Pastel Exhibition." *Art Amateur* 19 (June 1888): 3-4.
RETTIG, JOHN PAPERS. Archives of American Art, Smithsonian Institution, Washington, D.C.
RETTIG, JOHN Scrapbooks. 8 volumes. Cincinnati Historical Society.
ROSS, STEVEN J. *Workers on the Edge: Work, Leisure, and Politics in Industrializing Cincinnati, 1788-1890*. New York: Columbia Univ Press, 1985.
VITZ, ROBERT C. "Cincinnati Art and Artists: 1870-1920." Master's thesis, Miami University, 1967.
———. *The Queen and the Arts: Cultural Life in Nineteenth Century Cincinnati*. Kent, Ohio: Kent State Univ Press, 1989.
VOGELER, ADOLF G. *John Uri Lloyd: A Character Sketch*. Chicago: Office of the *Western Druggist*, 1897.
WASON, CLARENCE. "The Salon of the Champs de Mars." *Art Amateur* 29 (July 1893): 31.
Williams Cincinnati Directory. Annual volumes, 1880-1920.
WOMAN'S ART CLUB SCRAPBOOK. Cincinnati Historical Society.

CONCLUSION

GENERAL

ALBRECHT, FLORENCE CRAIG. "Volendam, The Artists' Village." *Scribner's Magazine* 41 (March 1907): 327-338.
BOWEN, MARJORIE. *The Netherlands Displa'd*. New York: Dodd, Mead & Co., 1927.
DEMAREST, D.D. "The Dutch in Kentucky." *New Amsterdam Gazette*. 6 (31 October 1889) p. 12, col. 1-2.
EDELMAN, HENDRIK. *The Dutch Language Press in America: Two Centuries of Printing, Publishing, and Bookselling*. Nieuwkoop: De Graaf, 1986.
GORE, JAMES H. *Holland, The Home of Peace*. New York: Holland America Line, 1913.
HOWELL, CHARLES FISH. *Around the Clock in Europe, A Travel-Sequence*. Boston & New York: Houghton Mifflin Co., 1912.
KENNEY, ALICE P. *Stubborn for Liberty: the Dutch in New York*. Syracuse: Syracuse Univ Press for the New York State American Revolution Bicentennial Commission, 1975.
KUIJLAARS, TON. *200 Years of Consulates of the Netherlands in New York, Boston, Philadelphia*. 1984.
LEEUW, HENDRIK DE. *Crossroads of the Zuider Zee*. Philadelphia & New York: J.B. Lippincott Co., 1938.
MADDEN, EVA. "In the Land of Windmills." *Harper's Bazar* 43 (August 1909): 759-765.
MEAD, EDWIN D. "The World's Debt to Holland in the Cause of Peace." *New England Magazine* 37 (October 1907): 232-240.
NORDHOLT, J.W. SCHULTE AND ROBERT P. SWIERENGA, eds. *A Bilateral Bicentennial: A History of Dutch-American Relations, 1782-1982*. Amsterdam: Meulenhoff Int., 1982.
OSBORNE, ALBERT B. *Finding the Worth While in Europe*. 1913; New York: Robert M. McBride & Co, 1923.
RAYMOND, ANDREW VAN VRANKEN. *Union University: Its History, Influence, Characteristics and Equipment*. New York: Lewis Publishing Company, 1907.
ROOSEVELT, THEODORE. *Theodore Roosevelt Cyclopedia*. Oyster Bay, NY: Theodore Roosevelt Association, 1989.
VLEKKE, BERNARD H. M. *The Netherlands and the United States*. Boston: World Peace Foundation, 1945.

WHITE, ANDREW D. "Hugo Grotius: the Founder of International Law." *The Chautauquan* 53 (February 1909): 411-417.

"A Word About Our Dutch Newspapers in the United States." *New Amsterdam Gazette* 3 (30 September 1885), p. 4, cols. 1-2.

CHILDREN'S LITERATURE

ABBOTT, JACOB. *Rollo in Holland.* Boston: Brown, Taggard & Chase, 1857.

BANKS, HELEN WARD. *The Boys' Motley.* New York: Frederick A. Stokes, 1914.

———. *The Story of Holland.* 1914; New York: Frederick A. Stokes Co., 1925.

Catalogue of Books in the Children's Department of Carnegie Library of Pittsburgh. 2 vols. Pittsburgh, 1920.

CHAMPNEY, ELIZABETH W. *Witch Winnie in Holland.* New York: Dodd, Mead and Company, 1896.

CHASE, JESSIE. *Mayken, a Child's Story of the Netherlands in the sixteenth century.* Chicago: A.C. McClurg & Co., 1902.

DAWSON, ARTHUR H. *Stories from Dutch History.* New York: Thomas Y. Crowell, 1913.

DEAN, IDA M. AND MARIAN M. GEORGE. *A Little Journey to Holland, for Home and School, intermediate and upper grades.* Chicago: A. Flanagan Company, 1902.

DODGE, MARY MAPES. *Hans Brinker or the Silver Skates.* Illustrated by Allen B. Doggett. New York: Charles Scribner's Sons, 1905.; Illustrated by George Wharton Edwards. New York: Charles Scribner's Sons, 1915.; Illustrated by Sears Gallagher. Boston: Ginn & Co., 1917.

———. *The Land of Pluck: Stories and Sketches for Young Folk.* New York: The Century Co., 1894.

ELSON, RUTH MILLER. *Guardians of Tradition: American Schoolbooks of the Nineteenth Century.* Lincoln NE: Univ of Nebraska Press, 1964.

FIELD, EUGENE. "Dutch Lullaby." In *A Little Book of Western Verse.* New York: Charles Scribner's Sons, 1890.

FIELD, WALTER TAYLOR. *Fingerposts to Children's Reading.* Chicago: A. C. McClurg & Co., 1907.

GRIFFIS, WILLIAM ELLIOT. *Brave Little Holland and What She Taught Us.* 1894; Boston: Houghton Mifflin Company, 1931.

———. *Dutch Fairy Tales for Young Folks.* New York: Thomas Y. Crowell Co., 1918.

GROVER, EULALIE OSGOOD. *Sunbonnet Babies in Holland.* Chicago: Rand, McNally & Co., [c.1915].

HALL, MAY EMERY. *Dutch Days.* New York: Moffat, Yard & Co., 1914.

———. *Jan and Betje, A Story of Two Dutch Children.* New York: Charles E. Merrill Company, 1914.

HENTY, GEORGE ALFRED. *By Pike and Dyke.* New York: Scribner's, n.d.

———. *By England's Aid or The Freeing of the Netherlands.* New York: A. L. Burt Company, n.d.

HEWINS, CAROLINE M. *Books for Boys and Girls.* Chicago: American Library Association, 1915.

JUNGMAN, BEATRIX AND NICO. *Peeps at Many Lands: Holland.* London: Black, 1908.

MCMANUS, BLANCHE. *Our Little Dutch Cousin.* Boston: L.C. Page & Co., 1906.

MOTT, FRANK LUTHER. *Golden Multitudes: The Story of Best Sellers in the United States.* New York: MacMillan Co., 1947.

OLCOTT, FRANCES JENKINS. *The Children's Reading.* Boston & New York: Houghton Mifflin, 1912.

OLMSTEAD, EMMA G. AND EMMA B. GRANT. *Ned and Nan in Holland.* Chicago & New York: Row, Peterson & Co., 1916.

PERKINS, LUCY FITCH. *The Dutch Twins.* school edition. Boston: Houghton Mifflin Company, 1911.

POST, MAY AUDUBON. *My Little Dutch Book.* London and New York: E. Nister and E.P. Dutton & Co., n.d.

SCUDDER, HORACE E. *The Bodley Grandchildren and their Journey in Holland.* Boston: Houghton, Mifflin & Co., 1883.

SEAMAN, AUGUSTA HUIELL *Jacqueline of the Carrier-Pigeons.* n.p.: Sturgis, n.d.

SINDELAR, JOSEPH C. *Nixie Bunny in Faraway-Lands.* Chicago: Beckley-Cardy Company, 1917.

SMITH, MARY ESTELLA. *Holland Stories.* Chicago: Rand, McNally & Co., 1913.

SOUTH CAROLINA DEPARTMENT OF EDUCATION. *List of Library Books Adopted April 23, 1909.* Columbia, SC: R.L. Bryan Co., 1909.

———. *List of Library Books and Supplementary Readers Adopted.* Columbia, SC: R.L. Bryan Co, 1923.

UPTON, BERTHA AND FLORENCE. *The Adventures of Two Dutch Dolls and a Golliwogg.* Boston: DeWolfe, Fiske, 1897.

———. *The Golliwogg in Holland.* London & New York: Longman's Green & Co, 1904.

DUTCH IMMIGRANTS

"Another Touch of Holland Coming to Pella." [overview of canal project]

Pella: A Touch of Holland (Spring/Summer 1997): 13.

BALDWIN, NICK. "Pella Style Remodeling Keyed to Old-World Theme." *Des Moines Tribune* 13 January 1966 in the Pella clippings file, Iowa State Historical Society Library, Des Moines.

BRINKS, HERBERT J. *Dutch American Voices: Letters from the United States, 1850-1930*. Ithaca: Cornell University Press, 1995.

DEJONG, GERALD F. *The Dutch in America, 1609-1974*. Boston: G.K. Hall, 1975.

HIGHAM, JOHN. *Strangers in the Land*. New Brunswick, NJ: Rutgers Univ Press, 1955.

LAGERWEY, W. *Neen Nederland, 'k vergeet u niet*. Baarn: Bosch & Keuning n.v., 1982.

LUCAS, HENRY S. *Netherlanders in America: Dutch Immigration to the United States and Canada, 1789-1950*. Ann Arbor: Univ of Michigan Press, 1955.

NOEL, LEON. "The Largest Estate in the World." *The Overland Monthly* 12 (November 1888): 480-94.

SWIERENGA, ROBERT P., ed. *The Dutch in America: Immigration, Settlement, and Cultural Change*. New Brunswick: Rutgers University Press, 1985.

THOMAS, CALVIN. "The Hollanders in America." *Chautauquan* 13 (May 1891): 205-209.

VERSTEEG, D. *De Pelgrim-Vaders van het Westen*. Grand Rapids: C. M. Loomis, 1886.

WABEKE, BERTUS HARRY. *Dutch Emigration to North America, 1624-1860*. New York: Netherlands Information Bureau, 1944.

WEBBER, PHILIP E. *Pella Dutch: The Portrait of a Language and its Use in One of Iowa's Ethnic Communities*. Ames: Iowa State Univ. Press, 1988.

WYCK, MILLIE VAN. *The Town of South Denver*. Boulder, CO: Pruett Publishing Company, 1991.

BOER WAR

B., S. "The Boer and the White Flag." *Harper's Weekly* 43 (9 December 1899): 1245.

BLAKE, COL. J.Y.F. *A West Pointer with the Boers*. Boston: Angel Guardian Press, 1903.

BOWEN, H.H. "American Public Opinion of the War." *The Nineteenth Century* 47 (May 1900): 744-752.

CRESWICKE, LOUIS. *South Africa and the Transvaal War*. 8 vols. Edinburgh: T.C. & E.C. Jack, 1900.

CUST, HENRY. "The Dutch in South Africa." *North American Review* 170 (February 1900): 198-211.

DAVIS, CECIL CLARK. *With Both Armies in South Africa*. New York: Charles Scribner's Son, 1900.

DAVITT, MICHAEL. *The Boer Fight for Freedom: From the Beginning of Hostilities to the Peace of Pretoria*. 3rd edition, revised. New York and London: Funk & Wagnalls Company, 1902.

DOYLE, A. CONAN. *The Great Boer War*. New York: McClure, Phillips & Company, 1900.

EASTON, E.E. "Inside the Boer Lines." *Harper's New Monthly Magazine* 100 (May 1900): 815-831; 101 (June 1900): 3-18; 101 (July 1900): 163-167.

HILEY, ALAN R.I., AND JOHN A. HASSELL. *The Mobile Boer*. New York: Grafton Press, 1902.

HILLEGAS, HOWARD C. "The Boer Girl of South Africa." *Ladies' Home Journal* 17 (January 1900): 6.

INTELLIGENCE OFFICER, THE. *On the Heels of DeWet*. Edinburgh: William Blackwood & Sons, 1902.

KRUGER, S. "Boer Women." *Harper's Bazar* 33 (20 January 1900): 46.

LACY, GEORGE. "Some Boer Characteristics." *The North American Review* 170 (January 1900): 43-53.

MILLARD, THOMAS F. "The Boer as a Soldier, his Peculiarities, his Weaknesses, and his Independence." *Scribner's Magazine* 28 (July 1900): 113-117.

MULANAX, RICHARD B. *The Boer War in American Politics and Diplomacy*. Lanham, Maryland: University Press of America, 1994.

STERNBERG, COUNT. *My Experiences of the Boer War*. London: Longmans, Green and Co., 1901.

VOIGT, DR. J.D. "The Afrikanders in Natal." *North American Review* 170 (February 1900): 212-24.

AFTER 1920

BARNICOAT, JOHN. *A Concise History of Posters*. New York and Toronto: Oxford University Press, 1979.

BASSMAN, ROBERT S. "Largest foreign company in America." *Europe* n.362, (December 1996): 24.

COHEN, DAVID STEVEN. *The Dutch-American Farm*. New York: New York University Press, 1992.

DANTO, ARTHUR C. *Mark Tansey: Visions and Revisions*. New York: Harry N. Abrams, 1992.

DUPARE, FREDERIK J. AND ARTHUR K. WHEELOCK, JR. *Johannes Vermeer*. Washington and The Hague: National Gallery of Art and Mauritshuis, 1995.

Encyclopedia of Associations vols. 1 & 2,

various editors. Detroit: Gale Research, Inc., 1970-1997.

GOODFRIEND, JOYCE D. *Before the Melting Pot: Society and Culture in Colonial New York City, 1664-1730*. Princeton: Princeton University Press, 1992.

Great Dutch Paintings from America. Zwolle: Waanders Publishers, 1990.

HOLLIS, RICHARD. *Graphic Design, A Concise History*. London: Thames & Hudson, 1994.

JANSSEN, ROEL. "Dutch banks in the US: Still Financing Growth in the New World." *Europe* n.362 (December 1996): 18.

JORGENSEN, JANICE, ed. *Encyclopedia of Consumer Brands*. 3 vols. Detroit: St. James Press, 1994.

Judith Leyster: a Dutch Master and her World. Zwolle: Waanders Publishers, 1993.

LEWIS, JOHN AND JOHN BRINKLEY. *Graphic Design with special reference to Lettering, Typography and Illustration*. London: Routledge & Kegan Paul, 1954.

MEGGS, PHILIP B. *A History of Graphic Design*. New York: Van Nostrand Reinhold Company, 1983.

Nederlandse Architectuur, 1880-1930, Americana. Zaandam: C. Huig for Rijksmuseum Kröller-Müller, 1975

NOOTER, ERIC AND PATRICIA U. BONOMI, eds. *Colonial Dutch Studies*. New York: New York University Press, 1988.

NORDHOLT, J.W. SCHULTE. *The Dutch Republic and American Independence*. Chapel Hill: University of North Carolina Press, 1982.

OLPIN, ROBERT S. "North American art, Dutch influences" and "North American painting, Dutch influences." In *Dutch Art: An Encyclopedia*, ed. Sheila D. Muller, 258-261 and 263-268. New York and London: Garland Publishing, 1997.

ORR, LYNN FEDERLE AND ELISE BREALL. "Exhibitions of Seventeenth-Century Dutch Art in American Museums and Public Galleries: 1888-1991." In *Great Dutch Paintings from America*, 494-98. Zwolle: Waanders Publishers, 1990.

PROKOPOFF, STEPHEN S., ed. *The Modern Dutch Poster: The First Fifty Years 1890-1940*. Cambridge, Massachusetts: MIT Press and Krannert Art Museum, 1987.

Rembrandt/Not Rembrandt in the Metropolitan Museum of Art: Aspects of Connoisseurship. New York: Metropolitan Museum of Art, 1995.

SCHAMA, SIMON. *The Embarrassment of Riches*. New York: Alfred Knopf, 1987.

SINKE, SUZANNE. "Tulips are Blooming in Holland, Michigan: Analysis of a Dutch-American Festival." In *Immigration and Ethnicity: American Society—"Melting Pot" or "Salad Bowl"?*, ed. D'Innocenzo, Michael and Josef P. Sirefman, 3-14. Westport, Connecticut: Greenwood Press, 1992.

SLIVE, SEYMOUR, et. al. *Frans Hals*. Washington: National Gallery of Art, 1990.

STAYTON, KEVIN L. *Dutch by Design: Tradition and Change in Two Historic Brooklyn Houses*. New York: The Brooklyn Museum and Phaidon Universe, 1990.

VEENENDAAL, A.J. *Slow Train to Paradise: How Dutch Investment Helped Build American Railroads*. Stanford, California: Stanford University Press, 1996.

INDEX

(Boldface indicates an illustration. The alphabetical list of artists in the appendix has not been indexed here. See pages 265-277)